THE OTHER ARAB-ISRAELI CONFLICT

MIDDLE EASTERN STUDIES, MONOGRAPH NO. 1
GRADUATE SCHOOL OF INTERNATIONAL STUDIES
UNIVERSITY OF MIAMI

The author and the University of Chicago gratefully acknowledge
the contribution of the University of Miami toward the publication
of this book. Information about future volumes in this series is
available from the Graduate School of International Studies, University of Miami, Coral Gables, Florida 33124.

THE OTHER ARAB-ISRAELI CONFLICT

Making America's Middle East Policy, from Truman to Reagan

Steven L. Spiegel

The University of Chicago Press
Chicago and London

STEVEN L. SPIEGEL is professor of political science at the University of California, Los Angeles. He is the author of *Dominance and Diversity: The International Hierarchy* (1972) and coauthor of *The International Politics of Regions: A Comparative Approach* (1970). He has edited several volumes, including *The Middle East and the Western Alliance* (1982) and has written extensively on international politics and the Middle East.

The University of Chicago Press, Chicago 60637
The University of Chicago Press, Ltd., London

© 1985 by The University of Chicago
All rights reserved. Published 1985
Printed in the United States of America
97 96 95 94 93 92 91 90 89 88   8 7 6 5 4

Library of Congress Cataloging in Publication Data

Spiegel, Steven L.
   The other Arab-Israeli conflict

   (Middle Eastern studies; monograph 1)
   Bibliography: p.
   Includes index.
   1. Near East—Foreign relations—United States.
2. United States—Foreign relations—Near East.
3. United States—Foreign relations—1945–   .
4. Jewish-Arab relations—1949–   . I. Title.
II. Series.
DS63.2.U5S62   1985   327.73056   84-16253
ISBN 0-226-76961-5

To Fredi

CONTENTS

PREFACE

The work on this volume began in the 1973–1974 academic year when I received a Guggenheim Fellowship to go to Washington to study the formulation of American policy toward the Arab-Israeli conflict. I stayed on the following year with support from the Twentieth Century Fund. I am grateful to both of these institutions for their support and to the UCLA Academic Senate Committee on Research. Several lectures derived from the manuscript were delivered at the University of Miami. I appreciate the financial support provided by the Graduate School of International Studies toward the publication of this volume.

It never occurred to me, however, that determining why U.S. policy evolves as it does toward the Arab-Israeli conflict would consume the energy and years that ultimately were expended. In Washington and on a trip in summer 1974 to Israel, Jordan, and Egypt, I conducted over three hundred interviews with bureaucrats, former officials, interest group executives, and foreign leaders. I studied documents, oral histories, memoirs. I am grateful to all those who were willing to share their time and experiences.

These discussions were an education, but they also sent me on an intellectual odyssey as I sought to distinguish between interested and effective parties in U.S. policy making. At first I had attempted to concentrate the study on crises, but I soon found they could not be separated from the full period of the administration in which they occurred. I wrote two hundred pages on interest groups and bureaucracies but finally had to discard them when they did not fit the story as it unfolded. An account of the activities of these groups and institutions is a volume yet to be written, but it would reflect the fascination of Americans with the Middle East more than why American policy evolves as it does.

Gradually, the themes and organization of the volume as it stands took shape as I realized that although groups, institutions, and foreign events influenced the context and constraints that do affect policy, it was the principal policy makers and their ideas about what policy should be that were the key to how policy is formulated on the issue. Thousands of Americans are involved with the Arab-Israeli issue and their sympathies diverge; many are active, but they do not make policy.

For those interested in U.S. policy toward the Middle East, I hope that this book will help explain the inconsistencies and changing fortunes that have marked the U.S. experience in the area. For those interested in U.S. policy making, I hope that this examination of several administrations on one issue will illuminate the policy process and perhaps stimulate several similar examinations on other issues. I am convinced that it is not possible to understand policy making adequately by examining only one crisis, one administration, or one aspect of an issue.

A word about footnotes. It has recently become commonplace either to dispense with footnotes or to include them only sporadically. Because my conclusions are sometimes controversial, I have tried to be scrupulous in including my sources for every point. The result may be overfootnoting, but I have compensated by dispensing with the usual bibliography, which seemed unnecessary in view of the completeness of the notes and the length of the volume. I hope that (with the exception of those interviews where the interviewee would not allow me to use his or her name) the reader will appreciate having the option of knowing the basis on which conclusions were drawn.

In any large research undertaking pursued over several years, there are always a great number of individuals who should be thanked for their assistance. Kathy Jackson helped pare the manuscript down when it appeared too long to be manageable. Carol Barker of the Twentieth Century Fund was a great source of encouragement at the start of the project. Arthur Abramson and Tina Kahn joined me in Washington. Art's fascination with the Truman era inspired me to become engaged in a period I had not previously studied seriously. Other students at UCLA were particularly helpful. Jody Myers organized the final push for footnote completeness, which was executed by Lisa Zemelman and Robert Pool. Bob's assistance on the later chapters was invaluable because of his ability to synthesize and to locate oft-forgotten material. Sandra Smith's dedication to detail and cross checks in the last stages of the manuscript were overwhelming. When the Reagan epilogue was added at the last moment, she was prepared to spend long hours in aiding me to complete the task rapidly. I deeply appreciate her devotion.

Many authors thank their spouses for assistance; I owe a special debt to my wife who played a unique role in the production of this manuscript. Fredi had to live with this project for a decade as we moved across the country and back and as the growing number of drafts cluttered every corner of the house. My problem in completing the manuscript was one of organizing the notes that I had collected into a coherent scheme. As I floundered desperately looking for the proper approach, she brought to the manuscript her keen sense of logic, organization, and clarity of perspective. Without the sometimes stiff doses of advice she offered, I doubt that the project would ever have been satisfactorily completed. I am particularly grateful that she advised against publishing the manuscript completed in November 1977.

It would also be unfair not to acknowledge the debt I owe to our three children—Mira, Nina, and Avi—who have grown up suffering with a sixth member of the family, "the book."

The Arab-Israeli issue in American foreign policy is a much discussed topic, but the reasons that the United States behaves as it does toward the problem is a subject less frequently addressed. I hope that this volume will help Americans improve their understanding of the process by which foreign policy is made on an issue that has become one of the major problems of our times.

Los Angeles
April 1984

CHRONOLOGY

Truman Administration

August 1945: Harrison Report

April 1946: Anglo-American Committee Report

July 1946: Morrison-Grady Plan

4 October 1946: Truman's Yom Kippur Message

18 February 1947: Britain turns the Palestine Question to the United Nations.

August 1947: United Nations Special Committee on Palestine (UNSCOP) Report.

29 November 1947: General Assembly votes to partition Palestine into Jewish and Arab states with Jerusalem internationalized.

19 March 1948: Ambassador to the United Nations Warren Austin announces United States support for trusteeship to replace partition temporarily in Palestine.

14–15 May 1948: Israel independence declared. The United States recognizes the new state eleven minutes after its independence.

15 May 1948: Arab states attack Israel.

17 September 1948: Count Folke Bernadotte, U.N. mediator, assassinated by Jewish terrorists.

February–July 1949: Ralph Bunche, new U.S. mediator, arranges armistice agreements between Israel and Egypt, Lebanon, Jordan, and Syria, respectively. The Arab states still refuse to recognize Israel's right to exist.

Eisenhower Administration

May 1953: Dulles tours the Near East and South Asia.

October 1953–1955: Eric Johnston seeks agreement among Arabs and Israelis for sharing the area's waters.

24 February 1955: Baghdad Pact is announced. It includes Britain, Iraq, Pakistan, Turkey, and Iran.

August 1955: Dulles announces new principles for Arab-Israeli peace efforts.

27 September 1955: Nasser announces the conclusion of an arms deal with Czechoslovakia.

December 1955: Nasser objects to terms of Western offer to finance the building of the Aswan Dam.

March 1956: Secret U.S. mediation between Egypt and Israel fails.

19 July 1956: United States announces it will not finance the Aswan Dam despite belated Egyptian agreement on terms.

26 July 1956: Egypt retaliates to America's reversal of the Aswan Dam offer by nationalizing the Suez Canal.

29 October 1956: As part of secret collusion with Britain and France, Israel attacks Egypt in the Sinai.

6 November 1956: War ends after American pressure on Britain, France, and Israel.

1 January 1957: Eisenhower Doctrine unveiled "to deter Communist aggression in the Middle East area."

1 March 1957: Israel agrees to withdraw totally from Sinai after U.S. pressure.

July 1958: Pro-Western Iraqi regime overthrown; the United States intervenes in Lebanon to prevent radical takeover.

Kennedy Administration

September 1962: United States' sale of Hawk missiles to Israel is concluded.

December 1962: Joseph Johnson mission to resolve Palestinian refugee problem fails.

December 1962: United States recognizes the new regime in Yemen.

Johnson Administration

16 May 1967: Sudden Mideast crisis erupts when Nasser orders the U.N. emergency force to withdraw from the Sinai.

5–10 June 1967: Six-Day War. Israel captures the Sinai, Gaza Strip, West Bank, and Golan Heights.

22 November 1967: U.N. Security Council passes Resolution 242: outline for Middle East settlement.

9 October 1968: Johnson announces that Israel will be allowed to purchase fifty Phantom jets.

Nixon Administration

March 1969: Nasser begins war of attrition along the Suez Canal.

9 December 1969: The Rogers Plan, United States' outline for peace settlement, is announced.

August 1970: Rogers arranges cease-fire along the Suez Canal, but Egyptian violations prevent projected talks.

September 1970: Jordanian civil war. Hussein defeats Palestinian guerrillas and invading Syrian troops. The United States and Israel maneuver to stop radical forces.

March–October 1971: Rogers fails to gain a limited agreement between Egypt and Israel.

July 1972: Sadat expels Soviet military advisers.

6 October 1973: Egypt and Syria surprise Israel in a two-front attack.

17 October 1973: Arab oil producers announce oil embargo and production cuts in retaliation for the American airlift to Israel.

22 October 1973: U.S.–Soviet sponsored cease-fire takes effect.

24 October 1973: U.S. "nuclear alert" to warn Soviets not to intervene to save the Egyptian Third Army in the Sinai.

17 January 1974: Egypt and Israel agree to disengagement accord mediated by Henry Kissinger.

29 May 1974: Syria and Israel agree to disengagement agreement mediated by Henry Kissinger after he spends thirty-three days in the Middle East.

Ford Administration

March 1975: Kissinger fails to conclude a second Egyptian-Israeli agreement and the United States announces a "reassessment" of Middle East policy.

1 September 1975: Kissinger mediates second Egyptian-Israeli agreement.

Carter Administration

March–July 1977: Carter meets separately with Mideast leaders; plans are made to convene a Geneva Conference for a comprehensive Middle East settlement.

1 October 1977: The United States and the Soviet Union jointly release a statement covering principles for convening a Geneva conference.

19 November 1977: Sadat shocks the world by visiting Jerusalem; new peace efforts are planned.

February 1978: Carter meets with Sadat at Camp David to stem Egyptian disillusionment with the peace process.

February 1978: The administration announces a Mideast arms package to Israel, Egypt, and Saudi Arabia.

5–17 September 1978: Camp David summit between Carter, Sadat, and Begin produces accords on the Palestinian question and Egyptian-Israeli peace.

March 1979: In a dramatic Middle East trip, Carter gains agreement between Egypt and Israel to final details of peace treaty.

May 1979: Talks between the United States, Egypt, and Israel on Palestinian autonomy on the West Bank and Gaza Strip begin. They were still in progress at the end of the administration.

Reagan Administration

April 1981: United States announces the sale of five AWACS jets to Saudi Arabia.

7 June 1981: Israel destroys the Osiraq nuclear reactor in Baghdad.

6 October 1981: Anwar Sadat is assassinated.

29 October 1981: U.S. Senate approves the AWACS sale.

15 December 1981: The United States suspends the new strategic cooperation agreement with Israel after the Likud government applies Israeli law to the Golan Heights.

6 June 1982: Israel invades Lebanon.

19 August 1982: Special U.S. envoy Philip Habib concludes agreement for safe departure of PLO fighters from Beirut. Reagan announces that U.S. marines will participate with French and Italian forces in protecting the PLO fighters in their departure.

1 September 1982: Reagan announces a new United States plan for Mideast peace calling for "self government by the Palestinians of the West Bank and Gaza in association with Jordan."

17 May 1983: Secretary of State Shultz concludes Israeli-Lebanese agreement but Syrian opposition prevents its implementation.

23 October 1983: Terrorist attack on U.S. marine headquarters in Beirut kills 241 Americans.

7 February 1984: Reagan orders U.S. marines to leave Beirut and redeploy offshore, ending the American role in the peacekeeping force.

1

THE PROCESS OF AMERICAN MIDDLE EAST POLICY MAKING

The Middle East—its inhabitants and disputes—has long fascinated and divided Americans. From the beginning of the American experiment, many in the New Jerusalem looked romantically on the aspirations of those who had once ruled the holiest of Biblical cities. In a country imbued with Old Testament protestantism, with a frontier ideology and a belief that miracles were possible, a Jewish return to Palestine was anticipated by many. "I really wish the Jews again in Judea an independent nation," wrote John Adams in 1818.[1]

Later, in 1891 (three years before Theodor Herzl, founder of the modern Zionist movement, began his campaign to establish a national homeland for the Jews in Palestine), William Blackstone of Chicago presented President Benjamin Harrison and Secretary of State James Blaine a memorial signed by 413 prominent Americans proposing that the Jews be restored to Palestine. In response, the American consul in Jerusalem reported to the State Department, "1. Palestine is not ready for the Jews. 2. The Jews are not ready for Palestine."[2]

This clash of views is a conflict older than the Arab-Israeli struggle itself, and just as intransigent. The battle is for Washington's favor. On one side are those concerned with the Arabs or the Israelis. Supporters of Israel, remembering the Holocaust, may place the survival of the Jewish state before all other considerations. Some Christians see the working out of a divine plan in the Jews' return to Palestine. Other observers focus on Arab rights or demands; they view the Palestinian refugees as a displaced people with the right to self-determination. Some Christians operate missions among the Arabs or have theological difficulties with the Jewish return to Palestine.

1

On the other side are nonpartisans who see the Middle East as part of larger, more global conflicts. These people favor the side that seems more compatible with the foreign policies they advocate. Disagreements occur over global views, or over tactics, but do not center on commitments to either Arabs or Israelis. For example, both President Eisenhower, whose overriding global concern was fighting communism, and President Carter, who favored detente with the Soviet Union, viewed the Arab states as crucial to the achievement of their aims in the Middle East. President Eisenhower considered the Israelis an impediment to his fight against communism, but President Nixon, with similar priorities, saw them as an asset.

To complicate the issue further, the Middle East is changing while American policy changes and there is no necessary connection between the two. A series of overlapping regional conflicts have pitted Arab against Arab and the Arabs against Israel. There have also been conflicts elsewhere in the region, in places such as Iraq and Iran; Turkey, Greece, and Cyprus; Ethiopia and Somalia. Within the Arab world rivalries have changed. In the 1960s, radical Egypt was in conflict with moderate Libya; in the 1970s, radical Libya was hostile toward moderate Egypt. A similar about-face occurred between Iraq and Egypt from the 1950s to the 1970s. Further, in the 1970s Iraq and Syria—whose regimes both originated from the Baathist party—were bitterly disputing which government was more ideologically pure. Today, Jordan and Saudi Arabia, ruled by the once fiercely competitive Hashemite and Saudi families, cooperate as moderate monarchies. Undermining the claim of Arab unity have been wars within their world, as over Yemen in the 1960s and Lebanon in the mid-1970s and among the Palestinians in the early 1980s. Even Israel has played a part in these intra-Arab conflicts, as in 1970 when it was prepared to aid Hussein's Jordan against radical Palestinian insurgents and invading Syrians, its support of the Christians in Lebanon after 1975, and its further entanglement in Lebanese politics after the June 1982 invasion.

American reactions to these regional developments are often confused and always involve multiple perspectives. Over the years, myths have developed among those with special concerns. These myths usually assume that American policy is being sabotaged by those of opposing views. For example, former Senator James Abourezk, an outspoken supporter of the Palestinian cause, has written:

> U.S. policy on the Mideast is virtually directed by Tel Aviv. So long as the public ignores U.S. Government actions in the Middle East, Israel will continue to dictate our policies there. When a politician gets no message from his constituents on a particular issue, he is completely free to vote and act as he chooses. Thus, the only real pressure on politicians concerning the Middle Eastern question comes from the Israeli lobby. Always capable

of raising money for political campaigns, the lobby enlists the active aid of American Jews in every state of the Union. It takes its orders from Israel and then lays down the party line to the American Jewish community in a variety of ways—newsletters, community newspapers, and synagogue speeches. American Jews want desperately to help Israel; so they rely on the Israeli lobby to tell them how. Highly organized, smart, and constantly alert, the Israeli lobby uses political intimidation if everything else fails.[3]

In contrast, in *The Plot to Destroy Israel*, author and veteran foreign correspondent Alvin Rosenfeld argues,

There are a great many groups the Arabs can use to "pressure and influence the decision-makers" in a country like the United States, where lobbying is an accepted method of political action. The use, however, by Big Oil of propaganda processed by the Arab belligerents has gone largely unnoticed. Few stockholders and few, if any, holders of oil company credit-cards know that their investments and the tanks of gas they buy may help finance the circulation of foreign propaganda aimed against Israel through tax-exempt foundations.[4]

These opposing assumptions about who influences American Middle East policy are widely held, but both radically oversimplify the process of policy formulation. Every administration confronts an array of conflicting perceptions and interests that must be balanced. Influences operate from at home and abroad, from within the government and without, during periods of crisis and quiet. Critical differences occur even within the chief executive's circle. Some pressures are consistent; others shift in particular presidencies according to the background, predispositions, and philosophies of the key players. The task of this book is to examine the experiences of each president who has dealt with the highly controversial Arab-Israeli question in order to understand what decision-making systems developed and what substantive policies resulted from the process. In conducting this examination, I seek to separate actual policy making from the mythologies surrounding the issue among partisans of different philosophies and preferences.

The Components of Policy

American policy toward the Arab-Israeli dispute involves three levels of decision making: the global, the regional, and the actual area in conflict. However, while these levels may be related for purposes of analysis, their relationship in the real world is constantly shifting. Any administration will always have global aims (for example, containment of the Soviet Union, human rights, free trade). Sometimes these aims seem to relate directly to the Middle East, as in Eisenhower's and Dulles's pursuit of the Baghdad Pact and Carter's pursuit of stability for energy supplies. At other times the Middle East is peripheral to the administration's main concerns, as it was to Truman's containment policy or Kennedy's multiple options doctrine. There will also be regional aims, such as the promotion of a pro-American Arab unity around the favorite of the moment or the attempt to build Iran as a protector of the Persian Gulf. Last, there may be specific plans for resolving the Arab-Israeli conflict, such as Eisenhower's Johnston Plan, Kennedy's Johnson Plan, and Nixon's Rogers Plan.

In any administration, the global perspective will be paramount. Regional objectives may sometimes conflict with goals related to Arab-Israeli differences but neither regional nor Arab-Israeli policy will contradict global objectives knowingly. To understand an administration, it is important to identify its global objectives, observe the degree and intensity of consensus, and analyze how the Middle East fits in. Every president begins with foreign policy priorities and objectives, however obscure and inarticulate. Most, if not all, of the president's major advisers share these primary notions; they pay attention to the Arab-Israeli dispute to the extent that it seems critical to their global aims. Of course, occupying an important place in the administration's global picture can aid either the Arabs or the Israelis. In the Ford administration, for example, Secretary of State Henry Kissinger and U.N. Ambassador Daniel Patrick Moynihan both saw the Middle East as a key element in their top priority effort to limit Russian influence. But Kissinger in his shuttle diplomacy pursued an evenhanded strategy and Moynihan believed in close American identification with democratic Israel. Similarly in the Truman era, Clark Clifford, the president's special counsel, advocated a new Jewish state to thwart Russian aims in the area where Secretary of Defense James Forrestal opposed a Jewish state that might draw Russian intervention and jeopardize essential energy supplies for the West.

Not only executive key officials (such as the president, the national security assistant, the secretaries of state and defense, the ambasador to the U.N., White House aides) see the Middle East in light of their global concerns. Others on the American political scene also approach the Arabs and Israelis from a global orientation. Many congressmen approach the area with ideologies (or rationalizations for perceived political necessities) that have global applications—the need to support Israel because of its anticommunism, its friendship with the United States, its status as a liberal democracy; the need to support the moderate Arabs because of their anticommunist and pro-American position or because of the need for stable energy supplies.

These arguments, frequently heard in congressional debates, reflect foreign policy priorities; both the Arabs and the Israelis are subordinated to other American objectives. For example, after the Vietnam War, ideologists on the left—especially within America's minority communities—identified with the third world in rallying against global inequality. Many viewed the Palestinian cause as part of a worldwide struggle between the oppressors of the "North" (here symbolized by the Israelis) and the oppressed of the "South" (played here by the Palestinians). The Arab-Israeli dispute temporarily became part of a global ideological conflict.

Until the fall of the shah and the Soviet invasion of Afghanistan, the Pentagon showed no primary interest in the Middle East. Throughout much of the post-1945 period, its missions concentrated on the European and Asian theaters, where most conventional forces abroad were stationed in opposition to the Soviet Union and China. In the late 1940s, Defense Department officials fretted that oil supplies would be threatened or opportunities for Russian influence opened if a Jewish state emerged. The Pentagon worried about having to expend scarce troops to rescue the Jews if the Arabs attacked. By the 1960s, however, some officials saw arms sales to Israel as a means of extending production runs and cutting unit costs. Later, the military planners came to favor arms sales to the Arabs for the same reason. During the Vietnam years, Israel shared with American intelligence and military officials its combat experience with Egyptian-manned Russian equipment over the Suez Canal. This cooperation, and not developments in the Middle East, increased the sympathy of many officers and analysts toward Israel. The 1970s brought new threats to energy supplies, causing Pentagon planners again to focus on the Middle East and Arab importance as they had in the 1940s.

Only one organized interest group has viewed the Middle East as a symbol of global ideological interests. American labor has consistently focused on the prominent role of labor in Israeli society and, particularly after the mid-1950s, applauded Israeli anticommunism and urged support for the Jerusalem government. Although labor's attitude has not been important to the American executive branch, unless it influenced the president's ideas or affected his political calculus, it has helped strengthen the prevailing support for Israel in Congress.

Those who focus on primarily the second level of policy making in the Middle East, regional concerns, concentrate on the structure of international politics there. These people, both analysts and participants, seek an American policy relevant to the cultural, religious, political, and economic trends in the area. Because the Arab states outnumber the other regional actors, such thinking focuses on the Arab role in the area. Analysts who argue from this view often stress the benefits of Arab unity (or, at least, low levels of inter-Arab strife), believing that an Arab consensus encourages a coherent U.S. Mideast policy. When tensions erupt within the Arab world, so do conflicts among adherents of a regional strategy, thereby dissipating their influence on American policy-making.

This regional approach to the Middle East dominates the State Department, especially within the Bureau of Near East and South Asian Affairs. Even during the Ottoman Empire and the period of French and British rule, the department sought to protect American commercial, educational, and cultural interests by maintaining at least correct relations with the party or parties thought to be dominant in the region.[5] The Zionists could never attain that position, and so it is not surprising the State Department's strategies have often been at odds with those of the Israelis. For similar reasons many intelligence officials, Near East analysts in the National Security Council, and involved officials in the International Security Agency (the Pentagon's "State Department") have usually favored the regionalist approach. By the early 1980s this view also prevailed among analysts at the offices of the Joint Chiefs of Staff.

Outside of government, oilmen and many scholars have taken a similar position. Over the years oilmen have sought to support stable, moderate, pro-American regimes in the Arab world. Any movement or leader espousing a doctrine of nationalization or producer-independence has been feared and opposed. Oilmen and diplomats have not always addressed precisely identical concerns, but their policy preferences have tended to coincide on the Arab-Israel issue. While the influence of petroleum industry representatives on specific policies has been minimal, their overall harmony of view with many bureaucrats has given the appearance of influence. This coincidence of perspective has been shared by construction companies, banks, and other businesses increasingly active in the area since the petro-financial revolution of October 1973.

Most students of the region also have focused on the Arabs as the area's dominant cultural and linguistic unit, which has led to increasing sympathy for the Arab world in American academia. This broad diplomatic, corporate, and scholarly regional consensus is best exemplified by the Middle East Institute in Washington where retired officials, leading corporate figures, and scholars engage in discussions, educational programs, and research.

The third way of thinking about American policy toward the Arabs and Israelis is taken by those who have a specific interest in the conflict itself and are largely unconcerned about either global or regional trends. The best known and most-noted example of this perspective is American Jewish support for Israel. Few American Jewish leaders offer global or regional reasons for backing the government in Jerusalem. Their support has deep religious and cultural roots reinforced by concern for Jewish survival in the wake of the Nazi extermination of one out of every three Jews in the world during the Second World War.

This support for Israel is expressed in myriad ways—backing of sympathetic political candidates, rallies and demonstrations on Israel's behalf, financial contributions, lectures and publications, communications to political leaders. The abundance of Jewish organizations brings diverse pressures to bear. For example, the American Jewish Committee deals especially with minorities and Christian clergy. The Anti-Defamation League of B'nai B'rith defends Jews (and Israel) against discriminatory practices. The American Israel Public Affairs Committee—the pro-Israeli lobby—supports legislation that favors Israel in

Washington, especially on Capitol Hill. The Conference of Presidents of Major American Jewish Organizations speaks on foreign policy issues concerning Jews (especially Israel) and deals directly with the executive branch.

Jewish strength arises from the thousands of individual Jews who are prepared to express their sentiments to politicians and officials. Intense concern in part compensates for small numbers. Moreover, Jews have neither a bureaucratic mission nor a profit motive. Their religious, humanitarian, and ethnic concerns often appear more altruistic and less self-serving to politicians than those of their adversaries.

Despite their small number, Jews also have a definite, though limited influence on the electoral process. They contribute more generously to political campaigns than any other ethnic group; they go to the polls in higher percentages; their largest concentrations of population are located in the states electorally crucial to any presidential race; they are active in politics, especially in presidential campaigns. Thus, few people who run for the presidency do not first meet with Jewish leaders to discuss political issues, particularly their attitudes toward Israel. Many candidates and some presidents have counted prominent supporters of Israel among their friends and devoted backers. Most presidents have attempted to maintain communications with the Jewish community. Most have named a White House aide, who has usually had other domestic policy assignments as well, to champion the administration's positions to Jewish leaders and organizations and to represent their views at the White House.

The respect and attention commanded by the American Jewish community in the executive and legislative branches is not always duplicated elsewhere. Because American Jewish spokesmen usually deal with Israel as a cause—almost an ideal—separate from all other foreign policy concerns, they are perceived, especially within the foreign policy community and the press, as partisans of a single special interest. This perception blunts their effectiveness despite the intensity of their efforts.

The American Arab community, approximately a million and a half strong, has not traditionally been intensely involved in political questions, in part because of the comparatively recent arrival of most of its members and their disparate origins (especially Lebanon, Syria, Egypt). However, with the greater interest in the Middle East generated by the 1967 Six-Day War and accelerated by the October 1973 War and the ensuing energy crisis, and with the renewed ethnic awareness of Americans generally, Arab-Americans have begun to speak out for the Arab cause, especially on the Palestinian question. Two groups well established by the early 1980s were the National Association of Arab-Americans, patterned after AIPAC, the pro-Israel lobby, and the American-Arab Anti-Discrimination Committee, the Arab-American counterpart of the Anti-Defamation League. Both groups seek to interest the American elite in Arab rights in Palestine. Although their groups are growing in importance, Arab-

Americans remain divided over issues like the war in Lebanon, which helps explain why they have had only a limited effect on the public debate on the Arab-Israeli dispute. Joseph D. Baroody, a past president of the NAAA, observed, "We can't represent the Arabs the way the Jewish lobby can represent Israel. The Israeli government has one policy to state, whereas we couldn't represent 'the Arabs' if we wanted to. They're as different as the Libyans and Saudis are different, or as divided as the Christian and Moslem Lebanese."[6]

Through the years some American groups have assisted cultural exchange with the Arab countries and promoted the Arab cause. Through speakers, literature, and films, they have attempted to aid Palestinian refugees and draw attention to their plight. These groups include Amideast (American Mideast Educational and Training Services, Inc., an outgrowth of the once-active American Friends of the Middle East), Americans for Middle East Understanding, and Americans for Near East Refugee Aid. The American Educational Trust and the American-Arab Affairs Council are two organizations founded in the early 1980s with headquarters in Washington; they have a special interest in promoting the Arab cause in educational institutions. More politically active groups devoted to the advance of the Palestinian cause include the Palestine Human Rights Campaign and the Palestine Solidarity Committee.

Since October 1973 several Arab governments led by the Saudis have set up an American-staffed Arab lobby to represent their cause in Congress. This lobby first demonstrated its clout when the sale of F-15 jets to Saudi Arabia was debated in the Senate in mid-1978 and was intensified during the controversy over the sale of five AWACS jets to Saudi Arabia in 1981. Prominent Americans who have worked as lobbyists for Arab governments in Washington include Fred Dutton (a former aide to both President John F. Kennedy and Senator Robert Kennedy), former Senator J. William Fulbright, and J. Crawford Cook—a public relations executive who is a close associate of the Carter administration's ambassador to Saudi Arabia, John West. Growing Arab leverage results not only from increasing numbers and organizations but also from the wealth available to key Arab governments since October 1973. American business people interested in promoting Arab ties have begun to balance the traditionally strong pro-Israeli influence in Congress.

Curiously, equally localized views of the Arab-Israeli conflict have pulled seemingly similar organizations in opposite directions. Clergymen, church leaders, and religious organizations have found in the Holocaust, in the Ecumenical Movement, or in anticommunism reasons to favor the Israeli side. Some religious leaders supported the Jewish return to Palestine as a fulfillment of biblical prophecy. On the other hand, the Arab case has been supported by those within American churches who are anxious to protect missionary activities in the Arab world or who are sympathetic to Arabs because of knowledge gained through missionary experience. The Arabs have also been favored by those eager to develop ties with Third World churches and by those who have taken up the cause of the Palestinian refugees. The emergence of a Jewish state has precipitated problems for theologians who considered the Jews as powerless in history because they had rejected Christianity.[7]

Leaders of American minority groups have also taken opposing views. Those influenced by ideologies of Third World solidarity, oppression, and inequality have favored the Arabs; but most minority politicians, party officials, and labor leaders have been sympathetic to Israel. Divisions within the black community were illustrated in August 1979 by the controversy surrounding the resignation of the U.N. Ambassador Andrew Young after he held an unauthorized meeting with the PLO delegate at the United Nations. This trend was accelerated by the support for a PLO state and PLO-Israeli dialogue by presidential candidate Jesse Jackson in 1984.

In Republican and Democratic party politics, global and regional arguments have been less important than winning elections. The pattern of Jewish personal interest, contributions, voting, and campaign service has usually earned support for Israel. But since October 1973 those sympathetic to the Arab cause, especially for business reasons, have also exerted influence, particularly through campaign contributions.

Finally, the most obvious and explicit expressions of conflict-centered concern come from the Arab and Israeli embassies in Washington, each seeking to gain support for its side. The Israelis have only one embassy, but they compensate with a large staff and contacts with a broad range of American society and institutions. Their own democratic system also gives them a better understanding of U.S. politics than their Arab counterparts have. The Arabs have far larger numbers and financial resources available for diplomatic functions, but they are hindered by the cultural gulf dividing them from most Americans, internal differences, and the tendency of their governments and the State Department to conduct major diplomatic business through American embassies in Arab capitals. Believing that their countries suffer from insufficient American understanding of Arab aims, the Arab embassies put major emphasis on educational and propaganda materials. The Arab League Information Office in six American cities reflects this concern. Arabs have not been as active on Capitol Hill as have their Israeli counterparts. Recently, however, Israelis have shown greater concern about "public relations" and Arabs have given increased attention to Congress and paid lobbyists.

All of the institutions, groups, and individuals who take a parochial view of the conflict risk seeming to be captives of a special interest. Advocates who argue from global or regional perspectives are likely to appear more consistent with general American national interests and are therefore likely to be more persuasive in the public debate. Public arguments do not always affect policy but they are important nevertheless for their impact on the views of present and future policy makers.

The Process of Policy

Events affect American policy, and partisans both inside and outside the U.S. government constantly seek to influence decisions. These factors alone do not account for the government's actions, however, and at times they may be inconsequential.

The president and his team largely decide which voices will have access to the higher levels of government, because the chief executive's central position allows him to determine the American approach to world affairs. Although particular crises may demand attention during an administration, each new president enters office with his own interests and these guide his choices of issues on which to concentrate.

The priority assigned to the Arab-Israeli dispute by the president and his key advisors determines how policy is made. If the issue is given low priority, presidential attention will be minimal and the influence of the bureaucracy, Congress, and the interest groups will increase. When the issue is important to the president, however, interested groups and agencies will have less access to the policy process unless the administration wants to use selected agencies or to get the reaction of specific groups for its own purposes. A specific group may also have special access to a particular administration. Public activity by interest groups does not necessarily translate into influence.

The critical factors determining the content of American policy are: the basic assumptions of the president, the individuals on whom he relies for advice, and the resulting decision-making system which converts ideas into policies. While presidents may translate similar objectives into differing tactics, all presidents enter the White House with specific assumptions that prove remarkably resistant to the effects of outside forces—interest groups, events and crises in the area, the bureaucracy.

Even elections do not determine American policy toward the Middle East, any more than do oil companies, missionaries, Congress, lobbies, the "Arabists" of the State Department, the press and media, crises, or historical precedents. All these elements are important constraints on presidential action and influences on presidential attention. Constraints and influences, however, do not necessarily alter opinions. Presidents meet every challenge on the basis of their predispositions, and here particular groups do help mold the beliefs that a president and his advisers bring to office. Yet in the end policy can be understood only by examining an administration's foreign policy priorities, philosophical assumptions, decision-making system, and key personalities.

Truman was the first president forced to deal with the Arab-Israeli issue in detail, but two of his predecessors—Wilson and Roosevelt—did address the Palestine question. Although the issue then was of minimal priority, because Israel was not yet established and most of the present-day Arab states were not independent, the experiences of Wilson and Roosevelt foreshadow the patterns that developed later.

Wilson first confronted the issue in fall 1917 when the British requested his advice and support on the Balfour Declaration. The president, a firm opponent of European imperialism, was suspicious of secret Franco-British treaties covering the Ottoman Empire. He was fascinated with the idea that a democratic Zionism might replace Ottoman despotism and create a haven for oppressed Jews in Palestine. The biblical overtones were not lost upon him. "To think that I the son of the manse should be able to restore the Holy Land to its people," he once told one Jewish leader.[8] Moreover, leading Zionists like Louis Brandeis and Rabbi Stephen S. Wise had access to the president and they also had a sympathetic public behind them: the American Federation of Labor and the Presbyterian General Assembly (encouraged by Blackstone) had already expressed support of the Zionist cause.[9]

Yet there were divisions within the administration. Many diplomats, including Secretary of State Robert Lansing, were loathe to alienate the Turks, who still controlled Palestine and were not at war with the United States.

Policy making within the administration was further confused by the position of Colonel Edward House, Wilson's most important aide, whom the Zionists regarded as a close ally. They often worked directly with him, but unknown to them he hoped to keep Turkey intact and in private conversations with Wilson took a position similar to that of the State Department.[10]

When a generally worded British request for American approval of a declaration in favor of a national home in Palestine arrived in Washington in September, House raised the issue with the president and helped elicit a reply urging restraint. Several weeks later the British again cabled the president, but this time they provided a specific proposed document and referred to intelligence reports that the German government might be considering a similar declaration. Even before American Zionist leaders could reach House to urge support, Wilson acquiesced with the proviso that American backing not be made public. In these critical deliberations which lent secret U.S. support to the release of the Balfour Declaration, the State Department, Secretary Lansing, and Zionist leaders all played only indirect roles. Decision making centered at the White House with the president himself at the center of the process.[11]

Wilson's approving the issuance of the Balfour Declaration demonstrates factors more pronounced later when the issue gained prominence in the United States. Here was a president who brought several existing beliefs to the problem—assumptions partly balanced by and partly contradicting specific foreign policy considerations. On the one hand, he was sympathetic to the Zionists and sought to please his (and their) British allies. On the other hand, he did not wish to alienate Turkey. Swirling around him were competing forces at home. Within his own entourage major figures took opposing sides (for example, Brandeis and Lansing) and, in the public forum and the bureaucracy, opinion ranged from sympathy for the Zionist cause to opposition by powerful groups. In this case the president's resolution of the issue satisfied many involved parties plus his own principles and needs. (The State Department, however, resented being bypassed). Soon, those in the government opposing Zionist aims would be strengthened by Protestant missionary and educational leaders who sought to protect their involvement in the Middle East by promoting Arab nationalism.[12] Nonetheless, Wilson's secret approval of the Balfour Declaration illustrates the president's central role; the critical function of key advisors; and the role of groups, agencies, and other countries in forcing presidential attention and in constraining the chief executive.

The experience of Franklin D. Roosevelt is more complex than Wilson's. Roosevelt himself was reserved in advocating Zionist aspirations—a matter of low priority throughout his presidency. With Hitler's oppression, the Zionist argument for a homeland in Palestine assumed new urgency, but Roosevelt seems to have felt that the European Jewish refugees could be settled in some exotic underinhabited location such as Northern Rhodesia, Kenya, Tanganyika, Cyrenaica (in what is now Libya), or the inhospitable Orinoco Valley of South America.[13] He was not unaffected by British opposition to an expanded Jewish presence in Palestine and by concerns in the State Department and among White House advisors that support for the Zionists might endanger oil supplies and America's lightly-guarded Middle East bases. The issue threatened to complicate relations with the Arabs and the British and hence, the war effort. In Roosevelt's case, then, a global preoccupation with the war was reinforced by regional concerns, including the fear of alienating the Arabs.

Yet the president was caught between his own cautious instincts and mounting congressional and public pressure to act on behalf of the Zionists. On March 9, 1944, for example, he authorized two prominent Zionist leaders, Rabbis Wise and Abba Hillel Silver, to issue a statement suggesting future American support for a Jewish national home. Then he congratulated Speaker Sam Rayburn for keeping the House in line *against* a resolution favoring a Jewish commonwealth in Palestine. A few days later he assured six Arab leaders that no decision would be made on the future of Palestine without full consultation with both sides![14] Similarly, during the 1944 presidential campaign, Roosevelt was pressured into promising to work for the establishment of Palestine as a free and democratic Jewish commonwealth in Palestine. We now know that the next day he approved the usual assurances dispatched by the State Department to the Arabs.[15] Public pro-Zionist statements after pressure balanced by secret assurances to Arab leaders constituted the pattern of the later Roosevelt years. At the very least, these contradictory promises to the two sides misled both.

The contradictions in Roosevelt's policy can be explained partly by the president's confidence that ultimately he could gain Saudi Arabia's support in a peace-making effort, perhaps to produce a Palestine trusteeship, binationalism, or some form of local autonomy. Roosevelt toyed with ideas inspired partly by his love of geography and his fascination with the land of the Bible. At times he envisioned an exclusively Jewish Palestine (with the Arabs bribed to leave) in the context of some kind of international trusteeship or regional federation with the Arab states.[16] However, on his way home from Yalta, he met King Ibn Saud on an American cruiser in the Suez Canal. Saudi Arabia had been the only noncombatant during the war years to receive lend-lease aid; therefore, Roosevelt expected the Saudis at least to listen to American views on Palestine. The president proposed a deal: in return for Saudi help in gaining Arab support to resolve the Palestine question, increased American aid would be forthcoming. The king rejected this notion out of hand and Roosevelt was apparently shocked by the vehemence of the Saudi monarch's opposition to Zionism—the king recommending instead that the Jewish refugees of Nazi oppression be granted the choicest homes and land of the defeated Germans. The president quickly relented and reiterated his previous promises that he would not adopt a policy hostile to the Arabs.[17]

When reporting on his Yalta trip to the Congress, he ad-libbed about his visit with the king, "Of the problems of Arabia I learned more about the whole problem, the Moslem problem, the Jewish problem, by talking with Ibn Saud for five minutes than I could have learned in an exchange of two or three dozen letters."[18] Then he told Judge Joseph Proskauer, the head of the American Jewish Committee, that "on account of the Arab situation, nothing could be done in Palestine."[19] That led the Zionists to wonder about Roosevelt's campaign pledge, whereupon the president assured Rabbi Wise publicly that he still supported a Jewish commonwealth in Palestine.[20] No sooner had the Zionists been assured than the president dispatched a letter prepared by the State Department to Ibn Saud repeating his pledge of full consultations. It was dated 5 April; the president died a week later.[21]

Here again we see the primacy of the president and his philosophy. In retrospect, Roosevelt's reaction to Zionism appears quite different from Wilson's. The president himself was more pragmatic, less romantic, and basically more skeptical. At home Roosevelt was exposed to more widespread political pressure on behalf of Zionism than Wilson had to endure, but the result was merely a series of sympathetic statements that masked the president's private agreement with the bureaucracy and the British that prudence was necessary in Palestine to protect Western interests. Throughout Roosevelt's administration Palestine was a mere detail; the exigencies of alliance and war demanded his attention. Certainly, no force within the administration could have suggested that this issue deserved attention that might have been devoted to winning the war. Given Roosevelt's penchant for procrastinating on complex matters, his answer to external and internal pressures was to put them off with contradictory promises—a tactical maneuver typical of his style. With the war ending, however, the arguments by partisans of both sides of the Palestine question increased in intensity. The president was too close to death to deal with them.

From Roosevelt, Truman inherited a context in which policy on Palestine was being formulated. The president was becoming the focus of countervailing pressures at home (primarily from Zionist supporters, including congressmen versus national security bureaucrats) and abroad (with the British and Arabs opposing Jewish aims). The temptation to become more involved in the Arab world and to promote its alliance with the West competed with the practical problem of handling the Jewish refugees who had survived the Holocaust. Gradually, the Palestinian and refugee problems became interconnected—a link FDR had tried to resist. With Roosevelt, however, the result of countervailing pressures was contrary promises leading to a growing confusion. Just what was American policy? Yet several factors already present under Wilson were reinforced by these experiences: competing views and pressures; a resulting focus on the presidency; recurring themes such as opposition to European imperialism (now in the form of the Jewish refugee question), advocacy of self-determination, a fascination with specific benefits offered by the area's prime rulers (first Turks; now Arabs).

The contradictory pressures that the new president would face were epitomized by an incident occurring a few days after he assumed office. When Rabbi Wise made an appointment to see him, Truman already had a memo on his desk from the secretary of state warning him not to make any public statements if Zionist leaders approached him before he had received the department's "background information on this subject" (revealing Roosevelt's secret commitments to the Arabs). [22] The State Department would soon discover that the new president was more receptive to different groups and arguments than his more calculating predecessor had been. Truman would also soon be forced to deal with the issue more frequently and to respond to more urgent pressure from more partisans than any previous president.

The transition again illustrates the role of the chief executive as creator of agendas: David Niles, who served both FDR and Truman, once remarked, "There are serious doubts in my mind that Israel would have come into being if Roosevelt had lived."[23] Whenever a new president arrives in the Oval Office, the system changes because he brings with him a new set of advisers and associates, a new background, different knowledge and predispositions, a new philosophy, a conception of his own interest, and a new attitude toward the proper policy roles of the bureaucracy, Congress, and interest groups. Each president sets the rules and helps determine the victors in the war for Washington that is waged between the Arabs, the Israelis, and their respective American supporters.

2

TRUMAN
Palestine on the Periphery

The Russians had been largely irrelevant to Roosevelt's Middle East policy and the European Jewish refugees had entered American considerations only
toward the end of his administration. These two factors, however, became critical in Truman's approach to the region. As allied troops defeated German armies, the full dimensions of the Holocaust were revealed and the plight of Jewish
survivors seeking to go to Palestine became a stirring issue. But as always, global
policy took priority. The new president's perspective was almost immediately
colored by the American national security elite's growing disenchantment with
the Russians. What came to be known as "containment" of the Soviet Union
became the hallmark of Truman's foreign policy. That containment concentrated on the areas along Russia's borders—eastern Europe, Asia, Turkey, and
Iran. For Truman, Palestine was a low priority nuisance.

The Truman Policy Setting

From the end of the war through 1948, advocates of different policies
toward Palestine undercut one another's position around a president occupied
with other matters. Pressure groups saw an opportunity to influence events because of Truman's lack of direct interest in the Palestinian issue, his loose decision-making style, and intense public interest. The pressure groups' public
prominence gave rise to the conventional wisdom that Truman was pro-Zionist
for domestic reasons.[1] Although he was sometimes responsive to domestic influence, it is astonishing that he was not more pro-Zionist, given the pressures on

him. The reason can be found in the strengths of the two competing forces in the administration as well as in his own attitudes.

Among those formally responsible for national security matters, not one major figure supported the idea of establishing a Jewish state. James Byrnes, the first secretary of state appointed by Truman, left the issue to his undersecretary, Dean Acheson, who adamantly opposed Zionist aims. Byrnes's successor, General George Marshall, firmly believed that a Jewish state could not be defended if the Arabs attacked. He shared the prevailing military view that using American troops to save the Jews would require mobilization, with accompanying disastrous effects at home and abroad. Since Truman tended to trust professionals assigned specific tasks, this opposition to Jewish statehood by key officials carried considerable weight with him.

Throughout this period other major figures in the State Department opposed Jewish statehood. They were led by Loy Henderson, the head of the Near East Division after mid-1945, who had served in eastern Europe for most of his career before becoming chief of the American legation in Iraq in 1944. Henderson was deeply anticommunist and believed that a Jewish state would impair American relations with the Arab world as well as open the area to the Russians. In this, he shared the unanimous view of Arabists and other officials assigned to the area. Other key State Department officials against Jewish statehood included Robert Lovett, Marshall's undersecretary; George Kennan, head of the policy planning staff; and Dean Rusk, head of the new office for handling the United Nations.

The diplomats were not alone in their opposition. The first secretary of defense, James Forrestal, strongly opposed a Jewish state because of the strategic location of the area and its oil; he believed the development could only aid the Russians. The vehemence of his position on Palestine increased an estrangement from the president that led to his resignation in early 1949 (later that year he committed suicide). In addition, Admiral William Leahy—Roosevelt's holdover adviser at the White House—adamantly opposed Zionist objectives. The intelligence agencies joined in the opposition of the State and Defense Departments, echoing their belief that the Jews could never hold out against the larger and better-equipped Arab forces in case of war.

The Zionists were not entirely without backing within the executive branch. There were two key pro-Zionist figures in the White House, Clark Clifford and David Niles; and throughout the bureaucracy, there were sympathetic individuals prepared to communicate important information to these officials. Niles held the position of Special Assistant to the President for Minority Affairs, but he seems to have dealt only with the Jews. Strongly committed to the Zionist cause, he was not only prepared to argue with the president in favor of a Jewish state but to counter the effects of the bureaucracy.[2] Special Counsel Clark Clifford, whose influence ranged broadly over foreign as well as domestic affairs, intervened heavily at key moments in 1948 on the Zionists' behalf.[3] Other figures who helped the Zionists included Benjamin Cohen, the counsel of the State Department; General John Hilldring, an official who sought to solve the European refugee problem by finding a home for the displaced persons; and Judge Samuel Rosenman, both before and after he left the White House Staff. The Zionists benefited frequently from the intervention of key outsiders, including the Zionist leader Chaim Weizmann, whom Truman respected as a grand historical figure; and Eddie Jacobson, his old haberdashery partner. Support was also given by illustrious figures of the time such as Eleanor Roosevelt and Reinhold Niebuhr, and Jewish leaders such as Rabbi Stephen S. Wise of the American Jewish Congress.

Despite a nearly united bureaucracy, the passion and numbers of Zionist activists weighed heavily in favor of their cause. They were intensely involved with Congress, the press, and both political parties. Many Democrats feared that administration positions against the Zionists would undermine the party in the elections of 1946 and especially the presidential election of 1948. Although public opinion was not as solidly pro-Zionist as it would be after the establishment of the state of Israel (many of the undecided became sympathetic to Israel only after independence), public rallies for the Zionist cause attested to its strength. Public opinion polls showed that Zionist backing was broad and far stronger than the almost nonexistent support for the Arabs.[4]

Arab supporters were present in the public arena and sometimes were powerful, but they were not effective politically. Oil company spokesmen, especially James Terry Duce of Aramco, vehemently opposed a Jewish state as did traditional centers of pro-Arab sentiment. These included former missionaries, scholars, individuals with business experience in the Arab world. During the Truman era, Arab sympathizers were also aided by the British government—especially its embassy and consulates in the United States, as London's conflict with the Jews of Palestine grew. The vocal Arab embassies often impressed State Department people by appearing en bloc. Until 1949, however, there was no Israeli embassy in Washington. The Zionists were represented only by Jewish groups and the Jewish Agency representative in Washington—Eliahu Epstein, who later became Israel's first ambassador to the United States.

The Zionists were also hindered by divisions in the Jewish community, which were later to diminish. State Department officials frequently cited the anti-Zionist American Council for Judaism or even the neutral American Jewish Committee in their contention that Jews were not united, by 1946, behind the Zionist cause. Public opinion polls suggested, however, that 80 percent of the American Jewish community did support a Jewish state in Palestine.[5]

Truman's Personal Stance

Truman was open to outside pressures, more from a sense of loyalty to personal friends and trusted aides than from a desire to manipulate domestic politics. He has been quoted as explaining to a group of diplomats in 1945, "I'm sorry, gentlemen, but I have to answer to hundreds of thousands who are anxious for the success of Zionism; I do not have hundreds of thousands of Arabs among my constituents," but this comment, if indeed it was made, was unusual.[6] The president repeatedly told the State Department not to consider "political factors" in deciding Palestine policy. Instances of similar positions dominate the record. For example, in early 1948, with pressure mounting, he told a high-ranking figure in the Democratic National Committee that he excluded politics from consideration of the Palestine question, and he said as much in a similar letter to a New York congressman in May.[7]

Truman was confronted with a very complex situation on a foreign policy issue that he did not view as central to his concerns. He was caught between an articulate public position that was supported by most of the Congress and some key White House staff and opposed by all but a few in the national security bureaucracy. The low priority given the Palestinian issue and the strong divisions within the government and American political system account for the inconsistency of the Truman administration in its Palestinian policy. At critical points, individuals who favored the Zionists and were respected by the president outweighed the efforts of cabinet officials and the bureaucracy. Truman's belief in regular channels helped defeat the Zionists and their allies in many specific battles, but his openness to information aided them at key junctures.

On the regional level, the administration's policy was a holding action. Support for Jewish statehood conflicted with the aim of maintaining solid relations with Arab regimes, which partly explains why support for a Jewish state came so slowly. Because the Arabs were not seen as directly involved with the Cold War or central to American foreign policy, however, those supporting closer American ties with them were at a basic disadvantage. Given the low global priority, Truman felt free to listen to various views. This openness allowed lobbies from within and without the executive branch to influence the president, and explains his inconsistency as he was persuaded first by one side and then the other.

Truman could be swayed in both directions because his own attitudes were so balanced. He had long been an avid reader of history and believed that he understood the plight of the Jews. His one major concern about Palestine— the Jewish refugees—was an issue that had developed in the European theater and, like the Marshall Plan, was related to European rehabilitation after the Second World War. But he did not believe that a Jewish state was necessary to rehabilitate the refugees. Truman suggested both publicly and privately that he was not about to send 500,000 American troops to create it. He supported Jewish statehood, and then unenthusiastically, only when there seemed no other way to achieve Jewish immigration into Palestine and when a Jewish state appeared to have been accomplished by the Jews themselves with no American assistance. If Congress had accepted liberalized immigration laws more rapidly, the president would have been satisfied to admit many refugees to the United States.[8] (He was, therefore, personally stung when the British Foreign Minister, Ernest Bevin, in June 1946, accused the Americans of agitating for Jewish immigration into Palestine because "they did not want too many of them in New York.")[9] Despite later mythology, Truman was no advocate of a Jewish state in Palestine before Israel came into existence.

Indeed, he frequently resented the entire matter. There are many records of his frustration at spending so much time on what he regarded as a peripheral matter. According to the diaries of Henry Wallace, at a period of particular pressure he exclaimed at a cabinet meeting in mid-1946, "If Jesus Christ couldn't satisfy them here on earth, how the hell am I supposed to?" He added later, "I have no use for them and I don't care what happens to them."[10] Similarly, in the summer of 1947 he responded to a telegram from Rabbi Wise with the tart remark, "There seem to be two sides to this question. I am finding it rather difficult to decide which one is right and a great many other people in the country are beginning to feel just as I do."[11] Truman was often bitter about Zionist pressures on him. Several months earlier he had written to the Bronx Democratic leader, Ed Flynn, "I have done my best to get [100,000 Jews into Palestine] but I don't believe there is any possible way of pleasing our Jewish friends."[12]

As a force outside the executive branch and the usual foreign policy channels, the Jews were reduced to the role of a special interest. Truman often viewed them and their congressional allies as pleaders of a cause distinct from the national interest. Yet the plight of the refugees always engaged his sympathy. Henry Wallace relates that when James Forrestal argued what was happening in Palestine was crucial to the American economy, Truman commented: "I don't care about the oil, I want to do what's right."[13]

Despite Truman's efforts to temporize and please everyone, neither the Arabs nor the Jews were satisfied with American policy. The Zionists gained limited American support for partition and immediate recognition of the Jewish state, but little diplomatic backing and no arms. The Arabs were fundamentally disappointed, but they and their supporters consistently foiled Zionist efforts to establish a coherent American policy favoring a Jewish state in Palestine.

Early Policy Developments

With the end of the Second World War, both the Arabs and Zionists had become more impatient; both wanted a state of their own—on the same territory. The Arabs argued that Palestine was their territory, that the Jews were only a minority, and that the British should turn the League of Nations mandate under which they administered the area over to an independent and sovereign Arab state of Palestine. For the Jews the situation was filled with special irony and pressure; one of the central tenets of Zionism was to create a haven for Jewish brethren—especially those suffering from oppression. The Jewish people had just suffered the destruction of six million, a third of their number worldwide, during a period when the British had closed the gates of Palestine to all but 15,000 a year—and even that number seemed soon to be diminished.

British policy for over a decade had sought to placate the Arabs in order to maintain bases, influence, and diplomatic friendship in the area. The new Labour government elected as the war ended was pledged to support Zionist aims, but it intensified the pro-Arab tilt on Downing Street. As the Zionists organized a program of illegal immigration, British policy continued to harden. The right wing of the Jews, whose main group was led by the former Polish soldier, Menachem Begin, began guerrilla operations against British installations and troops. In a pattern that would become familiar in the post-war world from Vietnam to Kenya, the colonial power alienated the moderates as it tried to counter the radicals. The mainstream Jewish population under David Ben Gurion turned against the British attempt to quell the uprising and London's firm stand against Jewish immigration and autonomy.

When Roosevelt died and Truman assumed office in April 1945, the impending explosion in Palestine was only beginning. The United States' immediate problem was dealing with the holocaust survivors who were being assembled in displaced persons' camps—many of which were under American military control. State Department policy favored returning all refugees to their original homes, but after the suffering they had endured, few European Jews were interested. Most sought to go to Palestine. Truman as a senator had said that the time to help the Jews with their Palestinian homeland was after the war. "We want to help the Jews," he wrote at one point, but "we cannot do it at the expense of our military maneuvers."[14] With the end of the war, helping the Jews meant addressing the refugee question.

In June 1945 the new president adopted a suggestion by David Niles and asked Earl G. Harrison, dean of the University of Pennsylvania Law School, to go to Europe to investigate the condition of the refugees.[15] Harrison's report—delivered secretly in August and later released to the public—created a storm by criticizing conditions in the camps, confirming the refugees' desire to go to Palestine, and recommending that 100,000 Jews be admitted immediately.[16] The issue of Jewish refugees in Germany had brought the United States into the Palestine question for the first time. Truman adopted the suggestion regarding the 100,000 and conveyed it officially to the British government.[17]

Here—almost by accident and without any clear direction—Truman began to enmesh the United States in the Palestine question. In a pattern repeated throughout the Truman era, no sooner had the Zionists achieved a victory than their opponents set out to reverse it. The British had no intention of acquiescing to Truman's request based on the Harrison report and thereby alienating the

Arab world. They countered with a delaying tactic by recommending an Anglo-American Committee of Inquiry. Despite the opposition of Zionist groups and many Democratic party officials, the president accepted this recommendation with State Department blessings, for it allowed him to avoid confronting the issue directly.[18]

The committee, consisting of six members from each country, spent the next several months traveling to Europe and Palestine. It finally produced a report in April 1946. The document adopted the idea of admitting 100,000 refugees and also called for easing land restrictions on Jews in Palestine originally promulgated in the 1939 White Paper. It also recommended a U.N. trusteeship leading eventually to a binational state composed of Arabs and Jews. Truman reacted favorably and particularly singled out the recommendation on the 100,000 refugees, which he passed along to the British government. London responded angrily to this suggestion, maintaining that the report should be taken as a whole. The Zionists accepted it unenthusiastically; and the Arabs were virulently opposed, demanding an independent Arab state in Palestine. The State Department and its bureaucratic allies sympathized with British insistence that the entire report be taken as a basis for discussion. Truman liked the idea of a binational state, but as he later commented, "The report showed me what to do, but not how to do it."[19] At all costs he wished to avoid American responsibility, politically or militarily, for the future of Palestine, although he did agree to finance the transportation of Jews from Europe.

With this attitude he accepted a British suggestion that an American cabinet committee meet with their English counterparts in London to evaluate the Anglo-American Committee of Inquiry. This tactic (the new committee was called the Morrison-Grady committee after its British and American chairmen) was a further example in the Truman era of one group stealing the other's thunder. The Anglo-American committee was hardly Zionist but it was prepared to respond to the Zionist demands. The American bureaucrats sent to London were more receptive to the opinions of diplomats and military officials in both countries, where there was a growing fear of potential Russian influence in the Moslem world should the Palestine controversy further exacerbate relations with the Arab regimes.

The individuals sent were not knowledgeable about Palestine. They quickly swallowed an old English idea for cantonization of the country. Although the Jews and Arabs were to be given semiautonomous provinces in specific areas, the plan produced by the Morrison-Grady committee actually would increase British authority in Palestine and give the Jews less control than they already had. As a consolation to the Zionists and in order to gain the president's backing, the committee appended the recommendation that 100,000 Jews were to be admitted to Palestine when Jews *as well as* Arabs accepted the plan.

The president did not completely understand the implications of the report but his policy advisers in the State Department were supportive. Since the plan did grant immigration to the 100,000, he was at first inclined to accept it and was incensed when the Zionists opposed the idea. A series of strained meetings between Zionist supporters (including several congressmen) and the president followed when details of the report were leaked to the press. At one meeting, for example, Truman complained that he was tired of pleas from special interests and wanted to hear people concerned about defending American interests for a change. "I'm not a New Yorker. All these people are pleading for a special interest. I'm an American."[20] Truman's interest focused on the refugee rather than the Jewish sovereignty question; hence the effectiveness of the bureaucratic maneuver to reverse the intent of the Anglo-American Committee by substituting the recommendations of a cabinet committee consisting of British and American officials.

In this tense atmosphere, Niles told Zionist leaders they should quickly produce an acceptable counterplan of their own. He also suggested to the president that perhaps the American members of the Committee of Inquiry should be asked to comment on the Morrison-Grady Plan. Both suggestions were followed, and the tide turned in mid-August. The Zionist Executive had been in session in Paris with Ben Gurion attending. (He was temporarily exiled from Palestine as the British were imprisoning Jewish leaders there in response to growing Jewish terrorism.) The Executive produced a compromise proposal, which Nahum Goldmann, the head of the U.S. section of the Jewish Agency, brought to Washington. Previously, the Zionists had claimed all of Palestine from the Jordan River to the Mediterranean for a Jewish state. Although the decision was controversial within the movement, in response to Morrison-Grady, the Zionist leaders meeting in Paris accepted the principle of partition into two states—one Jewish and one Arab.[21]

Meanwhile, the American members of the original Anglo-American Committee of Inquiry reacted angrily to the Morrison-Grady Plan; even the members unsympathetic to Zionist aims believed the bureaucratic group had gone beyond its jurisdiction in producing a new program for Palestine. The combination of this reaction to the Morrison-Grady Plan, obvious public and Congressional disapproval encouraged by the Zionists and their allies, Arab opposition to the plan because it did not advocate an independent Arab Palestinian state, and the favorable reaction in the White House to the idea of partition led Truman to reject the Morrison-Grady Plan. In using the 100,000 as bait, the opponents of Jewish statehood had failed to ensnare the Zionists with a resolution falling short of Jewish sovereignty in Palestine. The Zionists had produced an idea that seemed reasonable to a large number of interested American intellectuals, politicians, church leaders, and journalists. It also increased Jewish support for a Jewish state.

The events of the next two years flowed from this confrontation of August 1946, but the Zionist victory proved hollow. They had defeated British and American diplomats, but they still had nothing positive to show for their arduous activities. The Zionist switch to partition after the president's flirtation with Morrison-Grady showed that the White House had as much if not more influence on the Zionists than they had on the president. Political pressure was working in both directions.

With the failure of Morrison-Grady, the British sought meetings with Arabs and Jews in London in fall and winter 1946–1947. But the Jews did not attend because of poor British-Jewish relations in Palestine and British refusal to discuss partition. The Arabs continued to call for an Arab Palestine—their consistent position for a generation. The killing of British soldiers in Palestine was making the Jewish cause less popular in England, but in the United States the idea of partition was well-received and added to Zionist support.[22] As the congressional elections approached, congressmen and Democratic party leaders pressed Truman to make a statement, because one by Governor Dewey of New York was anticipated imminently.

On Yom Kippur in early October, Truman reiterated his support for the entry of 100,000 Jewish refugees into Palestine and acknowledged that the American public could accept partition. The effect of public pressure was clear in the timing of this statement. Although many suggested that the president had now announced himself in favoring a Jewish state, he had simply recognized the growing public acceptance of partition. He even called for a "bridging" of the gap between Morrison-Grady and partition. Governor Dewey, who was consistently more pro-Zionist in his pronouncements than Truman, issued his statement as expected and called for the admission of several hundred thousand refugees into Palestine.[23]

Truman's vacillation was drawing pressure from both sides—at home and abroad. First, he had called for the Harrison report and agreed with the Zionists in adopting as his own the demand for 100,000 surviving Jews to enter Palestine. Then, he accepted the British delaying tactic of an Anglo-American committee, which also featured the admission of 100,000 refugees into Palestine. Truman further confounded London by focusing on this recommendation, ignoring the qualifications. The British, in turn, pressed Morrison-Grady, but the Zionists gained public visibility with a counterplan of their own that scaled down their call for a Jewish state occupying all Palestine. The resulting favorable reaction to the idea of partition and the approaching congressional elections gained them a favorable-sounding presidential statement. This did not change the situation in Palestine, however, where severe limits on Jewish immigration continued, illegal and over-crowded Jewish ships were being captured and turned back by the British, and British-Jewish and Jewish-Arab tensions within the mandate structure intensified.

In fall 1946, while the British were conducting talks with the two sides in

London, the bureaucrats had again taken over American policy. Truman was relieved to avoid involvement, for he consistently remained apart and tried not to pressure London to avoid strains in the evolving Cold War alliance with Europe against the U.S.S.R.

Although the Zionists were temporarily stymied, their pressures continued. Frustration reigned on all sides in the United States. The president's private remarks of the time reflect his mood. His correspondence is filled with contradictory observations on the difficulties of pleasing the Jews, the need to provide a haven for the displaced persons, the tendency of underdogs to become arrogant after achieving power, and the need to get the refugees to Palestine in order to end the financial burden of feeding them. After almost a year and a half of working on the Palestine problem, he felt no nearer a solution than when he began.[24]

The U.N. and Partition

The British continued to meet separately with Zionist and Arab representatives in London in early 1947. During this period the Truman administration informed London privately that while it might decide to support partition, it would not guarantee this solution by armed force despite continued Arab opposition.[25]

When the talks in London broke down, a frustrated Bevin announced that the entire Palestine question would be turned over to the U.N. He then proceeded to blame American interference and domestic politics for the failure. Instead of escalating Anglo-American tensions over the matter, Truman resolved to use the dispute as a model for future U.N. intervention in international conflicts. He would support any resolution the General Assembly endorsed *as long as it was enforceable*. Once again, American policy waited on events during spring and summer 1947 as the U.N. Special Committee on Palestine (UNSCOP), of which the United States was not a member, retraced the path that British investigating commissions had followed for almost thirty years. The Zionists and their supporters bombarded the White House with letters and telegrams to seek explicit American backing of a Jewish state within Palestine, hoping to influence UNSCOP.

The president would not take a stand until UNSCOP had made its recommendations, which it did at the end of August. The committee unanimously rejected an Arab state in all of Palestine. A minority supported a federation which would give the Arabs veto power over Jewish objectives. The majority, however, proposed partitioning the country into two states—one Arab and one Jewish, a ten-year economic union between the two parts, and the internationalization of all Jerusalem. The Arab states continued to demand sovereignty over all of Palestine, and their American supporters urged opposition to UN-

SCOP. The Zionists disliked the UNSCOP solution for Jerusalem and the awkwardness of the proposed borders; they would also have preferred more territory for their state. Sensing, however, that a great historical opportunity had arrived, they accepted the plan. Their supporters in the United States were also strongly in favor.

The arguments swirling around Truman were fierce. Those opposing partition maintained, first, that a Jewish state would seriously—perhaps permanently—damage American relations with the Arabs, and the Moslem world as well. They claimed a cooling of the former American friendship with the Arabs had already set in. For this they blamed the Zionists. Second, they believed that the U.S. could not afford to alienate the Arabs because Europe depended on their oil, which was essential for the Marshall Plan; because American firms—especially oil companies—active in the area would be hurt; and because the U.S. needed military access to the region and the base at Dharan in Saudi Arabia. Secretary of Defense Forrestal was particularly concerned that an American energy crisis was pending; he once said, if a Jewish state comes into existence, "American motorcar companies would have to design a four-cylinder motorcar. . . ."[26] Third, opponents said that Arab opposition made partition unworkable and, if it were instituted, the Palestine problem would become a permanent feature of international politics. In the meantime, the United States would have to contribute militarily and financially. Fourth, they held that the idea of a Jewish state was contradictory to the U.N. Charter and American principles of self-determination; it would also increase tensions between Jews and Gentiles in the United States. Fifth, they argued that partition would lead to the growth of extremism in the Arab world. Sixth, the Russians would be aided by the chaos in Palestine that partition was sure to precipitate.[27] Some thought that the ensuing conflict would push the Arabs toward Russia. Others assumed that the new Jewish state would become a Soviet ally. In short, said the pro-Arab partisans and bureaucrats, give the moderate Arabs and Jews time to find common ground. The diplomats had in mind some form of trusteeship, a back-up position long held within the State Department should the mandate fail.

The pro-Zionist position was simpler and more forceful. Partition was equitable. It offered each side a state; it protected the holy sites of Jerusalem for members of all religions, and it provided a haven for the refugees in Europe as well. Many supporters of a Jewish state in the Middle East also maintained that it would be a bastion of democracy in the area and would therefore enhance America's new world role.[28] By supporting partition, Americans could be humanitarian, moral, and realistic at once. Further, an independent neutral body of the United Nations had produced the report. If the United Nations were to have a chance of success, its positions should be taken seriously. This argument had a powerful effect on Truman; for over two years he had believed that the

United Nations should resolve the Palestine issue.[29] How could the United States now reject the U.N. proposal?

An event in August had also affected public opinion in the Zionists' favor. When the Exodus, an overcrowded, illegal immigrant ship, tried to get to Palestine, the British discovered it and, falling into a political trap, sent it back to France. The passengers refused to disembark. The British retaliated by sending the Exodus to Germany; news coverage of this ironic voyage sealed public support for partition in America. In this atmosphere, together with the usual communications from congressmen and Jewish and labor leaders, it was not surprising that the administration supported the UNSCOP proposals.

It did so, however, in a subdued manner. The decision was announced by Herschel Johnson, the American delegate to the United Nations' ad hoc committee reviewing the UNSCOP report. When approving the statement, the president privately cautioned his advisors that any American aid on the plan was to be channeled through the U.N. to limit U.S. involvement.[30] To the amazement of most Washington experts, the Russians also supported partition, thereby placing themselves on the side of the Zionists. For the first time at the U.N., the United States and the Soviet Union were potentially on the same side against the British, despite the emerging Cold War. Suddenly, the two superpowers seemed to be competing for the Zionists' favor. The demands of the Jewish-Arab conflict in Palestine diverged from the administration's other global and regional exigencies.

In the State Department's view, American policy toward Palestine was deteriorating. Earlier in the year Secretary of State Marshall had been preoccupied with the Truman Doctrine and the Marshall Plan, both more central to the administration's concerns. Meanwhile, the conduct of American Palestine policy had been in the hands of Undersecretary Lovett, NEA leader Henderson, and the Office of Special Political Affairs under Dean Rusk. In May the Russian representative at the U.N. had hinted that his government might indeed consider partition if a binational state proved unworkable. This statement was not taken seriously. It was assumed that the Kremlin had decided to bargain for greater leverage with the Arabs—a classic case of bureaucratic persistence of mind set despite contradicting evidence. Meanwhile, NEA had been preparing different versions of a trusteeship plan but these ideas had, at least temporarily, been overtaken by events. The president could hardly propound them in the political atmosphere of the period.[31] Even Secretary of State Marshall—returning to the Palestine question at the United Nations in September—favored careful support of partition, although he still doubted that the plan would prove enforceable.[32] When Henderson and Wadsworth—two known opponents of partition—were appointed to advise Herschel Johnson, Niles persuaded Truman to appoint General John Hilldring—a known supporter of a Jewish state—in a similar capacity. The latter appointment was valuable to the Zionist position throughout the fall. The White House through Niles used Hilldring to circumvent the State Department and convey information directly to the U.N. delegation in New York.[33]

The State Department officials were now in something of a quandary. They fervently believed that the policy favoring partition would seriously damage American interests in the Middle East. Yet the public clearly backed partition and, after the UNSCOP report, opposing the policy forthrightly would mean compromising the U.N. itself. Therefore, the bureaucrats set about to undermine support for partition by indirect moves that would seem consistent with official American policy. During the ensuing battles, the influence of bureaucrats over the implementation (and, to a lesser extent, the formulation) of policy was dramatically demonstrated.

NEA first suggested that the United States recommend transferring the Negev, the southern desert area of Palestine sparsely inhabited by Bedouin, to the Arab Palestinian state. They based this proposal on the Negev's Arab population and on the desirability of creating a land bridge between the Arab states of North Africa through the Sinai and the Arabs of the Northeast through Jordan. As the diplomats well knew, this proposal would tell other United Nations delegations that American support for partition was lukewarm. To counter this proposal, the Zionists gained, with the help of the sympathetic British ambassador, a secret meeting for Chaim Weizmann with Truman on 19 November, the very day that the United States delegation was scheduled to present its recommendation on the Negev.[34] Weizmann so filled Truman with enthusiasm about the Jews developing the Negev and a southern port on the Gulf of Aqaba as an outlet to East Africa and Asia that the president phoned General Hilldring as a key meeting was about to begin. The general expressed his own doubts about American policy. In response Truman did not contradict State Department instructions but indicated that the United States should not make the proposal if it was alone in supporting the position. A confused Johnson and Hilldring then simply refrained from taking any stand at all and the idea was dropped. When the undersecretary of state complained to the president, Truman denied trying to interfere with the policy process.[35]

Truman continued to hope that somehow the United Nations would produce a fair resolution without involving either the president or the United States government. And yet the battle was so fierce even within America that often only the president could serve as arbiter. As suggested by the Negev incident, Truman was reluctant to play even this role, preferring instead to offer minimal tactical satisfactions to both sides without his being personally committed. This approach became more difficult as the vote on partition neared. As it did, events overcame any pretense of rational decision-making.

The State Department entourage again tried to reverse American support for partition in a memorandum from Henderson that Lovett read to

Truman. Playing on Truman's desire to remain uninvolved, the memo urged successfully that the president should restrain American lobbying on behalf of the plan. As Lovett reported Truman's instructions, "we were in no sense of the word to coerce other Delegations to follow our lead" in voting for partition.[36] The president had a somewhat naïve idea that international justice should run its course through the U.N. debate. The State Department, in contrast, hoped that American aloofness would either help defeat the resolution or limit Arab resentment against Washington, since the United States often lobbied in favor of issues it regarded as crucial.

The Zionists, on the other hand, had been urging a more active American role for weeks. As Truman noted in his memoirs, "some [extreme Zionist leaders] were even suggesting that we pressure sovereign nations into favorable votes in the General Assembly."[37]

On 25 November 1947, the Ad Hoc Committee approved the partition report one vote short of the two-thirds necessary for passage in the General Assembly. A mad scramble now broke out as both the Jews and Arabs intensified their efforts to influence votes through lobbying, bribing, even threatening delegates in New York and their governments back home.[38] The key to the battle was the position of the American government. In this struggle—which lasted four days until the final vote on the twenty-ninth—four distinct American policies emerged.

There was first the official policy of restraint enunciated by the president to the State Department and practiced by key State Department officials and Secretary of Defense Forrestal, who tried to convince the Democratic party chairman that he should stop linking Palestine with domestic politics.[39]

The second group represented White House officials such as Clark Clifford and the president's press secretary, Charlie Ross, who believed that the Truman administration would be faulted at home if partition failed. These officials lobbied for the plan by contacting representatives of wavering states and Americans with influence in the capitals of pivotal delegations.[40] If the president knew about the activities of these officials, he failed to stop them. Perhaps he assumed that his own aides would not "coerce" the delegations of other nations.

The third course was taken by David Niles, whose modus operandi seems to have been to act for the president as long as Truman had not ordered him against a particular action. In the crucial days before the final vote, he solicited favorable positions from other countries and was prepared to use the arm-twisting tactics that the president had abjured. In the name of the president, he also instructed specific officials (especially Herschel Johnson) to use such tactics if necessary. He encouraged Americans with high-level contacts in foreign capitals to use their leverage. Truman does not seem to have known precisely what Niles was doing.[41]

Finally, Zionist supporters were independently contacting foreign officials and prominent Americans who might influence other governments. These included Zionist leaders, congressmen, two Supreme Court justices, several members of the U.N. delegation, and prominent businessmen. These contacts angered Truman and made him feel that his instructions had been violated.

These contradictory activities resulted in a circus atmosphere and an inconsistent policy. The State Department assured Arab representatives that pressure tactics would not be used, but such methods were employed by other officials and private citizens over whom the State Department had no control. Despite the confusion in U.S. ranks, partition finally passed the General Assembly by a vote of 33–13—aided by the UNSCOP report, Soviet-American consensus, and general revulsion at the Holocaust.[42]

Truman complained to Lovett about press reports that individual Americans had exerted pressure for partition, but he was not known to have been unhappy when he was given the credit for passage by many journalists.[43] The president had been prepared to accept a favorable vote but not to take specific actions to achieve it.[44]

The State Department's Response to Partition

Even before the partition resolution passed, a proposed embargo on arms to the Middle East emerged through State Department channels. Because the Zionists were temporarily out of his favor and the issue seemed essentially bureaucratic, the president readily gave his approval to an embargo. Truman was told by the Near East division that sending arms would make war more likely, resulting in problems for American policy as Arabs and Jews killed one another and blamed the United States.[45] In practice, however, the embargo hurt only one side—the Jews. The Arab countries were gaining ample ammunition and equipment from the British.[46] From December onward the Zionists sought desperately to reverse the embargo, but the only U.S. arms sent on behalf of the Jews were secret supplies transmitted illegally by pro-Jewish partisans.[47]

The partition resolution escalated conflict in Palestine itself. Sporadic violence erupted, accompanied by protest attacks against American installations in Lebanon and Syria. Arabs began leaving Palestine immediately—first the aristocracy, later the peasants. "Volunteers" from the surrounding Arab countries began infiltrating the country as the British announced an early departure for 15 May and openly connived with the Arab side. Direct hostilities between Jews and Arabs began to occur, and until late March it appeared that the Arabs would easily win the probable war.

After the vote on the partition resolution, the president was tired of the issue and of pressure from Zionists—especially from the pro-Taft Republican leader, the fiery Rabbi Abba Hillel Silver. At one point the Zionists had even approached his mother and sister.[48] Enough was enough; he would deal no more with private pressures. He would concentrate on foreign policy issues more central to the national security. The pressure to gain a favorable U.N. partition vote had used up the Zionists' political capital with the president.

Unlike Truman, the bureaucracy saw that the partition resolution was just another battle, not the end of conflict. There was still no clear way to enforce the U.N. partition plan for Palestine. The Security Council would have to set out specific steps; British skepticism and Arab opposition would have to be overcome. Otherwise, the Arabs might attack and it was generally assumed—certainly in Washington—that the Jews could not successfully defend themselves. Then what? In January the Jewish Agency asked the U.N. for an international police force to implement partition. The entire executive branch and both its diplomatic and military community were opposed to the use of American troops: the U.S. was demobilizing; the funds were not available; American forces were already stretched thin from the developing Cold War with the Soviet Union; the Arabs would be permanently alienated and the Marshall Plan threatened. But so soon after the Holocaust, how could the Jewish residents of Palestine be left to a massacre? Could the United States sit idly by if the Soviets offered troops on their behalf? What if troops from both countries were authorized under a United Nations framework? Truman would favor using U.S. troops in Palestine only if that became necessary as part of a U.N. force.[49] But if the Russians were involved, their activity might lead to Moscow's presence in the area, threatening vital American interests throughout the region.[50]

The State Department was prepared with answers for these dilemmas. It held that partition could not be enforced, and, debatably, that the Security Council was not empowered to implement the General Assembly decision on Jewish and Arab states in Palestine (a position announced by Ambassador Austin in a speech to the U.N. Security Council 24 February 1948).

But if not partition, what? For years the department had an answer to that question—trusteeship. By early 1948 some form of temporary U.N. control over Palestine seemed a good interim solution. Officials at State preferred as an ultimate resolution some binational state that would allow self-expression to the Arab majority while also protecting minority Jewish rights.[51] Yet trusteeship could be sold as a step toward partition with the argument that the Jews could not win the seemingly inevitable military confrontation with the Arab states. The Jews "must be saved in spite of themselves," to borrow a phrase from the 1970s. Conveniently, the Russians were not members of the U.N. Trusteeship Council and so could not participate in a trusteeship, whereas they could become involved if the Security Council implemented partition.[52] Seemingly every quandary posed by partition could be resolved through trusteeship. As early as mid-January, when George Wadsworth, the American ambassador to Iraq, met with the president, he presented a memorandum arguing that a U.N.

trusteeship should be established over Palestine. According to Wadsworth, the president told him that "he himself saw alike with the State Department" and that previous efforts to reach an agreement had been aborted by "British bull-headedness" and "American Jews."[53]

Global concerns in early 1948 reinforced the trusteeship argument. Truman was occupied elsewhere, especially in the crucial period from late February to early March: the Czech coup, Stalin's pressures on Finland, General Clay's warning that war with the Soviet Union might be imminent, the worsening Berlin situation. In response, the president spoke before Congress calling for Universal Military Training, the restoration of Selective Service, and the enactment of the European Recovery Program. The administration also secretly resolved to order a limited mobilization if the Italian Communists won the vote scheduled for April and to intervene militarily if the communists sought to take over by force.[54]

The deepening confrontation with the Soviets in Europe strengthened the bureaucracy's arguments that partition was obviously unworkable. The State Department feared a worsening of Arab-American relations; the military feared it would be called upon to send troops; the CIA was convinced the Jews would lose. All were worried about the Russians and about oil. Trusteeship would impose an extended ceasefire while tempers cooled and a new compromise was sought.[55]

There was an alternative view—namely, that moves toward a Jewish state had proceeded too far to be turned back; that the Jews in Palestine and America would react with horror to the proposed trusteeship, thereby helping to undermine it; that the Arabs would not accept it; and that the idea would be seen by other U.N. member states as an American betrayal of its commitment to the UNSCOP report. Proponents of this view charged that turning back on partition represented capitulation to an Arab threat of force; they believed that the Arab states would continue selling oil to the United States in any event because "the Arabs need us more than we need them."[56] In short, they said, the United States should embrace partition, end the arms embargo, and oppose the Russians in the Middle East through support for the Zionists. If the Jews were allowed to buy their own arms, they could fight for themselves and take the United States off the hook. The leaders of the national security bureaucracy dealing with the issue—Marshall, Lovett, Forrestal, Henderson, Kennan, Rusk—and their staffs saw this position as folly. Those left to propound it, like Clifford and White House aide Max Lowenthal, had other major responsibilities, especially on domestic affairs, and were not regular foreign policy decision makers.

There had been other cases in which the State Department's major proposals on Palestine were questioned by Jews: Morrison-Grady, assignment of the Negev to the Arabs, restraint on lobbying for partition in the General Assembly. In each case there had been opportunity for other officials to enter the policy process (Niles, Clifford, Hilldring), to make opposing arguments, and to persuade the president.

As the State Department pressed in early 1948 for a new policy of trusteeship, five factors limited the influence of officials who favored partition: (1) Truman's preoccupation with foreign policy matters he viewed as more pressing; (2) the president's deep annoyance with the Zionists; (3) the personal involvement of Secretary Marshall; (4) a heart ailment suffered by Niles that kept him out of the office for several critical weeks until late March; (5) the president's approval, while he was vacationing in the Virgin Islands in late February, of key documents supporting trusteeship.

The day after the president returned from his vacation, the State Department sent him an outline of a proposed statement by Austin favoring a temporary trusteeship. Immediately, Clifford presented two papers to Truman favoring an intensified American effort for partition.[57] On the day the second paper was presented (8 March), Truman met with Marshall and Lovett. In that conversation the president *orally* approved the trusteeship option as an alternative if the Security Council could not agree on implementing partition.[58] As later events were to indicate, the president expected that he would be informed if and when the announcement would be made, while it never occurred to Marshall and Lovett that further checks with the president were necessary. Marshall immediately informed Austin that the president had approved the new policy statement "for use if and when necessary."[59] Due to the dynamics at the U.N., the date of 19 March was later set for arranging the new policy.[60]

In those ten days the influences on Truman began to change, tempering his support for the trusteeship option. Clifford strongly presented support for partition, citing legitimate American national security interests. The Zionists were aware of the negative trend in American policy, but when they sought to exercise influence they found the White House door closed, for in early 1948 Truman refused to see anyone representing them. The logical next step was to work through Chaim Weizmann, who had established a special rapport with Truman. Therefore, as Weizmann prepared to leave London for Palestine, the American Zionist leadership implored him to return to the United States. When he arrived in early March, Truman refused to see him.

In desperation, Zionist supporters began to explore innovative routes of access to the president. A group of B'nai B'rith leaders contacted Eddie Jacobson, Truman's old haberdashery partner, who then tried to arrange a meeting between Weizmann and the president. Jacobson's task was not easy, given the president's deep-seated resentment of pressures, but after a heated meeting he was finally able to persuade Truman to see Weizmann. The president met the aging Zionist leader secretly at the White House on 18 March. Weizmann appealed again for Truman's support and the President reiterated his backing of partition as long as the United Nations did not approve a temporary trustee-ship.[61]

Just as the State Department had no knowledge of this meeting, so Truman did not know that his U.N. ambassador was to make a speech at the Security Council on the next day, calling for a special session of the General Assembly to suspend its decision on partition and create a temporary trusteeship in Palestine when the British departed on 15 May. Zionists and their supporters reacted with unmitigated fury to this statement and many U.N. delegates who had backed the UNSCOP report were amazed. No one, however, was more stunned than Truman when he picked up his newspaper the following morning and read for the first time about the speech. Now the president's ire was turned on the antipartition bureaucrats just as he had been disgusted with the proparti-tion Zionists for the previous several months. Marshall and Lovett, whom he admired and trusted, happened to be out of town, so it was easier for the presi-dent to blame "the third and fourth levels of the State Department."[62] Clifford conducted an investigation, but since the president had approved the general outline of the policy it was difficult to assess blame.[63] Contrary to the letter of Truman's instructions, Austin's speech had been delivered before the Security Council had actually voted to reject enforcing partition. But it was made after the majority of the Council voiced opposition to the U.N. implementing parti-tion, so the spirit of Truman's instructions had been observed.[64] The president sent a secret message of reassurance to Weizmann through former White House official Judge Samuel Rosenman. A month later he asked Rosenman to tell Weizmann that if trusteeship was not adopted by the General Assembly, he would recognize the Jewish state when it was established. (The jubilant Weizmann kept the secret, but because of this message, in the chaotic days of early May 1948, when several Zionist leaders hesitated, the usually moderate Weizmann insisted that the Jewish state must not be delayed.)[65]

Yet, because his public ratings were already low, Truman did not reverse the actions of his own officials; to do so would make it appear that he could not control his own government. He also agreed to tighten the embargo, for the State Department insisted that some modus vivendi in Palestine might soon be possible.[66] Ending the embargo would have contradicted the trusteeship effort; and an embargo was consistent with the president's preference for American passivity. Indeed, Truman would have accepted trusteeship if it had been adopted at the United Nations. He probably did not understand that if it passed the General Assembly, trusteeship would legally have superseded partition; the future implementation of the latter plan would then have been unlikely.[67]

There are ironic lessons to be learned from the haphazard evolution of the trusteeship position. The closed policy process that Truman had followed prevented his predicting the firestorm that would erupt. The president often resisted an open decision-making system but it actually protected him in controversial cases like Morrison-Grady in 1946 and partition in 1947. The open system forced him to confront different views of particular policies so that he better understood the alternatives before him. In the trusteeship issue, the closed system resulted in anguish and public acrimony that the open approach he so thoroughly resented would have avoided. This result was unpalatable in an election year.

Recognition

In late March the tide of military and diplomatic battle turned in favor of the Zionists. In Palestine itself the Jews began to defeat the Arabs for the first time. By May, their chances of withstanding Arab armies appeared far better than they had in February. To the disappointment of American diplomats, the trusteeship idea was not well-received at the United Nations and was never adopted. To pass in the special session of the General Assembly, as the United States had requested, the idea would have required a two-thirds majority, which several factors made unlikely. Both Jews and Arabs opposed the idea and their inability to agree even on an American-sponsored U.N. call for a truce further reduced the likelihood of success. Trusteeship was widely perceived as a retreat from the General Assembly's advocacy of partition the previous November and as further evidence of American oscillation. Most important, it was generally assumed that trusteeship would have to be enforced by a U.N. peace force for which there was little enthusiasm. The British were opposed and American military readiness was painfully low.[68] Even a resolution calling for trusteeship only in Jerusalem had not passed when the Jewish state was declared.

Ironically, trusteeship under American sponsorship would have necessitated greater U.S. engagement than did the partition plan, despite State Department opposition to partition on grounds that it would lead to U.S. involvement. (The reasons for this apparent discrepancy were both global and regional: trusteeship would keep the Russians out of the picture because they were not members of the U.N. Trusteeship Council, and trusteeship would prevent establishment of a Jewish state—and so alienation of the Arabs and possible war would be avoided.) There were, however, serious practical problems with trusteeship from the outset. At one point Forrestal pointed out to Lovett that the 50,000 men, estimated as the American share of the U.N. police force, would represent most of America's ground reserve then active.[69]

With trusteeship languishing at Lake Success, American diplomats tried other options to forestall a Jewish state and war. In late April the head of the office of United Nations affairs, Dean Rusk, met secretly and separately with Jewish and Arab delegations in New York. He tried to secure a truce and acceptance of trusteeship, but the negotiations broke down when the Arab delegates at the U.N. (especially Foreign Minister Faisal of Saudi Arabia—the future king) refused to accept a temporary immigration quota during the period of a truce because it would have assured that the number of Jews in Palestine could grow.[70]

Rabbi Judah Magnes, president of the Hebrew University and still in favor of a binational state, was brought to the United States confidentially; he met with the president and tried to organize a group of prestigious Jewish leaders to back his position.[71] Zionist leaders refused an airplane furnished by the United States government to fly them, Arab representatives, and Western intermediaries to an island off Greece for secret talks if they would delay by ten days their declaration of independence.[72] There were rumors that tax deductible contributions might be revoked if warfare erupted and the Zionists were blamed.[73] But these efforts were too late; history was moving in another direction. The Zionists and their sympathizers were bombarding the president with pleas for support. One visitor to the White House in early May found Truman reading the Bible and the American Declaration of Independence.[74]

The two schools in the administration (pro- and antipartition) now prepared for the climax of their three-year-long debate. The two differing policies can be illustrated by a conversation between Rusk and Clifford on 8 May. As reported by Clifford, Rusk wanted to prevent either a Jewish or Arab state in Palestine when the British left the country. He hoped to do this by a truce; if that failed, he thought the votes were available in the General Assembly to approve a "simplified trusteeship" for Palestine as a substitute for the earlier partition resolution. In contrast, Clifford thought that "there was strong indication of actual partition now and we should be in a position to reconcile the two peoples . . . without creating a United Nations' legal substitute for partition." Therefore, he thought the chances of arranging a truce would be good after both states had been declared.[75]

In a telephone conversation with two members of the U.N. delegation (11 May), Rusk put the case bluntly: "The main thing across the way at the White House is if this thing is going to happen anyway why don't we go ahead and get credit for it and we are trying to break that off."[76] Yet Rusk realized he was unlikely to succeed: "Nevertheless, I don't think the boss [President Truman] will ever put himself in a position of opposing that effort when it might be that the U.S. opposition will be the only thing that would prevent it from succeeding."[77]

At first, Rusk's prediction seemed incorrect. A bitter meeting was held at the White House the next day, 12 May; the key participants included Truman, Marshall, Lovett, Clifford, and Niles. By now, antagonism had developed between Marshall and Clifford. As early as March, Clifford had told the president that he thought Marshall had known about Austin's trusteeship speech at the U.N.—an implicit accusation of disloyalty, a view rejected by Truman.[78] For his part Marshall resented Clifford's interference in foreign affairs, thinking him motivated by domestic politics. The flavor of this meeting is clear from the notes of a Clifford aide: "CMC was enraged—and Marshall glared at CMC. State has no policy except to 'wait.' "[79]

Under instructions from Truman to make a case that would convince Marshall, Clifford argued that since a Jewish state was going to come into existence in any case, the United States should recognize it before the Soviet Union did.[80] He recommended that the president announce his intention to recognize the new state at a news conference the next day. Lovett and Marshall vehemently disagreed because such a step would interfere with efforts at the United Nations, the nature of the Jewish state was not yet clear, and the announcement would seem a transparent effort to play politics and win votes in the next election. According to Marshall's own account, he told the president that if he "were to follow Mr. Clifford's advice and if in the elections I was to vote, I would vote against the President."[81]

The president approved Marshall's recommendations, but after the meeting Truman told his White House counsel that he had not yet lost the argument.[82] As Marshall recognized, the presence of Clifford, Niles, and Mat Connelly, the president's appointments secretary, already indicated the direction of Truman's thinking. The State Department had delayed the president, but since it could produce neither a truce nor approval of trusteeship, the argument against recognition weakened with every passing hour. The delay also gave the forces aligned with Clifford an opportunity to counter the arguments made against them by Marshall and Lovett. Clifford arranged for Eliahu Epstein, the Jewish Agency representative in Washington, to request recognition when the new state's independence was declared on Friday, 14 May—a declaration that would present the administration with a fait accompli.[83]

After meeting with Truman, Lovett, apparently uneasy about the morning's meeting, phoned Clifford. The two talked frequently until Friday, their discussions culminating in a private lunch. There Clifford informed Lovett that he and the president had been convinced by the arguments for delay on Wednesday, but with a vacuum about to occur in Palestine "a number of people" had pushed the President toward recognition. Lovett was reduced to arguing against "indecent haste"—asking for perhaps a day, even a few hours, on the ground that American missions in the Middle East should be informed. Furthermore, the U.S. delegation at the U.N. should be warned to prevent embarrassment; a U.S. truce proposal was being debated at a General Assembly session expected to last until 10 P.M.[84] According to Lovett's account, Clifford replied that the "timing of recognition was 'of the greatest possible importance to the President from a domestic point of view.' "[85] From the president's perspective it made little sense to hold back once the decision favoring recognition had been made. Thus, at 6:11 P.M., eleven minutes after the new state had come into existence, de facto recognition of Israel was announced at the White House.

The ultimate spectacle of policy division within the American government was displayed at the General Assembly: pandemonium broke out as the American U.N. delegation was arguing for one policy as the president opted for another.[86]

The Jewish state would have survived if Truman had waited a few hours, days, or even weeks. The most important implication of his act was domestic— it signaled to the antipartition forces that American policy favored Jewish statehood. Recognition had no popular domestic opposition. Still, the United States provided no practical assistance and the arms embargo remained in effect. Even a loan, which the Israelis requested almost immediately, was delayed by the bureaucracy until January 1949.[87]

As Palestine receded from the front pages and the number of issues requiring his attention diminished, Truman became more sympathetic to the new state. Once the Jewish state was a reality, many of the dangers predicted earlier by the antipartition forces did not come to pass. Rusk's report of a meeting he held with the president on 30 April indicates Truman's attitude. He expected both sides to accept a truce, he told Rusk. "If the Jews refuse to accept a truce on reasonable grounds they need not expect anything else from us." On the other hand,

> the President said our policy will not change. We want a truce. Tell the Arabs that our policy is firm and we are trying to head off fighting in Palestine. Remind them that we have a difficult political situation within this country. Our main purpose in this present situation is to prevent a war. He expressly stated his concern over the Russian aspect of this situation. He ended by saying "go and get a truce. There is no other answer to this situation. Good luck to you and let me know if there is any way in which I can help."[88]

But Rusk did not produce a truce. Two weeks later Truman accepted the new status quo, timing the announcement for maximum political benefit at home and the additional advantage of anticipating similar Russian action.

The President's Role

On this issue, which the president considered peripheral to his main concerns, Truman could be affected by groups, advisors, and events. It does not seem accidental that he moved toward trusteeship in early 1948 when the Zionists were less active and less effective. On 14 May, however, it was Clifford (not Marshall, Lovett, or Rusk) who was with the president when the decisions on recognition and its timing were made.[89] But we must remember that he determined who had contact with him. In February he had refused to see Weizmann; in May he talked often with Clifford about Palestine.

Truman was not indifferent to events. When the battle in Palestine went well for the Jews and the United Nations failed to back trusteeship, he simply recognized the situation for what it was—a Jewish state existed. If Truman could have achieved his goal of sheltering refugees by other means, he would have accepted that alternative. Indeed, given the weak American military readiness, he would probably have accepted an Arab victory as long as an alternative haven for the European Jews was found and the Palestinian Jews were not placed in physical jeopardy.

As for the argument that the Truman administration supported recognition because of the domestic Jewish vote, the records clearly show that Truman insisted privately as well as publicly that he would not be influenced by domestic politics but would act in the light of U.S. national security.[90] If his purposes had been otherwise, it would be difficult to explain continuing the arms embargo even after recognition, his early support for trusteeship, and his delay in supporting recognition. Only when the State Department ran out of options did Truman accept the momentum of circumstance.

Although domestic politics affected the timing of the recognition announcement by a matter of hours or even days, the decision was made because the state already existed. It seemed advisable to Truman to register American acceptance rather than leave the issue open to Russian initiative.

In early 1949, Israel's chief rabbi saw Truman and told him, "God put you in your mother's womb so that you would be the instrument to bring about the rebirth of Israel after two thousand years." Tears rose to the president's eyes.[91] The rabbi had repeated in hyperbolic form a view that became conventional after 1948, but Truman only gave Israel a legitimacy and prestige it might otherwise have lacked. He did not create the new Jewish state.

The Bernadotte Plan

In Palestine the surrounding Arab states attacked as soon as a Jewish state was proclaimed, but the Jews managed to hold their own for four weeks until the first of three U.N.-arranged ceasefires occurred. Once they had survived this first month, Russian-supplied Czech weapons and illegal shipments from the West strengthened the Israelis in their weakest area—arms.[92] It gradually became clear during summer 1948 that the Jews would be able to maintain their independence. Indeed, the question became how much territory they would control.

The official American policy in the area was to keep aloof. Washington sponsored a mediator appointed by the U.N. and adhered to a U.N. call for an arms embargo to the area. Behind the scenes, however, American representatives were actively engaged with both sides to achieve some way to stop the fighting—with the British, with U.N. mediator Count Folke Bernadotte, and at the U.N. itself.

The frustration of the times was caught in Ambassador Warren Austin's undiplomatic comment that the Arabs and Jews should "settle this problem in a true Christian spirit."[93]

After recognition, the Truman policy-making apparatus rapidly reverted to the same patterns of conflict that had preceded the establishment of Israel. Thus, the State Department and the White House soon were arguing over issues such as the timing of de jure recognition; the commissioning of a noted Zionist, James G. MacDonald, as (in effect) the first ambassador to Israel; and a $100 million loan to the new Jewish state. Clifford quickly won on sending MacDonald, who reported to the White House as well as the State Department. But de jure recognition and the loan were delayed until Israel's first elections in January 1949.[94]

The public and private controversy over the Bernadotte Plan illustrates these recurring conflicts. On 17 September 1948, Bernadotte was assassinated by Jewish terrorists. Shortly before, he had completed a report which had been sent to U.N. headquarters and had spawned rumors that led to his death. Unveiled at the United Nations, the report alienated both sides: the Arabs disliked it because it assumed a continuing Jewish state, the Israelis because it recommended turning over the Negev to the Arabs. Indeed, the spirit and content of the Bernadotte Plan so resembled the State Department ideas of fall 1947 that pro-Israeli spokesmen immediately accused the department of complicity. Although the British and Americans consulted secretly with Bernadotte and his assistant, Ralph Bunche, the ideas were Bernadotte's. His basic approach, however, was in line with that of the American bureaucracy.[95] Indeed, the United States had secretly played a role in Bernadotte's selection.[96]

As the U.N. delegations gathered for the annual General Assembly to be held in Paris, they expressed horror over the assassination of the organization's mediator. Many American diplomats were also bitter at what they perceived as the intrusion of domestic politics into their decision making during the previous year. In this atmosphere Marshall announced in Paris that the United States would support the Bernadotte Plan's proposals and "strongly" urged the "parties and the General Assembly to accept them *in their entirety.*"[97] This meant that Israel would have to relinquish the Negev.

The new American position set off a controversy like the storm of the previous March that had greeted Ambassador Austin's announcement favoring trusteeship. It actually began a few days after recognition, when Lovett told Truman that "resignations among the members of our delegation to the United Nations and the State Department" had been prevented only with "difficulty." Lovett reported that the president "was unaware of this and seemed much perturbed."[98] Throughout the summer Truman presided over continuing White House–State Department tensions concerning the loan to Israel, de jure recognition, and the MacDonald appointment. By mid-August, he admitted to Lovett that he would rather speak with him than Marshall on such subjects "because of their political implications."[99] Clearly, Truman saw that Marshall considered domestic politics to be interfering with the formulation of foreign policy. Yet, for its part, State was treading very carefully—informing the president, for example, about its reasons for delaying action on the Israeli loan request before acting.[100]

With the election campaign on and Truman the underdog, politics and policy could not possibly be separated. In July the Democratic party platform declared,

We approve the claims of the State of Israel to the boundaries set forth in the United Nations Resolution of November 29 [1947—the partition plan] and consider that modification thereof should be made only if fully acceptable to the State of Israel.[101]

Yet key figures in the State Department had been thinking throughout the summer of rearranging the 29 November resolution in ways similar to the Bernadotte Report.[102] The matter came to a head in a department letter to MacDonald in Tel Aviv on 1 September, responding to several critical questions he had raised about the administration's Palestine policy. After a meeting between the president and his secretary of state, Marshall was careful to gain Truman's written approval of the document, which contradicted the party platform:

. . . the U.S. feels that the new state of Israel should have boundaries which will make it more homogeneous and well-integrated than the hourglass frontiers drawn on the map of the November 29 Resolution. . .Specifically, it would appear to us that Israel might expand into the rich area of Galilee, which it now holds in military occupation, in return for relinquishing a large portion of the Negev to Transjordan.[103]

In keeping with this policy statement, Rusk's close aide, Robert McClintock, was secretly sent to Rhodes to consult with Bernadotte and a British emissary on the mediator's forthcoming recommendations. As McClintock reported to the department, there was little discussion on "matters of substance" because the three parties agreed. Except for the letter to MacDonald and a meeting with Marshall, Truman and his White House aides knew little about the specifics of the department's coordination with both the British and Bernadotte.[104] After the posthumous release of the mediator's report, newspaper accounts and Zionist accusations suggested actual American preparation of the report, and Lovett found it necessary to inform Truman that consultation and not coordination had occurred with Bernadotte.[105] He also instructed department officials to present false information to the press concerning McClintock's visit in Rhodes to maintain the appearance of independence about the Bernadotte document.[106]

It is not surprising that Truman was not involved in the details of this issue for it was not a high foreign policy priority. By late September he was in the Midwest on a campaign train fighting for his political life. Both Jacobson and Clifford were with him and, according to Jacobson's diaries, there was a feeling aboard the train that the secretary of state had seriously compromised the president's veracity by strongly endorsing the Bernadotte Plan before the U.N. General Assembly in Paris. Truman claimed that "he had nothing to do with the American Delegation at the U.N. approving the Bernadotte Plan—Marshall acted without consulting him."[107] In contrast to his public silence during the trusteeship controversy the previous March, Truman was determined to state publicly that he stood by the Democratic platform and his government's previous position. He wrote out a telegram to Marshall in Paris detailing a policy clarification that would have amounted to a disavowal of his secretary of state. The telegram was not sent. When Clifford telephoned Lovett about this plan between train stops, Lovett not only read him the letter to MacDonald "specifically approved by the President," but also indicated that the department had telegraphed a copy of the proposed Marshall statement to the president's train and "asked for instructions" if the president was "not in agreement."[108] No reply was received and therefore Marshall's Paris statement had been made. Clifford had not known about any of this.

Here lies the lesson of the Truman policy-making system. The State Department and White House aides favored different policies toward Palestine, but only the State Department was involved in routine business. State Department officials (Marshall and Lovett in particular) could gain the president's approval when the policies which they presented seemed reasonable to him. When White House aides had no chance to present alternative arguments or to suggest the political implications, a crisis would erupt with the public announcement of the policy. Once public, White House aides as well as congressmen, interest groups, and local politicians would pressure the White House. Unless the issue had sufficient priority to involve White House officials ahead of time (as in the case of recognition but not of trusteeship and the Bernadotte Plan), the system itself guaranteed political controversies in the domestic arena. The only way out of this trap was for the president regularly to confront either his foreign policy bureaucracy or the Zionists. Instead, Truman took a position between the two groups, favoring one or the other according to his own view of national security, his preoccupation with other matters, events in the Middle East, domestic politics, or arguments made to him by key aides.

The controversy over the Bernadotte Plan typifies policy making in the Truman system. Lovett dissuaded the president from releasing his repudiation of Marshall's stand on the grounds that the British had supported the plan only by prior agreement with the United States, and that representations on its basis had already been made to the Arab governments and Israel. Certainly, he argued, a dramatic reversal would seriously compromise American dealings with other governments. Instead, a vaguely worded statement was prepared in response to a telegram from Rabbi Wise.[109]

Now the State Department began an extensive behind-the-scenes effort to persuade Governor Dewey to keep the issue out of the campaign. A tentative agreement was reached with John Foster Dulles—Dewey's international affairs advisor—who was a member of the U.N. delegation in Paris.[110] Meanwhile, the debate continued within the administration. The president and his advisors were desperate to keep the Bernadotte Plan off the U.N. agenda until after the election—a difficult task after the American delegation had urged prompt attention to the issue. For its part the department sought to prevent the president from diluting American support for the Bernadotte Plan and attempting to retrieve the Negev for Israel. So anxious was the White House about the president's political position that Truman instructed the U.N. delegation in Paris not to issue pronouncements or take actions unless he personally cleared them.[111]

The State Department might well have forestalled a public presidential statement had Dewey not finally raised the issue. Elaborating on criticisms in the Republican platform of Truman's vacillation on Palestine and on the recent controversy over the Negev matter, he attacked the administration's apparent support of the Bernadotte proposals. To Truman his opponent had broken an implicit agreement against making Palestine a campaign issue. Clifford was delighted, for Dewey's criticism now freed the president to erase a serious political liability.[112] Truman quickly released a statement declaring that he stood "squarely on the provisions covering Israel in the Democratic platform," expressed the "hope" that the United States would soon aid Israel with financial assistance, and promised to grant de jure recognition as soon as a permanent Israeli government was elected.[113] A few days later he told a cheering crowd at Madison Square Garden that Israel "must be large enough, free enough, and strong enough to make its people self-supporting and secure."[114]

The State Department chafed under the restrictions that Truman had imposed. As the election neared, Lovett wrote Marshall, "Am told removal of restrictions on normal procedures may be expected next week when silly season terminates."[115] A Security Council resolution that the Israelis opposed but the American delegation had supported was nearing a vote.[116] Truman instructed Lovett that if it came to a vote before the election, the delegation should abstain. If the vote occurred afterward, they could vote for it, which indeed finally happened.[117]

After the election, the balance of forces within the administration began to move back toward the State Department. Just a few days after the president won his astounding victory, he reaffirmed a position that permitted consistency with the letter of his campaign commitment and the spirit of State Department preferences. Neither the Democratic party platform nor the president had ever promised Israel more than the frontiers encompassed by the original U.N. partition resolution. But the Bernadotte Plan proposed taking the Negev away from the new Jewish state although it had been granted Israel under partition. Truman's promise during the campaign to stand by the original plan came to symbolize his support of Israel's objectives. But the Israeli armed forces had also captured western Galilee, which had not been promised under partition, and the Israeli government wanted both—claiming need on the basis of security and right to the land as the victim of Arab aggression. As McClintock recalled the president's position, "If the Jews hold me to my contract, they will have to keep theirs."[118] Alternatively, the Israelis could keep western Galilee and give up the Negev, which is what the department wanted.[119]

This position rapidly came to seem unrealistic, because the Palestine war was moving in Israel's direction. The Israelis successfully invaded the Sinai at the end of 1948 and completed their occupation of the Negev the following March. Under these conditions, the United States was hardly in a position to dictate peace terms. The U.S. delegation to the U.N. General Assembly in Paris moved to accommodate policy to Israel's war gains, stressing direct negotiations rather than great power or U.N.-determined territorial positions.[120] In the end, a delicate U.N. balancing act allowed Israel to retain the Negev and all of Galilee, while discouraging the nation from taking more territory and encouraging the Arabs to enter negotiations. First, the United States and Britain coaxed Israel out of the Sinai, when Britain threatened to invoke a 1936 treaty with Egypt and enter the war on her side. The threat was delivered from Washington along with a stiff message signed by the president in which Israel was warned to remove her troops from the Sinai.[121] Then, in the first half of 1949, Ralphe Bunche, the new U.N. mediator, negotiated armistice agreements between Israel and four Arab states individually—Egypt, Lebanon, Jordan, and Syria. As with recognition, the key factor in U.S. decision making had been external events—mainly Israeli military victories.

Truman himself was caught in the middle of conflicting arguments within his administration. Even during the election campaign, when he indicated sympathy for Israel at Madison Square Garden, he had added: "I have refused consistently to play politics with the question of Israel. I have refused, first, because it is my responsibility to see that our policy in Israel fits in with our foreign policy throughout the world; second, it is my desire to help build in Palestine a strong, prosperous, free, and independent democratic state."[122] The problem repeatedly confronted by the president was that the State Department considered his two objectives irreconcilable. Those among his White House aides, personal friends, and political supporters who believed that a vibrant Israel would be consistent with national security interests were not in a position to conduct foreign policy on that basis—especially in ongoing contacts with the British, the Russians, the Arabs, and Israel itself.

Looking back, we can empathize with Truman's frustration in determining where national security lay. On the one side, he and his aides were influenced by the desire for reelection. On the other side, the professional diplomats were often wrong in their assessments (e.g., the ability of a Jewish state to survive) or unsuccessful in their maneuvers (e.g., trusteeship). In retrospect it is hard not to be amused with the need to cooperate with a British government whose foreign minister believed at the end of 1948 that Israel might be Communist "within five years."[123]

The Aftermath of the 1948 War

Although the armistice agreements did not end the belligerency between Israel and its Arab neighbors, they ended the first Arab-Israel war, fought over eight months between May 1948 and January 1949 with alternating periods of combat and U.N.-arranged ceasefires. The armistice lines at the end of the war became Israel's borders (although these boundaries were unrecognized by its neighbors) and included a larger area of Palestine than had been allotted to the Jewish state under the UNSCOP plan, plus half of Jerusalem. The bulk of the originally proposed Palestinian Arab state was captured by neighboring Arab countries: Egypt occupied the Gaza Strip and Jordan annexed the West Bank and the eastern half of Jerusalem. (Jordan's gains were also unrecognized by her neighbors.) With these precarious arrangements, the Middle East settled into a new uncertain status quo.

For the remainder of the Truman administration, Palestine was a minor issue, especially after the onset of the Korean War in June 1950. But as before, when an occasion arose, Israeli supporters appealed to the president over the heads of bureaucrats in the State Department. In this way Truman approved a loan to Israel despite the reluctance of the chief of the economic assistance program, approved de jure recognition of Israel after its first elections, supported American sponsorship of Israeli membership in the United Nations, and muted American backing of an internationalized Jerusalem under the partition plan.[124] When Israeli advocates began seeking economic assistance from Congress in 1951, Truman told FDR Jr. that they had not requested enough.[125] In February 1952, three days after a meeting with Jacobson, the president instructed the director of the Bureau of the Budget to increase economic aid to Israel for fiscal year 1953 from $25 to $80 million.[126]

Although bitter bureaucrats charged that Israel policy was ultimately made in the White House, they exerted wide-ranging influence during the extensive periods when the president was occupied with other matters. Despite the public perception, Truman did not always side with the Israelis, just as he had often opposed the Zionists before Israel's establishment.

An example of the president's delicate balancing can be found after 1948 in the aftermath of the Bernadotte Plan. As a consequence of U.N. maneuvering over the plan, a Palestine Conciliation Commission had been established, consisting of the United States, France, and Turkey. This commission convened a conference at Lausanne in spring 1949, attended by key Arab states and Israel, in an attempt to reach a peace settlement. The Israelis made it clear that even in return for peace they would not compensate the Arab states with territory gained in the 1948 war. They also refused to accept Palestinian war refugees back within their territory, arguing that they could not allow a fifth column within their borders. They were prepared to compensate Arabs for loss of their land and to reunite families separated by the war. They asked, "If we are accepting our refugees, why can't the Arabs do likewise?" The Arab states continued their adamant opposition to the creation of a Jewish state and refused to meet with the Israeli delegation. Nonetheless, the wrath of the American government fell upon the Israelis for their unwillingness to compromise on territory or refugees to facilitate negotiations. To the State Department and the president, the original boundaries of the partition plan—not the territories Israel now occupied—were the basis for negotiations. Controversy over the Bernadotte Plan had by no means abated.

The president shared the view that the Israelis were not sufficiently forthcoming. In one note to an American diplomat he stated bluntly, "I am rather disgusted with the manner in which the Jews are approaching the refugee problem." After White House validation, a key State Department letter to the Israeli government warned Israel to revise her diplomatic stands or "the U.S. Government will regretfully be forced to the conclusion that a revision of its attitude toward Israel has become unavoidable."[127] The president reported to one State Department official that he had told several Jewish leaders that "unless they were prepared to play the game properly and conform to the rules they were probably going to lose one of their best friends."[128]

Despite this tough talk from both the president and State, discussions continued with the Israelis and the Lausanne talks dragged on through most of 1949. In the end the Israelis did agree to accept 100,000 Arab refugees under American pressure, but most American diplomats believed the Israelis should have offered to accept at least 250,000—about one-third the total number. In the end, the talks disbanded in failure.[129] It was to be the last Arab-Israeli peace conference until a one-day meeting at Geneva in December 1973. As the Arab states and the Israelis failed to reach any agreements, the armistice lines remained intact with the Israelis in control of more territory than the State Department thought just. American efforts to pressure Israel into unilaterally offering territorial concessions had simply failed.[130]

In spring 1950, Israel's American friends began to demand arms for Israel in response to rumors of increased British shipments to the Arabs. The president was not opposed to the idea, telling Jacobson somewhat contradictorily that he was "not to worry, Israel would get plenty of arms if they needed them. Hopes they never will! . . . He felt confident that there would not be any new war in Israel."[131] Meanwhile, the president remained annoyed with continuing Zionist pressures on him. The idea of furnishing Israel with arms was aborted when Acheson went to Europe and an initiative from the Near East Bureau was officially announced. The United States, Great Britain, and France issued the Tripartite Declaration by which the three Western powers sought to limit arms shipments to the area.[132]

The Truman administration's last major Middle East initiative was the Middle East Defense Command, designed as a small-scale Near East "NATO." The Egyptians, considered central to the idea, quickly vetoed it, but a year later a new government in Cairo secretly showed some interest. The whole matter was left unfinished at the end of the administration.[133]

Conclusion

The Truman administration presided over a critical period of American policy concerning the Arab-Israeli dispute. Israel was established during this era, and patterns that began under Wilson and Roosevelt were solidified in ways dictated by circumstance, priorities, and the president's own style.

The president was confronted with conflicting global, regional, and local constraints. In the global arena, growing concern about Soviet objectives took Truman's attention away from the Middle East. One major aim of American policy was to ensure that, however the Palestine question was resolved, the Soviet Union would not benefit. Washington officials debated which options would yield the least influence to the Kremlin.

A further global constraint was Britain, which on most issues was America's closest ally. Palestine was a point of tension between the two governments not consistent with the rest of their relationship. The resulting anomalies were uncomfortable for both and continual efforts were made to overcome them.

Regionally, the Palestine question was a nuisance for it threatened to ruin American relations with the Arab world and disrupt oil supplies to the West. Nevertheless, the most immediate external constraints during the Truman era were local and occurred in the Palestinian arena itself. Here specific developments changed policy in Washington and the tactics of key officials. Whatever theoretical consequences of a Jewish state were debated within the administration, the Jews of Palestine declared their independence. The State Department expected them to fail and wanted to limit their success, but the Israelis won the war and occupied additional land.

Pressing even more painfully on the president was a full range of internal constraints. Truman could not ignore the electoral factor, especially as the 1948 presidential election became imminent, however sincerely he might seek to avoid the interrelationship between domestic politics and foreign policy. Beyond the political dimension, domestic pressures were divided with rough equality between two powerful coalitions favoring and opposing a Jewish state. To the Zionists and their supporters, a democratic pro-Western enclave in a politically unstable but crucial region would secure future American interests there. Opponents demanded that a Jewish state be prevented or at least limited in area. They argued that American interests in the region (relations with the Arab world, communications links, oil and its consequences for the success of the Marshall Plan) would be adversely affected by Israel's existence.

Reflecting these ideological divisions, two camps within the administration competed for the president's favor. White House aides thought State Department officials pursued their own preferences despite the president's interests; the charge of disloyalty to the president was not infrequent.[134] State Department officials saw their opponents as motivated solely by domestic politics and willing to sacrifice national security for political advantage. Thus, coordination was minimal.

Further dividing the administration, no channels existed to expose the president to both sides' views, and each group proceeded on its own. The president's approval of either side's actions was taken by its partisans as carte blanche. This system placed a premium on keeping one's opponents in the dark so that they could not prevail on the president to reverse course. Policy snafus abounded in such matters as partition, trusteeship, recognition, and the Bernadotte Plan.

The administration's openness to outside influences, the internal diversity, and the multiple channels of policy making became sources of internal conflict rather than ways of exposing the president to competing views. The appointment of James G. MacDonald as the first ambassador to Israel was a case in point. Pushed through by Clifford as a means of gaining independent information from the State Department, MacDonald was resented by the department and his authorization to deal directly with the White House weakened him at State.[135] Rather than increasing interchange between State and the White House, he became a further source of distrust. Truman contributed to the chaos by seeing advisers intermittently, as when he closed off the Zionists in early 1948 and relied on Clifford in May.

Indeed, the president swayed back and forth as internal and external constraints affected him. The outcome was a weak and inconsistent policy, which neither side could totally influence. Thus, the Truman presidency illustrates the central role of the person in the Oval Office. Truman's own ideas affected his response to events and advisors: his placing national security above partisan politics; his concern for refugees; his sense of the historical role of the Jews in Palestine; his desire to support the United Nations; his fear of increased Russian influence; his reluctance to use American troops in a dispute perceived as peripheral; his wish to prevent open warfare in Palestine. Frequently confused by the issue and the supporters of each position and often affected by the people most recently seen, this president tried to follow his own principles. Those advisors, agencies, and groups who appealed to the president in ways consistent with his beliefs most often succeeded.

Truman's inconsistency frequently led the administration to speak with two voices. For example, in fall 1948, the president approved a State Department policy document that was designed to give the Negev to the Arabs in return for Israel's keeping western Galilee, which it had occupied in the war. At about the same time, he signed a David Niles-authored letter to the Israeli president, Chaim Weizmann, that extolled the utility of the Negev for Israel.[136] So all-encompassing was this divergence that later presidencies can be analyzed by the degree to which they continued the duality.

One of the principal reasons for policy vacillations was the low priority assigned to the problem by the administration. Only when international events or domestic pressures forced his direct engagement did Truman deal with the matter. He had no overall goal; any solution that answered the needs of the Jewish refugees in Europe and brought peace to the region would have been acceptable. Unfortunately for Truman, intense public interest in the question turned a merciless spotlight on his inconsistencies.

In the war for Washington, the divided Truman administration is a model against which its successors can be assessed and understood. Most of the frustrations and issues that beset Truman recur in later administrations. However, only Harry S. Truman was forced to improvise and experiment. This distinguishes his approach to the Arab-Israeli conflict from those of his successors, a difference clearly revealed in the administration of Dwight D. Eisenhower.

3

EISENHOWER
The Failed Search for a Coherent Containment
Policy

It is difficult to conceive of two American administrations more different
in handling the Arab-Israeli dispute than those of Truman and Eisenhower.
Given the external, internal, and historical constraints that operate no matter
who is in power, the differences between the two presidencies are striking indeed. Eisenhower's inclinations, philosophy, and organizational preferences created a much different atmosphere from Truman's.

The Effect of Constraints

When the Republicans assumed office, the Palestine War had been over
for four years. All actors had adjusted to the new circumstances and Truman had
not been pressed by external events to deal with the subject during his second
term. But after the Korean War, the Middle East again attracted attention as it
had during Truman's first years. Now, however, the causes and motivations were
different. For Truman, external events and domestic pressures had required his
concern despite what he saw as issues of greater weight. For the "new look" of
the Eisenhower administration, however, the Middle East became significant
because of the altered Soviet-American competition. Constraints were presented by global and regional conditions and not by specific events in Palestine.

Global competition between the two superpowers had already extended
beyond the areas bordering the U.S.S.R., and the spread of the conflict would
become a major development during the Eisenhower era. As the Cold War
spread, the Middle East became more central to American foreign policy. "As

far as sheer value of territory is concerned there is no more strategically important area in the world,"[1] Eisenhower said of the Middle East during the campaign. As president, he saw the Arab world in particular as a significant arena for containing the Soviet Union.[2] According to John Foster Dulles, it was "high time that the United States government paid more attention to the Near East and South Asia."[3]

At the outset, the administration saw itself facing two broad external constraints in the Middle East. First, Britain's declining role in the area, and particularly the Anglo-Egyptian dispute over continuing English control in the Suez Canal Zone, was perceived as hindering American relations with the Arab world. Second, the Arab-Israeli conflict was viewed as blocking American influence and administration designs to contain the U.S.S.R. in the area. But the external constraint that would in the end most inhibit the administration's policies—Arab nationalism—was not seen as a potential impediment at all. Rather, it seemed merely an international condition to which U.S. policy could adjust.

Later events would appall and frustrate Eisenhower (e.g., the Czech-Egyptian arms deal of 1955; Nasser's nationalization of the Suez Canal and the subsequent Anglo-French-Israeli invasion of Egypt in 1956; the overthrow of a pro-Western government in Iraq, and an incipient Lebanese civil war in 1958). These developments impeded his regional foreign policy goals more than any confronted by his predecessor and they spread beyond the Palestinian conflict to engulf the entire area, extending ultimately to the two key European allies and the Soviet Union.

If foreign problems plagued Eisenhower more than they had Truman, domestic pressures were muted. There were several reasons. First, international conditions had changed. Since Israel's existence was not at stake and Middle East issues in the early Eisenhower years usually involved intra-Arab rather than Arab-Israeli conflicts, fewer people outside the American government took interest than in the early Truman period.

Second, the most vocal and public domestic pressure, the pro-Israeli forces, lacked the strength of both earlier and later days. Israeli backers had drifted into other interests after 1948 and later crises had not yet called them. With the Middle East issue on the back burner and Israel perceived as relatively secure, those concerned with the new state were concentrating their efforts on the economic assistance needed by Jerusalem to absorb immigrants and gain viability.[4] Not much energy was left for maneuvering in Washington. However disturbing administration actions might be, they were not quite dramatic enough to arouse large-scale political activities. In retrospect, the Eisenhower period was not the pro-Israeli camp's finest hour; it failed during these years in all its major objectives: to oppose the Baghdad Pact, gain arms for Israel, or achieve an American-Israeli defense pact.[5]

Third, the new president depended less on electoral politics than his predecessor. Unlike Truman, he did not have close Jewish friends who might influence him at critical moments and he was not dependent on Jewish support. Many of Israel's traditional constituency had backed his Democratic opponent, Adlai Stevenson (Jews, Labor, congressional liberals). In addition, he had made no campaign commitments on the Middle East because the issue played less of a role than in any other presidential campaign after 1944. Eisenhower's military status, his popularity as a hero, and his abstinence from conventional politics permitted him a diffidence toward the subject that would have been difficult for a senator, a congressman, or even a governor. One of Secretary of State Dulles's aides reports that Dulles saw Eisenhower's independence of the Jewish vote as an opportunity to strengthen America's position among the Arabs. At the end of 1953, for example, the tension between the administration and Israel's supporters was so acute that there were rumors (unfounded as it turned out) that the administration would investigate the American Zionist Council. Therefore, an independent lobbying committee was formed (which years later was renamed the American Israel Public Affairs Committee, or AIPAC).[6]

Fourth, the new president surrounded himself with individuals who were enthusiastic about the services Arabs might perform on behalf of America. Because of his military experience, the president believed in expert authority, a position which favored the Middle East specialists in the State Department. He trusted wealth and temporal power; his close friends were men of industry, oilmen, bankers.[7] This situation was reflected in official policy.

Fifth, since the new president thought that political pressures were improper, the Eisenhower team talked openly about the political impact of the pro-Israeli coalition, and indeed about domestic pressures generally.[8] For example, Robert Donovan reports that at a cabinet meeting in November 1953, Dulles reported on efforts to promote an Arab-Israeli peace.

> After Dulles had spoken, the President said that since foreign policy so often involves domestic policy as well, he was eager to have the Cabinet talk about it. The best policy at home, he said, was to do the right thing abroad even though this might temporarily alienate extremists in the United States. He cautioned the Cabinet against "playing politics" with foreign affairs. Obviously referring to Israel, which Dulles had just mentioned, the President said that he had been told of one case in which the Truman Administration had used foreign policy for domestic political advantage.[9]

In a statement of stunning prescience—revealing an ability to withstand domestic pressures two and one half years before Suez—Assistant Secretary of State Byroade sought to assure the Arabs that the United States would not allow Israel to embark upon "expansive aggression":

The Arab people wonder if the domestic political aspects of such a problem in the United States . . . might not make it impossible for us to live up to our intentions. I know the Arabs are wrong in this interpretation of the American people . . . America would back no state, including Israel, in a matter of expansive aggression and . . . its opposition would be equally strong regardless of which side started such a move. If this fact could be established in the Arab mind, we would have passed one of our greatest difficulties in dealing with them.[10]

According to the minutes of a conversation between British Prime Minister Eden and Secretary of State Dulles and their aides at the White House on 30 January 1956, the subject of an allied show of force arose. Dulles comments,

There might be some suspicion that any military plans developed might be related to Zionist efforts to involve the United States in fighting to support Israel, and there was substantial opposition to the U.S. being drawn into such an affair. Also, we had always played down American oil interests, and it would certainly not be popular if the impression should be given that we were risking military action to protect investments of American oil companies. Unless, therefore, military preparations were represented in their proper light—of reacting to a Soviet threat—it would not be easy to obtain support for the prospect of sending United States troops to the area.[11]

In his memoirs Eisenhower relates that some Republican party officials informed him at the height of the Suez crisis that he might lose the election if he persevered in his opposition to the Israeli invasion of the Sinai:

. . . their reason was simple: the Israelis had committed aggression that could not be condoned. Perhaps, it would be necessary for the United States, as a member of the United Nations, to employ our armed force in strength to drive them back within their borders. If this turned out to be the case, much of the responsibility would be laid at my door. With many of our citizens of the eastern seaboard emotionally involved in the Zionist cause, this, it was believed, could possibly bring political defeat. None of them, however, urged me to abandon my position. I thought and said that emotion was beclouding their good judgment.[12]

In concluding his chapter on Suez, he adds, "During the campaign, some political figures kept talking of our failure to 'back Israel.' If the administration had been incapable of withstanding this kind of advice in an election year, could the United Nations thereafter have retained any influence whatsoever? This, I definitely doubt."[13] Thus, domestic factors—and especially pro-Israeli influences—were discussed during the Eisenhower era, but they were presented as obstacles to be overcome rather than as factors in formulating policy.

Even though internal constraints upon Eisenhower were more limited than for Truman, the new chief executive would not remake history. The Republican president inherited a Middle East scene in which the United States was already committed to Israel's existence. Eisenhower told B'nai B'rith's Philip Klutznick in May 1953 that he was not sure, if he had been president at the time, whether he would have supported establishing the State of Israel but now that it was done, we would have to live with it. Dulles reported after a trip throughout the area in spring 1953 that the British, French, and Israelis were "millstones around our necks."[14] The policy Eisenhower and Dulles sought to pursue affected their perception of such constraints.

Philosophy

The president brought to the Arab-Israeli dispute a detached perspective. He had encountered the issue previously in North Africa, where early in the war he had confronted what he later called "the age-old antagonism between the Arab and the Jew." And as allied commander in occupied Europe, he was in charge of displaced persons, including the refugees of the concentration camps. Recalling one incident in his memoirs, he related, "From time to time, during all the post-war years, I had been visited by advocates of both Arab and Jewish causes. I had listened to complaints from all quarters, and one was no less eloquent than another."[15]

The president's belief in impartiality included a suspicion of Israeli motives. For example, when asked at a news conference in April 1954 whether he would consider granting military assistance to the Israelis in addition to the Arabs, he cautioned, "We are not rendering anyone assistance to start a war or to indulge in conflict with others of our friends. When we give military assistance, that is for the common purpose of opposing communism."[16]

This theme is reflected in his diary of 8 March 1956:

. . . there can be no change in our basic position, which is that we must be friends with both contestants in that region in order that we can bring them closer together. To take sides could do nothing but to destroy our influence in leading toward a peaceful settlement of one of the most explosive situations in the world today.[17]

He proceeded to recollect disdainfully a meeting he had held with two young Israelis "in 1946 or 1947" while army chief of staff. They sought arms, but Eisenhower remembered trying to talk to them "about the future of the region":

The two of them belittled the Arabs in every way . . . They boastfully claimed that Israel needed nothing but a few defensive arms and they would take care of themselves forever and without help of any kind from the United States. I told them they were mistaken—that I had talked to many of the Arab leaders and I was certain they were stirring up a hornets' nest and if they could solve the initial question peacefully and without doing unnecessary violence to the self respect and interests of the Arabs, they would profit immeasurably in the long run. I would like to see those young Israelis today . . . In any event, we have reached the point where it looks as if Egypt, under Nasser, is going to make no move whatsoever to meet the Israelites in an effort to settle outstanding differences. Moreover, the Arabs, absorbing major consignments of arms from the Soviets, are daily growing more arrogant and disregarding the interests of Western Europe and of the United States in the Middle East region."[18]

As suggested by this basic approach to the area, Eisenhower presided over a foreign policy toward the Middle East determined to "show sympathetic and impartial friendship" toward the Arabs and Israelis and to thwart Soviet advances.[19] Impartiality did not mean equality: to Eisenhower the Arabs offered assets, while Israel constituted a liability to American interests. Disappointed with his failure to resolve the Arab-Israeli dispute, he wrote in his diary,

The oil of the Arab world has grown increasingly important to all of Europe. The economy of European countries would collapse if these oil supplies were cut off. If the economy of Europe would collapse, the United States would be in a situation of which the difficulty could scarcely be exaggerated. On the other hand, Israel, a tiny nation, surrounded by enemies, is nevertheless one that we have recognized—and on top of this, that has a very strong position in the heart and emotions of the Western world because of the tragic suffering of the Jews throughout twenty-five hundred years of history.[20]

Surprised at a March 1954 news conference by a reporter's question on the Arab-Israeli dispute, the president at first waffled and then launched into his standard line on the subject:

There is, of course, so much emotionalism in the thing that you can't tell from day to day how it is going to come out. But I do say it is a case where both sides ought to restrain their partisans and their extremists, use a little bit of reason, and depend upon the judgments of outside people.[21]

Eisenhower followed his own advice and proceeded to provide ideas. Indeed, no administration has pursued a more careful, coherent, and consistent approach to the area. In this, the Eisenhower technique differed markedly from the improvisational Truman method. Eisenhower's administration had a global strategy that included a specific approach toward the regional arena and the Arab-Israeli conflict itself. Globally, its primary objective was to contain international communism and the Soviet Union (which were equated in this period).[22] According to Assistant Secretary of State Byroade, "The more Russia's aggressive moves are stalemated in Europe and the Far East, the more the danger grows for the Middle East."[23]

The Middle East was seen as critical because of its geopolitical importance and the value of its oil resources to Western Europe, a matter which Eisenhower frequently stressed in his public and private comments. For example, in a long and philosophical letter to Churchill in late March 1956—at a time when the Mideast was frequently being discussed at the White House—he wrote, "The free nations know, for example, that the prosperity and welfare of the entire Western world is inescapably dependent upon Mideast oil and free access thereto. This is particularly true of all Western Europe, and the safety and soundness of that region is indispensable to all the rest of us."[24] In late November at a meeting of top administration officials with the president, "There was discussion as to the relative importance of the Middle East and of Western Europe, culminating in statements by the President and Secretary Humphrey that the two must be considered together, and are together the most strategic areas in the world—Western Europe requires Middle Eastern oil, and Middle Eastern oil is of importance mainly through its contribution to the Western European economy."[25]

The regional approach followed logically from Eisenhower's goal of stopping the Russians in this critical area. Eisenhower and Dulles sought to make Iran and Turkey bulwarks against the Kremlin, and early in the administration they had the CIA engineer a coup that ousted Iranian nationalist-oriented premier Mossadegh and returned the shah to full power.[26] The neighboring Arab world fascinated and troubled the president and the entourage led by Secretary of State John Foster Dulles. If the Arabs could be organized against presumed Russian designs on the region, the Kremlin would be effectively blocked from a political or military thrust into Mideast areas away from its own borders.

The Eisenhower strategy toward the Arab-Israeli conflict also followed from these global and regional concerns. If the Arabs were an aid to the containment of communism, then the Israelis were "an impediment" because Israel symbolized Western imperialism to Arab leaders. Given these assumptions, a high level of disagreement between Jerusalem and Washington was not long in appearing. By early 1956, for example, Dulles was telling the Senate Foreign Relations Committee that the Israelis should rely for their national defense on "collective security" and the United Nations, not on arms alone.[27]

Privately, Dulles was even tougher. At a White House meeting in late March 1956, he told his colleagues that the Israelis were showing a much less arbitrary and truculent attitude in discussions with him, "since clear evidence has been given that we are not going to 'cave in' on the Israeli question."[28]

Almost a year later Dulles was telling congressmen, "The firmness of the U.S. position thus constituted the critical issue particularly since much of the world, including the Israeli government, believed Israel could in crucial moments control U.S. policy. Should the Arab nations see any confirmation of this belief, they would feel compelled . . . to turn to Russia. He added that this did not mean the United States had to follow an anti-Israeli policy."[29] Similarly, an oft-repeated theme in administration statements suggested that both sides were to blame for the conflict. One State Department official argued in fall 1955, "It would be easy if the situation were all black and white, but it's not. Extremists in Israel would like to expand their present boundaries. Arab extremists would still like to drive the million and a half Israelis into the sea."[30]

Eisenhower and Dulles were fully convinced that if only the Arab-Israeli dispute could be resolved, the Arabs would be prepared to align themselves with the United States against the Russians.[31] Although their approach to the Middle East formed a fully consistent strategy, it did not accord with the realities of the region. The strategy assumed that the Middle East nations had durable governments and that the Arab regimes agreed with one another on basic issues. It also assumed that the main disagreement in the Middle East was between the Arabs and Israel, and that the principal danger was outside Russian aggression. In these assumptions Eisenhower and Dulles were proven incorrect. Despite their careful analysis, the primary source of Middle East instability during the 1950s was within the Arab world. The main military intervention in this era was by the British, French, and Israelis in 1956, and by the United States in 1958.

In each case the interventions occurred because of developments originating in intra-Arab conflicts, even though Soviet meddling or Arab-Israeli hostilities might be blamed initially. Political instability within the Arab world was epitomized by friction between Iraq and Egypt. Iraq, led by King Feisal and his prime minister Nuri al Said, was close to the British and sought Western protection against the Russians and its own Arab enemies. The Egyptians were led by a team of army officers who had assumed power in a coup of July 1952, overthrowing the monarchy of King Farouk. Gamel Abdel Nasser, the new strong man, maintained nationalist and pan-Arab ambitions and regarded overt alliance with any Western power as, at the very least, a return to colonialism. Officials in the administration generally recognized the Egyptian government as the most critical Arab state, but the Nasser regime saw Washington and its policies as antithetical to the Egyptian revolution. Despite its cleverness, then, the new American policy could not cope with Arab disunity and nationalism.

From the outset, Eisenhower moved to stop the spread of communism through a series of pacts that would have created mini-NATOs around the world. Although it was successful only in South East Asia and the "northern tier" of the Middle East, this policy demonstrated the administration's preoccupation with thwarting actual and potential Russian designs and its failure to take seriously indigenous nationalist movements. On the contrary, the foreign policy of Eisenhower and Dulles was rooted in a moralism and legalism that had little appreciation of cultural distinctions and local, historical, and political dynamics. Rather, all international actors were divided into two camps—the free world and its Communist antagonists. Bilateral treaties, mutual security arrangements, congressional resolutions, United Nations votes, and collective security became code words for applying legal norms which did not exist to the chaos of international affairs. Such moral standards, however simplistic, gave American leaders a sense of certainty amidst the bewildering regional developments in this period.

This philosophy formed a coherent conceptual scheme with which the administration approached areas such as the Middle East. Their precepts also permitted the sweeping moral judgments that were later applied in particular cases, even when discrepancies arose. For example, when Dulles confronted Ambassador Eban over the Israeli invasion of the Sinai in 1956, he is reported to have admitted that he was not unhappy with Nasser's defeat: "I am torn, yet can we accept this good end when it is achieved by means that violate the UN charter?"[32] When Eisenhower referred to his distaste for recent Israeli actions, he claimed, "We do these things under the, you might say, policies laid down by the United Nations. We attempt to support the United Nations. We don't attempt to prejudge anything, but we do believe that the United Nations must be supported in all of these activities, and the thing will be carried out exactly as originally programmed."[33] This statement was not made during the Suez crisis, but in October 1953 during an earlier confrontation with the Israeli government. Discussing the Lebanese intervention in 1958, the president agreed with General Twining that "it was the right thing to do," but he added, "so long as the action rests on moral ground." The general observed, "If, however, our only argument is economic—saying that the life of the Western world depends upon access to oil in the Middle East—this would be quite different, and quite inferior to a purpose that rests on the right to govern by consent of the governed. The President said he is giving deep thought to finding a moral ground on which to stand if we have to go further."[34]

Decision Making

The decision-making apparatus of the Eisenhower Administration was the exact opposite of its predecessor, substituting a highly structured, tight chain of command for the multiple channels and chaos of the Truman era. The new procedures facilitated a uniform policy, but also severely limited the debate which had characterized the Truman method.

Eisenhower's military career had taught him to depend on the delegation of authority and to conserve his energy for only the most significant issues. Consensus was first to be reached by his subordinates; he would deal exclusively with broad policy outlines and critical problems. This system often resulted in his not understanding the internal policy debate which led to recommendations. Eisenhower's decision-making style permitted the emergence of a foreign-policy czar, and Secretary of State Dulles was careful to claim the role. He was never omnipotent, however, although the quip at the time was that Dulles carried the State Department around in his hat.[35] He always understood that he was the president's lawyer in foreign affairs and that he must maintain his client's confidence in order to retain his portfolio.[36] He could not forget his Uncle Lansing's failure to maintain Wilson's trust as secretary of state, and he was chastened by Eisenhower's early distance from him. Only by gaining the president's overwhelming respect did he emerge as preeminent adviser, a role that became even more central with Eisenhower's heart attack in September 1955.

Like his boss, Dulles believed that the Truman administration had favored Israel and that approaches should be made to the Arabs to right the balance. However, he believed that relations with the Arab states could be improved without abandoning "worthy policies which had led to the establishment of the State of Israel."[37] This concern seems absent in Eisenhower's private remarks and opinions.[38] Dulles's sympathies were in uneasy balance, with his biblical orientation and the Israelis' anticommunism on one side; weighing on the other side were the mild anticolonialism of the period, calculations of the Arabs' usefulness in thwarting communist advances, and a fascination with international organization manifested in the quixotic pursuit of a collective security arrangement for the Middle East. During the first term, Dulles's preoccupation with containing communism in the Middle East made him less interested in Israel. Later, Nasser's flirtation with the Kremlin increased Dulles's appreciation of Jerusalem as a potential anti-Communist instrument.

Dulles always "seemed deliberately to attract criticism to himself so as to deflect it from President Eisenhower."[39] Even though the administration had a president committed to impartiality, Dulles appeared to many Israel supporters as the spearhead of an anti-Israel campaign.[40] When criticism of Israel was deemed necessary, the secretary usually spoke; when praise or aid was warranted, Eisenhower ordinarily made the announcement. Further, because it was Dulles and his aides and not the president who saw pro-Israeli delegations, they were the ones to explain administration policy to unhappy critics. The State Department was indirectly responsible for the forming of the Conference of Presidents of Major American Jewish Organizations. Tired of seeing so many Jewish representatives with the same litany of complaints, Assistant Secretary of State for Near East Affairs Henry Byroade asked to see them all at one time in one group.[41]

Although Eisenhower was more involved in policy making than he pretended (except during periods of illness), his system of delegated authority isolated him from the rest of his administration. This pattern was reinforced by

Dulles's jealous guarding of his prerogatives as chief foreign policy adviser. Unlike Eisenhower, Dulles had difficulty delegating authority and tended to work alone.[42] This practice enhanced his extraordinary power but also increased the difficulty of criticism in a highly formal decision-making system.

This tendency toward isolation, especially when Eisenhower and Dulles became involved in an issue, created problems for all involved groups. For the Jews there was little access to the administration, except through Dulles on formal occasions—hardly the equivalent of the influence enjoyed through such figures as Clifford, Niles, and Jacobson during the Truman era. The "Jewish portfolio" in the White House did not exist. As the president once told the highest ranking Jew in the administration, Cabinet Secretary Maxwell Rabb, "no groups should have a caretaker."[43] Thus, under Eisenhower there was no channel for promoting the policies championed by Clifford and Niles during the battles over partition and recognition. Indeed, the options favored by leading pro-Israeli analysts received little consideration.

On the surface, the philosophy and decision-making technique of the administration favored the arguments usually put forth by the State Department. But the bureaucracy was not without its problems. Eisenhower's and Dulles's general policy regarding the Middle East was approved by many officials who were relatively insulated from outside groups and Congress. But they could no more "special plead" than the Israeli advocates. When bureaucrats disliked policies, they had no court of last resort in which to voice their criticisms. The diplomats were free to pursue their limited responsibilities and they were satisfied that Eisenhower's instincts were closer to their own than his predecessor's, but those seeking even closer relationships to key Arab states had no recourse if decisions went against them. And the secretary of state was ever-unpredictable.[44]

There was an extraordinary gulf between the higher echelons of the administration and the bureaucracy. Communication between Washington and the ambassadors was erratic or nonexistent, resulting in a low morale.[45] At times the State Department was allowed to go its own way and could function normally. But when Eisenhower and Dulles took over, as in the formulation of the Eisenhower Doctrine, the bureaucracy was likely to find itself looking on. However, despite this isolation and serious questions about their superiors' increasing anti-Communist preoccupations in the Middle East, the bureaucrats were happy with the administration's emphasis on experts and its rejection of domestic group pressures.[46]

One of the most intriguing aspects of the administration's decision making is that Arab disunity was soon reflected in serious divisions among those who believed in closer ties to the Arabs. Without the need to unite against pro-Israeli interference, two nebulous but conflicting camps emerged. On the one hand, those with global concerns wanted to support states prepared to align with the

Western powers.[47] On the other hand, those involved with regional relations argued that regimes ready to take a stance more independent of the West were the "wave of the future" and might ultimately present a better guarantee for American interests.[48] Conflict between these two groups rather than debate over partition constituted this administration's battle over Middle East policy. It was conducted within a highly formal system which did not allow the open disputes on fundamental goals that distinguished Truman's period.

One of those committed to a closer relationship with the Arab states— Allen Dulles, head of the CIA—occupied a peculiar position in administration decision making. Not only was he the secretary's brother but he had been head of the Near East Division in the early 1920s and he promoted an activist agency. Under his leadership, Mideast operatives under Kermit Roosevelt played an unusual role, one more inclined than Foster Dulles to stress the importance of Egypt—even when tensions with Nasser unfolded. For example, well before his brother, Allen Dulles sensed the possibility that Egypt might turn to the Soviet Union. As suggested by this case, despite their closeness his advice was not always determining.[49]

Although frustrated by their inability to control the actions of states in the Mideast, Eisenhower and Dulles did not feel, as Truman had, that they were spending undue time on it. They chose to focus on the area because they believed a threat of Soviet influence existed throughout the region.[50] Among the pre-1967 administrations, the Middle East ranked highest in priority for Eisenhower. The unfolding of a more active and clearly conceived American role in the area gradually emerged as a consequence of this increased attention.

The Origins of Policy

The new policy went smoothly with pro-Western Iraq, and an arms deal was concluded between Baghdad and Washington in April 1954. The United States was also anxious to offer economic and military aid to Egypt. Indeed, just before the Truman administration had left office, negotiations had been conducted with the Egyptians over a possible arms deal. The problem, however, was that the Egyptians were still threatening terrorist harrassment against the 80,000 British troops if Britain did not evacuate the Suez Canal zone. Eisenhower, the apostle of Anglo-American amity, could hardly resist British entreaties that he refrain from action. He agreed that the United States would delay economic and military aid to Egypt until a Suez deal could be reached and, behind the scenes, American officials worked on such an agreement. The resulting Suez arrangement was signed in October 1954 and, as promised, American economic aid to Egypt was announced shortly thereafter. Dulles had already proclaimed that the United States had been "favorably impressed by the plans of the present Egyptian government to concentrate on internal, social and economic development."[51] The Egyptians had suggested that cooperation with Washington would increase after the Suez Canal agreement.[52] Therefore, the administration assumed, as did the Egyptians, that arms would soon follow economic assistance.

However, Eisenhower and Dulles had a conception for containing the Russians that reached beyond arms aid to each major Arab country. They still believed a Middle East "NATO" was necessary. Referring to an Arab-Western defensive arrangement, Dulles had said after a trip he took to the Middle East in spring 1953, "We must . . . avoid becoming fascinated with concepts that have no reality."[53] The new idea was to create an organization of Middle East countries, especially those in the "northern tier" closest to the Soviet Union. In order to ease nationalist sensitivities, the British and Americans would not join. In April 1954, Turkey (member of NATO) and Pakistan (now in the new SEATO) had signed a bilateral treaty, which Eisenhower and Dulles hoped could be expanded to include several Arab states.

The most eligible first candidate for such an arrangement was Nuri's Iraqi regime, which seemed ready to use the West as a launching pad for its ambitions in the Arab world.[54] Dulles began maneuvering to lure Iraq into a Western defense pact as the British and Egyptians were agreeing on British withdrawal from their Suez Canal bases in fall 1954. But London—used to the Middle East as its sphere of influence—had even greater interest in a Western-oriented pact that included Iraq to replace its Suez Canal bastion.[55] While Dulles plotted, Prime Minister Anthony Eden moved toward arranging the pact in early 1955, preempting American efforts and astonishing the secretary of state. The British then joined the pact, but Dulles remained true to his amended conception that the great powers should stay out.[56] The secretary nevertheless kept the United States close to the alliance known as the Baghdad Pact, which at its peak, in the mid-1950s, included Turkey, Iraq, Pakistan, Iran, and Britain.

Those who dealt with Egypt and favored friendship with Nasser, like Kermit Roosevelt, head of Middle East operations for the CIA, were certain that supporting a regional pact would alienate the Egyptian leader. Since Nasser saw the Baghdad Pact as limiting newly-won Arab independence, many bureaucrats preferred emphasizing relations with Egypt, the most populous Arab country.[57]

Some American officials advocated cultivating the friendship of Iraq because they sought to create a Middle East defense organization or thought it best to collaborate quietly with the British. The Iraqi backers generally believed that favoring the Baghdad Pact would eventually lead to Cairo's acceptance of the arrangement. In addition to the president and secretary of state, Assistant Secretary of State Byroade backed the concept (until he arrived in Cairo as ambassador in February 1955), as did his successor, George Allen.[58]

This disagreement produced the worst of each policy alternative. Each bureaucratic group checkmated the other. Advocates of a strong relationship with Nasser could point to the danger of the United States joining the Baghdad

Pact, despite British entreaties. In turn supporters of the pact were able to block arms for Egypt since John Foster Dulles led this group. The pact was pushed, thereby alienating Nasser, who took an ever more antiimperialistic posture. But the United States did not give the pact complete symbolic backing because it failed to join even after Britain had. Furthermore, Nasser was led to expect arms by American representatives stationed in Cairo and many who visited from Washington. When he did not soon receive what he wanted, he began to consider turning elsewhere.[59]

There were many additional problems, the clash between the visions of John Foster Dulles and the ambitions of Gamel Abdel Nasser not the least among them. Differences over policy directions arose among officials, all of whom agreed that closer relations with the Arabs were necessary. They were stimied by competition within the Arab world itself, a competition that ultimately compromised the basis of the policy.

When difficulties arose in seeking the backing of Egypt as well as of Iraq for its regional designs, the administration did not see intra-Arab divisions but the Arab-Israeli conflict as the principal obstacle to its efforts. Two policy directions were pursued: greater distance from Jerusalem and closer relations with the Arabs. Both altered postures would result, it was thought, in decreasing Arab suspicion of American imperial designs. As Dulles put it at one point, "Our basic problem in this vitally important region is to improve the attitude of the Moslem States toward the Western democracies, including the United States. . ."[60] If American policy toward the Arabs and Israelis was adjusted, it was also thought that America could sponsor an Arab-Israeli settlement, which in turn would help Arab governments align with Washington.[61]

Disagreement arose between Israel and the United States over the administration's solicitude toward the Arabs, its level of economic aid to Jerusalem (which was soon decreased),[62] its opposition to Israel's policy of retaliatory raids into Arab territory, its refusal to sell arms to Israel, its criticism of Israel's decision to move her foreign ministry to Jerusalem, and its disinterest in discussing a bilateral treaty. The sharpest evidence of the new approach came when the United States suspended aid to Israel in October 1953. The suspension had been requested by the UNTSO (United Nations Truce Supervision Organization) chief of staff when Israel had refused to stop work on its hydroelectric project on the upper Jordan.[63] Israel soon caved in to American pressure and suspended work on the water project, whereupon the aid program was resumed.

Assistant Secretary of State Byroade made two speeches in spring 1954 in which he asked the Arabs to accept Israel "as an accomplished fact" and terminate the no-war, no-peace situation. But he called upon the Israelis to give up unlimited Jewish immigration (the raison d'etre for their state), to relinquish their hope for an early formal peace treaty, and to compensate Arab refugees.[64] Insensitively, one of the speeches was delivered before the American Council for Judaism, the only Jewish anti-Zionist group and an organization much resented by both the Israelis and other American Jewish organizations.

The Israelis and their supporters were also opposed to the idea of a Middle East defense pact, but their reasons were different from the Egyptians'. The Israelis feared that the pact would provide arms to their enemies and further isolate them. A title of a *Commentary* article of the time summarized the complaint: "Arms for Arabs—and What for Israel?"[65] Eisenhower's and the bureaucracy's view was simply that Arab arms would not be used against the Jewish state, that the balance of power still favored Israel, that it could gain necessary arms from other states, especially France, and that its best interests would be served by the administration's strategy.[66] Therefore, understanding of Israeli policy was minimal. During a March 1956 meeting, for example, Dulles spoke about "obtaining Israeli agreement to a more moderate stand and to territorial adjustments."[67]

There was little interest in the argument of Israel's supporters that creating distance between Jerusalem and Washington would harm American relations in the area by encouraging Arab challenges to the Jewish state and by increasing Israeli fears.[68] American leaders in this period were not anti-Israel but rather unaware of its needs and too fascinated with their own concepts to heed the argument that increased isolation would increase Israeli insecurity and the danger of overreaction. There were no changes in Eisenhower's "impartial" policy despite protests, meetings with congressmen, and the emergence of the new policy as an issue in the 1954 congressional elections.

The administration pattern of ignoring opposition was not limited to Israel; it also applied to American relations with Egypt. Congress in approving military aid to all countries had required that it be accompanied by an advisory mission, but Nasser would not consider even a diluted version of this affront to his independence.[69] Dulles gambled that the Egyptian president, like Nuri in Iraq, eventually would accept American terms and he delayed a favorable decision on arms to Cairo.[70] Those who pointed out that Egypt had Russia as an alternative to the United States were not seriously taken into account. The single channel between president and secretary of state and Dulles's tendency to be carried away with his own conceptions prevented an airing of alternative views. What made matters worse was that George Allen, the assistant secretary at the time, was a rather weak figure in bureaucratic interchange and loathe to challenge the Mid-East defense pact.[71]

Thus the Baghdad Pact leadership at the White House and the State Department triumphed over the Egypt-firsters in the CIA and State who warned in mid-1955 that Nasser was not bluffing about the Russians.[72] Nasser had recently suffered a staggering series of reversals: the signing of the Baghdad Pact over his vehement opposition; the embarrassingly effective February 1955 Israeli raid into Gaza in retaliation for lethal Fedayeen forays from that area; and growing Parisian opposition to his support for the Algerian rebels. But Eisenhower and Dulles thought they were being blackmailed by Nasser and assumed that he would not turn to the Russians for arms.[73] Britain and France had become seriously critical of Nasser's policies, so the prevailing concept in Washington was that he would eventually turn to the United States. Dulles and Eisenhower saw only a military threat in Russian involvement; they feared the Soviets would somehow conquer the area. They did not comprehend (since it had never occurred) that a regime might *choose* to deal with the Kremlin.

Instead of dealing with Nasser's growing impatience, the administration tried to lessen Arab-Israeli tensions. As early as fall 1953, Eric Johnston had been sent as a special envoy to the area to urge a plan for joint Arab and Israeli use of the Jordan River.[74] He had shuttled through the region during most of 1954 and 1955 to begin the reconciliation through this mutually rewarding endeavor, which would aid the Arab refugees by making more irrigated land available. This project—with its reliance on technical problem-solving to overcome seemingly irreconcilable political differences—was preferred by Eisenhower and his corporate associates. In the end, the Israelis cautiously acquiesced to the plan, but the Arab League rejected it, with Syria objecting that it would benefit Israel as well as the Arabs.[75]

Even before the Johnston mission failed, Dulles had pursued other avenues. The administration was already talking about promoting a "step-by-step reduction of tension" in the area, as Kissinger would do a generation later.[76] The secretary had created a State Department task force, which consulted with the British on ideas for settling the conflict. The concepts that emerged after months of study resemble the approach later pursued by President Carter. In a speech in August 1955 to the Council on Foreign Relations in New York, the secretary of state reported on these hitherto secret investigations, identifying three major issues in the dispute: the Arab refugees (later known as the Palestinian issue), the "pall of fear" on both sides (later known as the peace issue), and the absence of permanent boundaries between Israel and her neighbors (later known as the territorial issue). Dulles advocated refugee resettlement and repatriation, water development, permanent frontiers, and security guarantees.[77]

The Council on Foreign Relations speech was a precursor of a new peace initiative to be launched secretly. If the Arabs and Israelis could resolve their differences, then Egypt might well find association with the United States less threatening to its national integrity. Unfortunately, Dulles's speech was made after President Nasser had already decided to turn to Russian arms.[78] The Eisenhower approach to the area never fully recovered from this crushing blow. By the time the deal was announced as a Czech-Egyptian arrangement in late September 1955, American policy in Egypt had clearly failed. A belated attempt to send Kermit Roosevelt to change Nasser's mind achieved no results, nor did a last-minute disclosure that America would sell arms to Egypt on credit. To complicate matters further, the American government was in disarray because the president had just suffered a near-fatal heart attack.[79]

The inability of American leaders to believe that Egypt might turn to the Russians, despite repeated CIA warnings, illustrates one weakness in the Eisenhower decision-making structure: it could not process conflicting points of view. Once a policy decision was made, arguments and facts that contradicted it were simply ignored. The administration made the same mistake as the British Foreign Office, which was quarreling with Nasser over the Baghdad Pact and did not predict the Egyptian move toward the Russians.[80]

The decisions that followed the Czech-Egyptian arms deal reflect a second major weakness in Eisenhower's Middle East decision making: the rigid link between global and regional policies. The administration had planned to use the Arabs as a bulwark against Communist aggression. If Egypt would not join with the West against Communists, none of Eisenhower and Dulles's goals for the area could be achieved and a new policy would have to be formulated. Since neither bureaucracies nor statesmen are noted for flexibility once embarked on a particular adventure, and since an entire coherent global policy was at stake, it was assumed that the United States could persuade Nasser to return to the pre-September 1955 situation. Therefore Dulles, although skeptical that countries in the area could get "security through an arms race," sought to moderate the American stance toward the arms deal to accommodate Nasser: "It is difficult to be critical of countries which, feeling themselves endangered, seek the arms which they sincerely believe they need for defense."[81]

Instead of plotting an uncooperative leader's overthrow as the Eisenhower administration had done when challenged in Iran and Guatemala, Dulles sent emissaries to protest Nasser's decision and to persuade him to change his mind.[82] Subsequently, the administration sought a rapprochement by offering to help with the Aswan Dam and the Arab-Israeli conflict.

The Aswan Dam

The first administration response to an external challenge in the Middle East, then, was to reassert previous assumptions and policies. The regional strategy of trying to align the Arabs against the Russians was not altered by the Czech-Egyptian arms deal; neither was the strategy toward the Arab-Israeli conflict. The hope remained that if the Arab-Israeli dispute were settled, the Egyptians would cooperate with the United States.

As the administration's frustration increased, resentment against Israel grew. Jerusalem still needed arms from other Western allies, and arming Israel complicated the task of winning back Nasser. In October 1955, Dulles told a group of colleagues in his office, "We are in the present jam because the past administration had always dealt with the Middle East from a political standpoint and had tried to meet the wishes of the Zionists in this country. That had created a basic antagonism with the Arabs . . . It is of the utmost importance for the welfare of the United States that we get away from a political basis and try to develop a national non-partisan policy. Otherwise we might lose the whole area and possibly Africa."[83] In private talks with Anthony Eden in early 1956, Dulles complained that it was "extremely difficult" to get Arab help "in dealing with the communist problem" because "many Arabs often interpreted this as working with Israel." He told Eden that the administration needed a settlement of the Arab-Israeli dispute because "the United States could not get public support" for joining the Baghdad Pact until "we were able to offer a comparable security arrangement to Israel."[84] At a White House meeting on the subject, Dulles told his colleagues and the president that "the U.S. cannot join the Baghdad Pact without giving some security guarantee to Israel, and that if we were to do so, our action would quickly knock out Iraq."[85]

Resolving the Egyptian-Israeli dispute was essential. The president chose a trusted deputy, former Deputy Secretary of Defense Robert Anderson, to mediate directly between Nasser and Ben Gurion in an early form of shuttle diplomacy. It was hoped that a meeting between Egyptian and Israeli officials would result. Because it was thought that a resolution of the Egyptian-Israeli dispute would return Nasser to the pro-Western fold, the secret Anderson mission allowed the administration to offer generous aid to a country that had just made an arms deal with the Russians. In early 1956 Anderson traveled between Cairo and Jerusalem. His separate discussions with Ben Gurion and Nasser were so secret that for several years afterward few knew of their existence.[86] With close coordination between the Dulles brothers, CIA operatives in Cairo and Jerusalem handled arrangements. But conditions were not auspicious. The Israelis were disturbed by the potential effect of the arms deal on the regional balance of power. Nasser was disturbed by the continued progress of the Baghdad Pact. In the end, the parties could not agree on procedural questions, let alone the substantive matters that divided them.

This breakdown marked the end of the administration's effort to achieve a breakthrough in global and regional policies by resolving the conflict. There were sporadic efforts to revive the Johnston mission and even a new enterprise (in 1958) to encourage Arab-Israeli cooperation: Admiral Lewis Strauss wanted nuclear desalting plants in the area, built by an international corporation within the U.N. framework. But these efforts were half-hearted in comparison with earlier projects. The administration's Middle East strategy now concentrated on thwarting the Communist menace.

The failure of the Anderson mission also had serious implications for the offer to help finance construction of the Aswan Dam. In fall 1955, Undersecretary of State Herbert Hoover, Jr., the petroleum engineer and a hero of the 1953 intervention in Iran, had connected the Anderson mission to the Aswan Dam offer and won administration approval of both projects on this basis. Although there was no necessary relationship between the two enterprises, it was assumed that Nasser would comprehend that aid for the High Dam would strengthen his position at home and enable him to reach agreement with Israel.[87] As was common in this administration, all of this was neat and plausible, but trouble was bound to follow if Nasser did not play by the rules.

The Aswan project was proposed in mid-December, after obtaining British backing and support from the president of the World Bank, Eugene Black, who had recently issued a favorable report after two years of work on the project. Eisenhower had liked the idea since early 1953 at least. Dulles saw the dam as a means of limiting Egypt's ability to undertake military adventures with the new Russian arms, because its scarce resources would be committed to a constructive enterprise.

As soon as the offer was announced in late December, Nasser objected to the terms despite the agreement of his negotiating team. He feared Western restrictions on his capacity to purchase arms and make independent decisions affecting his economy.[88] With Nasser's nonacceptance, Washington's pro-dam coalition began to unravel. Some of the pro-Baghdad Pact aides, never fully convinced about Aswan, argued that Nasser was being rewarded for his recalcitrance on the pact and his flirtation with Russia. As early as the end of January, Dulles was telling Eden that "we might soon know whether our whole attitude toward Nasser would have to be changed."[89]

The turning point came in mid-March, when Anderson returned from his second trip to the Middle East and reported directly to the president and Hoover. Eisenhower noted ruefully in his diary, "Nasser proved to be a complete stumbling block. He is apparently seeking to be acknowledged as the political leader of the Arab world." In the American assessment, Nasser was reluctant to make any move toward Israel lest his popularity at home or in the Arab world be threatened. Not that the president held the Israelis blameless. He saw them as "anxious to talk with Egypt" but "completely adamant in their attitude of making no concessions whatsoever in order to obtain a peace." Their general slogan is "not one inch of ground," and their incessant demand is for arms "as a means of ensnaring the U.S. as a protector." But Eisenhower's real concern was to find a new strategy since it was painfully clear that Arab-Israeli reconciliation would not unite the area against the Russians. "It begins to look to me as though our best move is to prevent any concerted action on the part of the Arab states." Eisenhower sought to win over Libya and Saudi Arabia through aid to those countries and through concessions by London to Riyadh in a territorial dispute between the Saudis and one of the British Gulf protectorates. "If Saudi Arabia and Libya were our staunch friends, Egypt could scarcely continue intimate association with the Soviets, and certainly Egypt would no longer be regarded as a leader of the Arab world."[90]

By mid-March, aiding Egypt with the Aswan Dam no longer held a high priority within the administration. To the long-frustrated pro-Israel forces, the Aswan Dam was a focus of disenchantment with Eisenhower policies, and in an election year their views gathered increased political clout. Hardliners and conservatives who opposed neutralism were disdainful, a position that Dulles himself seemed to share on other issues. In addition, a group of "cotton senators" from the South opposed the dam because it would intensify competition with Egyptian cotton in fifteen to eighteen years. The dam also involved the sort of long-term financial commitment that Congress disliked. Both the House and Senate Appropriations Committees were negatively disposed, and made their positions clear at critical junctures.[91] At the very least, gaining support for the dam would require a congressional battle in an election year. Dulles had only limited political capital on the Hill and Eisenhower was still gradually recovering from his heart attack and preparing for his second campaign.

To further complicate matters, in mid-May Nasser recognized the People's Republic of China because he suspected the Russians might not prove trustworthy. This action added to Washington's disillusionment with the Egyptian regime.[92]

Rumors and conflicting stories further solidified opposition to the offer. A new Soviet foreign minister, Shepilov, was in Cairo in mid-June to help celebrate the last British soldiers' departure from the Suez base. Washington believed that he might have made an offer more favorable than the West's or, somewhat contradictorily, that Nasser was interested in the Western offer because he had been rebuffed by the Russians. In any case, Nasser "now gave the impression of a man who was convinced" that "he could play off East against West by blackmailing both."[93] As in the case of the Czech-Egyptian arms deal, both Eisenhower and Dulles deeply resented even the appearance of blackmail. There were reports that Nasser had concluded a second arms deal with the Russians, and this information intensified Washington's distrust, since administration officials believed that the deal was larger than it really was.[94] Reports of the arms purchase added to the administration's assumption that the basis for making the Aswan Dam loan had disappeared because the Egyptian cotton crop would be committed to paying for military equipment. According to the view prevailing in Washington, the Egyptian economy would not be strong enough to fulfill the obligations represented by the dam, and the resulting problems would lead ultimately to increased friction with Cairo.[95]

Among Eisenhower's entourage the only remaining proponent of the offer was the World Bank president, Eugene Black. After June meetings with Nasser, he believed that the Egyptians were still interested and could handle construction of the dam. When he returned to Washington, he found Dulles skeptical.[96] London, now totally disillusioned with Nasser, added its opposition. Since the initial Aswan offer had not been accepted, the two governments tentatively agreed by late June to drop the offer. They determined to let it wither quietly away, rather than make a formal announcement that could irritate Nasser.[97]

Ironically, the pro-American Egyptian ambassador to the United States quickly destroyed this strategy. Never has an Arab ambassador been more important to an American decision. At home to warn Nasser of America's negative reaction to his recognition of China, Ambassador Hussein coaxed the Egyptian leader into letting him return to Washington and accept the offer of the previous December without conditions. The Egyptians then informed the State Department of Hussein's mission, thereby forcing the administration to take specific action. (Behind the scenes, intelligence informed Dulles that the Egyptians expected a negative reply.)[98]

Recuperating in Gettysburg after a bout of ileitis, the president was briefed about Hussein's trip and, after a full discussion, made the final decision to revoke the Aswan offer.[99] The administration might have stalled, as in the arms deal the year before, but Ambassador Hussein wanted an answer. Furthermore, an explicit public response would gain credit with Congress and the public in an election year.

The meeting with the Egyptian ambassador was set for 19 July 1956. A statement was released at the same time that Dulles gave Ambassador Hussein the news privately. The meeting was unnecessarily tense, for Dulles reacted angrily to what he thought was Hussein's resort to blackmail when the ambassador intimated that the United States should not terminate the Aswan offer because otherwise the U.S.S.R. would pay for the dam.[100] Language concerning the inadequacy of Egypt's resources was included to explain the decision and indicate that it might one day be reexamined. The wording was not intended to insult Nasser, but it was likely to annoy him, a factor not seriously considered by the group around the secretary of state. The statement itself had been shown to Eisenhower that morning: "I looked at it and it seemed all right. Then I said, 'All right, go ahead'."[101]

The Aswan offer was reversed because of external and internal influences operating on the administration. Nasser's own actions in dealing with the Russians, in recognizing China, in blocking negotiations with Israel, and in refusing the initial offer undermined support even at the highest levels of the administration. Because the Aswan Dam offer required congressional funding approval, a positive Egyptian image was even more important than for other types of aid. In an election year the Eisenhower administration could not ignore the powerful coalition arrayed against it on the Aswan deal: the combination of pro-Israeli forces, cotton state senators, conservatives opposed to rewarding countries that depended on the Kremlin, and budget-minded congressmen who questioned the long-term financial outlay of the projected arrangement.

The Aswan reversal represented a victory for those domestic and bureaucratic interests who opposed a strong Egypt and for those who focused on the Baghdad Pact as the key to American strategy. The decision undermined the position of those who wanted to make Nasser central to Arab-American links. Henceforth, the Eisenhower administration planned to contain Nasser, not to bolster his strength. In March when the Anderson mission broke down, the president noted in his diary, "I suggested to the State Department that we begin to build up some other individual as a prospective leader of the Arab world—in the thought that mutually antagonistic personal ambitions might disrupt the aggressive plans that Nasser is evidently developing."[102] Cairo's recognition of China, rumors of stronger Soviet-Egyptian ties, and consolidated congressional opposition strengthened this resolve.

Regional tactics would now have to change: Nasser would have to be controlled rather than promoted. Before a new approach could be charted, however, Nasser suddenly took action which began the prolonged Suez crisis of 1956.

The Suez Crisis

In reaction to the Aswan Dam reversal, Nasser nationalized the Franco-British–owned Suez Canal Company. Eisenhower's first response was to send Dulles to London at the end of July to dissuade the allies from attacking. A prospective Franco-British intervention to recover the canal would have compromised American policy goals in the region.[103] Eisenhower and Dulles feared that intervention by American allies might make Washington appear "imperialist" and therefore less able to combat communism. At a meeting later in the crisis, "Secretary Dulles commented that he had been greatly worried for two or three years over our identification with countries pursuing colonial policies not compatible with our own."[104] Although determined to "contain Nasser," the American leadership feared that conniving at the Egyptian leader's demise might be interpreted in the area as antagonistic to Arab political needs.

For similar reasons, there was no desire to reward Israel with increased friendship. The administration ignored Israel's apprehensions about the increased fedayeen raids (which had precipitated her ill-considered Gaza raid of February 1955), the continuing Egyptian blockade of the Straits of Tiran, and the threat to the Egyptian-Israeli military balance posed by Cairo's Russian arms. It saw no link between these issues and Suez and therefore did not anticipate the Anglo-French-Israeli collusion.[105]

The administration focused only on the nationalization of the canal. Eisenhower and Dulles were preoccupied with preventing the war that the British and French so passionately wanted. Although the president opposed Egypt's action, he believed a compromise possible; his experiences at the more complex Panama Canal in the 1920s indicated to him that the Egyptians could handle the less difficult Suez passageway. Further, he believed that the Egyptian actions, however repugnant, did not merit military intervention. After all, the Suez Canal Company was supposed to revert to the Egyptians in 1968. Most important, he did not wish his record of peaceful foreign policies marred, especially before or during the reelection campaign in which he sought Republican control of both houses of Congress.[106]

Dulles, always the president's lawyer if more ideological and less practical, shared most of Eisenhower's views. But he was more thoroughly scandalized by Egypt's act, a threat in his eyes to property rights and the functioning of international legal arrangements.[107] He was by now involved with an anti-Nasser policy. There was also a difference in the functioning of the two: Eisenhower had the luxury of remaining at the White House or at his retreats, but Dulles shuttled between London and Washington (three times between 1 August and the end of September) and then to the U.N. in early October. Because of the notable difference in their perspectives and their tasks, Dulles sometimes seemed contradictory, sounding more sympathetic to the British and French position when he was away from Washington or in communication with them than when he was at home or in contact with the president. He was the one who had to deal with the British and French, calm their political and moral outrage, and confront their political and economic concerns.

Contradictions in the thinking of both Eisenhower and Dulles are revealed in the recently declassified minutes of a meeting held with congressional leaders in mid-August. On the one hand, both men compared Nasser to Hitler, with Dulles recalling "all our efforts to work with him until we finally became convinced that he is an extremely dangerous fanatic." The president for his part "wanted everyone to understand clearly that we do not intend to stand by helplessly and let this one man get away with what he is trying to do." On the other hand, the secretary told how he had warned the British and French against immediately using force because they "had not yet made their case." The president cautioned that an attempt to capture the canal would "get to be a long and tedious one, allowing the other fellow to hit and run." He believed that "we can't resign ourselves to underwriting the European economy permanently."[108]

It is no wonder then that Eden and French premier Guy Mollet were confused. They were determined to intervene and sought American approval for their action. Hence, they combed Dulles's statements for signs of implicit agreement, no matter how much he stressed a peaceful resolution of the Suez dispute. They also assumed that the United States would accept an intervention if diplomacy failed.[109]

In August Eden and Mollet went through the elaborate charade of an international conference in London on the canal's future because their generals had informed them that they needed six weeks in which to mobilize. Eisenhower and Dulles interpreted this strategy as prudence; it was simply a stalling operation. Years later Eisenhower suggested that he would have acquiesced if the British and French had acted immediately upon Nasser's nationalization.[110] As Eisenhower's later comment implies, the Franco-British justification for military force diminished as the canal continued to operate efficiently.

The outcome of the first London conference was a delegation to Cairo. Its leader, Australian Prime Minister Robert Menzies, was ideologically and personally the opposite of Nasser. This further impeded a mission that had no chance from the beginning. Dulles apparently realized the unlikelihood of success: he refused to join the delegation.

In early September, unknown to Washington, British and French guns were ready to strike. Dulles offered a slightly convoluted idea for a Suez Canal Users Association (SCUA). Somehow he managed to persuade Eden to explore the idea and even to suggest it as his own. The British leader continued to hope that Americans would accept military intervention.[111] More weeks were lost in diplomatic wrangle, and the French and British lost any pretext of international crisis as the European pilots withdrew and the Egyptians handled the canal efficiently on their own. In late September the allies shocked the secretary by bringing their complaints to the Security Council. When the Egyptians surprisingly accepted a proposed British compromise, Eden and Mollet added a rider negating the effect of the intended resolution and the Russians quickly obliged with a veto.[112] U.N. Secretary General Hammarskjold then sought to arrange talks and Nasser offered to negotiate personally with Eden and Mollet. Eisenhower had already expressed premature relief with the comment, "It looks like here is a very great crisis . . . behind us." Dulles expected the crisis to "wither on the vine."[113]

By this time the British and French were running out of excuses for attacking Nasser. The initial shock of his defiant act was abating, even in Western capitals. Paris therefore generated a new casus belli out of a problem hitherto unrelated to the crisis—the Arab-Israeli connection. The French, closely involved with Jerusalem over the previous two years with a virtual military alliance by the end of September, were well acquainted with Israel's fears of growing Egyptian strength.[114] However, French leaders were slow in revealing to their British counterparts the extent of their cooperation with the Israelis because of the British alliance with Jordan. To complicate matters still further, the Jordanians joined a defense bloc with Britain's enemy, Egypt (plus Syria), in mid-October.

In late 1955 Eden had suggested truncating Israel's territory; as late as mid-October 1956 his government was threatening to invoke its treaties with Jordan to attack the Jewish state for its harsh retaliatory raids against Jordanian-based fedayeen.[115] But once the French made the offer, Eden could not resist the opportunity to unseat Nasser, even if it meant collusion with the Israelis. The British were so concerned to protect their moderate Arab flank that Eden kept blocking a coherent plan, lest the collusion be discovered. His foreign secretary even suggested that the British attack an Israeli force to give credit to the story that the British and French were acting only to protect the canal and separate the Egyptian and Israeli armies.[116] The Israelis naturally refused to let their soldiers serve as cannon fodder for Eden's sensitivities.

The plan evolved by the three parties reflected their conflicting interests, dooming the cover story from the outset. They agreed that Israel would invade the Sinai and quickly land paratroopers near the Suez Canal. Then, the British and French would demand that the two sides withdraw from the canal area; when Egypt refused, they would have an excuse to attack in order to protect the waterway. To secure their lines, however, the Israelis demanded that air attacks on the Egyptians occur on the second day of the war, and the British and French agreed that the invasion of the canal area would come five days after the air strikes.[117]

As the British, French, and Israelis took the final step in their secret collusion, Dulles and Eisenhower had only tidbits of information: tension on the Jordanian-Israeli frontier, continuing Israeli mobilization, and Franco-British buildup in the Mediterranean, a suspicious termination of regular high-level communications with Washington by Paris and London, a sizeable growth in Israeli-French diplomatic radio traffic, a large increase in French Mystere pursuit planes for Israel beyond the number reported to Washington.[118] Two days before the Israeli attack, Eisenhower, who was in the hospital undergoing a pre-election checkup to prove his health good enough for another four years, warned Ben Gurion not to resort to force. "Israel and barium make quite a combination," he quipped to an aide.[119] The day before the Israelis attacked, Abba Eban, who had just returned from Israel but had not been told of the coming campaign, mystified the administration by playing golf. Summoned to see Dulles, he found the secretary staring at a huge map of the Israeli-Jordanian frontier.[120] Just hours before war, the administration was still in the dark.

Eight days before the election (29 October) the Israelis attacked as planned, in the Sinai—not against Jordan as the administration had suspected. During the first evening of meetings at the White House, the president made it clear that since the Tripartite Declaration and subsequent government statements committed the United States to aid a victim of aggression on either side of the conflict, we should "redeem our pledge" on behalf of Egypt.

The President said, in this matter, he does not care in the slightest whether he is re-elected or not. He feels we must make good on our word. He added that he did not really think the American people would throw him out in the midst of a situation like this, but if they did, so be it. Mr. Dulles said that one adverse result of this action may be a wave of anti-Semitism through the country, and general agreement was indicated.[121]

An appearance before the United Nations would be the first step, but that would not be enough, "We must take more definite action," Eisenhower argued. At one point "the President asked if a blockade would be effective." At another, "He said he did not fancy helping Egypt in the present circumstances but he felt our word must be made good."[122] The alternative was, "Russia is likely to enter the situation in the Middle East." Eisenhower even thought that support for Egypt might split the Arab world, with gains for the United States among the several countries "uneasy at Egyptian developments."[123] He determined to stop the Israelis before the war spread, offering Jerusalem a combination of carrot and stick—warnings if Israel continued and intimations of improved American-Israeli relations if the Israelis abruptly withdrew from the Sinai.[124] But the president's policy of distance from Jerusalem had decreased his leverage with Ben Gurion. He and Dulles were forced to condemn rather than control.

The frustration with the British and French was even greater. Although Dulles quickly suspected that London and Paris might have colluded with Jerusalem, there was hope that the British could be brought to support the American position. Eisenhower thought the British should be informed "that much is on their side in the dispute with the Egyptians, but that nothing justifies double-crossing us."[125] It soon became clear that the allies were presenting the United States with a fait accompli demanding American support and the fury at the White House knew no bounds. "The President said he did not see much value in an unworthy and unreliable ally and that the necessity to support them might not be as great as they believed." When his staff explained the disruptive effect of British and French actions upon European oil supplies, he turned acid tongued. "The President said he was inclined to think that those who began this operation should be left to work out their own oil problems—to boil in their own oil, so to speak."[126]

Eisenhower's resentment was deepened by the stunning shocks Washington was suffering. On the second day of the war, the British and French vetoed a resolution offered by the United States at the U.N. Security Council that called for Israeli withdrawal, no force by other states, and no aid to Israel. Then the British and French issued their planned ultimatum, giving both the Israelis and Egyptians twelve hours to withdraw ten miles on each side of the canal under the threat of a forceful intervention. In a telephone conversation with Eisenhower, Dulles called it "about as crude and brutal as anything he has ever seen."[127] When the Egyptians refused to accept the ultimatum, the British and French bombed their airfields (the French had already provided air cover over Israeli territory).[128] Because Eden wanted to protect the original cover story of a neutral intervention, the British and French expeditionary force was still several days away from a military capability on the ground.

With failure at the Security Council, the United States took the issue to the General Assembly. Dulles may have been slightly more antagonistic to

Nasser than his chief, but both believed that this crisis challenged the international organization.[129] If the violent use of force were allowed—no matter by whom—the United Nations would be undermined. In his speech at the General Assembly, Dulles argued, "The resort to force, the violent armed attack by three of our members upon a fourth, cannot be treated as other than a grave error, inconsistent with the principles and purposes of the Charter, and one which if persisted in would gravely undermine our Charter and undermine this organization."[130] The American resolution that the speech supported was rapidly passed, but hours afterward Dulles was afflicted with severe abdominal pains. He was taken to the hospital, where cancer was discovered. The secretary did not return to the State Department for several weeks and no other aide took his place as chief foreign policy advisor. Eisenhower, determined to restore the status quo ante bellum, was now alone at the helm.[131]

The Israeli attack had occurred on Monday, 29 October. By Saturday, 3 November, both Egypt and Israel had accepted a cease-fire, which the Israelis renounced two days later under pressure from the French and British who still wished to attack. So impoverished were Franco-British plans that they did not attack until Monday morning, 5 November; two hours later, the Israelis renewed their agreement to a cease-fire. By then they controlled the entire Sinai. Meanwhile, the disorganized Anglo-French invasion force had paratroop contingents on the ground, but amphibious forces were still twenty-four hours away. The cover story of neutrality was now blown, since the hostilities between Egypt and Israel had ceased.

Eisenhower was stunned at allied actions, revealing as they did both betrayal and incompetence. Punishment was required.[132] At least the Israelis had been effective. Besides, the British and French had committed their forces knowing full well that the Americans would have to bail them out if they got into real trouble with the Soviet Union. Although they relied on the United States, they had not even consulted Eisenhower and this riled the president most, leaving the Israelis further in the background.[133]

To complicate matters further, Hungary was in an uproar. At first it appeared that a Hungarian revolt had succeeded and a neutral government would come to power. The Russians had withdrawn their forces. But on Sunday, 4 November, the day before the Franco-British attack on Egypt, Soviet troops invaded Hungary with a vengeance. The forces of the new government quickly fell as the Russians reimposed a Communist regime. The United States watched helplessly, volunteering to assist any Hungarians who could flee across the Austrian border.

The United States had been challenged by friend and foe on the eve of a presidential election. No wonder that Eisenhower called the period beginning 20 October "the most crowded and demanding three weeks of my entire Presidency."[134] Eisenhower had to accept the inability of the United Nations and the United States to punish the Soviet Union for its acts in Hungary while remaining ready to deal firmly with the three errant democracies. It was an embarrassing double standard to uphold.

Shortly before the end of Mideast hostilities, the Russians suggested in a note to the president that the United States and the Soviet Union join forces to end the warfare in Egypt. The American response was to issue a White House statement calling a joint action with the Soviets "unthinkable." Eisenhower warned that any entry of new troops (i.e., the Soviets) into the area would be greeted by countermeasures from all members of the United Nations, including the United States.[135] Simultaneously, the Russians sent threatening notes to the British and French and an even more ominous letter to Israel.[136] Eisenhower did not rate the chances for Russian action as very high, but the letters from Moscow made his task of pressuring Paris, London, and Jerusalem easier.[137] Eden took the Russian letter less seriously than did either Mollet or Ben Gurion, but America's refusal to help arrest the decline of the pound sterling forced him to halt the Suez invasion on Tuesday, 6 November: election day in America. The French reluctantly agreed. Meanwhile, rumors abounded about possible Russian intervention (some observers later claimed that they were CIA-inspired). As a precaution, the president ordered steps to warn the Russians "without being provocative."[138] These steps foreshadowed actions that the United States would take on a more drastic scale at the end of the October 1973 war. As in 1973, Soviet-American preparations for a possible confrontation put pressure on the Israelis.

When it seemed as if the Israelis would not agree to withdraw without a settlement from the Sinai, Eisenhower, Hoover, and Rountree (the new Near Eastern assistant secretary of state) bluntly warned Jerusalem on 7 November of possible dire consequences: U.N. condemnations, attack by Soviet "volunteers," termination of all U.S. governmental and private aid.[139] As usual, the harsher warnings were uttered by the representatives of State, but the message was clear. Ben Gurion reluctantly announced on 8 November that the Israelis would withdraw, contingent upon satisfactory arrangements with the U.N. force then being established.

The British and French intended to exercise leverage on Egypt by maintaining their troops along the canal. However, the U.N. refused to allow clearance of the canal (blocked by the Egyptians early in the war) and the United States refused an emergency oil lift to Europe until troops were withdrawn. Key American officials were concerned that the Arabs might be alienated if the allies were aided prematurely through funds or by offsetting their oil shortages. At one point the president made it clear that as soon as the British and French initiated withdrawal, "we would talk to the Arabs to obtain the removal of any objections they may have regarding the provision of oil to Western Europe."[140] In this atmosphere British and French troops were out of Egypt by late December.

Throughout this period the Israelis sought to delay their own withdrawal in order to explain their actions and obtain greater support from the American populace. Israeli officials lobbied with bureaucrats, politicians, congressmen, prominent Republicans, elite leaders, and the American Jewish community. This effort succeeded by February in creating sympathy that had not existed in October. Jewish leaders—some of whom had questioned the Sinai invasion—now rallied to Israel's cause as its goals became clearer, more limited, and apparently more justified. After long consultation, the Israelis thought that State Department troubleshooter Robert Murphy was sympathetic to their position, that Assistant Secretary of State Rountree and U.N. Ambassador Lodge were not, and that Dulles himself understood their position on the Straits of Tiran.[141]

By early 1957, the Israelis still maintained positions in a small part of the Sinai overlooking the Straits of Tiran to protect their port of Eilat and in the Gaza Strip to block fedayeen raids. In the United Nations, however, pressure continued for total Israeli withdrawal. Unlike the 1947–1948 period when Truman faced a United Nations largely in favor of partition and a secretary general sympathetic to the emergence of the state of Israel, there was now general U.N. opposition to Israel's Sinai campaign and a secretary general opposed to Israeli use of force.

By early February the administration was in something of a quandary. On the one hand, there was talk at the United Nations of imposing sanctions on Israel if her troops remained in the Sinai. The administration could hardly acquiesce in the Israeli position without sacrificing its principles against the use of force and without jeopardizing a new effort to promote relations with the Arab world. On the other hand, the administration was not as independent as it had been during the war. There was now more congressional and public sympathy for Israel, as well as more criticism of Eisenhower's pressure on Israel after the United States' inability to counter Moscow's brutal suppression of the national uprising in Hungary.[142] Moreover, congressional support was required to approve a new Middle East program the administration was now recommending. Criticism of the administration for threatening Israel was coming from several congressmen, including the Republican and Democratic Senate leaders, William Knowland and Lyndon Johnson.[143]

Eisenhower and Dulles tried to ease their way out of the dilemma by coaxing Israel into a compromise, thus avoiding a controversial vote at the United Nations on sanctions against Jerusalem—an issue on which the administration could not conceivably avoid foreign and domestic opposition. Israel was offered an aide-mémoire in which the United States called for withdrawal from Gaza but accepted the Israeli claim that the Gulf of Aqaba "comprehends international waters."[144] Then, the administration offered a highly limited guarantee. The United States was prepared, on behalf of American vessels, to exercise the right of free and innocent passage through the gulf and "to join with others to secure general recognition of this right." When Dulles refused to make the American pledges more formal and broad, Israel did not accept the *aide-mémoire*.[145]

That was as far as the administration was prepared to go. U.N. Ambassador Lodge continued warning Eisenhower that a successful Arab U.N. resolution advocating economic sanctions against Israel was imminent.[146] Under the pressure of events at the U.N., the president's closest advisors (Dulles, Humphrey, Lodge) unanimously believed that Israel must withdraw immediately without further concessions or guarantees. Eisenhower therefore determined to push the Israelis back, even if it meant terminating all private American assistance (governmental aid had already been suspended when the Israelis invaded the Sinai).[147]

On 20 February the president met with congressional leaders, hoping to solicit bipartisan support in favor of pressure on Israel. The president spoke of clearing the Suez Canal and resuming oil supplies to Europe; he held out the possibility of renewed economic aid to Israel if it withdrew, and fretted about a possible increase of Russian influence with the Arabs if it did not. However, the congressional leadership refused to issue a joint statement with Eisenhower.[148]

The president thought the congressional hesitation petty and political, but several legislators found his position morally and politically wrong.[149] During the meeting key participants such as Johnson and Knowland repeatedly asked why Israel should be pressured over a sliver of Sinai when the Russians were not hampered over Hungary. Dulles and Lodge responded that the existence of the veto power created an "inbuilt double standard" and the U.N. would "never vote sanctions against either Russia or the United States."[150]

Lodge stressed that since the Suez crisis began, the Arabs had developed an "increased respect" for the United States; "he concluded that the Arabs would feel we have abandoned our position if we do not support some effective measures to accomplish Israeli withdrawal." The U.N. ambassador "referred several times to indications that Egypt would make concessions once Israeli withdrawal had been accomplished." However, the Israelis and their American supporters were skeptical of Arab intentions and sought firmer assurances that freedom of passage through the Straits of Tiran and a U.N. administration of Gaza would indeed occur. But the president refused to reward aggression and feared alienating the Arabs if major concessions were made to the Israeli government. He also distrusted Israeli objectives. In addition to assurances on Gaza and the straits, he thought the Israelis "wanted an absolute guarantee, such as a security treaty with the United States."[151]

As a consequence, those congressmen who sought to reassure the Ben Gurion government were not appeased. Unwilling to accept the president's position and unable to produce an alternative that he would accept, key congressional leaders recommended that the president take his case to the people. The president readily agreed to this and delivered a blunt television broadcast that evening in which he systematically rejected each argument made on behalf of Israel.

It was clear to the Israelis that they would have to withdraw after the president had committed himself so forcefully. They also knew that the United States, despite the administration's position, was more likely to compromise than the United Nations. Therefore, it was a matter of getting the best deal possible from Washington. Dulles and Eban met frequently, sometimes at the secretary's home. During the discussions, Secretary General Hammarskjold demurred on several key points that Dulles was ready to accept, forcing further Israeli concessions.[152] The secretary general's influence was balanced by the French, who helped arrange a final compromise.[153]

In order to convey the proper messages at the U.N., an elaborate performance was arranged between Eban and Dulles with the stage to be the General Assembly. When Israeli Foreign Minister Golda Meir made her speech before that body on 1 March, she indicated that Israel would withdraw totally from the area it had occupied, but that it expected the United Nations Emergency Force which had been assembled not to withdraw precipitously from the Gulf of Aqaba area. If Israeli shipping was forcefully interdicted, Meir announced that Israel would exercise its "inherent right of self-defense under article 51 of the Charter" to insure that passage. (This statement became the immediate casus belli in 1967.) The reference to Article 51 of the U.N. Charter had been suggested by Dulles himself.[154] Meir announced that Israel was withdrawing from the Gaza Strip on the assumption that UNEF, rather than the Egyptians, would exercise control "exclusively"—thereby preventing fedayeen raids because the United Nations would control Gaza.

As the Americans and Israelis had planned, Ambassador Lodge spoke immediately after Meir, but his statement surprised the Israelis. They thought that Dulles had committed the United States to "international rule in Gaza without the Egyptians" and anticipated that Lodge would make that position public. They expected him to reiterate Meir's statement, but instead he was vague. In reference to the straits, he called her assumptions "not unreasonable." On Gaza, however, he emphasized the 1949 armistice agreements and the role of the U.N. secretary general, thereby deviating radically from the Dulles-Eban agreements by not stating that the U.S. supported a U.N. administration in Gaza and opposed an Egyptian return.[155]

Whatever the reasons for the difference between Israeli expectations and Lodge's actual statement,* this stance helped the United States maintain its

---

*Dulles and not Lodge had made the private arrangements in the first place. The ambassador had been influenced by the tougher attitude toward the Israelis at the U.N. during the Suez period. Without a prepared script and under the influence of a different atmosphere at the U.N., he was more likely to present a different perspective; his constituency was not identical to the secretary's. It

credibility with sympathetic Arab regimes. A successful new American program in the Middle East was possible because the United States had brought Israel to withdraw without substantial public commitments in return.[156] Thus, the Eisenhower administration avoided the appearance of softening its tough stance against rewarding aggression.

Concerning the conflict itself, Israel had cause to voice fears that the blockade of the Straits and the raids from Gaza would resume. But for American global and regional policy, it was difficult to deal with the Israeli complaint and still initiate a new diplomacy with the Arab world. Since the United States had little leverage on Egypt, Eisenhower and Dulles assumed that once the Israelis withdrew, Nasser would cooperate with the United Nations; at least they thought that Hammarskjold had assurances from Cairo. At the critical meeting with congressmen on 20 February, Eisenhower had argued that "nobody liked the idea of sanctions, and he asked what could possibly be done to reach a settlement if it were not possible to encourage Israel's withdrawal to the 1949 line, especially since the Arabs assert that the withdrawal is the sine qua non of any settlement." Dulles added at the same meeting that Ambassador Eban had been informed privately "of the possibility that Egypt would accept, subsequent to Israeli withdrawal, some new form of administration of the Gaza Strip."[157]

Despite American expectations, the Egyptians assumed control over the district as soon as the Israelis withdrew from Gaza. Since UNEF remained on the border between Gaza and Israel, the fedayeen raids did not resume. After this thin compromise, the Suez crisis was finally settled and the administration could move forward, giving little further attention to the Arab-Israeli conflict other than commenting on Nasser's irresponsibility. Eisenhower believed that Nasser had violated an understanding with Hammarskjold and demonstrated "lack of concern for the good will of those powers which had so recently come to his aid," but the president still thought that the Egyptian leader was "within his rights according to the Armistice of 1949 and that, in any case, Israel had gained in world public opinion from her 'unconditional withdrawal' from the Strip."[158]

The withdrawal of Israeli forces had a different impact in the Middle East than in America. For both the Arabs and Israelis, the return to the original 1949 armistice lines was the sharp result of the diplomatic confrontation in the area. For the Eisenhower administration, however, the evacuation of the remaining Israeli forces from the Sinai was only an aspect of its global and regional aims. The withdrawal removed a nuisance, which had provoked policy contradictions and domestic conflict.

The methods employed in gaining Israeli withdrawal had profound im-

---

is even possible that he did not understand the significance of special words. Certainly it would have been preferable for Dulles to have made the statement himself, since he had been the American official most responsible for negotiating with the Israelis.

plications for the future American role in the conflict, as all Middle East participants drew lessons from the actions of the United States in 1956–1957. For
example, after the Six-Day War the Arabs were convinced that the proper
amount of threat and enticement would persuade the Americans to repeat their
1957 performance. By the same token, the Israelis became dramatically apprehensive at any sign of American pressure to make them withdraw from territory for, from their perspective, inadequate concessions. And after the
Egyptians failed to cooperate on Gaza in 1957 and on the straits in 1967, the
United States was itself less prepared to press the Israelis than it had been in
1957. Regarding policy formulation, the Suez crisis demonstrated that an administration unified in philosophy and structured to restrict diversity could effectively withstand external and internal constraints.

The lessons of Suez were intensified for the Arabs and Israelis because
many of the top leaders in each government remained. In 1967 participants such
as Nasser, Hussein, Meir, and Eban were still in positions of influence as they
had been in 1957. In the United States, whatever lessons were to be drawn from
1957 were less clearly perceived by a new set of leaders, although within the
American bureaucracy a fascination with a 1957-type solution remained. In
later years the formula would recur of initial Israeli withdrawals and a settlement
based on isolating and protecting Israel with a cordon sanitaire of U.N. forces
and guarantees.

With the final withdrawal of Israeli troops from the Sinai and Gaza, the
Suez crisis ended but it had been clothed in paradox. A conflict with Egypt over
Aswan had indirectly led to American confrontation with Israel; world indigna-
tion over a simultaneous Soviet intervention in Hungary had sharpened
Eisenhower and Dulles's impatience with their allies; and the Russians who confronted the United States over Suez actually functioned as an instrument of
American policy. The Suez crisis has special complexity as a crisis in America's
relations with her two oldest European allies, with the Arabs and Israelis, and
with the Soviet Union.

As American actions toward the Middle East in the months ahead would
demonstrate, a technological and legal approach was inadequate for the Arab-
Israeli problem. But the significance of Arab nationalism and Israel's social and
psychological isolation, which had led to the attack in the first place, was lost on
the American leadership. The administration was not content to delay pursuing
its anti-Communist aims until the Arab-Israeli dispute was resolved. Settlement
of the dispute was never an interest of itself but merely a step in the containment
strategy. As administration actions after the Suez war would make painfully
clear, Eisenhower and Dulles were concerned with manipulating the local scene
so that the individual parties would be useful in their global enterprises. Yet
without the British and French presence in the Middle East, America would
become more exposed and vulnerable.

A "New" Middle East Program

Despite U.S. opposition to the French, British, and Israeli military action, official American opposition to Nasser was mounting. As soon as the Anderson mission had collapsed the previous spring, Eisenhower had begun to discuss the possibility of grooming King Saud of Saudi Arabia as Nasser's rival. "It would begin to appear that our efforts should be directed toward separating the Saudi Arabians from the Egyptians and concentrating, for the moment at least, on making the former see that their best interests lie with us, not with the Egyptians and with the Russians." Though admitting that he "did not know the man," Eisenhower's interest was natural because of the Middle East oil factor. In a telephone conversation with Dulles in April, the "President said we still want to settle our differences with Saudi Arabia; wondered if there was any way we could flatter or compliment King Saud." Later in the conversation, the "President said again we must find some way to be friends with King Saud."[159]

Opposition to Nasser by now ran deep. In a meeting with the president three weeks before Israel invaded the Sinai, Under Secretary of State Hoover "referred to the visit of a group with one of our agencies on how to tackle Nasser. He questioned whether this is the time to attempt this. The President said that an action of this kind could not be taken when there is as much active hostility as at present. For a thing like this to be done without inflaming the Arab world, a time free from heated stress holding the world's attention as at present would have to be chosen."[160]

Eisenhower had another scheme for overthrowing Nasser. In a mid-December cable to Dulles at a NATO meeting in Paris, he told his secretary of state, "I am sure that they [our NATO friends] know that we regard Nasser as an evil influence. I think also we have made it abundantly clear while we share in general the British and French opinions of Nasser, we insisted that they chose a bad time and incident on which to launch corrective measures."[161] The president made clear that his method of satisfying Franco-British objectives was to "build up an Arab rival of Nasser . . . If we could build him up as the individual to capture the imagination of the Arab world, Nasser would not last long."[162]

Thus King Ibn Saud of Saudi Arabia was invited to Washington at the end of January. It was the first official visit by an Arab head of state; no Israeli leader was so honored during Eisenhower's eight years. When announced, the trip created a storm of public controversy, especially among supporters of Israel. Eisenhower proceeded with the visit but soon discovered that he did not have the right man for his purposes. Not surprisingly, the king understood his role better than the president; when he departed for Washington, he sent his brother to see Nasser. Eisenhower reported in his memoirs, "No political advances were realized in the talks."[163]

The collapse of the Saudi strategy left the administration with a program that rapidly became labeled as the Eisenhower Doctrine. The president believed that "an understanding with the Arabs" was necessary. Yet, because of British involvement, the Baghdad Pact itself no longer seemed a viable strategy. "The President thought that if the British get us into the Baghdad Pact—as the matter would appear to the Arabs—we would lose our influence with the Arabs."[164] Therefore, Eisenhower had in mind an expanded Middle East program to thwart Communist influence:

> The President thought that we are in a period in which we can strengthen our bilateral arrangements with the various Arab countries, not being so bound as in the past by the Arab-Israeli dispute. These might tend to bring Egypt into an appropriate role. He would be prepared to take bold constructive action in this regard.[165]

By mid-December he was telling Dulles, "I hope that our friends in Europe will see the necessity, as we see it, of beginning confidentially and on a staff level to develop policies and plans whereby the West can work together in making the Mid East secure from Communist penetration."[166] Shortly thereafter he was meeting with the congressional leadership on New Year's Day and telling them that "not until two weeks ago had any plans for the Middle East been put on paper." The president now recommended a program of economic and military assistance and he sought prior congressional agreement that American troops would be used should any country in the area request aid to thwart overt armed aggression from any nation controlled by international communism.[167]

As Dulles informed the assembled congressmen, "the United States would focus solely on the Russian threat, making certain of keeping clear of internal squabbles . . . The Secretary summarized the situation as one that could be met successfully by restoring confidence of security against any direct aggression and of protecting against indirect aggression through economic programs of a size not much larger than presently in being." To the president a resolution by Congress was needed because the "entire world" had to be put "on notice that we are ready to move instantly if necessary."[168]

The president's presentation to Congress triggered a general discussion with much criticism of the administration's part in the Suez crisis and its general Middle East policy. Some congressmen questioned why the Eisenhower Doctrine dealt with overt aggression from international communism, when many believed that national communism, or even more probably, Communist subversion in situations of local instability, were more pressing dangers. Others complained that the doctrine did not deal with the Arab-Israeli dispute; still others were concerned that it confused the Constitutional roles of the president and Congress in the declaration and conduct of war.[169]

Among the usual interested groups a unique diversity prevailed. Oilmen were at the time becoming worried that Nasserism would threaten their holdings in the area; they outspokenly supported the Eisenhower Doctrine. For similar reasons pro-Arab groups with strong cultural, educational, and religious ties in conservative Arab countries such as Lebanon and Jordan voiced support.[170] Many Egypt-firsters (including many officers in the Near East Bureau and the CIA) were skeptical, arguing that the doctrine would be anathema to Nasser and to all who sympathized with him, thereby dissipating the goodwill gained by the United States during Suez.[171] As before, the split within the Arab world was reflected among Arab supporters at home.

For the pro-Israeli forces, the doctrine was a relatively minor issue, and some confusion reigned. During congressional hearings on the subject, spokesmen for American Jewish groups generally supported the doctrine while seeing it as largely irrelevant to the Arab-Israeli conflict.[172] The Israelis initially suspected the doctrine.

The controversy over pressure on Israel to withdraw to the 1949 armistice line delayed Senate passage of the doctrine but that roadblock was overcome when the Israelis complied. With congressional approval, the president quickly signed and announced that the United States would collaborate more actively with the Baghdad Pact and join its military planning committee.[173] Like the Baghdad Pact before it, the doctrine was opposed by Egypt and Syria but Nasser's enemies in the Arab world welcomed it. In Lebanon and Jordan, however, the idea precipitated much domestic turmoil generated by Nasserite opposition to the arrangement. An American program designed to stop the Communists was rapidly becoming part of the "Arab Cold War."[174]

The Israelis were last to announce a reluctant acceptance. Abba Eban, who quipped privately that it was the "Doctrine of the Immaculate Assumption," lobbied with the Israeli Cabinet back home, arguing that the American guarantee ought to include Israel.[175] The Israeli military prowess shown in the Sinai campaign had raised eyebrows in the American bureaucracy, especially in the Pentagon. The Eisenhower Doctrine pushed the process of reassessing Israel along, almost imperceptively—for the first time the Israelis had become a part of a multilateral program sponsored by the United States.[176]

The Eisenhower Doctrine was rooted in the same assumptions as the Baghdad Pact, but it was designed for a situation in which the Russians had already broken through the "northern tier" that Dulles had sought to erect in the first term. The Eisenhower experience in the Middle East was now bathed in ironies. By scrupulously avoiding identification with the British and French during Suez, the administration so weakened them that a power vacuum was created—leading to Washington assuming the "imperialist" mantle in spite of itself. The policy that had hoped to resolve the Arab-Israeli dispute and promote Arab unity behind American leadership had turned away from those efforts.

Instead, the new concentration was on the Communist menace, and any instability in the area was perceived as originating behind the Kremlin walls.

The Eisenhower Doctrine Applied

During its first year the doctrine was invoked toward two countries—Jordan and Syria. In the early months of 1957, young King Hussein seemed threatened by various nationalist elements. The White House, seeing the trouble as instigated by Communists, invoked the doctrine and showed off the Sixth Fleet. The king finally staged a "kind of royal coup d'etat" and won out over other factions.[177]

Syria was the next little tempest in the Middle Eastern teapot. In mid-1957 Eisenhower and Dulles thought that the Damascus government might be succumbing to international communism because of its anti-American accusations, personnel changes in the government, and reports of Soviet arms shipments. Dulles bluntly stated the administration's view in a confidential memo to the president:

> There is evidence in Syria of the development of a dangerous and classic pattern. The Soviets first promise and extend aid, military and/or economic. With this aid they promote the control of any positions by pro-Soviet persons. The end result sought is that the country will fall under the control of International Communism and become a Soviet Satellite, whose destinies are directed from Moscow.[178]

In response, the usual instruments were used: the Sixth Fleet, a prestigious envoy, assurances and arms shipments to Syria's neighbors. The Domino Theory reigned supreme. According to Eisenhower, "with Syria firmly in communist hands, the other Arab nations could scarcely avoid a similar fate." Perhaps it would be necessary for Syria's neighbors to participate in an attack against her in order "to react to anticipated aggression . . ."[179] The conservative Arab regimes decided one by one that such an enterprise against Arab brethren was too "radical" an idea. Slowly, the Syrian crisis petered out; in 1958 the Syrian army coaxed Egypt into unifying with them in order to prevent the growth of communism in the country.[180] The United Arab Republic was born.

In the crisis atmosphere of the post-Suez era, Eisenhower and Dulles were no longer wooing the whole Arab world to gain allies in the conflict with the Soviet Union. Now they were intervening in intra-Arab affairs to assure that those individuals and forces inclined to reject Soviet influence either rose to power or remained in authority. The effort to co-opt Arab governments into the program for containing the Soviet Union had been replaced by a doctrine which projected the international hunt for communists into Arab politics.

Many pro-Arab oilmen cheered the new policy because they feared the rise of nationalist forces bent on massive nationalizations; but "evenhanded" types within the bureaucracy and without were worried about American acceptability in various "nationalist" Arab circles and became disenchanted with the administration's approach to Arab affairs. On the other side, pro-Israel forces could only marvel at the rapid transformation of the Eisenhower-Dulles team, who now fretted over developments in the Arab world and seemed less concerned with Israel as an obstacle to the attainment of American objectives.

Although the Eisenhower Doctrine was designed to combat international communism, it rapidly became an instrument against Nasserist Arab nationalism. The Egyptian leader remained an enigma in Washington through the 1960s. But in the late 1950s the various bureaucracies (especially in State and CIA) were busily debating the objectives and content of Nasser's policies and what the United States should do about them. Few in Washington were as critical of Nasser as Eisenhower and Dulles were. The president later admitted that by early 1958 the Egyptian leader's "exact political leanings were still something of a mystery" but that did not prevent him from concluding with Dulles that "If he was not a Communist, he certainly succeeded in making us very suspicious of him."[181] Matters reached such a state that at one point in this period Allen Dulles misunderstood his brother and thought he wanted Nasser assassinated.[182]

In early 1958, yet another crisis developed in the area, this time in Lebanon. The country's pro-Western president had designs on amending the constitution so that he could stay in office. In response armed mobs rioted, generally pro-Nasser and anti-American in tone. Nasser seemed to be encouraging the rebels, but there was no indication of Soviet involvement. Eisenhower and Dulles, however, saw red. "Behind everything was our deep-seated conviction that the Communists were principally responsible for the trouble . . ." By mid-May a false alarm occurred when intervention was considered. Foster Dulles favored "direct action," but his brother, Allen, was more cautious, "urging a delay of at least 24 hours." In the end tensions temporarily subsided. Meanwhile, Dulles reinterpreted a doctrine designed to protect states against the aggressions of international communism into a doctrine that permitted involvement in an internal civil war if the regime in power requested assistance. Congressional protests were ignored.[183]

The crisis in Lebanon seemed to be ebbing when, on 14 July, a swift military coup occurred in Iraq where the pro-Western government was ousted and its leadership brutally murdered. The Lebanese president immediately sought an American protective intervention.[184] Officials in Washington began studying the situation during the night to make recommendations, but the president was not waiting. By mid-morning he had already made up his mind to intervene in Lebanon where there was still a reasonable chance that the pro-

Western government could be saved. Dulles was supportive, and, of the key advisors with whom the president met, only Deputy Defense Secretary Quarles raised serious objections.[185] The mood of the day is reflected in conclusions emerging from a meeting of key officials with the secretary of state.

There was general agreement that the effects of the United States doing nothing would be:
1. Nasser would take over the whole area;
2. The United States would lose influence not only in the Arab states of the Middle East but in the area generally, and our bases throughout the area would be in jeopardy;
3. The dependability of United States' commitments for assistance in the event of need would be brought into question throughout the world.[186]

Allen Dulles told congressional leaders at the White House that in a discussion with the American ambassador King Saud's emissary had "demanded" that the Baghdad powers intervene in Iraq and Jordan or "what is the use of all these pacts?"[187]

The next day the Marines landed on the beaches of Beirut, greeted by the sunbathers and soft drink peddlers typical of calm beaches in mid-summer. Although American troops initially encountered sporadic gunfire, they did not engage in any serious combat and the situation in the country rapidly calmed.[188] Why had Eisenhower sent them? First, he had been inching towards a Middle East intervention since Suez, as crises occurred in one country after another. Second, after the Iraqi coup, he feared falling dominoes—Lebanon, Jordan, the Persian Gulf states. Iraq, rich in oil, had been central to Eisenhower's hopes for Western orientation in the Middle East, a position reinforced by his disappointment with King Saud. The coup would put at least $45 million worth of American military assistance in the hands of new leaders. They would also acquire access to the secret military plans of the Baghdad Pact and to the former Iraqi leadership's schemes for subversion in Syria. If the Iraqi coup could not be reversed (at the outset there were some in Washington who hoped that it might), Eisenhower wanted at least to contain it.[189]

The president would later ruminate, "In Lebanon the question was whether it would be better to incur the deep resentment of nearly all the Arab world (and some of the rest of the Free World) and in doing so risk general war with the Soviet Union or to do something worse—which was to do nothing."[190] This was strange reasoning indeed for the man who less than two years before had counseled his allies to be patient and allow the procedures of the United Nations to run their course. But by now Eisenhower was in a very different mood; antagonism to radical Arab nationalism had become more central and the president seems to have assumed that an anti-Western coup and the potential of more were threats of larger magnitude than the nationalization of the Suez Canal Company. In short, interests perceived to be vital to the United States were more important than those of the British and French.

In a farcical twist, the British and Israelis now found themselves cooperating with the Americans in another Mideast intervention: the British moved into Jordan with American acquiescence. Despite encouraging Western action, the Saudi Arabians (seeking nationalist support) refused to allow Britain to use their U.S. airbase for resupply. When the British requested overflight rights in Israel, Ben Gurion phoned Dulles to verify their American backing, not wishing to make the same mistake twice. Dulles received the call at 2:30 A.M. in Washington. There were difficulties, but the Israelis had now demonstrated their ability to assist the United States in a crisis.[191] Meanwhile, additional American forces were sent to the area to protect the regimes or territories of Jordan, Kuwait, and Saudi Arabia. As a final insurance, Eisenhower related, "I instructed General Twining to be prepared to employ, subject to my personal approval, *whatever* [translate thermonuclear] means might become necessary to prevent any unfriendly forces from moving into Kuwait. In the state of tension then existing, these measures would probably bring us no closer to general war than we were already."[192]

In response to a series of congressional questions, Eisenhower pondered whether the "impetus" for the intervention came "solely from Nasser, or through him from the Soviet Union." The president told General Twining, "he is so small a figure and of so little power, that he is a puppet even though he probably doesn't think so."[193]

Some congressmen were skeptical over the intervention. While the obedient mores of the times meant that the commander-in-chief's actions would be supported, there were potential constraints on expanding the adventure.[194] As it turned out, things went well. Eisenhower sent Deputy Under Secretary of State Robert Murphy to Beirut to mediate among the conflicting Lebanese factions, and he successfully arranged for new elections—held at the end of July in the Lebanese parliament. The last American troops were out of the country by the end of October, recording only one fatality.[195] Even in Iraq, the extraordinary Eisenhower luck prevailed. The days of British and American dominance in Baghdad were over, but the new regime (though nationalist) soon had ample difficulties with Nasser, Iraq's Communists, and the Soviet Union. Nasser's influence had not expanded after all.

Having acted forcefully, the American leadership now took a more relaxed attitude toward developments in the area. Whether or not Nasser was actually contained, Eisenhower was comforted by having finally acted decisively toward the Egyptian leader.[196] The catharsis of Lebanon allowed the president and his immediate entourage to deemphasize Middle East issues; once they paid less attention, competitors for influence both inside and outside the government could have more effect.

The policies favored by many bureaucrats and Israeli advocates ran counter to the thrust of American policy in the years following Suez. In 1957 and 1958, culminating with the Lebanese intervention, the United States had remained aloof from the two principal states in the Arab-Israeli theater—Egypt and Israel. The main sources of tension had been pro-Western states like Lebanon, Jordan, Saudi Arabia, and Iraq, and the possibility that Syria might fall to communism. Now the administration began a program gradually to strengthen relations with Israel and Egypt, which many outside the White House had been urging.

As usual, the pro-Israeli vehicle was Congress. The administration acquiesced in broader programs of economic and technical aid to Israel even while it discontinued economic grant aid on the basis of Israel's progress.[197] Pro-Israeli voices also focused on complaints about individual Arab policies—the Saudi Arabian refusal to allow Jews to serve at the American airbase or, indeed, to enter the country; the Arab boycott against American businesses dealing with Israel; the Egyptian refusal to allow Israeli nonmilitary cargoes through the Suez Canal despite agreements to the contrary. On these matters the pro-Israeli forces were quietly successful in gaining congressional backing. They achieved wider support for specific issues than had been the case before Suez, suggesting a new strength. They were not successful, however, in changing either the administration's passive approach to these matters or the policies of individual Arab countries.

Bureaucrats who remained committed to the Egypt-first posture saw their policies rejected consistently after Suez. For example, after the Aswan Dam reversal, a State Department–Pentagon–CIA paper had been presented to the National Security Council describing Nasser as the "wave of the future." It recommended beating the Soviets at their own game by giving Nasser economic and military support, but Eisenhower and Dulles had rejected it.[198] In the months following the Lebanese accommodation, however, aid to Egypt was resumed for the first time since Suez and then increased.

Several factors contributed to the shift. First, with the Middle East on the back burner, matters were left more to State Department officials responsible for the area. Many of them were anxious to see if improved relations with Nasser would bear fruit. Second, Nasser did not seem as threatening after Lebanon, an interpretation supported by deteriorating relations between Egypt and the Soviet Union in early 1959. Third, Dulles died in May 1959; he had already been replaced by his more mellow undersecretary, Christian Herter. Although the new secretary did not have his predecessor's influence with the president, he was more in tune with many of the administration's critics. He came to the office with a record of publicly expressed friendship toward Israel, but he was also more willing than John Foster Dulles to condone approaches to Egypt, as indicated by his approval of a PL-480 wheat sale to Egypt that had been opposed by Dulles.[199] Herter made it easier for the lower levels of the department to pursue a muted form of the original Egypt-first policy.

In these limited approaches, a basic split continued among those favoring strengthened ties with the Arab world. Although the Baghdad Pact policy had become unworkable, Nasser was still deeply distrusted by oilmen, some officials, and many pro-Arab partisans well disposed toward Arab conservatives. Many frustrated officials in Washington argued, however, that the only policy left to the United States was to improve relations with Cairo.

Conclusion

The Eisenhower administration had begun with a grandiose and comprehensive strategy toward the Middle East and had ended with reduced attention at the top and a muted approach overall. Indeed, no administration would attempt major initiatives toward the Arab world again until late 1969. In evaluating the record, policies, and decision-making style of the administration, the contrast is dramatic between its high hopes and great attention and limited results. For every Middle East policy problem, the policy had failed by the time Eisenhower left office. The Russians had not been prevented from breaking through the "northern tier" and establishing a base in the heart of the area. After the debacle at Suez, the Western position had seriously declined. Regionally, relations with a divided Arab world were more uneven than they had been when the Republican administration assumed office. Finally, no progress had been made in resolving the Arab-Israeli conflict and, indeed, a second Arab-Israeli war had been fought with a further hardening of the opposing positions.

Because of their failures, the Eisenhower strategy and tactics offer useful lessons. Eisenhower was the one president after Israel's establishment who confronted Jerusalem and demanded changes in Israeli policy (October 1953, November 1956, February 1957). In this approach, he pursued the very policy toward Israel long favored by advocates of improved Arab ties. Yet, the policy failed to block Russian gains and it did not achieve an enhanced American position in the Arab world. After Suez, relations with Nasser continued to deteriorate. Within two years the area's major pro-Western regime, conservative Iraq, had fallen to a nationalist military coup and American and British troops had to rescue the regimes in Lebanon and Jordan. Critics have argued whether these post-Suez debacles prove the press-Israel strategy ineffective or whether the failures occurred because the administration mishandled a workable policy. (Others, of course, have argued that Israel would never have invaded the Sinai if it had not been isolated by the effects of Eisenhower's policy.) The cause of American post-Suez frustration in the Middle East is debatable, but the record demonstrates that when heavy pressure on Israel was exercised, U.S. problems were worsened.

For the president himself, Israel was the reason for his problems. At the time of the Lebanon intervention, he told colleagues that "except for Israel we could form a viable policy in the area." The president of Ghana, Kwame Nkrumah, had recently told him that Israel was now tacitly accepted by the other countries of the region. "If this is true, it may be possible for us to find a way out. If our policy is solely to maintain the Kings of Jordan and Saudi Arabia in their positions, the prospect is hopeless, even in the short term." Dulles cautioned against regarding Arab unity as a "valid, permanent movement," but the president reiterated that he was trying "to get at the underlying Arab thinking. We must either work with it or change it, or do some of both. He recognized that they may act out of violence, emotion and ignorance. Our question is still how to get ourselves to the point where the Arabs will not be hostile to us."[200]

A few days earlier Eisenhower had told visiting British Foreign Secretary Lloyd that it was "essential that we be more skillful in identifying the interest of Arab nationalism with the free countries of the world and the Western point of view. The Communists had taken over this concept of nationalism and we must do a better job in winning the minds of the Arabs."[201] It is unclear how the radio stations and increased propaganda operations that Eisenhower had in mind would alter Arab attitudes toward the West, of which the Arab position on Israel was a part. Once the president had concluded, following the failure of the Anderson mission, that he could not resolve the issue, his strategy toward the region was seriously jeopardized. The president was essentially pessimistic, as he commented at the time of Lebanon: "The United States seems to have become anathema to the region . . ."[202]

By mid-1958, Eisenhower had ample reason for chagrin as he surveyed his Mideast policy. By attempting to maneuver between the conflicting interests of Egypt, Israel, Britain, and France, the administration had alienated all of them. Having seen clearly that the British and French position was on the wane and that an Arab-Israeli settlement would help secure American interests, the administration was unable to devise policies to please any party concerned.

The tactics devised by Eisenhower and Dulles to accomplish their goals, though unsuccessful, were not lacking in ingenuity. Indeed, despite later criticism of this administration for its passivity in many areas, it can be criticized for over-activity in the Middle East. In Eisenhower's first term, area leaders were treated to a dizzying array of initiatives, which ended finally in reneging on one of the projects—the Aswan Dam.

The one-dimensional nature of Eisenhower's policy making undermined its chances for success. Neither the president nor the secretary of state were exposed to sufficiently diverse views of American policy. For example, the two leaders were probably naïve in underestimating the intensity of feelings on both sides: first, the Israelis' psychological need for manifest support, and second, the

Arabs' hostility toward Israel and imperialism, both of which could easily include the United States. Certainly, there was little understanding of the area's cultural and historical dynamics.

Finally, only one perspective was represented in the administration: that disposed towards the conservative Arabs. Many critics of the administration believed that the United States had ignored and weakened Israel during the Eisenhower era. Others believed that the United States should have accommodated the new Arab nationalism. After the intervention in Lebanon and Dulles's death, these two competing views gained more credence. Only when the Eisenhower-Dulles team ended did a new approach evolve.

If any group of Americans involved in the Middle East was satisfied by the end of the Eisenhower administration, it was the oil company leadership. Eisenhower's policies had kept Israel at a distance, treated it with hardheadedness, and catered to the conservative Arabs at the expense of radical national movements. Although individual policies such as the Baghdad Pact and the Aswan Dam reversal did provoke disagreements among oilmen, Eisenhower and Dulles's policies pleased them more than any other single group. This convergence of perspective occurred because of a similar world view and overlapping concerns. The fear of a cutoff in Western Europe's Mideast oil supplies prompted interest in the area, but the administration's central focus was the threat of the Soviet Union and "international communism." The major policies of the era were designed to contain the Soviet Union—the initial opening to the Arab world, the Baghdad Pact, the Aswan Dam offer and the reversal, the Eisenhower Doctrine, the intervention in Lebanon. Even U.S. opposition to the British, French, and Israelis over Suez, seemingly motivated by opposition to the unnecessary use of force, was actually prompted by the fear that the allied action would enhance the Soviet position in the area. In the 1956–1957 period, Eisenhower and Dulles repeatedly referred to the danger of Russian gains within the Arab world if the Israelis did not withdraw from the territories that they had captured.

The decision-making style of the president increased the isolation of the White House. Even when Eisenhower sympathized with a particular policy recommended below, his system and style limited his exposure to advocacy—reinforced by the tendency of his first secretary of state to pursue policy decisions on his own without detailed consultation with his department. This isolation and inaccessability presented difficulties that those advocating alternative policies had to endure. The president's determination to pursue impartiality as he defined it and the highly structured closed system meant that most outside parties were either frozen out of involvement in high policy circles or acted on the periphery. The administration did not have the personnel and reserve to adjust adequately to developments. In the end, the first presidency to view the Middle East as a prime region of foreign policy concern produced a program coherent in its global, regional, and local objectives but rigid in formulation and content.

4

KENNEDY
The Issue on Ice

The Truman administration had been troubled by a protracted crisis in Palestine, which it saw as peripheral to its central policy concerns in Europe and Asia. It had an open decision-making style, and different interests competed for the president's shifting attention. The Eisenhower presidency was the opposite, treating the Middle East as a high priority concern and formulating policy within a highly structured decision-making system.

The short-lived Kennedy era is in many respects unique, combining traits exhibited by its predecessors in a very different mixture. As in the Truman era, the Middle East returned to low priority, domestic constraints were prominent, and open decision making prevailed. As in the Eisenhower era, there was a deliberate attempt to develop an innovative regional strategy for the Arab-Israeli dispute consistent with global concerns. The regional strategy, however, represented major changes in policy that were to have longstanding effects on the American future in the area. As in the Eisenhower experience, the initiative aimed at an Arab-Israeli settlement failed and the regional strategy was undermined by intra-Arab rivalries.

External and Domestic Constraints

With respect to external constraints, Kennedy presided over the quietest period in the Middle East since 1945. During his administration, Middle East matters had lowest priority since there was no major crisis in the region. Nasser was preoccupied with the United Arab Republic experiment until spring 1961. Even after the Egyptian-Syrian divorce, the Arab-Israeli theater seemed quiet in comparison with other periods, except for occasional incidents on the Syrian or Jordanian borders with Israel. By late 1962 an intra-Arab rivalry was developing over the future government in Yemen. As it was said at the time, the parties had placed the Arab-Israeli dispute "on ice." There was optimism that this temporary stability would become durable, that, if the stalemate continued, major agreements between the Arabs and Israelis could become feasible after a few years.

Chester Bowles, the president's ambassador to the Third World, encapsulated the mood of the times when he said in spring 1962, "The Middle Eastern nations . . . are becoming less focused on conflicts with their neighbors and more interested in their own internal development." In the region, "there is a kind of quiet political and economic relaxation which, with a measure of good luck, may gradually make for lessening tensions and greater opportunities for all concerned."[1]

The potential for Soviet-American confrontation in the area also seemed defused. The Soviet Union—having established a major breakthrough in Egypt, Iraq, and Syria—was suffering from the problem that had plagued the United States in the 1950s: dealing with competing Arab states. Although the Soviet base of influence seemed secure, its continuing problems with Arab clients seemed to present opportunities for the United States.

The lack of external constraints permitted new initiatives toward the area, which meshed well with the activism promised by the new American leadership. However, limited Middle East tensions also permitted reduced attention—a condition encouraged by a flurry of crises elsewhere (e.g., Cuba, Berlin, Indochina, the Congo).

While external pressures diminished under Kennedy, domestic constraints actually increased. His policy of making overtures to Nasser was under attack in Congress; and many in the bureaucracy, especially in the Pentagon, as well as leading figures in the oil industry, questioned the wisdom of appeals to Arab factions that could threaten pro-American oil producers, particularly Saudi Arabia. The severest domestic constraint confronting Kennedy in his Mideast policy came from the Jewish community. Kennedy was more prepared than Truman and Eisenhower to use the Israel issue for electoral purposes and, as the results of the 1960 presidential election demonstrate, he was more dependent on the American Jewish community than were his predecessors. With his Boston background, ethnic politics came naturally to Kennedy. As he often suggested in speeches and private conversations, he had an emotional attachment to Ireland; why shouldn't the Jews identify with Israel?[2]

As Kennedy emerged on the national scene during the 1950s, he had spoken more and more strongly about friendship toward the Zionist experiment.[3] This position was forced upon him in part by the deficits with which he began his presidential campaign. Despite Kennedy's ties to the Boston Jewish community, key Jewish figures nationally had close links with his principal opponents—Stevenson, Humphrey, and even Lyndon Johnson of Texas. Moreover, Kennedy's father had a reputation of sympathy for the German government as American ambassador to Britain shortly before the second World War. Kennedy himself was greeted with suspicion by many Jewish leaders because he allegedly had been "soft" on Joseph McCarthy, because he had failed to associate with Israel's friends in Congress during his years in the House and Senate, and because in 1958, as head of the Senate Foreign Relations African Subcommittee, he had criticized the Eisenhower administration for supporting the French against the Algerian rebels who were closely linked to Nasser. Reflecting these criticisms was a Jewish War Veterans report of December 1960 in which the authors complained that Johnson had backed Israel with actions; Kennedy only with statements.[4]

Aware of these complaints, Kennedy met thirty Jewish leaders on 8 August 1960 at the Hotel Pierre apartment of Abraham Feinberg in New York. Domestic questions and Arab-Israeli issues were the major topics discussed. On Israel the candidate listened to the Jewish leaders' complaints about the policies of the Eisenhower administration; his responses were positive but circumscribed. He made no sweeping promises, saying that Israel's economic and military strength should be maintained while admitting that he was not ready to commit the United States to providing those arms. Kennedy won over the Jewish leaders with his honesty; he would actually deliver more to Israel as president than he promised that day. What he did assure the prominent figures assembled was that if he gained the White House, he would discuss any problem that concerned them.[5] Access had been denied during the days of Eisenhower; for leading members of the pro-Israeli camp, this was a commitment to be valued.

Kennedy may have been circumspect in private; he was much less so in public. When the Zionist Organization of America invited both presidential candidates to speak at its national convention in late August, Kennedy accepted and Nixon refused. His ringing endorsement of the Zionist experiment, the strongest to that date of any presidential candidate, was exuberantly reported in the national Jewish press.[6] In preparing that speech, Kennedy had his staff draft two versions; he personally chose the stronger.[7] Kennedy argued that Israel "has not been merely a Jewish cause—any more than Irish independence was the cause merely of those of Irish descent. Because wherever freedom exists, there we are all committed—and wherever it is in danger, there we are all in danger. The ideals of Zionism have in the last half-century been endorsed by both parties and Americans of all ranks in all sections. Friendship for Israel is not a partisan matter, it is a national commitment."[8]

Later Kennedy would not regret his strong statements on Israel during the campaign. His razor-thin margin in the election meant that he was beholden to many groups and states for his victory, but the Jews had voted for him in astronomical percentages (over 80 percent); they had been critical to his victories in Illinois and New York. Unlike Eisenhower, Kennedy could please his domestic constituency—labor, liberals, Democratic party officials—with strong support for Israel.

Kennedy's interest in Israel went beyond foreign affairs. When Ambassador Stevenson denounced the Israelis in particularly harsh language for a raid into Syria in early 1962, the president nervously asked an aide, "Who are they blaming?" When he learned that Stevenson was being criticized by the pro-Israeli groups, he muttered in relief, "Better him than me."[9] Kennedy had not seen the speech, but he had approved the American vote at the Security Council censuring Israel for the raid even while the White House disavowed the president's involvement.[10] As president, Kennedy opposed the Israeli government on several key issues (e.g., Egypt policy, Jerusalem, refugee questions, UN votes, recognition of Yemen), but unlike Eisenhower, he differed cautiously because of domestic politics.

Even without political constraints, it is unlikely that Kennedy would have expended the energy necessary to confront Jerusalem, given the low priority of the issue. The White House, however, recognized the public relations value of positive administration actions. At one point in spring 1963, a letter critical of Israeli policies had been released by the State Department.[11] The NSC staff member on the Middle East soon reported to his chief that he had arranged with the appropriate State Department officials for the White House to clear before they were issued:

1. Those key letters to Congressmen, public statements, press briefings, etc. on Arab-Israeli problems which have major policy implications and could create domestic repercussions.
2. Major substantive policy proposals which bear substantially on the A-I situation and could create domestic repercussions when revealed.[12]

Philosophy

In approaching third world regions, the philosophy of the new Kennedy team differed in major respects from that of its predecessor. In contrast with Eisenhower and Dulles, Kennedy viewed these areas as centers of opportunity for advancing American power. His policy team took a decidedly more positive stance toward states seeking an independent path between East and West. They also advocated expanding economic development programs on both a bilateral and multilateral basis to bolster regimes and movements sympathetic to American values.[13] Yet the Kennedy team was not arguing against the policy of containing the Soviet Union, only that containment could be more effective if the targets of American largesse changed. If these methods were to fail, the administration would consider action to maintain compatible regimes either through the employment of U.S. forces or through military assistance to local parties. In many cases, then, the Kennedy administration was brought back to the policies pursued in the Eisenhower and Dulles era, with the major difference that the new president was opposing anti-American elements more energetically while employing a rhetoric and style more sympathetic to neutralists. Vietnam soon dramatized the anomaly of this new conception, for Kennedy's desire to align the United States with "progressive" forces competed with the objective of confronting Communist forces wherever a threat arose. This administration and its successor soon sunk into the worst of both worlds, cooperating with a series of right-wing dictators and aiding them against their adversaries in times and places of the local Communists' choosing.

The Middle East—although largely a sideshow during the Kennedy era—followed the patterns predominating elsewhere. In seeking "progressive" and popular nationalists in the Middle East, Kennedy chose Nasser as the only viable candidate. The sole alternative, feeble King Saud, was not seen as a "Kennedy-type."[14] With Nasser's nonalignment to be respected, not berated, the New Frontiersmen were more prepared than their predecessors to distinguish between radical Arab nationalism and Moscow-controlled communism. Seeking to prevent polarization of the area along East-West lines, they hoped to deflect Nasser's attention toward Egyptian domestic problems and encourage him to cooperate with the United States, which might result in Nasser's being more restrained toward Israel. Through Nasser, they would approach American relations toward the Arabs in a more positive framework.[15] For example, Bowles's secret report to the president on his February 1962 trip to Cairo was filled with optimism about the "extremely competent men" leading Egypt, as well as relaying private reassurances from Nasser that "the UAR will never attack [Israel] first" and "communism as a political or economic system is unworkable in Africa or the Middle East."[16] The Egypt-firsters, in political purgatory since the Aswan Dam affair, now emerged as a significant influence on American policy.

As in other regions, the new policy eventually confronted uncomfortable and compromising choices. Nasser did respond favorably to Kennedy's overtures, but the potential of a new American-Egyptian connection soon evaporated. Nasser's independent posture in foreign affairs and his pan-Arab ambitions led him to oppose conservative and pro-American Arab governments, forcing the administration to move toward defending the regimes favored by Eisenhower.

The uniqueness of the Kennedy policy did not lie solely in its initiative toward Nasser, for many officials had decried for several years American alienation from this largest and most important Arab country. Rather, Kennedy's political skill was shown in his ability to combine policies in new packages even when options were severely limited. In the Middle East, Kennedy pursued Eisenhower's impartiality, but he turned its assumptions upside down. Eisenhower and Dulles had distrusted Nasser and regarded Israel as an albatross. Kennedy instead balanced off competing regional and domestic forces by creating new ties to Cairo and embracing the Israelis. Before his administration, Israel had been treated by policymakers as an embarrassment to the United States. Now the president spoke openly of ties to the Jerusalem government and of its close relations to the United States. Kennedy accepted Israel as a positive force consistent with American ideals.[17] For example, in a message to the Zionist Organization of America's annual conference in mid-1962, he stated, "This nation, from the time of President Woodrow Wilson, has established and continued a tradition of friendship with Israel because we are committed to all free societies that seek a path to peace and honor and individual right."[18]

The area's temporary quiet facilitated this turnabout in American thinking. Kennedy had demonstrated that Israel could be celebrated—at least rhetorically—for its special connection to the United States without undue negative effects on America's policy in the region.

Decision Making

The decision-making approach of the administration paralleled this effort to create new relations with both Israel and the "nationalist" Arabs. There had been widespread criticism of Eisenhower for being so removed from the details of the policy process that his thinking remained uninformed by the debate within the bureaucracy and among his advisors. His strong dependence on one advisor, Dulles, was also much criticized. Kennedy entered the White House determined to break down Eisenhower's staff system, which he saw as deadening.

In the light of outside recommendations and his own personal style, Kennedy involved a wider variety of advisers than ever before in formulating policy, with the White House becoming more important as an arena of influence and debate. The National Security Council under McGeorge Bundy assumed the prominent role it has played ever since.[19] Kennedy's foreign policy apparatus offered access to an active, dynamic White House staff with pipelines to competing views.

Whereas Eisenhower had personally disliked having groups of Americans competing for influence over U.S. Mideast policy, Kennedy institutionalized the conflict in the White House staff. Robert Komer, an official whom McGeorge Bundy had hired from the CIA to deal with Third World matters, was noted for advocating an opening to Nasser's Egypt. Komer presented to the president the view prevailing at the State Department and the CIA. Available to advise Komer were several experts with experiences from outside the government. These included Phillips Talbott, the assistant secretary for Near East and South Asian affairs whose major experience had been in South Asia, and John Badeau, the ambassador to Cairo, an arabist with many years of experience in Egypt. Komer was also in close touch with officials who conducted relations with the Arab world within the State Department hierarchy.

On the other side of the policy fence, Kennedy asked Myer Feldman, his deputy special counsel, to play the role of conduit for the attitudes of Israelis, Jewish leaders, and congressmen inclined toward the Israeli position. Feldman, a Jew who made no secret of his attachment to Israel, had handled Israeli matters for Kennedy in the Senate where he had served as a legislative aide. His mandate was stronger than that of previous officials who had carried the "Jewish portfolio." Feldman's responsibilities extended to day-to-day operations. For example, in mid-1962 Feldman telephoned Talbott to ask why the State Department regularly sought to dissuade foreign governments from establishing their embassies in Israel in Jerusalem. His phone call did not change policy, but it did lead the department to make a full explanation to McGeorge Bundy.[20] In addition to Feldman, other pro-Israeli "insiders" and "outsiders" were available to feed into the White House system. They included Philip Klutznick, the former B'nai B'rith president and then one of Adlai Stevenson's assistants at the United Nations; Abraham Feinberg, prominent Democratic party fund raiser; Abraham Harman, the Israeli ambassador; and a number of pro-Israeli Democratic congressmen.

The arrangement covering Feldman and Komer had an essential asymmetry; except for Israel, Feldman dealt with domestic, not foreign, affairs. Komer, on the other hand, was a high-ranking member of the prestigious National Security Council staff. Feldman's selection suggests Kennedy's keen awareness of the domestic significance of the Israeli question.

It also demonstrates the president's preference for having direct information from individuals with opposing views. Both men often wrote memos presenting their positions and often argued before Kennedy personally, insuring that the president would be exposed to each side's arguments. The president, whose work schedule often included a long stay at his living quarters during the midafternoon and late working hours in the office, liked to conduct minidebates with aides on key issues late in the day. When an issue was being considered at Oval Office gatherings, Feldman and Komer (or, perhaps, Bundy) would argue different, sometimes opposing, sides of an Arab-Israeli question. Thus, this president, more than others, assured his exposure to all arguments at issue in any particular situation.[21]

Many observers have argued that the new president's inspiring new oratory veiled a preference for the old policies and established figures.[22] The selection process for secretary of state illustrates this anomaly. Senator J. William Fulbright, long noted for opposing many of Israel's policies, was actually Kennedy's first choice for the post. When the word leaked, civil rights proponents managed to kill the appointment. Robert Lovett, staunch opponent of the creation of Israel until the last moment in 1948, was then offered the job, but he turned it down because of ill health. When Dean Rusk was considered, Kennedy's staff did not realize he had been a prominent State Department opponent of Israel's establishment in 1948. Given the issue's low salience in this period, Rusk would probably have been chosen even had they known. Few except Israel's staunchest supporters and the officers of the Near East Bureau even wondered about Rusk's Middle East position. Rusk was also a protege of John Foster Dulles, suggesting a continuity at Foggy Bottom that applied to the Middle East as well.[23] When policy did change, the differences were often subtle and the locus for change was at the White House rather than the State Department.

Policy toward the Arab World

The new approach to Nasser can be illustrated by a statement by Under Secretary of State Chester Bowles in fall 1961:

Only a few years ago all thoughtful observers were clearly concerned about Soviet penetration into the Middle East. Many thought that Egypt, for example, was on the road to Soviet control. Yet today Nasser's nationalism fiercely combats internal communism and his relations with the U.S.S.R. grow increasingly cool. Although the situation in the Middle East remains unstable and unpredictable, the Soviet gains here run far behind their expectations.[24]

In attempting to arrange a new relationship with Nasser, Kennedy relied on a person-to-person, presidential gambit of direct correspondence. Instead of the dry State Department letters—"documents that sounded like treaties"—Kennedy had letters written in his own personal style. Several Arab leaders received them, but the central target was Nasser.[25] Dissatisfied once with an aide-mémoire that Badeau was to carry back to Cairo, the president called in a secretary and personally redictated it. Generally, the letters were "correct and polite, but very frank indeed"; yet, they created a "feeling" of dealing between equals. There still were no private arrangements or understandings. As Kennedy admitted at a mid-1962 news conference, "We continue to attempt to have good relations with the U.A.R., but I have received no information or assurances from President Nasser in regard to any future policy decisions which he might make."[26]

Future events were rapidly to confirm this description. In September 1962 Nasser released Kennedy's first letter and his own reply, an act that infuriated the president and began his disillusionment with his Egyptian counterpart.[27] Kennedy had cause to be embarrassed. Assuring Nasser that "our attitude continues to be based on sincere friendship," he stated as well, "I am also proud of the real encouragement which my government and the American people have in the past given to your aspirations and those of your countrymen, especially in the critical days of 1956."[28] These were not sentiments the pro-Israeli forces were likely to appreciate.

The substantive side of this "fresh effort" toward Egypt was increased aid, especially PL-480 wheat, which Kennedy sought in the face of a Congress progressively disillusioned with Nasser.[29] There were other signs of the intent to demonstrate "evenhandedness." For example, in April 1962 the United Nations Security Council condemned Israel (with the United States voting in favor) because of an Israeli retaliatory raid against Syria. Publicly, the president maintained a hands-off posture; privately, the president approved, according to Feldman, because he felt he could not reverse Rusk, Bundy, Stevenson, and others who were all in favor of a U.S. vote for condemnation.[30] Whenever United Nations votes arose on Arab-Israeli issues, the positive impartiality pursued by the administration was challenged. To vote against an Israeli position was to court the antagonism of Israel and its supporters; to vote against Arab objectives was to endanger the policy of new relations with the Arab world.

But Arab-Israeli tensions were not what led to the breakdown of the new Arab strategy. As with the early Eisenhower efforts, conflicts among Arab countries were the cause. For example, when Syria withdrew from the union with Egypt, the problem arose whether to alienate Nasser by recognizing the new regime in Syria or to alienate Damascus by failing to do so. In the end the United States waited until the Soviets had themselves extended recognition.[31]

The Arab conflict that broke the back of Kennedy's approach to Nasser occurred in little known, backward Yemen, still living under a theocratic medieval regime barely affected by the modern world. In September 1962 the autocratic ruler of the country died; a few days later pro-Nasser army officers staged a coup, ending ten centuries of the imamate. The revolt, however, was only partially successful, for the imam's son rallied his forces and retreated to the hinterland along the border with Saudi Arabia. A classic interventionist struggle evolved with the new regime in Sana, Yemen's capital, appealing to Nasser, while the royalist forces sought aid from Saudi Arabia and Jordan—two countries concerned that the defeat of yet another monarchy would threaten their regimes. Gradually, Nasser's "Vietnam" emerged. At first Russian-made planes flew in arms and military advisers. By mid-October, regular Egyptian troops were entering the country.

In Washington these events set off a policy debate lasting through the fall on whether or not to recognize the new regime. Many American diplomats at home and abroad favored recognition on the grounds that the new regime was bound to be better than its anachronistic predecessor. Here was one opportunity for the United States to side with an Arab regime committed to political progress.[32]

In the Near East Bureau under Phillips Talbott, some officials hoped that recognition would limit Nasser's involvement; others argued more bluntly that recognizing Yemen would give the United States more clout with Nasser and would make him more amenable. This argument was strengthened when Nasser seemed to promise Ambassador Badeau that Yemen would not be used as a base for attacks on neighboring Saudi Arabia and the British possession of Aden. Since intelligence reports predicted defeat for the Yemeni royalists, it was also hoped by some supporters of U.S. recognition that such a step would prevent the U.A.R. and the new regime in Yemen from involving the Soviet Union.[33] The key people backing recognition were Rusk and Komer.

A curious coalition opposed recognition, although their position was not coordinated. Major Pentagon officials and the British were opposed on the grounds that it would weaken the British position in Aden. Oil representatives and diplomats in Jiddah were opposed because they feared that the new Yemeni regime would threaten Saudi Arabia. Feldman and his allies were unenthusiastic and cautious; they came up with the idea that if recognition occurred, a quid pro quo should be demanded from Nasser, such as reducing anti-Israeli propaganda, but they did not make this recommendation in time for it to be acted upon. The decision to recognize came in mid-December. Afterward, pro-Israeli congressmen and groups were generally critical of the decision.

The arguments in favor seemed more powerful to the president because the republicans appeared to be gaining and the royalist opposition on Saudi soil to be waning. The argument that prevailed in Washington was that it would be preferable to accept a fait accompli and gain points for the new Arab strategy in the bargain. Before recognition was extended, the Sana regime responded to American inquiries by announcing that it would reaffirm Yemen's international obligations and would undertake to live at peace with its neighbors.[34]

Had the Yemen War ended soon afterward, with the anticipated victory of the republicans, the intended effect of recognition would have been achieved. Instead, the war dragged on and destroyed the new Kennedy approach to the Arab world, turning his policy into one like the old Eisenhower-Dulles defense of conservatives. It was one thing to flirt with Nasser as long as he remained at home and relied on propaganda to promote Arab unity. But Nasser was escalating his involvement in the Yemen, and the Saudis—who were supposedly aligned with the United States—felt threatened by his moves and were countering with support for the royalists. Several American diplomats and oilmen began to fear that the future of the Saudi regime was in jeopardy. Despite recognizing the Yemeni republicans opposed by the Saudis, the administration feared supporting Nasser against Jiddah lest Western oil interests and a major pro-American regime suffer.[35] Resolving this apparent contradiction in American policy meant ending the Yemen conflict as soon as possible by gaining a disengagement of all external forces.

In Jiddah and Cairo, the American ambassadors sought to persuade Nasser and Crown Prince Faisal (now in charge; he would become king in November 1964) to disengage. In Cairo, Badeau sought to convince Nasser that his long-term interests involved good relations with the United States, and these were being threatened by his Yemeni expedition. In Jiddah, Ambassador Parker T. Hart assured Faisal that the United States was behind his regime despite its recognition of the Yemeni republican government. Hart also encouraged him to cease his backing of the royalists. In early 1963 the administration encouraged mediators to arrange a settlement. It was hoped an effective U.N. emissary could be arranged, but with the situation further deteriorating, Ellsworth Bunker was appointed as a special presidential envoy.[36]

The ensuing strategy failed. Several State Department and White House officials had concluded that Nasser was too committed to the Yemeni republicans to withdraw precipitously and would if necessary extend the war into Saudi Arabia.[37] Moreover, if the war continued, some in Washington feared that both the U.A.R. and the new Yemen regime would invite Soviet military assistance. The way to attain U.A.R. withdrawal was to have the Saudis withdraw first. To encourage the Saudis along this path, Bunker would publicly reassure Faisal of American support and offer eight U.S. Air Force planes to help protect Saudi Arabia from the U.A.R. aircraft that were frequently raiding Saudi villages suspected of serving as royalist havens. The Pentagon, especially the Air Force, was opposed to this plan from the outset because the Dharan base in Saudi Arabia had been deactivated the previous year.[38]

There were other problems with this strategy. If the eight planes sent to Saudi Arabia represented a serious gesture, the Saudis might treat them as a factor in the war, thereby risking escalation and further American military involvement. If, on the other hand, the planes were intended as symbols, they might have a negligible effect on Saudi diplomacy. The strategy also depended on Nasser's placing at least as high a value on relations with the United States as the Kennedy administration placed on him. Shortly, the Kennedy team would discover that their influence was limited in both Arab capitals.

Once Bunker had presented the planes to Faisal and returned to Washington, it was clear that Secretary General U Thant was reluctant to continue a mediation likely to fail. Therefore, Bunker was sent back to the area to try for an agreement between Nasser and Faisal. After engaging in shuttle diplomacy between the two capitals, Bunker produced an agreement for disengagement, but it broke down—in part because the deal was rooted in an American initiative and did not fulfill the political aims of both parties, and in part because the United States preferred U.N. observers rather than its own personnel to supervise the withdrawal.[39] By the time the U.N. observer team began to arrive in the

Yemen, nearly three months had passed since the agreement had been signed and it was already disintegrating.

The war in Yemen dragged on. There were other agreements between Nasser and Faisal—in August 1965 and August 1967.[40] Neither was more successful than the first, but the Six-Day War so severely weakened Egyptian forces that they never again attained a similar strength and their evacuation was completed by December 1967. Subsequent Yemeni republican governments turned out to be more moderate than other nationalist regimes in the area. In the long term the United States had limited the Yemeni conflict without a threat to Saudi Arabia, but in the meantime American efforts to establish a new relationship with Nasser were ruined. When Lyndon Johnson became president in late 1963, the atmosphere had been poisoned. In Washington, Nasser's reputation had plummeted. The Yemen War had forced the United States into the old role of protecting conservative Arab regimes against the more progressive, a role that the Kennedy administration had determined to avoid. The president grew more skeptical of Nasser's motives before his fateful trip to Dallas. Although some officials continued to explain Nasser's actions as motivated by domestic Egyptian politics, others became disillusioned as well. Those who had argued that Nasser was "the wave of the future" found it much harder to gain adherents.[41]

Symbolically, JFK had planned to invite both the Israeli prime minister and the Egyptian president to the White House in 1964. King Saud had visited Kennedy in early 1962 and Crown Prince Faisal had followed later in the year. Neither set of talks was successful. Meanwhile, plans for the Israeli visit went forward and Levi Eshkol arrived in June 1964; the invitation to Nasser was never delivered. Badeau later ruminated ruefully, "I am sure that Nasser didn't understand what made America tick . . . I felt that it would do a great deal to make our relations more understanding if he would just come to this country and see it and talk with businessmen and so forth. So I worked very hard toward that end and I would have gotten it had not the Yemen war broken out and that put the end to it."[42]

By the time that Kennedy died, his initial policy lay in shambles, the fear of falling Arab dominoes having surmounted the hope of a new relationship with a progressive nationalist. A few bureaucratic pockets still cherished the Egypt-first strategy, but as a national policy, it was moribund and would not revive fully until 1973. By spring 1963, the administration was concerned about the internal turmoil in Jordan, believed to be inspired by Nasserist sympathizers.[43] As in the Eisenhower era, intra-Arab tensions had undermined an American administration's plans for a new foothold in the Arab world. The Kennedy experience is all the more representative because it occurred when the Arab-Israeli dispute was relatively quiescent.

When the Yemeni crisis destroyed the approach to Nasser, no new policies were waiting to replace it. Kennedy's assassination removed a leader who might have developed alternatives; his successor was uninterested.

Policy toward Israel

A major breakthrough in Middle East policy under Kennedy was the concept of improving relations with the Israelis even while flirting with Israel's major adversary of the time, Nasser of Egypt. Administration personnel repeatedly argued that there was no contradiction here. In describing a luncheon meeting he had held with an Israeli official in early 1963, Komer reported:

> I further queried the generally critical Israeli attitude about our Nasser and Yemen policies, both of which I saw as quite in Israel's interest. It was Soviet arms, not U.S. wheat or development credits, which enhanced the threat to Israel; nor was this arms flow indirectly dependent on U.S. aid. On the other hand, to the extent that Nasser felt a vested interest in good relations with us, he would obviously be on good behavior toward Israel lest he jeopardize this interest. I further argued that since we and the Israelis had a joint interest in the preservation of Pro-Western regimes in Jordan and (paradoxically) even in Saudi Arabia, our Yemen disengagement policy made real sense from the Israeli point of view.[44]

The president presented this new philosophy to Foreign Minister Golda Meir at a late December 1962 meeting in Palm Beach. There the policy of combining close ties with Israel with initiatives toward the Arab world was stipulated more clearly than on any public occasion during the Kennedy era. According to the minutes of the meeting,

> The United States, the President said, has a special relationship with Israel in the Middle East really comparable only to that which it has with Britain over a wide range of world affairs. But for us to play properly the role we are called upon to play, we cannot afford the luxury of identifying Israel—or Pakistan, or certain other countries—as our exclusive friends, hewing to the line of close and intimate allies (for we feel that about Israel though it is not a formal ally) and letting other countries go. If we pulled out of the Arab Middle East and maintained our ties only with Israel this would not be in Israel's interest.
>
> To be effective in our own interest and to help Israel, the President continued, we have to maintain our position in the Middle East generally. Our interest is best served if there is a group of sovereign countries associated with the West. We are in a position then to make clear to the Arabs that we will maintain our friendship with Israel and our security guarantees.[45]

The Kennedy administration reassured the skeptical Israelis that the United States could support them with the Sixth Fleet in the event of local instabilities.[46] In the meeting with Meir, the president stated, "I think it is quite clear that in case of an invasion the United States would come to the support of Israel. We have that capacity and it is growing."[47]

Kennedy's administration supported these cordial remarks with substantive policies. During this period the Israelis had two major requests of the United States: for the sale of Hawk missiles and for a satisfactory allocation of Jordan waters, an issue left over from the termination of the Johnston mission in the mid-1950s. Kennedy backed Israel's contention that it could unilaterally implement its part of the Johnston plan despite persistent Arab opposition.[48] But the Hawk missile deal represented the most important policy innovation of the period. For the first time, the United States agreed to an arms deal with the Jewish state. This new relationship with Israel had major long-term implications for American policy toward the Arab-Israeli dispute.

Israeli concern over Russian arms shipped to Egypt and Iraq had led it to ask for the anti-aircraft Hawk missile late in the Eisenhower era. When Kennedy saw Ben Gurion at the Waldorf Astoria in May 1961, the Israelis renewed the request, but Israel was given the standard answer compiled by the State Department with the aid of the Pentagon.[49] The United States would not become engaged in the Arab-Israeli arms race. But the Israelis and their supporters persisted. Feldman responded with a memo for the president in which he pointed to a basic contradiction in American policy—the administration was committed to a balance of arms in the Middle East, but it was not prepared to redress the imbalance caused by Russian aid to the Arabs.[50]

After debates at the White House between Komer and Feldman, the president had the two investigate whether any other allied weapon system could counter the Russian arms effectively. The British wanted to sell Israel their own anti-aircraft missile, the Bloodhound, and were opposed to American competition. The White House concluded between mid-1961 and mid-1962 that no alternative to the Hawk would satisfy Israel's legitimate security needs.[51]

Kennedy knew the implications of this conclusion. Although the Hawk was still classed as a defensive weapon, its sale could begin a new American activity in the area and could well hinder Kennedy's dialogue with Nasser on Arab nationalism. Yet the critical problem remained that neither the Russians nor the Egyptians were interested in an arms limitation agreement. The Israelis could not acquire weapons elsewhere to effectively counter the Russian arms. When Ambassador at Large Chester Bowles met with Nasser in Cairo in February 1962, the Egyptian leader rejected the idea of a private understanding with Israel on limiting the size of each side's military forces.[52] Defense Department evaluations confirmed that the Middle East balance of power might soon favor the Arabs. There were persistent reports in this period, for example, that German scientists were aiding the Egyptians with the development of missiles.[53]

In June 1962, Assistant Secretary Talbott reluctantly informed the American ambassadors to the Middle East of the impending sale. If the Israelis were indeed falling behind in the arms race, what option was there? Even the dubious ambassadors to the Arab countries had no effective counterargument. As one of the participants later recalled,

> We had a long debate at this meeting as to whether this sale should be made, of the Hawks. The eventual conclusion of the meeting was a reluctant agreement that it was all right, it should be done. The Ambassadors to most of the Arab countries were very dubious, very nervous about it, but on the basis that it was a strictly defensive weapon and that the Israelis in fact appeared to be falling behind at the time in the arms balance and needed some support, that this was probably the least offensive type of arms that we could furnish—the least offensive to the Arabs—that we should go ahead with the proposed sale of Hawks.[54]

This decision, which would basically alter the American-Israeli relationship, was made then not because of domestic politics but because of the policy commitment to a regional balance of power, which the administration believed in jeopardy because of Russian arms shipments to Iraq and Egypt.[55] The White House decision-making structure, which gave the pro-Israeli spokesman a voice in the process itself, did allow key arguments to be made that led to a successful conclusion of the arms deal. In the Eisenhower administration it would have been extremely difficult, if not impossible, for pro-Israeli forces to have initiated such a process.

While domestic politics did not influence the basic decision, they did influence its announcement. Since the congressional elections of 1962 were soon to occur, Kennedy was encouraged to set a deadline for the decision. Once he decided to sell the Hawks, he sought to receive credit in the domestic political arena. The White House leaked the information to several Jewish leaders and some of the congressmen most active in lobbying for the sale. An article soon appeared in the *New York Times* announcing the deal.[56]

The department immediately sent a telegram to relevant embassies indicating that the possible sale was "not a change or reversal of long-standing U.S. policy. The U.S. intends to continue to avoid becoming a major supplier of offensive or sophisticated weapons to parties to the Arab-Israeli conflict. It is [a] single decision designed [to] meet [a] specific need for an improved air defense." U.S. ambassadors in most Arab capitals were told they could reply affirmatively if they were asked whether the Hawk would also be sold to the Arabs.[57] In keeping with the administration's effort to keep Egyptian support, a high-ranking official in the Near East Bureau had already informed Nasser personally. As a consequence his press was surprisingly quiet when the word became public.[58] Several weeks later, Badeau reported that the U.S. government had "come off as well as could be hoped on this one."[59] Other American ambassadors were more apprehensive. The American embassy in then conservative Libya reported that the sale "could serve as [a] catalyst to bring together vocal Libyan Arab nationalists in [an] anti-U.S. and/or anti-U.K. attack." Protests from disparate Arab regimes such as Jordan, Syria, and Iraq were also reported.[60]

Still the president maintained the pretense of no military aid to Jerusalem. In April of the next year, questioned about military assistance to Israel, he stated, "As you know, the United States has never been a supplier of military equipment directly to the Israelis. We have given them economic assistance."[61] In the strictest sense, the statement was accurate, but as all the principal actors well knew, the Hawks for Israel had already been ordered. Indeed, the Hawk issue had prompted a first-ever U.S.-Israeli meeting in July 1962 to review the regional arms balance, a process later continued in fall 1963 when the Israelis requested several new weapons.[62]

The Kennedy system also promoted economic assistance to Jerusalem. When the Israelis sought to finance the Hawk deal by a long-term low-interest loan, the Pentagon demurred because it preferred rapid payments and a State Department paper likewise argued that the Israelis could afford to pay immediately. But Feldman discovered that the Australians had made special arrangements with Washington for financing weaponry. Marshalling his arguments that Israel could not afford strict terms and it deserved a better deal because it did not receive military grant aid, Feldman used the Australian arrangement as a model and persuaded the president to overrule the Pentagon. This decision was significant because it set a precedent for later weapons arrangements.[63] Similarly, when various nonmilitary types of foreign assistance for Israel were discussed, AID and the State Department were invariably arrayed against the pro-Israeli camp (congressmen, Jewish leaders, the Israeli ambassador, Feldman). In the end, the president usually overruled the aid bureaucracies and substantially increased the sums for Israel.[64]

There was another face to the administration's Israel policy, however; in return for the largesse extended, it sought Israeli cooperation with American objectives and problems. Kennedy was cordial but explicit in his meeting with Meir. His argument was essentially that the United States and Israel were engaged in a partnership, with responsibility on both sides:

In the Middle East we have the twin problems of being historically and obviously associated with Israel and, especially in this Administration, building on that association through our actions with respect to the Jordan waters, Hawks, and aid, while at the same time we have other responsibilities in the Middle East. Israel, the United States and the free world all have difficult survival problems. We would like Israeli recognition that this partnership which we have with it produces strains for the United States in the Middle East.[65]

The new policy of an extended hand toward Jerusalem, therefore, anticipated a quid pro quo. Kennedy was forthright in his mixture of friendship and expectation: "This country is really interested in Israel, the President said, as he is personally. We are interested that Israel should keep up its sensitive, tremendous, historic task. What we want from Israel arises because our relationship is a two-way street. Israel's security in the long run depends in part on what it does with the Arabs, but also on us."[66]

Despite his stress on Israeli responsibilities and American expectations, the concentration on partnership and informal alliance with Jerusalem represented a milestone in American thinking toward the Israelis. Certainly, neither Truman—with his low security interest in Israel—nor Eisenhower—with his view of Israel as a hindrance to American interests—could conceivably have made the statements presented by Kennedy in his Palm Beach meeting with Meir. Even though they were made privately, Kennedy knew that they would soon leak. Ten months later he reaffirmed his commitments to Meir in a letter to the Israeli prime minister.[67] Just as the administration had appealed to the Arab nationalists, its policies toward Israel were leading toward an era of cooperation between Jerusalem and Washington.

The Johnson Plan

As Meir and Kennedy acknowledged to each other, delicate diplomatic differences still existed between the two governments—especially on how to settle the Arab-Israeli dispute. According to the president, "a settlement might seem impossible to achieve, but it is equally impossible to let this dispute run on and blow up."[68] Their specific differences included the questions of how to deal with the U.N. and how to deal with the refugees, both of which came to a head in the extended discussions in 1961 and 1962 over the Johnson Plan.

Most new presidents seek some step toward facilitating an Arab-Israeli peace. Given the quiet of the period, Kennedy was content to provide opportunities for bridgebuilding between Arabs and Israelis (in matters such as water projects, desalinization, mixed armistice commissions, refugee problems, none of which succeeded although they were not vigorously pursued). The president had been particularly concerned with the Arab refugees. As early as February 1957, in addressing a meeting of the National Conference of Christians and Jews, Kennedy had said:

Let those refugees be repatriated to Israel at the earliest practical date who are sincerely willing to live at peace with their neighbors, to accept the Israeli Government with an attitude of *civitatus filia*. Those who would prefer to remain in Arab jurisdiction should be resettled in areas under control of governments willing to help their Arab brothers, if assisted and enabled to earn their own living, make permanent homes, and live in peace and dignity. The refugee camps should be closed.[69]

In an interview with an Israeli newspaper in summer 1960, "Kennedy stressed the importance of the refugee issue."[70] In repeated private discussions with Dean Francis Sayre of the Washington Cathedral and Feldman shortly after the inauguration, he took a personal interest in the problem.[71] After White House consultations, an exploratory mission through the United Nations was chosen to mask the American initiative in case of failure. The long dormant Conciliation Commission for Palestine was chosen. Although it required cooperation with the other two members, France and Turkey, using the commission permitted the American special representative to serve as a United Nations official. Joseph Johnson, president of the Carnegie Endowment, was selected after discussions among White House aides; he was asked to produce resolutions on the refugee issue that might be considered at the United Nations with the support of all involved parties.[72] In planning for the enterprise the president, Feldman, Bundy, Komer, Rusk, Talbott, Arthur Schlesinger, Jr. (White House liaison with Adlai Stevenson), Stevenson, and U.N. Secretary General Hammarskjold all seem to have been involved.

In September 1961, Johnson embarked on a fact-finding mission to the area. With several Arab leaders, discussions were "realistic and quiet" in tone, but they were "relatively vague."[73] When he reached Israel, however, Johnson found that Ben Gurion and other Israeli leaders feared that the mission would give the refugees a free choice to return to Israel where they would serve as a fifth column against the Jewish state. Returning to New York, the U.N. special representative prepared a report and invited the comments of the major involved parties. The Israelis did not provide suggestions for revising the draft, but the Arabs did. To the consternation of Foreign Minister Golda Meir, some of these were accepted in the final report by Johnson.[74]

By now, Meir and Johnson were developing what was by all accounts a mutual antipathy.[75] In his first report, Johnson suggested in a general way that the refugee question could be handled step-by-step as an issue isolated from the rest of the Arab-Israeli dispute. Even this tentative recommendation was attacked by Arab delegations, who stressed that the only solution for the refugee question was the right of unqualified repatriation.[76] Nevertheless, Johnson's mission was renewed by the appropriate organs of the U.N. in early 1962.

The special representative now set about implementing some ideas for refugee resettlement. Traveling to the Middle East once again, he found the Israelis highly skeptical about his notion of a pilot project to involve what he vaguely called a "relatively small number of refugees."[77] He anticipated that the refugees would first be asked to indicate their preferences for future residence. The Israelis thought that this formula would result in large numbers seeking repatriation, and they wanted to limit the numbers that they would have to accept. They also feared that once the plan was put into effect, the refugees would be propagandized by the Arab governments (especially Egypt) to return to Israel as a means of undermining its security.[78] In the Arab countries Johnson found that many were opposed to the pilot project on opposite grounds from the Israelis. The Jordanians, in particular, feared that few refugees would seek repatriation in Israel and that they would be saddled with internal turmoil. This issue embarrassed the Arabs because they had been urging a U.N. effort on the refugees for several years before 1961. The Jordanians explicitly told Johnson to discount their speeches to the General Assembly.[79] With the Israelis seeking information on specific numbers and the Jordanians seeking to abort the effort by provoking Arab opposition, Johnson's efforts appeared in danger.

Johnson's own position remained anomalous. He performed as a quasi-independent agent, paid by the United Nations and the Carnegie Endowment rather than the United States government.[80] Yet his ties to the American government were, to put it mildly, close. For example, at one point the American ambassador in Israel asked the State Department to permit him to convey a message to Israeli Foreign Minister Meir rather than travel to the vacationing Ben Gurion (and thereby attract more attention) in order to maintain the "U.N. character" of Johnson's mission.[81] Johnson himself, a former member of the State Department, did not take instructions from the U.S. government but spent "more time negotiating with U.S. officials than with Israel or the Arab states, since he believed only the United States was in a position to underwrite the financial burden of a settlement and bring effective pressure to bear on Israel should that be necessary."[82]

At home the issue set off internal wrangling. A project that had begun as a White House initiative now had a new supporter, the Near East Bureau. Many officials there began to see the Johnson plan as a key that might open the tightly shut door of Arab-Israeli settlement.[83] When Israeli supporters noted who was supporting the plan, their suspicions grew, because of their disagreements with these officials on other issues.

The number of involved parties and drafts was increasing to the ultimate detriment of the project, but Johnson persisted during summer 1962. He did not return to the Middle East but maintained contacts with representatives of the parties in New York and with U.S. officials.

By August Johnson's next draft was ready and he presented it at the

White House to several key administration officials, including the president, Rusk, Feldman, Komer, and Bundy. Kennedy was skeptical; he feared a repeat of the previous year's pressures from pro-Israeli partisans after the Israelis had been angered by Johnson's alterations in the draft report. He thought neither the Arabs nor Israelis would accept the plan. The strongest advocate was Robert Strong, Talbott's deputy for Middle East affairs. Despite his doubts, Kennedy finally decided to go ahead with the project by sending Feldman to Israel to gain Ben Gurion's acceptance.[84]

The plan was to have Feldman send a coded message if the Israeli response was positive enough to merit approaching Nasser (Strong was waiting in Cairo). The trip itself was cloaked in secrecy. The press was told that Feldman was going with his wife to vacation on Rhodes and had accepted a "long-standing invitation" from the Weizmann Institute to see Israel for the first time.[85]

The basis of Feldman's approach in August was the quid pro quo that Kennedy would outline to Meir months later at their meeting in Florida. As prearranged in Washington, Feldman opened the first meeting by announcing to an astounded Ben Gurion and Meir, "The President had determined that the Hawk missile would be made available to Israel." As he later recalled, they were "ecstatic."[86] The State Department was also pleased that Ben Gurion did not seem interested in escalating the regional arms race. Feldman reported that Ben Gurion had said that "he would gladly agree to no missiles at all if Nasser could agree to arms limitations and controls."[87]

But Feldman then made requests of the Israelis. He first gained their word that they had no plans to make weapons grade material at their Dimona nuclear reactor (discovered by American intelligence only in late 1960) and that they would allow the United States to inspect it.[88] The prime issue in the discussion, however, was the Johnson Plan. It was clear from Feldman's talks that the Israelis feared that the Arabs and especially Nasser would sabotage the plan by propagandizing the refugees or would refuse admission to those who sought to resettle in their countries if they accepted the plan at all. Neither Johnson nor the American government would accept any conditions because that "would be contrary to [the] basic approach of [the] Johnson Plan which is to begin a procedure in which it is hoped the parties will cooperate in good faith but without prior specific commitment. Ben Gurion will realize there is no prior agreement being sought from Israel that it will repatriate those who opt for repatriation. It is asked only to examine such repatriation applications in good faith."[89] After a six-hour meeting with Meir, Feldman was discouraged by continuing Israeli skepticism. He relayed to Washington his conclusion: "I do strongly advise that we not commit ourselves to support of the Johnson Plan until we get Arab reaction and that Nasser be informed that it is a part of the Plan's intention that no attempt be made to influence refugee votes."[90]

The involved State Department officials, however, refused to be dismayed. They instructed Strong and Badeau to deal with Nasser. They ordered him informed about the Hawk missile decision and Ben Gurion's arms limitation offer.[91] Regarding the Johnson Plan, the department cabled,

> our study of Feldman's useful exploratory talks in Israel leads us [to] conclude that although Israel's leaders are understandably hesitant to state *carte blanche* [their] acquiescence in [the] implementation [of the] Johnson Plan equally they have apparently NOT repeat NOT found in Plan sufficient hazards to Israel to justify its immediate rejection. Objections put up by Ben Gurion and Mrs. Meir seem to us essentially diversionary. In short, we have come out of this phase just about where we might have expected. Having explored preliminary reactions on one side without meeting rejection, we think similar exploration should be carried out on other. By these we are NOT repeat NOT necessarily committed finally to proceed with Johnson Plan at this time. Rather, we will have facts on which this Government can determine whether [it is] worthwhile [to] commit [the] US to [the] Plan and [to the] attempt [to] proceed [with] its implementation.[92]

The seeds of later controversies over the Johnson Plan can be found here in the State Department's optimism and misreading of the depth of Israeli concern.

When Nasser's response to the Johnson Plan was noncommittal, many officials at the State Department interpreted his failure to reject the idea as positive.[93] The president again was skeptical. Perhaps his correspondence with the Egyptian leader accounted for the mild response? Johnson was authorized to present the plan at the U.N. session.[94] But the plan was changing! As before, Johnson continued to refine his draft. Some of the alterations were discussed with State Department officials, whose enthusiastic expectations were rising. A few slight changes might make it easier for the Arabs to accept; and, at the Near East Bureau, it was generally believed that the Israelis would acquiesce in these alterations.[95]

However, Golda Meir was livid upon reading Johnson's report at the United Nations in September. When Feldman arrived in New York to meet with her, the two of them counted sixty-two changes from the draft that they had discussed in Israel, a draft that Ben Gurion and Meir did not expect to be altered. The Israelis believed that the original version provided safeguards against their having to absorb too many refugees; now these assurances (some implicit) were absent.[96] There were statements that Israel had the right to reject any Palestinian it chose, but now there was stand-by authority for the U.N. to grant the person entrance into Israel if Israel's rejections were found to be inadequate.[97] Meir, of course, saw this latter point as infringing on her country's sovereignty. Johnson later said publicly that all states in the area—Arab as well as Israel—should have the final say as to whether or not permission would be granted for individual refugees to enter.[98]

But the Israelis were not convinced by these assurances; they believed that the United Nations could not conduct a fair election among the refugees and that it could not shield the refugees from Arab propaganda. They saw the entire project as biased against them. During the fall Meir continued to meet separately with both Rusk and Feldman; although she said Israel would publicly reject the plan, if necessary, the discussions continued.[99]

Meanwhile, the Arab states were uncomfortable because the plan resembled their previous public statements. But since the Jordanians and the Syrians were not satisfied with the proposal, and the Egyptians and Lebanese were prepared to back Jordan's stand, the Arabs hoped that Israel would reject the plan and save them the embarrassment of having to do so. Therefore, they gave Johnson an indefinite reply. With parts of the plan beginning to leak in early October, Syria surprised all the participants by publicly rejecting it early that month.[100]

America found itself in limbo, its plans foiled once again by internal Arab divisions. The State Department pressed the White House to push the plan, which many officials believed would force the governments of the area to accept it. The State Department also tried to convince the administration that the Israelis and Arabs would adopt the plan if enough political capital was spent; Near East Bureau officials sought to convince the Israelis that the refugees would accept compensation rather than return in large numbers to Israel. But events were moving against the State Department position. Both the Israelis and Arabs were opposed to the plan and the pro-Israeli forces were mobilizing against it as rumors—only partly accurate—began to spread. American policy drifted through the fall, but in early December the president made his decision; the plan would be "buried."[101]

At his Florida meeting with Mrs. Meir shortly afterward,

the President noted that obviously Israel cannot accept a flood of refugees. The Arabs have their troubles too. Maybe no compromises are possible. But he did not think we should give up on refugees. They are costing the United States money and they cause great damage to the prospects of peace. What we were trying to put together may have been impossible. Israel needed reassurances. The Arabs obviously could not make advance commitments. Our judgment, however, was that the great majority of refugees would resettle. We have not made any progress on the Johnson Plan and that is gone. But we should keep trying. He is not convinced that it is impossible.[102]

In these comments we are treated to a revealing and unusual glimpse of Kennedy, his views and his modus operandi toward the Arab-Israeli dispute. The conversation demonstrates major differences with the Israelis over the role of the United Nations in the Arab-Israeli dispute, the resettlement of the refugees, and the immediacy of the refugee crisis itself. The comments also assume that Israel has major obligations that it can fulfill by a more forthcoming approach in negotiations.[103] Even though he shelved the plan, Kennedy accepted Johnson's interpretation that the Israelis bore the greatest responsibility for the breakdown of discussions. Today, however, documents indicate that the Arabs were as responsible as Jerusalem for the failure of Johnson's proposals.[104] Here Kennedy's impartiality is demonstrated: he accepted the State Department interpretation of events but he killed the plan.

By order of the president, the plan itself was never published in order not to embarrass the participants and to keep future options open. But Johnson did publish an article in 1964 describing its contents. First, he argued that the wishes of the refugees should be given priority. Second, the refugees could not have unconditional free choice if the legitimate interests of the states involved were to be safeguarded. Third, he called for the United Nations to take an active role in implementing the plan. Johnson went on to suggest that Israel's existence could not be threatened by the returning refugees. He proposed that the refugees' wishes be ascertained in an environment isolated from external political pressures. They were to be made to understand that they might not get their first choice; the implications of the available options were to be explained to them, including what it would be like to live in a Jewish state.[105]

Johnson expected four concepts to dominate the procedures: First, there would be no public document but rather a tacit "acquiescence" in the practical measures to be undertaken. Second, he anticipated that repatriation and resettlement would occur simultaneously so that the first family returning to Israel would move on the same day as the first family resettling in an Arab country. Third, all governments involved would have the right to disengage themselves—that is, "to *refuse further* cooperation" if they became dissatisfied with the procedures. Fourth, the process would occur gradually over an extended period so there would be no slip-up in the machinery for resettlement.[106]

Johnson concluded that neither the Arabs nor Israel would get everything they wanted:

> Both would have to give up something. Israel would continue to exist as a state with a predominantly Jewish population. The refugees would not be recompensed in full for the injustices they have suffered, and only a handful of them would return to the actual homes they left a decade and a half ago. Arab politicians would have to abandon a propaganda weapon they have cherished for those years. Israel, for her part, would have to take in some refugees she does not want, without any prior agreement on the number (which . . . I am convinced would, under the procedures I propose, be very small, fewer than one-tenth of the total of the refugees and their descendants). And she would do so without obtaining what she wants on other specific issues.[107]

But the Israelis feared that the numbers would be far larger, questioned the possibility of a "free choice," and thought they had had a prior agreement on the numbers they would have to admit. On the other hand, the Arabs thought they would have to accept most of the refugees with little gain in the diplomatic battle with Israel.[108] Since the Johnson approach insisted on not clarifying in advance where the process would lead, each party concluded that the outcome would be unsatisfactory to its own interest.

Key officials in the Department of State viewed Johnson's efforts very differently, as was shown in an exceptional laudatory briefing paper prepared for a presidential meeting on Johnson's departure from the U.N. post in early 1963. Johnson is pictured as having "a remarkable wisdom and patience" and his work is described as "splendid." He is also praised for having maintained his U.N. identity while simultaneously operating in a "most harmonious relationship with the Department of State." The Arab written reply to his plan is labeled "the highwater mark of Arab realism on this problem."[109] Within the Near East Bureau, the notion continued that if the Israelis could just be persuaded that the plan was in their interests, the Arabs would acquiesce.[110] Several officials recommended putting genuine pressure on Israel, or at least making support for the plan a condition for granting the Hawks, economic aid, or other acts in support of Israel.[111] None of these ideas was approved, but genuine bitterness toward the Israelis over their attitude toward the plan remained in the Near East Bureau for years.[112] The plan was not buried easily. As late as 1969, its remnants can be discerned in the refugee section of the Rogers Plan.

Conclusion

In evaluating the Kennedy record on the Arab-Israeli dispute, four features stand out: the successful development of a new decision-making structure and a new policy toward Israel, balanced by the failure to implement a new Arab policy and the inability to begin settling the Arab refugee question. The initiatives and methods were novel; the results resembled those obtained by other administrations.

Kennedy's Middle East policy never had to surmount the crises other presidents faced in the area. His experience suggests that policy changes need not await a crisis, and that the best atmosphere for experimentation may be relative calm. But Kennedy's presidency also teaches that novel directions in American policy cannot succeed without the active involvement of the highest levels of an administration.

5

JOHNSON
An Unwanted Diversion from Vietnam

The Johnson era offers a study in contrasts: The president's knowledge and skill in domestic affairs marred by his inexperience and lack of confidence in foreign policy. An overwhelming outpouring of sympathy and support after the assassination of John Kennedy and the president's landslide victory over Barry Goldwater in 1964 eroded by the national trauma over Vietnam. A man who saw himself as committed to peace abroad, prosperity at home, and the advancement of minorities destroyed by the war, rioting in America's ghettos, and increasing violence and tension in American society. A president who repeatedly implored, "Let us reason together," undermined by a growing credibility gap, a widespread perception that he was untruthful in his conduct of affairs— especially in Vietnam. Johnson's Middle East policy shows similar contrasts: the adventurism of Vietnam in contrast to a prevailing caution in Arab-Israeli affairs; a reputation for pro-Israel sentiment and associates balanced by severe differences with Jerusalem and a reluctance to act decisively during the May 1967 crisis.

External and Internal Constraints

Johnson policy in the Middle East cannot be understood apart from the Vietnam imbroglio and the Six-Day War. Each conflict set priorities in the administration's global and regional policies and each determined the context in which existing assumptions became specific Mideast programs.

At the outset of the Johnson administration, after the Cuban missile crisis and the military buildup of the Kennedy years, the United States seemed exceptionally powerful relative to the Soviet Union. Many authors began to write about a pax Americana or a "unifocal" international system.[1] In the Middle East the United States faced relative quiet. Yet, in 1966 with Washington preoccupied with Vietnam, conflict was growing in the region. The Yemen War was dragging on, draining the Egyptian economy and Nasser's political capital in the Arab world. Internal Arab tensions were rising as the Arab countries became divided between radical nationalist states tied to the Soviet Union, like Egypt, Syria, and Iraq, and conservative regimes, like Saudi Arabia, Jordan, Lebanon, and Libya, dependent on American arms and backing. As was traditional in Arab politics, the Palestinian issue was being used to overcome divisions. Steps were taken to divert water from the Jordan River and thereby ruin Israel's new water project, to create a Palestine liberation army, and to strengthen Arab military cooperation in the "war" with Israel. The Arab regimes competed to demonstrate hostility toward Israel, with accompanying incidents on the country's borders drawing Israeli retaliation against suspected terrorist strongholds.

External pressures on the United States from the Arab-Israeli dispute altered radically with the Six-Day War. Washington believed that the war worsened the Arab-Israeli problem by increasing regional instability, inviting confrontation with the Soviet Union, encouraging radicalism, and threatening vital oil supplies. The area demanded presidential attention and the president's perspective changed accordingly. As late as November 1966, Johnson said at a news conference, "We are increasingly interested in the African Continent and the Middle East. Our reports give us a reason to believe that things are going as well as could be expected." By contrast, in a commencement address in May 1968, the president linked the Middle East with Vietnam: "Today in two areas of danger and conflict—the Middle East and Vietnam—events drive home the difficulty of making peace."[2]

The Six-Day War also altered the way in which the conflict was seen. Before 1967, administrations viewed settling the dispute as important to national interests (as in Eisenhower's first term), but the efforts to achieve settlement were coordinate or subordinate to regional objectives (as under Truman and Kennedy). Now efforts to resolve the Arab-Israeli dispute became central to American policy toward the area.

Johnson began with an absence of constraints unprecedented after U.S. involvement with the problem began in 1945. Congressional pressures were largely dormant, except for the issue of aid to Egypt, which was suspended in early 1967 after a period of declining sums.[3] The State Department was hardly in a position to press the White House for new initiatives or programs. By early 1967 the Near East Bureau was a dispirited place. Assistant Secretary Talbott had left in 1965, replaced by the retiring Raymond Hare for one last year of service; the post had then been vacant for several months before finally being filled by the ambassador to Egypt, Lucius Battle, in April 1967. During late 1966 and early 1967, the State Department Policy Planning Council did not have a member assigned to the Middle East.[4]

Johnson did not have to worry about the oil industry. As senator from Texas, he had learned long since how to retain the backing of oilmen. As Harry McPherson, a key White House aide, later recalled,

> What he has done, what he was doing in the Natural Gas Act of 1956 was to do just enough to keep them off his back down in Texas, to keep a lot of oil money from going against him in the next election whatever that was— Presidential or Senatorial or whatever. *He was never a friend of the Oil and Gas Industry . . .* , He had no desire to become an apologist for the industry.[5]

In any case, industry influences on him had always been domestic and had not interfered with his pro-Israeli posture in the Senate.

Even anti-Israeli pressures from companies with Middle East interests were restricted in this period because of the threat to Saudi Arabia from Nasser. Thus, the issue of petroleum moved Johnson against Nasser, Israel's chief adversary.

⌈The Jewish community also contributed to the president's permissive environment.⌋ Ever since he had championed Israel's cause when the Eisenhower administration pressured Israel in February 1957, Johnson had been received favorably by Jewish groups and leaders. Throughout his career, he was surrounded by prominent Jewish figures who shared his commitment to social liberalism as espoused, for example, by the American labor movement.[6] Lacking any crisis in the region, the president was safe from this quarter.

Vietnam and the Six-Day War radically altered the domestic forces operating on Johnson. Vietnam became a constraint that poisoned executive-legislative relations and created suspicion within the liberal, antiwar wing of the Jewish community, which had previously supported the president. The June 1967 crisis escalated these trends. The Near East Bureau was resuscitated and its role enhanced by the salience of the issue. In oil circles the Middle East scene was transformed: a weakened Nasser no longer threatened the conservative Arab sheikdoms. Now Arab concentration on Israel made an intimate American relationship with Jerusalem more troublesome. Meanwhile, the Jewish community—traumatized by the threat to the Jewish state in May 1967 and exhilarated by the electric Israeli victory—became more involved with Israel than ever. The war led to more press and media coverage, accelerating public involvement. During his last eighteen months in office, Johnson and his Middle East policy were buffeted by a storm of pulsating domestic pressures.

Global and Regional Perspectives

The Indo-China conflict plagued Johnson's administration. Its actions there characterized its approach to foreign affairs. The Johnson era brought to fruition the globalism implicit in the Truman Doctrine, Dulles's pacts, and Kennedy's rhetoric. Inherent in the Johnson approach was an interventionism in which the United States would involve itself anywhere and any time to contain the Communist menace and define an American world order.

Two comments made by Johnson in 1966 illustrate the attitude of the times:

> Surely it is not a paranoid vision of America's place in the world to recognize that freedom is still indivisible—still has adversaries whose challenge must be answered.[7]
> We have steadily resisted Communist efforts to bring about by force and intrigue a world dominated by a single ideology. Our convictions, our interests, our life as a nation demand that we oppose, with all the strength that we can muster, any effort to put this world in anyone's straitjacket.[8]

In early 1965 the United States intervened in the Dominican Republic to halt what was regarded as a Communist-inspired rebellion. Dean Rusk justified the effort with the argument that there were more Communists behind the forces backing Juan Bosch than the number of right-wing extremists who had originally backed Hitler.[9] If a handful of Communists anywhere around the world could draw an American intervention, then containment had fully evolved. Dulles's theories of ubiquitous external threats were meshed with the multiple options of Kennedy's defense policy to produce a foreign policy in which the United States would involve itself at will around the world.

In the optimistic days following the Cuban missile crisis and the Johnson landslide, the president and his aides could well assume that historical forces were on their side. On the one hand, this perception generated a willingness to negotiate arms control with the Soviet Union and begin the process later known as "detente." The nonproliferation treaty of 1968 was in this respect the crowning achievement of Johnson's foreign policy.

On the other hand, a sense of enhanced strength also led to the belief that the United States had the power to stop all Communist threats and this power should be used while history was on America's side. Thus, the optimism of power coexisted with a fear of weakness.[10]

Given these perceptions, it is not surprising that Johnson retreated from Kennedy's attempt to deal with nationalists. Instead, like Thomas Mann, the assistant secretary of state for Latin American affairs, officials tended to equate even a left-leaning government as threatening to American interests if Communists were perceived to be involved.[11]

Johnson's statement that he wanted to bring his domestic "Great Society" to Vietnam to create a TVA for the Mekong delta reflected the new mood.[12] All was possible: guns and butter in the federal budget, the uplifting of America's ghettos, and the modernization of less developed countries aligned with the United States. The optimism and rigid anticommunism of the mid-1960s was reinforced by several key advisors surroundng the president: Thomas Mann, Walt Rostow, who replaced Bundy as the NSC adviser in 1966, and Dean Rusk, a secretary of state who had been restrained under Kennedy but flourished under the Johnson system.

These global perspectives were critical for the Middle East. In an antinationalist climate favoring governments clearly identified with the United States, few sympathized with the policies of the Egyptian regime. The Yemen War continued, with its threat to the Arab oil sheikdoms. Nasser continued to aid the Congo rebels against the American-backed government there. Black African students protesting American actions in the Congo burned the USIA library in Cairo on Thanksgiving Day 1964 while Egyptian officials looked on. Shortly after, the Egyptians shot down an American plane owned by a friend of President Johnson. In November 1966 Cairo seized the assets of the Ford Motor Company after a dispute with the firm over customs duties. Nor was the president enchanted with Nasser's flirtation with the Vietcong. When a misunderstanding with the American embassy arose over the delivery of wheat, Nasser— not realizing how much assistance he was actually receiving from the United States—angrily declared, "Whoever does not like our conduct can go drink up the sea. If the Mediterranean is not sufficient, there is the Red Sea, too."[13]

Clearly the Egypt-first approach was dead.[14] The new administration accelerated Kennedy's moves to improve relations with the region's conservative regimes, many of which seemed threatened by Nasser's pan-Arabic pretensions. There were, however, no continuing initiatives toward the Egyptian leader of the sort that Kennedy might have pursued, although there were occasional tentative efforts at a more positive policy toward Cairo.[15] Each of these projects was dropped after a short period, usually because the Egyptians rejected them.

In April 1965—just when the Vietnam and Dominican Republic crises were emerging—Komer wrote a memo to Bundy urging that the president resist congressional amendments limiting aid to Cairo: "Mac, believe me when I stress my conviction that *we've got to have some room to maneuver with Nasser if we're going to avert a major crisis in the Middle East.* I may not know my Congress but I do know my Arabs. You and I were the ones who began clamping down on UAR aid back when NEA was still breathing euphoria."[16]

While the perils of the unraveling American-Egyptian connection were clear, they were overshadowed by more pressing crises. Kennedy had begun to return to the Arab conservatives reluctantly, but Johnson embraced them willingly. This approach was ideologically consistent with concern over oil and with the administration's tendency to favor antiradical, pro-Western regimes.

If Johnson altered Kennedy's Arab policy, he reinforced Kennedy's relationship with Israel. In every interchange—economic and military aid, summitry, cooperation between middle level bureaucrats in intelligence and defense—Johnson cemented a more intimate connection between Jerusalem and Washington. Like Truman, Johnson had a biblically based religious background that reinforced his sympathy toward Israel. As he told a B'nai B'rith meeting in Washington in 1968, "Most, if not all of you, have very deep ties with the land and with the people of Israel, as I do, for my Christian faith sprang from yours. The Bible stories are woven into my childhood memories as the gallant struggle of modern Jews to be free of persecution is also woven into our souls."[17] It is difficult to imagine Eisenhower, Kennedy, or Nixon making a similar statement.

In addition Johnson could easily identify with the Israelis as pioneers, hard workers, self-made men and women. As he told Prime Minister Eshkol in 1964:

> The people of Israel have labored long and hard to make of their ancient land a highly developed and most modern nation. Their achievements are remarkable. Toil and sweat alone are not responsible for such success. The spirit and the dedication of your people, Mr. Prime Minister, have been the inspiration for their labor. . . We welcome you here tonight . . . as representative of a country for which we have great admiration and affection.[18]

Johnson also saw Israelis as sharing a common heritage with the United States. Toasting Israeli President Shazar at the White House in 1966, he argued that ". . . Our Republic, like yours, was nurtured by the philosophy of the ancient Hebrew teachers who taught mankind the principles of morality, of social justice, and of universal peace. This is our heritage, and it is yours."[19]

By contrast, Johnson saw the Arabs as culturally different and their experiences as alien to his own. Thus, toasting King Hussein in 1964, Johnson focused on the differences with America in a stereotypical injunction, "In Jordan, he and his people have brought that ancient land of the camel, the date, and the palm to the threshold of a bright and a hopeful and a modern future."[20]

Johnson tended to see the Israelis fighting the Arabs as a modern-day version of the Texans struggling with the Mexicans. The analogy between the Alamo and Massada was not far below the surface. The Israeli conversion of a barren desert into a fertile agricultural land reminded him of projects he had sponsored along the Pedernales.[21] When Prime Minister Levi Eshkol visited the LBJ ranch in January 1968, the president immediately referred to their common interests in irrigation and had his pilot fly the prime minister and his party over the area as he recited the statistics of his own water projects.[22] That evening Johnson effusively celebrated the Israeli-American relationship with unprecedented cordiality:

> Our peoples, Mr. Prime Minister, share many qualities of mind and heart.
> We both rise to challenge. We both admire the courage and the resourcefulness of the citizen-soldier. We each draw strength and purpose for today from our heroes of yesterday. We both know the thrill of bringing life from a hard but a rewarding land.
> But all Americans—and all Israelis—also know that prosperity is not enough—that none of our restless generation can ever live by bread alone.
> For we are equally nations in search of a dream. We share a vision and purpose far brighter than our abilities to make deserts bloom.
> We have been born and raised to seek and find peace. In that common spirit of our hopes, I respect our hope that a just and lasting peace will prevail between Israel and her neighbors."[23]

As suggested by the greeting to Eshkol, Johnson's experience with domestic issues propelled his sympathy toward Israel. He had fought beside many Jews in battles for liberal social causes. The Texas populist recognized in the New York Jew a fellow outsider in relation to the "Eastern establishment." Johnson easily transposed this empathy for the American Jewish community to Israel.[24]

As he told the B'nai B'rith convention in September 1968,

> It is quite natural that American Jews should feel particularly involved with Israel's destiny. That small land in the eastern Mediterranean saw the birth of your faith and your people thousands and thousands of years ago. Down through the centuries, through dispersion and through very grievous trials, your forefathers clung to their Jewish identity and clung to their ties with the land of Israel. . . History knows no more moving example of persistence against the cruelest odds. . .[25]

Israel symbolized the foreign policy issues the president preferred: problems of economic development and external hostile forces. A domestically oriented president found in Israel a country and issue he could comprehend and identify with.

Further, Johnson saw the Israelis as loyal to him, a crucial factor to this president. Nasser delivered insulting speeches, supported anti-American causes from the Congo to Puerto Rico, and flirted with the Vietcong. The most prominent Egyptian newspaper, El Ahram, even published a cartoon at one point that seemed derogatory to Mrs. Johnson.[26] The Israelis, on the other hand, were reliable and never attacked him. Quite the contrary: many Israelis seemed to understand the reasons for his Vietnam policies, and the president appreciated their willingness to defend his policies to many of their American supporters.

Where both Eisenhower and Kennedy had planned their strategies for dealing with the Arab-Israeli dispute, Johnson evolved his basic policy through experience. Eisenhower had favored pro-Western Arab parties exclusively, alienating both Egypt and Israel in the process. Kennedy had sought to embrace the nationalist Arab leader, Nasser, and the Israelis as well. Johnson moved American policy closer to the Israelis and the conservative Arabs out of ideological predisposition rather than strategy. Johnson's policy emerged as an improvisational reaction to events. His basic approach was set even before the critical Six-Day War.

Decision Making

The decision-making approach of Johnson's presidency reflected many factors: his ignorance of foreign affairs and preference for domestic politics; his ideological globalism and anticommunism; his prime experience in the Senate as parliamentary leader; the split within the administration between those who favored Kennedy's style and policies and those who owed primary allegiance to the new president. Johnson's decision-making system reflected his preoccupation with loyalty and reliability among his aides, his suspicion of those who might still be attached to Kennedy, and his lack of administrative skills. In contrast to the Kennedy era, there was little effort to organize the administration for conducting foreign policy. Rather, the new administration found itself dealing ad hoc with crises.

Never able to overcome his parliamentarian's preference for the behind-the-scenes deal, Johnson's approach to the substance and procedures of foreign policy were enmeshed in personal fears and insecurity, eventually leading to his downfall over Vietnam. The president failed to replace Kennedy's White House–centered system, and foreign policy formulation became more diffused. As crises or key issues emerged, high officials took charge, depending on their available time and interest and the president's preferences. The more central the issue to the administration's concerns, the higher the official who became the "fireman."

The problems that arose came directly from Johnson's distinctive style. On especially difficult questions, the president preferred to solicit advice from as many trusted associates as he could in person or by telephone. For example, at a particularly dramatic moment in the Middle East crisis of May 1967, Johnson kept a nervous and impatient Israeli foreign minister waiting while he assembled his key foreign policy aides and asked each for advice.[27]

Joseph Sisco, the head of the International Organization Bureau, spoke of "very spirited debates on the Middle East" in the National Security Council.

"If there was one point at issue, he would go around the table and ask every man to express himself, and he'd hear them out and hear them out very patiently, I thought."[28] As Earle Wheeler, the chairman of the Joint Chiefs of Staff for much of the presidency, later recalled,

> President Johnson, as you no doubt know, likes to get the views of any number of people before he makes a decision. There was nothing unusual at all for him to say, "Well, now, I called" so and so, and so and so, and so and so last night. These would be people all around the country. [He was] just taking their pulse you see, to find out what their reaction was to this situation or that situation. He was a great telephone user. So was President Kennedy, I might add. He liked to get a number of views. He was a good question-asker. His method of doing business was contrary to that of President Kennedy who liked to see things in writing. He absorbed things quickly in writing. President Johnson preferred to use, I imagine, the system that he developed when he was majority leader on the Hill, [that] of getting people in a small smoke-filled room and boring into a subject until he had picked your brains, and I suppose, examined all of the facts of the problem, before he would make up his mind to do something.[29]

Roche put it succinctly, "He was not isolated in the White House. He had those damned telephones of his going all the time."[30] As Wheeler later added to his analysis, "Mr. Johnson was used to operating in the congressional way. In other words, in dealing with a group, a relatively small group of senior senators, [he was used to dealing] by personal persuasion, and argumentation, and as he said, talking things out, arriving at a decision and then going ahead and pushing it through to legislation, as might be required. So he operated when he was President very much in that same manner."[31]

The central decision-making forum that evolved from 1965 onward was a luncheon on Tuesdays that was attended by the president, the secretaries of state and defense, the CIA director, the chairman of the Joint Chiefs of Staff, the president's assistant for national security affairs and other close associates in and outside government. Johnson relied on outside advisers and personal friends, several of whom were invited to policy meetings or even the Tuesday lunch.[32] At one time or another this circle included Abe Fortas, Clark Clifford, Dean Acheson, McGeorge Bundy, George Ball.[33] Clark Clifford, describing the system of 1968, observed that "as far as important national security questions were involved, like the war in Vietnam and other problems we had over the face of the globe, those discussions and the decisions were made" in this group.[34] He continued,

> That's where those things were talked out. If we needed anybody else, somebody might be brought in to brief us, but the President learned if you

begin to talk about very important policies and begin even to make preliminary decisions, when you got a whole group together like the National Security Council, you'd be almost sure to get a leak. But with this small group of five men—that's the luncheon group that he'd have luncheon with once a week—then we'd meet sometimes day after day after day, steadily on important security problems. I think he never had a leak.[35]

This informal approach to making foreign policy helped blur the lines of authority.[36] On matters outside Vietnam, such as the Middle East, it was often unclear who had the prime responsibility for policies.

In regard to openness and accountability, this informal system also had a contradictory effect. On issues like Vietnam in which the president and his key advisors were intensely involved, heavy outside criticism had little influence. Policies might be altered only after internal dissent, as in the famous bombing halt of March 1968. Even here the president resisted change.[37] On the other hand, the informal Johnson system actually encouraged a high degree of openness on lesser issues. The president himself, unsure and susceptible to a variety of views, would be open to contrasting perspectives.[38] Thus the Johnson system, when it was not dealing with a central issue like Vietnam or the intervention in the Dominican Republic, was quite open to bureaucratic, congressional, and private interest groups.

The Middle East was one of the lower priority matters, where the president's policy options were not set even though his attachment to the Israelis and his preference for conservative, pro-Western Arab regimes were clear. Therefore, after mid-1967 when the Near East Bureau had been rejuvenated under Lucius Battle, the impact of the bureaucracy on the White House was more effective, especially with the onset of the 1967 crisis. The Pentagon also began to show an interest in the Middle East after the Israeli victory; their experiences in battle against Russian arms could be translated into lessons for Vietnam.

The contrast between decision making on Vietnam and the Middle East can be illustrated by an incident that occurred early in the May 1967 crisis. Dean Rusk, appearing before the Senate Foreign Relations Committee to report on events in the Middle East, received a clear message from Senator Fulbright and his colleagues that they would not condone the unilateral intervention of American troops. The committee's stance reinforced Rusk's policy preferences and those of the key figures in the administration. It therefore had an enormous impact on American conduct during the crisis, even though other congressmen, more sympathetic to U.S. intervention, later made statements (disparate though they might have been) encouraging forceful U.S. action.

Fulbright had opposed American policy in the Dominican Republic and Vietnam and by now his committee and the administration were almost constantly at loggerheads. Rather than oppose the committee on yet another issue, the administration in this case bowed to influence from its congressional adversaries.

In further contrast to Vietnam and the "Tuesday luncheon" style of decision making, the number of players involved in Middle East policy was exceptionally large, larger than in previous administrations, especially Eisenhower's. Lucius Battle later said of the Six-Day War period, "I think there's always a tendency in moments of hot crisis that you find too many people trying to cook the stew. There was a bit of that in this one."[39] The unusually large numbers involved in noncrisis periods reflected high interest running through the administration. Since avenues of influence were often blocked over Vietnam, some officials took the greater opportunities to affect policy in the Middle East.

On the one hand, those involved with policy at the highest levels included many with typical bureaucratic roles: Rusk, McNamara and then Clifford as secretary of defense, Walt Rostow at the NSC, Battle and his colleagues at State's Near East Bureau. In addition, when Komer joined the Vietnam policymakers in 1966, he yielded responsibility for South Asia and Near East Affairs on the National Security Council to his former deputy, Harold Saunders. Although a quieter, more retiring person, Saunders was a careful, effective civil servant who was to outlast all other participants in the issue. Over a decade later he would still play a prominent role in Arab-Israeli affairs for the Carter administration.

On the other hand, the administration was filled with people sympathetic to Israel on grounds of culture, politics, ideology, and religion. From Vice-President Humphrey on down, key members who had been part of the "old Left" Democratic liberal-labor alliance had backed Israel solidly, viewing the Jewish state as expressing the same humanitarian outlook that had produced Democratic party programs from the New Deal to the Great Society. This group included John Roche and Ben Wattenberg, two speech writers on the White House staff, and Sheldon Cohen, chief of the Internal Revenue Service. Even in the usually "evenhanded" national security apparatus, there were officials who fit into the pro-Israeli framework: Arthur Goldberg as American ambassador to the United Nations and Eugene Rostow as undersecretary of state for political affairs.

One of the president's assistants, Harry McPherson, became the first and only non-Jew to hold the Jewish portfolio when Feldman departed in early 1966. McPherson was less central in the role than Feldman had been because there were more people around the president who already expressed sympathy with Israel and because he had less experience with the issue. As McPherson himself recalled, "Throughout my time here . . . I've been a conduit for the Jewish community in the United States. Why, I don't know. I knew a lot of its leading members before I became Special Counsel and it seemed natural for me to do it."[40]

Those from outside the government with particular interest in Israel included a local Texas Jewish businessman, James Novy, who had contributed to Johnson's first campaign in 1937 and continued in contact with him.[41] In addition, there was Ed Weisl, a prominent New York lawyer, Democratic party regular Abe Feinberg, Arthur Krim of Paramount Pictures (whose wife was Israeli and who later purchased a ranch near Johnson's in Texas), and David Ginsberg, a prominent Washington lawyer who had included the Israeli embassy among his clients. Even the Israelis themselves had a contact near Johnson. Ephraim ("Epi") Evron, the number-two man at the Israeli embassy, was occasionally invited to the ranch for a weekend. McPherson later noted, "I got to know and to become an intimate friend of the Israeli Minister here [Ephraim] Evron, who developed one of the most unusual friendships with an American President, I suspect, that any Minister has ever developed."[42]

In an increasingly isolated administration, in which loyalty and a common world view were cherished, many insiders were "believers" in Israel, even though their primary responsibility was domestic. Their prominence gave the administration a pro-Israel cast in the eyes of partisans concerned about American Middle East policy. Yet, the sentimental attachments of these insiders were usually irrelevant to policy. Most officials sympathetic to Israel did not play a role in foreign policy. Johnson's style and background made his White House similar to Congress in its dealings with Israeli affairs: much sympathy, many interested parties, much latitude for "constituency" influence. However, the administration included various figures who took a diplomatic point of view and who often differed with the advocates of Israel. It is possible for the bureaucracy to shut out the pro-Israeli forces, as occurred under Eisenhower, but the pro-Israeli forces can never exclude the bureaucracy from policy making.

As this disparate decision-making system only begins to suggest, Johnson was unpredictable. He demanded complete loyalty, especially from his friends, and when pressured he could react in the most unexpected ways, as the following three stories illustrate.

The first suggests the close rapport between Johnson and Evron. As noted earlier, the Israeli minister was occasionally invited to the ranch for the weekend. At one point LBJ took him on a typically wild Jeep ride around the ranch with the Secret Service in hot pursuit. On this particular ride the president overturned the Jeep and landed in a ravine; both Johnson and Evron had to be dragged out.[43]

The second incident involved the Jewish War Veterans. The president privately believed that Israel was like South Vietnam, a small country threatened by outside aggression. He was therefore perplexed by the opposition of many prominent Jews to the Indochina War, especially because there was a written American commitment to South Vietnam as there was not for Israel. "Dammit, they want me to protect Israel, but they don't want me to do anything in Vietnam," he is reported to have said on several occasions.[44] While discoursing with Eban in late 1968 on the dangers of an American isolationism that would allow Israel to "go down the drain," he said, "A bunch of rabbis came here one day in 1967 to tell me that I ought not to send a single screwdriver to Vietnam, but on the other hand, should push all our aircraft carriers through the Straits of Tiran to help Israel."[45]

At one point in fall 1966 the president made the mistake of expressing his views to the head of the Jewish War Veterans. The veteran agreed with Johnson completely and promptly reported the discussion to the press. A political flap ensued, because the president appeared to be threatening to withdraw or at least reduce American support for Israel unless key American Jews reversed their opposition to the war. McPherson organized consultations at the White House with key members of B'nai B'rith and a statement was released denying any link between Middle East and Indochina policy. The incident illustrates, however, the delicate state of Johnson's thinking by late 1966. Although the president vehemently denied linking policy in these two areas, he remained incredulous that people who supported Israel would not see the Vietnam situation as analogous.[46]

A third story, told by speech writer John Roche, illustrates the peculiar Johnson style. Early in the May 1967 crisis, the president had decided to speak on the Egyptian closing of the Straits of Tiran. Dissatisfied with a State Department draft, he phoned Roche in the middle of the night to have it rewritten in a manner more sympathetic to the Israelis. Yet, as Jewish groups pressured him the next day, he played what Roche recalls as "one of his little malicious games." He began reading to Israel's supporters the State Department draft. The Israeli ambassador phoned Roche from Vice President Humphrey's office to complain; neither the ambassador nor the vice president had the slightest notion that the president had decided upon a more favorable statement. Johnson instructed those who did know (W. Rostow, Roche) not to tell anyone, including Humphrey.[47]

All three stories point to a highly emotional, mercurial president for whom personal loyalty was paramount. It would always be difficult to predict what his reactions might be. For Johnson, the formulation of policy was more informal and idiosyncratic than for most other occupants of the Oval Office. His approach to both the Arabs and Israelis must be seen in this context.

The Evolution of Policy before May 1967

American policy before the Six-Day War took on three main avenues: (1) an unsuccessful attempt to persuade Nasser to limit his arms acquisitions; (2) a subsequent effort to arm the conservative Arab states (especially Jordan) threatened by Nasser's pan-Arabism; and (3) increased military assistance to

Israel to balance the Russian aid for Arab radicals and American aid for Arab conservatives.

Repeated administration efforts to persuade Nasser to restrain his arms policy are shown in the record as it has been revealed over the years. For example, in a May 1964 cable to the American ambassador in Cairo, the department instructed:

> We particularly wanted you to emphasize mischievous role of UAR missile program in pushing arms rivalry to new and dangerous levels, as covered in previous guidelines. . . Moreover, we think it important he [Nasser] be made to realize, in a way he will not resent, fact that he must shoulder large share responsibility for arms race in general. His periodic openings of "icebox" door (cite cases) has let out blast of cold air that put great psychological pressure on Israelis to obtain deterrent. We are not trying to justify Israeli actions to him; we are merely explaining them and his responsibility."[48]

Similarly, in summer 1963 and fall 1964, John J. McCloy, the former chairman of the board of Chase Manhattan Bank, met with President Nasser to initiate an arms limitation program. The reasons for the meeting were not made public at the time. In its first effort, the State Department was satisfied by a letter from Nasser assuring Johnson that "the UAR would not introduce or develop weapons of total destruction."[49] In McCloy's second mission, he proposed a freeze on current Egyptian missiles; in this case the department's low expectations of success were confirmed.[50]

Use of a secret and private envoy often reflects poor relations with a country and little hope for genuine achievement. Indeed, McCloy's two missions occurred against the backdrop of deteriorating relations with Cairo. On the other hand, relations with Jerusalem were improving in this period. Keeping to Kennedy's plan to meet Prime Minister Levi Eshkol in spring 1964, Johnson was expansive in presiding over the first official Washington visit by an Israeli prime minister, a visit conveniently scheduled in an election year. At one point, the president turned to Eshkol and smiled, "Some say that we are alike. Well, that's not at all bad."[51]

The Israelis sought another major change in American arms shipments toward Israel—the purchase, for the first time, of an offensive weapon: tanks. Defense and intelligence experts confirmed Israeli need of a counter to Soviet arms shipments to the UAR, although Pentagon officials preferred that the Israelis get their tanks from Germany or Britain. State Department officials argued against the sale on the grounds that the regional balance of power still favored Israel. At the White House, Feldman supported Israel's case; Bundy wanted to swap the tanks for an agreement that Israel would not develop missiles and atomic weapons.[52] In the end, Johnson agreed to help Israel secure the tanks from other sources; but, if necessary, the United States would supply them it-self.[53] The Israelis for their part agreed to the inspection of their nuclear facili-ties.[54] During private meetings, the president sweetened the atmosphere with several reassuring comments, saying, for example, that Israel could always count on the United States in an emergency.[55]

The Israelis preferred German tanks if they could not acquire them di-rectly from the United States. Indeed, they had already established a secret arms arrangement with West Germany that had been operating for about five years.[56] Chancellor Ludwig Erhard arrived on a scheduled visit to the United States soon after Eshkol departed, and he was the next to receive the Johnson treatment. However, despite his country's arms arrangement with Israel, the reluctant Ger-man leader feared that if a tank sale to Israel were discovered, Arab states would seek diplomatic relations with East Germany. But he could not resist the per-suasive American president and finally agreed to sell Israel both tanks and sub-marines. By January 1965 the news had indeed leaked out; several Arab states threatened to break relations with West Germany and recognize its East German foes. In February the Germans cut off supplies to Israel and the Johnson admin-istration finally completed the deal itself.[57]

Meanwhile, Nasser's continued plans for a united Arab command were stimulating countermoves by the United States. The keystone in the policy of checking Nasser was Jordan, which threatened to seek Soviet supplies if it did not receive them from the United States.[58] To the administration, it seemed necessary to make a stand in Amman against the influence of both Cairo and Moscow. Yet major military assistance to Jordan, an Arab state bordering Israel, raised political and military problems. Aid to King Hussein, combined with accelerating numbers of Russian weapons to Egypt, Syria, and Iraq, could unset-tle the Arab-Israeli military balance.

Ironically, the desire of the United States to balance these Russian sup-plies by supplying arms to friendly Arab regimes led to a dramatic increase in arms for Israel. The new relationship did not evolve easily, as a reluctant Wash-ington bureaucracy resisted every move. Since increased arms for the Israelis seemed politically and militarily necessary, the objective was to keep the sales as limited and secret as possible.

Having decided to increase arms sales to Jordan, the administration sent the undersecretary of state for political affairs, Averell Harriman, with Robert Komer to inform the Jerusalem government of this decision in early 1965. The mission asked Israeli help in selling the idea to Israel's American supporters and offered new assistance "if Israel met certain conditions."[59] Anyone who sup-poses that Israeli-American relations have always been conducted in harmony will be astonished by the acrimony of these discussions, the minutes of which have since been released.

In the American view, failing to send U.S. tanks to Jordan would result in a dramatically larger supply of Russian weapons going to Amman:

Governor Harriman stressed that the President's interest in Israel was undiminished; he was keenly concerned about Israel's security. The President accepted the need for Israel to have an adequate deterrent. We realized that this Jordan business was a shock to Israel, but the dangers to Israel would clearly be greater if we did not help Jordan.[60]

On behalf of Johnson, Harriman requested that Eshkol "put these matters into proper perspective for the key leaders of the [American Jewish] community. This was an essential part of our relationship."[61] In other words, the Israelis were asked to head off a domestic political crisis for the president.[62] In return, "For the first time the President was willing to consider the direct sales of military equipment Israel needed, at an appropriate time with appropriate coordination of the publicity problem. This represented a major change in U.S. policy."[63] Harriman quickly added that the United States still preferred that Israel acquire arms from other Western sources.

At all this, Prime Minister Eshkol and Foreign Minister Meir exploded. First, they demanded simultaneous and public supplies of weaponry and in larger numbers than Jordan was receiving. Harriman and Komer were adamant that they would not publicly announce any direct arms sales to Israel. According to Harriman, "Whenever it was done there would be an explosion" in the Arab world. Second, the Israelis demanded that Americans enter the current dispute over Jordan waters on their behalf. At the time the Arabs were threatening to divert the Jordan headwaters within their territories and thereby reduce Israel's water supply. The dispute went back to the Johnston Plan, which the United States considered functional even without explicit multilateral agreement. The administration had been supporting Israeli rather than Arab claims to water rights. However, Harriman and Komer made it clear that the United States wanted Jerusalem to counter the Arab diversion plans by enlisting the U.N. to "develop world opinion" on Israel's side. Under no conditions would the administration countenance "preemptive action," even if the U.N. had considered the matter and failed to act. Meir then accused the United States of reversing its commitment and Harriman suggested that she was "sneering" at the Security Council.[64]

When the two sides later exchanged different memoranda of understanding, the disputes continued. Eshkol asked, "Did the U.S. really think Israel had deterrent superiority? Mr. Komer replied yes. The prime minister said, 'Then we are lost.'" As the discussions continued, Eshkol complained, "You leave me with nothing." When Harriman reiterated the need to supply arms to Jordan, the prime minister retorted, "Then don't ask us; you are a world power." (At this point the prime minister, in an aside, asked Shimon Peres what he thought of the U.S. paper. Peres responded, in Hebrew, "No good.") The Israelis wanted to discuss their military needs, but Harriman insisted that was for the future; he had come only to obtain Israel's agreement to the Jordan arms deal. To one

Israeli, the American paper "would be the most secret piece of paper in Israel. It was so terrible that he did not want anyone else to see it."[65]

The disagreements were sufficiently far-reaching that Komer was forced to stay in Israel to try for an accord after Harriman left. Peres reports of Komer, "On more than one occasion he would ring me at three or four in the morning with a brain wave."[66] Finally, however, secret agreements were reached. The Israelis did communicate informally with their American friends about the Jordanian arms deal and the United States did agree to sell Israel combat aircraft if comparable weapons could not be obtained from West Europe. The arms and water issues were separated, but the Jordan water dispute remained, with the United States seeking to influence the involved Arab states diplomatically in order to head off precipitous Israeli action.[67]

Over two months after the Harriman-Komer meetings in Jerusalem, a discussion between Israel's Ambassador Harman and Assistant Secretary Talbott in Washington reveals the continuing discord and the bureaucratic resistance to a new arms pipeline for Israel. The ambassador maintained that Komer had told the Israelis that the American promise on planes was "not intended to 'fob us off.' If Israel could not obtain planes from Western Europe, it could do so from the U.S." Yet, Harman complained, the Israelis were already being "fobbed off." Having informed the administration that Israel had failed to find suitable European aircraft, the embassy "had been told that no decision had been reached to sell planes. This was difficult to understand since there was no room for misinterpretation of the agreement." Unknown to the Israelis, Rusk had cabled Talbott in Israel a month earlier that the United States preferred West European suppliers: "While we wish to avoid specific discussion on bombers or attack aircraft, we do not think this is what Israel needs for defense or what we would wish to sell."[68]

At the meeting with Harman in Washington, Talbott suggested that "he was not sure that our response [on arms] would be pleasing to Israel." He then counterattacked by warning Israel not to use force over the water issue, specifically referring to incidents along the Israeli-Syrian border and linking this problem to the arms.[69]

The discussion over specific planes dragged on for several months, but in February 1966 agreement was finally reached that the United States would sell 48 Skyhawk bombers to Israel. The deal was announced in May. With the 210 tanks sold in 1965 (40 had earlier been received from West Germany), the Harriman-Komer talks marked a turning point in American-Israeli relations and in the U.S. role in the Middle East. Despite the clashes in specific conversations, the outcome was never in doubt. Once the United States sought to balance the mounting Russian arms aid to Cairo, Damascus, and Baghdad by supplying arms to the conservative Arabs, increased military assistance to Israel was inevitable despite official hesitations. First, the American commitment to a continued Arab-Israel arms balance demanded no less, especially as European arsenals could not match the Russian assistance to the radical Arabs. Second, the administration was committed to providing regimes friendly to the United States with arms and military assistance. During the Johnson administration, arms aid rose from $44.2 million in 1963 to nearly $995.3 million by 1968.[70] Third, a congressional leak in October 1967 revealed that not only Jordan but several other conservative Arab regimes were being supplied with arms. These states included Libya, Morocco, Lebanon, Saudi Arabia, and Tunisia.[71] In this context, aid to Israel could hardly be avoided, given "the recurrent and vehement public Arab threats to Israel's security."[72]

Fourth, there remained a fear that "if Israel is unable to obtain its valid conventional arms requirements, those in Israel who advocate acquisition of nuclear weapons will find a much more fertile environment for their views.[73]

Fifth, as Johnson recognized in pressuring Eshkol to support his decision on arms for Jordan, pro-Israel feeling was a continuing domestic constraint. For example, in a March 1964 memo to the president, Komer discussed proposed assistance for an Egyptian monument that he described as a "cultural matter, which feelers indicate would not create any political problems here." Although Johnson and his associates would certainly expect political controversy if Israel were not aided at all, the administration had wide latitude on the timing, terms, and quantities of arms transfers. And, as in Kennedy's Hawk missile decision, the deal could be justified without reference to domestic politics.[74]

Between 1964 and 1967, America increased aid to the opponents of the Soviet Union and the adversaries of Soviet clients in the region. Yet neither the price nor the priority of such assistance was high. The dollars expended were minimal in comparison with the sums committed in Indochina. And key officials were not eager to see Middle Eastern affairs given greater importance. For example, in 1966 an interdepartmental group called the Holmes Committee under the chairmanship of Eugene Rostow, the new under secretary of state for political affairs, investigated Soviet encroachments in the area of the Middle East and the Indian Ocean. Its report argued for intensified American efforts to thwart growing Russian influence throughout the region, but its recommendations were unwelcome to Johnson's Vietnam-dominated higher circles. Regarded as overly alarmist, the report was buried at the National Security Council level in early 1967.[75] Thus, administration policy in the Middle East by early 1967 amounted to an attempt to bolster pro-American regimes while avoiding intensified commitments and any diplomatic programs.

For months signs warned that the Middle East was drifting toward crisis, but they could not be addressed seriously by an administration so preoccupied with Vietnam. It is not clear, however, that even without the distraction of Indochina the signals would have been properly perceived.

In February 1966 an unstable leftist regime assumed power in Damascus, but it faced worsening ethnic and political divisions. Its answer to its woes was to pursue a "war of liberation" against the Israelis, increasing the number of raids on Israeli territory, the worst onslaught in ten years.[76] Israel took out its frustration in a major retaliatory raid against the Jordanian village of Es-Samu in November 1966; an attack against Jordanians suspected of collaborating with terrorists was considered less likely to escalate than one against Syria. In response, Arthur Goldberg (speaking at the United Nations on behalf of the administration) deplored the use of force by both sides.[77] Terrorist activity continued, but the worst incident before May 1967 occurred on 7 April when the Israelis shot down six Syrian Mig-21s with no loss to themselves.

In early 1967, Battle, departing Cairo for Washington to assume office as the new assistant secretary of state for Near East affairs, repeatedly warned of Nasser's growing entanglement in Arab politics and his growing economic woes at home, especially in the wake of the Yemen War. Battle suggested that Nasser

> needed a diversion and something to cover this internal difficulty, that he could heat up the Yemen crisis with a view possibly toward undermining the Saudi Arabian situation in the hopes of getting some of the oil money that existed there or in Kuwait. He could go the other way and try to undermine by subversive action the regime in Libya, also a very rich regime where he had a great many Egyptians who were functioning there as teachers ostensibly and in other ways; or, lastly he could heat up the Arab-Israeli situation.[78]

To Battle a new conflict with Israel seemed least likely, because it would offer Egypt no economic gain.[79]

In late April a crisis developed in Yemen when two American AID officials were seized by Egyptian soldiers and the secret papers in their possession confiscated. Dean Rusk, once a proponent of aid to Nasser, was so thoroughly annoyed that he considered breaking diplomatic relations with Egypt, but the quiet minicrisis was papered over when the two Americans were released.[80]

Here we see the situation that would explode into a new Middle East crisis in the following month: Egyptian-American relations at a new low, suspicions of Nasser rising in Washington, and a new American ambassador to Cairo not yet arrived. Meanwhile, the administration was preoccupied with Vietnam and its relations with Congress were deteriorating as its credibility diminished over Indochina policy. Into this context came the events of May 1967, forcing the Johnson administration to switch its attention from Southeast Asia to the Middle East.

The May 1967 Crisis

The situation in Washington was confused because the crisis itself was so unexpected and complex that it demanded focus and an ordered decision-making system, neither of which existed in the Johnson administration. The disjointed American reaction to the 1967 crisis can be divided into three phases.

The first period began on 16 May when Nasser suddenly ordered a limited withdrawal of the United Nations Emergency Force that had been stationed on the Egyptian-Israeli border since 1957. Although Nasser appeared to be responding to Russian reports that the Israelis were preparing for war against Syria, he had received such warnings from Moscow twice during the previous year and knew them to be false.[81] Several countries participating in the U.N. force were reluctant to retain men in place under those conditions and, indeed, some U.N. troops were physically evicted by the Egyptians. Secretary General U Thant responded in a way that "shocked" and "puzzled" the American president.[82] Instead of adopting the stalling procedures that Hammarskjold had designed a decade earlier for just this contingency, he informed Nasser that he interpreted his request as a demand for total withdrawal. Meanwhile, in response to Nasser's moves, the Israelis began to mobilize.

The administration reacted to these events by trying to gain time and prevent hostilities. Reminiscent of Truman in 1947 and 1948, Johnson recalls in his memoirs, "As far as possible, I wanted the main thrust of our diplomacy to be through the United Nations. At the same time, I was prepared to use American influence in any way that might be effective and helpful."[83] During this period the president sent individual letters to Nasser, Eshkol, and Kosygin urging diplomacy, and he supported the secretary general's plan to go to Cairo for discussions with the Egyptian leader.[84] The Israelis, however, were already impatient with the low-key American response to Nasser's moves; the administration had rejected their request for public support and even suggested that the UNEF troops be moved to the Israeli side of the armistice lines.[85]

By the last day of this stage of the crisis, 22 May, Israeli ambassador Harman was complaining to Battle that the American approach actually invited Nasser to interfere with free passage in the Straits of Tiran. On the same day, Johnson ordered the Sixth Fleet to the eastern Mediterranean.[86]

Later on 22 May Nasser announced a blockade of all Israeli shipping and strategic goods bound for Israel through the Straits of Tiran.[87] This act led to a second and more serious stage of the crisis. The declaration was technically an act of war, and the Israelis had held since 1957 that they would take military action to maintain their free access to the port of Eilat. The administration's first reaction was to gain a forty-eight hour delay from the Israelis and to seek consultation preceding any use of force. To avoid a repeat of the Suez crisis tensions with Washington, Jerusalem decided on 23 May to acquiesce in the president's appeal. They sent Foreign Minister Eban to Washington, assuring a delay in hostilities for several days.[88]

Meanwhile, Johnson could no longer avoid a public reaction to Nasser's actions, which led to the 23 May speech drafted by the State Department and rewritten by Roche.[89] In the speech Johnson reaffirmed the long-held American position that the Gulf of Aqaba was an international waterway and said that a blockade of Israeli shipping was therefore illegal. Yet the president did not declare overt support of Israel, nor did he suggest a solution to the crisis.[90] While Eban saw President de Gaulle and Prime Minister Wilson in Paris and London en route to Washington, the administration sought a plan to convince the Israelis that reversing the blockade could be achieved without military action.

In preparing its moves, Johnson and his advisers were largely free of key public pressures. For example, Jewish leaders issued a statement pledging support of "whatever action may be necessary to resist aggression against Israel and to preserve peace." It would have been impolitic for Jewish groups to call for either an Israeli attack or unilateral American action and they were, therefore, left to press the administration to "do something"—a vagueness which allowed flexibility.[91]

To further the administration's objective of avoiding unilateral American or Israeli military action, key officials seized on a British suggestion for a two-stage multilateral approach. First, a public declaration would reaffirm the right of free passage through the Straits of Tiran. Then, a naval task force would sail through to Eilat and challenge the blockade. Each stage would involve as many nations as possible. The recommendations were consistent with the commitments made to Israel in February 1957 and now reaffirmed by former President Eisenhower himself.[92]

When Eban arrived in Washington on Thursday, 25 May, President Johnson was in Montreal, ostensibly to participate in United States Day at Expo '67 (he was actually seeking Canada's participation in the multilateral fleet proposal).[93] Eban was scheduled to confer with State Department officials in preparation for his meeting with Johnson the next day, after which he planned to return to Israel. He had hardly arrived in Washington when an incident occurred that altered the atmosphere of his visit and affected American-Israeli relations throughout the remaining crisis.

Upon deplaning, the foreign minister was greeted by Ambassador Harman, who showed him a cable he had just received from the prime minister's office in Jerusalem. This message suggested the danger of an imminent Egyptian attack.[94] Israel's chief of military intelligence, Aharon Yariv, had already participated in writing a cable directly to Eban "for his eyes only," which spoke only of "indications pointing to offensive intentions." But Eban never saw this cable and the Israeli delegation acted on the basis of the more disturbing message.[95]

The foreign minister, therefore, sounded an alarm that was not taken seriously by U.S. experts and (unknown to him) even by his own intelligence service. His message caused American officials to suspect the Israelis of undue nervousness or deviousness; the president himself was annoyed with the added pressure.[96] At the very least the new message undermined the talks during

Eban's twenty-four hours in Washington. It also exacerbated the gap between Israeli alarm and American preference for established diplomatic procedures.

The timing of the visit further impeded Eban during his Washington stay; he had come because of Israeli urgency and to avoid the 1956 error of acting without an "understanding" with the American Government. But the administration, caught off guard by the unexpected crisis, had not reached definitive conclusions within its own ranks, a task made more difficult by Johnson's collegial approach to foreign policy. Before Eban's arrival, the secretaries of state and defense had prepared an option memorandum in which they argued that the United States should assume responsibility rather than "unleash" the Israelis. Building on the British suggestions, they envisioned three stages. First, United Nations efforts were to be exhausted. Second, the declaration by maritime powers would be attempted. Third, if all else failed, the international flotilla would sail through the Straits of Tiran.[97] On the evening of Eban's arrival, he was presented with this American plan at the State Department. The discussions became more tense when officials spelled out the plan to seek congressional and U.N. Security Council approval before taking action. They also stressed congressional preference for a multilateral framework.[98] The Israelis were interested in speed, but American officials were content to warn the Egyptians not to use force while asking the Russians to urge similar restraint on Cairo. If the Egyptians were not going to attack (as all officials in Washington believed), why were the Israelis in such a hurry?

Eban and his entourage demonstrated their nervousness by seeking a broad American declaration that an attack on Israel would be considered tantamount to an attack on the United States, a NATO-type commitment that Johnson—now observing constitutional amenities to the letter after his Vietnam experience—was not about to consider.[99] The first round of talks ended with the Israelis concerned about the vagueness of American plans and the delays involved in going before the United Nations, and Johnson and his aides annoyed about the Israeli alarm over what they considered an improbable Egyptian attack.

The second day of Israeli-American talks reinforced this divergence. Eban first met at the Pentagon with McNamara, Joint Chiefs of Staff Chairman Wheeler, CIA Director Helms, and other aides. U.S. military and intelligence officials made it clear that they did not expect the Egyptians to attack and that, even if they did, the Israelis would win. The Pentagon did not believe that time, at least in the short run, was working against Israel, and indeed they argued that it was the overextended Egyptians who were becoming more vulnerable as the days progressed.[100] When the discussion turned to the "Red Sea Regatta," the foreign minister could hardly be encouraged. As one Pentagon official later recalled, "We didn't have much to discuss because there wasn't much to the plan." McNamara revealed his own doubts when he asked whether a warship would have to escort every Israeli vessel through each time one sought to navigate the Gulf of Aqaba to or from Eilat. It was a haunting question, but the idea for a flotilla was the Americans', not the Israelis'.[101]

That afternoon Eban and his colleagues waited nervously for the president while, unknown to the Israelis, Johnson met with his principal foreign policy advisers to decide what he could tell the Israeli foreign minister. This was the only large scale meeting during the crisis; it included almost all the major foreign policy figures of the administration—Humphrey, Rusk, Eugene Rostow, Wheeler, Helms, Battle, and Sisco (head of State's U.N. bureau)—as well as four private advisers to the president—Abe Fortas, Cyrus Vance, George Ball, and Clark Clifford. The meeting continued the divergence between the American and Israeli positions and the administration's reluctance to support Jerusalem. Rusk prepared a memo for discussion in which he recommended that the president take a "positive" position on the multilateral fleet proposal but make no final commitment to Eban. At the same time, it was thought that the U.N. force should be reconstituted along both sides of the Israeli-Egyptian frontier. If Egypt refused the proposal, perhaps Israel might accept it—even though the Israelis had always adamantly opposed a U.N. force on their side of the border because they distrusted U.N. personnel and argued that it was the Egyptians and not they who allowed terrorists to cross the border. As all this was happening, Rusk suggested that economic and military aid might be offered Israel to offset the burden of continued mobilization. At the meeting, however, Wheeler argued that Israel could remain fully mobilized for two months without an undue burden.[102]

It is clear that the Johnson administration and the Israelis viewed the February 1957 commitments to Israel differently: in Jerusalem Dulles had committed the U.S. to use force if necessary in reopening the straits, whereas in Washington Dulles had only recognized Israel's right to use force under the provisions of Article 51 of the U.N. Charter.[103] This difference affected American and Israeli perceptions during the 1967 crisis, and increased Israeli skepticism about American or international guarantees in the years following the Six-Day War. In typical Johnson style, the president asked each adviser for views at this critical meeting, but the discussion centered on the multilateral force, which Johnson called his "hole card" in his talk with Eban.[104]

While the American team deliberated, the Israeli group around Eban became tense about the White House failure to set a meeting with the president. The foreign minister had completed his business in Washington except for this crucial session. In some desperation, Evron was sent to the White House and, with Walt Rostow, finally arranged the meeting, a matter complicated by Johnson's fear of premature publicity. This fear had been rekindled when Canada's Pearson publicly discussed their meeting of the previous day.[105]

As these arrangements were being completed, the president phoned Rostow and, learning that Evron was there, asked to see him immediately. The Israeli envoy's full report of this meeting was later published. At this session Johnson told Evron that any American involvement encouraging force would require congressional approval. Apparently he had in mind something like the Gulf of Tonkin Resolution, which he had interpreted as granting him the power to take action he thought necessary in Vietnam. In order to gain congressional support, he had to await the report of U Thant's visit to Cairo and explore action through the United Nations, however unlikely the prospect of success. He described his hopes for a multilateral force, but stressed that he would not be hurried by the Israelis into precipitous action. Israel as a sovereign government could choose to act unilaterally, but if it did so the inevitable damaging consequences would be its responsibility. Johnson usually personalized matters and in this meeting, "He emphasized several times that Israel could depend on him."[106]

When the president finally met Eban, he repeated this message. He and McNamara reassured the foreign minister that three separate intelligence teams had examined the Mideast balance of forces and concluded that, as Johnson put it, even "if the UAR attacks, you will whip hell out of them."[107] As General Wheeler, who was not present at this particular meeting, later put it,

I told [the president] that our best estimate was that if there were a war, that the Israelis would win it in five to seven days. He asked me to go back and check this out and talk to him about it again. I did, and I came back and told him exactly the same thing—that there's just no question; that the way the two sides lined up in the air and on the ground, the Israelis would win; that if the Israelis preempted the UAR, the war would be shorter and their losses would be less than if the contrary happened and the Arabs had preempted the Israelis.[108]

Repeated intelligence estimates from the DIA, the CIA, and armed forces intelligence agencies had reaffirmed Israeli superiority. The president, indeed, had been so skeptical of these reports that, as Wheeler suggests, he had ordered reassessments—pointing out that overly optimistic intelligence estimates had ruined his policies in Vietnam.[109] The result was that an initial estimate of a seven-day Israeli victory was changed to ten.[110] Therefore, the president assured Eban of his backing but insisted on exploring every possible diplomatic channel to assuage American public opinion. According to Eban's notes of the meeting, the president said, "I have spent hours of work on this and I have the determination; but it is essential before anything else to thrash this out in the United Nations and to try to work out some kind of multilateral group. Other nations can and should help. There should be no doubt about my objective. It is to get Israeli shipping through the Gulf." And he added later, "I am not a feeble mouse or a coward and I am going to try. What is needed by the United States is a group [of nations], five, or four or less, or if we could not do that, then on our own."[111] Revealingly, he suggested that Vietnam made him skeptical of acting without congressional backing, and he wanted to be sure in this case that congressmen did not find "excuses to turn tail and run if the going got rough." At the climax of the conversation Johnson stated "very slowly and positively," three times, an aphorism that the State Department had prepared: "Israel will not be alone unless it decides to go alone."[112] Ambiguously, this statement could be interpreted to mean, "If you think you can go on your own, do so, but if you need us, you will have to act according to our timetable." Yet the aide-mémoire the president handed Eban before he left made the message clear: "We cannot imagine that Israel will make this decision."[113]

Despite such careful orchestration, Johnson must have felt that he was not offering enough to Eban, who left Washington immediately afterward for Israel. At the meeting with his advisors earlier in the day, Johnson had argued that he could not commit himself to use force because of congressional sentiment. As he left, "he wondered out loud if he would regret on Monday not having given Eban more today."[114] After Eban departed, he told his advisors, "I failed. They're going to go."[115] Later that evening, Johnson asked Roche over to his office.

Walt [Rostow] was there. I have a feeling someone else was there. I forget. Anyway, he had some of that poisonous low-cal Dr. Pepper, and I had a cup of coffee. He said, "What do you think they're going to do?" He told a little bit about his visit with Eban. You know he was a great mimic, Johnson was. He did a take-off on Eban, a little miniature Winston Churchill . . . and he said, "Now, what do you think they're going to do?" We . . . sat around and talked about what we thought the Israelis were going to do. Somebody, I forget who it was, said, "They'll wait." It wasn't Walt. I didn't think so either. I said, "I think they'll hit them." He said, "Yes, they're going to hit. There's nothing we can do about it." He knew his customers—very, very, penetrating intelligence.[116]

The cautious formulation of carefully worded messages reflected the ambivalence with which key officials approached the crisis. Nonetheless, American policy succeeded in the near term. It was not only the Johnson-Eban meetings that made the Israelis delay a move against the blockade and Egypt's troops in the Sinai. Two American communications received in Jerusalem shortly after Eban arrived home temporarily helped turn the tide toward restraint. First, the U.S. ambassador delivered an official State Department account of the Eban talks in Washington so that no misunderstanding would occur. This message confirmed Eban's version of the meetings, for the State Department reported that the president had told the foreign minister "of his determination to make the international maritime plan work." The report also confirmed that Johnson had agreed to make "every possible effort to assure that the Straits and the Gulf would be open to free and innocent passage."[117]

The second message was a presidential letter that reported Soviet warnings against military action and repeated the injunction given Eban, "Israel just must not take preemptive military action and thereby make itself responsible for the initiation of hostilities."[118] But the critical part of the message was an addendum from Rusk in which he reported that Britain and America were planning the military aspects of the multilateral force, with Canada and Holland already agreed.[119] The Israeli Cabinet concluded that if the Western community would establish the international status of the waterway through action, Israel could avoid force. The Cabinet, therefore, decided on Sunday, 28 May, to withhold action for a time, which Eshkol later explained in a message to Johnson as "a week or two" during which the Israelis expected the Red Sea Regatta to sail through the Straits.[120] The administration interpreted this time frame broadly, assuming that the Israelis would not take matters into their own hands until about 11 June. In the course of the next few days Israeli diplomats in contact with the administration seemed to confirm this interpretation.[121]

The crisis now entered its critical third stage, extending from Monday, 29 May until the following Monday, 5 June, when the Israelis attacked in the Sinai. Three factions emerged within the administration, each offering different prescriptions. Eugene Rostow led the first group, which pressed for the multilateral force. This policy option came closest to the declared aim of the administration, but the practical problems and the disappointing reaction from other governments regarding the declaration and the maritime force helped undermine Rostow's position.[122] His problem was that there was actually little enthusiasm for the maritime force in the administration, even though many officials felt compelled to support the notion in the absence of alternatives. Rostow was later criticized by several colleagues for excessive zeal in advocating the Red Sea Regatta although later accounts of the Israeli decision-making process show that only this initiative kept the Israelis from attacking. Nevertheless, personal differences among those working on the issue and serious questions about the multilateral force and Rostow's actions contributed to the confusion emanating from Washington.[123] In turn, Rostow seems to have felt the idea was sabotaged. He claims the president "wanted to get this thing [the multilateral force] into motion; we were held up by naval planning. The defense department people were planning it as if they were going to open up the second front in Normandy."[124]

Lucius Battle led a second faction, centered in the State Department's Near East Bureau, which favored pursuing diplomatic options in order to protect American relations with Arab countries. To this end Charles Yost, former ambassador to Syria, was sent to Cairo to help with details. Robert Anderson, who was in Egypt on business, arranged a visit to Washington by Egyptian Vice

President Mohieddin for 7 June, with the hope that some alternative to war or a multilateral force could be found. Once the agreement had been reached with Cairo on 31 May for the vice presidential visit, key officials, including Johnson and Rusk, leaned toward this alternative to avoid use of the multilateral naval force.[125]

The third group, centered in the Pentagon, did not so much favor any policy as oppose American military activity of any kind. Because of their preoccupation with Vietnam, both military and civilian officials sought to avoid another foreign involvement. The proposed international force seemed to them impractical and many feared that the confrontation would escalate as had the Vietnamese enterprise. Many high-ranking officials in the Pentagon assumed that Israel would act in any case and, armed with the optimistic intelligence reports, believed Israel could easily handle her Arab opponents. The Pentagon opposition to American action was sufficiently determined and its confidence in Israeli superiority sufficiently great that by the eve of the war a secret paper was written in the International Security Agency, recommending that the Israelis handle the situation and take preemptive action if they chose to do so.[126] Before this paper could be transmitted to higher authorities, the Israelis took matters into their own hands.

The competition among these three groups produced a stalemate in American policy. Differing basic attitudes within each group contributed to the confusion. Most diplomats involved with the Middle East at the State Department wanted to prevent deterioration of relations with Arab countries. At one point Yost reported from Cairo, for example, that serious consequences for American relations with the Arab world would follow if the United States used force to open the Egyptian blockade.[127] Most officials at the Pentagon fretted about overextending the American military if action in the Gulf of Aqaba were required. At the White House a predeliction for caution was mixed with a strong sense of obligation to Israel.

In Congress, sentiment strongly favored Israel, but there were no policy prescriptions and much opposition to intervention. Key senators on the Foreign Relations Committee, like Fulbright, Mansfield, and Stennis opposed unilateral American action. But others urged the use of force, including three Vietnam doves (Edward Kennedy, Robert Kennedy, and Oregon's Wayne Morse). Senator Stuart Symington, for example, suggested that a choice had to be made between the Middle East and the Far East, and that he favored the Middle East as meaning more to the United States and its allies, "politically, economically, and mutually."[128] The House appeared more ready than the Senate to approve some type of American action. In this complex international situation, Congress was too divided to take any initiative.

Washington's hesitant actions and cautious statements soon conveyed to Jerusalem a sense of an administration divided. The Israeli government was becoming impatient as its forces remained mobilized, Arab unity continued to grow, and the U.S. commitment to a multilateral force appeared to ebb. The administration's inability to quickly assemble an international force to open the gulf sent signals of weakness to both the Arabs and the Israelis. And the declaration on free passage of the straits as finally formulated was timid: it did not mention force but simply pledged the signatory governments "to cooperate among themselves and to join with others in seeking general recognition" of the international right of passage through the Gulf of Aqaba waterway.[129] Its effect was further weakened when the U.S. ambassador to the U.N., Arthur Goldberg, introduced the American draft resolution on 31 May as an endorsement of U Thant's call for a "breathing spell" to release tensions. He argued that the resolution would not prejudice the ultimate claims of any party.[130] Nonetheless, on the eve of the war only six countries besides the United States and Israel had agreed to sign the declaration, and only five others appeared to study it. These numbers fell short of the forty or fifty that had been discussed and promised to the Israelis.[131]

As this disappointing reaction demonstrated, the administration had gained no international support for a maritime force. Only the Australians, Dutch, and British were willing to join. In his memoirs, President Johnson wrote that American action would have been taken if necessary, but at the time the administration had not prepared the public for such an event.[132] It was one thing to think of principles, commitments, rights; it was another to think of arms and a second-front war.

The president thought that he could use military force, even if multilateral, only with the support of Congress, and he did not think he would gain such backing until other alternatives had been explored. He also saw this approach as proper strategy. "I was opposed to using force until I was persuaded that every other avenue was blocked." This method meant, however, that considering the naval force and a presidential approach to Congress—which might have stayed Israeli action—was delayed as "other avenues" were followed, like the visit of the Egyptian vice president (with some discussion of a Cairo trip by Humphrey). Johnson was devoted to this approach because of his Vietnam experiences. Because he saw South Vietnam and Israel as similar issues, he mistrusted the conversion of "Congressional Vietnam doves" into "Israeli hawks" and discounted many statements backing Israel as merely "political."[133] He was convinced that only a deliberate course would gain congressional backing, no matter what individual congressmen said.

The Israelis reacted to U.S. caution by exerting ever-increasing pressure for the Americans to take a definite position, but such pressure on Johnson was liable to backfire. As John Roche notes in reference to another 1967 Mideast crisis story, presidents hate pressure. "The theory 'If you don't like the heat, stay out of the kitchen' sort of thing [is] nonsense. Maybe Truman was that way, but the fact is that they [presidents] hate being pressured, even though you think it's par for the course."[134]

The Israelis could hardly avoid noticing that the Johnson administration was avoiding an active response to the crisis. On 31 May Rusk denied in a congressional committee hearing that the United States was planning any unilateral military action.[135] The same day the White House received a letter from Eshkol in which he referred to "the assurances that the United States would take any and all measures to open the Straits of Tiran to international shipping." Walt Rostow swiftly called in Evron to declare that the president was disturbed, since such a commitment would go beyond the president's constitutional authority. Evron protested that the sentence accurately reflected the president's statements to Eban and had been a major factor in the Israeli decision not to attack.[136] Whoever was correct, the lesson of the story is startling. If Israeli and American officials could not agree on what they had said to each other a few days earlier, their collaboration was indeed tenuous.

Meanwhile, the Pentagon sent every signal possible that the United States would not become involved. The Sixth Fleet, still the dominant factor in the Mediterranean, would need reinforcements to undertake serious military activity; reserves were not called up. The fleet's strike forces were also positioned at a safe distance from the area; the Marine batallion landing team in the Mediterranean was on shore leave at Malta on the day the war began, three days from either Egyptian or Israeli ports. The *Intrepid,* a small aircraft carrier caught in the Mediterranean during the crisis while awaiting permission from Nasser to pass through the Suez Canal, left the area on 31 May despite a Russian announcement the previous day that the Kremlin was sending additional ships to the Mediterranean. If anyone had doubts, the Pentagon repeatedly announced no plans to test the blockade.[137] The American position weakened further when Prime Minister Wilson cooled toward the multilateral force; the British had more equipment in the area than the United States had.[138]

An incident with even greater effect on the Israelis occurred when Eshkol sent Meir Amit, the chief of Israel's counterintelligence agency, the Mossad, to the American capital on 30 May to assess American support. Surveying the military and intelligence services in Washington with which he was better acquainted, Amit rapidly perceived that the Red Sea Regatta was not receiving their support and appeared unlikely ever to sail. This implied that the United States could accept Israel's taking matters into its own hands. His conclusions were conveyed to his government and reinforced their inclination to take unilateral action.[139]

There was a certain irrelevance about American-Israeli contacts during the days leading up to the war. The Israelis began to realize that the maritime declaration and naval escort were less useful than they had originally thought. Nasser might outwit the Americans by defusing the crisis and allowing ships to pass. Then, months later, he could renew his blockade. McNamara had already raised the question whether the Americans could provide a permanent naval escort. Even if such an enterprise were politically, diplomatically, or militarily feasible, it would represent a massive political defeat for the Israelis. More important, a naval escort in the straits would not resolve the problem raised by the massed Egyptian troops in the Sinai. These troops had become the major concern to the Israelis, and it was clear that no solutions were coming from Washington or elsewhere.[140]

Nonetheless, if the naval force had appeared more effective, with plans progressing and international support growing, it is improbable that the Israelis would have dared attack, especially with the memory of the Sinai campaign still fresh. As late as 28 May, Dean Rusk's strong words of reassurance and hints of imminent Western action had swayed the Israeli Cabinet. In the days that followed, this message from Rusk began to seem inaccurate; by 2 June he was telling Harman that "nothing had been firmly decided."[141] The Israelis began to discuss preemptive action among themselves and with the United States. By 2 June several American ambassadors in Arab countries and Evron, in a conversation with Walt Rostow, were arguing that it would be more favorable to American relations with the Arabs and the Russians for the Israelis to act on their own. The United States should not participate in a confrontation with Egypt. There is no evidence that Johnson accepted this view, however.[142]

Divisions within the Johnson administration and declining support from other states finally sank the international flotilla. Although the military professionals opposed it as provocative or ineffectual, the show of force could have demonstrated to the Israelis that their grievances could be redressed without military combat. Yet, as Battle notes, the issue of the regatta "was very much an open one at the time the war began."[143]

In this context, it was not a good time for the Egyptian vice president to come to Washington. Nor were matters helped by the rumor that the Egyptians would propose taking the dispute to the International Court of Justice and the United States might accept this proposal.[144] Although the administration hoped by dealing with the Egyptian official to forestall Israel's attack and protect relations with the Arab world, neither goal was achieved. Instead the Israelis suspected America's willingness to safeguard their rights and interests, even though they were informed of the proposed trip before the 3 June public announcement.[145]

As the Israelis quickly realized, the vice presidential visit was well suited to Nasser's strategy. Despite his private and public protestations that he would not be the first to use force, Nasser expected to recover and emerge victorious after Israel struck the first blow. Meanwhile, the vice presidential visit could attain by diplomacy what might be lost in war.[146]

The significance of the proposed vice presidential visit can also be gauged by developments in the region. The offer of dialogue stands in sharp contrast to Nasser's provocative statements. On 28 May he asserted at a press conference, "Israel's existence in itself is an aggression"; the next day he was telling his national assembly, "If we are able to restore conditions to what they were before 1956, God will merely help and urge us to restore the situation to what it was in 1948 (prolonged applause)."[147]

Nasser was backing these statements with actions. In addition to massing troops in the Sinai, he signed a joint mutual defense pact with King Hussein (lately Cairo Radio's "Hashemite whore") on 30 May, leading to a joint command with the U.A.R., Jordan, and Syria. Iraqi and Egyptian troops began arriving in Jordan on 3 June; a defense pact between Cairo and Baghdad followed the next day.

These developments altered the crisis over Israeli rights in the Gulf of Aqaba to one involving the very existence of Israel. American leaders, with the optimistic intelligence estimates in their pockets, ignored these danger signs, but no Israeli government could. Nor could Israel easily maintain the general mobilization of its citizen army, which had been called at the outset of the crisis; with every passing day this mobilization weighed heavier on the Israeli economy and psyche, a factor about which the American government was at best non-chalant. The American government thought it had Israeli assurances that they would not act for another week, but, even then, the pressures on Israel demanded more relief than Washington was offering. The weak declaration of maritime freedom, the poor international response to the naval escort, the hesitation and division in Washington—all convinced Jerusalem that it gained nothing by waiting and might soon confront a much stronger Arab foe. Johnson increased the Israeli leaders' disquiet in his last letter before the war, when he wrote of his determination to preserve the peace, but added, "Our leadership is unanimous, the United States should not move in isolation."[148]

The 3 June announcement of the impending vice presidential visit to Washington coincided with the end of an Israeli political crisis over the leadership of Levi Eshkol. The crisis was resolved by 1 June, when the right-wing opposition led by Menachem Begin was offered two positions in the Cabinet as ministers without portfolio. Eshkol relinquished the defense ministry (which he had held simultaneously with the prime ministership) and offered the post to Moshe Dayan.

As the Israelis moved toward war, official Washington recognized that hostilities might be imminent but thought a few days remained before military activity could begin. The mood in Washington on that last weekend before the Israeli attack is illustrated by a cable sent by Rusk to the American ambassadors in the Arab capitals. He urged them to "put your minds to possible solutions which can prevent war," warning that the Israelis might be nearing a decision to use force. He said, "It will do no good to ask Israel simply to accept the present status quo in the Strait, because Israel will fight and we could not restrain her.

We cannot throw up our hands and say, in that event, let them fight, while we try to remain neutral." The secretary stated bluntly, "We cannot abandon, in principle, the right of Israeli flagships to transit the Strait." Yet, he also urged them to remain "evenhanded" if war did break out.[149]

Revealed here is the passivity and sense of inevitability with which the administration approached the crisis. As much as key officials sought to avoid war, they gave even higher priority to avoiding unilateral American military involvement. Washington was unsuccessful in preventing an Israeli attack because it was preoccupied with Vietnam and divided within itself. Moreover, this was not perceived as a case of imminent Communist takeover, the only type of threat to which the Johnson administration had responded actively in the past.

When the president takes charge in a crisis or when he becomes involved, outside groups become less significant. In this crisis Israel's American supporters were left strangely on the sidelines. They wanted to see Israeli security preserved but given the atmosphere of the times, they could not call for unilateral American action or Israeli preemption. In a sense, some of the problems that inhibited Johnson inhibited them. Vietnam had created a political atmosphere in which any military action, however limited, could not be easily contemplated.

While a crisis often limits the role of outside groups, Washington bureaucrats still exercise influence even if high ranking figures are making the major decisions. Despite poor Egyptian-American relations and low administration attention to Arab affairs, key officials were still able to affect the developing American reaction more than domestic groups sympathetic to Israel could.

Johnson's own memoirs best reveal the cross-cutting objectives, internal pressures, and contradicting sentiments that hobbled American policy in the days before the Six-Day War.

> I have always had a deep feeling of sympathy for Israel and its people, gallantly building and defending a modern nation against great odds and against the tragic background of Jewish experience. I can understand that men might decide to act on their own, when hostile forces gather on their frontiers and cut off a major port, and when antagonistic political leaders fill the air with threats to destroy their nation. Nonetheless, I have never concealed my regret that Israel decided to move when it did. I always made it equally clear, however, to the Russians and to every other nation, that I did not accept the oversimplified charge of Israeli aggression. Arab actions in the weeks before the war started—forcing UN troops out, closing the Port of Aqaba, and assembling forces on the Israeli border—made that charge ridiculous.[150]

This sympathy mixed with regret prevailed in the Johnson White House at the onset of the Six-Day War; it explained the president's handling of the crisis during the war and efforts for peace in its aftermath. Rusk and others in the

State Department who had counted on the Egyptian vice president's visit to make a difference were surprised and upset at the Israeli attack. Many in the administration felt at the time that the Israelis had cut off a possible diplomatic solution.[151] General Wheeler told the Johnson Library that "nothing stands out in my mind other than the fact that Mr. Johnson was determined, if possible, to avert war in the Middle East." Washington feared that once a war began, its consequences would be unpredictable.[152]

The Six-Day War

The war, however, was rapid and decisive when it came. The Israelis attacked on Monday morning, 5 June, destroying most of the Egyptian air force on the ground. They proceeded quickly to conquer the Sinai Peninsula and the Gaza Strip. On the first day, the Israelis sent a diplomatic message to Hussein asking him not to attack them in turn; he did so and rapidly lost Jerusalem and the West Bank. On the fifth day the Israelis removed the Syrians from the Golan Heights from which they had terrorized the kibbutzim below, a situation which hastened the war. The Golan Heights, including the town of Quneitra, were captured when the war ended at midday on 10 June.

President Johnson and his associates spent much of the week monitoring each development. The White House remained concerned about the attitude of Congress. Battle was sent to brief fifty-one senators on the first evening of the war. Upon his return,

> The first question the President asked was what I thought the Senate believed at that moment. And I said, "It's impossible to tell, Mr. President." I said, "If I had to guess, I think you'd find them split about even between some kind of U.S. intervention and some have an attitude that is roughly 'don't get involved.'" I said "I think very few would be in favor of the interjection of American military—of manpower—into this situation. Arms are another question.[153]

The president was spared deciding how to involve the United States by the speedy Israeli victory. If the signals the White House received from Congress throughout the crisis were confused, the White House's attempts to ascertain congressional opinion were hardly systematic. Meetings between the president and the congressional leadership could have been arranged, but they were not.

Earlier that first day, the hotline to Moscow was used for the first time, and it was used again on several occasions throughout the week. The administration quickly assured the Kremlin that it was not involved in the fighting, indicating its surprise at the outbreak of war and its wish to end hostilities. At first the United States sought to arrange in the Security Council a cease-fire resolution that would call for Israeli withdrawal to the original armistice lines *and* removal of Egyptian forces from the Sinai.[154] By the time the Russians would accept a simple cease-fire in place, Jerusalem had nearly conquered the entire Sinai peninsula, the Gaza Strip, and the West Bank. When the Egyptians and Jordanians finally accepted the cease-fire, they had lost those areas.

Some Washington officials hinted to the Israelis that they would not oppose punishing Syria for its role in instigating the war. Johnson seems to confirm this position when he writes, "We did know Israel's military intentions toward Syria, and the situation remained tense on June 9."[155] However, the next day the administration pressed Israel diplomatically for a cease-fire on the Golan Heights while confronting the Soviet Union over Israel's advances. With large amounts of equipment and advisers stationed in Syria, the Russians were concerned about Israeli intentions toward their client and specifically its capital, Damascus. The Russians not only broke relations with Israel but, in a particularly harsh message over the hotline, demanded that Israel cease operations immediately or they would take "necessary actions including military." Johnson ordered the Sixth Fleet maneuvered close to Syria and was later to see this as a Cuban missile crisis of his own. However, the war appears to have ended before any actions by either superpower were necessary or had time to be effected. Meanwhile, U.S. maneuvering in the United Nations gave Israel the few additional hours needed to complete its objectives.[156] In recalling the war, General Wheeler later claimed, "I never had any [worry about intervention on the part of the Soviet Union], because I didn't think that they would. It's contrary to their practice to intervene in things like that. Of course, this is something you have to take into account. But it wasn't anything that really worried me a great deal."[157]

The Russians and Americans were also in contact on the fourth day of the war regarding the accidental Israeli attack on the USS *Liberty*, an intelligence ship operating off the Sinai coast. The Sixth Fleet command did not suspect Soviet involvement, but for almost a half hour the Pentagon believed that it might have been a Kremlin attack. Secretary of Defense McNamara later remarked, "I thought *The Liberty* had been attacked by Soviet forces—thank goodness, our carrier commanders did not launch immediately against the Soviet forces, who were operating in the Mediterranean at that time."[158]

While American planes came to the aid of the ship, the president cabled Kosygin by the hotline to inform the Soviets of American actions and intent. In any event, the *Liberty* incident, taken with U.S.-Soviet confrontations over the Golan Heights, at the U.N. and on the hotline, gave to American policy makers a much keener sense of connection between the Arab-Israeli conflict and the superpowers' relationship than they had had previously.[159] Speaking in late 1968, Eugene Rostow told the Johnson Library that the president "feels in many ways it's [the Middle East] a more dangerous crisis than Vietnam, because it can involve a confrontation with the Russians, not the Chinese."[160]

This new sense of connection between the conflict and global arenas was strengthened as regional policy became less important as a consequence of the war. Arab hostility to the United States following Israel's victory blocked the development of any new Arab policy. On the second day of the war, Nasser accused the United States and Britain of aiding Israel in its attacks on Egypt. Despite vehement American denials, most Arab states eventually broke diplomatic relations with the United States, six on that day. Kuwait and Iraq immediately embargoed all oil shipments to the United States and the United Kingdom. The United States was not yet sufficiently dependent on foreign oil, and the producers not yet sufficiently organized, for the embargo to have any measurable effect on Western economies.

The false Egyptian accusation of U.S. complicity in the attack drew strongly negative reaction from the American public and key elites. Even within the Near East Bureau there was bitterness toward Nasser.[161] Battle argued in 1968 that if the war had been prevented and Nasser

had been given a free victory, I think the result from our point of view would have been even worse than what we have now. His own power in that part of the world would have been increased markedly; the tendency toward polarization within the area between East and West, between Arab and Israeli, could have been as great as today. And we would have found ourselves in a situation that would have been quite intolerable for everybody.[162]

The disruption of diplomatic relations would be felt for years afterward in American contacts with the Arab world. Once key Arab representatives were absent from Washington, the influence of their countries was bound to diminish.

By contrast, Israel gained in public approval and Washington favor after its electrifying victory. Although Vietnam had inhibited U.S. support before the war, Israel's success now inspired many at a time of American frustration and low morale. And American decision makers no longer looked on Jerusalem as a weak client in need of protection.

The position of the United States as interested bystander was illustrated by a curious incident on the first day of the war. The State Department press officer described the American position as "neutral" in "thought, word and deed." When the president heard about the remark he was livid. One White House source later recalled, "I have never seen him more upset." Johnson ordered Rusk to make a statement distinguishing between neutrality and indifference; Rusk added, "Indeed, indifference is not permitted to us." Johnson suggests in his memoirs that neutral "was the wrong word." Theodore Draper's question, however, remains apt: "If the United States wasn't 'neutral' what was it?"[163]

This incident symbolized the contradictions of the Johnson administration position once the war erupted. On the one hand, many key officials, including the president, were quite sympathetic to Israel. Yet they were also interested in preserving relations with the Arab world and in maintaining peace, or at least stability, in the area. Therefore, their relief at not having to intervene on Israel's behalf did not mean that they acquiesced in Israel's territorial gains. This dichotomy would later generate tension with Jerusalem and shape the Johnson diplomacy of the postwar period.

Diplomacy in the Aftermath of War

The Six-Day War increased both the external and domestic constraints on the administration. It raised the global importance of the Middle East and accelerated efforts at some kind of Arab-Israeli settlement. These changes have led most observers to argue that the Six-Day War altered American policy.[164] Yet, although the administration adjusted its tactics to the new setting, it acted from the same assumptions and policy framework that had operated before the war. It remained markedly passive in the wake of regional events; it experienced sharp policy disagreements with Israel balanced by de facto permissiveness; and it showed a continuing preference for conservative Arab governments mixed with sporadic hope that somehow relations might be resurrected with the radicals, especially Egypt. The pattern of parallel connections with the conservative Arabs and Israelis, established by the sale of arms to Jordan and Israel before the war, continued afterward. Although it was now considered a major crisis area, the Middle East was still subordinate to Vietnam in administration concerns.

During the Six-Day War, Johnson brought McGeorge Bundy back into the administration to bring order into the decision-making process. Bundy acted to clear up the factional differences and crossed signals such as were demonstrated in the State Department's announcement of American neutrality.[165]

The first challenge for the Bundy team was to determine how the administration should react to the war. The Arabs, with Russian backing, were seeking to regain at the United Nations what they had lost on the battlefield. When unable to pass the one-sided resolutions in the Security Council, the Kremlin called for a special emergency session of the General Assembly. Premier Kosygin and the heads of several governments friendly to the U.S.S.R. flew to New York for the meetings, which convened on 19 June. In a speech in Washington the same day, Johnson unveiled his own approach, in which the United States would not press Israel to retreat from her territorial gains without Arab diplomatic concessions. The speech, drafted by the Bundy task force, was designed to appeal to a broad spectrum of interested parties. It did not include a major U.S. diplomatic initiative. An activist approach was not likely to succeed at the time and might be controversial at home, especially if it implied pressure on the

Jerusalem government. While reflecting Israel's postwar popularity, the speech also presented principles that could appeal to conservative Arabs.[166]

Basically, Johnson agreed that the Israelis should withdraw from the territory they had occupied, but only in return for a peaceful settlement. "Certainly, troops must be withdrawn; but there must also be recognized rights of national life, progress in solving the refugee problem, freedom of innocent maritime passage, limitation of the arms race, and respect for political independence and territorial integrity."[167] This view became widely accepted in the American government, but there was great divergence on what Arab concessions should be required for Israeli withdrawals. Officials concerned about U.S. relations with the Arab world advocated total Israeli withdrawals in return for Arab commitments to nonbelligerence. These officials were prepared to accept great power guarantees to supplement Arab promises. Pro-Israeli groups, on the other hand, demanded concrete acts by the Arabs demonstrating good faith—actions like trade and travel that would break down the barriers between the two sides. Such groups would require the Arabs to accept Israel's legitimacy. Most thought Israel should be allowed to keep some captured territory in a peace settlement. Different interpretations of "negative" and "positive" peace would be a major area of disagreement among Americans for the next several years.

Certainly, Johnson's statements on a possible peace settlement lent themselves to differing interpretations: "Clearly the parties to the conflict must be the parties to the peace. Sooner or later, it is they who must make a settlement in the area. It is hard to see how it is possible for nations to live together in peace if they cannot learn to reason together."[168] Did that mean that the two parties would be expected to sit down together, as the Israelis and their supporters hoped, or that they should deal only through intermediaries, as the Arabs and their American sympathizers insisted? Over the next several years, few would agree on this point, either in Washington or in the region itself.

A further matter at the center of debate in Washington was what level of armament to provide for the Israelis and America's Arab friends. Johnson had named arms limitation as one of his five principles for a peaceful settlement and the United States had embargoed arms to the Arabs and Israelis at the outbreak of war. However, when the Soviet Union refused to limit arms and rearmed its clients in the area, the United States faced the familiar problem of how to balance Russian weapons with arms to Israel as well as to the friendly Arab regimes. After 1967, Israeli defense needs not only became more critical to American-Israeli relations, but also were necessarily intertwined with American diplomatic efforts to resolve the Arab-Israeli dispute.

With Premier Kosygin in New York for the United Nations General Assembly session, a summit conference seemed logical and even unavoidable. Hastily arranged for the college town of Glassboro, New Jersey, it occurred on 23 June and 25 June. But the American and Russian leaders were interested in different subjects: the one in strategic arms, the other in the Middle East. "Each time I mentioned missiles, Kosygin talked about Arabs and Israelis," Johnson summarized.[169] The summit conference ended without any concrete agreements on the Middle East.

At the U.N. meanwhile, the Israelis suggested a willingness to discuss an early withdrawal from most of the captured territories, but the Arabs sought total and unconditional withdrawals. The Russians tried to gain a General Assembly resolution supporting the Arab demand but they were rebuffed.

The Johnson administration through Ambassador Arthur Goldberg at first supported the basic Israeli position, but the president and key administration officials were dismayed by the virtual Israeli annexation of East Jerusalem in July. With the General Assembly session nearly complete, Goldberg and Russian foreign minister Gromyko reached agreement on a draft resolution calling for the Israelis to withdraw "without delay" in return for a vague declaration of nonbelligerency.[170] To the Israelis this resolution was thoroughly unacceptable because it did not provide for direct negotiations or even mention the word *Israel.* It provided only a few easily dismissable words concerning peaceful arrangements in return for actual Israeli withdrawals back to the original pre–Six-Day War boundaries. American acceptance of this draft indicated that profound differences existed between the American and Israeli governments over the objective of diplomatic discussions and basic negotiating tactics.

It is not clear that the president would have given final approval for American backing of this resolution; before any steps could be taken, the Arab states flatly rejected it. In retrospect, this move was a great diplomatic blunder, for the Arabs would never again be offered so favorable an international resolution backed by the two superpowers. After the special session of the General Assembly, an Arab League conference was held at Khartoum in August; there the Arab states definitely rejected the implications of their military defeat, insisting there would be "no peace, no recognition and no negotiation" with Israel.

Despite Arab objections, however, the thrust of international diplomacy favored some form of United Nations resolution, a move reinforced by Washington's wish to remain in the background and Moscow's frustration. The next opportunity for discussions came in the fall at the annual U.N. General Assembly. Efforts were now focused in the Security Council, and this time, behind the scenes, King Hussein of Jordan hinted that he and perhaps Nasser might accept a U.N. resolution.[171] By November, Ambassador Goldberg was discussing a broadened resolution to balance the stances of both Arabs and Israelis, while remaining ambiguous enough that each could interpret the resolution as it saw fit. Goldberg met separately with the Egyptian, Jordanian, and Israeli delegations at the Waldorf-Astoria Hotel. This was one of those rare situations in which the U.N. ambassador becomes central to American policymaking. As

Sisco observes, "Both President Johnson and Secretary Rusk gave a great deal of latitude to Ambassador Goldberg in trying to work out this framework in the November 1967 resolution."[172]

Near the end of the discussions, the British, who had better relations with Cairo than did the United States, sponsored the negotiations. Their delegate, Lord Caradon, continued shuttling among the various delegations and produced the final document. Whatever the final sponsorship, Resolution 242, which passed the Security Council unanimously on 22 November, was the Johnson administration's finest achievement in Arab-Israeli diplomacy. It provided the framework for future negotiations and its very existence stands as a milestone in the attempts to reach a Middle East settlement: it was the first agreement to involve both the Arabs and Israelis, even indirectly, since the armistice accords of 1949. The Johnson administration had ample reason to be satisfied, for it played a central role in negotiating the resolution, and the principles providing for a settlement reflected those announced by President Johnson after the war.

The approach affirmed positions valued by each side. For the Arabs, it called for Israeli withdrawals "from territories occupied in the recent conflict." For the Israelis it called for an end to the state of belligerency and insisted on the right of every state in the area to be acknowledged as sovereign and to "live in peace within secure and recognized boundaries." The resolution affirmed freedom of navigation through international waterways (of concern to Israel), and called for a just solution to the refugee problem (of concern to the Arabs).

The language of the resolution lent itself to varying interpretations. Concerning content, for example, did the resolution call for total Israeli withdrawals from the territories it had occupied? In the negotiations the Russians and Arabs had repeatedly sought to have the word *all* or at least *the* inserted in the reference to Israeli withdrawals. On behalf of Israel, the American delegation had continued to support the original phrase: "Withdrawal of Israeli armed forces from territories occupied in the recent conflict." At the last moment Johnson rejected Kosygin's call for an interpretation applying the phrase to "all" the territories.[173]

This language led to a disagreement among key American officials whether the United States had intended to suggest by the vagueness of the wording that the Israelis could keep "insubstantial" areas limited to minor border adjustments or whether, after a peace settlement, they could keep a larger portion of the territories captured in 1967. In later years, men like Dean Rusk and Lucius Battle would take the more restrictive interpretation, Eugene Rostow and Arthur Goldberg, the more lenient. The strict interpretation was generally preferred within the bureaucracy and among most Arab supporters; the lenient one preferred in Congress and among Israel's backers.[174]

In regard to diplomatic procedures, varying interpretations were also quite common. Before serious negotiations would begin, the Arabs sought an

Israeli commitment to complete withdrawals from the territories captured in 1967. Indeed, many Arab diplomats later claimed that they had accepted the resolution because the American negotiators had led them to expect imminent Israeli withdrawals after it was signed.[175] But in the Israeli view, no withdrawals would take place until peace negotiations had been completed, and Jerusalem sought to involve the Arabs in face-to-face negotiations where final boundaries would be discussed as well as other disputed issues.

Despite the ambiguities, Resolution 242 represented the growing American involvement in detailed Middle East negotiations, and thus it foreshadowed later developments. In the immediate context, however, the resolution actually diminished the American role because, under British urging, it called for a special representative to implement its agenda. The secretary general appointed Gunnar Jarring, the Swedish ambassador to the Soviet Union. During the remainder of the Johnson era, Jarring frequently shuttled between the various capitals as the central Middle East diplomat. This arrangement suited America's desire to leave the issue to the United Nations and was consistent with the Johnson administration's preoccupation with Vietnam diplomacy in its last year, especially after the president announced at the end of March 1968 that he would not run for reelection.

When Johnson was asked at a news conference what he was doing personally to reduce Mideast tensions, his answer indicated how his administration was leaving the initiative to others during this period. He gave a rambling discourse on how Battle and Goldberg were "working on the general problem everyday" and referred to his five points of the previous June. The president declared, "We are trying to help with the Jarring mission wherever we can."[176]

By the end of summer 1968, however, incidents along the Suez Canal were increasing and it became clear that Jarring's mission would not produce dramatic results. The conditions existed for a renewed U.S. diplomatic initiative. This episode began with a Russian note proposing one-sided complete Israeli withdrawals for minimal Arab commitments. The United States rejected the note but, while discussing it, Secretary of State Rusk repeatedly asked the new Israeli ambassador Yitzhak Rabin, "Isn't it enough for Israel and the Arabs to sign a joint, multilateral document?"[177] Rabin reiterated the Israeli desire for specific treaties with individual neighbors to establish normalized relations. Yet at the fall 1968 meetings of the General Assembly, Rusk presented to the Egyptian foreign minister "seven points" for a possible peace agreement between Egypt and Israel without apprising Jerusalem of the contents or even the existence of a plan.[178]

Since the United States had no diplomatic relations with Egypt at the time but had close relations with Israel, the document and the way it was handled again revealed great diplomatic differences between the United States and Israel after the 1967 war. Except for making withdrawal part of a package as envisioned by the Israeli interpretation of Resolution 242, Rusk made no effort in his "seven points" to move toward direct negotiations or even elementary steps of normalization. Instead, Israeli withdrawals were to be exchanged for an end to hostilities in some as yet unspecified form. As further incentive to Jerusalem, the document also would have assured Israeli use of the Suez Canal and forbade Cairo to demand withdrawal of a U.N. force in the Sinai. As further incentive to Cairo, the Near East Bureau revived the old idea from the Joseph Johnson mission that the refugees could state their preferences for repatriation or resettlement.[179]

The American stand was still unacceptable to the Egyptians, however, who wanted to devise procedures so that they would not have to acknowledge Israel's existence in signing any possible documents. As this indicates, any serious negotiations that might have resulted would likely have widened the considerable chasm between the Israelis and the Americans. But the chief concern of the State Department was to rebuild relations with several Arab states.[180] This objective was already leading to a distinct American negotiating position designed to occupy the nebulous ground between the two sides. Eugene Rostow put it succinctly to the Johnson Library: "Our only hope is that in the end we'll get peace under our resolution and under our auspices, which ought to restore our position in the Middle East."[181]

This approach revealed the persistence of a bureaucracy intent on rebuilding American-Arab relations. As the Rusk initiative demonstrated, high ranking department officials were disinclined to support Israel's territorial conquests and demands for bilateral peace treaties. The secrecy with which diplomacy is often conducted enabled the bureaucrats to disregard Israel's supporters in Congress and the public.

Arms Aid in the Aftermath of War

Public interest in Israel and its cause had been dramatically increased by the trauma and exhilaration of May and June 1967. According to opinion polls, sympathy for Israel rose to an unprecedented 55 percent in the few weeks during and after the war, while those committed to the Arab side remained at about 4 percent.[182] At first, however, this support had mostly superficial effects. It was apparent mainly in increased fund raising, more travel to Israel, and attendance at celebrational events around the country.

Despite Israel's enhanced popularity, the administration embargoed all arms to the Middle East following the war (including spare parts, ammunition, and contracted arms) to encourage Moscow to reciprocate. The Russians were not interested in any arms agreement or in stopping their huge arms shipments to their Arab clients, so the administration again confronted the problem of arming Jordan to keep King Hussein from dealing with Moscow. Nor could arms deliveries be resumed to Amman without resumption to Jerusalem. Therefore, by late September, the Israelis were assured that the Skyhawks agreed upon in 1966 would be delivered on schedule. In late October the decision was announced, and it was also acknowledged—for the first time publicly—that five pro-Western Arab states would receive military equipment ordered before the June war. The process that operated during the administration's February 1965 dealings with the arms issue reappeared: fear of Russian arms causing an imbalance of regional power and concern that Jordan might turn to the U.S.S.R. led to increased arms sales to both Jordan and Israel after a severe controversy with Israel. In 1965 the controversy occurred over the idea of arms for Jordan; in 1967 Israel and the administration differed over the embargo.[183]

In the arms arena, several factors gave the Israelis and their supporters a stronger position than in the diplomatic area. First, the American commitment to a regional balance of power meant that arguments for arms were stronger than arguments about territorial disposition and peace settlements. Second, with the French supply route closed, the Israelis and their American backers could argue that only the United States could provide the required weapons. Third, it has always been easier for Israel's supporters to campaign for material assistance than for diplomatic support—especially because the Constitution grants Congress the responsibility for appropriating funds.[184]

Moreover, on arms issues Jerusalem initiates the process by making a request, which alerts members of the pro-Israeli camp to the existence of a discussion. They can then solicit support in Congress and from friends in the Pentagon, appealing directly to the president over the heads of State Department and Defense Department opponents. On diplomatic issues, however, pro-Israeli forces may not learn of a State Department initiative until too late in the decision-making process to do anything but react. And on more intricate diplomatic issues, the president is more likely to listen to foreign policy experts than to outside interest groups.

The political atmosphere created by Vietnam was favorable to providing increased arms for Israel. If many antiwar partisans began to favor the Arabs after the Six-Day War because they saw Jerusalem as too closely tied to American "imperialism" and too prone to use force, conservatives and military officials became more sympathetic to the Israelis for just the opposite reasons. Israel had shown traits that most Americans admired and respected: self-reliance, democracy, anticommunism, successful pragmatism, idealism. The Israelis had achieved a spectacular military victory when the United States had been frustrated on the battlefield. Most important, the Israelis were now positively contributing to U.S. security: their combat experience and capture of Russian equipment provided information important to the American military in Vietnam. The closure of the Suez Canal also impeded the supply of Russian arms to Indochina. President Johnson secretly approved an increased exchange of information with Israeli intelligence, while cooperation with the Arab states reached a new low.[185] To the discomfort of most American diplomats in the area, Israel clearly opposed Russian objectives whereas the most prominent Arab states were aligned with Moscow.

These altered conditions provided established supporters of Israel with new arguments. Moreover, Israel's new conservative sympathizers were more likely to agree with its military approach to conducting foreign policy and with the need for advanced weaponry.

The new balance of domestic forces was tested by an Israeli request to purchase Phantom jets in 1968. It was a classic case of competition between traditional opponents in the Arab-Israeli dispute. The bureaucracy almost unanimously opposed the sale; backers of Israel were mobilized, and the two fought for the president's support.

The first skirmish ended at the Johnson ranch in January 1968, where Prime Minister Eshkol was a guest. In those days an invitation to the ranch was a sign of particular friendship, practically reinforced by cordialities between the president, the prime minister, and their wives. The atmosphere was even friendlier than during Eshkol's first visit in 1964.

The meetings were not designed for symbolic pleasantries, however: the issue under serious discussion was the Phantoms. As the Israelis looked on in stunned silence, Johnson quizzed an obviously skeptical Rusk and McNamara about technological and diplomatic details. Finally, the president indicated that the Israelis would receive the planes if an arms limitation agreement could not be reached with the Russians. In order to ensure that the Israelis would not suffer from the delay, however, he decided that the Israeli order for fifty jets would be placed in the production line so that they could be delivered on schedule if necessary. Informally, however, the "promise" of the jets was less tentative; at one point Johnson is reported to have told a worried Evron, "Awh, Eppie, you know I'm going to give you the Phantoms. . ."[186]

The communiqué released at the end of the meetings was the strongest granted by a U.S. president to Israel until that point. Not only did Johnson agree "to keep Israel's military defense capability under active and sympathetic examination" but the president and prime minister "declared their firm determination to make every effort to increase the broad area of understanding which already exists between Israel and the United States. . ."[187]

The bureaucracy did not take this declaration as final. As the year proceeded, the various involved agencies moved almost unanimously against the decision to sell Israel the jets. The State Department, especially the Near East Bureau, argued that sale of the Phantoms would further hinder relations with the Arab states and complained that these costs were not offset by any particular benefits to the United States. Many officials also felt that the Israelis did not need the Phantoms because their forces were already superior; and they disputed

Israeli estimates of Soviet shipments to Arab parties.[188] Many argued that selling Israel these arms would hinder diplomatic negotiations; some believed that the Israelis were not cooperating with Jarring and had delayed their explicit acceptance of Resolution 242; others wanted Israel to withdraw totally from the territories occupied in the Six-Day War as a condition for receiving the jets.[189]

Many in the Defense Department, especially at ISA, opposed the sale as a destabilizing factor in the regional balance of power. Moreover, parts of the Pentagon—especially at ISA—agreed with the view that the Israelis did not require the weapons for defense. Several officials felt that the Phantoms should be withheld until the Israelis agreed to the nuclear nonproliferation treaty, then a major American foreign policy issue. The Israelis were reluctant to sign and ratify the treaty and in the end never did so.[190]

CIA analysts also thought that Israel did not need the weapons, but the agency did not represent a policy position, in keeping with its bureaucratic function.[191] The only major official to favor selling the jets was General Earle Wheeler, chairman of the Joints Chiefs of Staff. He believed that the net effect of Israeli aircraft losses and Soviet resupplies to the Arabs "was that Israel was being placed in an inferior military position," an assessment confirmed by his own analysts. Wheeler provided information to help Johnson determine how many Phantoms the Israelis should receive.[192]

In the face of the bureaucratic opposition, the pro-Israeli forces mounted a campaign of their own in 1968. In the Jewish community, every major organization stressed the importance of the jets in its political or educational activities (depending on the nature of the group). A variety of non-Jewish organizations also endorsed the sale, including Americans for Democratic Action, the American Legion, and the AFL-CIO. In several of these cases, Jewish groups either instigated or encouraged the action, but in each organization underlying support was clear from the lack of opposition when pro-Phantom resolutions were presented to executive bodies. Indeed there was no concerted public opposition to the sale.[193] As usual AIPAC was active. It obtained statements supporting the sale from every presidential candidate and successfully lobbied for favorable planks at each party convention.[194]

For their part the Israelis continued to deal directly with the White House, State Department, and Pentagon. In early 1968 Jerusalem sent Yitzhak Rabin, its former chief of staff, as ambassador to Washington, believing that an emissary with military experience could better persuade the American government to sell the Phantoms.

The White House had hinted that the president wanted congressional support before proceeding with the sale (even though at the time no action by the legislative branch was necessary for an arms sale). In coordination with AIPAC, Representative Bertram Podell (D.-N.Y.) sponsored a "sense of the House" resolution favoring the sale. In the next ten weeks more than a hundred representatives signed or associated themselves with the resolution, while a number of senators expressed themselves in favor.[195]

In mid-July the Foreign Assistance Act of 1968 came to the House for debate and Representative Lester Wolff of New York offered an amendment that practically ordered the president to sell "not less than 50" Phantom jets to Israel.[196] The amendment passed the House as part of the Foreign Aid Bill. Wolff had acted on his own without consulting AIPAC, his congressional colleagues, or Jewish leaders.[197] However, with the amendment enacted, the forces supporting the sale to Israel were suddenly strengthened. The White House indicated to congressional contacts and American Jewish community representatives that it opposed the language of the amendment but not its substance. After considerable debate on this point among those urging the sale, I. L. Kenen (then leader of AIPAC) informed the Senate Foreign Relations Committee that a more general "sense of the Congress" resolution would be satisfactory. Kenen understood that challenging a president by making action mandatory would jeopardize the campaign for the jets.[198] Senator Frank Church then offered a substitute measure indicating congressional support for the sale of supersonic jets to Israel. This amendment passed the Senate on 31 July as part of the Senate version of the Foreign Aid Bill; with both the administration and Israeli advocates supporting it, the Senate-House conference committee approved the Church amendment as part of the revised bill just before Congress adjourned for the Republican and Democratic conventions.[199]

On 8 September candidates Nixon and Humphrey both made statements supporting the sale at the B'nai B'rith convention in Washington.[200] President Johnson spoke shortly thereafter, emphasizing the need for an arms limitation agreement with the Soviet Union and not dealing with the jets. A few days later the Zionist Organization of America held its annual convention in Washington. During its meeting a report in the *New York Times* suggested that the administration had decided not to sell the jets to Israel and would instead pursue an arms limitation agreement and further efforts for Arab-Israeli settlement with Soviet leaders. The next day Vice President Humphrey urged that the sale was "now a necessity" and Richard Nixon sent a message to the convention repeating his earlier statement.[201]

In the wake of statements and appeals from Congress, George Christian, the president's press secretary, declared that the *Times* article was "completely inaccurate" and that the president had not decided the question: he suggested that the Johnson-Eshkol communiqué of January was still operative. Meanwhile, AFL-CIO president George Meany and the annual convention of the American Legion similarly urged President Johnson to sell Israel the jets.[202]

When Congress reconvened in mid-September, the conference committee's version of the Foreign Assistance Authorization Act of 1968 moved rapidly through both Houses. During debates several congressmen repeated their support of the sale and seventy senators signed a letter to that effect. On 9 October, when President Johnson signed the act, he indicated that he had "taken note" of the "sense of Congress" resolution within the bill on the sale of planes to Israel. He said that "in the light of the expression of the 'sense of Congress' " he would ask the secretary of state "to initiate negotiations with the government of Israel and report back to me."[203]

Consistent with the policy set forth at his ranch in January, Johnson acted only after two meetings between Gromyko and Rusk made it clear that Moscow would not support an arms limitation agreement in the area at that time. The Russians had demonstrated their disinterest during the summer by offering more arms to the U.A.R. Less than twenty-four hours after Gromyko left for Moscow, Johnson announced that he was initiating formal negotiations on the sale. Other factors likely weighed on the president: after the Soviet invasion of Czechoslovakia in August, a summit conference was hardly likely; moreover, both presidential candidates and large majorities in Congress had now endorsed the arms sales. Johnson was too much the politician to ignore the assistance the sale announcement could give Humphrey. He also was inclined to act on controversial questions after Congress had given him support. This after all had been his position in the days preceding the Six-Day War. Finally, he himself had virtually promised the jets to the Israelis in January. Because of these factors, the opposition of bureaucracies in the executive branch was surmounted.[204]

Events now moved rapidly. Israeli–State Department discussions began on 14 October. When Eban visited Washington a week later, he found the president asking him to tell Eshkol that "Lyndon B. Johnson had kept his word" on the Phantoms. Rabin, however, thought Eban's meetings with Rusk suggested that the administration was stalling. Nonetheless, approval for the purchase was given to Jerusalem on 7 November and on 28 December the administration announced that the first Phantoms would arrive in Israel in late 1969.[205]

Still the bureaucracy tried to delay. Shortly before the president ordered the sale concluded, Rusk sent the Israeli ambassador to the Defense Department where Rabin spoke with ISA chief Warnke. Warnke wanted Israel to accept conditions in return for the Phantoms. According to Rabin, Warnke told him that the United States wanted Israel to sign a document consenting "to a U.S. presence and supervision of every Israeli arms-manufacturing installation and every defense installation engaged in research, development, or manufacture— including civilian research institutes such as the Weizmann Institute of Science and Israel's universities. . . I told Vornike [sic] that any state that agreed to sign such a shameful document would be forfeiting its very sovereignty!"[206] After the many disputes with the Johnson administration over arms, the Israelis apparently were used to wrangling with the bureaucracy on matters later reversed by the White House. Rabin promptly began successful lobbying efforts with "Israel's Democratic supporters."[207]

Conclusion

The recurring pattern in the Johnson administration's dealings with the Middle East is striking. A decision to sell more and better arms to Israel and Jordan in 1965 and 1966 was balanced by faltering efforts to maintain PL-480 wheat sales to Egypt. The proposal for a multilateral fleet to break the blockade of the Straits of Tiran during the May 1967 crisis was balanced by the agreement to bring the Egyptian vice president to Washington. Refusal to bring pressure on Israel to return to its original borders in summer 1967 was balanced by a yearning for agreement with Moscow on arms supplies to the area and support for a U.N. resolution over diplomatic details. The sale of Phantom jets to Israel in 1968 was balanced by Rusk's "seven points." Moves to maintain relations with conservative Arab states reflected a basic desire to support pro-Western regimes. These pursuits were often tentative because the administration's policy was not to take the initiative, even after the Six-Day War raised the importance of developments in the area.

Given its preoccupation with Vietnam, its high level of improvisation, and its lack of a formal decision-making process, the Johnson administration found both coordination and conception difficult. Johnson was not insulated from differing views, as Eisenhower had been, and his efforts to improve relations with the Arabs were not part of a structured plan, like Kennedy's. Rather, Johnson was affected by differences within his own administration and within the country at large. Unable to produce a new approach after the Six-Day War, the president often spoke as if the five principles cited in his speech of 19 June 1967 and U.N. Resolution 242 constituted his entire Middle East policy.

Before 1967 the Middle East in general and the Arab world in particular had largely been neglected in American policy making, and at the time of the conflict, U.S. officials were caught off guard. Afterward, caution and restraint marked their approach. Even U.N. Resolution 242, a worthwhile achievement, seemed improvisational in comparison with the carefully devised strategies of Johnson's successor. As it evolved, Resolution 242 provided an agenda about whose substance the parties differed. The administration gave little thought to the role the United States would play after the resolution had passed. If Eisenhower and his staff had erred on the side of grandiose conceptions, Johnson and his entourage suffered from the opposite: passivity, avoidance, and lack of imagination.

The record, however, should be seen in perspective. Even if Vietnam had not preoccupied the administration, it would still have been difficult to foresee Nasser's actions and their consequences before May 1967. After the Six-

Day War, the shock of defeat and the dominance of the Arab world by radical forces made acceptance of imaginative approaches difficult. The Johnson team wisely held back from imposing a settlement after the Six-Day War and insisted on an interconnected resolution of all matters in dispute. Israel would not be forced to withdraw without a peace agreement. But the Johnson team offered no conception of a genuine peace—no prescription for normalization and no ideas for initiating Arab-Israeli contacts.

As the Eisenhower experience demonstrated, activity and imagination do not necessarily guarantee a convenient meshing of ends and means. Passivity and patience can be virtues in particular situations. The Johnson approach, however, was made up of two irreconcilable strategies: one favored by the bureaucracy and pro-Arab supporters, the other by Congress and many of Johnson's political associates. Johnson found it harder than most presidents to resolve the two strains and therefore adopted both to the confusion of all involved parties. Thus, a diplomacy divergent from Israel's was balanced by growing arms sales to the Jewish state. In this sense, the president's approach was similar to Truman's and the resulting confusion in American policy was also analogous.

In the end, as in Vietnam, the unfinished plate was left for Republican successors. Sentiment and concern had proved no substitute for innovation, skill, and willingness to set priorities. In this way Johnson's Arab-Israeli policy was no different from the administration's approach in other regions, especially in Southeast Asia.

6

NIXON
The State Department and the National Security
Council in Conflict

Although one was a Democrat and one a Republican, Johnson and Nixon shared a basic belief in an active global foreign policy. They reviled critics who opposed U.S. involvement in Vietnam and lamented the declining American consensus in foreign affairs. They also distrusted the bureaucracy, especially the "liberal" State Department, and were preoccupied with preventing leaks to the press that upset their plans.

But these apparent similarities masked critical differences. Johnson's prime concern was domestic politics, epitomized by his concept of the "Great Society" to aid the disadvantaged and the poor. Nixon, on the other hand, saw foreign policy as his strong suit, showed little concern for less fortunate groups, and sought to limit federal spending and the U.S. government's role in local affairs. Johnson was basically gregarious and tried to compensate for his inexperience in foreign affairs with endless consultations. Nixon, on the other hand, craved privacy for decisions and writing; he hated personal confrontations. Although he had traveled widely and was fascinated with the intricacies of diplomacy, his personal traits and work habits often led him to seek isolation. Unlike the Johnson foreign policy system involving several key figures, the Nixon approach was highly structured, with power flowing directly to the White House. By design, fewer key officials influenced policy; even the secretary of state during the first term was often a spectator. Nixon's calculated policy was in sharp contrast to Johnson's frequently visceral responses to ongoing developments.

Domestic and External Constraints

Middle East developments drew increasing American involvement but global problems competed for presidential attention. During the period following the Six-Day War, the stability imposed by the Israeli victory proved fleeting. Palestinian terrorism increased. Airline hijackings designed to harrass Israel became media extravaganzas and Syrian and Jordan-based guerrillas staged frequent raids on the Jewish state. The Palestinians directly threatened the regime of King Hussein in Jordan. Israel responded to Palestinian forays with retaliatory raids, and the cycle of violence escalated. Just as the Johnson administration was ending, the Israelis retaliated for an airline hijacking in Athens with a spectacular raid on Beirut airport, destroying planes but inflicting no casualties.

The military situation on the Israeli-Egyptian frontier was also becoming critical as the number and severity of incidents increased. The Egyptians initiated a war of attrition along the Suez Canal in March 1969. Until August 1970 Israel and Egypt fought a bitter and gradually escalating series of battles there. Occasionally spectacular attacks, increasingly sophisticated arms, and mounting casualties on both sides provided a chilling backdrop to American diplomatic initiatives during the first eighteen months of the Nixon administration.

To make matters worse, in September 1969 King Idris's conservative pro-American monarchy in Libya was overthrown in an army coup. The new regime immediately made clear its anti-American bias. Virulently Islamic, pan-Arab, and radical in tone, it gradually developed a foreign policy aligned with the Soviet Union. At first, some U.S. officials welcomed the new leadership as more progressive, but others feared that the Libyan coup might foreshadow the overthrow of other pro-Western regimes unless steps were taken to ameliorate the Arab-Israeli dispute. The desire to aid moderate Arab regimes against radicals further pressured the Nixon administration, especially when the Libyan regime challenged Western oil interests.[1] There was also a growing tendency, especially in the State Department, to see all Mideast problems as part of the Arab-Israeli conflict, not as isolated problems to be handled with different strategies.[2]

Despite these Mideast pressures, global considerations and problems elsewhere distracted Nixon and Kissinger. Initially the top priorities of the administration included establishing a new relationship with the Soviet Union that might resolve many outstanding issues, like Vietnam and the Middle East.

Ending the war in Vietnam, however, was of necessity the "most pressing foreign problem."[3] It remained a major burden throughout the first term as the war expanded into Cambodia and "Vietnamization" led to the gradual withdrawal of American troops. Developing a new approach toward a hitherto hostile China was directly related to the administration's ideas for mending relations with the U.S.S.R. and resolving the Vietnam War. At the outset, efforts were also made to refurbish contacts with America's European and Japanese allies.[4]

The administration gave high priority to dealing with the instabilities of the Middle East, except when other issues were perceived as more critical. No administration, including Eisenhower's, had entered office with a conception of the Middle East as being more important to American interests. This tension between perceived importance and time available for attention was to become a leitmotif, leading to a dichotomy in policy throughout the first term.

Domestic pressure, like external constraints, operated in opposing directions. Nixon claims in his memoirs that advocates of Israel's cause did not greatly influence his domestic policy:

> From a political standpoint, my approach to the question of civil rights for black Americans was similar to my approach to the question of Israel. In each case, I was in the unique position of being politically unbeholden to the major pressure group involved, and this meant that I was more readily trusted by opposing or competing groups; this, in turn, meant that I had more flexibility and freedom to do solely what I thought was the right thing.[5]

But his resentment of pro-Israel pressures may be revealed more accurately when he complains later about "the unyielding and shortsighted pro-Israeli attitude prevalent in large and influential segments of the American Jewish community, Congress, the media, and in intellectual and cultural circles."[6]

As early as March 1969, Israeli foreign minister Abba Eban recalls, Nixon "took me into the Rose Garden for a few moments, despite the cold March winds, to ask me earnestly why 'Israel's friends' in America did not have more faith in his concern for Israel's interests. He assured me that he would never let Israel down." Referring to the White House tapes, Eban adds, "I did not understand, until some years later, why the Rose Garden was regarded as a more intimate arena than the Oval Office."[7] Although Nixon did not gain substantial Jewish support until the 1972 presidential campaign, he had always had Jews around him—from Los Angeles lawyer Mandell Silverberg and controversial adviser Murray Chotiner at the beginning of his political life to his defender, Rabbi Baruch Korff, at the end of his presidency. Nevertheless, Kissinger relates that "the President was convinced that most leaders of the Jewish community had opposed him throughout his political career. A small percentage of Jews who voted for him, he would joke, had to be so crazy that they would probably stick with him even if he turned on Israel. He delighted in telling associates and visitors that the 'Jewish lobby' had no effect on him." Still, Kissinger maintains, Nixon acted "on almost all practical issues" from an "unsentimental geopolitical analysis" that led him "to positions not too distant from ones others might take on the basis of ethnic politics."[8]

The Nixon camp, however, did not ignore domestic politics. During the 1968 campaign, Nixon insisted on a more pro-Israel speech than most of his staff wanted. He told speech-writer William Safire, "You'll see. There won't be a single vote in this for me. They'll cheer and applaud, and then vote for the other guy; they always do."[9] Despite this cynical analysis, Nixon was well aware that a Jewish vote for him was really two votes, because it reduced the opposing vote and could make the difference in key states in a close election. Nixon actually received one percentage point less of the Jewish vote in 1968 than in 1960, but in 1972 the Committee to Reelect the President (CREEP) created a special office for attracting American Jews.[10] This effort initiated a new Republican pitch for Jewish votes. There were two parts to the appeal: (1) Nixon was a strong backer of Israel and (2) Republicans took the conservative positions on social issues like quotas, mandatory busing, and crime that concerned many Jewish voters.[11] Nixon was well aware of the new strategy, as suggested by a note to one of his Jewish aides on election night in 1972, "We even carried Brooklyn." But, according to the Watergate tapes, he had cautioned chief of staff H. R. Haldeman the previous June not to send daughter Julie to museums or other art centers: "The Arts, you know—they're Jews, they're left wing—in other words, stay away."[12]

The move to portray Nixon as a defender of Jewish interests occurred only after four years of pressure from the Democratic-controlled Congress, which criticized administration policies as antagonistic to Israel. Where Eisenhower had a strong electoral mandate and faced no intense public interest in the Middle East to block his own inclinations, Nixon, and later Ford, were never in so strong a position. The Democratic Congress repeatedly criticized administration policies toward Israel and pressed for a different administration policy through legislation, resolutions, letters, and speeches. Led by Senator Henry Jackson, a presidential candidate in 1972 and 1976, the pro-Israel congressional forces emerged as a domestic constraint that could not be ignored in the policy process.

Nixon, like Johnson before him, was "annoyed that a number of the senators who were urging that we send more military aid to save Israel were opposing our efforts to save South Vietnam from Communist domination."[13] For example, a group of seven antiwar senators, including the eventual 1972 Democratic presidential nominee, George McGovern, wrote the president in May 1970 to urge selling more Phantom jets to Israel, maintaining that "there are fundamental differences between the situation in Indo-China and the situation in Israel."[14] Nixon, however, held adamantly that the conflict with the Soviet Union was indivisible and that his opponents could not choose where to confront the Kremlin. In a memo to Kissinger he wrote, "We are going to stand up in Vietnam and in NATO and in the Middle East, but it is a question of all or none. This is it cold turkey, and it is time that our friends in Israel understood this."[15]

In particular, Nixon's delay in selling Jerusalem increased numbers of Phantom jets in 1969 and 1970, and Secretary of State Rogers's plan to settle the Arab-Israeli dispute led to much public acrimony.[16] In response, Nixon was prepared to separate himself from the State Department when it was under fire from Congress and the press as antagonistic to the Israelis. In fall 1969, for example, Nixon " . . . was not yet ready to press Israel, largely for domestic reasons." But there were exceptions to this pattern. For example, when Jewish War Veterans groups demonstrated in March 1970 against visiting French President Pompidou because of the sale of French jets to Libya, the administration held up action on Israel's application for Phantom jets. "I don't want to see any more Jews about Israel in my office for at least—I don't know how long . . ." Nixon is reported to have blurted to Haldeman in irritation. There was a temporary halt to routine congratulatory messages for Jewish dinners, yearbooks, and bar mitzvahs.[17]

The president also saw himself as constrained by the executive branch. He was suspicious of the "liberal" bureaucracy and the State Department in particular, as well as the nebulous "Eastern establishment." In his memoirs Nixon tells how through the first months of his administration he unsuccessfully "urged, exhorted, and finally pleaded with my Cabinet and other appointed officials to replace holdover Democrats with Republicans who would be loyal to the Administration and support my programs." Kissinger confirms Nixon's "distrust of the existing bureaucracy" and recalls the president's early conviction that the "influence of State Department must be reduced." Nonetheless, because of matters of priority, Nixon put Middle East policy under the control of the State Department at the outset of the administration.[18] This structure led to policies that provoked criticism from Congress.

During the Nixon first term, oil did not greatly affect policy in Arab-Israeli matters. The major international oil companies, however, felt growing pressure from their Arab partners after the Six-Day War and became more vocal in supporting Arab views. Aramco in particular did not hesitate to tell Pentagon officials, congressmen, and industrial leaders visiting Saudi Arabia that the image "of the United States has more or less collapsed in the aftermath of the 1967 Arab-Israeli War" and that "as a direct consequence of our identification with Israel, Soviet influence in the Middle East—which was practically non-existent in the mid-fifties—has burgeoned . . ." The Senate Committee on Multinational Corporations was given a summary of "typical" Aramco messages to visiting officials; it ended with the recommendation that the United States "adopt a neutral position in the Arab-Israeli dispute and a pro-American rather than pro-Israeli policy in the Middle East."[19]

The companies backed Nixon heavily in 1968; one congressman compiled a list of 413 persons in the oil business who contributed $5.7 million to the president's 1972 campaign. Gulf contributed generously to Nixon's campaign and made a 1971 secret gift of $100,000 to place them "on the inside track." Nonetheless, oilmen were consistently unable to affect the administration's foreign policy. Rawleigh Warner of Mobil told Anthony Sampson, "We could always get a hearing, but we felt we might as well be talking to the wall." During the first term oilmen met with Nixon and Kissinger about Middle East policy only once, in early December 1969. Warner reports that Nixon was "very sympathetic" to mollifying the Arabs and "explained that the one group to which he was not indebted for his election was the Jewish vote." Still the company leaders remained displeased after the meeting.[20]

Despite their largesse, U.S. oilmen lacked clout in diplomatic Washington.[21] In mid-1973 the majors did not succeed when they conveyed a message from King Faisal of Saudi Arabia that the United States would be punished if it did not alter its policy toward Israel. They also failed in maintaining U.S. government support for negotiations with the oil producers in 1970 and 1971 and in preventing U.S. military aid to Israel during the October 1973 war.

The U.S. government had long separated diplomacy from oil industry matters. The majors found it much easier to gain domestic benefits from the administration, as in their campaign to get quotas on oil imports reduced and then abolished. Success ironically came in April 1973, in a changing market that generated the energy crisis six months later. Seen in this light, Nixon's policies did indeed aid the international oil companies, whose profits soared as their prices quadrupled. The companies with international interests recognized the benefits of looking after their own concerns without meddling too obviously in diplomacy and drawing poor publicity. One executive confided that oil companies gave lower priority to foreign policy, even during extreme crisis, than to improving their position in the domestic marketplace.[22]

Nixon was not as free from domestic constraints as he often pretended. The State Department, the oil companies, Congress, and American Jews all pressed him in different directions. However, the divisions among those seeking to influence him often gave him ample room to pursue his own policies.

Philosophy

Never before or since the Nixon-Kissinger era have America's international affairs been as consciously conceived and executed with such experience in world politics. The decision-making process was infused with ideological presuppositions. To the new president and his national security adviser, the Soviet Union was central to American problems worldwide. Although they recognized the growing domestic opposition to the Vietnam War and the global increased restraints on the unilateral exercise of force, the new team still believed in an activist American foreign policy. They designed a strategy to confront the Kremlin directly (even forcefully) when the Soviets challenged, while tempting the Russians with increased cooperation, trade, and even economic assistance when they "behaved themselves."

Emphasizing world balance of power and determined to pursue a careful, analytical foreign policy, Nixon and Kissinger relied on three approaches to achieve their goals: power politics, linkage, and detente. Power politics meant that the classic American choice between ideals and self-interest in the conduct of foreign policy was replaced by a stress on *realpolitik* and *raison d'etat*. Little importance was attached to traditional policy-making concerns like human rights, legal niceties, and moral standards in international affairs.

It was Nixon and Kissinger's notion that all matters in conflict with the Soviet Union would be interlinked; the Russians would not be accommodated in one arena (e.g., SALT) without settlement in another (e.g., Vietnam):

> During the transition period Kissinger and I developed a new policy for dealing with the Soviets. Since U.S.-Soviet interests as the world's two competing superpowers were so widespread and overlapping, it was unrealistic to separate or compartmentalize areas of concern. Therefore, we decided to link progress in such areas of Soviet concern as strategic arms limitation and increased trade with progress in areas that were important to us—Vietnam, the Mideast, and Berlin. This concept became known as linkage.[23]

The concept also turned out to be more plausible in theory than in practice, but Nixon and Kissinger always perceived Russian behavior in the global context. Teaching the Kremlin how to conduct itself in ways acceptable to Washington became a major objective of the period. Once the Russians began to play by American rules, then detente would be possible.

The policy approach to the Middle East was similarly structured in a logical and comprehensive fashion. The basic goals to which Nixon and Kissinger aspired were: "to reduce Soviet influence, weaken the position of the Arab radicals, encourage Arab moderates, and assure Israel's security."[24]

The view prevailed throughout this administration that resolving—or at least ameliorating—the Arab-Israeli conflict was central to improving the American position in the Arab world. Only thereby could the United States avoid a confrontation with the Soviet Union during a crisis or the expansion of Russian influence in the no-war, no-peace situation. Many in the State Department believed that Johnson had been too passive in addressing the Arab-Israeli dispute and too willing to rely on the United Nations special representative, Gunnar Jarring.[25]

Yet the new goal posed a dilemma that became central to policy differences during the first term: if an Arab-Israeli settlement was essential for American success in the area, what if an Arab-Israeli accord could not be achieved? Within the administration, two answers were current. Those whose principal effort was improving relations with the Arab world saw pressure toward a settlement as essential. Those who concentrated on the Soviet Union, however, devised a secondary strategy to pursue until a settlement could be reached. American policy in the area would be seriously handicapped if there were no means of combatting Soviet influence other than Arab-Israeli accord. Therefore, the second policy proposed building up individual states in the area to serve as proxies for the United States.

This second posture was consistent with the "Nixon Doctrine" enunciated in a 1969 presidential speech made on Guam and applied at the time to Southeast Asia.[26] The idea was to ease the U.S. out of past entanglements by building up the states of the area to assume the role. In the Middle East, the focus was on proxy states that would further American purposes without need for U.S. troops. As the first Nixon term evolved, two states seemed particularly able to play this role in the Middle East: Iran and Israel. According to this theory, with the aid of American advisers and materiel, Iran was to replace the British in the Persian Gulf. For domestic, political, and economic reasons, the Wilson government had announced in 1968 that it would depart the Gulf by 1971, even though Britain had maintained peace in the area for 150 years. Rather than pressure the British to remain, the administration focused on the shah, who was deemed a stable, pro-American bastion, ready to serve American interests.[27]

The notion that supporting Israel would contain the Soviet Union became especially important at the White House after the Israelis cooperated with the United States in the Jordanian crisis of September 1970 and helped to thwart an attack by the Russian-backed Syrian regime. Many in Washington thought that Israeli strength would deter an Arab attack, allow time to initiate negotiations, and, indeed, move the Arabs toward a settlement. Presumably, once the Arab states concluded that they could not engage the Jewish state militarily, they would accept diplomacy as the only option.[28]

The concept that Iran was important for containing the Soviet Union in the Middle East was not contested in the Nixon administration. However, the notion that Israeli strength would actually encourage negotiations with the Arabs was seriously doubted in the State Department and the Pentagon, even as a temporary measure. Indeed, many thought that this strategy would undermine efforts for an Arab-Israeli settlement.[29] As the prospects of settlement became more bleak, controversies within the administration increased over whether to pursue the primary or secondary approach.

Decision Making

During the Nixon administration's first term, high-ranking officials engaged in an unprecedented and prolonged controversy over Middle East issues. The debate involved the national security adviser and the secretary of state. Their differences had their origin in the decision-making system created by the new president. Because of his suspicions of the bureaucracy, Nixon appointed Henry Kissinger as national security adviser with instructions to design a president-centered approach. Nixon later wrote that "from the outset of my administration . . . I planned to direct foreign policy from the White House."[30] The flow of memoranda and committee reports through the National Security Council system provided the president with various options, putting policy formulation in a broader context than had been available to previous presidents. Yet the system ultimately broke down because Nixon and Kissinger demanded power over all issues that concerned them.

Of the post-1945 foreign policy approaches, Nixon's White House–centered system was most similar to Kennedy's, but there were differences because of contrasting presidential styles. Kennedy preferred discussions with favored aides and outside advisers, while Nixon tended to withdraw in isolation where papers could be studied, speeches written, and issues resolved. Nixon's trait was bound to center policy at the White House and increase the influence of the president's entourage, especially since the president used White House assistants to convey his decisions. Kissinger made a conscious effort to strike a balance between what the new team considered the untidy informality of the Kennedy-Johnson years and the arid formality of the Eisenhower era. During the first term, the system leaned toward the Kennedy rather than Eisenhower model in its reliance on contacts outside the formal structure. Yet Nixon, like Eisenhower before him, came progressively to rely on a foreign policy czar and became isolated from the rest of the decision-making system.[31] Kissinger describes the evolution of this system in his memoirs:

> Eventually, though not for the first one and a half years, I became the principal adviser. Until the end of 1970 I was influential but not dominant. From then on, my role increased as Nixon sought to bypass the delays and sometimes opposition of the departments. The fact remains that the NSC machinery was used more fully before my authority was confirmed, while afterward tactical decisions were increasingly taken outside the system in personal conversations with the President.[32]

For all their common global perspectives, however, the relationship between Nixon and Kissinger was, in the latter's term, "wary," "close on substance, aloof personally." Nixon described their relationship similarly: "Henry, of course, was not a personal friend. We were . . . associates but not personal friends; not enemies but not personal friends."[33]

Although their relationship had recently become more distant, secretary of state William Rogers was, by contrast, an old friend of the president's and a former attorney-general under Eisenhower. Despite his inexperience in foreign affairs, he was chosen for his negotiating skills.[34] This selection guaranteed that Nixon and Kissinger would be unchallenged in dominating the foreign policy system. Rogers, however, expressed his views and sought vigorously to ascertain what policies were being prepared without his knowledge. His competition with Kissinger became a dominant pattern in the first term. According to Nixon, "Rogers felt that Kissinger was Machiavellian, deceitful, egotistical, arrogant, and insulting. Kissinger felt that Rogers was vain, uninformed, unable to keep a secret, and hopelessly dominated by the State Department bureaucracy." In this struggle Rogers was clearly weaker, for his inexperience in foreign affairs limited his ability to pursue policy independent of the bureaucracy or to differ effectively with the more knowledgeable NSC adviser. His cabinet post assured a greater physical and psychological distance than Kissinger's from a president who distrusted the foreign service.[35]

The disagreements between Kissinger and Rogers frequently made Nixon uncomfortable. He found their disputes distasteful because of the need to overrule one of them, a factor that became significant in Mideast policy where both men were involved.[36] This competition confused the administration's otherwise structured foreign policy process by interrupting coordination and allowed foreign governments to play off one government unit against another. Such division led to growing tension among the key foreign policy officials.[37] Nowhere was this process clearer than in the Middle East.

Neither Kissinger nor Rogers assumed office with expertise in Middle East problems. At the outset of the administration, Kissinger had never visited an Arab country but had been to Israel three times. He was already in office when he first heard of the U.N. Resolution 242 formula and admits thinking that the speaker was "pulling my leg."[38] Rogers, for his part, was so uninitiated in Middle East problems that when he was first briefed about the various State Department bureaus, he reportedly exclaimed, "Why, that's all the Middle East? You fellows do have a large area on your hands."[39]

Developments after they entered office rather than preconceptions about the Arab-Israeli dispute caused these two key policy makers to differ over the Middle East. Their different offices, personalities, backgrounds, and philosophies also fueled policy disputes. Kissinger the strategist saw foreign affairs in global perspective, viewing the Middle East in light of the conflict with the U.S.S.R. and other continuing questions, such as Vietnam and relations with the Third World. Adopting at first a hawkish policy toward the Soviets, Kissinger was inclined to share the Israeli view that only through strength in Washington and Jerusalem could the Western position improve in the area.[40] With the Kremlin and the premier Arab state, Egypt, growing closer, Kissinger sought improved relations with countries in the area willing to associate with the United States against the Soviets and regional radicals. Conditions for promoting an Arab-Israeli settlement would improve only when America and Israel demonstrated strength against Russian and radical pressure.

Rogers had a contrasting perspective on the conflict. The major influences on him seem to have been: (1) legal training that encouraged him to act as a judge weighing each side; (2) State Department influence that pointed him toward a regional perspective and a concern for improving relations with Arab states; (3) his emphasis on negotiation that led toward accommodation with the Soviet Union and countries aligned with the Kremlin. As a result, Rogers's emphasis was on the primary policy of the administration: pressing for some kind of Arab-Israeli settlement. Conflict with Kissinger on other issues further exacerbated their differences over the Middle East.

The question arises why Nixon had Rogers concentrate on the Middle East, when Kissinger was responsible for other major foreign policies. According to the participants themselves, there were several reasons for the presidential assignment. First and most important, the NSC had too many other matters to handle and Nixon seems to have believed that the Mideast problem could be dealt with by the State Department. After all, the secretary of state needed some special area of foreign policy: "Primarily . . . I felt that the Middle East required full-time and expert attention. As I told Kissinger, 'You and I will have more than enough on our plate with Vietnam, SALT, the Soviets, Japan, and Europe.' "[41] But why pick the Middle East for "exclusive" assignment to Rogers? The president preferred to distance Middle East policy from the White House because he believed its chance of success was slim and because he feared the reaction of Israel's supporters to U.S. initiatives. Moreover, the Middle East was easier to assign to the State Department than any other issue because Joseph Sisco, the new head of the Near East and South Asian Affairs Bureau, was the most dynamic assistant secretary of state of the time. An accomplished bureaucratic infighter, Sisco was adept at maneuvering between the key figures of foreign policy during this period. As Kissinger admits, "In the end, [Sisco] probably spent as much time mediating between Rogers and me as between the Arabs and Israelis."[42] Still another key factor was Kissinger's Jewish background. The Johnson administration had been much criticized in the Arab world for its three prominent Jews: Arthur Goldberg and the two Rostows. Nixon has written that he thought Kissinger's Jewishness would "put him at a disadvantage" in trying to reopen diplomatic relations with the key Arab states. Kissinger claims that Nixon "suspected that my Jewish origin might cause me to lean too much toward Israel."[43]

Despite his involvement in other issues, Kissinger seems to have resented his early inferior role in Middle East affairs. In his memoirs he laments being unable to block the Russians in the area, recounts fundamental policy disagreements with Rogers, and explains that at first he could only plan for the Middle East or "force deliberations into the NSC framework." He complains, "Until the end of 1971 I was not permitted to conduct diplomacy except in rare periods of acute crisis . . ."[44] Kissinger bridled at his unaccustomed secondary position, while Rogers—realizing that the Middle East represented a unique opportunity to emerge from Kissinger's shadow—pressed for diplomatic success to prove his and his department's effectiveness before a skeptical president. The result was recurring division worsened by absence of the direction that usually flowed from the White House. The unusual latitude granted the State Department was marred by occasional White House interference that further damaged the policy's efficacy.

Despite the dominance of Kissinger and Rogers, other officials played important roles in policy making. The most important was Melvin Laird, the new secretary of defense. In the Pentagon, it was often said that Laird was concerned lest American policy become so strongly committed to Israel that it would result in a confrontation with the Soviet Union.[45] Meanwhile, Harold Saunders retained the position he had held under Johnson as the key official dealing with the Middle East on the National Security Council staff. Compared with later periods, Saunders played a backstage role that even led one commentator to conclude mistakenly that he was no longer significant in policy making.[46] He was, however, overshadowed by Sisco.

Nixon appointed Charles Yost as American ambassador to the United Nations. Yost was a professional diplomat with previous experience in the Middle East as ambassador to Syria and as emissary to Nasser during the 1967 crisis. Because he tended to reflect traditional State Department attitudes, his views generally reinforced Rogers's. When Nixon replaced him in late 1970 with the more politically sensitive and compatible George Bush, rumors blamed the change on Yost's attitude on the Middle East. Certainly, Rogers had lost an important ally. In any case, Yost's philosophy as revealed in his memoirs differed markedly from Nixon's and Kissinger's in taking a conciliatory and accommodationist attitude toward the Third World and the Communist states.[47]

During the first Nixon term, several individuals pressed for policies sympathetic to Israel. Kissinger himself often championed many positions advocated by Israel's supporters. Although he may have been influenced by his Jewish background and his family's flight from Germany in the 1930s, he was more motivated by his rivalry with Rogers and his global perspective, as later events were to demonstrate.[48]

Several more peripheral figures were advocates for Israel. The Jewish portfolio itself was not held by a single person. The one closest to that position was Leonard Garment, a high-ranking domestic adviser, but speechwriter William Safire never made a secret of his pro-Israel leanings. Neither, however, was a member of the inner circle like White House aides Haldeman, John Ehrlichman, Ronald Ziegler, and Dwight Chapin.[49]

Rita Hauser, the U.S. delegate to the U.N. Human Rights Commission, also had a reputation for sympathy to the Israelis. In addition, Max Fisher, a prominent Republican industrialist and national Jewish community leader, functioned as intermediary between the Jewish community and the White House. Although he was the most powerful Jewish leader associated with the president, Fisher shunned any official role in the administration and remained aloof from policy details in order to save his political capital for use during crises in Israeli-American relations. Therefore, his influence varied, depending on timing and circumstances. One of the more unusual roles in the administration was played by Attorney General John Mitchell, who, as a private adviser to the president, seemed to influence Nixon on Israel's behalf—apparently for reasons of domestic politics. The Reverend Billy Graham also played a pro-Israel role.[50]

One other individual was relevant in the Mideast policy process during the Nixon administration: the Israeli ambassador, Yitzhak Rabin. In 1966, Rabin, then chief of staff of the Israeli Defense Forces, was the only high-ranking Israeli official to befriend a visiting private citizen, Richard Nixon. It was a stroke of good fortune for Israel. When he was about to become president, Nixon recalled Rabin's attentions with gratitude. Nor was Rabin acting insincerely. Privately, he thought that Nixon's global and strategic view of negotiating with the Soviets from strength, like Israel's attitude toward the Arabs, was more consistent with Israel's needs than Hubert Humphrey's more conciliatory global posture.[51] The rapport that Rabin established with both Nixon and Kissinger made him invaluable in Israel's effort to gain increased economic, military, and diplomatic support from the United States. His role demonstrates that a foreign ambassador in Washington can influence the policy process.

Standing above this process and internal administration disputes was a president with contradictory impulses toward the Arab-Israeli dispute, the Arabs, and the Jews. Nixon wanted to revive relations with the Arab countries but also to use Israel against the Soviet Union. He sought major diplomatic initiatives that involved appeals to the Arab states but did not want to alienate Israel or its supporters at home and their congressional allies. He had taken the unusual step for his administration of using the State Department as policy maker to avoid the political and diplomatic consequences of failure and policy reversals, but he frequently undercut the authority he had bestowed on Foggy Bottom.

When Nixon assumed office, American relations with the Arab world were at a new low and he was determined to upgrade them. After he had visited the Aswan Dam in the early 1960s he had told Nasser, "Today I have seen

America's greatest mistake." In his resignation speech in August 1974, he referred to his advances in the Arab world and did not mention Israel.[52]

On the other hand, William Safire has revealed that Nixon admired the Israelis—their patriotism, their nationalism and "guts," their work ethic, their understanding of his Vietnam policies, their "moxie." The Israelis reciprocated with a genuine admiration for Nixon as the first president who looked on them as a strategic advantage for American interests.[53] Naturally, they preferred to be an asset rather than a ward. They sought to deal directly with the administration rather than develop indirect contacts through American Jews. Nixon also preferred this, because he had never established a strong relationship with the American Jewish community.

Because of the increasing priority of Mideast issues, Nixon was the first president to develop ongoing relationships with several Israeli leaders. These contacts covered the spectrum between cordial summit meetings and severe White House criticisms of Jerusalem. Kissinger aptly summarizes the peculiar Nixon position in describing the first White House meeting between the president and Prime Minister Golda Meir: she hailed him ". . . as an old friend of the Jewish people, which was startling news to those of us more familiar with Nixon's ambivalences on that score. But it gave him a reputation to uphold, and in the event he did much for Israel if not out of affection then out of his characteristically unsentimental calculation of the national interest." But Kissinger interprets that calculation narrowly: "He favored a strong Israel because he did not want the United States to have to fight Israel's battles. . . ." Nonetheless, Nixon was on occasion severely disillusioned with the Israelis, writing a note on one Kissinger memo, "I am beginning to think we have to consider taking strong steps unilaterally to save Israel from her own destruction."[54]

Meetings between Nixon and Meir were almost always successful; Rabin observes that "her rapport with Nixon was often truly extraordinary." On the other hand, Nixon noted in his diary in early 1973, "I feel that some way we have got to get the Israelis moved off of their intransigent position. Needless to say, we can't move to the all-out Egyptian or Arab position either, but there is some place in between there where we can move."[55]

Above all Nixon was preoccupied with global politics and this affected his policy toward the Middle East. On one of Kissinger's memorandums he noted, "'Even handedness' is the right policy—but above all our interest is— what gives the Soviet the most trouble—don't let Arab-Israeli conflict obscure that interest." Since he believed the Soviet Union had been the political victor in the Six-Day War, he disagreed with Kissinger's view that the Arab radicals would eventually realize that only the United States could produce progress in the talks. Writing on another Kissinger memorandum, he stated, "The Soviets know that Arabs are long on talk. We have been gloating over Soviet 'defeats' in the Mideast since '67—and State et al. said the June war was a 'defeat' for

Soviet. It was *not*. They became the Arabs' friend and the U.S. their enemy. Long-range this is what serves their interest."[56]

Like Eisenhower before him, Nixon sought to mitigate the Soviet threat by improving relationships with the Arabs. "It was clearly in America's interest to halt the Soviet domination of the Arab Mideast. To do so would require broadening American relations with Arab countries."[57] But Nixon took a different approach from his mentor. Even though at difficult times "he leaned toward the [State] departmental views that Israel's policies were the basic cause of the difficulty . . ." he insisted that the Arabs make major changes toward the United States. Like Kissinger, he had come to question Eisenhower's policy during the Suez crisis, because it left the United States alone in facing Russia and because "in retrospect I believe that our actions were a serious mistake. Nasser became even more rash and aggressive than before, and the seeds of another Mideast war were planted."[58] Thus, Washington could not cater to the Arab radical leaders even while making overtures to them. The difficulty of defining this policy would lead to many tactical differences among top officials during the first term.

Unlike Eisenhower, Nixon used Israel to counter the Soviet Union, although like Eisenhower he wanted Israeli diplomatic concessions to gain closer relations with the Arab states and limit Soviet influence throughout the region. This strategy differed markedly from the policy during the Kennedy-Johnson years. It took Israel to be more central to American interests, and it more seriously expected Israeli cooperation in return for largesse. As Nixon wrote to Kissinger at one point, "Our interests are basically pro-freedom and not just pro-Israel because of the Jewish vote. We are *for* Israel because Israel in our view is the only state in the Mideast which is pro-freedom and an effective opponent to Soviet expansion. We will oppose a cut-and-run policy either in Vietnam or Cuba or the Mideast or NATO or any place else in the world. This is the kind of friend Israel needs and will continue to need. . . ." Nixon's attitude toward Mideast diplomacy was reflected in another private comment. When Kissinger admitted at an off-the-record news conference that the American aim was "to expel" the Soviet pilots and combat personnel from the area, Nixon noted in preparing for another news conference that the Soviets could be expelled "by peace settlement."[59]

To this president diplomacy itself was a means to a higher global end. "What I was trying to do . . . was to construct a completely new set of power relationships in the Middle East—not only between Israel and the Arabs, but also among the United States, Western Europe and the Soviet Union."[60] This objective was more sweeping than any that other presidents had undertaken in the area and represented the closest link between global and regional politics yet designed.

At the same time, strategy before the Yom Kippur War was inchoate and not vigorously pursued. It still reflected competing objectives at home and abroad that rested on an elementary machismo, an insistence on absolute loyalty from friends, and a focus on the Soviet Union as the unifying force in international politics for the United States. As Nixon wrote in his diary:

. . . Mrs. Meir, Rabin, et al., must trust RN completely. He does not want to see Israel go down the drain and makes an absolute commitment that he will see to it that Israel always has "an edge." On the other hand, he must carry with him not just the Jewish constituency in New York and Pennsylvania and California and possibly Illinois which voted 95 percent against him, but he must carry with him the 60 percent of the American people who are in what is called the silent majority, and who must be depended upon in the event that we have to take a strong stand against Soviet expansionism in the Mideast. Only when the Israeli leaders recognize this fact are they going to have any kind of security which will be reliable. . . . We are going to be in power for at least the next three years and this is going to be the policy of this country. Unless they understand it and act as if they understood it beginning now, they are down the tubes.[61]

Global politics in general and balancing Soviet efforts in particular remained Nixon's motivation in dealing with the Mideast even as he sought an Arab-Israeli settlement, reduced influence for Arab radicals, better relations with Arab moderates, and new support from American Jews. Nixon's concentration on the Soviet Union as the key challenge to American interests, combined with more intricate relations with Israel and new overtures to individual Arab states, resulted in a more complex strategy than those pursued previously. The problem facing the president throughout the first term was that his strongly divided policy apparatus could not handle the complexity. The outcome was an inconsistency and chaos atypical of this administration's conduct of foreign affairs.

The Rogers Plan: The First Initiative

The dangers and confusions were clear even before Nixon took office. William Scranton, the former governor of Pennsylvania, toured the Middle East on a fact-finding trip for the president-elect. When he crossed the Allenby Bridge from Jordan to the Israeli-occupied West Bank, he declared that U.S. policy in the area should be more "evenhanded" than before, by which he meant that the United States should "take into consideration the feelings of all persons and all countries in the Middle East and not necessarily espouse one nation over some other." Scranton's statement was widely interpreted as signaling a new pro-Arab approach. Scranton, however, had not intended to set a new policy. In his private report to the president-elect, he argued that American policy should take better account of Arab needs; otherwise, the Russians would make major progress in the area. But he also urged that the United States continue its strong commitment to Israeli security. Whatever the former governor intended, a spokesman for Nixon quickly disassociated him from Scranton's remarks.[62]

Nixon himself sent mixed signals in his early public statements. On the one hand, he reassured Israeli defense minister Dayan of his support at a meeting they held in mid-December.[63] On the other hand, at his first presidential news conference he made it clear that he would not continue Johnson's passive policy. Nor would he back Israel in its quest for direct Arab-Israeli negotiations. He called the Middle East a "powder keg" and dwelt on the danger of Soviet-American confrontation if the area should explode again.[64] For the Israelis such talk raised the specter of an imposed peace.

In the first few weeks of the administration, a consensus developed for taking novel diplomatic steps in the area. Several factors encouraged an initiative: (1) increased fighting along the Suez Canal, (2) State Department urging, (3) proposals by the Soviet Union for Big Two talks and by France for Big Four talks,* and (4) a Nixon campaign pledge to take a new approach. The French and Soviet proposals for talks carried weight because Nixon sought closer ties with De Gaulle's France, and he wanted to use the Middle East as "a lever to ply loose some Soviet cooperation on Vietnam."[65] State unanimously favored a major initiative in which the United States would sponsor a settlement and force Israeli concessions in order to reach it. This approach was intended to reduce Soviet influence and improve Arab-American relations. Kissinger disagreed. He maintained that the administration should be more patient and encourage negotiations between Jordan and Israel because both were aligned with Washington. He also questioned whether State's concept of negotiations could succeed. Even if it did, he argued that countries associated with Moscow should neither benefit from American efforts nor should the Kremlin be allowed credit for any progress.[66]

The thrust toward a more active policy was powerful. Kissinger attempted to thwart it by recommending to the president that both the French and Soviet suggestions be accepted; he hoped that two formats would restrain momentum and prevent the State Department from moving rapidly toward certain failure.[67] The ploy was not successful. Under the veil of encouraging the stalled Jarring mission, Charles Yost was soon meeting with his British, French, and Russian counterparts at the U.N., and Joseph Sisco held conversations with Soviet Ambassador Dobrynin in Washington during spring and summer 1969.

*The Big Two meant the United States and the U.S.S.R.; the Big Four meant France and Great Britain in addition.

Involved State Department officials like Sisco, Rogers, and Undersecretary of State Elliot Richardson advanced toward an agreement on general principles with the Soviets for settling the conflict.[68]

The Israelis and their supporters looked upon this process with growing alarm. To them the Soviets were acting as dutiful lawyers for the Arabs, while American representatives were negotiating on their own terms and only later informing Israeli officials about the progress of the talks.[69] In the Big Four talks the Arabs had two spokesmen: the French as well as the Russians. Moreover, the Israelis believed that the general principles the United States was developing and showed Eban on a visit in mid-March could only cause tensions between Jerusalem and Washington, because they moved Washington toward supporting the 1967 borders with only "minor" changes. To the Israelis, this was a concession made at their expense.[70]

Rogers announced the new framework at a late March appearance before the Senate Foreign Relations Committee. He declared that the United States would now play a more active role in Mideast diplomacy, emphasized that changes in the 1967 lines "should not reflect the weight of conquest," and reminded his audience that U.N. Resolution 242 affirmed "the need for a just settlement of the refugee problem."[71] Many American bystanders sympathetic to the Israelis thought this reliance on U.S. formulas inappropriate for promoting talks between the Arabs and Israelis. As early as mid-February, a congressional delegation was calling on the president to express its concern. This pattern accelerated over the next several months, with growing numbers of letters signed by senators and congressmen, for the most part opposing a peace imposed on Israel. Key administration officials met with both congressional delegations and Jewish leaders.[72]

Secretary of State Rogers in particular had difficulty mollifying these groups and soon got the reputation of being "a tiger with the Jews." In her memoirs Golda Meir recalled Israeli frustration with Rogers: "I suspect that he never really understood the background to the Arab wars against Israel or ever realized that the verbal reliability of the Arab leaders was not, in any way, similar to his own. I remember how enthusiastically he told me about his first visit to the Arab states and how immensely impressed he was by Faisal's 'thirst for peace.' As is true of many other gentlemen I have known, Rogers assumed— wrongly, unfortunately—that the whole world was made up solely of other gentlemen."[73]

In these early forays, Kissinger was not allied with the delegations opposing the State Department even though he was also critical. Rather, he represented a third point of view. He feared that the State Department's plan would place the burden on the United States "for producing all the substantive proposals and for bringing the Israelis around." Kissinger sought to deny any gains to Russia. "A good definition of an equitable settlement is one that will make both sides unhappy. If so, we must have Soviet help, and the Soviets must share the blame for pushing an unpalatable solution." Kissinger did not oppose America's precipitating a settlement, even if it interfered with Israeli demands for direct negotiations, but he wanted to try this procedure only after careful preparations and after radical Arab leaders had been brought to look to the United States and not to the Soviet Union: "The State Department wanted to fuel the process of negotiations by accepting at least some of the Soviet ideas to facilitate compromise. I wanted to frustrate the radicals—who were in any event hostile to us—by demonstrating that in the Middle East friendship with the United States was the precondition to diplomatic progress." Nasser's continued demands for U.S. support against Israel, his unwillingness to resume diplomatic relations with the United States or to show diplomatic flexibility of his own despite new Nixon administration concessions to him, further confirmed Kissinger in this stance. Kissinger makes clear in his memoirs that he was prepared to extract concessions from Israel, but only if "the Arabs showed *their* willingness to reciprocate. . . ."[74] He would define and judge this willingness himself. The differences between his standards and Jerusalem's inevitably generated controversy with Israeli leaders after October 1973.

As discussions proceeded and the Russians sought more specific explanations of the United States position, Rogers pressed for presidential authority to declare privately that the United States would insist that Israel return to the pre-1967 borders with Egypt. The president demurred during spring and summer 1969, but he was caught between his own desire for progress, Kissinger's warnings, the State Department's enthusiasm for a rapid negotiating process, his unwillingness to "flatly" overrule his secretary of state, and a mounting number of incidents along Israel's frontiers, especially along the Suez Canal. The result was a classic drama played out between a cautious, somewhat confused president and a determined bureaucracy. At one point Kissinger was told by Attorney General John Mitchell that "the President had no preconceived notions on how to proceed."[75]

Nixon's solution was to restrict State's flexibility but permit it to proceed. Gradually, restraints on making specific proposals to the U.S.S.R. eroded. In response, State Department officials moved negotiations forward, usually by inching closer to concrete positions likely to attract the Arabs, such as endorsing the 1967 borders. By mid-September Nixon brought John Mitchell into the discussions and sought his advice on the domestic implications of American actions and proposals. The result was a more skeptical president, who asked Rogers and Sisco, "Do you fellows ever talk to the Israelis?" Nixon subsequently told his NSC adviser, "The summit and trade they [Moscow] can have but I'll be damned if they can get the Middle East." Kissinger claims that Nixon was "restless with State Department steam roller tactics," but the president also believed that something had to be done. Thus he rejected both State Department calls for pressure on Israel and Israel's apparent preference for joint American-Israeli firmness to make the Arabs negotiate.[76]

In the midst of these deliberations within the administration, Golda Meir, having assumed office the previous March after the death of Levi Eshkol, arrived in September 1969 for her first visit to Washington as prime minister. The mood of the talks was cordial. Nixon aide Ronald Zeigler was humming the theme from Exodus in the wings as the president compared the prime minister to the Biblical leader, Deborah, in his toast at a White House dinner. Nixon spoke about Israel as "a remarkable story," commenting "how they have made the land bloom."[77]

According to several accounts, Nixon gave his Israeli visitors the impression that he did not share the State Department's enthusiasm for the talks then in progress. He reinforced their hopes by including Kissinger rather than Rogers in his private session with Meir and by establishing a special channel between Kissinger and Rabin to sidestep the State Department.[78]

The Israeli negotiators, however, were interested in more than restraining the State Department's experimental diplomacy. They also sought additional arms supplies and aid, especially more Phantom jets.[79]

On the U.S. diplomatic stance and military assistance, Nixon spoke in reassuring generalities, supporting Meir without specific commitments. To the Israelis' consternation, however, false rumors circulated in Washington shortly after the talks that they had accepted a "software/hardware" formula. The rumor had Nixon and Meir agreeing that Jerusalem and Washington would trade Israeli diplomatic concessions for increased American military assistance.[80]

The flap revealed a continuing tension in American policy that became chronic during the Nixon era. If military assistance and diplomacy were indeed to be linked, although neither the Israelis nor the State Department realized it at first, Israel had as much leverage as the United States. With American anxiety over maintaining negotiations, the Israelis could require U.S. aid commitments before offering any diplomatic concessions.

The Israelis and Americans soon found themselves in a mutually dependent relationship accompanied by recurring and serious disagreement. Although he does not mention it in his memoirs, Kissinger carefully manipulated aid to Israel to produce both trust and insecurity in his client. The intent was to encourage flexibility in diplomatic negotiations by not giving Israel everything it wanted. The "hardware/software" flap was a rare surfacing of this conflict.[81]

A further distinctive characteristic of this administration was the president's effort to exploit internal administration disagreements in dealing with both the Israelis and the Arabs. Once each side had its "friends," the president could balance the competing parties while appearing sympathetic to all. This pattern was particularly clear when the first phase of Nixon policy toward the Middle East culminated in the Rogers Plan.

After Meir left the United States, the State Department moved to achieve the basis for agreement on the 1967 frontiers in return for Arab security guarantees to Israel. Finally, a Nixon preoccupied with Vietnam allowed Sisco to present the formula to Dobrynin in late October. At the same time he had Mitchell and Garment privately convey to Jewish leaders his doubts about State Department policy and his assurances that Israel's interests would be protected.[82] When the Kremlin and Nasser surprised State's key people by not accepting the formula, Rogers and his aides, determinedly pursuing diplomatic success, decided to present it publicly. Regional developments seemed to demand an initiative. Tensions were increasing between Jordan and the PLO over growing Palestinian strength in Hussein's kingdom; along the Suez Canal, the war of attrition intensified. Colonel Qaddafi had clearly brought Libya to the side of Arab radicals. In November, even after seeing Rogers's proposals, Nasser had called the United States the "number one enemy of the Arabs."[83] American diplomats worried that U.S. interests would be seriously compromised in the area if the administration did not seize the initiative before an Arab League conference scheduled in late December. Oil executives had been warning the administration that American policy must change or the conservative Arab camp would be weakened, American petroleum interests threatened, and Soviet influence increased.[84]

In the resulting speech of 9 December, the secretary of state revealed a framework that became known as "the Rogers plan." It proposed a basic tradeoff in which Israel would withdraw from occupied territory and the Arabs would agree to some contractual arrangement guaranteeing a permanent peace with Israel. Rogers declared American policy to be "balanced" between the Arabs and Israelis. Consistent with its State Department origins, the new formula came closer to Arab positions than had public U.S. policy since the Six-Day War. For example, although the secretary of state did not echo the Arab insistence on Israel's withdrawing to the 1967 frontiers, he came close by suggesting that alterations in the 1967 borders should be "insubstantial" and only for "mutual security." Similarly, regarding peace, he continued State Department refusal to call for either normalization or direct negotiations. Although the "binding agreement" that Rogers advocated implied Arab obligations that they were not then prepared to make, it was not the formal peace treaty demanded by the Israelis. Rogers further alarmed Israel by (1) raising the refugee question, as in the Johnson Plan, and (2) advocating that Israel and Jordan should participate "in the civic, economic and religious life" of Jerusalem.[85]

At the Big Four talks in New York a few days later, Yost presented proposals on an Israeli-Jordanian settlement. Although not public, his proposals came even closer to the Arab view. Basically, Israel would return to its pre-1967 frontiers in exchange for guarantees, improved access to the holy places in Jerusalem, and an agreement prohibiting violence across the Jordanian border. Although the proposals considered that the two governments would formally recognize each other's sovereignty, territorial integrity, political independence, and right to live in peace, Israel would have to accept back some Arab refugees.[86]

Although the Nixon era was noted for presidential control over the national security bureaucracy, the Rogers Plan was a rare but dramatic exception. Rogers announced the new approach on the day before the NSC was scheduled to decide on future American policy in the Middle East.[87] Kissinger's statement that State preempted the NSC is supported by a meeting that he and Nixon had arranged in anticipation of the NSC discussion with several corporate and banking leaders, including David Rockefeller, John McCloy, and Robert B. Anderson. Nixon and Kissinger would hardly have planned to discuss future Mideast initiatives with such prominent corporate figures if they had already decided to announce a new policy.

The announcement of the Rogers Plan recalls the State Department's backing of trusteeship in March 1948. As on that occasion, a storm of public protest descended on the White House. But this president did not react with anger at the State Department preemption. He had just met with corporate leaders who were likely to welcome the Rogers Plan, as Truman had just made private commitments to Weizmann. Nixon, like Truman, was not prepared to overrule his secretary of state. Nixon, like Truman, sought to distance himself from the State Department on the issue while allowing the policy to go forward. Truman let the arms embargo to the area continue; Nixon permitted Yost to present the Jordanian policy paper in the Four Power talks. Nixon, like Truman before him, would have acquiesced had State's policy succeeded. In both cases the policy did not succeed and the department's failure ultimately led the president to adopt altered policies. Nixon, like Truman, sent secret messages to assure an Israeli leader that he would not strongly pursue the State Department policy. Truman sent Judge Samuel Rosenman to Weizmann; Nixon instructed Leonard Garment to convey private assurances to Meir that "we would not press our proposal."[88]

Nixon reinforced the divergence between State and White House when he failed to endorse the Rogers Plan publicly or back it politically. In late December he gave an impromptu audience to Rabin and offered vague assurances. His first "State of the World" message, released in February, diverged from Rogers's statements in its emphasis on the Soviet threat and the need for direct Arab-Israeli negotiations.[89]

Even more dramatically, Nixon appeased a meeting of nearly a thousand Jewish leaders in Washington at the end of January. They protested the Rogers

Plan after an unsuccessful meeting with the secretary of state several weeks earlier. Nixon had Max Fisher read a presidential message that did not disavow the Rogers Plan but assured the audience that the United States would not impose a peace settlement, saying that "an agreement can be achieved only through negotiations between [the parties]." The message even hinted that a favorable response to Meir's request for additional Phantoms and Skyhawks might be forthcoming. Though Nixon did not contradict his secretary of state, his tone was more sympathetic to Israeli complaints than Rogers's recent statements had been.[90]

The president, however, did not scrap the plan even though it was rejected by all relevant parties—the Arabs, the Israelis, and the Russians. He had been pressured for such a statement by diplomats and oil executives before its release and afterwards by congressmen and Jewish leaders opposed to it. There was a perceived need for a symbolic statement in which the United States recognized the justice of certain Arab arguments, and there was little likelihood that such a diplomatic initiative could succeed. Nixon therefore chose a skillful balancing act. He accepted Rogers's position but also accepted Kissinger's skepticism in failing to back it politically:

I knew that the Rogers Plan could never be implemented, but I believed that it was important to let the Arab world know that the United States did not automatically dismiss its case regarding the occupied territories or rule out a compromise settlement of the conflicting claims. With the Rogers Plan on record, I thought it would be easier for the Arab leaders to propose reopening relations with the United States without coming under attack from the hawks and pro-Soviet elements in their own countries.[91]

This strategy raised serious difficulties in working with Israel. Indeed, the Yost proposals, presented on 18 December, had an even more debilitating effect on the Israelis than Rogers's speech did. Two days before they were presented, Eban was in Washington to protest the Rogers Plan. He strongly urged the United States to avoid similar action in relation to Jordan lest private Israeli-Jordanian contacts be torpedoed. Twenty-four hours later, Eban met with Kissinger and received the impression that his representations were being taken seriously. The next day Rabin was informed that the United States had presented the Yost proposals a few hours earlier. In the meetings with Rogers and Kissinger, the Israeli representatives had been kept in the dark. It seems that Nixon approved the Yost proposals on the day Eban met with Kissinger, and the State Department in its enthusiasm presented them within twenty-four hours.[92]

The Rogers speech and the Yost follow-up at the U.N. were the most comprehensive U.S. effort yet to deal with the Arab-Israeli problem. Only Dulles's 1955 speech to the Council of Foreign Relations and the accompanying background study (on which it was based) rivaled this initiative in breadth, and the issues had become more important since. In both cases, the proposed peace fell short of full normalization of Arab-Israeli relations and would require major Israeli concessions on refugees and territories. Unlike in 1955, however, American policy was split between the supposedly official stand of Rogers and statements emanating from the White House such as the "State of the World" message and the Nixon letter to Fisher. The confused signals caused by this internal division were soon answered by confused actions of Mideast governments.

Repercussions of the Rogers Plan

After the new State Department approach, Israel initiated deep penetration raids into Egypt. The raids, an effort to end the war of attrition along the Suez Canal, proved to be a major blunder. Ambassador Rabin repeatedly urged them and thought they would strengthen Israel's hand, but there is no evidence to substantiate his claims that the administration was pleased. So seriously had Washington's relations with Israel deteriorated that even as well-informed and well-connected an ambassador as Yitzhak Rabin misinterpreted American intentions, an error encouraged by his personal commitment to the raids.[93]

It is surprising that at first the administration leveled neither public nor private criticism at Israel, but Washington's leverage on Jerusalem was reduced after the Rogers Plan was announced and some early Israeli military successes were spectacular (e.g., the capture of an Egyptian radar site, the transport of sophisticated equipment back to Israel).[94] However, in mid-February the Israelis accidentally hit an Egyptian factory on the outskirts of Cairo, inflicting about 150 casualties and drawing a U.S. condemnation. Nasser seemed unable to thwart the Israeli raids, but two weeks before the factory attack, the Russians had decided to respond. In late January, the Egyptian leader had traveled secretly to Moscow where the Russians agreed to supply Cairo with advanced Soviet anti-aircraft missiles to stop the Israeli raids.[95] For the next several weeks, in letters and in personal exchanges between Russian and American diplomatic representatives, there were numerous hints of possible new Russian arms to the Egyptians. Kissinger wondered if Soviet combat personnel would be sent to Cairo as well.[96]

Given the prevailing view at State and Defense that "Israeli intransigence" caused the problem and that Israel maintained clear air superiority, there was no inclination to consider new, large-scale aid to Jerusalem despite pleas from the Israelis, their supporters in Congress and the Jewish community, and Kissinger. Among the various arguments in favor of sending the Phantoms and Skyhawks, Kissinger's was typical. He held that such aid would reassure Israel and demonstrate American readiness to stand up to any Russian and radical Arab challenges that might emerge.[97]

In the wake of the controversy over the Rogers Plan, Nixon had announced at the end of January that a decision on arms to Israel would be made "within the next 30 days." The context and the deadline suggested a positive response. Yet within the government there was little support for the Israeli request. Nixon himself believed that Israel's policies caused the difficulties. He hoped to avoid giving the Russians a reason to increase aid to the Arabs, and he thought that arms restraint might further the resumption of U.S. diplomatic relations with Egypt and Syria.[98] A positive response to the aid request was therefore unlikely.

In early March an unrelated incident strengthened the case against a new Phantom sale to Israel. On his visit to the United States, French President Pompidou was harrassed in Chicago by members of the Jewish War Veterans protesting his recent arms deal with Qaddafi's Libya; he in turn threatened to leave the country prematurely. Nixon, afraid that the demonstrations would ruin his efforts to improve Franco-American relations, was incensed. Further infuriated with the New York governor and the New York City mayor for their snubbing of the French leader (Nixon reportedly told his aides "Let'em get their planes from Rockefeller and Lindsay!"), he took the step unprecedented in his monarchial presidency of substituting for Vice President Agnew at a New York dinner honoring Pompidou.[99]

The day after the Chicago demonstrations against Pompidou, the White House dramatized the president's pique by announcing on a Sunday that the decision on Israel's receiving additional aircraft would be postponed. Once this delay was ordered, officials who opposed increased sales were able to rally support. It was the 1968 Phantoms decision in reverse, as public pressure backfired and the bureaucracy persuaded the president that Phantoms for Israel were not yet essential. In late March Secretary Rogers announced the "interim decision" not to sell the jets, and Israel's supporters could do little but bide their time.[100]

When Rogers made his announcement, the Israeli and American governments had already learned that the Soviets had sent highly sophisticated anti-aircraft missiles and personnel to Egypt with larger increments on the way. This aid was unprecedented to a non-Communist country. Despite their knowledge of the Russian moves and Kissinger's muted warnings, Nixon and the major agencies still opposed changing the policy framework.[101]

In private, however, the president moved in a somewhat different direction. He instructed Kissinger to inform Rabin that some of Israel's aircraft losses in the war of attrition would be replaced and that the balance of forces would be maintained in Israel's favor. The NSC adviser made it clear that the administration sought to move decisions on Israeli arms to the private arena.[102] Nixon reiterated this point in a somewhat emotional meeting with the Israeli ambassador and, according to Rabin, added:

Whenever you request arms—particularly planes—all the media sound off about it and everyone waits for the administration's decision. That's a superfluous and harmful dramatization of the matter. Some sections of the administration are strenuously opposed to supplying arms to Israel at this time. I won't identify them, but believe me, they have spared no effort in trying to convince me. You can be sure that I will continue to supply arms to Israel, but I shall do so in other, different, ways. The moment Israel needs arms, approach me, by way of Kissinger, and I'll find a way of overcoming the bureaucracy.[103]

Later in the meeting, Nixon responded to Rabin's continued pleas with the comment, "You can be sure you'll get your arms. I only want to go about it in a different way."[104]

Despite these private assurances, the administration's response to the Russian foray into Egypt was uncharacteristically muted, especially considering its penchant for seeing every major Kremlin action as a direct challenge. The reaction is even more startling in light of Kissinger's revelation in his memoirs that the reason for the more conciliatory private attitude toward Israeli arms requests was not the Soviet initiative in Cairo but Moscow's diversionary tactic in March of proposing an undeclared cease-fire along the Suez Canal. According to Kissinger, the administration hoped to gain Israeli acceptance of the cease-fire proposal by softening its reluctance to replace Israeli aircraft losses; the cease-fire idea later evaporated because of Russian moves.[105]

In the end, the administration did not react to the Kremlin arms initiative. In part, it was involved with other crises; the president was preoccupied with the emerging crisis in Cambodia and the threatened second Senate rejection of an appointee to the Supreme Court. Nixon was also beginning his secret move toward a Soviet summit, which colored his approach to Kremlin activities in Egypt for the next several months.[106]

With the president's attention elsewhere, bureaucratic calculations were most important in the early lack of response to Russian moves in Egypt. The bureaucracy generally thought that the Israeli raids had precipitated the Soviet move and that the military balance favored Israel, a typical example of analysis meshing with preference. Instead of supporting increased military aid to the Israelis as a signal to the Russians, discussions within the bureaucracy centered on how to induce greater Israeli flexibility. The result was that the United States conveyed no serious concern about Moscow's activities in Egypt and Russian escalation followed.[107]

The next several months were marked by Washington's continuing preoccupation with Indochina and policies toward the Soviet Union, while within the administration the conflict between the NSC and the State Department intensified. Kissinger accepted State's criticism of the Israeli raids at the beginning of 1970, but he believed they had become irrelevant in the face of a Russian challenge. With continued Soviet expansion in Egypt, Jerusalem suspended its deep penetration raids at the end of March and complained about America's failure to respond to the buildup.[108] Finally, the Israelis discovered that Russian pilots were actually flying defensive missions over Egypt's cities, thereby seriously intensifying Moscow's involvement and leading to possible confrontations between Israeli and Soviet aircraft. The administration still did not act because the news of this escalation arrived at the White House in late April just as the president was moving toward a decision on Cambodia. Indeed, the news about Egypt seems to have influenced his decision on Cambodia, suggesting the need to demonstrate American seriousness in withstanding Russian pressures. Because the immediate crisis confronting Nixon was in Southeast Asia rather than in the Middle East, he responded to the crisis in Cambodia first.[109]

During the next several weeks Washington was preoccupied with domestic and international controversy following the Cambodian invasion, a controversy intensified by the killing of four students at Kent State University. "Not until Watergate was Nixon so consumed and shaken; he was not prepared to add to his problems."[110] Without White House direction, the administration's response continued to be cautious because Nixon and Kissinger were the only key administration officials disposed to see the Soviet escalation in Egypt as a challenge to the United States. Bureaucrats in the intelligence, defense, and diplomatic communities saw the Russian action as a situation calling for Israeli concessions.

Nixon did authorize Kissinger to inform Rabin secretly that he would now supply new planes to Israel. This message was reiterated in a meeting between the president and Eban in late May. Nixon also told the Israeli foreign minister that Washington would begin to push actively for a cease-fire. Rabin's account of the meeting reflects Nixon's inconsistent response to Mideast events. He reports the president as saying, "Everytime I hear of your penetrating their territory and hitting them hard, I get a feeling of satisfaction. I agree with you that the Soviets and the Egyptians are putting us both to the test." Then he proceeded to talk about a political solution. Additional jets were not forthcoming, because in the absence of a public announcement or an approval of specific numbers, bureaucrats opposed to an arms deal were able to delay it.[111]

Meanwhile, many in Congress attacked the timid administration response to Russian activities in Egypt. In May, seventy-three senators spanning the political spectrum from Goldwater to McGovern signed a letter to the secretary of state that stated, "Your decision in March to hold in abeyance the sale of additional jet aircraft to Israel . . . has failed to induce the Soviet Union to exercise reciprocal restraint with respect to the army of the U.A.R. and other Arab states."[112]

The Second Rogers Initiative: "Stop Shooting, Start Talking"

With the State Department controlling specific tactics in this period, congressional pressures were ignored. Rogers embarked on his second major peace initiative—the so-called "stop-shooting, start-talking" project—which called for a ninety-day Egyptian-Israeli cease-fire along the canal, accompanied by indirect talks through Jarring. Despite Kissinger's complaints that this proposal did not address the growing problem of Russian combat troops in Egypt, the plan proceeded with the approval of a president loathe to clash with his secretary of state and a bureaucracy whose key members outside the NSC were largely united. While the Egyptians first responded to the initiative with silence, the Meir government stopped just short of outright rejection. The Israelis' enthusiasm did not increase when Secretary Rogers informed Rabin that U.S. arms supplies depended on their "positive response" to the new diplomatic efforts. [113]

At this point, the internal differences within the administration erupted publicly. In an anonymous press backgrounder for which he was by then famous, Kissinger took a position very different from the State Department's. "We are trying to expel the Soviet military presence, not so much the advisers, but the combat personnel, the combat pilots, before they become so firmly established." [114]

In the fresh aftermath of Cambodia, the remarks provoked an immediate public controversy over their meaning, and a White House spokesman quickly indicated that the United States did not intend to expel the Russians by force. [115] However, Nixon announced his renewed concern with the Middle East in a television interview on 1 July, threatening action if the Soviet Union upset the balance of power in the area. He reiterated American determination "to maintain Israel's strength vis-à-vis its neighbors," called Syria aggressive and charged that it wanted to "drive Israel into the sea," and suggested that Israel was entitled to "defensible borders." The last point implied Israel should not have to withdraw totally from the territories won in the 1967 war. By the end of the month, seventy-one senators had endorsed the president's remarks. [116]

The secretary of state, who was in Europe at the time, saw the statements by Nixon and Kissinger as compromising his peace efforts. But an even greater threat to Rogers's proposals was the Soviet missile complex that had been moved close to the Suez Canal, creating the possibility of Soviet-Israeli confrontation. Kissinger reports, "I instituted urgent planning with unenthusiastic agencies who were still mumbling about forcing greater Israeli flexibility in negotiations irrelevant to the problem we faced." [117]

At this unlikely moment in late July, the Egyptians accepted Rogers's proposals, although with qualifications. The administration now tried to get Jerusalem's acquiescence. The Israelis had made it clear that they regarded

Rogers's cease-fire idea as a ruse, a risk hardly worth taking, and an agreement that the Egyptians would likely violate.[118]

Two weeks of negotiations with Israel ensued in which private assurances were conveyed, many of them by letter from the president, regarding future American stands toward peace negotiations and arms. Some of these assurances contradicted similar secret communications with the Arabs. Once Nixon publicly promised the Israelis that the cease-fire would not result in an Arab military buildup, the skeptical Meir government felt it had little choice but to accept Rogers's initiative.[119]

The apparent agreement by Egypt and Israel (as well as Jordan) to a cease-fire and indirect talks represented the first diplomatic breakthrough of an administration attacked at the time for its bellicosity. Moreover, the agreement appeared to vindicate Rogers's policy, which had been much criticized by Kissinger, Congress, and Israeli supporters. In his memoirs Nixon gives Rogers and Sisco the credit for this accomplishment.[120] The vindication was especially crucial to Rogers because this was the only major issue over which the State Department had prime authority.

Once Israeli acceptance had been gained, the conceptions that had dominated the administration's Mideast policy began to undermine the achievement. The State Department still saw the Israelis as the impediment to agreement. Certainly, Jerusalem was skeptical of the State approach. Therefore, the principal American objective was to implement the cease-fire before either party (most likely Jerusalem) could change its mind. When the Israelis shot down four Russian-piloted MIGs at the end of July, Washington's desire for speed was intensified. This State Department concern overrode the need to make cease-fire arrangements clear and verifiable in order to avoid violations or accusations of violations. The cease-fire was rushed into effect on 7 August without completing negotiations about what actions were prohibited and without completing arrangements for verifying compliance.

With the Russians and Egyptians placing missiles ever closer to the Suez Canal, monitoring the cease-fire became essential to place the peace process on a solid foundation. However, since the State Department team had predetermined that the first outcome of the negotiations would be Israeli withdrawal from the vicinity of the canal, it was concerned with neither the Soviet missile movements nor the Egyptian ability to cross the canal under missile protection. A withdrawal by the Israelis, whom the diplomats believed had caused the problem anyway, would obviate the need to monitor Egyptian and Soviet military maneuvers.

This analysis failed to comprehend that the Israelis would never negotiate if (1) the Egyptians would gain bargaining leverage by committing cease-fire violations and (2) the United States would not back Israeli positions with military and diplomatic assistance. Agreement to the cease-fire had strained the limits of Israeli flexibility. At the time, however, their agreement under pressure suggested to the State Department that Jerusalem could be pressed for even greater concessions as the peace process unfolded.

From the beginning, negotiations had been marked by much background wrangling with the Israelis over the framework of the political talks as well as the cease-fire arrangements.[121] When the Israelis complained almost immediately about Egyptian violations, U.S. officials were in no mood to listen. Egyptian violations of the agreements would undermine the Rogers strategy. Therefore, many in the bureaucracy involved with the Middle East did not want to admit that the violations had occurred. Typically, Secretary of Defense Laird said in mid-August, "I think the important thing for us is to move forward toward negotiations and not debate what went on twelve hours before or twelve hours after." About the same time Nixon reminded Rabin that the American people were in a "peace mood" and urged, "Israel must not permit herself to be blamed for refusing to negotiate." The president years later defended the American response on the grounds that even a violated cease-fire "established the United States as the honest broker accepted by both sides."[122] Although the president approved a rapid delivery of more sophisticated missiles for Israel, American restraint in the face of the initial violations may have encouraged the Egyptians to place more missiles closer to the canal.[123]

Evidence of violations mounted that simply could not be ignored. In an effort to salvage the peace process, the State Department released statements that protested weakly. By the end of August, Rogers was accusing Kissinger at a San Clemente meeting with the president "of seeking to foment a crisis by being so insistent on ceasefire violations." But American intelligence was gathering clearer evidence of increasing violations. Intelligence experts demonstrated to a dubious secretary of state how accurate the most sophisticated technology allowed intelligence analysts to be.[124]

Egyptian violations continued despite American and Israeli protests, and the Israelis announced that they would not return to the Jarring talks. Nixon ordered the sale of at least eighteen more Phantom jets to compensate Israel for the canal violations, hoping that building their military confidence would forestall an Israeli preemptive attack along the canal. The decision was made on 1 September at a meeting between the president, Kissinger, Rogers, and Sisco in San Clemente.[125] Hours later, the military procurement authorization bill was passed in the Senate containing an amendment offered by Senator Henry Jackson giving the president almost unlimited authority to provide Israel with arms to counter Soviet weapons in Egypt.[126] Jackson, increasingly concerned over Soviet involvement in Egypt, emerged as a major Israeli supporter on Capitol Hill.

The new military assistance could not compensate for the missile systems moved up to the canal, a development that eventually made feasible the Egyptian attack in October 1973. Like the first Phantom arms decision by Johnson, this one was made after disappointment with Russian actions, under congressional pressure, and despite bureaucratic opposition in the State Department and the Pentagon, especially on the civilian side. What was different was the crisis atmosphere in which this decision was concluded.

The new Israeli-American arms deal had barely been confirmed publicly when a delegation of ten Arab ambassadors met with Secretary Rogers in an attempt to stop the sale. Instead, the new military aid to Israel was being expanded and accelerated because of a crisis in Jordan. For months, while the administration had been intent on Cambodia and arranging a Suez cease-fire, internal conditions in Jordan had been deteriorating. Palestinian guerrillas had been acting beyond the king's control, backed by 17,000 Iraqi troops who had been in the eastern part of the country since the 1967 war. By 1 September two attempts had been made on Hussein's life and soon—to the horror of the State Department—the Jordanians had twice asked about Israeli intentions in the crisis, implying that if matters reached the boiling point they would acquiesce in Israeli intervention. Ironically, these inquiries were occurring just as Israel agreed to discuss with Jordan the future of the West Bank in then projected Jarring talks.[127]

The Jordan Crisis—September 1970

The new emergency erupted suddenly on 6 September when a group of radical Palestinians, worried that Rogers's initiative might somehow succeed, embarked on a spectacular multiplane hijacking. Worldwide attention focused on an abandoned airfield in northern Jordan where the guerrillas brought one Swiss, one British, and one American jet. They demanded a wholesale release of Palestinian terrorists held by the British, German, Swiss, and Israeli governments, while the innocent passengers suffered squalid conditions in the planes on the airfield. Although there was private squabbling among the four governments over how to proceed, American pressure succeeded in achieving a united public front.[128]

Washington at first concentrated on three objectives: (1) maintaining King Hussein's power during this further Palestinian challenge to his authority; (2) saving the hostages; (3) preventing the British, Germans, and Swiss from making separate deals with the terrorists. Within the administration, familiar divisions rapidly emerged. Rogers believed that the United States could do nothing. Nixon took the opposite position: he saw the crisis as an opportunity to crush the guerrillas in Jordan once and for all. If the Iraqis or Syrians intervened or it became necessary to move against the fedayeen, he preferred a unilateral American rather than Israeli response. Kissinger recognized the logistical difficulties of a U.S. intervention in Jordan, with military operations continuing in

Southeast Asia. These military problems explain why Secretary of Defense Laird and Chairman of the Joint Chiefs Moorer sympathized with Rogers's cautious approach. Indeed, Nixon directly ordered Laird to have American planes bomb guerrilla hideouts in Jordan. Laird, claiming bad weather as an excuse, failed to carry out the president's order. He recalled: "The Secretary of Defense can always find a reason not to do something. There's always bad weather."[129]

Despite the difficulties of intervening, Kissinger feared that the American position in the region would be undermined and "the entire Middle East would be revolutionized" if the king's authority collapsed because of the hostage crisis. The potential negative effect on the U.S. position was further heightened by Israel's reduced military effectiveness along the Suez Canal after Egyptian violations of the U.S.-approved cease-fire. Therefore, Kissinger devised a two-stage strategy for both action and protection against military failure. If the hostages needed to be evacuated, American forces would be used. But if Syria or Iraq were to intervene on behalf of the fedayeen, the United States would condone an Israeli response and America's primary role would be to deter Soviet action against the Israelis.[130]

As the president continued to insist on sole American intervention, Kissinger had two sets of contingencies prepared—for U.S. and Israeli intervention respectively—to protect the president from his "tendency toward impetuous declarations that he never expected to see implemented."[131] Kissinger's initiative suggests again how a determined NSC adviser can guide a president.

The Washington Special Action Group (WSAG), designed by the Nixon team to monitor international crises, met to work out strategy at least once a day for the seventeen days of the crisis. Kissinger was chairman and members included Sisco, the deputy secretary of defense, the undersecretary of state, the chairman of the Joint Chiefs, and the CIA head.[132]

Using this committee brought deliberations away from the State Department and into the White House, where the president stood by to accept recommendations and make decisions. The crisis therefore marked a turning point in the administration's approach to Arab-Israeli problems; for the first time the center of Mideast policy making shifted from the State Department to NSC.

While the United States increased its armed forces in the area and the Sixth Fleet maneuvered in the eastern Mediterranean, Rogers continued to maintain that Washington could do nothing and sought to calm the crisis atmosphere. Nixon remained determined to use American ground troops if necessary and to keep Israel out of the conflict. Kissinger for his part believed that "once we were embarked on confrontation, implacability was the best as well as the safest course."[133] Meanwhile, tension continued to rise: the three planes were blown up; the European governments freed seven Arab prisoners, and the guerrillas released some three hundred hostages and dispersed the rest in refugee camps in and around Amman. The last group of fifty-four was not released until the end of September.[134]

Finally, on the night of 15 September, the tenth day of the crisis, word arrived in Washington from the American ambassador in Amman and from the British government of a possible move by the king against the Fedayeen. Since the entire WSAG was attending a dinner in Virginia for the secretary of defense, the team helicoptered back to the White House for consultations. When the president received a report the next morning, he angrily questioned the necessity of an emergency WSAG meeting, nevertheless stressing his desire to avoid confrontation if possible but to use American forces if necessary. At this point Nixon was concerned that a crisis could disrupt his plans for a summit in Moscow. He then left to campaign in the Midwest on behalf of Republican candidates in the forthcoming congressional elections.[135]

The next day (17 September) Hussein finally ordered his army to move against the Fedayeen. The WSAG responded by encouraging the king with an intensified military buildup in the Mediterranean. In a telephone conversation with Kissinger, Nixon exulted from Chicago, "The main thing is there's nothing better than a little confrontation now and then, a little excitement." He then suggested to a group of astonished newspaper editors, in an "off-the-record" meeting, that the United States might intervene in the crisis—a statement that immediately created headlines around the world.[136] Kissinger had not recommended this statement and saw it as another of the president's "impetuous declarations." Nonetheless, he claims to have used the growing impression by the British and others that the United States might act precipitously as a means of persuading the Soviets and the Arab radicals not to seek Hussein's overthrow.[137]

Domestic reaction to the president's declaration was not positive but seemed irrelevant. The king was winning easily, since Iraqi forces did not intervene on the guerrillas' behalf as Washington had feared. The U.S.S.R. seemed to be seeking a way out of the crisis. Therefore, the situation in Jordan was not a major topic of discussion in an 18 September meeting of Nixon and Meir in Washington.[138]

Two days later Syrian tanks invaded Jordan. Key U.S. officials, anticipating an Iraqi invasion or a Fedayeen victory, were caught by surprise. Analysts have argued ever since whether the Syrians were acting with the Russians, but both Nixon and Kissinger had no question; knowing the Damascus government's close relationship with Moscow, they saw this development as a test by the Soviet Union. Their apprehension and determination were intensified by intelligence reports suggesting that the Soviets were building a nuclear submarine base in Cuba.[139] Just as news of Russian pilots in Egypt had redoubled Nixon's resolution to act in Cambodia the previous spring, so now the news of developments in Cienfuegos Bay reinforced his belief that the Soviet Union must be convinced of the administration's firmness.

Nixon and Kissinger thus took a global view of the impending crisis.

According to their recollections, Kissinger saw it as a challenge that "had to be met" because it would determine whether the Russian-backed radicals or the American-supported moderates would control the area. Nixon's position was even stronger:

> We could not allow Hussein to be overthrown by a Soviet-inspired insurrection. If it succeeded, the entire Middle East might erupt in war: the Israelis would almost certainly take preemptive measures against a Syrian-dominated radical government in Jordan; the Egyptians were tied to Syria by military alliances; and Soviet prestige was on the line with both the Syrians and the Egyptians. Since the United States could not stand idly by and watch Israel being driven into the sea, the possibility of a direct U.S.-Soviet confrontation was uncomfortably high. It was like a ghastly game of dominoes, with a nuclear war waiting at the end.[140]

The Syrian attack occurred on Sunday, 20 September, and the administration immediately issued a tough public statement, conveyed a stiff note to the Russians, secretly reassured King Hussein, and ordered conspicuous manuevers of American forces at selected locations to signal U.S. determination. It was still assumed, however, that either U.S. or Israeli forces would have to be deployed in Jordan. Therefore, the WSAG met all night Sunday to prepare a strategy. Although the president had informed Kissinger that he had changed his mind in favor of Israeli rather than American intervention, the NSC chief asked him not to reveal this new position to the WSAG so they would consider all remaining options.[141] As these WSAG deliberations began, a message arrived from Hussein requesting immediate air strikes. This communication reinforced the American preference for Israeli action. Rogers had decided to remain at home and be informed of developments by telephone, leaving the way clear for Kissinger to exercise his increased authority. In Rogers's absence, Sisco joined Kissinger to apprise Nixon of WSAG decisions. These included recommendations that certain American forces be placed on alert to demonstrate U.S. seriousness, especially if there was any doubt whether the Israelis would act. According to Kissinger, "In my view what seems 'balanced' and 'safe' in a crisis is often the most risky." Therefore, a leader "must be prepared to escalate rapidly and brutally to a point where the opponent can no longer afford to experiment."[142]

On this Sunday evening, Nixon approved the recommendations while bowling in the basement of the Executive Office Building and the decision was made on the alley to consult with the Israelis for the first time.[143] An "Israeli option" had been considered over the previous several days on the assumption that Israel would act in its own interests if Jordan were invaded. Kissinger called Rabin out of a New York dinner in honor of Prime Minister Meir. In this conversation he sought Israeli intelligence concerning the extent of the Syrian advance, but Rabin shrewdly guessed that the Americans had in mind Israeli air strikes on Syrian positions. The conversation had to be interrupted; unknown to Rabin an urgent new message had arrived in Washington from Hussein requesting immediate air strikes. After Rogers agreed that the United States should endorse Israeli air strikes in light of Hussein's requests, Kissinger and Sisco returned to the bowling alley and got the president's approval.[144]

The president arrived in Kissinger's office as the latter again phoned Rabin in New York to assure him that Washington "would look favorably upon an Israeli air attack" if the next morning's reconnaissance required it. Kissinger also offered "to make good the material losses" and "to do our utmost to prevent Soviet interference." After consulting with Meir, Rabin phoned back to report Israeli doubts that air strikes would be sufficient, and he promised to consult further after Israeli reconnaissance over the battle zone. As Meir returned to Israel, the White House arranged to fly Rabin back to Washington.[145]

At this point Nixon, Kissinger, and Rogers were united in supporting Israeli air strikes if necessary. (Yet there were serious differences within the administration. These disputes are suggested by Nixon's late night rejection of a Defense Department calculation that the Soviets might retaliate against Israel with air strikes if the Israelis acted.)[146] By Monday dawn, this three-way unity was undermined when Rabin phoned to say that ground forces might indeed be needed. Kissinger woke the president and urged him to consult with his senior advisers on a response, but the president instead decided to approve Israeli use of ground forces. The NSC chief nevertheless consulted with key advisers anyway and found predictable differences. Sisco agreed with him and with Nixon; Rogers and Laird were more cautious. Finally, the president agreed to an early morning NSC meeting and heard Rogers's objections. "Nixon finally decided that Sisco could inform Israel that the United States agreed to Israeli ground action in principle, subject to determining the King's view and consultation prior to a final decision."[147]

The Israeli mobilization, combined with American deployments, conveyed the message of imminent intervention to Damascus and Moscow. The Israelis, however, occupied the unusual position of acting in close coordination with Washington. Cautiously, they sought repeated clarifications from the administration.[148] The delay while Washington and Jerusalem consulted provided King Hussein's forces opportunity to rally, presumably bolstered by Washington's assurances and Israeli and American maneuvers.

Meanwhile, the Soviet chargé d'affaires in Washington conveyed his government's concern about the emerging crisis. On Tuesday, 22 September, the third day of Syrian intervention, Kissinger appeared at an Egyptian party "to show that our policy was not anti-Arab." The Soviet chargé stopped him and publicly expressed Kremlin opposition to the Syrian action, thereby implying that the United States had overreacted. In the midst of the party, Kissinger insisted that the Syrian tanks must withdraw; a cease-fire in place was insufficient.[149]

Although the Jordanians appeared victorious, the Syrian forces did not withdraw. When the crisis remained unsettled on Wednesday morning, Kissinger and Rogers disagreed whether to revoke the commitments to Israel. The president accepted Kissinger's point that a conflict between Jerusalem and Washington might lead the Syrians and Russians to question U.S. resolve concerning Syrian withdrawal from Jordan. That afternoon the point became moot when the White House received confirmation that the Syrian troops were departing. The Syrian invasion had been at best ineffective. Not only had the Jordanians, the Israelis, and the United States rallied to thwart it, but conflict within the ruling Ba'ath party had led the head of the Syrian Air Force, Hafez Assad, to decide not to enter the war. According to one report, U.S. diplomats and intelligence officials learned that he even sent secret assurances to Hussein. Under these conditions the Syrian intervention was doomed from the outset.[150]

The crisis over Jordan in September 1970 was a central experience in Washington's dealing with the Arab-Israeli dispute during the Nixon first term. It established precedents for American-Israeli relations and exacerbated the differences between the White House and the State Department over Mideast policy making. At the White House, the crisis was seen as a major diplomatic victory in a global and regional confrontation with the U.S.S.R. The Kremlin had been shown that Washington could thwart Moscow-sponsored designs. The administration had demonstrated to both Arab radicals and moderates that the United States could effectively back an Arab ally in a crisis and that close association with the Soviets could not assure success. From this perspective, the Israelis gained prestige from the effectiveness of their maneuvers, their caution in not acting precipitously, their willingness to cooperate with the White House, and their loyalty (especially compared to the skepticism of the European allies). At the State Department, however, the crisis was not seen as a global watershed thwarting Soviet moves in the area or as a regional turning point establishing Israel's usefulness. Rather, State saw the crisis as a diversion from the Arab-Israeli settlement that would transform the U.S. role in the area.

The sharper divisions within the administration would be reflected in Mideast developments over the next year. More important, the crisis appears to have led to a shift: the president became more sympathetic to Kissinger's perspective and more prepared to use Kissinger in Arab-Israeli diplomacy.

These contrasting attitudes toward the crisis were also reflected in academic and journalistic analyses. Some accounts stressed the administration's skill in crisis management, in thwarting Soviet designs, and in manipulating regional events. Others questioned whether the Jordan crisis in fact presented a Soviet challenge, citing particularly the nonparticipation of the Syrian Air Force under Hafez Assad (who would soon seize control of the government) and the haphazard entry of Syrian forces into northern Jordan. From this perspective, Nixon and Kissinger had overreacted.[151]

The crisis also reveals Nixon and Kissinger's penchant for granting secret assurances to gain specific tactical objectives. This aspect of their policy style has been more fully explored in relation to countries such as Vietnam, Cambodia, Chile, and Iran. The success of Hussein's forces obviated the need to complete the Israeli deal and so the record of the negotiations is left unfinished. If more specific assurances or written agreements between the two sides had been required, however, they undoubtedly would have involved behind-the-scenes backing for Israel and would have involved very few officials. This is suggested by Nixon's willingness to approve Israeli ground forces on the phone with Kissinger from their respective bedrooms at 5:00 A.M.[152]

In the light of the Yom Kippur War three years later, many observers have since argued that the 1970 crisis led Nixon and Kissinger to rely too heavily on the Israeli deterrent. According to this view, by depending on Israel to prevent hostilities, they reduced the impetus for major diplomatic initiatives. The September 1970 crisis encouraged the White House to let Israel assume responsibility for defending itself in the absence of a settlement as long as it had sufficient arms. This attitude made it difficult to accept the possibility of a successful Arab attack in October 1973.[153]

Yet the period following the 1970 crisis also coincided with major administration initiatives toward the Soviet Union, China, and Vietnam; with Egyptian disarray after the death of Nasser following the crisis; and with Arab disunity as exemplified by Jordanian instability that lingered well into 1971. By 1972, it was an election year in the United States. Even if the Jordan crisis had not occurred, the administration probably would not have pursued a major Mideast settlement and spent the time and political capital necessary for dramatic achievements during the remainder of the first term.

Although the Israelis exaggerated the lasting significance of their collaboration with the White House during the crisis, in later years they could cite a specific case in which they helped conduct American policy in the Middle East. Meanwhile, on a personal level, the crisis reinforced the close working relationship between Kissinger and Rabin and the mutual respect between Nixon and Meir. Israel's supporters and opponents now saw a White House more sympathetic to Israeli aid requests and arguments. However, Nixon and Kissinger's major goal remained to thwart Soviet objectives in the area and not to befriend Israel.[154] For Kissinger this meant creating situations where individual radical Arab states would see it in their interest to deal with the United States rather than Russia. Nonetheless, the partly accurate perception of new appreciation of Israel at the White House led to increased sympathy for the administration from some Israeli supporters. This development received considerable public attention during the 1972 presidential campaign.

Finally, the temporary transfer of authority from the State Department to the White House highlighted the different operative approaches before and after the crisis—and the increased inconsistencies of U.S. policy. Thus, the State Department's reluctant response to Egyptian violations of the Suez cease-fire was followed a month later by a forthright reaction to the Jordan crisis at the White House, followed in turn by State Department efforts to achieve a diplomatic breakthrough. These internal contradictions reflecting a divided administration with differing centers of authority in crisis and normal periods confused observers at home and abroad. In the end, the Israelis had an ill-founded confidence that they could ultimately count on White House intervention on their behalf. The Arabs dealing with the administration were frustrated by the failure of State Department-sponsored initiatives.[155]

These elements led to the miscalculations and explosions of October 1973. Meanwhile, after September 1970, the earlier State Department pressure for diplomatic settlement led to another Rogers initiative.

The Third Rogers Initiative: The Try for a Partial Settlement

After the Jordan crisis, the administration first endeavored to have the Israelis return to the suspended Jarring talks. This feat was accomplished in December by combining continued reassurances (particularly in a letter from Nixon to Meir encouraged by Rogers) with increased arms sales, the latter reflecting Israeli popularity in the Democratic-controlled Congress.[156]

During the fall, Congress clarified that Senator Jackson's original amendment to the military procurement bill included the sale of ground weapons as well as aircraft to Jerusalem. For the first time, Israel could purchase military equipment totally on credit and, in addition, the administration could sell Israel any conventional weapons required.[157] In this climate the administration took advantage of Israel's popularity on Capitol Hill by attaching to Israeli aid bills funds for less popular countries like Cambodia, Taiwan, and South Korea. Only when the president acted against Israel did he receive complaints from Congress.

Without White House clearance, Sisco had been urging Jarring to use the Rogers plan as a basis for new discussions. The impasse in the talks continued as the Israelis insisted on total peace and the Egyptians on the complete withdrawal of Israeli troops from the Sinai. Neither demand was acceptable to the other side. In frustration, Jarring in early February acceded to repeated American suggestions and altered his mediating role by presenting questions to the parties that recalled the original Rogers formula.[158]

Not surprisingly, this approach infuriated the Israelis. They objected to Jarring's questions and saw any procedure that did not lead to direct negotiations as interfering with peacemaking. Rogers in turn shared with Rabin his misgivings about what he saw as Israel's "evasiveness" and "negative" attitude.[159]

Egypt, under its new leader, Anwar Sadat (who was almost universally regarded as an interim appointment), responded to the Jarring initiative by becoming the first Arab state to agree formally to sign a peace agreement with Israel at the end of the peace process. Nonetheless, since the two sides remained at odds over all other issues (borders, refugees, content of peace) and since the U.N. mediator himself had become controversial, Jarring's diplomatic gamble resulted in the end of his mission.

Problems in negotiating were complicated by the continuing split within the American government. Jarring and the Egyptians were encouraged by the State Department to believe that the Rogers Plan was indeed the basis of U.S. diplomacy, but the White House did not approve these assurances beforehand.[160]

The gap between the two offices, however, was more a matter of style, timing, and priorities than of substance. Nixon and Kissinger were also displeased with the Israeli response to Jarring and soon afterward, in separate conversations between the NSC adviser and Rabin and the president and Israeli president Shazar, both Americans obliquely hinted that military assistance could be used as leverage to encourage increased Israeli diplomatic flexibility. Yet Nixon, preoccupied with other issues, was not prepared to undertake the monumental effort necessary to impose the Rogers Plan on the Israelis. In his annual State of the World message released the day before Israel's reply to Jarring, he came closer than ever to identifying himself with the Rogers Plan.[161]

The diplomacy conducted by State could not be carried through. Since its implementation depended entirely on pressuring Israel, the divisions at high levels of the American government made the policy as it was then envisioned unworkable. Because key officials insisted on persevering even without full presidential support and in the face of Kissinger's opposition, the outcome left both sides frustrated: Israel with the effort itself and Egypt with the unsuccessful initiatives.[162]

The failure to progress toward the comprehensive Rogers Plan led the United States, Egypt, and Israel to seek an interim settlement. The effort had begun even before Jarring's endeavor had foundered. Sadat had floated the idea of an interim accord in which Israeli troops would be removed from more than half of the Sinai in return for the reopening of the Suez Canal.[163] The concept was based on a Dayan suggestion of two months earlier, but Dayan proposed only that the Israelis withdraw a few kilometers on their side, enough to allow the Egyptians to clear the canal. Sadat insisted that Egyptian troops cross to the Israeli side of the canal. He linked the interim arrangement to Israel's commitment to return all territories captured in 1967 and to accommodation with the Palestinians.[164] Jerusalem regarded these elements as dangerous and suspected Egyptian motives. But Washington saw Sadat's initiative as a major breakthrough.[165] These differing interpretations in the three capitals marred discussions over the next several months. Such differences further exacerbated divisions within the administration.

During spring 1971, discussions of an Egyptian-Israeli interim accord dominated Mideast diplomacy. This development included three milestones: (1) it was the first discussion since the 1967 War to take a piecemeal rather than an overall approach to an Arab-Israeli settlement; (2) it marked replacement of the U.N. by the United States as the major mediating instrument; and (3) Henry Kissinger emerged as a factor in negotiations. These new conditions were evident in a mid-March 1971 visit by Foreign Minister Eban to Washington. The president had asked his NSC adviser to consider negotiations. On this occasion Kissinger complained angrily to Eban and Rabin about the lack of specificity and focus in Israel's proposals. But the Israelis were having an even harder time with Rogers. When Eban conducted an unprecedented closed meeting with forty United States senators, Rogers responded by holding the first closed session with the entire Senate that any secretary of state had held since the Second World War. Israel's position was convincingly presented as inflexible.[166]

This beginning was inauspicious. There were even serious differences between Cairo and Jerusalem whether the agreement that they were seeking was "interim" (the Egyptians preferred this word because of its tentative connotation) or "partial" (the Israeli preference that suggested a concrete accord). Without pausing to clarify these questions or improve the U.S.-Israeli relationship, Rogers launched his third initiative for a limited settlement along the canal. When the Israelis tried again to formulate proposals, Kissinger told Rabin he found their suggestions so inadequate that he would not become involved. He declared that Israel had not made enough concessions or taken specific enough positions to allow serious negotiations. As Kissinger had quickly realized, Jerusalem and Cairo were still far apart on the nature of Israeli withdrawals in the Sinai, the corresponding pledges of nonbelligerence that Egypt would offer in return and Egyptian demands for Israeli concessions on the Palestinians.[167]

Rogers, however, was more optimistic; despite Kissinger's skepticism, Nixon approved the secretary's trip to Egypt and Israel to explore an agreement.[168] This trip in early May 1971 was the first by a secretary of state to the Arab-Israeli arena since Dulles's fact-finding visit in spring 1953, but the timing was inopportune. Forty-eight hours before Rogers arrived in Egypt, Sadat arrested his vice president, Ali Sabry, upon learning of an attempted coup against his government. Since Sabry was generally assumed to be the Soviet favorite among the Egyptian leadership, American officials anticipated a possible new policy direction in Cairo. Indeed, after discussions with Sadat, both Rogers and Sisco were encouraged in their belief that the Egyptian president actually sought a settlement. He also seemed to be interested in better relations with the United States and in reducing his dependence on the Soviet Union. Rogers and Sisco even got the impression that the new Egyptian president would begin expelling the Russians if the United States could obtain an "acceptable" peace settlement from the Israelis.[169]

The two Americans were therefore hopeful when they arrived in Jerusalem, but the secretary quickly found himself in a "sharp" and "animated" disagreement with Meir over Sadat's intentions. When he met with the full Cabinet, he was also displeased at having to listen to several ministers discuss Jewish history, American policy, and the required conditions of a settlement. The secretary of state contributed to the tension. When taken by air to see Sharm el Sheikh, he refused to fly directly over Israeli-occupied territory, lest this act be interpreted as showing American support for the Israeli position.[170]

Later in the visit, Sisco met with Defense Minister Dayan, the most vocal and innovative Israeli advocate of a limited approach. As a result, the atmosphere of the talks with Meir and the Israeli Cabinet improved so much that Rogers sent Sisco back to Cairo with a summary of Dayan's ideas, which Sadat seemed to view favorably.[171]

The secretary was now more hopeful. During the first staff meeting after his return to Washington, he leaned over to Sisco and laughingly suggested, "We may still come to share the Nobel Peace Prize!"[172] Kissinger's view was more negative. "Rogers's trip had no result except to get Dayan in some trouble at home when the differences between his government's position and his own became publicly known."[173]

Subsequent events quickly undercut whatever progress Rogers may have made. First, a Soviet-Egyptian Friendship Treaty was signed in Cairo after a hastily arranged trip by President Podgorny. It was weaker than documents that the Russians were signing during this period with other countries. The treaty suggested Soviet concern over the downfall of their Egyptian protégé, Sabry, and over Sadat's imprisonment, against Soviet wishes, of their closest allies among Nasser's successors.[174]

In Washington the usual differences between Rogers and Kissinger emerged. Rogers thought that the treaty might lead Sadat to be more flexible because the Russians had strengthened his hand. Kissinger, on the other hand, wished once again to delay the settlement process to avoid rewarding a Soviet client. Nixon stood ambivalent between his advisers, but he appeared not to share Kissinger's suspicion of the peace process. He wrote on one of Kissinger's memoranda, "We must not allow this [the Friendship Treaty] to be a pretext for escalation of arms to Israel. We should assist only in response to incontrovertible evidence of Soviet military aid which we evaluate as significantly changing the balance of power."[175]

Sadat's emerging dissatisfaction with the Soviets was signaled by a curious event in July. A pro-Communist coup in the Sudan was reversed through Sadat's aid when he flew loyal Sudanese troops from the area of the Suez Canal to Khartoum in Russian-built planes. The White House felt it was still too early to act on the basis of a potential shift in Cairo.[176]

These confusing signals on the future of Soviet-Egyptian relations were accompanied by a devastating U.S. diplomatic error, which destroyed whatever enthusiasm may have existed among the Egyptians and Israelis for an agreement. Internal divisions over the strategy for peace were not restricted to the Israeli and American governments. The Egyptian foreign minister, Mahmoud Riad, was opposed to the interim settlement approach. Sadat therefore dealt with the American government through other officials. During the ongoing discussions that followed the Rogers visit to Cairo, Donald Bergus, the U.S. representative in Cairo (in the continued absence of diplomatic relations), told Egyptian officials that their ideas could be expressed more positively. With their agreement, he produced a memorandum for them to consider. Egyptian diplomats rewrote his ideas in a more negative style but when their formal position on an interim settlement was presented in early June, it was similar to the original Bergus draft. When the foreign minister learned of the Bergus or "phantom" memorandum— as it was being called—he leaked its contents to Joseph Kraft, the American journalist who happened to be visiting Cairo in late June. Kraft promptly revealed the information in a 27 June column in the *Washington Post*.[177]

The result was an uproar affecting not only the Egyptians and Israelis but the continuing Kissinger-Rogers dispute as well. The Israeli embassy complained immediately to the State Department. The Israelis could not believe that Bergus would have acted without some authority, especially because Sadat had been attempting for weeks to maneuver the United States into furnishing a specific written position. Since the Israelis had previously conveyed their vehement opposition to the positions in Bergus's notes, the incident heightened Jerusalem's suspicions of American moves.[178]

The Egyptians were disillusioned when the United States did not endorse their position, as the bogus Bergus memorandum had led them to expect. Instead, the State Department disavowed the Bergus note as formal American policy.[179] Sadat now proclaimed 1971 as "the year of decision," suggesting that war might occur by the end of December if some settlement had not been arranged.[180]

Kissinger also doubted that an experienced diplomat like Bergus would act without his superiors' approval and he was furious that the White House had been uninformed on the developments surrounding the discussions. It appears that Rogers had not authorized the memorandum beforehand, but since it did represent his department's general approach, he tried to move negotiations toward the next round of discussions quickly after the news leaked.[181]

The secretary of state now proposed sending Sisco to Israel to work on an interim settlement. Kissinger resented the posing of this new suggestion on the very day, 1 July, that he was leaving for China on the famous secret trip that produced Nixon's visit to Beijing the following year. While on this trip, he persuaded the president to delay a decision until he could be present, and as an excuse Nixon scheduled an NSC meeting on future Middle East strategy for Kissinger's return. At that meeting Rogers pressed for the Sisco trip, Nixon complained about the pro-Israeli lobby, and Laird opposed further sales of advanced aircraft to Israel.[182] Since the Sisco trip was the only major idea then being considered for continuing the discussions about an interim settlement, it was approved.

Sisco failed to make progress in Jerusalem. The Israelis had little reason to ease their negotiating stance after the Bergus memorandum. Several weeks earlier, Jerusalem had requested an additional 40 Phantom jets to counter ever-increasing Russian arms in Egypt and the Soviets' expanding role there.[183] Sisco now suggested that the United States would not only sell Israel the 40 planes but 110 jets over a three- to four-year period. This was the first time that the United States even hinted of a long-term arms commitment to the Israelis, but the quid pro quo demanded by the administration was that Jerusalem accept the State Department's interim settlement. The conditions included a larger pullback than the Israeli Cabinet would accept, agreement to a token Egyptian force stationed on the Israeli side of the canal, and a two- to three-year cease-fire rather than a permanent one. The Cabinet turned Sisco down. Since no new Phantoms were scheduled to be delivered after 1 July 1971, the administration, in effect, imposed another embargo on Phantom sales to Israel.[184]

Kissinger opposed this concept of withholding arms until Israel altered its negotiating stance, feeling this policy would raise Arab expectations while making Israeli concessions even more difficult to obtain.[185] Whenever Washington had tied weapons sales to a particular Israeli diplomatic stance, as in 1968 and 1970, the Israelis had responded that they would not alter their position until the arms were promised.[186] The linkage of American arms with Israeli flexibility was a psychological and diplomatic trap for each American administration, resulting in frustrations for both Washington and Jerusalem. Although Kissinger understood this situation in 1971, he took the same ineffective stance in 1975.

In summer 1971, the State Department had adopted the Sisco approach because the Rogers team was running out of options for resolving the deadlock. Sisco admitted to Rabin that—based on Dayan's position—State had concluded that Israel would agree to a substantial withdrawal and had so informed Sadat. The Egyptian president soon accused Rogers of misleading him with false optimism.[187]

In an almost desperate effort to avoid a stalemate, Rogers presented in early October a six-point proposal to the U.N. General Assembly balancing the positions of both sides. The problems confronting the secretary of state were impressive: each issue of the limited settlement along the canal raised other problems. Where would the new lines be located and how long would they last?

What would be the connection between this accord and a final settlement? How long would the cease-fire along the canal be? What type of authority would replace the Israelis as they departed? Would it include Egyptian military and civilian personnel and would the U.N. have a presence? Who would control evacuated territory? If the canal were reopened, would the Israelis have navigation rights? If agreement were reached, what would happen next? On all issues in dispute Rogers assumed an evenhanded posture, pleasing neither side.[188]

The Emergence of Henry Kissinger

As the third Rogers initiative failed, Henry Kissinger became actively involved in Arab-Israeli diplomacy for the first time. Nixon was interested in preventing Mideast-oriented disturbances at home or abroad during an election year, and he therefore directed Kissinger to suppress any crisis. Thus, after fall 1971, Rogers no longer directed the administration's approach to an Arab-Israeli settlement alone.[189]

Kissinger abandoned Rogers's attempt to create conditions for a specific agreement. Rather, he wanted to draw the Arabs and Russians into protracted discussions until one or both moderated their stances. Where Rogers used leverage to gain Israeli concessions as a first step, Kissinger began by exploring Soviet interest in moderation. Kissinger was also more skeptical about an interim settlement, believing that it would take almost as much pressure on Israel to achieve the limited settlement discussed in summer 1971 as would be required for an overall agreement. If a partial accord was the only alternative, the NSC adviser favored an even more limited agreement that would not outline a final settlement.[190]

The effect of this changed perspective was more confusion in American policy. While Rogers still sought Israeli concessions, Kissinger held behind-the-scenes discussions with the Russians and explored secret Egyptian contacts. The State Department hinted that Israel would not receive further Phantom jets without concessions on the interim settlement, while the Soviets increased their assistance to the Egyptians. Kissinger's intensified involvement meant that two diplomatic strategies for the Middle East were being pursued simultaneously, and each was undercutting the other.

Nixon and Kissinger had reason to appear conciliatory. In July Nixon had made the stunning announcement that he would visit Beijing the following February, and he continued to hope that in response to discussions on the Middle East, the Soviets would be more helpful over Vietnam. Therefore, as Rogers's latest initiative petered out in fall 1971, Kissinger's new effort to discuss the Middle East with the Soviet Union seemed a chance worth taking. The Soviets, who were already dealing with Kissinger on other issues, were first to realize the new order in Washington. The Kremlin wanted Kissinger and

Dobrynin to take up the subject in their "back channel," especially as Moscow was in effect the intermediary between Washington and Cairo. Months of sporadic talks ensued, in which it emerged that the Soviets would not take a stand different from the Arabs.[191]

Kissinger's occasional pre-summit discussions with the Soviets complicated relations with the Israelis beyond their disputes with Rogers. When speaking to Rabin, Kissinger repeatedly held that a partial agreement required prior Soviet-American consensus and that specific Israeli proposals were inadequate, again raising Israeli fears of an imposed peace. Although he personally believed the Soviet proposals were unacceptable, the NSC adviser nonetheless asked the Israelis to consider them seriously (although their rejection was foreordained). Tensions were inevitably raised, although Kissinger regularly assured the Israelis, as Rogers had not, that all proposals would be coordinated between Jerusalem and Washington.[192] This tactic illustrated Kissinger's negotiating style: to raise needless negotiating difficulties that could be discarded or used as concessions when convenient.

As Rabin and Kissinger developed their own back channel, American-Israeli discussions intensified. As a consequence, arrangements were made for another Nixon-Meir summit to be held in early December 1971. By this time a turning point had occurred; Sadat had visited Moscow in October and received promises of increased military assistance. This announcement caused consternation in Washington. Ironically, Sadat's dissatisfaction when the Soviets did not fulfill their pledges later exacerbated his disillusionment with Moscow.[193]

A familiar pattern reappeared. First, Rogers indicated publicly that the administration would reconsider its limits on military assistance to Israel in light of the Russian announcement. Second, majorities in both houses of Congress endorsed resolutions calling for increased assistance to Israel.[194] Third, the Israelis announced that they would not participate in American-sponsored "proximity" talks* with Egypt until another arms deal with the United States was concluded. Fourth, the Egyptians strengthened the Israeli case by repeating statements that 1971 would be the "year of decision."[195]

Near the end of November a group of eight senators from both parties met with Secretary of State Rogers to urge the sale of more Phantom jets to Israel. Rogers was unsympathetic: further sales would impede the peacemaking process and increase the Israeli "intransigent attitude." One senator was incensed and bluntly informed Rogers that he would take the issue to the president. Rogers was confident: "That is your privilege, but I am sure that the President will back me up."[196]

Thus a divided Washington greeted Prime Minister Meir at the begin-

---

* Proximity talks had Egyptian and Israeli delegations located separately but nearby, as U.S. representatives shuttled between them. Rogers had proposed the talks in October to facilitate negotiations on a limited settlement.

ning of December on a trip that became a turning point in American-Israeli relations. In a conversation with Kissinger, the prime minister intimated that her position on key points in the interim settlement was more flexible than before.[197] At their meeting, the Israeli and American leaders achieved a major understanding, with the details added in follow-up discussions between Meir and Kissinger and then between Sisco, Rabin, and other officials over the next several weeks. There were several consequences of these discussions, which relegated Rogers to a reduced role.

1. The United States agreed to supply Israel with new Phantoms and Skyhawks over three years to avoid the controversies that erupted when short-term deals expired. This arrangement became the first long-term arms deal between Washington and Jerusalem.

2. Both sides decided to concentrate on a limited rather than overall settlement of the dispute with the Arabs, with the understanding that this would not bind Israel to the Rogers Plan.

3. Consideration of an interim settlement would henceforward be conducted on the two tracks preferred by Nixon and Kissinger: one public and one secret. On one track Sisco would conduct proximity talks between Egypt and Israel. Secretly, Kissinger and Dobrynin would explore Soviet attitudes towards the Middle East. The Americans viewed the secret meetings as necessary in the light of the forthcoming Moscow summit, but Nixon and Kissinger promised that the discussions would not result in an accord opposed by the Israelis or in pressure on them to accept the superpowers' deal.

Meanwhile, Rabin and Kissinger would also continue secret discussions, although there was still no secret channel between Kissinger and the Egyptians. This weakness was highlighted when the Egyptians refused in February 1972 to join the projected proximity talks.[198]

The new intertwined arrangements with Israel had a variety of motives. First, there were signals to be conveyed to the Russians and the Egyptians. Nixon wanted to hold a position of strength at the Moscow summit. The Kremlin had been escalating its assistance to Egypt while Sadat continued to threaten war, hardly enhancing U.S. credibility. Nixon felt that an unrelated international development had given him an opportunity to demonstrate his determination. In late 1971 India, backed by Russia, had taken advantage of an internal Pakistan crisis to create Bangladesh by force. The Indian case was popular in the United States, especially in view of past oppression of the Bengalis within the eastern sector of the Pakistani state and the suffering of Bengali refugees within India. But, in the jargon of the time, Nixon and Kissinger "tilted" toward Pakistan. They saw the crisis as a test between the two superpowers and, given the Pakistani government's assistance in establishing contacts with Beijing, they saw supporting Pakistan as a means of strengthening the new relationship with China.

In Nixon and Kissinger's view, the Middle East and South Asia were related. On the one hand, supporting Pakistan demonstrated to the Kremlin that if it backed the Egyptians in a war against the Israelis, the American response would be "even sharper." On the other hand, an understanding with the Israelis (and especially a long-term arms deal) signaled U.S. seriousness both to Moscow and Cairo. Indeed, Sadat later gave Soviet preoccupation with South Asia and the American response to that crisis as the reason he allowed 1971 to pass inconclusively. The Russians could not increase their assistance to him because of their involvement in the Indian-Pakistani crisis. [199]

Second, the new arrangement with the Israelis vindicated Kissinger's view that withholding arms from Israel to encourage flexibility actually toughened Jerusalem's stand in negotiations. According to this argument, labeled "killing Israel with kindness" by opponents, only a confident Israel would make the concessions necessary for an Arab-Israeli agreement. [200] Besides, as Kissinger pointed out, the Israelis received their arms anyway, after political disputes had weakened the U.S. role in negotiations. [201]

For their part, the Israelis were anxious to involve the White House in the peace process. They sensed greater sympathy in Nixon and Kissinger than in Rogers, even though Kissinger made it clear to Rabin that he entered only the negotiations that might succeed and that Israel would have to make difficult concessions if he became engaged. [202]

Third, in the light of Rogers's failure, increasing arms to Israel fit Nixon and Kissinger's global policies. Both leaders used arms sales to gain support from foreign leaders. Arms sales became a logical instrument of the Nixon Doctrine as the president sought to pursue an active international role in a period when Vietnam cast a pall over foreign activity. The Israelis and some of their supporters saw Nixon's largesse in 1972 as high-minded generosity. Yet the policy was in the pattern of Vietnamization, as were similar major increments in arms sales to Iran and Cambodia. The results in these countries proved to be disastrous. As the number of Middle East countries receiving arms from the United States proliferated over the next several years, the benefits to Israel ultimately diminished.

Indeed, given the way that the Nixon administration functioned, only internal divisions explain the delays in major arms sales to Israel. Rogers and Laird hesitated to sell arms to Jerusalem in large quantities, fearing that the Arabs might become more antagonistic to American policy; the Israelis might become less flexible in peace discussions and possibly launch a preemptive attack in a crisis; and the regional military balance of power might be changed. Nixon also worried that arms sales to Israel might have negative effects on reestablishing diplomatic relations with the Arabs, but Kissinger believed that limited but steady arms sales would lead to greater Israeli flexibility and serve as signals to the Russians and Arabs. Only when his view finally prevailed in late 1971 was a long-term arms deal possible.

Fourth, Kissinger emerged victorious because by the end of 1971, Nixon was more receptive to his arguments. Rogers had failed to win an interim settlement and the president wanted the area free of domestic and international controversies in an election year.[203] Moreover, various factors reinforced the new approach toward Israel: the impending Moscow summit, the Indian-Pakistani war, Sadat's threats, Russian assistance to Egypt, Kissinger's emerging involvement in Mideast matters and his novel strategy.

In this context, domestic politics supported an arms deal made for geopolitical reasons. Many congressmen vociferously called for more assistance to Israel, a cry dangerous to ignore in a presidential campaign. Increased aid to Israel might also earn Jewish votes and, even more likely, funds from major Jewish contributors, especially because it might give key leaders who wanted to support Nixon an excuse for doing so.[204]

After the arms deal with Israel, emerging political conditions favored the president in his reelection campaign. Senator George McGovern, the eventual Democratic nominee, frightened many prominent Jews, including major Jewish contributors, by his dovish record on defense spending, his antimilitary stance in foreign affairs, his positions on some domestic issues, and his criticism of Israeli reliance on military force for security.[205] In the critical California primary in June, Hubert Humphrey made an issue of the South Dakotan's supposed waffling on Israel. Nixon's delighted reelection committee began to cite his close working relationship with Israeli leaders and the record of the president's aid to Israel—the highest amounts of any administration to that point. Ignoring the administration's frequent differences with Jerusalem and the role played by a Democratic Congress in pressing for the increased aid, the Republicans now argued (with September 1970 as evidence) that Nixon (unlike McGovern) would support Israel strongly in another Mideast crisis.[206]

Ambassador Rabin seemed to agree. In a June interview on Israeli radio, he praised Nixon's address to Congress upon returning from the Moscow summit. Rabin noted that Nixon had gone further than any previous president in vocal support for Israel. Rabin was accused of supporting Nixon for president and interfering in U.S. domestic politics. He responded that he was only stating "a fact" and that he had also expressed gratitude to senators and congressmen who had supported Israel.[207]

This controversy focused even more attention on the issue of Nixon's sympathy for Israel against McGovern's. When the votes were counted in November, more Jews supported the president than in 1968 (39 percent vs. 17 percent), but Jews and blacks (89 percent for McGovern) were the only two discernible ethnic groups that voted a majority for the Democratic candidate.[208]

As the election campaign unfolded, behind-the-scenes controversies over Mideast diplomacy continued with the Israelis. Before the Moscow summit, Kissinger continued to pursue his contacts with the Israelis and the Russians. The Israelis were treated to hints of secret deals between Moscow and Washington. Rabin recalled, "Everytime I approached Kissinger he seemed to have changed his tune—alternately soothing me and subtly threatening that heaven alone knew what would happen in Moscow." Even as Kissinger conveyed his displeasure at supposed Israeli inflexibility, he was eliciting concessions from Rabin and Dayan on an interim settlement that contributed to the first Egyptian-Israeli disengagement discussions after October 1973.[209]

At the May 1972 Moscow summit, Kissinger concluded that the Russians would not alter their rigid backing of all Arab demands. Therefore, he successfully used the pressures of a summit format to get "the blandest possible formulation in the communiqué." The result was gratitude from the Israelis, who had been led to fear a possible sellout of their interests, and fury at the Kremlin from Sadat, who thought with good reason that the superpowers had endorsed the status quo.[210] In the declarations signed at the end of these meetings, the United States and the Soviet Union agreed to inform each other of potential local conflicts in order to dampen regional instabilities and limit any confrontations of their own. These declarations clearly fit the Middle East and would restrict Sadat's ability to consider war as long as Russian troops were on his soil.[211]

While negotiating with Gromyko in Moscow, Kissinger already knew that he was progressing toward a new relationship with Egypt. Nearly two months earlier Sadat had asked for secret, high-level talks with the White House, bypassing the two countries' foreign ministers. Kissinger invited the Egyptian president to send an emissary to Washington after the summit. Sadat responded several weeks later that a messenger would come only if and when the United States wished to discuss new approaches in the area.[212]

This ambiguous epistle was followed shortly by the shocking mid-July news that Sadat was abruptly expelling Soviet military advisers from his country and resuming control of the military installations the Russians had occupied. The effectiveness of Kissinger's strategy—especially the delays at the summit—may have been confirmed beyond his expectations by this act, but as Kissinger himself noted in a lengthy analysis for the president, the eviction could also mean that the Kremlin would have less ability to restrain future Egyptian offensive operations.[213] The prime conclusion of all Washington analyses, including Kissinger's, was that Sadat's dramatic step had bought time (at least until after the presidential election) to consider a new policy initiative.[214] There seemed ample opportunity to explore the new channel with Egypt and prepare for general, face-to-face meetings in a "spirit of goodwill," rather than honor the original Egyptian proposal of discussing specific new ideas.[215] In the end, Hafez Ismail, Kissinger's Egyptian counterpart as Sadat's national security adviser, did not come to Washington until February 1973, the trip delayed from the previous fall by the administration's preoccupation with events leading to the end of the Vietnam War in January.

With Ismail's trip set, Nixon was becoming frustrated with Kissinger's leisurely pace. As he noted in his diary on 3 February in what he labels "the first of several similar notes":

I spoke to Henry about the need to get going on the Mideast. I am pressing him hard here because I don't want him to get off the hook with regard to the need to make a settlement this year because we won't be able to make it next year and, of course, not thereafter with '76 coming up. He brought that up himself so apparently the message is getting through. What he's afraid of is that Rogers, *et al.* will get a hold of the issue and will try to make a big public play on it and that it will break down.[216]

By the end of the first Nixon term, there was reason for concern about differences between State and the NSC over the Middle East. Kissinger was now pursuing his own initiatives, as in the back channel with Egypt, without the knowledge of the State Department. The latter, however, was proceeding in diplomatic efforts without informing the White House. For example, the White House did not know about key discussions taking place in mid-1972 to get the Egyptians to agree to proximity talks. (Sadat rejected the proposal in June, but the State Departments efforts continued.) The result of this divergence was that foreign governments—especially Egypt's—had a better notion of competing U.S. government positions than the administration itself. Sadat, for example, could select the American proposals and agency he preferred. Moreover, State and the NSC each received routine information from unsuspecting American field representatives that revealed efforts pursued by their adversary unit within the administration.[217]

This disarray may have given the governments of Egypt and Israel alternatives when they became disillusioned with regular diplomatic channels. Yet it is difficult to agree with Kissinger when he claims in his memoirs, "strangely enough, except for the nervous strain on the participants, our procedures did no damage."[218] Although it perhaps could not have been prevented, the United States did not avert the Mideast war in October 1973, which proved costly to American interests. The divisions within the Nixon administration certainly contributed to this failure by confusing local parties and hindering development of a coherent American policy that might have more thoroughly addressed the problems in the area.

Conclusion

In reviewing the record of the Nixon first term in the Arab-Israeli dispute, the feature that stands out is the fierce competition between the secretary of state and the NSC adviser. No previous administration had endured such a high-level and prolonged dispute on Arab-Israeli matters among the president's key aides. Debates within previous administrations over issues like the birth of Israel, the Baghdad Pact, the Johnson Plan, or the Red Sea Regatta were not of the same magnitude or duration as the Rogers-Kissinger confrontations. When differences occurred under Truman, Kennedy, and Johnson over Arab-Israeli policy, the dissenters were usually White House operatives responsible for domestic affairs. Clifford, Niles, Feldman, Roche, McPherson, Eugene Rostow, or even Goldberg possessed neither the authority nor the inclination to challenge the secretary of state or to conduct their own diplomacy. Each might act at moments of crisis in specific channels—as did Niles over the partition vote at the U.N., Clifford in confronting Marshall over recognition of Israel, Feldman on aid issues, or Roche in rewriting a State Department speech during the May 1967 crisis—but only under strict presidential restraints. None of these officials could act as a second secretary of state, which became Kissinger's role as the first term neared its conclusion. Under Eisenhower, bureaucratic debate never reached the highest administrative echelon.

In the first Nixon term, Mideast policy was contested by two decision-making teams with different strategies, overseen by a president who could not decide which approach he preferred. As suggested by the ease with which Kissinger later moved into the State Department, Nixon, Rogers, and Kissinger all shared a similar goal: progress toward an Arab-Israeli settlement as a means of improving relations with the Arab states and of reducing Soviet influence and the chances of Soviet-American confrontation in the region.

The deep divisions were over how to achieve these goals. The secretary of state's strategy was regional; it was designed to confront the major problems between the Arab states and Israel. Impatient to move forward, Rogers often saw the Israelis as the major impediment and was prepared to withhold arms to extract concessions. For Rogers, concern with Russia was secondary to the immediate goal of an Arab-Israeli agreement. At one point, for example, he even hinted that as part of the guarantees for a settlement, the United States would consider the participation of Russian soldiers in a Mideast peacekeeping force.[219]

Kissinger, less involved with the area, took a more relaxed attitude toward reaching a settlement, believing that only when the Russians or one or more of the key Arab states had moderated their stance could progress be made. Central to Kissinger's policy were reducing Soviet support for Arab ambitions and expelling the Russians from primary involvement with key states. Both these objectives seemed possible when the Russians accepted vague wording at the Moscow summit and Sadat ejected their military advisers from Egypt several weeks later. Therefore, Kissinger was prepared to build up Israel's strength, which he later saw as a major factor in Moscow's 1972 summit restraint.[220] He was reluctant to press a settlement until Moscow had been weakened, lest the Kremlin receive the credit among Arabs for diplomatic success.

Nixon seems to have supported the views of both men in part. Like Kissinger, he saw the Soviet threat in the area as central and was prepared to condone, on particular occasions, increased arms sales to Israel without major changes in Jerusalem's diplomatic posture. However, he also shared Rogers's desire to move forward and was prepared to approve repeated State Department initiatives, especially in the light of his determination to improve relations with the Arab states. Like Rogers he was frequently dissatisfied with Israeli diplomatic positions, a view shared by Kissinger as he became more intensively involved. On the other hand, the president's perspective on the international role of military force was closer to the views of both Kissinger and the Israelis than to Rogers's emphasis on the legalities of negotiation.

In addition to unresolved conflicts in the president's own views, his reluctance to confront individuals directly compounded the confusion over American policy. The president could complain privately about specific Israeli acts and policies, but in meetings with Meir and Rabin he was usually "cordial, courteous, and vague."[221] In like fashion, he repeatedly avoided overruling Rogers on specific initiatives, especially because he had made the Mideast Rogers's responsibility. Even when the secretary of state announced the "Rogers Plan" before rather than after a scheduled NSC meeting to review Mideast policy, he acquiesced in Rogers's position. Similarly, even when the Egyptians violated the Suez cease-fire arranged by the secretary of state, the president did not move rapidly to overrule Rogers's cautious response to a challenge that threatened the secretary's greatest achievement at Foggy Bottom.

The outcome of these internal differences and the president's own ambivalence was a stunning series of turnabouts. The administration that more than any of its predecessors cooperated with the Soviets in the Mideast through the Big Two and Big Four talks, by the end of its first term threatened the U.S.S.R. in Egypt, the country of most significant influence in the area (after having confronted Moscow starkly over Jordan in September 1970). An administration that openly withheld arms to Israel in spring 1970, even after increased Russian involvement in Egypt, was by early 1972 concluding the first long-term arms arrangement with Jerusalem. An administration that openly issued a comprehensive plan for reaching an Arab-Israeli settlement (the Rogers Plan) found itself by the end of the term secretly discussing negotiations to initiate a mere interim settlement on the Suez Canal.

Of course, all U.S. administrations have suffered inconsistencies: given the complex policy choices faced by the United States in the Middle East, they are inevitable. Any administration, no matter how organized, would have had problems in developing an effective policy toward the area in the wake of the Six-Day War, the Arab frustrations it produced, and the continuing Vietnam War. Nixon and Kissinger's efforts to create new international relations, symbolized by the summits in Beijing and Moscow, further reduced the time and energy available for the Middle East. Nixon clearly anticipated that the Middle East would be the major area to be addressed after Vietnam, and late in the 1972 campaign he promised a new Mideast peace initiative after the election.[222] Yet the differences in personality, tactics, and style between the secretary of state and the NSC chief, and their conflict over who would control Middle East policy, assured fundamental inconsistencies in policy—compounded by the president's ambivalence. Middle East policy during the first term was thus conducted with a marked lack of coherence, in contrast to other issues that went through the orderly Nixon decision-making apparatus. In the term shared by Nixon with Gerald Ford this decision-making confusion evaporated.

7

NIXON AND FORD
The Kissinger Shuttle at Center Stage

After Nixon's second election, events at home and abroad dramatically altered the formulation of foreign policy, especially toward the Middle East. For the first several months of the second term, the Rogers-Kissinger schism continued. In August the president announced that Kissinger would replace Rogers as secretary of state and remain NSC chief, thereby ending the schizoid policy that had undermined Mideast strategy in the first term. Watergate began to absorb the president's attention, leaving him less involved in conducting foreign policy; this further strengthened Kissinger's domination, making him the most powerful secretary of state since John Foster Dulles.

On 6 October 1973, a coordinated Egyptian-Syrian surprise attack on Israel altered the Middle East political landscape. Suddenly, worldwide pressure came to bear on the administration's Middle East policy and, for the first time, the Arab-Israeli dispute became America's highest foreign priority. In the months that followed, Kissinger seemed obsessed with the Mideast and he spent an enormous amount of time there. As Watergate ate away at his presidency, Nixon abdicated American diplomacy to Kissinger. When Gerald Ford became president in August 1974, foreign policy changed less than between any administrations in the post-1945 era. Kissinger pursued the same strategy under both presidents.

Domestic and External Constraints

The October War completed the transformation of the Arab-Israeli dispute from a nuisance into a conflict central to American diplomatic and strategic concerns. The war led to a Soviet-American confrontation, as in the wars of 1956 and 1967, and provoked a crisis in the Western alliance, as had the wars of 1948 and 1956. The Arab embargo and the later quadrupling of OPEC oil prices trumpeted the world-wide energy crisis, which emerged as the compelling international problem of the 1970s. Suddenly, columnists began analyzing the effect of Middle East oil and the Arab-Israeli dispute on issues as diverse as the economic recession and U.S. relations with the Third World. Regional and global politics overlapped and Arab-Israeli negotiations were treated as critical to global foreign policy.[1] The Middle East demanded constant attention, with the result that decisions were made by top rank officials. Never had an administration felt more pressure to resolve the conflict.

Domestic pressures during these four years confused the administration. At first Nixon was in the comfortable position of not having to seek reelection, but once Watergate threatened the president's political survival, the domestic scene influenced foreign policy making. On the one hand, Nixon could not afford to alienate important groups (such as the American Jewish community) whose opposition might further weaken him. On the other hand, the Arab-Israeli crisis allowed Nixon to demonstrate the "indispensable" diplomatic skills that might yet save his presidency. He needed a major foreign policy success, and if he pressured Israel hard enough, he might achieve one. The war had demonstrated that an Arab oil embargo could cause economic dislocations in the United States, Europe, and Japan. Many politicians and bureaucrats feared that another well-timed embargo would devastate the American economy and cripple the political fortunes of anyone in power at the time.

This fear offset traditionally strong pro-Israeli sentiment. The recession of 1974–1975, accompanied by hysterical prophecies of imminent economic collapse, reinforced the concern that the West was hostage to the Middle Eastern oil producers.[2] As important as this fear was, the oil crisis also produced opportunities for American business. The petrodollars flowing into the accounts of Arab regimes created an enormous market for American goods and services. The value of U.S. exports to the Arab states, for example, increased 675 percent between 1972 and 1976.[3] Not only oil companies but construction firms, bankers, entrepreneurs, real estate and investment interests, educational institutions, and former government officials rushed to cash in on the new Arab market. In 1975 the United States actually had a trade surplus with the Arab states.[4] Expressing support for the Palestinians or the Arab cause in general proved one's trustworthiness to the Arabs (as always), but now the pool of those dealing with the Arab states increased.[5] More U.S. corporations than ever before had incentive to question U.S. support for Israel.

The growing attention paid to the Arab world by journalists, politicians, and businessmen provided opportunities for Arabs to express their views on the conflict with Israel. These new conditions gave Arab representatives and their supporters more importance in Washington, especially after the reestablishment of U.S. diplomatic relations with Egypt, Syria, Algeria, and the Sudan. In June 1975, Gerald Ford became the first president to see an official delegation of Arab-Americans.[6] Congressional visits to the Middle East now included mandatory stops in several Arab countries as well as Israel. Anwar Sadat began in 1975 to hold frequent meetings with visiting American dignitaries, especially congressmen.[7]

The October War strengthened the Arab case within the policy making community. Many officials in the diplomatic and intelligence communities had warned that another Mideast war would occur unless drastic diplomatic steps were taken, and they now enjoyed greater credibility. Their belief that the national interest demanded closer ties with the Arabs, even if it meant forcing Israeli concessions, gained greater acceptance throughout the bureaucracy.[8] Some of the officials closest to the Israelis—especially at the Defense Intelligence Agency—were removed after the war because it was thought that their prediction of no hostilities showed that they had been too influenced by their Israeli contacts.[9] In an unrelated development, the controversy over CIA domestic surveillance caused the retirement of the program's chief, James Angelton, the official with strongest ties to Israel in the Agency.[10] The Israelis even suffered in the Pentagon, where their image as effective fighters had been tarnished by their early war losses; some officers resented the loss of equipment sent to Israel during the emergency.[11] The chairman of the Joint Chiefs of Staff, George Brown, said in a Duke University lecture in October 1974:

> in answer to the question of would we use force in the Middle East, I don't know. I hope not. We have no plans to. It is conceivable, I guess, it's kind of almost as bad as the "Seven Days in May" thing, but you can conjure up a situation where there is another oil embargo and people in this country are not only inconvenienced and uncomfortable, but suffer and they get tough-minded enough to set down the Jewish influence in this country and break that lobby.
>
> It's so strong you wouldn't believe now. We have the Israelis coming to us for equipment. We say we can't possibly get the Congress to support a program like that. They say, "Don't worry about Congress. We'll take care of the Congress." Now this is somebody from another country, but they can do it. They own, you know, the banks in this country, the newspapers . . . you just look at where the Jewish money is in this country.[12]

That the chairman of the Joint Chiefs of Staff could make such a statement demonstrates that the pro-Israeli forces were weaker than they had been before the war. They were weakened both by the perceived increase in Arab strength and their own lost credibility. Their major argument had been torpedoed; Israeli strength had not deterred the Arab assault. Kissinger, who needed a weaker Israeli lobby in order to negotiate more flexibly, was soon giving private discourses on Israel's eroded support in Congress. By 1975 the image of an intransigent Israel had become current among policy figures and academics, and even the public opinion polls reflected a temporary drop in support for Israel.[13]

Yet the assumption of growing Arab strength and declining Israeli influence was balanced by examples of Arab weakness and Israeli resilience. Along with enhanced Arab respectability and clout came resentment at the oil embargo and the increase in oil prices, acts widely seen as economic belligerence toward the United States.[14] Although Iran and Venezuela had actually led the battle in OPEC for raising prices, the Arab producers were blamed in the American media.[15] Calls for the military to seize the Mideast (i.e., Arab) oilfields even led Ford and Kissinger to warn producers that the West would not tolerate economic "strangulation."[16] Though weak and contrary to the major thrust of U.S. policy, these warnings reflected American discomfort at an unaccustomed dependence on foreign powers.

U.S. firms eager to do business with the Arab oil producers also developed serious public relations problems after 1973. The major American oil companies found themselves under severe pressure over the suddenly discovered energy crisis and their huge profits. Polls immediately after the embargo showed that the oil companies were blamed for gasoline lines and shortages caused by the crisis. The investigations of the Senate Committee on Multinational Corporations under Frank Church uncovered embarrassing examples of companies assisting the Arab embargo.[17] Some business firms selling to the Arabs found themselves under attack from the Anti-Defamation League, which claimed that the firms were violating the civil rights of American Jews when they complied with the Arab boycott of Israel.[18] Participation of American business in the Arab boycott became a major issue in the 1976 presidential campaign, and engendered considerable legislative action on Capitol Hill.[19]

Meanwhile, Israel's war losses at the Pentagon were not uniform. Many officials sensed the political advantages of aligning with the Jewish community. Several prominent Jewish leaders argued in favor of increased defense expenditures when they discovered the dearth of U.S. weapons available during the war. Moreover, Israeli experiences in fighting against the latest Russian materiel provided important lessons for American military planners.[20]

Established patterns of Jewish political participation also proved difficult to break down. The October War undermined the intellectual framework within which all Israeli supporters had operated, and it led some Jewish groups to question Israeli diplomatic strategy. One group, Breira ("choice" in Hebrew), became much stronger among intellectuals and academics who believed that Israeli diplomacy had not been sufficiently flexible in recent years. This controversy, coupled with the traumatic effects of the war, led pro-Israeli organizations to intensify their activities. Threatened by new Arab successes at home and abroad and progressively unable to fathom the machinations of Henry Kissinger, Jewish groups redoubled their efforts. These activities culminated in a fierce public relations campaign in spring 1975. In a public letter, seventy-six senators questioned the administration policy of confronting Israel.[21]

The crucial factor favoring Israel's supporters was that Ford, unlike Nixon, could run for election in 1976. He could not ignore the political implications of the Mideast crisis. Nixon had foreseen Ford's difficulties with Israel's supporters in Congress and the Jewish groups; indeed such tension was a by-product of the Nixon approach to the Arab-Israeli conflict. He had had similar problems himself (on a smaller scale) in early 1970 over the Rogers Plan and his resistance to selling Phantom jets to Israel. In the 3 February 1973 entry in his diary, Nixon had noted

> Henry has constantly put off moving on it [the Mideast] each time, suggesting that the political problems were too difficult. This is a matter which I, of course, will have to judge. He agreed that the problem with the Israelis in Israel was not nearly as difficult as the Jewish community here, but I am determined to bite this bullet and do it now . . . The Mideast he [Kissinger] just doesn't want to bite, I am sure because of the enormous pressures he is going to get from the Jewish groups in this country.[22]

Because of the increased politicization of the Arab-Israeli problem, both candidates in the 1976 presidential campaign promised broadened assistance to Israel.[23] Arab gains in Washington did not seriously diminish Israel's popularity with the American people or its strong support among American Jews. Thus, a pattern first noted in 1944 had again surfaced: the tension between political promises in a presidential year and the pressures on pragmatic policy makers after the election. The increased attention given the Arab-Israeli dispute by government, media, and interest groups intensified the usual divisions on the issue. Henry Kissinger confronted a more complex domestic scene as well as more severe external constraints after October 1973.

A final complication in the administration's dealing with the American Jewish community in this period was the Jackson amendment that would link most-favored-nation status for the U.S.S.R. to a more liberal Soviet emigration policy. While Jewish organizations partially agreed with administration policy toward the Middle East, they disagreed with Nixon, Ford, and Kissinger (who opposed the amendment) on the best means of securing increased Jewish emigration from Russia. Kissinger believed that an increase in the whole detente relationship, including trade ties, would be most likely to achieve the common goal.[24]

Philosophy

The administration reaction to the Yom Kippur War was distinctive: after the most important Mideast crisis that the U.S. had ever encountered, the

U.S. government did not alter its basic approach, only the time it would spend on it.[25] Nixon, Kissinger, and Rogers had sought to thwart the Soviets and the Arab radicals with an Arab-Israeli settlement; they had differed only over tactics. The war was unexpected and challenged existing assumptions about the Arabs' poor fighting abilities, the accuracy of Israeli intelligence, and the invincibility of the Israeli military. The most immediate lesson of the war was that U.S. involvement in the peace process must intensify. Washington could no longer avoid making an Arab-Israeli settlement central to its global diplomacy.[26]

Consistent with his prewar policy, Kissinger hoped U.S. influence could be increased by interim agreements that skirted the fundamental questions. Therefore, he tried as far as possible to avoid the thorny issues: the Palestinian question, the final Israeli borders, and the nature of the peace after the negotiations. The disengagement accords between Egypt and Israel in 1974 and 1975 reflected precisely Kissinger's 1971 strategy: (1) a limited approach weakly connected to a comprehensive settlement; (2) both sides accepting American involvement in return for a willingness to make major concessions; (3) American sponsorship of diplomatic interchanges that reduced Soviet engagement and so gave Washington rather than Moscow credit for success. The war and Sadat's interest in improving relations with the United States gave Kissinger the opportunity to achieve this strategy.

The consistency of the administration becomes clearer when its strategy is weighed against the alternatives suggested by its critics. Several analysts called for a policy of confrontation with the Arab oil producers. The administration might have refused to sponsor Arab-Israeli negotiations until the Arab embargo was lifted and production cuts restored. It might have taken a harsh stand against any country that practiced "economic blackmail" against the United States. In the extreme it could have considered a military takeover of key Arab oil fields.[27]

On the other hand, many authorities sympathetic to the Arab world advocated a policy closer to the European and Japanese response to the crisis: a call for the Israelis to accept a Palestinian homeland and self-determination on the West Bank and the Gaza Strip. This approach would have involved economic, military, and diplomatic pressure on Israel to gain total Israeli withdrawal to her 1967 borders in return for a rapid lifting of the embargo. As Senator J. William Fulbright, the outgoing chairman of the Senate Foreign Relations Committee, put it in a speech in November 1974, even after the embargo's suspension: "The United States has done as much for Israel as one nation can do for another. We—and we alone—have made it possible for Israel to exist as a state. Surely it is not too much to ask in return that Israel give up East Jerusalem and the West Bank as the necessary means of breaking a chain of events which threatens us all with ruin."[28]

For several reasons, neither of these strategies was seriously considered after October 1973. First, they were not consistent with the previous policies of an administration that had sought to balance ties with Israel against the efforts to improve relations with the Arabs. Just a few months after challenging the United States through the Yom Kippur War and the oil embargo, the Arabs returned to business as usual and developed an enormous two-way commerce with America. Arab diplomats seemed exceptionally interested in improving relations. Here was a temptation Nixon and Kissinger could not resist. Pressing Israel would also clash with their past policy, which had avoided confrontation with Jerusalem, in line with Kissinger's belief that pressure only made the Israelis more stubborn.

Second, both alternative policies contained high risks and political costs. Confronting the Arabs could lead to serious economic consequences at home and a major crisis with the Soviet Union abroad. The policy could work only if backed up with the threat of military force, but it was unclear whether a military action would succeed, and Congress and the American public were clearly ill-disposed to a new military adventure. Confronting Israel would lead to a political uproar at home and dubious prospects abroad: the Arabs might raise their demands and the Israelis would likely become unpredictable and resistant to U.S. persuasion.

Most important, from October 1973 onward, this administration was by Nixon's own account preoccupied with the president's survival.[29] Unstable situations do not encourage risk taking and the supposedly bold policy pursued by Kissinger was actually the safest available option. By the time that Nixon resigned, the policy was too well established, it was too late in the term to redesign it, and the new president was too inexperienced in foreign affairs and too passive in style to break with the past. Besides, Kissinger's Mideast policy seemed successful. Only in mid-1975 did the administration flirt with confronting Israel, but the experiment failed. As Kissinger himself had predicted, there was heavy pressure from pro-Israeli forces at home and Jerusalem showed no sign of knuckling under quickly. The new strategy would have required prolonged confrontation with Israel and additional major concessions from the Arabs to succeed. Therefore, the administration rapidly reverted to the original approach and did not depart from it again.

Despite broad consistency of policy before and after October 1973, Kissinger had to acknowledge the energy and financial crises created by the oil embargo and the quadrupling of prices. For these issues the administration had two answers: First, it pursued an ambitious program for cooperation among the major Western industrial powers, with the establishment of the International Energy Agency and periodic summit meetings among key Western leaders. Issues discussed in these forums included developing a strategic oil reserve for use in emergencies, plans to share scant supplies in case of a crisis, conservation measures to reduce dependence on Middle East petroleum and means of cooperating to fight inflation.[30] Second, the administration tried drawing key Arab states into America's political and economic orbit. That would, it was believed, create powerful disincentives for future oil embargoes; the Arab oil producers would have more to lose from a future confrontation with the United States. For this purpose a joint economic commission was created with Saudi Arabia in June 1974. (This soon necessitated joint commissions with Egypt, Jordan, and Israel as well.)* The new Saudi-American interdependence was marked by a 1000 percent increase in U.S.-Saudi trade between 1972 and 1976, a 1974 arrangement to sell several billion dollars worth of U.S. treasury bonds to the Saudis, a marked rise in U.S. technical assistance, and a dramatic growth of American arms sales to Riyadh, all paid for with Saudi petrodollars.[31]

The linkage between this commerce and Kissinger's handling of the Arab-Israeli dispute remained unclear. On the one hand, trade could be seen as reinforcing the diplomatic process: such interdependent relations with the Arab states might support U.S. diplomatic efforts. On the other hand, the attempt to improve relations with the oil producers could be a wholly separate enterprise, unrelated to Arab-Israeli matters.

The administration deliberately confused the Arabs on the relationship between oil decisions and Arab-Israeli diplomacy. For tactical reasons, administration officials publicly denied that any link existed while privately acknowledging that it did. Thus, Sisco claimed on 25 January 1974, "The Arab-Israeli dispute is not the cause of the energy problem. The resolution of the Arab-Israeli problem is not going to eliminate our energy problem or the energy problem of Europe and the principal consumers throughout the world."[32] A year-and-a-half later Kissinger still publicly denied any connection between the two issues: "I think it would be extremely dangerous for the United States to let its foreign policy be determined by oil price manipulation. We have refused to discuss our political objectives in relation to the price of oil and we will continue to do so."[33]

But the real thinking of American officials can best be discerned from meetings and memos. As early as 2 November 1973, at a meeting of Kissinger's rump NSC, the Washington Special Action Group (WSAG), Kissinger linked the oil embargo to the need to pressure Israel and deliver "a moderate program" to the Arabs. A few days later Nixon made an even stronger statement to his cabinet (while Kissinger was in Cairo): "The President said . . . in connection with energy that it might be necessary to apply pressure on Israel to avert a serious oil shortage . . . He said it might be necessary for the U.S. to go to the U.N. and perhaps to apply other kinds of pressure on Israel. He hoped it would

---

*Joint commissions were also established in 1974–75 with India, Iran, and Tunisia, but the Saudi commission was the most important; for example, it had the only full-time staff.

not be necessary . . ."[34] Kissinger confirmed that the oil embargo influenced American policy in a secret memo to Nixon on 19 December 1973, in which he admitted that Israel had to be persuaded to attend the Geneva Conference to help relieve oil pressure on the United States.[35]

Later Kissinger tried turning the linkage against the Arab oil producers by threatening not to mediate with Israel if the producers did not lift the embargo. In a letter to Syrian President Assad on 5 February 1974, Kissinger said he would not proceed with the Syrian-Israeli disengagement talks until the oil embargo was lifted.[36] The Arabs called this bluff, and Kissinger continued shuttle diplomacy; the following month, however, they suspended the embargo.

Throughout the period of the embargo, American officials misunderstood the nature of the threat they faced.[37] They believed, like most of the American public, that the embargo had caused the shortages and the lines at gas stations. In truth, the embargo had only a psychological impact. Production cutbacks caused the shortages and made possible the price rises that hurled the West into a recession. Thus Kissinger mistakenly directed his diplomacy toward ending the embargo and did not pay enough attention to the larger problems caused by the production cuts and attendant price rises.

American strategy was hampered by a perception of limited options. If it was not possible to confront any major party in the area with military or economic pressure, the United States would have to accomplish its objectives by diplomatic skill. Unable to use the stick, Washington would have to find carrots for all those who would participate in the peace process. On the surface the United States seemed to have considerable leverage with both sides. It could apparently give or deny arms to Israel and dangle the prospect of peace. The Arabs stood to gain increased trade, economic and military aid, arms sales, and restoration of territories lost in 1967. But manipulating rewards and punishments was complicated by the area's long-standing enmities and the unpredictable acts of revenge that both Arabs and Israelis could enact in response to pressure. The negativism and defeatism sweeping the United States after Vietnam and Watergate, and the shock of realizing dependence on foreign energy supplies, encouraged caution and passivity. Kissinger was forced to maneuver accordingly.

There was, therefore, a headlong quality to Kissinger's Arab-Israeli diplomacy: it would have to keep moving and developing or it would fall. His arrangements also assumed that the Arab-Israeli question was central to America's problems in the area and that a settlement would improve the security of oil sources. Since it was likely that reaching a settlement would take many years, the United States would have to devise clever tactics to maintain the cooperation of every major competing party in the area. Here lay the genius and the danger of the approach. Success depended on devising a never-ending succession of effective tactics. To the extent that Kissinger was the indispensable instrument, the policy would collapse without his driving force. (One major change of the Carter administration was to abandon movement as a strategy and instead seek an overall settlement that would avoid the need to manipulate each party.) In the period between 1973 and 1977, Kissinger, Nixon, and Ford relied on diplomatic momentum and the carrots of trade, aid, and arms sales. Their aim was to expand the American role in the region at the expense of Russian influence. This would lead, they believed, to uninterrupted oil supplies as long as the new diplomatic process could be maintained. Their approach assumed that solving the Arab-Israeli dispute was not possible during their tenure.

Decision Making

Although the philosophy toward the Middle East during Nixon's new term remained largely the same, the decision-making system was altered. For two years (fall 1973–1975) Kissinger was both secretary of state and National Security Council chief. Even after his deputy, Brigadier General Brent Scowcroft, replaced him as the national security assistant in fall 1975, Kissinger remained the dominant force in the administration's foreign affairs. Kissinger's power may well have surpassed even John Foster Dulles's, because of Nixon's preoccupation with Watergate during his last year in office and Ford's lack of experience.

In his account of the period, H. R. Haldeman fills in the background on the Kissinger-Rogers transition. After Nixon's reelection, Kissinger yearned to replace Rogers with a more docile secretary of state, preferring to maintain the NSC adviser's position as the true seat of power without having to assume the administrative burdens of the State Department. Having decided in favor of Kissinger over Rogers, Nixon determined that Kenneth Rush, then ambassador to Germany, would be the new secretary. Kissinger supported the decision, but Rogers refused to resign and indicated he would wait for about six months. Nixon relented. By August, when Rogers finally did agree to leave, the president was in such trouble over Watergate that he felt a more prominent figure than Rush was needed. [38]

Nixon told David Frost that he would not have appointed Kissinger secretary of state if he had been able to find another candidate able to work with Kissinger as an equal. He had considered appointing John Connally, but conflict between Kissinger and the strong-willed Connally seemed inevitable. Since he sought to avoid creating another version of the Rogers-Kissinger feud, he could think of no alternative to appointing Kissinger himself to the post. Kissinger recognized that this choice was distasteful to a president who hoped to claim for himself much credit for his foreign policy successes. [39]

From November 1972 onward, the highest levels of the administration knew that Rogers was a lame duck. This stalled U.S. diplomacy until fall 1973.

It is ironic that Kissinger's tenure at Foggy Bottom was during a period when the Middle East was the leading international issue the country faced. As the first Jew and first immigrant to hold the post, this secretary of state was an unlikely choice to mediate the Arab-Israeli dispute. Despite Nixon's early concern about Arab suspicion of Kissinger's background, the president eventually understood that his NSC adviser also faced potential bitterness from what Kissinger delicately called his "co-religionists" whenever he made demands on Israel.[40] For the Arabs Kissinger's Jewishness was a continuing source of suspicion, while to the Jews his cordial relations with several Arab leaders raised uncomfortable questions.

By 1973, however, other factors worked to balance and overcome these constraints on Kissinger. With the conclusion of the Vietnam War, he became a media star, folk hero, and reputed diplomatic wizard. A nation gained prestige when Kissinger took interest in its problems. Sadat therefore actively sought to enmesh Kissinger in the Mideast peace process. On the Israeli side, Kissinger had won the trust of Meir, Eban, Dayan, and Rabin.[41] Whatever the controversies and crises during negotiations, he could at least count on this established confidence.

Despite the abstraction of his academic writing and speech, Kissinger followed a pragmatic approach in office. It was not accidental that he popularized terms like *maneuver* and *momentum, flexibility* and *firmness,* because these words aptly describe his tactical approach to diplomacy. Even his conception of detente with the Soviet Union ultimately broke down over continuing disputes with Moscow (as in the Middle East) and over conflicting conceptions of what was meant in the first place.[42]

The new decision-making structure of the administration facilitated his "lone ranger" diplomacy because Kissinger needed only to gain the president's approval on delicate points requiring U.S. commitments. Watergate made Nixon's support inevitable because by October 1973 he needed diplomatic accomplishments as an argument for continuing in office. Kissinger's overwhelming authority was a by-product of the president's weakness.

This decision-making structure altered the outside influences on the administration by excluding alternative views. The Rogers-Kissinger feud had provided two channels for disenchanted outsiders. Now protests could be registered only by going to the public or to Congress. As a result, administration policies met earlier and more vocal attacks than would have occurred if interested groups had believed that they had other channels through which to influence events. Thus, in summer 1973, when Kissinger had defeated Rogers, the oil companies felt unable to get a hearing from the administration and mounted a public campaign for policies more favorable to the Arabs. In 1975 the pro-Israeli forces staged a vehement campaign against Ford and Kissinger's "reassessment" of U.S. policy.[43] During a similar dispute in 1970 over arms sales, Israel's supporters perceived that Nixon and Kissinger differed with Rogers, and they moderated opposition to administration policy to avoid alienating the White House. With the single Ford-Kissinger channel, once administration policy had moved against Israel no alternatives were available except public protest.

Kissinger's relationship to the Arab-Israeli dispute now altered radically. As long as Rogers had been secretary of state (no matter how diminished his role), Kissinger could choose when and how to become involved. Once he was both secretary of state and NSC adviser, he had complete responsibility for the issue under the president and he could rarely blame other officials for errors, policies antagonistic to Israel, or unpopular decisions. This problem was somewhat mitigated by Kissinger's effectiveness with the press. However, his constant efforts to appear in a favorable light created confusion about what was actually happening in the administration. The controversy over who delayed arms shipments to Israel during the October War was a typical Kissinger-era dispute over what positions the president's advisers had taken. [44]

In his shuttle diplomacy between the Arabs and Israelis, Kissinger's power derived from his being the only person who knew what stances both sides had taken in particular circumstances. Even the two presidents depended on his reports. By the Ford era, he conceived and conducted policy and then informed the president of the negotiations in order to receive presidential approval. [45] When Dulles negotiated in London to avert a crisis over Suez, he had to satisfy a president with strong views. The British leaders had the alternative of communicating with Eisenhower directly, an option that on occasion they exercised. This heavy constraint was not present when Kissinger dealt with the Arabs and Israelis. Yet Kissinger's flexibility in international dealings ultimately damaged his domestic position; he became the target of all those disenchanted with specific administration policies. He became a political issue in the 1976 campaign.

The historical novelty is that two successive presidents within the same term depended on the same foreign policy czar. The disintegration of Nixon's presidency increased Kissinger's responsibilities, but it also gave Nixon a personal stake in Middle East diplomacy. He sought concessions from the Israelis, upon whom the United States had the most leverage, and he wanted previously anti-American Arab states to align with Washington. The flirtation with these regimes was analogous to his dramatic transformation of American relations with China, an initiative enormously popular at home. Nixon's hurried trip to the Mideast in June 1974 was meant to have the same political impact as his trip to China in 1972.

If Nixon's dependence on Kissinger was rooted in the Watergate crisis, Ford's dependence was a product of the new president's inexperience and admiration for Kissinger's expertise and finesse. John Hersey spent a week in spring 1975 observing the Ford White House; he was told that final decisions on foreign affairs were made by the president "in consultation" with Henry Kissinger:

". . . in the formulation of settled policy, this President, who had a minimal exposure to foreign affairs before he came to office, heard only one voice . . ." Hersey was told that "nobody, but nobody" attended foreign policy meetings between the president and the secretary of state, except Kissinger's deputy, Brent Scowcroft, and "occasionally" the secretary of defense. From the outset, Kissinger and Ford spent at least an hour every morning discussing the world's problems.[46]

In the novelty of Ford's position as the nation's first unelected president, Kissinger provided continuity and experience in the sensitive national security area. There had always been distance between Nixon and Kissinger, as both have testified, but Ford and Kissinger had a warm personal relationship. In his memoirs Ford wrote that "there never was a conflict of any significance between us." The claim, even if overstated, revealed the extent to which Kissinger dominated the foreign policy scene in the Ford presidency.

> It would be hard for me to overstate the admiration and affection I had for Henry. Our relationship began on solid, unshakable ground and grew even better with the passage of time . . . Our personalities meshed. I respected his expertise in foreign policy and he respected my judgment in domestic politics . . . I think we worked together as well as any President and Secretary of State have worked throughout our history."[47]

Kissinger had strong and well-developed views on foreign affairs; Ford's notions were not well-formulated beyond a bland Republican anticommunism. Kissinger's sense of history as a scholar and diplomat was incomparably superior to Ford's. Hersey writes, "The reach of Gerald Ford's historic memory was short indeed; back beyond the year 1949, when he entered Congress, it seemed to fall into a black hole."[48]

Ford was straightforward, perhaps naïve, certainly not underhanded. When writing about the pardon of Richard Nixon, he said, "Throughout my political life, I always believed what I was told. I was truthful to others; I expected others to be truthful with me," and later, "I'm not by nature suspicious of people or their motives . . ."[49] Many have noted Ford's passiveness both as a personal trait and in his approach to policy. After observing Ford at close range for several days, Hersey wrote, "His was a 'glacial caution.' Calm and healthy and relaxed as Ford appeared to be, one got the impression in the end that his was a passive Presidency. It was almost as if he were letting decisions happen to him."[50]

Ford assumed the presidency with a reputation of staunch support for Israel throughout his years in Congress, and this support had more effect after he became minority leader in 1965. He had not only spoken frequently at many Jewish gatherings such as UJA and AIPAC meetings but he also lent his name as cosponsor to numerous resolutions, statements, letters, and aid legislation favorable to Israel.[51] Thus, on various occasions in 1967 and 1968, he criticized the Johnson administration for its delay in selling Israel Phantom jets, for "dilly-dallying" on aid to Israel, and for confusing the American commitment to Israel by "inaction." Once the Republicans took over the White House, Ford's sense of duty, his devotion to party, and his position as a minority leader in the House made him slow to criticize the Nixon administration during its quarrels with Israel's supporters in Congress.[52] Thus, during the first term he proposed the "establishment of a 'hot line' between Washington and Jerusalem," promised that the United States "will not let Israel down," repeatedly urged the immediate sale of additional Phantom jets to Israel in mid-1970 when the Nixon administration delayed the sale (without criticizing the administration directly), and called for extending military credits to Israel (as well as to Lebanon and Jordan).[53] During the controversy over the sale of French jets to Libya, he said,

> We shall do everything we can in the interest of peace and stability in the Middle East. But we will do more than talk. The United States cannot and will not stand by and watch the military balance turn against Israel. We will not let the situation deteriorate because of ill-advised policies of other governments."[54]

Nevertheless, when Ford entered the White House, he adapted rapidly to his new role. In February 1972 he had become the first nationally prominent Republican to call for the United States to recognize Jerusalem as the "historic and lawful capital of Israel" by moving its embassy there from Tel Aviv. "To continue with the present arrangement might tend to indicate that there is something temporary about the location of Israel's capital. This situation does not encourage the Arabs to translate the present cease-fire arrangement into a permanent and lasting peace." When asked about this position at a news conference three weeks after taking office the new president declared, "that particular proposal ought to stand aside."[55] In other words, a prominent congressman could advocate a major new policy direction but a president would have to be more cautious.

More clearly reflecting a shift in his thinking was Ford's attitude toward the Arab-Israeli territorial question as minority leader and as president. In Congress, Ford had repeatedly called for direct negotiations between the parties and his public refrain was that Israel "should not withdraw from one inch of occupied territory unless there is a credible evidence that such action will produce a real peace treaty."[56] Yet during his presidency, the dominant theme of American policy was that Israel should repay American largesse during the October War with unilateral territorial concessions that would facilitate the peace process. Particularly ironic is a statement Ford made in April 1971, before an annual AIPAC policy conference. He claimed that Washington should not force

Israel to "negotiate with the U.S. rather than Egypt on the territorial question."[57] Four years later, President Ford allowed just such a disagreement with Israel to replace peace negotiations with Egypt and he conducted a highly controversial "reassessment" of American Middle East policy.

He made many positive statements about Israel before he became president, but one looks in vain throughout Ford's memoirs to find positive comments about Israeli policy during his presidency. Prime Minister Rabin is described as "dour," and "a tough negotiator"; Ford "wasn't sure how flexible Rabin could be." Sadat, in contrast, ". . . combined a professional soldier's erect posture with an aristocratic air of elegance, deep-set eyes and a quiet, thoughtful voice . . . he was very precise in everything he said." Ford also relates how he "admired" King Hussein's "personal courage" and "leadership."[58]

The focus was on the Israelis rather than the Arabs as the cause of America's diplomatic difficulties. Ford believed,

> For the past twenty-five years, the philosophical underpinning of U.S. policy toward Israel had been our conviction—and certainly my own—that if we gave Israel an ample supply of economic aid and weapons, she would feel strong and confident, more flexible and more willing to discuss a lasting peace. Every American President since Harry Truman had willingly supplied arms and friends to the Jewish state. The Israelis were stronger militarily than all their Arab neighbors combined, yet peace was no closer than it had ever been. So I began to question the rationale for our policy. I wanted the Israelis to recognize that there had to be some quid pro quo. If we were going to build up their military capabilities, we in turn had to see some flexibility to achieve a fair, secure and permanent peace.[59]

Ford thus reveals an unclear historical perspective on America's previous role in the region. Truman and Eisenhower did not conclude major arms deals with the Israelis. Ford also discounts Arab refusal to accept Israel's existence during the previous quarter century as a cause of the conflict. He also maintains an exaggerated view of Israeli military strength at a time when most analysts had concluded that Israel had lost the October War in a political sense and could actually lose the next war on the battlefield.[60]

In short, after years of pro-Israeli rhetoric in the House, Ford adopted a tough stance toward Jerusalem once he occupied the Oval Office. The explanation for this abrupt transformation is that Ford's attitudes and policies were molded almost completely by Henry Kissinger. The "arms for flexibility" formula as enumerated by Ford had been advocated since the first term by the secretary of state; in those days it was called "hardware for software." Kissinger also determined Ford's perceptions of individual events. In discussing a February 1975 visit to the Middle East by his secretary of state, for example, Ford demonstrates how his perceptions were colored by Kissinger's frustrations with Israel's delicately balanced cabinet government. It was Kissinger who reported Israeli toughness and Egyptian flexibility. "Egyptian President Anwar Sadat, he said, was trying to be flexible and to accommodate the Israelis' concerns about their security. The Israelis, however, while encouraging our efforts to push for a lasting peace, were being very tough in their demands . . . Despite these obstacles, Henry told me that nothing was more critical than a new Sinai accord."[61]

Here we have a clear example of how the secretary of state's influence prevailed in the administration. Alexander Haig, Nixon's chief of staff during his last year in office, conveyed messages between Nixon and subordinates and was trusted by the Israelis, who on occasion dealt with him when they were trying to reach the president.[62] Under Ford, however, challengers to Kissinger arose, but their foreign policy views varied and they could not gain the president's confidence. The two dominant challengers were Secretary of Defense James Schlesinger and U.N. Ambassador Daniel Patrick Moynihan. Since the latter months of the Nixon era, Schlesinger had questioned Kissinger's conception of detente and conciliatory dealings with the U.S.S.R.[63] Schlesinger had his disagreements with Nixon, but he had more profound difficulties with Ford, who found him arrogant and resented his efforts to question Kissinger's policies.[64] Schlesinger was fired in November 1975 and replaced by the administration's chief of staff, Donald Rumsfeld, a close associate of the president.

The U.N. ambassador, ABC newsman John Scali, served from late 1972 to 1975. "Scali . . . came to detest Kissinger and Kissinger held Scali in utter contempt," one observer wrote.[65] Scali was followed by Moynihan, who rapidly became the most colorful figure in the administration. Moynihan questioned what he considered Kissinger's optimism about accommodation with the U.S.S.R. and, with rhetorical flourish, attacked the Third World-dominated politics at the U.N. He became famous for his forceful resistance to the "Zionism is racism" resolution of fall 1975. He denounced the U.N. as a "theatre of the absurd" and commented that "the General Assembly has repeatedly been the scene of acts we regard as abominations."[66] Moynihan's outbursts gave Israel's supporters something to cheer, thereby deflecting criticism from Ford and Kissinger, but his spectacular speeches had little policy significance. In early 1976, he resigned from the administration after disagreeing with the State Department over its minimal support for his tough rhetoric at the U.N. and later that year ran successfully for the U.S. Senate from New York. He was replaced by William Scranton, a member of Ford's "kitchen cabinet." Scranton's lower-key style and readiness to consider new avenues of contact with the Arab states matched the Ford-Kissinger philosophy.

Other officials strengthened the administration's accommodationist approach toward the Arab world. The chairman of the Joint Chiefs of Staff, George Brown, stirred public controversies with comments about the inordinate influence of the pro-Israeli lobby and with later suggestions that Israel was a liability to American interests.[67] William P. Clements, the deputy secretary of defense, a

Texas oil drilling contractor before coming to the Pentagon, was favorably disposed to the Mideast oil producers, and his relations with Schlesinger were poor, leading to a division at the Pentagon during the Schlesinger years (1973–1975) that Kissinger exploited to enhance his own authority.[68] Melvin Laird, the former secretary of defense and congressional colleague of the president, was a member of the kitchen cabinet and since his days at the Pentagon had consistently voiced concern that too close a relationship with Israel could lead to confrontation with the U.S.S.R. These officials were part of a business-oriented atmosphere concerned with the threat of a new embargo, American dependence on Arab oil, Arab petrodollars, and the new markets in Arab lands. Nevertheless, the formulation of policy and the conduct of diplomacy were still monopolized by Henry Kissinger.

The "Jewish portfolio" was handled in a unique way in the Ford White House. Max Fisher, who had already served under Nixon as an intermediary between the American Jewish community and the Israelis and between American Jews and the administration, became more crucial as a "close" and "old friend" of the president's.[69] However, this system left him much weaker than Niles or Feldman, the various figures under Johnson, or the combination of Garment, Safire, and Kissinger under Nixon. David Lisey, a young Jewish Republican, served in the newly created Office of Public Liaison. His function was to keep contact open with the Jewish community, but he suffered from his junior staff status. Fisher could not deal with details in the daily routine because he was outside the administration. In any case, as the Dulles era demonstrated, it is extremely difficult for someone in the White House to deal with Israeli affairs when a czar reigns over the foreign policy apparatus. When there is only one foreign policy channel to the president, the influence of an extra-bureaucratic adviser is likely to be negligible.

All those who sought to influence U.S. policy suffered from a similar constraint: the dominance of Henry Kissinger. The pro-Arab forces, such as Arab-American groups and oil companies, suffered the same limitations as their pro-Israeli counterparts: they could try influencing government officials or public discussion, but their efforts might prove irrelevant as long as Henry Kissinger remained the central figure who would have to be convinced. Arab and Israeli embassies suffered a similar fate. The number and influence of Arab representatives in Washington increased, while the new Israeli ambassador, Simcha Dinitz, was even granted a direct phone line to Kissinger's office.[70] This "hot line" however, did not bestow on Dinitz greater influence with the secretary of state. On the contrary, Kissinger used it to exercise leverage over the Israelis, refusing to answer it when he was angry with them.[71]

During the Nixon-Ford term, most key bureaucratic positions were occupied by individuals who had been dealing with the issue for several years. Since Kissinger dominated both the State Department and the NSC, a high degree of teamwork developed between the two agencies. The Middle East was the number one problem; individuals working on it were likely to be promoted. Thus, when Kissinger moved to the State Department, Sisco was elevated to under secretary of state for political affairs and replaced at the Near East Bureau in turn by Alfred (Roy) Atherton, described by the *New York Times* as "soft-spoken but acute in his judgments . . . probably the department's top Middle East specialist."[72] Harold Saunders finally left the White House after a dozen years on the NSC Middle East desk to become Atherton's deputy and eventually head of the State Department's intelligence and research bureau. He was replaced at the NSC by Robert Oakley, a foreign service officer with previous experience in the Arab world. There were no major changes when Brigadier General Brent Scowcroft, Kissinger's deputy, became NSC chief in late 1975; by then the major accomplishments of the administration's Mideast diplomacy were complete.

After the October 1973 War, other agencies became engaged in Mideast issues, especially the Treasury Department, the new Federal Energy Agency, and the Department of Commerce. As they spent their oil money on American goods, various Arab governments stepped up their traditional demands for complying with their boycott of Israeli goods. The Saudis continued to refuse entrance visas to several American Jews working on projects in the kingdom. Under both Nixon and Ford, however, issues such as recycling petrodollars, energy price levels, and the Arab boycott were peripheral to American Mideast diplomacy. Rather, the administration's primary goals were to strengthen ties with moderate Arab states, wean the radical states away from the Soviet Union, progress toward settling the Arab-Israeli dispute, and guarantee an ample flow of oil from the area. A Pax Americana would, Kissinger assumed, usher in a new era of manageable stability, a "new regional structure," as he preferred to call it. Kissinger's key instruments became shuttle diplomacy, negotiations and agreements, arms sales, financial aid, and contracts for economic cooperation with other states. Kissinger left the working out of details to Pentagon, Treasury, Commerce, or lesser State Department officials.

During the four Nixon-Ford years, the Mideast issue achieved an unprecedented priority because of the October 1973 War and the energy crisis. As a consequence, a larger number of agencies dealt with the Mideast, but they remained weak compared to Henry Kissinger.

Prelude to October 1973

Nine days before beginning his second term, Richard Nixon jotted down some notes to himself on his goals for the next four years. The three top foreign policy aims were: "Russia—SALT; China—Exchanges; Mideast—Settlement."[73] Nixon by now had accepted the notion of a limited settlement as a means of initiating the peace process. He wrote in his diary in early February 1973: "The interim settlement is, of course, the only thing we can talk about—that's the only thing the Israelis will ever go for—and the Egyptians are just simply going to have to take a settlement of that sort—or the Arabs are—with the assurance that we will do the best we can to get a total settlement later."[74] A few days later he wrote Kissinger that this approach would do for the public track, but private negotiations should aim at secret talks leading to an overall settlement: "The time has come to quit pandering to Israel's intransigent position. Our actions over the past have led them to think we will stand with them *regardless* of how unreasonable they are."[75]

With the American role in the Vietnam War ending and the new approaches to China and the U.S.S.R. in place, there was discussion in the administration over whether to concentrate next on Europe or the Middle East. Nixon noted to himself, "Henry needs to have another great goal. Haig feels strongly that it should be Europe. Henry, I noticed, had picked up this theme in my last talk with him. I kept hammering, however, with Haig the necessity of doing something about the Mideast."[76]

Nixon soon wrote a prophetic memo to Kissinger, predicting, "This thing is getting ready to blow."[77] The first manifestation of the president's interest in exploring an Arab-Israeli settlement was a series of visits to Washington from late February onward by King Hussein, Hafez Ismail (Sadat's adviser), and Golda Meir—a period labeled "Mideast Month" in Washington. These discussions differed from earlier diplomatic efforts in that Kissinger (not Rogers) took charge.

Egypt and Israel were already the center of attention. The meeting with Ismail culminated Kissinger's longstanding effort to establish a dialogue with the Egyptian government. The two men explored each other's views in extended secret discussions over a weekend in surburban New York.[78] Ismail delivered a polite ultimatum demanding Israeli withdrawal from all conquered territories in exchange for an end to belligerency. The only hopeful sign was his hint that Egypt would negotiate with Israel separately, and might reach agreement before the Syrians and the Palestinians. Kissinger found little reason for optimism. Nevertheless, he told Rabin that he was very impressed with Ismail's views.[79] The pressure was therefore on the Israelis when Meir arrived in Washington at the end of February.

The prime minister's meetings at the State and Defense Departments were tense. The Americans sought Israeli diplomatic concessions; Israel wanted new military and economic assistance. By the time Meir met the president at the end of her visit, a new formula had been arranged between Rabin and Kissinger: the Israelis would permit Kissinger to explore a new approach with Egypt in which Israel would accept Egyptian sovereignty over the entire Sinai in exchange for an Israeli security presence on some Egyptian territory.[80]

Since the administration's strategy was to arm Israel heavily to promote its confidence during the peace process, a new arms deal with Israel was decided on soon after Meir's visit. The decision leaked prematurely and discouraged the Egyptians.[81] The State Department subsequently learned of the secret Kissinger/Ismail talks from Arab diplomats, and a State representative—Alfred Atherton—sat in on Kissinger's next secret discussions with Ismail near Paris in May. By now, however, Sadat had decided to go to war and Ismail was unresponsive.[82]

With the failure to move the Egyptians, a critical lull descended over American diplomacy. The impending October 1973 Israeli election made the Labor government unlikely to undertake any new directions. As has been widely noted, Kissinger was reluctant to enter negotiations unless he thought they could succeed, and the prospect of an early Egyptian-Israeli settlement did not appear bright. He still seemed to fear too great a public involvement in the Arab-Israeli issue because he was Jewish. Moreover, Israel had little incentive to bargain seriously, for its military superiority appeared secure for several years. Thus, in summer 1973, Kissinger lacked leverage. How could he sponsor successful talks when the Israelis had nothing to gain and the Arabs had nothing to offer? As he told Meir after the war, "My aim was to gain time and postpone the serious stage for another month, another year."[83]

After the summits and protracted negotiations to end the Vietnam War, hesitation overtook the White House. Since 1969 Kissinger had taken a more leisurely approach to Mideast negotiations than had either Nixon or Rogers, and the failure of Rogers's efforts certainly reinforced his inclination to be patient. The State Department and the intelligence community warned that renewed conflict was likely if the stalemate continued, but the warnings were not convincing because Israel enjoyed military dominance and Sadat had ousted his Russian military advisers.[84] To Kissinger an Israeli preemption seemed the greater peril. This danger would increase if negotiations were conducted abruptly. The hawkish tone of the Israeli election campaign promoted caution, and Kissinger proceeded slowly. He erred in assuming that he had until 1974 to produce diplomatic results (although in this he was encouraged by King Hussein, who did not know that Egypt and Syria planned to attack Israel in the fall).[85]

However important these factors were in rationalizing hesitation, it was the transition itself that accounted in large measure for the doldrums of American diplomacy in mid-1973. After all, Kissinger turned immediately to Arab-Israeli negotiations as soon as he became secretary of state in September. Until he assumed office, the decision-making process was in disarray. Nixon, who had frequently pressed for action on a Mideast settlement and could have been expected to do so in mid-1973, was occupied with Watergate. In late February the Senate appointed a select committee to investigate the Watergate incident and on 23 March, Judge Sirica read a letter from James McCord, one of those convicted in the break-in of the national Democratic party headquarters, in which McCord alleged direct White House involvement in the burglary. Two days before, the young White House counsel, John Dean, had warned Nixon that Watergate was a "cancer" on the presidency. At the moment when Nixon might have pushed for a new Mideast initiative, his attention was elsewhere.

This comparative quiet was interrupted by the second Soviet-American summit in Washington and San Clemente in late June 1973. The summit was not so dramatic as the first, but the personal relationship between Nixon and Brezhnev was markedly warmer. Brezhnev appeared to enjoy himself, especially after Nixon gave him a Lincoln Continental. The most important document signed was entitled "Agreement for the Prevention of Nuclear War," which committed both sides to consult with each other on problems that might lead to nuclear war, including wars that might break out over Third World conflicts. The agreement contained enough escape clauses that when the October War broke out less than four months later, the Russians could claim they had not violated it.[86] Many Americans believed otherwise.

At the end of the conference, Nixon and Brezhnev and their chief aides flew to San Clemente. After a full day, Brezhnev, who had insisted on staying at the Nixon home, said after dinner that he was tired and would go to bed early. Shortly after, Nixon himself retired, only to be summoned by Kissinger back to a meeting with Brezhnev, Dobrynin, and Gromyko. Claiming he could not sleep, Brezhnev launched into a three-hour discussion of the Middle East. His primary objective was to coax Nixon into agreeing to principles close to Arab positions. When the president refused to accept what would be an "imposed peace" at Israel's expense, Brezhnev hinted that he could not "guarantee" that war would not resume.[87]

The late evening rendezvous seemed a typical example of Soviet heavy-handedness. The Russians, however, must have at least suspected Egyptian war plans—since February, they had been sending more advanced equipment than ever to Cairo. But Nixon and Kissinger took the hint of Mideast war as an attempt to persuade them to accept Soviet principles. In the communiqué signed the day after the midnight meeting, the two sides simply recorded their differences over the Middle East.[88]

A development that impressed Washington more profoundly in mid-1973 was the emerging energy crisis. For years senior officials had concentrated on SALT, Vietnam, the U.S.S.R., China, and Arab-Israeli diplomacy. Energy issues were left to lower-ranking officials and the oil companies. By the time Nixon and Kissinger began to pay attention to the problem, it was almost too late.

For several years, OPEC (the Organization of Oil Producing and Exporting Countries, founded in 1960) had sought to increase the revenues of its members. In 1970, its golden opportunity arrived. The Western industrialized countries had become dependent on Mideast oil and spare productive capacity in the United States had declined to zero.[89] This meant that, for the first time, any cutbacks in Middle East oil production could not be made up from American supplies. Muamar Qaddafi was the first to seize this opportunity. As early as January 1970, he began to pressure the independent companies operating in Libya. He first threatened to withdraw the concession of Occidental Petroleum, the most vulnerable of the independents. Exxon refused to help Occidental and Occidental had to accede to Qaddafi's price demands. Qaddafi soon forced the other independents to agree to similar price rises and then he went after the majors, including Exxon.[90]

The State Department was not prepared to help. At a critical meeting between the oil companies and federal officials, including Under Secretary of State U. Alexis Johnson and head of the Office of Fuels and Energy, James V. Akins, the company representatives were informed that the U.S. government had little influence with the Libyan government, that Qaddafi's demands were "reasonable," and that the Palestinian problem was central to the difficulties the companies faced.[91] The State Department's conciliatory attitude toward the Libyan government contrasted sharply with the confrontational approach that the White House took toward the Syrians and Russians in the September 1970 crisis at the same time. As a Senate committee later concluded, "With no prospect of U.S. government support, companies which had not already reached a settlement with the Libyans did so." Just as the company representatives had predicted, however, accepting Qaddafi's terms led to escalating demands.[92]

Until September 1970, the oil companies had favored taking a firm stand with the OPEC countries, negotiating with them as a group to avoid being "picked off one by one in any country."[93] They also tried to avoid leapfrogging, an OPEC negotiating tactic in which an agreement with one country (or a group of producers) would be followed by a better deal with a second country, after which the first country would demand that its terms be renegotiated and so on in a never-ending spiral. In order to negotiate as a group, the oil companies gained a Justice Department waiver from antitrust prosecution for a showdown meeting with OPEC in Teheran in early 1971. OPEC, however, tried to force the companies to bargain with a subcommittee of the six Persian Gulf producers so that it could leapfrog its way to higher oil prices. The State Department sent Under Secretary of State John Irwin II to communicate the administration approach to the governments of the gulf. Newly appointed, inexperienced, and uninformed on oil policy, Irwin was persuaded by the shah to abandon the "elaborately worked out strategy" designed by the oil companies with the apparent approval of the State Department.[94]

Without American government support, the company position rapidly collapsed. The companies reversed themselves and negotiated with the OPEC subgroup of gulf states, who promised five years price stability in exchange for higher prices.[95]

The coordination between the oil companies and the State Department failed because of divergent objectives. Each oil company wanted to avoid rising prices and to preserve its share of the retail market, the time-tested strategies for survival in the cutthroat oil industry. If one company had to pay more for its oil concession than its rivals, its retail share or its profits would rapidly decline. However, the primary goal of each company in negotiating, even more than preventing price increases, was to preserve its concessions and crude volume. A company that lost its concession—as Occidental almost did in Libya in 1970— would be eliminated from the oil game.

The State Department, on the other hand, wanted to preserve close American relations with the producing states, especially the conservative Persian Gulf regimes of Iran, Kuwait, and Saudi Arabia. Far from resisting the price rises, the State Department may actually have favored them. James Akins, then head of the department's Office of Fuels and Energy, told a Senate subcommittee, "The cost of production in the United States is very high for oil . . . and the cost of alternative fuels is very high, and to say that the cost of oil should be very low in the Persian Gulf because the cost of production of the oil is very low is very nice as far as consumers would be concerned, but I don't think you are going to get any oil producer to admit that this has any validity."[96] Certainly the State Department was unwilling to risk confrontation over fifty cents a barrel. Without the backing of the U.S. government, the oil companies would not endanger their concessions. They capitulated in Teheran (and, as it turned out, actually profited from surrender). No one—not the State Department, the oil companies, the academic analysts, or even the producing nations—foresaw in 1971 the stunning consequences the Teheran Conference would have for the Western economies.

Irwin may have been ill-prepared for his mission, but the outcome was consistent with the intentions of Nixon and Kissinger. They planned to use the shah as the guardian of the gulf when the British relinquished the role later in the year. Whether or not administration policy makers actually preferred the price rises, as some have charged, the increases enabled the shah to purchase the arms necessary to his new role of regional overlord.[97]

The Teheran agreement of February 1971 promised five years of stability in the international oil trade, but the ink was barely dry when the agreement began to come apart. Having demonstrated that the oil companies and the U.S. government were vulnerable, the OPEC countries pressed on. A month after Teheran, Libya got a better price than the gulf states, which brought new demands from other OPEC members. During 1971 and 1972 the pattern continued: Libyan gains followed by new demands from other OPEC countries. Negotiations were soon replaced by the unilateral actions of individual producing states; they competed to see who could squeeze more from the oil companies and the West.[98] It was here that the energy crisis first became entangled with the Arab-Israeli dispute.

The "Israeli matter" was a factor from time to time in oil negotiations, especially when Qaddafi wanted to justify threats of nationalizations.[99] When he sought higher prices, he employed broader anti-Western rhetoric, including suggestions that Libya had been cheated in the past. As the vulnerability of the companies became clearer, however, a competition between Arab moderates and Arab radicals developed over oil prices and participation agreements, and anti-Israel rhetoric was often added to the Arab demands. Fundamentally, however, the oil supply crisis had nothing to do with the Arab-Israeli dispute.

Once the Arabs tied oil to politics, the companies—especially Aramco—grew alarmed. By January 1973, Aramco executives were concerned enough to say in a private briefing paper, which they hoped to convey to Secretary of the Treasury George Shultz, that "failing a new and successful peace initiative, [the] best hope for continued stability of supply of Arab oil, which will become increasingly vital to [the] U.S.A., is adoption by [the] U.S. government of [an] 'even-handed' approach to [the] Arab-Israeli conflict so often promised by President Nixon and Secretary Rogers."[100]

A growing public debate ensued. M.I.T. economist, M. A. Adelman wrote in *Foreign Policy* that there was no real oil shortage, only inadequate policies by the oil industry and the State Department. This broadside caused Akins to respond in a rival quarterly that not only was the shortage real but unless American policy in the Middle East changed, the Arabs could penalize the United States for its close association with Israel.[101] Perhaps it was a self-fulfilling prophecy, but it did not take long to come true.

In a May 1973 meeting in Geneva with Aramco officials, King Faisal did what he consistently had maintained he would never do: he wedded oil to politics. Simply put, Faisal wanted to pressure the American government to produce Israeli concessions on the Palestinian question, including withdrawals to the 1967 lines. According to a confidential account of one of the participants:

> Saudi Arabia is in danger of being isolated among its Arab friends, because of failure of the U.S. Government to give Saudi Arabia positive support, and that H.M. is not going to let this happen. "You will lose everything" (concession is clearly at risk.) Things must do (1) inform U.S. public of their true interests in the area (they now being misled by controlled news media) and (2) inform government leaders—and promptly (time is running out and "you may lose everything.")[102]

The oil companies immediately complied with the king's wishes. The next week Aramco officials made the rounds in Washington and met with key personnel including Assistant Secretary of State Joseph Sisco, Kissinger's deputy General Scowcroft, and Acting Secretary of Defense William Clements. At each stop Aramco spread the Saudi message. However, skeptical bureaucrats pointed out to the oilmen that Saudi Arabia had in the past successfully resisted greater challenges from Nasser than any the kingdom faced now. According to the Aramco officials, "The impression was given that some believe H.M. is calling wolf when no wolf exists except in his imagination. Also, there is little or nothing the U.S. Government can do or will do on an urgent basis to affect the Arab-Israeli issue." Unknown to the complacent bureaucrats, the Saudis were at that moment coordinating their activities with Cairo and had prepared large quantities of oil to be shipped to Egypt for the Arab attack. It never occurred to anyone at Aramco to report this obscure fact to Washington: they thought it happened because Libya had just stopped shipping oil to Egypt.[103]

Faced with unresponsive government officials, the oil companies tried another approach. They sponsored advertisements and public letters emphasizing the dangers of too much support for Israel. In late June, Mobil warned in a newspaper advertisement, "In the last analysis, political considerations may become the critical element in Saudi Arabia's decisions because we will need the oil more than Saudi Arabia will need the money.[104] A month later, Otto Miller, head of Socal (Chevron), wrote to the company's approximately 300,000 stockholders and employees about increased American dependence on foreign oil: "It is highly important at this time that the United States should work more closely with the Arab governments to build up and enhance our relations with the Arab people. . . . There must be understanding on our part of the aspirations of the Arab people, and more positive support of their efforts toward peace in the Middle East."[105] A storm of protest from Jewish groups greeted this letter. When thousands of credit cards were returned, Aramco officials in Saudi Arabia used the protests, and press reports about them, to prove their efforts on the Arabs' behalf.[106]

The oilmen would have been surprised to discover that their view was not very different from that of Washington policy makers. In summer 1973, National Security Council memoranda were calling for more distance between Washington and Jerusalem.[107] Similarly, significant elements of the intelligence community had by now locked onto the oil problem. That Aramco failed to influence U.S. policy immediately can be seen as evidence of Washington's complacency. But the oilmen were not objective observers; their advice was easy to ignore. Nonetheless, the Aramco warnings were part of a growing number of danger signals reaching Washington in mid-1973. These messages were not yet strong enough to affect the highest levels of the government, but the administration's perspective was rapidly changing.[108]

The intelligence community had been asked in the spring to appraise the possibility of war in the Middle East. The consensus was that the possibility was less than even, but the State Department's Bureau of Intelligence and Research (INR) disagreed, arguing, "If the UN debate of next week produces no convincing movement in the Israeli-Egyptian impasse, our view is that the resumption of hostilities by autumn will become a better than even bet . . ."[109] Among other indications, this agency had received a report that Sadat had told a confidante that Nixon and Kissinger were individuals who required a demonstration of military power to believe that a leader was serious. There were also signs of possible military preparations in Egypt. By the fall, however, INR grew more sanguine, expecting the Arabs to concentrate on the oil weapon, at least for the short term.[110]

Any suggestion that the Israeli and oil questions were linked would immediately increase Arab leverage on the United States. It would also alarm the Israelis, making them reluctant to consider concessions. Therefore, the State Department denied any linkage between oil and the Arab-Israeli dispute. As early as 29 March Assistant Secretary Sisco told a group of editors and broadcasters of the department's "serious doubts" that the Arab-Israeli dispute would interfere with producer-consumer relations.[111] On 30 April, Secretary of State Rogers denied before the Senate Foreign Relations Committee that increasing U.S. dependence on Mideast oil was changing U.S. Mideast policy. Similar statements were repeated at intervals throughout the summer.[112] Yet the president himself said at a 5 September news conference that Arab oil producers did tie oil to the Arab-Israeli dispute and that he had for that reason instructed Kissinger to "put at the highest priority moving toward . . . the settlement of that dispute."[113] At the same time he warned Arab producers that precipitous price rises and expropriations would lead to lost markets. He also denied that Arab oil pressure would change American policy toward Israel. Here, a month before the Yom Kippur War, he proceeded to outline the policy that has erroneously been regarded as the U.S. reaction to developments *after* October 1973:

> Israel simply can't wait for the dust to settle and Arabs can't wait for the dust to settle in the Mideast. Both sides are at fault. Both sides need to start negotiations off dead center. That is our position.
>
> We are not pro-Israel, and we are not pro-Arab, and we are not any more pro-Arab because they have oil and Israel hasn't. We are pro-peace and it is the interest of the whole area for us to get those negotiations off dead center. And that is why we will use our influence with Israel, and we will use our influence, what influence we have, with the various Arab States, and a non-Arab State like Egypt, [*sic,*-presumably Iran] to get those negotiations off. Now, one of the dividends of having a successful negotiation will be to reduce the oil pressure.[114]

Despite his disavowals, Nixon admitted here that he thought American Arab-Israeli diplomacy *was* related to the oil question, that the United States did have more leverage on Israel than on the Arab states, and that successful diplomacy would reduce oil pressure. Although these three themes are hallmarks of post-October 1973 U.S. diplomacy, they were consistent with previous Nixon policy and had been arrived at *before* the war.

As the president's remarks only indirectly reflect, by late summer 1973, he had grown frustrated with the Mideast diplomatic stalemate. Many diplomats were urging at the time a more active American approach. Some were so concerned at the stagnation that they would have welcomed a conflict, even an Israeli victory, as long as it resulted in movement. More important, the thinking of American analysts and diplomats was dominated by historical analogies with the Six-Day War and the Jordanian crisis of September 1970. Thus, Israeli maneuvers, preemption, and victory were the possibilities that they envisioned. Russian analysts, in contrast, assumed that the Arabs would attack first if war were renewed.[115]

During his first two weeks as secretary of state, Kissinger met with Arabs and Israelis at the annual United Nations General Assembly session in New York. With the Arabs he sought to demonstrate his willingness and ability to mediate. By the end of the period Kissinger scored a breakthrough when foreign minister Al-Zayyat indicated Cairo's possible interest in the long-delayed Egyptian-Israeli proximity talks. Kissinger was hopeful that discussions could begin a few weeks later, after the scheduled Israeli elections.[116]

Thus, on the eve of the Egyptian and Syrian attack on Israel, the administration had already shown it intended a step-by-step approach, beginning with an Egyptian-Israeli limited accord. The war would alter the psychological atmosphere, the urgency of the discussions, and the tactics of American diplomacy, but it would not change the overall strategy.

The October War

Throughout the crisis Nixon and Kissinger tried to impose their fixed conceptions on a situation that did not entirely fit. They believed Israeli strength would deter an Arab attack. They believed the Arabs would not fight Israel for more than a few days without suffering a crushing defeat. They believed an oil embargo would not be imposed, or, if imposed, would not "have any lasting impact."[117] They believed that the Soviets would play by the rules of detente as defined in Washington. In all these assumptions they were wrong. Thus, the crisis period was filled with false starts as Nixon and Kissinger reacted to events on the basis of mistaken expectations and then were forced to compensate. The administration tried to manipulate events so as to further Nixon's strategy of early September. The resulting mixture of determination and improvisation created confusion and tactical inconsistency, but it also led to an activist policy.

Nowhere was the gap between fact and preconception clearer than in the failure of the Washington intelligence community to assess accurately the meaning of Arab military buildup. One hour after the Egyptians and Syrians had attacked, the Watch Committee, a special intelligence group that advised the National Security Council in a crisis, concluded,

We can find no hard evidence of a major, coordinated Egyptian-Syrian offensive across the canal and in the Golan Heights area. Rather, the weight of evidence indicated an action-reaction situation where a series of responses by each side to perceived threats created an increasingly dangerous potential for confrontation. The current hostilities are apparently a result of that situation . . . It is possible that the Egyptians or Syrians, particularly the latter, may have been preparing a raid or other small scale action.[118]

Had the intelligence community concluded between 3 and 5 October that the Arabs were about to attack, American leaders might have been able to avert the conflict, its accompanying oil embargo, and a near Soviet-American confrontation. American action in the Cuban missile crisis, for example, was possible because President Kennedy was warned in time. In the October War, the intelligence community also influenced events, but by failure rather than success. Analysts with strong ties to the Israelis were inclined to accept their friends' confidence. According to one report, on 4 October "the group closest to the Israelis—the Pentagon's Defense Intelligence Agency—still disputed even the threatening nature of the Arab build-up."[119] But the Arabists in the intelligence community had other blinders on. They assumed that Sadat was too involved in improving his economy and building a new Arab front with the moderate oil producers to go to war.

Nixon later complained, "The news of the imminent attack on Israel took us completely by surprise. As recently as the day before, the CIA had reported that war in the Middle East was unlikely . . ." Kissinger pointed out in his 12 October press conference that the prediction errors were not due to lack of information but to false assumptions which caused incorrect analysis. In his memoirs he concludes that the problem was intellectual, a failure to ask the right questions about the confusing Soviet and Arab moves.[120] The day before the war the National Security Agency—able to monitor Egyptian communications from a secret base in Iran—discovered information that implied an imminent attack, but analysts in the intelligence community missed the significance of the data.[121]

The problem of faulty assumptions in Washington began with the intelligence failure, which had four basic causes. First and most important, American intelligence depended on the Israelis, who were thought to have a superior operation, especially in Egypt and Syria. It had always been assumed that because the Israelis would suffer most from error, they would be accurate. Certainly experience seemed to confirm the presumption. As Nixon later told David Frost, "What surprised me the most was, I know they [our intelligence community] were cooperating totally with Israel intelligence and the Israelis have fantastically good intelligence and their intelligence told us there was not going to be an attack."[122] As Israeli-American contacts had increased after 1967, Israeli intelligence was consistently accurate; the immediate Israeli identification of Egyptian violations along the Suez Canal in August 1970 stood as an impressive precedent. When the Israelis had made mistakes, they had always erred on the side of caution, as in their overestimation of the Egyptian armed forces before 1956 and their agitated expectation of an Egyptian attack in late May 1967. American officials had become accustomed to what they often thought were Israeli exaggerations of Arab military readiness and Israeli pessimism about Arab intentions. The Americans had become used to calming the Israelis at times of crisis—in order to downgrade Israel's weapons requests. The bureaucracy's reflex was to reassure the Israelis, not to alert them to their own dangers.[123]

Second, official Washington was prisoner to past experience; the Arabs were not thought capable of matching Israeli military strength. Therefore only a few isolated analysts thought the Arabs might initiate hostilities. As Kissinger noted in his memoirs, "Our definition of rationality did not take seriously the notion of starting an unwinnable war to restore self-respect."[124]

The third reason for misinterpreting the factual data was the clever Arab deception. Arab diplomats—even as important a figure as the Egyptian foreign minister—were not informed of the impending assault. They behaved at the United Nations as though eager to resume diplomacy under Kissinger's auspices, which led the new secretary of state to believe that diplomatic progress was imminent for the first time in two years.[125]

Fourth, the progress of detente in 1972 and 1973, as confirmed by summits in Moscow and San Clemente, led Nixon and Kissinger to believe that the Russians would honor their commitment to inform the United States of impending conflict in the Middle East. Nixon later said that if the Russians knew about the Egyptian and Syrian attack "and did not inform us, that would have been, I think, a very great breach of all of the understandings we had."[126] Yet there are indications that the Russians did know of Arab plans at least three days beforehand.[127] In the week before the war, they ferried nonessential technicians and dependents out of Damascus as well as Cairo, leaving some American analysts to conclude that the Syrians were now imitating the Egyptians in expelling their Russian advisers. In addition, during the two to three weeks before the war, the Kremlin shipped ammunition to Syria and Egypt in huge quantities. Soviet tanks and anti-aircraft missiles enabled Sadat to achieve his breakthrough in crossing the canal. (As early as April, Sadat had uncharacteristically expressed satisfaction with Russian supplies of arms.)[128]

When Sisco burst into Kissinger's Waldorf Towers suite on 6 October at 6 A.M. (New York time) with news that war was imminent, Kissinger's mistaken orientation continued for several hours. He attempted to prevent hostilities by contacting key Arab governments and the Russians, believing that the whole military confrontation reflected Arab fears of an Israeli preemptive attack.[129] When Ambassador Keating was summoned to Meir's office on the morning of the war, he discovered that she had already decided, despite pleas from her chief of staff, not to launch preemptive air attacks in order to gain U.S. diplomatic support and military resupply during the war.[130] Kissinger warned Israel's acting ambassador, Mordechai Shalev, not to preempt, instructed Keating to warn Meir again, and after reviewing Keating's report of his first meeting with Meir, told Eban that he wanted it clear that the decision not to preempt was an Israeli decision relayed to the United States "after it had been taken."[131]

As Kissinger returned to Washington from New York on Saturday afternoon and Nixon from Key Biscayne on Sunday evening, their false assumptions continued. Given the confident Israeli prediction of an overpowering counteroffensive and signs that the Soviets feared imminent Arab defeat, Nixon and Kissinger expected a quick, sweeping Israeli victory.[132]

Many in the administration were not pleased by such a prospect, with its promise to replay the diplomatic results of 1967—Arab humiliation and reaction against the United States, a precipitous decline in U.S. influence, greater instability in the area, and increased difficulty in fostering negotiations. Hampered by poor intelligence from the battlefield and unaware of what was happening, the administration at first condemned the Arab attack and proposed a cease-fire status quo ante. Although this position initially appeared to favor the Israelis, it was thought that it would soon seem partial to the Arabs, after their armies had been routed.[133] According to Secretary of Defense Schlesinger, "There were two premises to our initial policy: that Israel would quickly defeat its foes, and that the U.S. should maintain a low profile and avoid visible involvement."[134]

As a result, no one in the Washington decision-making group was particularly worried about Israeli security during the first three days of the war. Israeli requests for resupply of specific lost equipment were not huge and not thought urgent. Kissinger agreed to allow a few high priority "consumables"—mainly Sidewinder air-to-air missiles—to be picked up by Israeli planes.[135] The decision marked the first time during an Arab-Israeli war that the United States did not impose an arms embargo on all belligerents.

By Monday and Tuesday, 8 and 9 October, it began to appear that the war would last longer than had been anticipated. The Israelis were not so successful as had been expected. Their sudden weakness strengthened the temptation to manipulate the war and create stalemate, thereby providing an opportunity for U.S. diplomacy and expanding U.S. influence in the area. Nixon was later explicit in admitting the American objective:

I believed that only a battlefield stalemate would provide the foundation in which fruitful negotiations might begin: Any equilibrium—even if only an equilibrium of mutual exhaustion—would make it easier to reach an enforceable settlement. Therefore, I was convinced that we must not use our influence to bring about a cease-fire that would leave the parties in such imbalance that negotiations for a permanent settlement would never begin.[136]

In order to be effective, this strategy required dexterity, delicacy, and deception, a skillful balance of relations and contacts with all parties involved. It could succeed only with one man as the key decision maker.

It was Nixon's style to maintain some distance from involved officials (as in September 1970), and October 1973 was also a time of domestic crisis; the president's attention was constantly diverted.[137] Therefore, Kissinger was left with extraordinary latitude in conducting U.S. policy. It would be difficult to imagine a similar situation occurring in the open and often leaky Carter apparatus, the collegial Johnson system, or the more formal Truman structure.

As the war continued during the first week, the problem confronting the administration was to retain the confidence of Israel and its supporters at home without ruining the possibility of reopening relations with the Arab world. The Arabs had to be convinced that the United States was doing little for Israel while the pro-Israeli lobby had to think that the U.S. was doing a great deal. Nixon later described this contradiction: "While we had to keep the interest of the Israelis uppermost during this conflict in which they were the victims of aggression, I hoped that we could support them in such a way that we would not force an irreparable break with the Egyptians, the Syrians and the other Arab nations."[138]

How to accomplish this contradictory task became the tactical question of the crisis. On the one hand, Nixon and Kissinger had to deal with various pro-Arab forces: the Arab world itself, emboldened by its attack and growing oil leverage; the oil companies, who feared that an embargo and possible loss of their concessions would follow Washington support of Israel; and the State Department bureaucracy, which sought to avoid repeating the post-1967 Arab alienation from the United States. On the other hand, the administration had obligations to Israel: Jerusalem had been promised that additional American arms would be available in a crisis.[139] The most important consideration in the Nixon-Kissinger calculus, however, was U.S. military credibility. Israel need not achieve a 1967-style victory, but the United States could not allow one of its most visible allies to be intimidated. It could not allow the Arabs to score a clear success with Soviet arms against American arms, since that would influence the perceptions of governments throughout the world. The U.S. had to be seen as a superpower that would back its friends firmly.

During the war, American policy toward the Soviet Union was uncharacteristically ambivalent. As in September 1970, Nixon was more inclined to see Soviet complicity than was Kissinger.[140] But the approach to Moscow had become more complex for both of them. Because of the agreements reached at the two summits of 1972 and 1973, the two U.S. leaders had a political and psychological stake in a smoothly functioning detente. Although Nixon suspected that the Soviets had had foreknowledge and Kissinger thought the Russians "stopped short of encouraging the war but made no effort to halt it," they did not picture the war as a confrontation with the U.S.S.R. or approach it like the September 1970 Jordan crisis. Somewhat contradictorily, key administration officials feared that the Russians might intervene if Israel humiliated the Arabs or that a major resupply of Israel by the United States might lead to a large Russian program favoring the Arabs.[141]

By Tuesday the Israelis had smashed the Syrian advance on the Golan Heights and had counterattacked, but only after heavy losses in Israeli aircraft.[142] In the Sinai, however, the hastily devised Israeli counteroffensive failed. The Israeli Defense Forces had not yet adapted to the new Egyptian tactics, which used infantry-operated antitank missiles to overwhelm Israel's armored thrusts.[143] There would be no significant change on the Sinai front for the next five days.

The fourth and fifth days of the war, 9 and 10 October, were the turning point in how key policy makers perceived the conflict. Originally, the American decision-making group had hoped to prevent a catastrophic Arab defeat and the resulting damage to American interests. On Tuesday, 9 October, however, Israeli ambassador Dinitz brought shocking news: Israeli losses in the Sinai were staggering; Egypt had the best of the fight so far. American belief in Israeli invincibility, an article of faith just hours before, was shattered. As Kissinger later wrote, "What Dinitz was reporting would require a fundamental reassessment of strategy."[144] Ironically, Israel's setbacks prompted Kissinger to raise his sights for postwar diplomacy: he saw an opportunity for the United States to nudge the intractable conflict toward solution.

In the new circumstances, the NSC decided on Tuesday to press for a cease-fire in place, and sought to involve the U.S.S.R. in this effort.[145] The Soviets expressed some interest, as they had been pressing Sadat since the first day of the war to accept such a cease-fire. None of the combatants would accept the idea, however; the battle for the Sinai could still go either way.[146] Meanwhile, the administration grew suspicious of the U.S.S.R. when Brezhnev urged the Algerians to become militarily engaged.[147]

As a military stalemate developed in the Sinai, U.S. and Israeli objectives began to diverge markedly. For the American leadership, the stage had been set for a workable cease-fire before the Israeli forces could recoup and the Russians could begin to reequip their Arab clients. The Israelis, however, were determined to reassert their military dominance.

As early as Sunday evening, 7 October, Kissinger had told Dinitz that Israeli El Al jets could start picking up military supplies at U.S. depots, as long as their markings were painted over.[148] This operation began the next day. By late Monday, however, the Israeli counterattack in Sinai had foundered and Dinitz requested much larger quantities than the El Al planes could transport. Nixon notes that on Tuesday, 9 October, "I met with Kissinger and told him to let the Israelis know that we would replace all their losses and asked him to work out the logistics for doing so.[149] By late Tuesday, Kissinger had informed Dinitz, with whom he was speaking several times a day, of the president's decision.

The problem with the president's decision, however, was that it was open-ended. Moreover, it had been communicated only to Kissinger, which meant that the secretary of defense was not at this stage receiving direct instructions from the president. How and when and in what quantities the Israelis would receive these weapons was caught up in bureaucratic confusion. During the next seventy-two hours—over Wednesday, Thursday, and Friday—the Israelis remained frustrated while the administration sought means of supplying them quietly, if possible, without alienating the Arabs. Kissinger informed Dinitz that Pentagon reluctance to ship the arms was causing the delays.[150] The explanation seemed plausible. Kissinger had worked closely with the Israelis for nearly five years, but the Defense Department was now run by two new officials whom the Israelis had reason to suspect: Schlesinger, a convert from Judaism, and Clements, a Texas oilman.

Unknown to Dinitz, however, the reality was more complex. Kissinger was using the stalled arms to force Israel to accept a cease-fire in place to end the war in military stalemate.[151] The secretary of state was determined, however, that Israel should at least regain the prewar lines on the Syrian front before the cease-fire came into effect; he could not allow the appearance of an unqualified Arab victory on both fronts. For this reason, he stalled on the cease-fire initiative until Friday, 12 October, by which time Israeli forces were well into Syria but were still mired in the Sinai. In order to help the White House withstand the pressures of Israel and her American supporters while he waited for the optimal moment, Kissinger blamed the Defense Department for the delays.[152]

The actual situation in the Pentagon was more convoluted than Kissinger portrayed. The initial indifference of Schlesinger and Clements's lack of sympathy toward the Israelis was shared by many line officers, who feared that their commands would be stripped of arms for Israel. In contrast, Air Force chief George Brown and his intelligence head, George Keegan, worked on their own authority throughout the week to prepare a military airlift in case the president should order it. The Chief of Naval Operations, Admiral Elmo Zumwalt, was openly favorable to the Israeli requests. Chairman of the Joint Chiefs, Thomas Moorer, embodied these conflicting attitudes: on the one hand, he favored a military airlift to resupply Israel from the outset of the war, but on the other hand, he admitted late in the war that he found the Israelis "difficult" and hoped they would not receive all items on their "wish list." The Pentagon, then, was a melange of policy impulses awaiting clear direction.[153]

As the new secretary of state sought to persuade the Arabs and Israelis to agree to a cease-fire and to involve the Russians in that effort on Wednesday, Thursday, and Friday, the president was largely removed from the scene. Shortly after Nixon ordered the resupply of Israel "in principle" on Tuesday, he met with his vice president and heard officially that Agnew had decided to resign. The decision was made public the next day. Therefore, during the three critical days as Kissinger sought a cease-fire, Nixon was plunged into meetings over a new vice president. On Friday he was further harassed by a Court of Appeals ruling that ordered him to release nine tapes sought by Special Prosecutor Archibald Cox. Thus, the president was not closely involved in the Mideast crisis during this period, and he continued receiving his information from Kissinger mainly by telephone. For example, he wrote that he "had been checking almost hourly with Kissinger," on how the resupply effort was proceeding. Nixon claims to have favored increased arms shipments to the Israelis and to have objected when his secretary of state informed him that the secretary of defense was delaying them.[154]

Both Kissinger and Schlesinger admitted after the crisis that arms to Israel had been delayed during this period. Schlesinger protested to interviewers several months later, "Your suggestion that the Department of Defense was . . . dragging its heels in resupplying Israel is wrong; there is a difference between dragging your heels and having your shoes nailed to the floor by national policy."[155] Kissinger told a news conference on 25 October 1973: "Throughout the first week we attempted to bring about a moderation in the level of outside supplies that were introduced into the area. . ." Schlesinger was more straightforward when he told reporters at a news conference the next day that "the United States delayed, deliberately delayed, the start of its resupply operations hoping that a ceasefire could be implemented quickly."[156]

Kissinger was powerful enough to create bureaucratic shields against criticism. In his memoirs he admits to deceiving Israeli Ambassador Simcha Dinitz on occasion to preserve their personal relationship: "When I had bad news for Dinitz, I was not above ascribing it to bureaucratic stalemates or unfavorable decisions by superiors." That seems to have been Kissinger's tactic when he informed Dinitz that the arms for Israel had been delayed by Defense Department "foot dragging."[157]

In the intervening three days, the NSC and the Pentagon quarreled over means of quietly resupplying the Israelis; the administration was still far from considering a direct airlift. In each case the Pentagon raised questions about methods that seemed as impractical as they were original. The painted-over El Al planes simply could not carry enough supplies, and the operation was no longer secret: crews loading supplies for Israel had been photographed in Norfolk, Virginia.[158]

It was suggested that Israel might charter regular commercial planes. A check with Lloyd's of London revealed that the insurance to enter a war zone was almost as high as the cost of the planes themselves. Next, the NSC asked the Department of Transportation to charter civilian aircraft, but American companies were also unwilling to fly into a war zone. Even if their pilots consented and their planes survived, they could soon become targets of Palestinian terrorists. They took the reasonable attitude that if the American government was too timid to act, why should they? The government has authority to commandeer civilian aircraft, but only when a national emergency has been declared. That action would have involved more political and diplomatic problems than sending materiel in military aircraft.

By Friday, 12 October, it was clear that military aircraft would have to be used. Nixon phoned Schlesinger in their only direct contact of the week to order materiel shipped to the American base in the Azores, where it would be picked up by the Israelis. This scheme avoided a direct airlift to Israel, but it was a logistical nightmare. No permission had yet been gained from the Portuguese. Worse yet, American aircraft would have to deliver hundreds of tons of materiel to a military airport in the Azores where it would then be transferred to another island for Israeli pickup.[159] And where would Israel get the planes needed to haul the materiel from the Azores?

Meanwhile, a president weakened by the growing Watergate crisis confronted the persistent Israeli ambassador, Simcha Dinitz, and pro-Israeli forces more vocal than in any previous crisis. As Israel's situation appeared more grim, business, labor, religious, and congressional leaders bombarded the White House on Israel's behalf. Senator Javits and the Reverend Billy Graham, for example, communicated directly with the president despite his relative seclusion.[160]

Matters became critical for Israel on 12 October. The Israelis had been promised that Phantom jets would be flown secretly to Israel to replace those lost in battle, but even this operation had not yet begun. In contrast, a Russian airlift of arms to Cairo and Damascus, begun gradually on Wednesday, had reached massive proportions by Friday.[161] Meanwhile, the danger of a Jordanian attack remained. The United States had exerted pressure over the previous three days to keep King Hussein out of the war despite entreaties from the Saudis, Egyptians, and Syrians that he order his army into the conflict. The administration had gone as far as to warn Israel not to attack Jordan. In the end Hussein did commit a crack armored brigade, but it did not see action until 16 October, too late to make a difference.[162]

With the tension increasing late Friday in Washington, the only way to avoid a direct military airlift to Israel was through a cease-fire. Kissinger feared that American forces resupplying the Israelis would alienate the Arabs, ruin hopes for diplomatic progress after the war, and lead to an oil embargo against the United States. Yet neither Kissinger nor the American public could countenance an Israeli defeat. The Israelis had already suffered grievously in casualties and loss of materiel. Prime Minister Meir had telephoned the president several times pleading for arms and even offered at one point to fly secretly to Washington to see him, an offer Nixon gently rejected.[163] On Thursday Meir had even raised the possibility of an Israeli defeat. Since the Israelis were now eighteen miles outside Damascus and in the midst of transferring troops to the Egyptian front, Meir hoped she could trade Israeli gains in Syria for Egyptian advances in the Sinai. By Thursday Kissinger had coaxed Meir into accepting a cease-fire in place.[164] It seemed that Kissinger's strategy was working perfectly. The war could end without a direct American airlift to Israel; the basis for future diplomacy would have been established, and American oil interests in the Persian Gulf would remain secure.

Although Russian radio broadcasts had urged other Arab countries to join the fray and Arab producers to embargo oil, the Soviets also indicated a willingness to accept a cease-fire in place by abstaining if a cease-fire resolution was brought to the Security Council. They would not introduce it. The United States could not introduce such a resolution, since that would give the impression that its ally, Israel, was suing for peace. Thus it became necessary to find a country not involved in the fighting to propose the ceasefire resolution, and Kissinger chose the British, who now maintained solid relations with both sides. But the British embassy in Egypt had reported that Sadat opposed a military standstill, so Britain sent its ambassador to query Sadat, who had to be roused from sleep. The proud Egyptian leader bluntly refused the cease-fire.[165]

Kissinger learned of the incident Friday evening (in Washington) and was furious with London for having sought Egypt's approval before introducing the resolution to the U.N.[166] Kissinger's whole strategy depended on presenting Sadat with a fait accompli. Sadat could then tell his Arab brethren that he had never wanted the cease-fire but had reluctantly acquiesced to both superpowers. Kissinger erred in failing to convey this clearly enough to the British. The British diplomats failed to perceive that this strategy would have ended the war without the consequences they feared. The Soviets erred in refusing joint U.S.-Soviet sponsorship of the cease-fire resolution. That move would have sent an emphatic signal to the belligerents, made British cooperation unnecessary, and secured terms favorable to the Soviet ally, Egypt, which would then have appeared victorious with Soviet arms. But Sadat's was the greatest diplomatic blunder of this stillborn initiative, and indeed, of the entire war. Exultant with success in the war's first week, Sadat foolishly threw away his only chance to quit while ahead.

When a desperate Dinitz met with Kissinger late Friday evening (after Nixon had announced that Ford would be the new vice president), Kissinger was prepared to consider the urgent Israeli request for arms. The pessimistic tone of Meir's recent communications had alarmed him. It was not impossible that Israel would resort to nuclear weapons if the situation worsened. Therefore, about midnight, an anxious secretary of state phoned Schlesinger, who was in bed, and asked him to arrange the resupply.[167] Upon his arrival at the Pentagon, the defense secretary consulted with other officials and decided on a direct military airlift. Since he did not trust Kissinger, Schlesinger phoned the White House chief of staff, Alexander Haig, to clear his decision with Nixon. Only afterward did he phone Kissinger. To hide the full extent of U.S. assistance, the secretaries of state and defense agreed that the planes would fly at night. However, many officials still believed, because of the poor American intelligence from the battlefield, that the Israelis were being deliberately pessimistic in order to obtain larger arms quantities for stockpiling.[168] The Pentagon therefore recommended to the president that only three C-5A military transport planes be used. Kissinger favored a slightly larger number. Nixon insisted that all available aircraft should be used immediately: "My reaction was that we would take just as much heat for sending three planes as for sending thirty." To clear up any confusion in the Pentagon about his intentions, he told Kissinger, "Goddamn it, use every one we have. Tell them to send everything that can fly!!"[169]

Kissinger still was concerned to protect diplomatic options. According to Nixon, Kissinger suggested that "politically it would be . . . perhaps . . . dangerous for us to send a greater number [of planes] and . . . it would . . . destroy the chances for negotiations in the future if our profile was too high." Nixon, always more prone than Kissinger to activism and risky policies, wanted to send a clear message to Moscow and believed that what mattered was not the number of planes but making the airlift "work."[170]

The consequence of this decision, which included flying additional Phantoms and Skyhawks directly to Israel, was that the Israelis were emboldened to seek victory. The supplies and equipment may not have decided between victory and defeat, but they were crucial to Israel's morale. Certainly the airlift permitted the military planners to make free use of supplies and weapons since they would be replenished. The magnitude of the airlift over the next several weeks was awe inspiring: several hundred individual missions and thousands of tons of equipment, an enterprise larger than the Berlin airlift of 1948–49.[171]

The first week of the war had important consequences for the administration's decision-making structure: it clearly placed Henry Kissinger at the helm of U.S. Mideast policy. Nixon agreed with his secretary of state on the need to create an atmosphere for diplomacy, and only he could order the massive airlift. Yet, within that broad framework, Kissinger worked out tactics and strategies while the president agonized over the growing domestic turmoil around him. Kissinger had no genuine rival. Thus, U.S. strategy—to end the war without a clear victory for either side and before a resupply of Israel became necessary— was conceived and executed at the State Department and the NSC without close presidential involvement. In his memoirs Nixon does not even mention an impending cease-fire as a factor in his diplomacy: his focus was on countering Soviet actions. Spending nearly full time on the problem, Kissinger moderated his chief's preoccupation with the Russians and planned the cease-fire initiative.

His plans did not include coordination with the allies. Kissinger was furious with his NATO partners for refusing to provide bases for U.S. forces and for balking at U.S. leadership lest they incur the wrath of the Arab oil producers. Turkey allowed Soviet planes to overfly its territory to resupply the Arabs but refused permission for U.S. planes to use American bases on Turkish territory. Kissinger had wanted to use U.S. bases in Britain for the flight of SR-71 intelligence craft over the Mideast, but he became so disgusted with British caution that he cancelled the project.[172] Prime Minister Heath later denied that the United States had ever asked permission, implying that it would have been granted. In any case, not sending the intelligence aircraft hindered U.S. efforts to monitor the war and made policy making difficult. The Spanish, not in NATO but close allies nonetheless, made it clear that U.S. bases on their soil would not be available for use on behalf of Israel. The Germans allowed flights from the major U.S. airbase at Ramstein until they became public on 24 October; the Bonn government then asked Washington to end all shipments immediately.

Only the Portuguese agreed to help, after enormous pressure was applied, allowing American transports to use the Azores for refueling. When the first planes took off from the United States, the Portuguese had not yet agreed to the use of their bases.[173] The U.S. had considerable leverage on Portugal because of the controversial Portuguese colonies remaining in southern Africa. In order to gain Portuguese cooperation, Kissinger wielded his familiar carrot and stick. In Nixon's name he bluntly turned down a Portuguese request for military equipment as a quid pro quo for the use of the Azores air base and "threatened to leave Portugal to its fate in a hostile world." But he also agreed to help Portugal avoid sanctions against its African colonial policy in the United Nations and the U.S. Senate.[174] Thus, when the moment arrived for action, America's allies were trembling before Arab oil threats and Washington was forced to act alone. Relations with the allies remained bitter for months afterward.

There had been no other Mideast war in which domestic support for Israel—especially arms resupplies—was as pronounced, unified, and vocal.[175] By the time Dinitz met with Kissinger late Friday night, the Israelis and their supporters were about to mount an intensified public campaign for military resupply. The State Department had been informed that Senator Jackson would deliver a major speech Sunday night blasting the administration for the delays. Holding back support for Israel could have cost the president support in the Watergate crisis.[176]

The record suggests, however, that domestic constraints were peripheral during the crisis. Nixon and Kissinger made the decision to resupply Israel because of the massive Soviet airlift and Sadat's refusal to accept the cease-fire. They sought to end the war without a clear-cut victory for either side; that goal now demanded aid to Israel. The decision was finalized by Nixon early Saturday morning. Despite administration efforts to keep the airlift secret by flying the planes at night, they were held up by crosswinds over the Azores and did not arrive in Israel until Sunday morning.[177]

By Monday, word of the airlift began to leak out. At first, the Arab reaction was surprisingly mild. Kissinger had sent secret messages to Sadat and Faisal explaining that the airlift would increase U.S. influence over Israel for an "equitable peace settlement."[178] On Wednesday four Arab foreign ministers met with Nixon and Kissinger. Both men cautioned the Arab representatives against linking a cease-fire to a total settlement, urging them to accept an unconditional cease-fire to be followed by active U.S. diplomatic efforts on a step-by-step basis. The meetings appeared warm and friendly.[179] The same day a letter from King Faisal reached the White House. It asked that the United States immediately terminate shipments of arms to Israel and called upon Israel to withdraw to the 1967 lines; otherwise, U.S.-Saudi relations would become "lukewarm." To give force to Faisal's words, the next day (17 October) the Arab oil producers announced that they would cut production by 5 percent a month until Israel had withdrawn from the territories captured in 1967, a threat they never pursued.[180]

The Arabs by now had ample reason for frustration, for the battle had turned. On Saturday and Sunday (13 and 14 October) the Israeli Defense Forces had crushed an Egyptian offensive aimed at breaking through toward the Sinai passes. As soon as the Egyptian armor tried to advance beyond its SAM-umbrella, it fell easy prey to Israel's deadly Phantoms and Skyhawks.[181] On Monday 15 October, Israel began a crossing of its own to the Egyptian side of the canal.

Friday afternoon, 19 October, Nixon requested an appropriation of $2.2 billion to cover the cost of the airlift. The move, unprecedented in size and scope, also represented an unusual executive initiated request for Israeli aid. The announcement incensed Faisal and led the Saudi king to announce an embargo on oil shipments to the United States. The other Arab producers soon followed his example.[182]

This dramatic step by Saudi Arabia lent urgency to Kissinger's efforts to end the war rapidly before the Israelis could win decisively, a development that would again destroy American relations with the Arab states. Administration actions now had to take account of increased Western dependence on Arab energy sources as well as the early Arab military successes; these factors created the perception of increased Arab power throughout the crisis.

Arab producers had threatened to use the oil weapon even before the war. By 15 September OPEC felt secure in its improved position because of the "tightening supply situation" and demanded a renegotiation of the 1971 Teheran agreements. The first meeting was scheduled for Vienna on 8 October, where the OPEC members (led by Iran and Saudi Arabia) demanded a 100 percent increase in posted prices.[183] By then the October War was two days old.

The major American oil companies active in the Middle East had not ignored these developments. On 13 October, a few hours after Nixon had secretly approved the airlift for Israel and a full six days before the embargo, John J. McCloy, the chief lawyer for Aramco, had a letter hand-delivered to President Nixon at the White House. Kissinger also received a copy. The letter was signed by the chairmen of Aramco's four constituent companies: Mobil, Exxon, Chevron, and Texaco. These gentlemen said bluntly:

> We are convinced of the seriousness of the Saudis and Kuwaitis and that any actions of the U.S. government at this time in terms of increased military aid to Israel will have a critical and adverse effect on our relations with the moderate Arab producing countries . . . In the present highly charged climate in the Middle East, there is a high probability that a single action taken by one producer government against the United States would have a snowballing effect that would produce a major petroleum supply crisis.

The four chairmen went on to suggest that if American interests suffered, the Japanese and Europeans, still highly dependent on Middle East oil, "may be forced to expand their Middle East supply positions at our expense." In other words, the United States should not support Israel lest the competitive position of the U.S. companies with the Japanese and Europeans be harmed. The letter concluded: "Much more than our commercial interest in the area is now at hazard. The whole position of the United States in the Middle East is on the way to being seriously impaired, with Japanese, European and perhaps Russian interests largely supplanting United States presence in the area, to the detriment of both our economy and our security."[184]

There was no response to the letter other than a two-sentence note of acknowledgment from Chief of Staff Haig, to whom it had been originally presented. There is no evidence that the companies pursued the matter further. Otto Miller of Socal (Chevron), one of the signatories to the letter, later told the Church committee that he could not remember any other occasion when such a letter was sent to the president.[185] Senator Church charged in a newspaper interview, "The letter appeared on its face to be from the American companies . . . but it was in fact the work of the Saudi Arabian government. And . . . after they had sent the letter, they reported back to Saudi Arabia that they had done as they'd been told, that they had followed their instructions."[186] Whether or not the letter to Nixon was a direct result of Saudi initiative, Saudi pressure had clearly influenced the company executives. On 25 October 1973, an internal Aramco cable contained the following comment:

> My other contact indicates great satisfaction with Aramco and Americans in taking pro Arab stand and he further remarked to effect that stateside companies also apparently [are] with [the] Arabs more than before. After I remarked that these things have been difficult and that cutbacks not good for our business he remarked, "we hope to reward you," and I took this in context of future growth.[187]

During this period Aramco supplied the Egyptians and Iraqis with oil, helped to enforce the ensuing Arab embargo against the United States, and refused to supply the American military in the area in accordance with Saudi instructions. According to the Aramco Chairman Frank Jungers, "The important thing was to give the immediate image of being *with* the [Saudi Arabian] government, not trying to fight it."[188]

The concerns and behavior of the oil companies were not important to Nixon and Kissinger, and the companies had no direct impact on policy during the war. Nor were Nixon and Kissinger seriously concerned about threatened price increases and threatened production cuts. They were, however, worried about the possible effects of the embargo and anxious about relations with Moscow.

During most of the second week of the war, Sadat did not realize the extent of the Egyptian military disaster. Premier Kosygin traveled to Cairo on Tuesday, 16 October, to show Sadat aerial photographs demonstrating the seriousness of the Israeli crossing.[189] As soon as Kosygin had completed his trip, the Kremlin sent an urgent message to Washington suggesting immediate consultations either through a Gromyko visit to Washington or a Kissinger trip to Moscow. Schlesinger advised Kissinger to stall for a few days to gain leverage on Moscow and to teach the Russians a lesson for their destabilizing actions during the crisis.[190] Nixon and Kissinger, however, saw a second opportunity for concluding the war. The Israelis would soon achieve an overpowering victory and with it would come dangers of confrontation with the U.S.S.R. and destruction of U.S. relations with the Arabs.

Kissinger told Dinitz that his real reason for the Moscow trip was to gain extra time for the Israelis to complete their operations.[191] Actually, the secretary wanted to fly to Moscow so he could negotiate on his own, unfettered by the Watergate turmoil. By this point Kissinger had gathered enough power in his hands to act without consulting the NSC. In this sense Kissinger had greater negotiating power than Gromyko would have had in Washington. The secretary of state received a message en route to Moscow in which Nixon informed him that he had told the Russians that Kissinger was authorized to conclude the negotiations for a cease-fire without the president's further approval. Kissinger was horrified. Nixon had just deprived him of the capacity to stall. As he wryly observed in his memoirs, "History will not record that I resisted many grants of authority. This one I resented bitterly; it was a classic example of how 'full powers' can inhibit rather than enhance negotiating flexibility."[192]

By the time that Kissinger received this message, two other developments had increased the urgency of the situation. First, the Arab oil embargo had been announced against both the United States and the Netherlands on Saturday, 20 October. This oil supply crisis gave new incentive for diplomatic actions. Second, the Middle East crisis reinforced Nixon's predisposition to fire the Watergate Special Prosecutor Archibald Cox (who was seeking the court-ordered release of selected tapes); he wished to convince Brezhnev that the president controlled his government. As he plotted his move that crucial Saturday afternoon, Nixon asked Leonard Garment, "If I can't get an order carried out by my Attorney General, how can I get arms to Israel?" With Kissinger in Moscow, Nixon argued that he had no choice about Cox. Aide Patrick Buchanan replied as Garment had: there was no choice, the president must fire Cox.[193]

When Nixon confronted Attorney General Elliot Richardson, however, he used the Middle East war to argue that Richardson should delay his resignation for several days until the crisis eased. Richardson later told Theodore White that the president "was desperately concerned about the Middle East situation . . . Brezhnev and his colleagues in Moscow could not conceivably understand the specific defiance of his orders by Cox in that afternoon's press conference. It was like the 1970 action in Cambodia—he wanted to show Moscow and Peking his determination, and he would pay the necessary domestic price to do it."[194]

As Nixon saw the interplay between domestic and foreign policy, presidential credibility with the Kremlin required that Cox be fired and Richardson remain. But Richardson refused to accept the president's argument. Within a few hours Nixon announced Cox's dismissal and the departure of Richardson and his deputy, William Ruckelshaus, who had also refused to fire Cox. The "Saturday night massacre" brought down what Haig called a "fire storm" upon the president. The vehement national reaction made the protest about the Cambodian invasion seem mild. Within three days the president capitulated and turned over the disputed tapes, but his position would never be the same. During the remainder of his term, as the Middle East continued to be the central foreign problem, Nixon would be preoccupied with self-preservation.[195]

Thus, when Kissinger began negotiating in Moscow, the burdens on Washington had increased dramatically as Nixon's mandate crumbled. By cable Nixon then ordered Kissinger to work with the Soviets *to impose* a comprehensive peace on the Middle East. Kissinger was outraged. The whole thrust of

American strategy had been to separate a cease-fire from any kind of specific political solution. Then Kissinger planned to initiate some form of step-by-step diplomacy that would have the benefit of excluding the Soviets from negotiations and reducing their influence in Egypt and Syria. To change course suddenly in the midst of a difficult negotiation in Moscow was something Kissinger refused to consider. He stridently rejected Nixon's orders.[196]

Working with the Russians to impose a solution based on some shared notion of "justice" ran counter to the Nixon-Kissinger philosophy. And the Russians were in no mood for prolonged haggling. They quickly agreed to a cease-fire resolution tied only to Security Council Resolution 242. This document was soon passed by the Security Council as Resolution 338 and became the legal basis for ending the October 1973 Mideast war and the framework for the negotiations that followed.

The first part of the resolution called for a cease-fire within twelve hours of its adoption by the Security Council. The second paragraph called for the implementation of Security Council Resolution 242, "in all of its parts." This statement was far different from Sadat's earlier insistence that any cease-fire require Israeli agreement to a long-term settlement, including Israeli withdrawal behind the 1967 lines.[197] But by pressing for some agreement, it held out the hope that the war Sadat had initiated would spark a move toward settlement and Israeli withdrawals. The phrase "in all of its parts" suggested that all sections of Resolution 242 would be considered as a package, so that Israel would not have to withdraw until it knew what it would receive in return from individual Arab governments. The third paragraph called for immediate negotiations between the parties, a major concession to the Israelis, but the phrase "under appropriate auspices" was an escape clause that allowed the Arabs to avoid face-to-face negotiations with Israel.[198]

The Israelis first received word of the Soviet-American agreement when a stunned Dinitz was summoned to the White House to meet with Haig early on Sunday afternoon, less than two days after Kissinger had left for Moscow. Israel had not been consulted but had simply been presented a fait accompli. In one last attempt to stall the cease-fire, Meir telephoned President Nixon Sunday evening and asked for extra time, but Nixon turned her down.[199]

The Israelis now had little choice. The Cabinet accepted the cease-fire, but the military remained frustrated. Meir's only consolation was that Kissinger would visit Tel Aviv on his way home from Moscow. Sadat, considering the disposition of the battlefield, had even less flexibility than the Israelis, but he is reported to have gained a critical concession from the Russians: they themselves would guarantee, if necessary, the observation of the cease-fire.[200]

On his five-hour stay in Israel on Monday, 22 October, Kissinger tried to soothe Israeli concerns. He claimed that the Soviets had orally agreed to the exchange of prisoners within seventy-two hours of the cease-fire, and he emphasized that the Arabs had now agreed to negotiations with Israel for the first time and without insisting on prior Israeli withdrawals to the 1967 lines. He steered Israeli thinking toward a Geneva Conference under Soviet-American auspices. Curiously, he hinted to the Israelis that he might tolerate a few hours "slippage" in the cease-fire, as though the emotionally devastated Israeli leadership would take comfort from a few extra hours of turning the screws on the Egyptian Third Army.[201]

If the secretary of state left Israel confident that the cease-fire would hold with only minor violations (which his actions seemed to contemplate), it is surprising that so experienced a diplomat could so ignore the realities on the ground. The armies of Egypt and Israel had ended in formations so entangled as to dizzy the imagination, presenting an almost overpowering temptation for the Israelis to close their trap on the Egyptians. Amazingly, Kissinger and the Russians had made no provision for enforcing the cease-fire or even for returning U.N. observers to the canal area to oversee possible violations.

It is hard to reconcile Kissinger's failure to provide for supervision of the cease-fire with his generally hard-nosed philosophy. Did he believe that his word was enough to hold back the Israeli Defense Forces, that they would not take revenge on the Egyptians who had inflicted so much punishment on Israel? If so, Kissinger's estimate of his own power far exceeded his understanding of human emotions. Kissinger's failure to work out with the Soviets a method for supervising the cease-fire proved to be his gravest diplomatic mistake of the crisis, an omission that resulted two days later in a nasty U.S.-Soviet confrontation.

After rapid approval by the Security Council, the cease-fire went into effect on schedule early Monday evening, 22 October, Middle East time. It did not last twelve hours. Shortly after the cease-fire began, Egyptian artillery violated it; there is no evidence that the infractions were ordered by Cairo. Nevertheless, the frustrated Israelis took rapid advantage. By Tuesday evening, they had captured the territory covering the remaining escape routes for the Third Army. No supplies could now reach that force without Israeli approval. If the Third Army remained trapped, it would soon have no choice but surrender.[202]

Kissinger returned to Washington at 3:00 A.M., on Tuesday, 23 October, and the next morning he had barely settled into his office when Soviet Minister Vorontsov was on the phone complaining of Israeli advances. The secretary of state was deeply concerned. He had assured the Russians that the Israelis would abide by the cease-fire; in fact, Kissinger now drafted and Nixon approved a sharp cable to Brezhnev in which he assumed "full responsibility to bring about a complete end of hostilities on the part of Israel."[203] The whole incident threatened to destroy America's improving relations with Moscow and Cairo. The Russians might conclude that he had not dealt honorably with them in agreeing to the cease-fire or perhaps that he had "colluded" with Israel (as Brezhnev soon implied in a hot line message to Nixon), further undermining trust. The new Israeli successes would ruin the possibility of improving relations with Egypt, especially since President Nixon had promised Sadat that a cease-fire would not lead to the starvation of his Third Army.[204]

Thus, Kissinger sought to induce the Israelis to spare the Third Army. At one point he telephoned Meir directly and then, to demonstrate his reliability to the Russians, he cooperated with another resolution passed by the Security Council on Tuesday evening, Resolution 339, which would have the parties return to their original cease-fire positions and place U.N. observers on the scene.[205]

By Wednesday morning, 24 October, the Israelis were in a position to turn back an Egyptian Red Cross convoy from Cairo carrying medical supplies and blood plasma for the Third Army. Now desperate, Sadat called upon the Russians and Americans to enforce the cease-fire by sending their own forces. The news of Sadat's appeal reached Washington at 3:00 P.M., and American intelligence sources soon spotted (or thought they had spotted) Soviet military moves indicating possible Russian intervention. The most frightening indicators were Ambassador Dobrynin's statement (about 7:25 P.M.) that in Moscow "they have become so angry they want troops," and the CIA's report that the Russian airlift to Egypt had stopped abruptly, implying that the air fleet was being reassembled to move Soviet troops into Egypt to enforce the cease-fire.[206]

While the U.N. Security Council debated Sadat's call for sending super-power troops to the war zone, a message from the Kremlin arrived at the White House about 10:00 P.M. It profoundly alarmed key officials. In it, Brezhnev said: "Let us together . . . urgently dispatch Soviet and American contingents to Egypt . . . I will say it straight, that if you find it impossible to act together with us in this matter, we should be faced with the necessity urgently to consider the question of taking appropriate steps unilaterally. Israel cannot be allowed to get away with the violations."[207]

By 11:00 P.M., Kissinger assembled a rather abbreviated Washington Special Action Group consisting of Schlesinger, William Colby (the CIA director), Thomas Moorer (the chairman of the Joint Chiefs), Haig, and Scowcroft. The group called for an American military alert that would increase the world-wide readiness of both conventional and nuclear weapons. It was potentially the most serious confrontation with the Soviet Union since the Cuban missile crisis of 1962. Yet the vice president had just resigned, and the president stayed upstairs in the White House, as was frequently his custom at late night meetings. He was "as agitated and emotional" as Kissinger had ever heard him, and the group communicated with him through Alexander Haig.[208]

No one from this harried group in the White House basement doubted that a dangerous crisis was imminent and that an alert was appropriate. Although some journalists asserted at the time that the alert was a sham to distract the public from Watergate, this was not the case. There were, however, some subtle differences of concern among the participants. Despite his supposed faith in detente, Kissinger appears to have considered Russian action possible, especially because he thought they could not tolerate another decisive Israeli victory. Despite his skepticism about detente, Schlesinger has since hinted that he thought the possibility of Soviet forces "being en route" was low. Still, he thought that the United States must demonstrate it could act firmly, even with its domestic crisis.[209] Nixon argues that he ordered the meeting in anticipation of a military alert, but he did not formally ratify the committee's decisions until three hours afterward.[210]

A Soviet threat had become a ritual at the end of each Arab-Israeli war. In 1956 the Russians seemed to threaten the destruction of Israel while calling on the United States to join them in a peacekeeping force. But Eisenhower doubted their statements. In 1967 they had warned that they might use military force if the Israelis did not cease their moves on the last day of the war, but the administration believed that they could not intervene. Compared to these previous events, the Russian note on the night of 24 October, 1973 was sober. As former assistant secretary for Near East affairs, Lucius Battle, later wrote, "The Brezhnev note of October 24th did not strike me as being as threatening as earlier flares signalled it to be. Compared to Russian notes that I have read in past years, it was relatively mild—at least as reported in the press."[211]

The Russians had moderated their rhetoric as their capacity for action had increased. Their airborne military capabilities had grown dramatically since 1967. Kissinger and his colleagues had to recognize that the Russians could intervene, and this basic ability appeared to justify American action, even if Russian action was not imminent. Ray Cline, then head of INR, later wrote a memo to Kissinger. When he was unable to deliver it, he published it: "I regret that you never advised your State Department intelligence arm that you had a problem nor asked us for an opinion on the evidence of Soviet intention to intervene with troops in the Mid East. Certainly the technical intelligence evidence available in the INR did not support such a Soviet intervention."[212] The Pentagon also doubted whether the Soviet messages were anything more than "an initial test of American nerves."[213] But in the Nixon-Kissinger system, only the fears and intuitions of the powerful few counted, and there was the key to the alert. Months afterward Kissinger would refer to the alert as "our *deliberate* over-reaction," but at the time the men in the White House basement did not believe that they could ignore signs of possible Russian activity and Brezhnev's blunt warning. As one State Department official put it, "You know, it didn't make any difference if you thought they [the Soviets] would intervene or not, a threat had been made. The United States had to react."[214] The objective in the alert was to deter Russian activity, because American policy makers saw themselves as weaker than in previous Mideast crises.

The alert was not intended to become public. However, it was not realistic to expect secrecy. One leak occurred when an airman sped to his base at seventy miles per hour and was stopped by a police officer who asked, "Where are *you* going so fast?" "I'm going to a nuclear alert," replied the airman. "Now I've heard everything," responded the bemused policeman. "Okay, call my base." The policeman did. The base confirmed the alert, the airman sped off, and the officer called the local radio station.[215]

The subsequent events exemplify the Nixon-Kissinger style: a demonstration of force or potential force followed by conciliation. This pattern held in Vietnam, for example, when the Christmas bombing of the North in 1972 was followed by an agreement and American withdrawal. On the night of the alert, Kissinger drafted a message to Brezhnev, and Nixon approved it through Haig. It denied Israeli violations, affirmed the American intention of preserving the cease-fire, and indicated that the United States would accept a U.N. observer and peace-keeping force of troops from any state other than the five permanent members of the Security Council. The letter also included a stern warning that the United States "could in no event accept unilateral action" by the Soviets.[216]

The observer concept was accepted by the Russians late Thursday morning and the Security Council rapidly established an emergency force, the first in the area since the 1967 war, in Resolution 340. But the new arrangement could last only if the Israelis spared the Third Army. Therefore, just as Eisenhower used Russian threats to pressure Israel in 1956 and Johnson insisted on an end to the 1967 war when he received a threatening Russian note, Kissinger now used the military alert to force Israeli cooperation. Accounts differ on the combination of threats used: the threat of terminating U.S. aid, allowing the Russians to supply the Third Army, or even the U.S. supplying the Egyptians.[217] No one, however, disputes that Kissinger threatened Israel. He told Dinitz that the United States would not allow Israel to destroy the Third Army, and that unnamed elements in the Pentagon (presumably Schlesinger and Clements) were advocating that American planes fly supplies to the trapped Egyptian troops. Kissinger thus portrayed himself as Israel's protector against an antagonistic bureaucracy, as he had throughout the war. Nixon's message to Golda Meir was even tougher. He paraphrased the "Godfather": "We gave 'em an offer . . . that they . . . could not refuse."[218]

At a news conference on the morning after the alert, Kissinger presented his position: "The conditions that produced this war were clearly intolerable to the Arab nations, and . . . in a process of negotiations it will be necessary to make substantial concessions." The next day he finally persuaded the Israelis to allow the resupply of the Third Army. He thereby thwarted a decisive Israeli victory and achieved the military stalemate for which he had worked throughout the war.[219]

Despite impressions created by the initially confused American response to the crisis, Kissinger achieved his primary objective—a viable basis for future negotiations—only because he knew how the war should end and what the American role would be afterward. Thus, his previously developed strategy, not an improvisational adjustment to new circumstances, allowed Kissinger to maneuver successfully. In this sense America's role in 1973 was the opposite of its role in 1948, 1956, and 1967, when U.S. leaders had reacted with no clear notion of what conditions they wanted after the crisis.[220]

Kissinger's position at the pinnacle of power within the administration permitted this single-mindedness. He was largely free from bureaucratic constraints and the internal rivalries that often prevent the formulation of coherent policy. Nor was he encumbered by the president. At a news conference called to discuss the "Saturday night massacre," Nixon used the alert to justify his continuation in office, declaring, "It was the most difficult crisis we've had since the Cuban confrontation of 1962." Ignoring the failure of detente to prevent the crisis, Nixon argued that the new relationship he had established with Brezhnev provided a "basis of communication," implying that, as a consequence, he was uniquely capable of handling such situations.[221] In fact, however, Kissinger handled the major developments in the war with only sporadic presidential guidance. Nixon's most important decision of the crisis was the full-scale airlift to Israel, but Kissinger had previously struggled to create conditions for a cease-fire that would make the airlift unnecessary. The secretary of state's trip to Moscow further established his control over American diplomacy: he was able to decide *unilaterally* on the cease-fire terms. In the delicate discussions among Egypt, Israel, and the Soviet Union that followed the cease-fire, Kissinger was clearly in charge.

This position enabled him to withstand pressures from inside and outside the administration, despite Nixon's ebbing political power. Indeed, because Nixon's authority was disastrously undermined, it was difficult to criticize his diplomatic lieutenant without risking the total compromise of the conduct of U.S. foreign affairs. Israel's supporters might grumble about the delays in the airlift, and the major oil companies might find the airlift threatening to their interests, but Kissinger pursued his policy freely. It was hard to criticize a man who was flying around the world working for peace.

Throughout the crisis Sadat initiated frequent communications with Kissinger and the president—a move they reciprocated as they explained to Sadat the reasons for the airlift and the alert.[222] In these communications, Sadat consistently held out the possibility of better relations with Washington after the war and conveyed his own interest in a peaceful settlement with Israel. The improved contact between Washington and Cairo proved critical. During the war, it had encouraged Nixon and Kissinger to work at preventing a total Israeli victory. By the end of the war, the United States had finally attained diplomatic leverage with Cairo and Jerusalem, the dream of American leaders for a generation. But the United States also faced its worst economic crisis since the Great Depression and the most severe loss of faith in its leadership ever. This mix of strengths and weaknesses would become central to Kissinger's conduct of U.S.-Mideast diplomacy.

The Aftermath of October 1973

The war had a startling effect on the activities, arguments, and positions of all involved parties. The pro-Israeli camp was suddenly thrown on the defensive. Its cherished assumptions had been compromised and its close connections with the administration severed. Pro-Arab forces were stronger but had yet to be tested.

Arab political strength also increased because of the alliance between Egypt and Saudi Arabia. This coalition created a united front between the Arab country with which Washington had established the closest relations after the Second World War—Saudi Arabia—and the Arab state it had been most anxious to win over during the same period—Egypt. This combination helped Kissinger's diplomacy and increased Arab influence on the United States because both the richest and the most powerful Arab countries were now developing close relations with Washington. Nixon and Kissinger were presented with an opportunity no American administration could refuse: Sadat's offer to restore American primacy in the Middle East. His willingness to trust the United States made Kissinger's policy possible.

The main Mideast diplomatic effort during Nixon's remaining days in the presidency was to unravel the tangled military situation that Kissinger himself had helped create. The very first step epitomized this process. The Egyptians made a political concession—face-to-face talks between opposing generals— and the Israelis made a tangible concession—the passage of one convoy of non-military supplies to the Third Army.[223] The talks began on 27 October in a tent in the Egyptian desert on the canal's west bank at Kilometer 101. In addition to an Egyptian and Israeli general, the Finnish commander of the U.N. force was also present. That the talks were held at all proves Egyptian desperation and American pressure on the Israelis. For days the Kilometer 101 meeting dealt with the details of resupply and possible disengagement, but what mattered were talks with Henry Kissinger in Washington.

Both Nixon and Kissinger knew the importance of Egypt in Middle East politics. Nixon called Egypt "the key to the Arab world." Now Kissinger tried to manipulate the military stalemate toward a political disengagement in which both sides would gain. He later told Mohamed Heikal after the war, "If we want to solve a critical conflict, the point we start from must be the point at which each party feels it has obtained something and that to stop there is not a defeat for it."[224]

Kissinger's objectives in the talks were highly complex: (1) to win the

Egyptians away from the Russians and to nudge them toward a settlement with Israel; (2) to demonstrate to the Arab oil producers that his mediation would help resolve a twenty-five year old conflict; (3) to convince the Israelis that they would gain more by relying on his diplomatic skill than by resuming the war; and (4) to maintain the backing of Israel's supporters at home. Kissinger's first step was accepting Sadat's offer to fly to Cairo. His second step was to meet separately at the end of October with Ismail Fahmy (soon to be named Egyptian foreign minister) and Golda Meir in Washington. Both Egypt and Israel were eager to talk and the United States held the pivotal position. Fahmy had arrived in Washington without waiting for an invitation and Meir also initiated her trip.[225] These meetings were the first practical application of Kissinger's postwar approach, an early form of what later became shuttle diplomacy.

The meetings with Fahmy were characterized by surprising public and private amity for two countries so recently opposed. The Egyptian emissary proposed a return to the 22 October cease-fire lines and ultimate total Israeli withdrawal from the Sinai in return for a state of nonbelligerency. Kissinger tried to convince him that the Egyptians should seek a more immediately attainable objective. Since he felt the original cease-fire lines were impossible to reproduce and a broader agreement was presently beyond reach, Kissinger argued for a "long range strategy" in which disengaging the forces of both sides would serve as a first step. The most important result of Fahmy's visit was to convince Nixon and Kissinger that Sadat was committed to a settlement.[226]

They presented this conclusion to the skeptical Golda Meir on 1 November. In the talks with the Israeli prime minister, however, Nixon and Kissinger found a leader heartbroken by her country's ordeals, simultaneously grateful for the airlift and resentful of U.S. diplomacy. The gratitude was expressed in her meeting with Nixon: "There were days and hours when we needed a friend, and you came right in. You don't know what your airlift means to us."[227] She listened impassively as the president outlined his goal of improved relations with Egypt and Syria, offered the opinion that Sadat wanted peace, and indicated that Israel would have to concede territory. Nixon stated flatly that the United States would not permit the destruction of the Third Army. The prime minister's resentment and anger were saved for Kissinger. At the usual dinner, the atmosphere was "chilly, if not hostile" and the secretary of state was incensed. Mrs. Meir argued with Kissinger about his actions in Moscow during the war. Kissinger unsuccessfully urged her to allow an Egyptian-controlled corridor to the Third Army, while she adamantly insisted on the return of Israeli prisoners of war, which, she reminded Kissinger, he had led the Israelis to believe would occur soon after the cease-fire.[228]

A new pattern now emerged. The secretary of state wanted a new relationship with the Egyptians and Syrians as an entrée for U.S. influence and interests in the area. He could offer economic aid and the prestige of American attention, but his major bargaining point was the prospect of Israeli concessions. The Israelis, however, insisted that Kissinger's achievements should not be made at their expense, despite his arguments that Jerusalem would benefit from increased U.S. influence in the area and the resulting restraint on the Arabs. Kissinger soon found himself complaining about the Israelis' intransigence and the "diplomatic Ghetto" in which they lived.[229] In the Arab world, Kissinger's efforts were equally complicated by distrust of the United States. Kissinger overcame these obstacles masterfully.

His trip to the Middle East in early November 1973 was the first of eleven he would take over the next two years, and his first visit to any Arab country. He was always accompanied by a substantial State Department team, which usually included Sisco, Saunders, and Atherton. Kissinger frequently met with major leaders alone, however, and only he had full knowledge of all the negotiations.

In these trips he achieved a position in Arab-Israeli negotiations unknown since the days of Ralph Bunche, who had gained the confidence of both sides. To the Egyptians he offered the fruits of the victory they had frittered away. To the Israelis he offered relief from the traumas of war, the possibility of a more secure position, and the return of their prisoners of war. The last was almost an obsession in a tiny country whose size and culture meant that few families were untouched by war casualties.

What was the secret of his success? It was not the one confided months earlier to Italian journalist, Oriana Fallaci: "The main point stems from the fact that I've always acted alone. Americans admire that enormously. Americans admire the cowboy leading the caravan alone astride on his horse . . . a wild West tale if you like."[230] This self-characterization was more than a little specious. Kissinger's diplomatic triumphs were possible because he commanded the power and prestige of the U.S. government. In the Mideast, he never went anywhere alone; he fashioned many of the key compromises from other people's ideas. Nevertheless, by 1974 Arabs and Israelis alike admired the self-styled Lone Ranger. In November 1973 Kissinger and the "senior official" who seemed always nearby began a dizzying round of talks. For months the State Department seemed a traveling air show, whose electronic gadgetry and journalistic glitter served one man. Formulation of American Mideast policy seemed to rest on the experiences and beliefs of Kissinger on his gallant Air Force charger.

When they first landed in Cairo, the U.S. team was uneasy about the politically unknown world they were about to enter. Nonetheless, the meetings between Kissinger and Sadat were a huge success. The secretary of state met the Egyptian leader for the first time alone and achieved what Kissinger later called one of the "dramatic breakthroughs" of his diplomacy.[231] Sadat accepted the recommendation that Kissinger attempt a broader disengagement and not expend his political capital on recreating the original 22 October cease-fire lines.

The Egyptian leader also accepted a basic "six point" agreement devised by Kissinger and his team.[232] A corridor to allow the resupply of the Third Army and Suez City would be exchanged for Israeli prisoners of war. The decision to restore full diplomatic relations between the United States and Egypt was made "in principle." According to Sadat, "The first hour made me feel I was dealing with an entirely new mentality, a new political method." For his part Kissinger was impressed that Sadat seemed a person with whom he could do business.[233]

As Kissinger proceeded with his trip, Sisco and Saunders went to Israel for approval of the "six points." Prime Minister Meir complained about several details and finally got concessions to assure that military supplies would not be smuggled to the Third Army. Through Kissinger she also obtained Sadat's oral agreement for lifting the Arab blockade of the Bab El Mandeb straits, which lead into the Red Sea and the Gulf of Aqaba.[234] Meir accepted the agreement on 10 November, and it was signed by Israeli and Egyptian generals at Kilometer 101 the next day.

Kissinger also visited Saudi Arabia on this first trip, just as he would on each of the following ten as secretary of state. Riyadh, of course, was not directly involved in Arab-Israeli negotiations, but the United States had courted the Saudis since the 1930s. Now the oil crisis had greatly increased their importance and made King Faisal the symbol of the new era. Kissinger tried to persuade Faisal to lift the embargo as soon as diplomatic progress could be demonstrated.

The secretary of state felt the irony of his role acutely when he dealt with Faisal. Saudi Arabia was notoriously antagonistic towards Jews, and Faisal had particularly strong feelings on the subject. Even Kissinger once labeled Faisal "a religious fanatic," and suggested to a reporter privately that the king hated Jews as well as Zionists.[235] Faisal regularly informed visitors—including Nixon and Kissinger—that Communists, Jews, and Zionists conspired to take over the world. "Israel is advancing communist objectives," Faisal told Kissinger at their first meeting, and he made much of the facts that Karl Marx had been Jewish and that Golda Meir was born in Russia.[236] Yet Faisal did not object to negotiating with this powerful American Jew and, like Sadat, he accepted Kissinger's strategy of step-by-step diplomacy. On this first trip, however, Faisal adamantly refused to lift the oil embargo until Israel returned to her 1967 borders.

After this journey to the area, Kissinger focused on convening an Arab-Israeli peace conference under Soviet-American sponsorship to arrange for disengagement with Egypt and Syria. Meanwhile, the military talks at Kilometer 101 had made substantial progress, which disturbed Kissinger. He believed that if an Egyptian-Israeli agreement occurred in isolation, it would be more difficult to extend the talks beyond disengagement with Egypt, and the United States would lose its central role. As Kissinger later explained, "Our strategy depended on being the only country capable of eliciting Israeli concessions, but also on our doing it within a context where this was perceived to be a difficult task." Therefore, he subtly moved both sides toward the Geneva forum and away from more direct military talks.[237] Geneva had two other advantages: it would keep the United States in a position to gain credit with Arab oil producers for successful negotiations, and it would not force all Arabs to accept direct bilateral talks with Israel before the process began.

Having decided on the Geneva forum, Kissinger set the stage for his next Mideast trip. He knew that Sadat was willing to attend, and he had ascertained from a meeting with Dayan in Washington that the Israelis wanted to withdraw their exposed troops from the west bank of the canal. This advance information was typical of Kissinger's approach: because of his unique contact with all parties, he could manipulate both sides and postpone agreements until he was ready to take credit for them. Before his December trip, for example, he urged Dayan to slow the pace of Israeli concessions in order not to raise Arab expectations; he wanted the Arab leaders to appreciate the difficulty of achieving a disengagement.[238]

The goal of Kissinger's second trip was to arrange a peace conference in Geneva, sponsored by the United States and the U.S.S.R., chaired by U.N. Secretary-General Waldheim, and attended by Israel, Egypt, Syria, and Jordan. The first item on the agenda would be an Egyptian-Israeli disengagement agreement. Kissinger's second objective was to persuade the Arabs to lift the embargo. On this December trip he asked Sadat to help convince Faisal that the embargo had accomplished its purpose. He wrote Nixon: "I told Sadat that without your personal willingness to confront the domestic issue nothing would have been possible. Sadat promised me he would get the oil embargo lifted during the first half of January and said that he would call for its lifting in a statement which praised your personal role in bringing the parties to the negotiating table and making progress thereafter."[239] Thus, whatever he might say in public, Kissinger's actions demonstrated to the Arabs that oil and Arab-Israeli diplomacy were indeed linked.

Nixon was less subtle. He wrote Sadat in December that he hoped to promote the peace process but the oil embargo could ruin the effort: "Therefore, Mr. President, I must tell you in complete candor that it is essential that the oil embargo and oil production restrictions against the United States be ended at once. It cannot await the outcome of the current talks on disengagement."[240] While Kissinger was in the Middle East, reports appeared that Nixon had made a shockingly blunt public comment linking oil with his Mideast diplomacy. He had told a group of governors: "The only way we're going to solve the crisis is to end the oil embargo, and the only way we're going to end the embargo is to get the Israelis to act reasonable. I hate to use the word blackmail, but we've got to do some things to get them to behave."[241]

This statement was exactly what the Arabs wanted, and it reinforced the logic of their oil embargo. The war would have increased U.S. diplomatic involvement in the Middle East even without the embargo. However, the Arab oil producers wrongly interpreted Washington's urgency as a selfish reaction. The two American leaders' statements in public and private confirmed this impression. After all, had not Sadat and Faisal received visits from Kissinger and messages from Washington seeking an end to the embargo, implying that refusal might weaken Nixon still further and contribute to his removal from office? Rather than giving the impression that the United States was strong and could not be blackmailed, Nixon and Kissinger confirmed the Arabs' hope that the oil embargo would lead directly to Israeli concessions.[242]

On his December trip, Kissinger became the first secretary of state since Dulles to visit Damascus, but he was unable to persuade Assad to attend the Geneva Conference. The Syrian leader wanted a disengagement agreement, including the entire Golan Heights, to precede the conference and Kissinger knew he could not possibly induce the Israelis to accept.[243] In Israel he found the Israelis worried about Sadat's insistence on Palestinian involvement, concerned about the degree of U.N. engagement, and anxious to obtain a list of prisoners of war held by the Syrians. Kissinger's method of resolving these issues typified the approach he would use over the next two years.

First, two messages arrived from the president urging the Israelis to go to Geneva and threatening a loss of U.S. support if they did not.[244] Second, Kissinger spent hours with Meir or with her "kitchen cabinet" or with the entire Cabinet trying to satisfy them on particular details. Finally, the Israelis were persuaded to accept U.N. chairmanship of the conference.[245] Third, Sadat was persuaded to withdraw his proposal for inviting the Palestinians. Fourth, since the Israelis still worried over the PLO, Kissinger secretly agreed to a memorandum of understanding by which the United States would veto any future participation of the PLO in a Geneva conference without Israeli consent.[246] This was to prove the most lasting of the arrangements he made in preparing for the conference. Fifth, Kissinger coaxed the Israelis into accepting the return of Syrian villagers to Israeli-controlled areas if Assad would release a list of prisoners of war before the conference. This was Israel's condition for attending the Geneva conference with Syria. In the end, the issue evaporated when Assad refused to attend the opening session.[247]

In negotiations Kissinger relied on charm, threats, the prestige of his office, his ability to focus world attention on the negotiations, and the advantage of having the most information. Moreover, the shuttle style was tailor-made for a man willing to endure gruelling days, sleepless nights, wretched food, and marathon discussions of six or eight hours at a time. His December trip set the pattern for future shuttles. After a six-hour meeting with Assad (originally scheduled for two-and-a-half hours), Kissinger arrived in Amman at midnight for dinner with King Hussein.

Compared with the preparations, the actual convening of the Geneva

Conference on 21 December 1973 was anticlimactic. All the diplomats present had agreed that the initial two-day meeting would be largely ceremonial. When the conference convened, the Israeli and Arab delegates met in the same room, but the Arabs still refused direct contact with the Israelis. They would not shake hands with them or exchange pleasantries. They would not even allow their tables to touch, and Fahmy vetoed Waldheim's suggestion for a joint cocktail party.[248] All that was left was a series of formalities and speeches. The war-delayed Israeli elections were to be held ten days later and the Israeli government could make no decisions in the interim, so the negotiations quickly adjourned until January. Few imagined that the conference would never reconvene.

Kissinger was still concerned with an Egyptian-Israeli disengagement, even at this comprehensive Geneva forum. When Dayan came to Washington in early January to discuss the subject, he brought with him the concept of Egyptian and Israeli zones separated by a U.N. area in the Sinai; these ideas soon formed the basis of the accord.[249] By the time of Dayan's visit, both sides had powerful incentives to reach a rapid agreement. Israel was suffering from the severe economic pressure of continued mobilization, the disheartening possibility of renewed warfare with Syria, and the diplomatic pressure of Arab oil strength. Sadat needed to save the Third Army and demonstrate that the war had gained territory for Egypt in order to continue to claim victory before his people.

Thus, when Dayan asked Kissinger to the Middle East to help achieve disengagement, Sadat readily agreed. When Kissinger arrived in Cairo in mid-January, Sadat asked him to complete the disengagement agreement during that trip without returning to Geneva.[250] When he learned the Israelis also wanted quick results, Kissinger began shuttling between Aswan and Jerusalem, carrying proposals and counterproposals back and forth. This method worked so well that it replaced the Geneva Conference. The negotiations began to falter over Israel's demand for nonbelligerency or some practical commitment to peace, such as Egypt's reopening the canal and rebuilding the canal cities, which would make war less likely. Kissinger therefore devised a two-tier system. Publicly, both sides would conclude an agreement for troop disengagement along the Suez front; the United States would produce a draft based on the Egyptian and Israeli drafts. Privately, each side would receive a "memorandum of understanding" listing its private assurances to Kissinger.[251]

As a result the negotiations appeared less direct, a face-saving concession to Sadat, in return for private commitments which locked Egypt into de facto nonbelligerence. The new approach was consistent with Kissinger's cautious and practical tactics. He avoided defining the end of negotiations, an approach that differed markedly from Rogers's attempts to outline a comprehensive solution. Like that of all previous American diplomatic efforts, Kissinger's concept of peace was limited. As he put it at Geneva, "A peace agreement must include these elements, among others: withdrawals, recognized frontiers, security arrangements, guarantees, a settlement of the legitimate interests of the Palestinians, and a recognition that Jerusalem contains places considered holy by three great religions."[252] This description foresaw no future in which diplomatic, commercial, and social barriers between the Arabs and Israelis would be broken. Kissinger aimed merely at the absence of armed conflict, the only approach he thought would lead to quick results. It did. The two-tier system produced the first disengagement accord just six days after he left Washington.

Ironically, the Egyptian-Israeli disengagement accord resembled the Suez "interim" arrangement considered in 1971. But after the war, both sides made significant concessions. In order to avoid past recriminations, both sides accepted American reconnaissance (through satellites and aircraft) to monitor compliance. In 1971 Israel had not been willing to allow any Egyptian troops across the canal. Egypt had insisted on a substantial Israeli withdrawal from most of the Sinai and a commitment to abandon the other territorial gains of 1967. Now, however, Israel relinquished its holdings on the canal's west bank and only withdrew from a tiny area of the Sinai (approximately twenty miles along the length of the canal). Israel also settled for seven thousand Egyptian troops on its side (the east bank). This meant Egypt would have to withdraw troops, since fifty thousand Egyptian soldiers had remained east of the canal at the end of the war.[253]

The agreement created three militarily limited zones on the east bank— an Egyptian area closest to the canal, an area occupied by a U.N. peacekeeping force, and an Israeli zone on the other side. Israel retained the strategic Gidi and Mitla passes. In the two forward zones, the Egyptian and Israeli forces would be thinned out. In order to protect Sadat against the charge of having agreed to a permanent Israeli occupation of the Sinai, a time limit of six months was established on the U.N. peacekeeping force. In secret, the Egyptians committed themselves to clearing and reopening the canal and to rebuilding its adjacent cities. Moreover, Kissinger assured the Israelis that Sadat would allow ships containing nonmilitary cargoes bound for Israel to pass through the reopened canal. But Sadat would not commit himself to a date.[254]

This confusion over reopening the canal illustrates Kissinger's tendency to adjust his arguments to a particular moment and his preoccupation with closing a deal. These traits explain why Kissinger achieved an initial success that proved difficult to sustain. His energies were devoted to specific, highly circumscribed agreements accompanied by secret oral and written understandings often interpreted differently by opposing sides. During the October War, Kissinger had very specific aims and achieved them, but his postwar negotiations were conducted with little consideration for where they might ultimately lead.

Kissinger was adept at using previous failures to advantage in present negotiations. He admitted to the Arabs that he had erred in not being more active in diplomacy before the war, but then he cautioned them that they could translate their limited military gains into tangible results only by cooperating. In Jerusalem he chastened the Israelis for relying on military deterrence. It had not worked, and he declared his acquiescence in it to have been a mistake. For both Arabs and Israelis, he drew the same conclusion: the time had arrived to depend on his diplomacy for solving the twenty-five year dispute. [255]

Nixon and Kissinger had always been prepared to use military and economic aid as tools of diplomacy, and they resurrected the old "hardware—software" formula during the disengagement discussions. Those states that they considered cooperative would be rewarded; those considered uncooperative would suffer. In a written memorandum that was part of the Egyptian-Israeli disengagement accord, Kissinger promised Israel that he would "make every effort to be fully responsive" to Israel's long-term equipment needs, but during the Syrian-Israeli negotiations that followed the Egyptian-Israel accord, Nixon and Kissinger hinted that the amount of aid to Israel would depend on her concessions. Soon Kissinger discussed increased economic aid and even military assistance to Egypt. Meanwhile, in the spring the administration requested from Congress increased aid to Egypt and Jordan and a special fund to use if Syria were forthcoming in the disengagement accords. [256] This aid created strings Kissinger could pull if Egypt, Syria, Jordan, or Israel adopted a hard line in negotiations. Clearly, however, the strings were more likely to be pulled on Israel because of its greater dependence on the United States.

After the Egyptian-Israeli disengagement accord, Kissinger returned home, and despite gas lines and Nixon's deteriorating authority, he received almost universal praise. The *New York Times* called the accord a "notable achievement" and complimented his "extraordinary diplomatic skill." The *Los Angeles Times* extolled the accord, saying that it "could well be the prelude to the most significant political development in the last quarter century." And the *Chicago Tribune* lauded Kissinger for his "diplomatic coup," even while expressing doubt that the agreement would hold. [257] At this juncture neither the State Department, Congress, the Jewish community, nor the oil companies criticized Kissinger's policy. All the major countries of the area also endorsed the accord. Iraq and Libya, always hostile to American initiatives, advocated continuing the oil embargo and stepped up their attacks against Sadat's policies.

Kissinger's signals to the Arabs seemed to imply that oil and diplomacy were separate unless diplomacy succeeded, in which case the oil embargo should be lifted. Thus, on 3 January, before his third trip to the Middle East, the secretary of state said: "We cannot engage in negotiations with the Arab governments about the specific terms that we will support in negotiations in order to get the embargo lifted, because it would make our foreign policy then entirely subject to the producing nations' decisions and would set up an endless cycle."

When he returned to Washington after the accord had been reached, however, Kissinger admitted, "We have had every reason to believe that success in the negotiations would mark a major step forward ending the oil embargo. . . ."[258]

When Kissinger claimed that the United States would not be coerced by Arab oil blackmail, he was not convincing. The Arab oil ministers could read about the sharp public outcry in the United States in the *New York Times*. As the American people blamed their own government and the oil companies, oil blackmail seemed to be working. After all, within weeks of the oil embargo, the U.S. secretary of state was calling on Arab leaders every month and promising progress toward peace and stability in the Middle East. Moreover, the embargo and the resulting shortages had made possible the quadrupling of world oil prices and the largest, most sudden transfer of wealth in the history of the world. All this had been accomplished without the slightest hostile action by the United States. Arab radicals could plausibly argue that the embargo should continue.

The Arab producers decided in early February that they would not lift the embargo until there was evidence of diplomatic progress between Syria and Israel. This unexpected step angered Nixon and Kissinger, but they could not carry through on previous threats to terminate the diplomatic process for three reasons: (1) they feared another war without a Syrian-Israeli disengagement; (2) the search for agreements was now the centerpiece of U.S. diplomacy and stopping the effort would destroy Nixon's rationale for remaining in office; and (3) Nixon and especially Kissinger wished to continue the fiction that oil and diplomacy were not linked.[259]

Therefore, on his fourth Mideast trip in late February, Kissinger dangled the prospect of sophisticated U.S. technology before the eager Saudi princes. As he had done in December, he offered the Saudis advanced military equipment and aid in developing an industrialized plant if they would end the embargo.[260] This offer was the precursor of the joint Saudi-American economic commission arranged later in the year and led to massive arms sales later in the decade.

The trip also allowed the secretary of state to strengthen his growing ties with Sadat, on whom he was increasingly dependent for advice and support with other Arab leaders. A policy of coordination with the Egyptian leadership, long the dream of U.S. statesmen, was now becoming reality. As a symbol of the new amity, the U.S. and Egypt announced the resumption of full-scale diplomatic relations while Kissinger was in Cairo.

On this trip Kissinger also made progress in the difficult negotiations between Jerusalem and Damascus. Assad had already accepted a complex U.S. plan in early February in which he would trade a list of Israeli prisoners of war held in Syria in return for a "serious" Israeli disengagement proposal. When Kissinger handed over the list to Golda Meir, however, he found that the Israelis proposed a three-stage zonal disengagement similar to the one on the Israeli-Egyptian front, except that Israel wanted all three zones to be located on Syrian territory captured in 1973. Israel was, in effect, proposing to keep some new territory. Kissinger feared that if he actually presented these ideas to Assad the talks would collapse, so he told Assad that the Israeli ideas were not worth presenting. Instead, in effect he made a side deal with Assad: Syria could hope to regain "a bit" of the territory Israel had captured in 1967, but Israel could not be induced to dismantle any of her Golan Heights settlements.[261] This move at least allowed the negotiations to continue. Meanwhile, Syrian artillery continued to shell Israel across the cease-fire lines, inflicting casualties daily and maintaining pressure on both the United States and Israel. Israel, of course, returned the fire, and a war of attrition continued throughout the spring.

The existence of an Israeli withdrawal proposal gave the oil producers a justification for suspending the oil embargo in mid-March. Faisal seemed to imply, however, that the embargo might be reimposed if an Israeli-Syrian disengagement accord was not reached within two months.[262] Nixon responded by publicly linking peace and oil when he told the National Association of Broadcasters in Houston on 19 March:

> Now, as far as our policy in the Mideast is concerned, we seek a permanent peace as an end in itself. Whatever happens to the oil embargo, peace in the Mideast would be in our interest and in the interests of the whole world.
>
> As far as the oil embargo is concerned, it is in the interest of those countries that imposed it, as well as the United States, that it be lifted. The two should go parallel. Inevitably, what happens in one area affects the other, and I am confident that the progress we are going to continue to make on the peace front in the Mideast will be very helpful in seeing to it that an oil embargo is not reimposed.[263]

Both Syria and Israel had powerful incentives to reach agreement on the disengagement of their forces. Israel needed her prisoners of war back and relief from the war of attrition; Syria needed to show territorial gains, however miniscule, from the war and to remove the Israeli guns from so near Damascus.[264]

The hatred and bitterness between Israel and Syria, however, ran deeper than the hostility between Israel and her other Arab neighbors. Syria was also closer to Moscow, and as Kissinger's experiences had already demonstrated, Assad was more difficult to handle than Sadat, Hussein, or even Faisal.[265] To make matters even more difficult, President Assad's tough negotiating stance did not augur well: he had opposed lifting the oil embargo and had intensified the war of attrition along the cease-fire lines. His army was not threatened by envelopment as the Egyptian Third Army had been.

Therefore, in preparing for the talks, Kissinger devised three steps. First, he wanted to isolate Syria from the other Arab states so that, if the talks failed and Syria was seen as unreasonable, Assad would not have broad Arab backing.[266] Second, he sought to keep the Soviet Union out of the talks. The Soviets could logically argue that they should participate because they were Syria's patron. Kissinger, however, persuaded Assad that shuttle diplomacy had proved more effective than the Geneva forum and that the Soviets could contribute nothing to the process. Kissinger also took pains to mollify the Soviets by meeting regularly with their foreign minister, Gromyko, to keep him abreast of developments. Third, he arranged for Dayan and the chief of Syrian military intelligence (Hikmat al-Shihabi) to come separately to Washington to share their latest ideas on the disengagement.

Thus, the concept of the accord was completed on 13 April in Washington.[267] All that seemed to remain was for Kissinger to go through the ritual shuttle, the act of political theater that would focus world attention on the antagonists and provide the crucial psychological pressure. And the two sides had to agree on where to draw the line.

Drawing the line between Syria and Israel proved to be the most difficult task of Kissinger's Mideast diplomacy thus far. The antagonism between the two peoples proved so deep-rooted that the governments of the two nations could make concessions only after agonizing, physically painful harangues at the secretary of state. Each concession had to be torn from the flesh of a nation and delivered to its mortal enemy. Israel could be under no illusions that Syria would make peace (as it could hope in the case of Egypt) or even implicitly accept the permanent existence of the Jewish state. The most Assad would grant was a formalized, stable cease-fire. For all these emotional reasons, the chief foreign policy officer of the United States spent thirty-four tense, grueling days persuading the leaders of two small nations to endorse an agreement both desperately needed.

Meanwhile, the leadership in both the United States and Israel fell into disarray. In Washington the Watergate crisis marched toward its conclusion, and the word *impeachment* appeared daily in the press. Nixon's focus on foreign policy and his practice of it made him think that somehow a diplomatic achievement might rescue him. He pressed Kissinger hard and used extremely tough language with Golda Meir.[268] He was, of course, unable to deal similarly with Syria as Washington had little influence there. The secretary of state remained in the Mideast because Nixon desperately wanted a triumph; Watergate actually increased the chances for a Syrian-Israeli disengagement accord.

In Jerusalem the Yom Kippur War crisis had led to the political downfall of Meir and Dayan and the designation of a new Labor party cabinet, including Yitzhak Rabin as prime minister; Rabin's rival, Shimon Peres, as defense minister; and Yigal Allon as foreign minister. Meir stayed on as a caretaker, but the new team would take office as soon as the Syrian disengagement was complete. Rabin, Peres, and Allon participated in several of the meetings with Kissinger, and their presence made agreement among the Israelis, who usually differed with each other in any case, even more difficult. Fortunately, however, Meir, Dayan, and Eban—all leaving Cabinet positions after years of service—were determined to achieve an agreement.

The Syrians were not easy to handle; one of their regular practices was to raise new demands after agreements had seemingly been reached. Not surprisingly, negotiating sessions frequently lasted several hours. "Every issue was contested with a tenacity that I find unequalled in my experience," Kissinger later complained. Often frustrated and suffering from sleepless nights, Kissinger would resort to his keen sense of humor to lighten the tension. Using hard-line Foreign Minister Kahddam as his foil, he quipped at one point, "I'll take Kahddam back with me. He can convince Golda."[269] Kissinger believed that Assad had to come away from the negotiations with more land than he had before the war; he could not accept a deal that legitimized the new cease-fire lines.

Kissinger's frustration with the Israelis was also considerable. Their meetings declined into acrimonious lectures from the U.S. secretary of state. After discussing the hills above Quneitra for what seemed like an eternity, Kissinger angrily told the Israeli negotiating team, "Such bargaining is not dignified for an American Secretary of State. I am wandering around here like a rug merchant in order to bargain over 100 to 200 meters! Like a peddlar in the market! I'm trying to save you, and you think you are doing me a favor when you are kind enough to give me a few more meters. As if I were a citizen of El Quneitra. As if I planned to build my house there!"[270] He had to deal delicately with Assad, but with the Israelis he could vent his emotions in furious shouting matches, berating them for their press leaks and battering them with speeches about diplomatic isolation. Kissinger tried to convince the Israelis that their concerns about Golan Heights security were less important than the benefits to Israel from maintaining the negotiations. At one point he reportedly told them, "Remember what this is all about . . . to keep the negotiating process alive, to prevent another round of hostilities which would benefit the Soviet Union and increase pressure on you, on us, and [on] Sadat to rejoin the battle . . ." Later in the negotiations, he is said to have exclaimed, "You're always looking at the trees, and you don't see the woods! If we didn't have this negotiation, there'd be an international forum for the 1967 frontiers."[271]

The atmosphere deteriorated further when twenty-four Israelis (most of them children) were killed by Palestinian terrorists on 15 May at a school in the village of Ma'alot, an incident that followed the killing of eighteen Israelis in the town of Qiryat Shemona on 2 April. These raids were intended by radical Palestinian groups to prevent serious Arab negotiations with Israel. Nonetheless, Kissinger and the Israelis pressed on. The raids only emphasized the consequences of failure.

Three times the talks nearly collapsed, but Nixon kept pressing his secretary of state to continue. On one occasion a final communiqué was prepared in

Damascus, but Assad suggested that Kissinger try one last time. Meanwhile, the secretary had Nixon put pressure on the Israelis and sought to employ the Egyptians, Algerians, and Saudis to persuade the Syrians.[272] The talks proceeded, with details being reconsidered even after tentative agreement. A deal was finally struck on 29 May, after Kissinger's thirteenth round trip between Jerusalem and Damascus.

The Israelis gained an exchange of prisoners of war and relief from the war of attrition on the Golan Heights in exchange for the territory they had conquered in 1973 plus the town of Quneitra, capital of the Golan, which the Syrians agreed to repopulate with civilians (a promise that they did not keep). This arrangement was a double compromise. Syria had initially demanded the whole Golan Heights, and Israel had initially insisted that the whole buffer zone should be in territory taken from Syria in 1973. Five zones were established, with two zones of thinned out forces on either side of a neutral zone occupied by a U.N. force. This force was similar to the force in the Sinai but had less authority. Israel wanted Assad to promise to control Palestinian guerrilla raids from Syria, but it settled for U.S. political support for Israeli reprisals and preventive strikes.[273]

Almost everyone saw the agreement as a remarkable success, but the difficulty of reaching it raised serious doubts about future Syrian-Israeli negotiations. The incentives for both sides might not be so great in the future. Moreover, it was doubtful that the Syrians and Israelis would again have a mediator who was as clever, powerful, and energetic as Kissinger. If under favorable conditions, Jerusalem and Damascus could barely agree to stop shelling each other, separate their troops, and exchange prisoners, the prospects for future Syrian-Israeli agreements were not bright. At the time so much general relief greeted the agreement (several times the press had reported that the talks were failing) that few were willing to criticize Kissinger's Middle East diplomacy.

Immediately upon Kissinger's return to Washington, a presidential trip was hastily sandwiched between the Syrian-Israeli disengagement accord and the next scheduled Moscow summit. Nixon was determined to use Kissinger's success to strengthen his tenuous hold on the presidency. He wrote in his diary afterward, "We must have gotten some lift from the trip, although it seems almost impossible to break through in the polls."[274]

The circumstances were not auspicious for a delicate presidential foray into Middle East politics. Nixon suffered from phlebitis in his leg. His doctor advised him to stay off his feet and, if possible, not to take the trip at all. In Washington, the president's lawyer, Fred Buzhardt, suffered a heart attack as the House Judiciary Committee moved closer to recommending impeachment. Kissinger had just returned from a month in the Mideast, so there had been no time for new planning and little accomplishment could be hoped for. Instead, Nixon might create misunderstandings and commit diplomatic gaffes. Perhaps the president thought he could shift credit for the disengagement accords from Kissinger to himself by taking the trip. Perhaps he believed that a trip could accomplish in 1974 what his trip to China had achieved in 1972: greater stature and domestic respect. (As he had been the first to visit China, Nixon became the first American president to visit each of the countries except Egypt; Roosevelt had attended the Cairo Conference in 1943.) He later claimed that his hurried excursion was necessary to the momentum of the peace process.[275]

For Kissinger the trip was particularly frustrating. He had returned to Washington expecting praise for his diplomatic achievement but had instead been accused of ordering illegal wiretaps on his subordinates. His response was emotional. He threatened to resign. It was not surprising that Kissinger appeared sullen and exhausted after his recent travails.

In Egypt Nixon received a tumultuous welcome—twice as many people greeted him along the Egyptian parade routes as live in Israel. While he signed agreements with Sadat for increased economic aid and cultural exchange, the most surprising agreement was the offer to sell Egypt a nuclear reactor.[276] Sadat still had a friendship treaty in force with the Soviet Union. Even though the Israelis were quickly offered a nuclear reactor of their own, their concern about the possible military use of any reactor increased their nervousness about American policy.

As friendly as he found the Egyptians, Nixon was particularly impressed with Assad. He later wrote in his diary, "The man really has elements of genius, without any question." He knew that the Syrians wanted to play off the United States against the U.S.S.R., but he believed that they could be weaned away from the Soviets if America could help with the return of their land and provide them with economic aid. During his visit, the United States and Syria announced that they would resume full diplomatic relations. One reason Nixon may have found Assad so cooperative was that he told the Syrian leader much that he wanted to hear. During their conversations, Nixon declared that the purpose of U.S. policy was to push the Israelis back, step by step, until they "fell off" the Golan Heights.[277]

Similarly, Nixon made promises in Jordan about a future Israeli disengagement on the West Bank. He had also told Sadat that his goal was to restore the 1967 Egyptian-Israeli border and involve the Palestinians in negotiations. Kissinger had been much more cautious in his promises throughout the previous months of negotiations. He had told the Arabs that he could not predict what withdrawals might emerge from the negotiations, although he implied that Israeli withdrawals would be substantial if not complete. The secretary of state had explained, however, that he would not repeat Rogers's error of announcing a plan. Nixon made sweeping commitments privately, but they fell short of an official public commitment to the 1967 borders and there was no way for his listeners to know whether the shaky U.S. government would be able to fulfill secret promises.[278]

Although the Israelis could not have known precisely what Nixon said in private to the Arabs, they were suspicious. Nixon observed, "Our reception in Israel, although warm by ordinary standards, was the most restrained of the trip." With the Israelis, Nixon explored their requests for economic and military aid but made it clear that he expected further concessions from them, beginning with the Jordanian frontier. He was typically unpredictable. In an informal meeting in Golda Meir's living room, Nixon told his astonished listeners that there was only one way to deal with terrorists. Then he stood up and acted out the use of a machine gun.[279]

Nixon's fascination with what he later called the "tremendous potential of the new role of the United States as a force for peace in the Arab world" led him to moderate his past support for Israel. Even before the trip, he told Jewish leaders that "hardware alone to Israel was a policy that made sense maybe five years ago but did not make sense today . . ." Therefore, "I made it clear there is going to be no blank check in our conversations with the Israelis although, of course, I expressed sympathy for their military needs and, of course, enormous respect for their bravery, etc."[280] By the time the trip was over, he was talking to congressional leaders about his goal of balanced aid to the Israelis. As he put it in his diary, "With the congressional leaders I stepped out a little bit ahead of Henry in indicating that we would make Israel strong enough that they would not fear to negotiate, but not so strong that they felt they had no need to negotiate. I would add to that, Israel should also be strong enough so that their neighbors would not be tempted to attack them, and would have an incentive to negotiate."[281] Nixon was obviously preparing to press Israel for concessions on the West Bank.

The trip was not without comic moments. When Syrian jets rose to greet Air Force One, the president's pilots initially feared that they might attack and took appropriate evasive maneuvers, shaking up everyone on board. After a surprise toast from Nixon at the state dinner in Israel, Golda Meir responded, "As President Nixon says, Presidents can do almost anything, and President Nixon has done many things that nobody would have thought of doing." This drew howls of laughter from the press corps listening to the speech in an adjoining room.[282] Finally, in his memoirs, Nixon provided a somewhat incongruous commentary on his visit to Saudi Arabia:

Faisal saw Zionist and Communist conspiracies everywhere around him. He even put forward what must be the ultimate conspiratorialist notion: that the Zionists were behind the Palestinian terrorists. Despite this obsession, however, and thanks to his intelligence and the experience of many years in power, Faisal was one of the wisest leaders in the entire region.[283]

The trip was a bizarre episode in a period of intense U.S. domestic turmoil and involvement in Middle Eastern politics. It was followed by a similarly fabricated exercise when, six days after returning to Washington, Nixon journeyed to Moscow. He returned to the United States in late June. On the eve of his Mideast trip, he had recorded in his diary a theme that would soon be widely accepted in official Washington: "Whether Israel can survive over a long period of time with a hundred million Arabs around them I think is really questionable. The only long-term hope lies in reaching some kind of settlement now while they can operate from a position of strength, and while we are having such apparent success in weaning the Arabs away from the Soviets into more reasonable paths."[284]

Here Nixon echoed the theme from the days of the Rogers Plan: U.S. diplomacy could awaken a new era in U.S.-Arab relations, block Soviet inroads in the area, and thereby guarantee Israeli security in the long run. Nixon had never deviated from this broad strategy. Throughout his years in office, he maintained an impressive consistency in approaching the Arab-Israeli conflict. The Yom Kippur War allowed him to implement his strategy and the oil embargo made the Mideast America's most immediate foreign policy concern, but neither of these epochal events changed the administration's basic direction. After Nixon's resignation on 9 August 1974, Kissinger pursued the same strategy under a very different president and in the midst of a rapidly changing Arab world.

The Ford Era: The Second Egyptian-Israeli Disengagement Agreement

All sides involved in the peace process had been fortunate that no other international crisis had distracted Kissinger's attention between the October War and June 1974. Watergate had actually pushed America into greater involvement in the area. One of the key problems with the Kissinger shuttle was that it depended on this delicate balance of international and domestic factors. The man who was both NSC adviser and secretary of state had to devote an enormous amount of his time to Arab-Israeli matters and spend lengthy periods outside Washington. He could not do so forever.

It was now necessary to move beyond the separation of forces to a new kind of agreement. The two disengagement accords were only a formalized redeployment of troops at the end of a war. By summer 1974, however, domestic and international constraints limited the time Kissinger could devote to Arab-Israeli matters. The hastily arranged presidential trip, although justified as a means of moving toward genuine peace negotiations, was actually motivated by Nixon's shaky hold on his office. The third U.S.-Soviet summit and the Cyprus crisis in July diverted attention from the Middle East. As the president moved toward possible impeachment or resignation, it took all of Kissinger's time just to keep U.S. foreign policy afloat. A new diplomatic initiative was unthinkable.

Nonetheless, both Nixon and Kissinger had proposed to confront the thorny issue of the West Bank after the Syrian-Israeli disengagement. Certainly, this course of action had logic on its side. Without a Jordanian-Israeli disengagement agreement, Jordan might seem to be the loser for not entering the war and for its close association with the United States. That relationship made King Hussein a more deserving recipient of American mediation and Israeli territorial concessions than either Sadat or Assad. During the previous months of shuttle diplomacy, Kissinger had placated Hussein by repeatedly promising that his turn would come after the first two disengagement agreements.[285]

Yet there were several major difficulties in negotiating with Amman. First, since Israel and Jordan had not fought in 1973, negotiations were less pressing. Second, negotiations over the future of the West Bank raised the issue of where the PLO would fit in. Since September 1970, the PLO had understandably regarded King Hussein as an enemy, and any Jordanian-Israeli disengagement agreement threatened to shut the PLO out of the process. Because it regarded itself as the legitimate ruler of any territory that Israel would relinquish west of the Jordan, the PLO would undoubtedly condemn any arrangement between Amman and Jerusalem. King Hussein was only now breaking out of his four-year diplomatic isolation in the Arab world by developing closer relations with Syria. A limited peace that Israel could accept would almost certainly be opposed throughout the Arab world. It would result in renewed isolation for Hussein and would weaken his longstanding claim to the West Bank. (In the period before 1967 when Jordan had held the West Bank, no Arab country had recognized its claim to sovereignty). Yet Hussein's claim could also be weakened by the emerging PLO, which professed to speak for the Palestinians of Jordan.[286] The rival objectives between the Hashemite kingdom and the PLO continued to impede negotiations. Third, the West Bank posed more severe ideological and security questions for Israel than did the Sinai or Golan Heights. Unlike these areas, the West Bank was part of the original British mandate for Palestine. Important Israeli political groups held that the territory they called Judea and Samaria belonged to the Jewish people for religious and historical reasons. It was also an area critical to Israel's security. At one point north of Tel Aviv, Israel had been only nine miles wide before 1967. Therefore, the new prime minister, Yitzhak Rabin, soon adopted Golda Meir's promise that any withdrawals from the West Bank would have to be approved by new Israeli elections; this would inevitably inhibit the Israeli negotiators.

If the Israelis were wary about negotiations with Jordan, they were adamantly opposed to dealing with the PLO. The Israeli information minister, Aharon Yariv, suggested on 12 July that Israel might deal with Palestinian guerrilla organizations that rejected terrorism and acknowledged "the existence of the Jewish State here in Israel."[287] He was quickly rebuked by Prime Minister Rabin, who spoke for the consensus that Israel should not deal with the PLO because of the organization's terrorist methods (the PLO had, for example, taken responsibility for the killing of the sixteen children in Ma'alot) and its proclaimed goal of replacing Israel with a "democratic, secular" state of its own. If talks between Jordan and Israel appeared difficult, talks between Israel and the PLO appeared impossible. Israel would not consider a separate Palestinian state west of the Jordan and would not talk to the PLO; the PLO would accept nothing less than a state and would not recognize Israel's right to exist.

Nevertheless, a "senior State Department official" hinted on 11 July that high-level contacts between the United States and "Palestinian organizations" might develop in the next several months. Despite this statement and later hints, however, Kissinger avoided including the PLO in the peace process. Doing so would only hurt Jordan, a close American ally, increase the difficulties of dealing with Israel, and possibly bring about closer Russian involvement in the talks. Moreover, Kissinger believed that the moderates in the PLO could not accept the existence of Israel without touching off a bloody Palestinian power struggle. Thus, no agreement between the PLO and Israel seemed remotely possible. Kissinger's determination to avoid hopeless enterprises encouraged him to reject the PLO option, at least for the moment.[288]

Rabin was not interested in discussions about the West Bank because he believed that Egypt, the premier Arab country, should be the focus of negotiations. The more agonizing issues should be left until after the Egyptian issues had been settled. Thus, his suggestions for concessions in the Sinai were more detailed and realistic than his proposals for the West Bank. What dismayed Kissinger most of all, however, was that the new Israeli government was inherently weak. The defense minister, Shimon Peres, coveted Rabin's position and publicly disagreed with Foreign Minister Yigal Allon on vital matters, including the future disposition of the West Bank.[289]

Despite its doubts and weakness, Rabin's government secretly considered giving back to Jordan a small salient around the town of Jericho. Hussein would gain the civil administration of the area, but the Israeli military would remain nearby. Rabin also considered expanding the salient to include the Nablus area. At Camp David in late July, Kissinger suggested to Allon that perhaps the U.N. could take over Jericho as part of a limited withdrawal.[290] These tentative discussions ignored Rabin and Sadat's desire to take up the Egyptian front next, whereas Kissinger and Hussein sought to establish the principle of Jordanian rule over the West Bank to block the PLO claim. As a warning to the Israelis, the State Department had already dropped a hint—whatever the later disclaimers— that unless Israel reached agreement with Hussein, the United States might deal with the PLO.[291]

To deflect these pressures, Israel proposed a final settlement with Jordan in late July. In exchange for peace, Israel would withdraw from the largest portion of the West Bank but retain East Jerusalem, a security border on the Jordan, and several other key areas. There was no chance that Hussein would accept these terms. His government, like Israel's, was inherently weak. Challenged by the PLO, courting Syria, and attempting to forestall assaults on his throne from radical Iraq and Libya, Hussein had little freedom to maneuver. That was precisely why Rabin wanted to deal next with Egypt. He believed that only Sadat was strong enough to reach a *political* settlement.[292]

Although no one could have known it at the time, Richard Nixon's resignation was fortunate for Israel. Before the October War, Nixon's instincts had led him to support Israel despite frequent doubts about policies of the Meir government. After the war, however, Nixon's concern about the oil crisis and his desperate need for diplomatic victories tempted him to solve his problems at Israel's expense. Nixon had always yearned to push Israel into a comprehensive peace with the Arabs. Several times during his tenure, he had ordered subordinates to cut off aid to Israel in retaliation for some affront from Israel or American Jewish leaders, but his aides understood perfectly well that his orders were to be ignored. After the October War, however, Nixon's desire to force a comprehensive solution upon Israel intensified.[293]

Kissinger strongly believed that such a strategy would fail. He still thought he could coax Israeli concessions through use of the carrot and the stick, but his influence with Nixon had eroded. Their communications increasingly passed through Chief of Staff Alexander Haig. Nixon continued to hope for some spectacular success—a sudden end to the oil embargo, a trip to the Middle East, a comprehensive solution to the bitter conflict of a quarter century—that would save his presidency. Thus, by the time that Nixon resigned, his strategy preferences and Kissinger's diverged markedly.[294]

With no foreign policy experience and without Nixon's anxieties, Ford accepted Kissinger's step-by-step strategy with little resistance. In the new president's first weeks in office, four Mideast leaders visited Washington: King Hussein, the Egyptian and Syrian foreign ministers, and Prime Minister Rabin. With the disengagement process over, the major parties to the Arab-Israeli dispute were now scrambling to assess the new president and to influence the next steps that Kissinger contemplated. The Russians complained frequently about U.S. policy, but Ford and Kissinger successfully deflected their demands for greater involvement and a return to Geneva. Ford was at least as vocal as Nixon about keeping the Soviets out.[295]

Once again, Kissinger was very much in charge of policy and ready to continue his shuttle diplomacy. It was clear after the Hussein visit that the United States favored a Jordanian-Israeli agreement before another Egyptian-Israeli accord, although discussions might begin with Egypt while the Jordanian negotiations continued. Nonetheless, all parties knew that the Kissinger style demanded one step at a time because the secretary of state could not personally handle more than that.

When Rabin arrived in Washington in mid-September, disagreement had already developed between his government and the new Ford administration. Rabin was preoccupied with Egypt and, if he mentioned Jordan at all, it was in the context of an overall settlement. Kissinger was convinced that Amman would not consider a comprehensive deal. Ford was disappointed in the talks. He found Rabin a "tough" instead of a "flexible" negotiator, and he thought Rabin's toast at the state dinner was not sufficiently conciliatory.[296] Despite his years in Washington, Rabin was prone to use blunt language; with him, controversies that might have been papered over with niceties immediately came to the surface. Ford and Kissinger were not pleased that Rabin used his Washington trip to confirm reports that he favored an Egyptian accord instead of a deal with Jordan.[297] His statement only advertised the differences between Israel and the United States.

Ford and Rabin did not develop the rapport that had existed between Nixon and Meir. Rabin, unlike his American counterpart, later claimed to have been pleased with the meetings. In Rabin's account, Ford and Kissinger agreed with him on the direction of negotiations and agreed to Israeli arms requests. In contrast to Ford's acid recollection of the meetings, Rabin offered a warm anecdote. He had been expected to dance with Betty Ford at the state dinner while the president was dancing with Leah Rabin. When he told Mrs. Ford that he couldn't dance, she grabbed him and whisked him onto the floor anyway with the comment that she had once been a dance teacher. Finally, Kissinger cut in. "If he had never done anything else for Israel, I would still be eternally grateful to Kissinger for that small mercy," Rabin wrote.[298]

The outcome of these Washington discussions was that Kissinger would return to the Middle East in October. Ford indicates that the American disagreement with Rabin led to the trip, whereas Rabin recalls a consensus between Israel and the United States. Rabin expected Kissinger to discuss the details of an Egyptian agreement.[299] Actually, Kissinger was most concerned about a forthcoming Arab summit and was anxious to forestall any developments that would lead to greater PLO influence.

Kissinger had reason to be disturbed by the direction of Arab politics. In late September, Sadat had reneged on a promise to Hussein and joined Syria in recognizing the PLO as the sole representative of the Palestinian people. The Arabs also gained overwhelming passage of a U.N. General Assembly resolution inviting the PLO to participate in its annual discussion of the Palestinian question in November.

On this shuttle, his seventh trip to the area in less than a year, Kissinger could do little to persuade the Arab states not to support the PLO. He privately obtained what he thought were assurances from Faisal and Sadat that the Arabs would not annoint the PLO at their forthcoming summit.[300] He also sought to persuade Israel and Jordan to demonstrate some progress, however limited, toward an agreement. That obstacle proved insurmountable. All parties were afraid to take any action before the Arab summit meeting.

When the Arab League met at Rabat in late October, Kissinger was shocked when the moderates endorsed an independent Palestinian state "on any Palestinian soil that is liberated" from Israeli occupation and recognized the PLO as the "sole legitimate representative of the Palestinian people." This meant that the Arabs endorsed the PLO and not Jordan as the negotiator for the future of the West Bank and Gaza. Sadat had sought a more ambiguous outcome, but Syria and Saudi Arabia were among the most vigorous supporters of the PLO.[301] Once he saw that Arab opinion was overwhelmingly against him, even King Hussein acquiesced, but he was bitter for months afterward.

The plans of yet another administration had been ruined by internal Arab conflicts. Kissinger's Middle East diplomacy never recovered from the blow dealt at the Rabat Summit. Rabat demonstrated that the Arabs would not follow Kissinger's script. Appointing the PLO to negotiate for the West Bank made sense from the perspective of intra-Arab politics, but as a pragmatic strategy it was disastrous. By cutting off the possibility of Israeli-Jordanian talks, the Arabs lost the opportunity to gain Israeli agreement to the principle of withdrawal from the West Bank, a principle that would have been no small Arab achievement. The Arab strategy intended that Kissinger press the Israelis hard in the months ahead, but instead it separated Sadat, the Arab leader most interested in further negotiations, from the rest of the Arab world.

Emotions ran high in the new atmosphere. Kissinger had hoped to postpone Israeli-Palestinian negotiations until a later stage. Now the Palestinian issue had been thrown like a monkey wrench into his strategy. When Yasir Arafat came to New York to address the U.N. General Assembly in early November, a hundred thousand Israeli supporters protested in New York City, and similar demonstrations were held around the country.[302] The ensuing Arab-sponsored anti-Israeli campaign in the United Nations acted to rally the pro-Israeli forces, only now emerging from the shock of the Yom Kippur War.

Rabin concluded from Rabat that he could not trust Sadat. In July the Egyptian leader had promised to back Hussein as the ruler of the West Bank if the Jordanian monarch would recognize the PLO as representing all the Palestinians outside of Jordan. By September, Sadat had abandoned Hussein and jumped on the PLO bandwagon. To Rabin the lesson was clear: "If Sadat was capable of breaking an agreement with a fellow Arab leader, how was he likely to treat an agreement with Israel if other Arab states placed him under pressure?"[303] This made Kissinger's task more delicate.

Yasir Arafat's vision of a democratic secular state in all of Palestine made clear that the PLO did not accept the U.N. partition resolution of 1947, let alone Resolutions 242 and 338. The Rabat decision, Arafat's speech, and continued high oil prices were bound to diminish the domestic popularity of a shuttle diplomacy dependent on Israeli territorial concessions and on an American secretary of state haggling with both sides over delicate details. Before further damage could be done, Kissinger moved to maintain diplomatic momentum by obtaining any type of agreement. He had no choice but to turn to another Sinai accord, the course that had been favored by both Sadat and Rabin for months.

After Rabat, however, Kissinger had little confidence in the new Israeli government. He thought Rabin had proven stubborn, shortsighted, and wrong in his West Bank assessment. As a warning to the Jerusalem government, the secretary encouraged Ford to answer a question at a news conference in a way calculated to disturb Israel: "We of course feel that there must be movement toward settlement of the problem between Israel and Egypt on the one hand, between Israel and Jordan or the PLO on the other, and the problems between Israel and Syria in the other category."[304] Never before had any American president publicly acknowledged the possibility of Israeli-PLO negotiations. It was taken as a strong signal in Israel.

Kissinger tried to pick up the pieces of his Mideast diplomacy on yet another trip—his eighth—in November. He faced a new impediment: a visit by Brezhnev to Cairo, scheduled for January, with its implicit threat that Sadat might return to the Soviet fold if displeased by the progress of the peace talks. Serious negotiations could not proceed until the results of Brezhnev's visit could be assessed.

Meanwhile, Kissinger grew displeased with the demands Rabin was making for the next round of negotiations. The Israeli leader had devised a new slogan, "A piece of peace for a piece of territory." His notion was that Israel should not enter into further agreements with Egypt unless Israeli withdrawals were accompanied by Egyptian political commitments. Rabin sought a statement of "nonbelligerence" between the two sides, but Kissinger tried to convince him that Sadat could not pledge nonbelligerence as long as Israel retained a part of the Sinai. Kissinger tried to persuade Rabin to accept steps that were the equivalent of nonbelligerence, such as an end to the Egyptian boycott of Israeli goods and a lessening of Egypt's anti-Israel propaganda. As usual, Egypt and Israel were far apart on how much withdrawal Egypt could expect in return for reduced hostility.[305]

Rabin tried out new ideas in response to Kissinger's pressure, but he used interviews with journalists as the medium for his message. In early December Rabin gave an interview in which he admitted that nonbelligerence was not a realistic objective for negotiations. He bluntly revealed Israel's strategy: Israel would try to use an agreement to separate Egypt from Syria and would try to delay the negotiations as long as possible to get closer to the 1976 U.S. presidential elections, when Israel would have more political leverage on the United States. This astonishingly candid statement was followed a few days later by the visit to Washington of Foreign Minister Yigal Allon, who brought the official

Israeli negotiating proposals. They included a call for Egyptian nonbelligerence, the very idea the prime minister had publicly termed unrealistic, in exchange for minor Israeli withdrawals.

Both Ford and Kissinger told Allon that Israel's "ten points," as they were called, did not go far enough. These points were obviously a ploy, a statement of Israel's desires rather than proposals Egypt might accept, so Allon privately asked Kissinger to inform Sadat that the Israeli position was flexible. Instead, the secretary of state simply forwarded the ten points to Egypt as they were, then used the predictable Egyptian rejection to pressure the Rabin government to make more concessions. The whole sequence of events undermined the trust between the Israelis and Kissinger and convinced the secretary of state that Israel's ruling troika was diplomatically inept and internally divided.[306]

At the end of December, the Brezhnev visit to Cairo was cancelled, suggesting serious problems between Sadat and the Kremlin. The Egyptian president had lost one of his trump cards and would be forced to negotiate from a weaker position. Nevertheless, he kept up a stiff and uncompromising negotiating stance. Syria and the radical states were pressuring him not to conclude another separate agreement with Israel, so Sadat maintained that he needed favorable terms to justify breaking the Arab consensus. He also needed tangible results to show that his tilt toward the United States and abandonment of the Soviets had been wise. Kissinger was sympathetic to Sadat's domestic and intra-Arab constraints and was inclined to accept his claim that even to consider another deal with Israel was a major concession.

Kissinger's strategy remained unchanged: he sought to buy Arab friendship with Israeli concessions. The goal was a new regional order with increased American influence and greater stability in Arab-Israeli relations, both of which developments Kissinger saw as being in Israel's long-term interest. Therefore, he believed, Israel ought to make the concessions necessary to successful agreements. Kissinger's rationale for Israeli concessions did not differ markedly from those of Dulles and Rogers before him. This secretary of state, however, was tactically more clever than his predecessors, and he could spend more time on the negotiations, because the problem was now in the forefront of U.S. concern.

Sadat's major demands in this phase had been return of the Abu Rhodeis oilfields and the Gidi and Mitla passes, the key strategic prize of the Sinai through which moved all ground forces east or west. The Israelis had steadfastly refused to relinquish either. Soon after he had invited Kissinger back to the Mideast in February, Rabin unexpectedly gave another interview in which he volunteered (without concessions from Sadat) to give up the passes and the oilfields in return for a commitment "not to go to war, not to depend on threats or use of force and an effort to reach true peace."[307]

Kissinger thought this an unfathomable blunder; major concessions should be made through him as the central mediator. Rabin had freely offered concessions that could not now be traded for Egyptian flexibility or used to improve Kissinger's standing with Sadat. Although Kissinger expected the talks on his February trip to be "exploratory" and the two sides to make minor concessions, differences remained profound. Still, both parties clearly sought an arrangement. Therefore, in mid-March the secretary returned to the area for what he believed would be the decisive shuttle for a second Egyptian-Israeli agreement.[308]

Kissinger's decision to return to the Middle East in March 1975 proved a major miscalculation. It was an error that grew from the contradictions of Mideast shuttle diplomacy as it had developed since October 1973. During Nixon's first term, Kissinger's diplomatic successes had involved negotiations in which the United States was a participant—talks with Vietnam, China, and the U.S.S.R. In each of these meetings, Kissinger had been able to make major concessions at the critical moments. When he became mediator instead of participant, he assumed that the parties—especially the Israelis on whom he had greater leverage—would conduct themselves in a similar manner.

After October 1973 Kissinger seemed to regard the Israelis almost as if they were the United States or South Vietnam in the Vietnam negotiations. The problem with the U.S. analogy was that Kissinger could not negotiate for Israel, nor was Jerusalem in as weak a position in its negotiations as Washington had been in Vietnam (or had perceived itself to be). The problem with the South Vietnam analogy was that Saigon had not had Israel's military power and internal strength. Indeed, Kissinger's lectures to the Israelis often ignored—to their irritation—Israel's growing military superiority.[309] Kissinger's recurrent fury toward Jerusalem stemmed from his different view of Israel's interests, which led him to expect Israel to make concessions he might have made in their shoes. He believed that the concessions asked of Israel were trivial. According to Edward Sheehan's reconstruction of the decisive meeting in Jerusalem, Kissinger argued, "Don't misunderstand me. I'm analyzing this situation with friends. One reason I and my colleagues are so exasperated is that we see a friend damaging himself for reasons which will seem trivial five years from now . . ." And later in the conversation, "I'm not angry with you, and I'm not asking you to change your position. It's tragic to see people dooming themselves to a course of unbelievable peril."[310]

The Mideast negotiating process had developed a definite pattern since October 1973. First, Kissinger assessed both sides' positions in exploratory shuttles or meetings with key leaders in Washington. On a later decisive trip, the United States advanced proposals for closing the gap, exchanged memoranda of understandings with each party to ease the way, and shepherded the parties to a final agreement. But the two previous negotiations involved the mere disengagement of troops and Richard Nixon had pressed hard for them to demonstrate his foreign policy prowess. Now Egypt and Israel were being asked to take practical steps toward resolving a conflict at least a quarter-of-a-century old, and President Ford was not as desperate for an agreement as Nixon had been. In addition, the shuttle approach demanded that all sides agree on the decisive moment. Because both Egypt and Israel had compromised in the past, Kissinger assumed that any negotiating stance could be altered when the time came. But in March 1975 neither Cairo nor Jerusalem shared Kissinger's assessment that the decisive moment had arrived. Neither was ready to make the necessary concessions. On the contrary, both sides stood to gain from a breakdown of the talks. The collapse of negotiations made Rabin a hero in Israel for resisting American pressure and improved Sadat's standing in the Arab world.

Kissinger may have miscalculated in part because of pressures from outside the Mideast. His handling of the Indochina settlement became suspect as the three pro-Western governments of the area weakened in the face of Communist assaults. Serious problems for the United States had also developed in Portugal, after a recent leftist coup, and in Turkey, where a congressional ban on military assistance over the Cyprus issue had infuriated Ankara. Relations with the U.S.S.R. also deteriorated in early 1975. The popularity of both Ford and Kissinger declined in the polls and Congress asserted itself over the details of foreign policy. The United States fell deep into the worst recession in thirty years. Thus, the administration needed a diplomatic victory, and the Egyptian-Israeli negotiations appeared the most likely opportunity. Yet his other concerns limited Kissinger's time. He had spent an entire month on the Syrian-Israeli disengagement, but on this March 1975 trip Kissinger simply could not stay longer than eighteen days. If he had been working under similar constraints in May 1974, a deal between Damascus and Jerusalem probably would not have been struck.

A further constraint on the ill-fated March 1975 shuttle was that the two sides were still far apart when Kissinger departed for the region. They disagreed over the extent of Egyptian commitment to nonbelligerence, the extent of Israeli territorial withdrawals, the duration of the accord, and Sadat's refusal to let Israel retain control of a critical electronic intelligence gathering facility at Umm Khisheiba. As long as the Egyptians would not agree to a declaration of nonbelligerence and take practical steps toward peace, the Israelis would not withdraw from the strategic Gidi and Mitla passes.[311]

Kissinger clearly believed that the Israelis were the ones who should have compromised and he made his distress with them known during the trip. He complained to Arab leaders that the Israelis were intransigent and had sought "to bring me down." He also disagreed with the Israelis to their faces. In the climactic meeting at the end of the discussions, Foreign Minister Allon commented, "The Egyptians really didn't give very much," whereupon Kissinger launched into the central thesis of his Mideast diplomacy: *any* agreement was in both American and Israeli national interests:

An agreement would have enabled the United States to remain in control of the diplomatic process. Compared to that, the location of the line eight kilometers one way or the other frankly does not seem very important. And you got all the military elements of non-belligerency. You got the "non-use of force." The elements you didn't get—movement of peoples, ending of the boycotts—are unrelated to your line. What you didn't get has nothing to do with where your line is . . . ."[312]

The crisis in American-Israeli relations after the breakdown of the March 1975 shuttle was a direct outgrowth of Kissinger's frustration with the new Israeli Cabinet. Near the end of the trip, Kissinger tried to change the Cabinet's bargaining position by prompting President Ford to send a harsh letter to Jerusalem. Ford bluntly stated,

I wish to express my profound disappointment over Israel's attitude in the course of the negotiations . . . Failure of the negotiations will have a far-reaching impact on the region and on our relations. I have given instructions for a reassessment of United States policy in the region, including our relations with Israel, with the aim of ensuring that over-all American interests . . . are protected. You will be notified of our decision.[313]

Since this letter appeared similar to President Nixon's rough correspondence during the Syrian-Israeli negotiations, the Israelis assumed, despite his denials, that Kissinger was behind the correspondence. Rabin in effect called the secretary of state a liar.[314] The talks ended the next day.

Kissinger's credibility with the Israelis had reached a new low. He warned them that the breakdown of the shuttle would end step-by-step negotiations. They would then face a return to Geneva, increased Russian and European involvement, more world pressure on behalf of the Palestinians, and "a linkage between moves in the Sinai and on Golan." Foreign Minister Allon asked why the talks couldn't simply start again after a few weeks had elapsed. The Israelis were even prepared to have Kissinger return to Egypt immediately, but both Sadat and Kissinger believed that the talks could not continue without further Israeli concessions. Rabin admitted in his memoirs that the Israelis "no longer believed that there was any hope." Not even dire warnings to the Israelis could produce an agreement.[315]

Kissinger thought the breakdown would weaken U.S. standing in the Arab world and strengthen the Russian position. He warned the Israelis that when these expected dire circumstances came about, "I can't promise you anything about American policy."[316]

The secretary of state did not handle failure easily, and the March 1975 shuttle was not one of his finest hours. The termination of the talks was unusually emotional: Kissinger visited Masada, where nine hundred Jews had committed suicide rather than surrender to Roman legions, and then broke into tears when he left Israel the next day. He had promised the Israelis that neither side would be blamed for the talks' demise, and they had therefore agreed that one-sided stories would not be offered to the press. Yet in a private talk before the negotiations collapsed, Kissinger accused the prime minister of having misled him about Israeli withdrawals. Rabin insisted that he had made it clear: only in return for an end to belligerency would he consider total withdrawals from the passes. That Jerusalem was his last stop was a further signal that Kissinger would hold Israel responsible for the talks' collapse. As soon as he departed, the secretary of state, in his role as a "senior official," released stories complaining about Israel's intransigence and Rabin's weakness.[317] A major crisis in American-Israeli relations began almost immediately.

On this tenth shuttle, Kissinger made various errors. First, before he set out, he concluded that Cairo and Jerusalem were closer to agreement than they actually were. During the shuttle he raised the negotiations to an importance they should not have had and so increased the cost of failure. Second, the harsh letter from President Ford to Prime Minister Rabin backfired and locked the administration into a conflict with Israel. Third, Kissinger became a victim of his own rhetoric. He seems to have believed that failure on this particular shuttle would be disastrous for both the United States and Israel. He refused to consider the likely possibility that, after a cooling-off period for both sides, a deal might yet be struck. Finally, Kissinger underestimated the negative influence of Rabin's domestic difficulties and the pressures of intra-Arab politics on the negotiations.

The secretary of state himself had become an issue in the talks, an old problem with Kissinger. In Egypt he saw himself as a supplicant, but in Israel he acted as a patron. He thought he had greater leverage on Israel and expected greater concessions there; this was bound to lead to tensions between the two countries. The explosion in March 1975 was ignited by a proposed Sinai deal in which the interests of Jerusalem and Washington clearly diverged. Israel was expected to relinquish the passes and the oilfields in return for nothing tangible, while Washington reaped profit by gaining influence in the area.

Kissinger now came to feel that the Israelis had been intransigent and that their divided government had not had a strong leader since Golda Meir. His frustration with the Rabin Cabinet led to weeks of wrangling between Jerusalem and Washington. Ford made good his threat to "reassess" U.S. relations with countries in the Mideast. While Israeli military supplies already in the pipelines were not cut off, no new arms deals were concluded.* Meanwhile, Kissinger

---

*Deliveries were also slowed, but it was never clear whether this was a deliberate policy or a consequence of short supplies and tardy production schedules resulting from a bottleneck that occurred at the same time as the reassessment.

asked State Department and Pentagon bureaucrats known to be skeptical of close American relations with Israel to produce studies exploring future options.[318] He ostentatiously met with experts and former officials known for their criticism of Israel, including George Ball, Charles Yost, John J. McCloy, and William Scranton.

Ford wrote in his autobiography that he was "mad as hell" at the Israelis but demonstrates that his anger was based on Kissinger's assessment of the talks.[319] The president's fury had been building for weeks; as early as February Kissinger had told him that Sadat "was trying to be flexible and to accommodate the Israelis' concern about their security. The Israelis, however, while encouraging our efforts to push for a lasting peace, were being very tough in their demands." Ford's view of the March shuttle was similar. "Again the Egyptians bent over backward. Again, the Israelis resisted." While he "didn't doubt for a minute" that Rabin "really wanted peace," Ford thought that "he didn't seem to understand that only by giving do you get something in return." Ford accepted Kissinger's assessment at the conclusion of the talks: "Henry was deeply disappointed by the Israeli attitude. He was worried that Sadat, who had gone along with many of our suggestions, would never work with us again."[320] Kissinger could depend on the new president to follow his recommendations.

As the discussions continued at the State Department, three options were suggested. The first would make the most radical change in American policy. The Geneva Conference would be reconvened and the United States would announce a peace plan in which Israel would be asked to return to the 1967 borders (perhaps with minor adjustments) in return for international guarantees of security. The Soviet Union would enter these negotiations, which would put pressure on Israel. Most of the experts, academics, and officials favored this option, which brought both Ford and Kissinger to consider it. To get public backing for such a policy, Ford would have to make a major speech over the heads of Israel's supporters in Congress and the country. The president hinted that he might indeed make such a speech to his old friend Max Fisher, head of the Jewish Agency and the key Republican contact with the Jewish community. Ford knew the message would be conveyed to the Israeli government.[321] The second option was a major deal between Israel and Egypt—an Israeli withdrawal from most or all of the Sinai in return for a nonbelligerency agreement or full peace.[322] Finally, the third option was a return to the step-by-step process in an attempt to reach agreement on the Egyptian-Israeli talks that had broken off in March. Other alternatives considered included a Soviet-American imposed peace, quickly rejected as not viable and against U.S. interests, and a total withdrawal from the peace process, also rapidly rejected.

During the reassessment, Ford saw a variety of public figures known for views ranging from pro-Israeli to pro-Arab (e.g., former Under Secretaries of State Eugene V. Rostow and George Ball, former Supreme Court Justice Arthur

Goldberg, and J. William Fulbright, former chairman of the Senate Foreign Relations Committee.) The president's private criticisms were aimed at the pro-Israeli forces, which gave their opponents hope that he would adopt the Geneva option. He was reported to have told friends, "All my life I fought for Israel and now when I need understanding from them I get a refusal." He warned publicly and privately throughout the spring that lack of diplomatic progress would lead to another war and another oil embargo.[323] Whether it was accurate or not, this doomsday rhetoric pressured Israel because it revealed Arab leverage on the United States.

The reassessment triggered a vehement response among the pro-Israeli forces and brought about their first major confrontation with the Ford administration.[324] Their efforts culminated in a letter from seventy-six senators calling for undiminished economic and military aid to Israel. The letter shockingly undercut the entire thrust of the administration's "reassessment":

> We believe that preserving the peace requires that Israel obtain a level of military and economic support adequate to deter a renewal of war by Israel's neighbors. Withholding military equipment from Israel would be dangerous, discouraging accommodation by Israel's neighbors and encouraging a resort to force . . . Within the next several weeks, the Congress expects to receive your foreign aid requirements for fiscal year 1976. We trust that your recommendations will be responsive to Israel's urgent military and economic needs. We urge you to make it clear, as we do, that the United States, acting in its own national interests, stands firm with Israel in the search for peace in future negotiations, and that this premise is the basis of the current reassessment of U.S. policy in the Middle East.[325]

Any document that brought together such disparate senatorial voices as Ted Kennedy and Barry Goldwater, Frank Church and Paul Laxalt, Walter Mondale and Strom Thurmond was bound to challenge the administration's Mideast diplomacy. It was the most powerful dissent to Kissinger's efforts in the Mideast since he had embarked on step-by-step diplomacy, and it was accompanied by several public statements that clarified the senators' opposition.[326] Ford and Kissinger blamed the letter on the pro-Israeli lobby, but the fact that three-quarters of the Senate had signed suggests serious congressional uneasiness over the administration's inclination to hold Israel responsible for the breakdown of the talks. Ford thought the letter would make the Israelis less willing to compromise and he bitterly resented the pressure. "It really bugged me," he wrote in his memoirs, and he also blamed the Israelis for it: "There was no doubt in my mind that it was inspired by Israel . . . I thought they were overplaying their hand. For me, that kind of pressure has always been counterproductive. I was not going to capitulate to it."[327] Like Ford's sharp letter to Rabin, the letter from the seventy-six senators offended the recipient; it made the president more determined to continue the reassessment.

Yet Congress and the president actually sought the same objective, if not in the same style. Ford and Kissinger, adopting the old Rogers approach that Kissinger had once opposed, were prepared to take a tough stand with Israel until an agreement could be reached. The overwhelming majority in Congress were not concerned with strategy but were opposed to denying aid. Kissinger agreed in substance with many of his congressional critics in that he did not want to include the Russians in negotiations and he sought to put off the Palestinian question. Kissinger's desire not to deal with the U.S.S.R. was strengthened when Moscow initiated preliminary discussions aimed at reconvening the Geneva Conference and failed even to gain the support of the divided PLO.[328]

Israeli and Egyptian preferences and the lack of other viable options, not domestic pressures, moved Kissinger and Ford back to the step-by-step process. A Geneva Conference would be too cumbersome, give too much influence to Arab radicals and the U.S.S.R., push the United States off center stage, and probably fail. The second option, a full-scale Egyptian-Israeli agreement, would be more difficult to attain than a limited arrangement and even if achieved would alienate Egypt from the Arab world. Thus, Congress and the pro-Israeli lobby pressed Kissinger and Ford onto a road they would have traveled in any case. Nevertheless, congressional interference, prompted by the pro-Israeli lobby, limited the administration's flexibility in handling both sides.

Meanwhile, dramatic events around the world shook American confidence. Three days after Kissinger left the Middle East in March, King Faisal of Saudi Arabia was assassinated. During April and May, as the reassessment proceeded, Cambodia, South Vietnam, and Laos fell to Communist forces. The first simmerings of civil war in Lebanon emerged. In the Mayaguez incident the administration used marines to free an American merchant vessel captured by Cambodian troops. Although the Mayaguez gunboat diplomacy was hugely popular in the United States, Ford and Kissinger still needed a diplomatic success to prove the new team capable of substantive achievement. In these circumstances the two men felt irresistible pressure to pursue any diplomacy that might succeed.

The actions of both Egypt and Israel encouraged a return to step-by-step diplomacy. In late March Sadat had stunned the diplomatic community by announcing that he would reopen the Suez Canal on 5 June—the eighth anniversary of the beginning of the Six-Day War—with or without a second Sinai accord. Israel responded by unilaterally withdrawing troops from the limited force zone established under the 1974 disengagement accord. These unilateral steps by Sadat and Rabin demonstrated their wish to reestablish negotiations through Kissinger.

The administration signaled that it might resume step-by-step diplomacy in early May, before the letter from seventy-six senators was even received. Ford announced that in June he would meet with Sadat in Salzburg, Austria, and with Rabin a few days later in Washington. The ostensible reason for these meetings was to get information from both leaders for the reassessment, but clearly if the meetings produced new ideas Kissinger would be encouraged to return to the step-by-step process. Ford later indicated that a meeting with Sadat was scheduled first as a subtle pressure on Israel.[329]

By all accounts, this first meeting between Sadat and Ford was a major success. A cordiality between the two presidents developed and they discussed economic and military aid to Egypt. Ford would not publicly advocate a return to the 1967 frontiers, but he repeated Nixon's promise of the previous year to work for that goal. In the absence of new ideas from the United States or Israel on the interim negotiations, Sadat produced a suggestion that proved critical. He proposed that the Umm Khisheiba surveillance station be operated by U.S. civilians rather than Israelis. Ford and Kissinger seized on the idea, but decided to keep it secret until the meeting with Rabin.[330]

During Rabin's visit to Washington in June, Ford toyed with the Israeli prime minister. At the outset, the president announced he favored the Geneva option even though the discussions quickly turned to the details of an Egyptian-Israeli accord. Kissinger in subsequent meetings used Geneva as a threat whenever he believed Rabin was not sufficiently flexible about an Egyptian-Israeli deal. "Geneva" of course implied to Rabin that the United States would use the conference to support a return to the 1967 frontiers. Rabin agreed to a new and deeper Israeli withdrawal line; Ford and Kissinger endorsed Sadat's insistence that Israel withdraw completely from the passes. The president presented the idea of U.S. civilian technicians in the buffer zone as an American concept. He believed that Rabin might reject such a suggestion by Sadat who would then be embarrassed in the Arab world when it leaked to the press. Rabin left Washington with the impression that he had "heard—and voiced—a lot of tough talk" during his visit. Ford "sensed that we were about to make progress." Once again, the two leaders perceived their meetings very differently.[331]

In the end Ford's optimism proved the more accurate perception. After the Washington summit of June, discussions proceeded on several issues. First, the Israelis suggested an even stronger U.S. role than Sadat had recommended—a military presence in the passes. When Dinitz brought this idea to Kissinger, the secretary of state was skeptical. Congress would surely oppose any new Vietnam-type commitments. According to Rabin, Ford opposed using United States military units but seemed willing to accept an American civilian presence. By mid-July the Israeli and American governments were discussing various plans for civilian intelligence stations in the passes after a suggestion by Israeli defense minister Peres.[332]

Kissinger met secretly with Yitzhak Rabin while both visited West Germany in July. In an ancient German castle, the two agreed to a plan for Egyptian and Israeli intelligence stations in the Sinai passes. The meeting took place in a climate of confusion, because the Americans had installed special loudspeakers that emitted obnoxious bleeps and whistles to thwart any electronic record of the clandestine conversation. "It was, indeed, a very advanced system that precluded anyone's overhearing our conversation, principally because the bleeps and whistles made it impossible to converse," Rabin recalls. Kissinger justified the maddening racket by saying, "You never know how many Soviet spies are lurking here."[333] If Nixon had installed this system in the White House he might still have been president in 1975. He might also have been deaf.

Despite the racket, Rabin accepted Kissinger's recommendation of a limited U.S. role: Israel would man Umm Khisheiba under an American flag, and the United States would build a similar station for the Egyptians. The United States would also build and man four smaller intelligence gathering stations. The intelligence gathering stations served as a face-saving device for the Egyptians because they concealed the continued Israeli presence in the passes. The U.S. presence also assured both sides that the other could not attack without warning; the United States would provide information to both. Kissinger remained skeptical about the idea of involving Americans. "It's a mistake," he told the Israelis later on his August shuttle. "There will be a reaction in the United States to this kind of thing."[334]

The negotiations were carried out in summer 1975 by a triangular long distance substitute for the Kissinger shuttle. Except for the Rabin-Kissinger meeting in West Germany, Ambassador Dinitz dealt with Kissinger in Washington for the Israeli Cabinet and U.S. Ambassador Eilts in Cairo conveyed Kissinger's messages to Sadat. The secretary of state refused to mount another shuttle unless assured of success. Nevertheless, he remained central to communications with both sides. This new variation helped protect Kissinger from the domestic Israeli and intra-Arab politics that had derailed his March shuttle, and allowed him to participate without using so much time and political capital.

In these summer negotiations both the Israelis and Egyptians agreed to the intelligence stations and the American presence. Sadat agreed to three annual renewals of the mandate for the U.N. Sinai peacekeeping force, thereby resolving another issue. More complex was the continuing dispute over the depth of Israeli troop withdrawals in the passes. After the June summit in Washington, Rabin had infuriated Ford and Kissinger by informing them that his Cabinet had not approved the withdrawal lines he had drawn there.[335] The Israeli general staff soon prepared a plan detailing a new line of withdrawal to the eastern end of the passes; this line eventually became the basis of the agreement. The haggling on this question did not end until Kissinger's shuttle at the end of August.

In preparation for the August shuttle, American experts produced a huge relief map of the Sinai based on satellite photographs and topographic investigation on the ground. Since the map revealed every ridge and hill, it contributed greatly to the bargaining. Kissinger promoted a disposition of forces that would let the Egyptians claim the Israelis were out of the passes and let the Israelis argue they retained a toe-hold. This helped satisfy pressures on the leaders of both countries.

Kissinger's manipulative skill extended to procedure as well as substance. In their Germany meeting, for example, he had asked Rabin not to reveal how far Israel would withdraw; he would convince Sadat at the appropriate time that Israel had conceded reluctantly. He used this technique in reverse when he withheld Sadat's concessions from the Israelis.[336]

The Israelis showed a new flexibility after the Ford-Rabin summit in June because they had resolved to accept American diplomatic, military, and economic assistance instead of Egyptian concessions. Through their conflict with Jerusalem, Ford and Kissinger had revealed how desperately they wanted an agreement. Since Ford had bluntly predicted a war and oil embargo if an accord was not reached, and Kissinger seemed to affirm this fear by the time and effort he devoted to the problem, making a second Sinai accord the administration's highest priority, Jerusalem felt it had considerable leverage. If Egypt refused peace in return for Israeli concessions, then at least the United States could be made to pay a high price in the form of military and economic aid to Israel.

As in the Vietnam talks or the agreements with the Kremlin, Kissinger seemed willing to sweeten the pot for those he saw as recalcitrant, even after he had punished them. In the Vietnam accords, for example, he first punished Hanoi with the Christmas bombing of 1972 and then promised economic assistance a few weeks later. In this case Israel was first threatened by the reassessment and then rewarded with aid commitments to induce agreement.

The extent and nature of compensation to Israel proved the most delicate subject on Kissinger's shuttle at the end of August. Kissinger engaged in the familiar haggling over details with the Egyptian negotiators (Sadat, as usual, dealt only with broad principles). In Israel, right-wing groups staged large-scale public demonstrations chanting "Jew-boy" and "Kissinger go home." Kissinger's visits to Jerusalem included physically taxing marathon discussions: "Five hours might be spent discussing a stretch of sand one hundred meters long." The haggling over the passes continued until the last moment, when the Israelis agreed to a final withdrawal. The last session to complete the "Memorandum of Agreement" between the United States and Israel lasted from 9:30 P.M. to 6:00 A.M. on 31 August. Rabin recalls, "as the hours wore on, participants on both sides dropped out of the discussion, so that by the end it had become a dialogue between Kissinger and me against a chorus of snores all around." Assistant Secretary of State Atherton, who phrased the details of the memorandum while Kissinger shuttled, did not sleep for two nights before the "Memorandum of Agreement" was finished on 1 September.[337]

The content of the accord was announced that day. Israel agreed to withdraw from the Abu Rhodeis oil fields and the Gidi and Mitla passes. Buffer zones, U.N. forces, and a U.S. civilian presence to supervise the intelligence-gathering stations were items included in the published text. (In the end there were eight stations—one each for Israel and Egypt, plus three manned and three unmanned U.S. stations.)[338] The two sides agreed not to use force or the threat of it in resolving their conflict and Egypt publicly consented to nonmilitary cargoes passing to and from Israel through the reopened Suez Canal.[339] Although several congressmen questioned the desirability of a U.S. civilian presence in the Sinai, few Americans found fault with these provisions. It was the Israeli/American Memorandum of Agreement which became most controversial.

In that memorandum, the Ford administration agreed to most of the aid Israel had requested (about $2 billion) for the forthcoming year. It agreed to consult regularly on Israel's long-term economic and military assistance needs, to request such assistance in Congress annually, to compensate Israel economically for the oil lost by relinquishing Abu Rhodeis, and to help Israel meet "normal requirements for domestic consumption" if it could not gain supplies on its own. Kissinger also agreed to review the Israeli request for F-16 jets and to "undertake a joint study" of selling Pershing ground-to-ground missiles with conventional warheads. This item raised eyebrows when it leaked to the press because the Pershing had originally been designed for nuclear weapons. It annoyed Sadat because he had not been informed as he had about the other provisions of the memorandum; some Egyptian officials suspected additional secret clauses. (In the end Congress showed no inclination to provide the Pershings and Israel settled for the shorter-range Lance, designed for conventional warheads.)

Ford later justified the generous arms assistance commitments in the following terms: "Nothing was more important to the Israelis than their own military security. If we provided the hardware, we could convince the Israelis that they were secure. Then they might be willing to accept some risks in the search for peace."[340] Ford thus described the strategy that he had rejected during most of 1975 and that Kissinger had advocated during the first term, a strategy that assumed Israel would be flexible if "armed to the teeth." The opposite approach, articulated during the first term by William Rogers and pursued during 1975 by Ford and Kissinger, was to hold Israeli arms requests "in abeyance" on the theory that only an arms delay would lead to Israeli flexibility. In reality neither strategy worked. Israel showed flexibility only when a favorable deal could be struck, and that depended more on Arab attitudes than on Washington's arms policies. In its impatience for agreements, however, the administration flipped between these different strategies, attempting to manipulate Jerusalem through arms sales.

The politically oriented elements of the memorandum were less controversial, though intriguing. The United States accepted the Israeli position that the next agreements with Egypt and Jordan would be final peace settlements, in effect ruling out an interim agreement with Jordan. Washington also agreed to "consult promptly" with Israel after any threat to its "security or sovereignty by a world power," that is, the U.S.S.R. This concept had been discussed all summer; at one point Israel had asked for a U.S. commitment to automatic military intervention in case of Soviet attack. Kissinger insisted that Congress would never accept such wording, and the compromise merely obligated the United States to do what it already would have done.[341]

In the light of later events, the clauses on a future Geneva Conference assumed special importance. The United States agreed that it would "concert action" with Israel in preparing for the conference, bound itself to consult with Israel on additional participants, and agreed that "the participation at a subsequent phase of the conference of any possible additional state, group, or organization would require the agreement of all the initial participants," thereby giving Israel veto power over PLO involvement. These sections demonstrate how much Kissinger would concede to gain Israeli approval of Sinai II. If the United States stuck to this agreement, it would negate a return to the Geneva Conference. The Arabs would not go without the PLO and Israel would veto PLO participation. If the Geneva Conference *did* reconvene, Washington agreed that it would "insure" that the "substantive negotiations" would be conducted "on a bilateral basis"—directly between Israel and each Arab neighbor. Most crucial for later developments, the United States pledged not to "recognize or negotiate" with the PLO as long as the organization "does not recognize Israel's right to exist and does not accept Security Council Resolutions 242 and 338." Here too the United States promised a unified strategy with Israel, thereby restricting America's ability to speak independently with the PLO. This clause would become the most politically significant section of the agreement; it represented the most important U.S. concession.[342]

Kissinger's assurances to Egypt were briefer. He promised to consult Egypt if the Israelis violated the agreement, to aid Egypt with money and in building her early warning station in the Sinai, and to begin the diplomatic process toward another Syrian-Israeli agreement.[343]

Kissinger controlled the U.S. position in the talks. He not only conducted the negotiations but on the last night decided when the deal had been struck and phoned the president only when the documents were about to be initialed. The written commitments also reflected Kissinger's style—a complex of formal and informal declarations to induce agreement. These commitments often proved ambiguous when the time came to fulfill them. Many of the supposedly "mind-boggling" promises to Israel were irrelevant as long as Israel could get its own oil or as long as the U.S.S.R. made no direct threat to Israeli territory.[344]

It was also typical of Kissinger's style to include informal commitments in the agreement. Thus, in addition to Sadat's public concessions to Israel, he reportedly agreed to limit anti-Israeli propaganda and Egyptian participation in the boycott of companies dealing with Israel.[345] Kissinger also assured Rabin that Sadat had pledged to abstain from battle if Syria attacked Israel. He assured Sadat that Israel would not attack Syria and that he would try to involve the Palestinians in the peace process.[346] These oral commitments eased the suspicions of both sides and provided a model for what Kissinger wanted: serial agreements.

Unlike the 1974 disengagements, the second Egyptian-Israeli accord was criticized from many sides. In Israel critics on the right believed that Israel had been tricked by the secretary of state into relinquishing the passes and the oilfields for mere paper agreements that did not accomplish Israel's goals of non-belligerency and direct negotiations. In the Arab world a vocal opposition, led by Syria's Assad, attacked the agreement as a separate peace between Israel and Egypt.[347]

The reaction in America was colored by the events of the previous several months. Kissinger and many supporters of Israel had engaged in several major disputes: the "reassessment," the letter from seventy-six senators urging the administration not to withhold arms for Israel, and the Ford administration's faulting of Jerusalem whenever the talks reached an impasse. Despite his effort to maintain ties with Jewish leaders, Kissinger's relations with them had deteriorated after reports in fall 1974 that he had delayed arms sales to Israel during the Yom Kippur War.

These tensions reached a crisis during summer 1975, when the administration announced that it would sell mobile Hawk anti-aircraft missiles to Jordan. This proposed arms deal was vehemently protested on Capitol Hill, where pro-Israeli congressmen campaigned intensively against it. They argued that the absence of an air defense had prevented Hussein's entry into the October War; an American-supplied missile umbrella could allow Hussein to wage war against Israel. The king was growing closer to Syria despite years of hostility and Syria's close relations with the U.S.S.R.

The State Department answered that the arms deal would not jeopardize Israel's security and was essential to keep Hussein from accepting Russian arms. When Senate hearings revealed that the Joint Chiefs unanimously favored selling only six batteries of missiles instead of fourteen, congressional opposition grew so intense that the administration withdrew the proposal temporarily to avoid an almost certain congressional veto.[348]

The pro-Israeli lobby was highly vocal on the issue. It was successful in part because the administration's timing seemed inappropriate; the "reassessment" supposedly had not been completed. Israel's friends in Washington were more effective in changing policy in this case than during the "reassessment," but on this issue the testimony of the Joint Chiefs had turned the tide. The pro-

Israeli forces would fail later in blocking arms for Arab countries when there was no comparable Pentagon dissent.

After much wrangling and bitterness, a deal on the Hawk missiles was finally struck in September, after the Sinai accords. The pro-Israeli forces stopped opposing the sale in exchange for an agreement that the fourteen missile batteries would not be mobile and could not be transferred to other countries without U.S. permission.

Despite the previous controversies, the pro-Israeli congressional forces who opposed Kissinger throughout the summer defended him after Sinai II. They applauded the pact and its addenda as a model for future agreements and argued that if Congress refused to station U.S. civilians in the Sinai, the Mideast would again sink into chaos.[349] Nevertheless, rumors circulated in Washington that Kissinger privately complained that Israel's backers were not working hard enough for a favorable congressional vote. Because Jerusalem was now vociferously behind the agreements, the public debate focused on Israel; few commented on the benefits for Egypt and the fact that Sadat rather than Peres had originally suggested an American presence in the Sinai.

The press now largely supported the accords. The *New York Times,* for example, opined that the monetary cost was "relatively small" compared with another war and a new oil embargo. Columnist Joseph Kraft wrote that questioning the American presence was "an intellectual embarrassment . . . it confused intercession with intervention on one side and mixes up what the United States did in Vietnam with the contributions made regularly to peacekeeping by, say Sweden."[350]

Many in Washington who had urged Kissinger in the spring to try for a comprehensive solution now had difficulty accepting Sinai II. They thought it too costly in political commitments, increased economic assistance, and sophisticated weaponry for Israel. If such assistance was required for one small step toward Middle East peace, what would the cost be for a series of steps? Former Under Secretary of State George Ball complained, "Time is worth buying only if it works on the side of peace—and in this case, that is doubtful."[351] Senator Adlai Stevenson of Illinois lamented because the Sinai accord was not linked to an over-all peace plan and thus accomplished too little to justify its costs.[352] Former Senator J. William Fulbright argued, "The total direct cost of this pullback, in foreign aid alone, will come to $12.9 billion (over 5 years). This turns out to be some $7.5 million for every square mile of sand to be given up by Israel, but more per square mile than we paid for all of Alaska back in 1867. It staggers the imagination to contemplate what an agreement on the Golan Heights might cost." But Fulbright used numbers loosely; much of this aid would have gone to Israel and Egypt without an agreement. The real additional cost of Sinai II was modest, perhaps no more than several hundred million dollars.[353]

Officials within the U.S. bureaucracy and even some congressmen also opposed parts of the accords. Some in the State Department were concerned about the political commitments Kissinger made to Israel; these same officials joined with Pentagon, CIA, Treasury, and Office of Management and Budget officials to oppose the new aid. Some congressmen wondered whether the two hundred civilian technicians might lead to another Vietnam.[354]

Despite these questions, Congress had no choice in the end. Legislators could not see an alternative to accepting the agreements and were not prepared to assume responsibility for a crisis in the area if one resulted from their failure to back the accords. After a month's debate, Congress approved the agreements overwhelmingly. The civilian technicians took their posts in the Sinai and the issue of "another Vietnam" evaporated.

The End of Step-by-Step Diplomacy

The main problem confronting Kissinger after the approval of Sinai II was where to go next. All routes seemed blocked. Jerusalem reluctantly acquiesced in Kissinger's plan to sponsor another limited accord between Israel and Syria, but Rabin was willing to consider only "cosmetic" withdrawals in the Golan Heights, no more than a few kilometers in depth. The secretary of state may have thought this only a negotiating ploy, but in any case Assad killed the plan. He refused to participate despite Kissinger's urging and tied future peace steps to progress on the difficult Palestinian question.[355] Now Kissinger's maneuverability was constricted. He had promised Israel that future negotiations with Jordan and Egypt would aim at a final peace treaty, an objective that he had never addressed and that his strategy was not designed to achieve. Therefore, Kissinger proceeded with limited efforts in several directions, hoping that one would open a new diplomatic avenue. None of these possibilities developed, but they were addressed by Kissinger's successors.

The secretary of state first raised a trial balloon, suggesting an "informal" meeting involving the United States, the U.S.S.R., the Arabs, and the Israelis. Such a meeting could set the agenda for a Geneva Conference and decide how to tackle the Palestinian issue. But only Israel seemed interested, and the idea quickly faded away.[356]

Kissinger then directly addressed the Palestinian question for the first time. Because of the greater prominence of the Arab-Israeli dispute and because of the energy crisis, public awareness of the issue had increased in the United States since the October War. A growing number of specialists thought that progress on the Palestinian problem might prevent another oil embargo, production cuts, and perhaps even price rises. One example of this new interest was the wide-ranging hearings on the Palestinian question held by a subcommittee of the House Foreign Affairs Committee in fall 1975. The hearings took place during an emotional period. The United States vehemently opposed the "Zionism is racism" resolution passed by the U.N. General Assembly in mid-November. Only two days after the U.N. had voted and Ambassador Moynihan had denounced the U.N. as "morally repugnant," Harold Saunders, now deputy assistant secretary of state for Near East and South Asian affairs, testified at the House Foreign Affairs Committee hearings that the Palestinians were the "heart" of the Arab-Israeli conflict. "The issue is not whether Palestinian interests should be expressed in a final settlement, but how. There will be no peace unless an answer is found." Most controversial in Saunders's statement was its tone and thrust. It presented the Palestinian question and the PLO in a more central, positive light than had any previous statement by a major U.S. official. Saunders suggested in the course of his address that "we do not at this point have the framework for a negotiation involving the PLO." Two paragraphs later, however, he added, "It is obvious that thinking on the Palestinian aspects of the problem must evolve on all sides. As it does, what is not possible today may become possible."[357]

To Israel and her supporters, of course, the central issue had always been Arab refusal to recognize the legitimacy of the Jewish state. Kissinger received complaints from them about the "Saunders document," and in response downplayed its significance and denied that he had been involved in its preparation. It made no sense, however, that in an era of a supremely powerful secretary of state, a careful official like Saunders would make a sensitive statement without approval. In fact, Kissinger had carefully edited the document and cleared its wording with President Ford.[358] The Saunders document suggested that the Israel-American memorandum signed just two months earlier would not hamstring U.S. diplomacy, but the incident further undermined Kissinger's credibility with Israel and her American supporters.

Kissinger shortly plowed new ground on the Palestinian question when the United States allowed the PLO to participate in a U.N. Security Council debate on the Middle East. The United States voted against seating the PLO but did not veto its participation, holding that the question was procedural rather than substantive (and thus U.S. veto power could not be exercised). However, the decision not to veto came from Washington and was reportedly opposed by Ambassador Moynihan. Israel refused to attend the Security Council debate. In the end, the United States vetoed the pro-Palestinian resolution that emerged. The exercise was designed to demonstrate that the United States was willing to hear Palestinian aspirations but would not accede to demands that threatened Israel.[359]

Still another signal was sent in March when newly appointed U.N. ambassador William Scranton delivered a speech to the Security Council criticizing Israeli policies in East Jerusalem and the West Bank. He argued that "unilateral measures" taken by Israel would not "prejudge the final and permanent status of Jerusalem" to be "determined only through the instruments and process of negotiation, agreement and accommodation." He then addressed the issue of Israeli settlements and labeled "substantial resettlement of the Israeli civilian population in occupied territories, including East Jerusalem" as "illegal . . . Indeed, the presence of these settlements is seen by my Government as an obstacle to the success of the negotiations for a just and final peace between Israel and its neighbors."[360] These halting gestures toward the Palestinians did not constitute a new diplomatic strategy; Kissinger even refrained from identifying publicly with them.

Meanwhile, Anwar Sadat demonstrated continued interest in improved relations with the United States and, after Sinai II, the two countries grew closer than ever. In late October 1975, Sadat became the first Egyptian leader to visit the United States. In an act of considerable symbolism, he was invited to address a full session of Congress, an honor never granted to an Israeli leader. (After some controversy, it was agreed that Rabin would be granted a similar opportunity in January.)[361] Privately, the Egyptian leader sought increased U.S. economic aid and the beginning of military assistance.[362] The administration agreed to some of his requests for economic aid and in March it announced plans to lift the arms embargo and to sell Egypt six C-130 Hercules transport jets. Administration spokesmen made it clear that they intended to send more military equipment if Congress did not object strongly.

Despite opposition from Israel and its supporters, Ford, Kissinger, and the new secretary of defense, Donald Rumsfeld, favored the Hercules sale. They argued that such a program would not affect the Egyptian-Israeli military balance and that America must reward Sadat for his moderation and rejection of the U.S.S.R. This argument was reinforced in March when the Egyptian president abrogated the 1971 fifteen-year Treaty of Friendship with Moscow.[363]

Israel's advocates feared, however, that the six transports would soon be followed by American weapons to Egypt. They pointed out that Egypt was already purchasing arms from European suppliers and that escalating American, French, and British shipments to other Arab countries like Saudi Arabia could be transferred to Egypt in a crisis. The outcome of the controversy was a compromise between the administration and congressional critics: Congress would not interfere with the sale but there would be no further military deals with Egypt *in 1976.*[364]

Sadat's October trip to the United States was followed by Rabin's visit in January. Kissinger and the prime minister agreed to explore future deals with Egypt, Syria, and perhaps Jordan to end the state of belligerency in exchange for Israeli withdrawals from a major part of the Sinai and the Golan Heights and perhaps even of the West Bank. Ford approved a list of arms for Israel that Kissinger claimed was $500 million more than the amount recommended by the National Security Council.[365] This display of amity, rare during Ford's administration, was clouded in Washington and Jerusalem by controversies erupting from internal conflicts in both governments. The Israeli leadership had not co-ordinated its request for future arms and their list made many in Washington wonder why the Israelis wanted such a large quantity of highly sophisticated weaponry. In a swipe at his rival, Peres, Rabin called the Israeli wish list "frivolous" and "unworthy of consideration" in an interview with Israeli journalists.[366] The episode diminished Israeli credibility in Washington.

Meanwhile, the United States was moving the start of its fiscal year from 1 July to 1 October. That left three months as a transition quarter. The Israelis thought they had an agreement from Kissinger to receive $500 million during the three months and the secretary of state seemed to confirm this when he publicly supported their claim. But the Office of Management and Budget deleted the sum from the aid request with the president's approval. This deletion resulted in a rare display of differences between Kissinger and Ford. A compromise was finally reached with Congress in late June, but the haggling spotlighted Israeli-American tensions. Another corrosive event occurred in mid-March when a CIA report was leaked (presumably by anti-Israeli bureaucrats) that concluded Israel had more than ten atomic bombs.[367]

Schlesinger and Moynihan, out of the government, attacked the administration for its attitude toward Israel. In a major speech at AIPAC's annual conference in May, Schlesinger decried what he called the "Vietnamization" of Israel, charging that administration policies were turning Israel into another South Vietnam (which had fallen to the Communists the previous year).[368] With Moynihan gone, the administration had no spokesman noted for pro-Israeli views. The absence of an alternative voice in foreign policy helped concentrate all political attacks on Kissinger. The new U.N. ambassador, Scranton, had coined the phrase "evenhandedness" eight years earlier and, unlike Schlesinger and Moynihan, was not battling the secretary of state. When Scranton articulated U.S. opposition to Israeli policies in occupied territories, he was widely regarded as Kissinger's mouthpiece.

The administration could cite substantial achievements to Israel's supporters: the disengagement accords, Sinai II, increased aid to Israel, and Sadat's entry into the Western camp. But Ford and many of his advisers feared another oil embargo and assumed the Democrats would nominate a candidate like Hubert Humphrey with appeal to Jewish voters, so they did not feel compelled to favor Israel. After all, Jewish votes were not significant in the Republican primary battles with Ronald Reagan.

Past administrations, of course, tried to avoid disputes with Israel's partisans during an election year, but now that the Middle East had top priority, it was difficult to stifle all controversy about the region. Thus, the Ford administration chose 1976 to ask for unprecedented military sales to Saudi Arabia (which would amount to $7.5 billion before the year was out). Early in the year, the administration concluded a deal to sell Sidewinder air-to-air missiles to the Saudis. By summer it was back with requests for additional weapons, including the devastating Maverick air-to-surface and TOW antitank missiles.[369] Until now, the pro-Israeli forces had largely overlooked the transfer of arms to Saudi Arabia. When it became clear that the administration would sell hundreds of lethal weapons like Mavericks, Sidewinders, and TOWs, however, AIPAC began an intensive campaign against them. Through summer and early fall, the controversy boiled. The administration argued that transfers to other Arab countries would not occur and that the sales were necessary to bolster Saudi defense. Privately, many officials suggested that the Saudis would be unable to use advanced weapons without American assistance (which could be withdrawn in an emergency).[370]

Critics charged that some of these missiles could conceivably be transferred to Egypt, Jordan, and Syria where they could be adapted to French, Soviet, or U.S. weapons, thereby enhancing Arab war-making capacity. The following exchange between Congressman Benjamin Rosenthal (D.-N.Y.) and Assistant Secretary of State Atherton during hearings in June typifies the tone of these discussions:

MR. ROSENTHAL. In the last 2 years, Saudi Arabia didn't have the advantage of this massive buildup of $5 billion worth of equipment. Now they really have the merchandise.

MR. ATHERTON. I think it is misleading to characterize this as a massive buildup.

MR. ROSENTHAL. How would you characterize $5 billion worth of military equipment?

MR. ATHERTON. First of all, it started from a very low base, almost no modern equipment. Second, it is not all equipment. A very large percentage of it, something in aggregate, as I recall, close to 80 percent of it is not equipment.

MR. ROSENTHAL. Some of this equipment is the most sophisticated missiles yet developed on the Earth, isn't that correct, sir?

MR. ATHERTON. The only missiles that we are talking about at this point are the Mavericks, which are designed as an integral part of the F-5's which we have been providing to the Saudis.[371]

The pro-Israeli congressmen remained unconvinced; even after getting Ford and Kissinger to agree to reduce the number of weapons, they still fought to eliminate the deal entirely. One witness at the hearing, Professor Alan Dowty of Notre Dame, summed up with prescience: "Many of us share a very definite concern that this particular sale is but a prelude for further sales, that it comprises in fact but the tip of an iceberg of frightening proportions."[372] At that time Congress had twenty days to veto an arms sale. After much maneuvering and bitter debate, time ran out on the pro-Israeli coalition and the reduced Saudi sale was automatically approved.

By June 1976, the pro-Israeli lobby confronted a new coalition that favored huge arms sales to the rich oil producers. This coalition included aircraft and missile manufacturers who sought additional markets, Pentagon officials who wanted larger production runs to reduce unit costs, diplomats who wanted good relations with the Arabs, and Treasury, Defense, and State Department officials who saw an opportunity to recycle petrodollars by providing military infrastructure and advanced arms to the Persian Gulf states.[373] This new alliance outweighed the influence of the pro-Israeli lobby on the question of Arab arms sales.

Another controversy unusual in an election-year was the Arab boycott of Israel. The Anti-Defamation League of B'nai B'rith filed suit and later sought legislation to force the Commerce Department to reveal which firms had complied with the boycott. This issue became a major factor in the Carter-Ford campaign. Under attack from Jimmy Carter, Ford suddenly announced in the second presidential debate that the Commerce Department would identify companies that had cooperated. The next day Commerce Secretary Elliot Richardson announced that this was not possible. Ford then looked ignorant of the policies of his own administration, an embarrassing mistake.

Outmaneuvered by Kissinger, outmanned and overburdened by the number of relevant issues, many in the pro-Israeli lobby lost faith in the administration and became convinced that only a new president could reshape U.S. policy in the Mideast. For example, according to the AIPAC Washington letter, *Near East Report*, of 6 October 1976, "Friends of Israel in Washington were bitterly disappointed over the adamant Administration opposition to effective anti-boycott measures attached to the Export Administration Act and to the move in Congress to block further sales of lethal Maverick air-to-ground missiles to Saudi Arabia."[374]

It was clear to all, including the secretary of state, that a new diplomatic strategy was necessary.[375] By 1976 Kissinger's vaunted shuttle diplomacy had stalled. Arms sales and new trade relationships, especially with Egypt and Saudi Arabia, had replaced diplomacy as the means for extending U.S. influence. Any major steps in 1976 were difficult because of (1) the election campaign and the president's bitter primary struggle with Ronald Reagan, (2) Kissinger's controversial position—attacked by both the Republican right and the Democratic left, and (3) the Lebanese civil war that stole Arab attention.

The Lebanese civil war had violently escalated in early 1976. A rough alignment of Christian Lebanese and conservative Moslem forces fought against Islamic nationalists, leftist radical movements, and the PLO. Neighboring Syria originally supported the radical Moslem alliance by allowing Palestine Liberation Army forces under its control to enter the country, but by mid-March Syria's position was beginning to change. When the Moslem and leftist coalition appeared to be victorious in early June, the Syrians—who had been united with Lebanon under the Ottoman Empire and still claimed the country as their own—aided the conservative Christian coalition, to the amazement of all involved. Assad apparently wanted to create a balance of political forces in Lebanon that would assure his dominance and prevent a complete PLO-leftist victory. A radical Lebanon would be difficult to control and might even threaten Syria's security by involving it in conflicts with Israel or by aligning with an antagonistic Arab coalition.

The Syrians drew attacks throughout the Arab world, from moderate Egypt to radical Libya and Iraq, for their intervention in Lebanon. Only Jordan, which sought to preserve its newfound friendship with Syria and had itself crushed a PLO insurgency in 1970, supported Assad's Lebanese policy. Meanwhile, the Israelis worried that they might soon face Syrian forces on their northern border as well as on the Golan Heights. They signaled through intermediaries that they would attack if the Syrians crossed into southern Lebanon, and they provided aid and services to the Christians across the "Good Fence" marking the border between the two countries. Astoundingly, these acts placed Syria and Israel on the same side in the Lebanese civil war.

The administration observed these developments with confusion, perplexed by the seemingly contradictory political and religious coalitions in Lebanon. Kissinger's first inclination was to see the conflict in Arab-Israeli terms and he sought to prevent Israeli and Syrian military intervention lest another Arab-Israeli war ensue. [376] When the Syrians intervened on behalf of the Christians, the secretary of state saw Syria as a force for stability and expressed muted support of Syria's role. Perhaps he hoped this would bring Syria back into the peace process. Yet America also maintained contact with the PLO during this period to ease the evacuation of U.S. citizens located in PLO-controlled zones. [377]

The controversy over the Syrian intervention in Lebanon shattered the little unity left in the Arab world after Sinai II and fragmented domestic attitudes in the United States toward the administration's Mideast policy. Many critics of Kissinger, most pro-Israeli, complained that he should have drawn the United States closer to the Christian-Israeli coalition. Others argued that he should have publicly endorsed Syria's intervention as a means of stabilizing the area and renewing the peace process. Some analysts declared that the root of the Lebanese civil war was the Palestinians' desire for their own state. Even the Arab-American community was split.

The Lebanese war illustrates the difficulties confronted by U.S. policy makers in 1976. In 1958 Eisenhower had intervened in Lebanon to prevent a Communist takeover that he thought might follow escalation of the civil war. In the post-Vietnam period, however, military intervention was unthinkable. By now U.S. leaders recognized that Middle East conflicts were too complex to be reduced to the "Communist versus anti-Communist" equation. Allowing Israel to threaten intervention, as it had during the Jordan crisis of September 1970, also seemed undesirable. The United States was less prepared to be associated with Jerusalem after October 1973 and, compared with September 1970, the Soviet role seemed vague. Most important, perhaps, there was no event to trigger an American response comparable to the Iraqi coup in 1958 or Syria's invasion across the Jordanian border in 1970. Because so many factions in changing coalitions confronted one another within overlapping territories, the situation on the ground in Lebanon was more resistant to specific military action than the earlier cases. Finally, after the 1973 October War, the United States had developed a policy to urge settlement of the Arab-Israeli dispute. All events in the area were assessed through the prism of this policy. Since the Lebanese civil war did not fit any of these expectations, the secretary of state found it difficult to formulate a response. It was easier to confront the problems of southern Africa. Kissinger soon embarked on a new round of shuttle diplomacy regarding the problems in Zimbabwe and Namibia.

Conclusion

Kissinger presided over an extraordinary era in U.S.–Middle East diplomacy. For the first time, management of the Arab-Israeli dispute became America's top foreign policy priority. Kissinger successfully manipulated events to increase U.S. influence in the Mideast, decrease Soviet influence, and show the first progress toward a settlement since 1947.

Because he so completely dominated the national security bureaucracy and because Nixon and Ford let him handle the negotiations, Kissinger could make decisions on the spot. This flexibility often made the difference between success and failure. Kissinger's dominance also vastly improved the coherence of American policy: the U.S. government was not divided internally as it often had been. Although Kissinger hesitated at times, once he had decided on a strategy, he pursued it until it succeeded or failed. Even when harshly criticized, as he was by the pro-Israeli camp in spring 1975, Kissinger retained a remarkable diplomatic flexibility owing to his verbal agility and generally excellent media relations.

The other side of his autocratic style was that Kissinger's opinions and prejudices were paramount; contrary ideas rarely received a hearing. Even when outside consultants were approached, as during the 1975 reassessment, they served as instruments for pressuring Israel rather than as genuine contributors to the diplomatic process.

Through his central position, Kissinger succeeded in controlling not only the American policy-making apparatus but also the negotiations. The parties could communicate with one another only through him, which allowed him to present each side's views in a way that would create the response he wanted. Although this technique yielded spectacular results in the short run, in the long run it stretched Kissinger's credibility to the breaking point. The March 1975 shuttle failed in part because Prime Minister Rabin believed that Kissinger had lied to him. After September 1975, Syria's President Assad demonstrated his loss of faith in the U.S. secretary of state by refusing to continue the process.

Nevertheless, the shuttle technique suited Kissinger's talent for breaking insoluble problems into smaller component disputes that could be settled. The theory behind this process was that each successful step would create momentum for the next. This theory seemed to work until after military disengagement agreements had been negotiated following the October War between Israel and her two Arab antagonists. Once negotiations turned to political accommodation, the momentum was lost. Kissinger spent the critical year between 1974 and 1975 wheedling Israel and Egypt to negotiate a costly and limited substitute for genuine peace.

Perhaps the failure of the Rogers Plan made Kissinger refuse to take a public position on the substance of negotiations, fearing to become a target for both sides. But his largely amoral tactical approach could not cope with the larger issues. Unlike incoming President Jimmy Carter, he would not demand that the Arabs accept normal relations with Israel or that Israel accept the legitimacy of Palestinian rights. In the absence of such a stance, it was doubtful that Kissinger's step-by-step process could ever wrestle with the deep social and cultural divisions between Israel and the Arabs, with the underlying moral issues in the dispute, or with the Palestinians. As step-by-step continued, Kissinger's policy options grew fewer.

Bold in style, Kissinger was extremely cautious in policy. His entire approach was to maintain a process. He had neither the vision nor the courage to transform the issue, to make a "psychological breakthrough" of the sort Sadat would later achieve in Jerusalem. For all Nixon's talk about "toughing it out" and not appearing a "helpless giant," Nixon and Kissinger conducted Mideast diplomacy with dashing tactics but strategic caution. Even their boldest action of the October War, the nuclear alert, was followed by acquiescence in Soviet demands for resupply of the Egyptian Third Army.

U.S. diplomacy during and after the October War was conducted to achieve quick, if limited, diplomatic successes. This method fit Nixon's and Kissinger's style and was calculated to bolster the president's domestic mandate. Although the Watergate crisis prompted Kissinger to press for diplomatic triumphs, it also paralyzed the U.S. government at a crucial moment during July and August 1974. By the time President Ford had settled into office, the countdown to the Arab summit at Rabat had begun and the diplomatic initiative had passed to the Arabs.

The new president's limited experience in foreign affairs led him to rely excessively on Kissinger's counsel, further concentrating power in the hands of the secretary of state and all but eliminating countervailing influences within the American government. In his memoirs Ford wrote that he never had a major disagreement with his secretary of state; this unanimity was possible because he allowed Kissinger to make most foreign-policy decisions.

Kissinger's autocratic system contributed to his critical error in March 1975, when he mistakenly concluded that an Egyptian-Israeli accord was possible. This miscalculation led to the policy "reassessment," which in fact was a powerful attempt to pressure Israel. The reassessment alienated the pro-Israeli camp in the United States and created false expectations among the Arabs. Rabin and Ford exchanged tough talk during June 1975, but after the rhetoric subsided, U.S. policy returned to its original path. The opposition of the pro-Israeli lobby was less important than several other factors in leading Kissinger to return to step-by-step diplomacy: the process was the best suited to Kissinger's cautious strategy and the most likely to produce an agreement. After Kissinger returned to the Mideast to conclude the Egyptian-Israeli agreement in August 1975, step-by-step diplomacy was exhausted and the United States was left with no further diplomatic options. The civil war in Lebanon confounded American policy makers and further encouraged American caution.

Despite deficiencies, Kissinger's achievements in the Middle East were, on the whole, impressive. In the end Nixon and Kissinger achieved their principal goals: (1) they created the conditions for and initiated a new Arab-Israeli peace process, beginning with a limited settlement; (2) they consolidated Egypt's move away from Moscow and toward Washington; and (3) they improved the American diplomatic position in the area at the Kremlin's expense.

What was most lacking at the end of Kissinger's tenure was a new conception. Perhaps he could have supplied it if he had remained in office. He had successfully exploited the opportunity provided by the October War to initiate shuttle diplomacy. Perhaps Ford's reelection would have given Kissinger the opportunity to direct the parties onto a new track, but we will never know. The American electorate decided that the chance to foster peace would fall to Jimmy Carter, who chose a different approach to the problem.

8

CARTER
Pursuing a Lasting Peace

Kissinger had so dominated Arab-Israeli diplomacy that it was unclear whether the movement toward peace could continue in his absence. Some observers, fearful that the new Democratic administration would fumble the opportunity, called for Kissinger to stay on as a special Mideast envoy. But Carter had sharply criticized him during the campaign. It was inconceivable that Kissinger's secretive, autocratic methods would mesh with Carter's more forthright style.

Although Carter voiced strong support for Israel, he had not even outlined the direction he might take when he assumed office in January 1977. Most of Carter's plans were undefined. Exhausted and disillusioned by Vietnam and Watergate, the American people had bet on a political outsider who offered himself as uncorrupted by special interests and traditional politics. Like McGovern before him, Carter had taken advantage of a reformed delegate selection process. Rather than identifying himself with particular ideas, he stood for efficiency, openness, and integrity—"I will never lie to you."

The foreign policy attitudes of politicians who have not previously made foreign affairs decisions are difficult to predict when they become president. Since their views are likely to be less informed, they are likely to be more than usually influenced by the people they surround themselves with.

Carter selected associates who would pursue a common Mideast strategy, working against all odds to achieve a comprehensive solution to the Arab-Israeli dispute. When events swamped that strategy, they tackled the Palestinian problem as a way to approach a general Mideast peace.

It was a considerable challenge for a former state governor, inexperienced in international politics, to become president at a time when the focus of U.S. global policies was on the Mideast—dominated by ancient hatreds and loyalties, swept by a religious fervor unknown for centuries in the secular West, and possessed of the lion's share of the world's most precious commodity. It seemed almost fated when poorly understood events in some of the world's oldest societies eventually sealed his political doom.

Domestic and External Constraints

On the surface Carter began his presidency with limited internal constraints. Jewish disillusionment with the Ford-Kissinger team and Carter's pro-Israeli statements reinforced the usual large Jewish majority in favor of the Democrats.[1] Although the new president did not have close ties with the American Jewish community, his vice president, Walter Mondale, did. Moreover, Israel's supporters were likely to avoid conflict with the new administration as long as it did not publicly confront Israel. The pro-Israel lobby was still reeling from the traumatic October War, the disturbing 1975 reassessment, and Kissinger's unfathomable maneuvers that the lobby at times supported and at other times opposed. Further, businesses selling to the Arab oil producers were likely to have less influence because business typically has less power over a Democratic administration and because commercial relationships with the Arabs were now routine.

Despite initial favorable relations with Israel's supporters, the administration believed that it must differ with Jerusalem to prevent major oil production cuts and price rises. The Carter team expected the Israelis to cooperate with its initiatives because it felt beseiged by Arab radicals like Syria and Iraq and inhibited by the growing political, economic, and financial clout of Saudi Arabia. After all, the Saudis had greater leverage over the United States than the Israelis did.

This outlook fueled tensions with Israel and its supporters throughout Carter's term, but its detrimental effect on the administration's domestic backing was exacerbated by tactical errors and clumsiness. The Carter team seemed to court adversaries and alienate allies at home and abroad. Carter habitually revealed his intentions toward the Mideast prematurely, thereby squandering precious political capital and drawing sharp criticism before it was necessary to do so.

Carter and the Georgian aides who surrounded him had had little experience with the national Jewish community. They had difficulty understanding its yearnings and fears. Relations were worsened by the Carter team's inability to accommodate those who disagreed with them—a trait reflected in its problems with Congress and in the 1980 reelection campaign.

Carter repeatedly sought aid from American Jewish leaders in pressing

Begin to make concessions. The administration also wrongly anticipated that some of the policies pursued by the Begin government, which took office in May 1977, would be opposed by major American Jewish groups. Many Jewish leaders did have misgivings about Begin's tactics, but the administration's heavy-handedness toward Israel drove them to support Jerusalem, right or wrong. Snafus, leaks, and misstatements constantly kept Israel's supporters aware that the administration was at odds with Jerusalem and with their own preferences for U.S. policy. Although Carter achieved the Camp David accords and the Egyptian-Israeli peace treaty, the recurrent tension between Jerusalem and Washington negated the approval that he might have received from American Jews.[2]

As had happened before, the first new presidency to follow a crisis entered office prepared to develop new policies to deal with the changed conditions. Carter's programs for settling the Arab-Israeli dispute included skepticism of Israeli policies and a new interest in the Palestinian question. Reacting to the October War of 1973 and the oil embargo, the Carter administration also proposed a program to develop energy resources. The president called it the "moral equivalent of war," but critics noted the acronym, MEOW. When Carter could not get his program through Congress, he saw placating the foreign oil producers as the only alternative. At one point the administration even postponed purchases for the strategic petroleum reserve—essential to U.S. national security—because the Saudis objected.[3] Thus, the major internal constraint on the administration was self-imposed: the fear of Arab sanctions against the United States. This fear shaped the administration's foreign policy so that a perceived external constraint—Arab oil leverage—became internal pressures. The administration assumed that it was under constant pressure from the Saudis, a pressure that now appears to have been greatly exaggerated.[4]

This administration, more than its predecessors, saw itself at the mercy of conditions beyond its control. It feared the Arabs for their oil power, resented American Jews for their lack of support, and disliked Begin for his rigidity. The result was that it underestimated Israel's capacity to sabotage its policy and overestimated Arab leverage. Therefore, this administration was continually shocked by outside developments: the surprising election of Menachem Begin in May 1977, President Sadat's stunning visit to Jerusalem the following November, the fall of the shah of Iran in early 1979, the hostage crisis, the Soviet invasion of Afghanistan, the wars between the two Yemens in 1979 and Iran and Iraq in 1980.

Before 1977, even administrations giving the Middle East a high priority were distracted by other international crises or by developments at home. After 1973 the Nixon administration was preoccupied by Watergate. Although the Arab-Israeli issue was important under Ford, it was still subordinate to Kissinger's global foreign policy objectives. The Carter administration was the first to concentrate on the Middle East, which it understood as the Arab-Israeli dispute.

Americans had traditionally equated the Middle East problem with the Arab-Israeli conflict, an assumption reinforced for a quarter century by relative quiet in countries like Iran, Turkey, Afghanistan, and Ethiopia. During the Carter administration, this quiesence ended. Ironically, it was not the Arab-Israeli dispute that was to prove the greatest constraint on the administration's policy in the area. Its greatest problems occurred from non–Arab-Israeli issues like the fall of the shah, the ensuing renewal of gas lines, trebling of oil prices, the hostage crisis, and the Soviet invasion of Afghanistan.

Philosophy

The Carter administration was prepared to endure domestic pressures to advance a program that, because of its well-developed philosophy, it believed was mandated by external constraints. This philosophy, which linked the Arab-Israeli conflict to America's destiny in the region and even around the globe, is the key to understanding its actions.

In 1976 many Democratic party critics of Henry Kissinger charged that he was insensitive to human rights, to the plight of emerging countries, to North-South relations, to the pursuit of ideals in international affairs, and to the role of economics in international politics. Against the background of these criticisms, the Carter administration's ideas soon crystalized into the following policy.

First, the administration deemphasized relations with the Soviet Union; the U.S.-Soviet relationship was no longer the organizing principle of American foreign policy. As Carter put it in his first significant foreign policy address at the Notre Dame commencement in May 1977: "The unifying threat of conflict with the Soviet Union has become less intensive even though the competition has become more extensive."[5] A benign interpretation of the Soviets and their proxies in the Middle East and Africa resulted. The principal objective of Kissinger's diplomacy—an intricate network of cooperative *and* competitive relations with the U.S.S.R.—was laid aside. This produced an erratic American policy toward Moscow, because the Soviets or their clients occasionally engaged in local activity that even the tolerant Carter administration could not stomach.[6]

Second, this lessened concentration on the Soviet Union resulted in a diminished preoccupation with worldwide communism as a threat; there was an early unsuccessful effort to normalize relations with Cuba and Vietnam. The administration was also willing to deal with pro-Soviet and anti-American regimes, and it flirted with radical black African governments while deemphasizing American relations with South Africa.

Third, Carter stressed the importance of the Third World in international politics. National Security adviser, Zbigniew Brzezinski, was fond of discussing "new influentials" such as India, Brazil, Nigeria, Venezuela, and Saudi

Arabia.[7] As Carter announced at Notre Dame, "We will cooperate more closely with the newly influential countries in Latin America, Africa and Asia. We need their friendship and cooperation in a common effort as the structure of world power changes. . . . We know a peaceful world cannot long exist one-third rich and two-thirds hungry."[8] As a result, the United Nations again became a locus of American diplomacy.

The fourth component of the new strategy was a disinclination to use force to achieve diplomatic objectives. The only military operation of the administration was the aborted rescue attempt of the hostages in Iran in April 1980 and that occurred five months after the provocation. The contrast with Kissinger's modus operandi was stark indeed. The administration also sought to apply its philosophy to other countries by limiting arms sales and the proliferation of nuclear weapons. The president declared, "We've fought fire with fire, never thinking that fire is better quenched with water. This approach failed, with Vietnam the best example of its intellectual and moral poverty."[9]

Less reliance on the use of force meant a greater emphasis on international interdependence, economic matters, and the dynamics of North-South relations. These concerns were reinforced by the energy crisis, which led many policy analysts and academic observers to conclude that economics was more important than military power in international affairs.

These policies were accompanied by an intensive human rights campaign. The administration sought to defend victims of torture, political imprisonment, and civil liberties violations around the world. According to the president, "We can no longer separate the traditional issues of war and peace from the new global questions of justice, equity and human rights."[10] The human rights campaign illustrated the Carter administration's rhetorical and public diplomacy, in sharp contrast to Kissinger's demonstrations of military power and behind-the-scenes negotiations.

The Carter approach toward "new influentials" and nationalist regimes was directed at governments which had not been close to Washington. Therefore, it was bound to cause tensions with many traditional friends. It often seemed that American policy was following (Groucho) Marx's dictum: "I would never join a club that would accept me as a member." For example, regimes that had violated human rights were easier targets for pressure when they had relationships with Washington than when they did not. Ironically, this syndrome extended even to Communist states: the Kremlin, in contact with many American officials, was criticized but China was not. After all, the administration hoped to normalize relations with Beijing and in any event had little influence there.

The Middle East served as a model for the administration's global conceptions. As part of deemphasizing conflict with the Kremlin, the Soviet Union was seen as an ally in achieving an Arab-Israeli settlement. With a diminished concern over communism and a desire to win over previously anti-American regimes, the administration began to woo Syria, Iraq, Algeria, Libya, and the PLO. Since the human rights issue was pressed against regimes with which the United States had influence, the administration soon found itself at odds with the two countries that had previously been America's most reliable allies in the region—with Iran, over the degree of freedom allowed by the shah, and even with Israel, over a more limited issue—settlements on the West Bank.

Since the Palestinian question had come to symbolize Third World aspirations, it is not surprising that the administration proceeded further than its predecessors in identifying American policy with the objective of a Palestinian homeland. U.S. diplomats repeatedly sought to associate the United States with U.N. Security Council resolutions that would enshrine the new approach and were even prepared to encroach upon U.N. Security Council Resolution 242, the centerpiece of Middle Eastern diplomacy for over a decade.

The oil question now replaced the U.S.S.R. and anticommunism as Washington's preeminent concern. Not since the era of FDR had oil held the top priority. It was therefore appropriate that Carter, like Roosevelt, sought Saudi aid on the Palestinian issue and oil supplies.

OPEC was seen as an instrument of a united and determined Arab nation rather than as an international cartel responsive to economics. Therefore, a comprehensive Arab-Israeli settlement was perceived as the means to stabilize the oil supply and avert an even more acute global energy crisis. As Brzezinski wrote in a 1975 article: "It is impossible to seek a resolution to the energy problem without tackling head-on—and doing so in an urgent fashion—the Arab-Israeli conflict. Without a settlement of that issue in the near future, any stable arrangement in the energy area is simply not possible."[11]

Each new administration since the birth of Israel had tried some initiative, however limited, to solve the Arab-Israeli dispute. But Carter saw Middle East peace as the equivalent of world peace. As he toasted Crown Prince Fahd at a May 1977 White House dinner, ". . . there is an increasing realization that peace in the region means to a great degree a possibility of peace throughout the world."[12]

This integration of global and regional approaches favored State Department interpretations of Mideast affairs. For the first time, the State Department, NSC, and the president all agreed on the Palestinian question, the Soviet Union as a participant in the peace process, and the Saudis as playing an important role in the area. This philosophical unity allowed coherent decision making but provoked conflict with those who disagreed, especially Israel's supporters.

Decision Making

Despite their differences about the Soviet Union and other areas of foreign policy, Secretary of State Cyrus Vance and National Security Adviser

Zbigniew Brzezinski did not differ in their approach to the Arab-Israeli dispute. It was their styles and roles that were fundamentally dissimilar. Vance was a conciliator. Personally congenial and self-effacing, he remained the chief negotiator on Arab-Israeli affairs through the Egyptian-Israeli peace treaty and was always far more involved in the details of peacemaking than was Brzezinski. Despite his solid relations with the Israelis, he was frequently as critical of them as was Brzezinski. His penchant for negotiation and compromise led him on several occasions to recommend secret dealings with the PLO.[13] Brzezinski, arrogant and bombastic, was prone to confront those he opposed. Although his Mideast view was much the same as Vance's, Brzezinski was constantly at odds with the Israelis and their supporters. In his memoirs, for example, he places Begin in the same category as Qaddafi, Khomeini, and Brezhnev as leaders who exploited what he saw as the State Department's excessive faith in compromise.[14]

Other major administration figures included Andrew Young and his successor Donald McHenry, the two black U.N. ambassadors who supported Third World causes. The articulate and controversial Young often overstated the administration's policy. By contrast, Harold Brown, the administration's defense secretary, was a quiet, unassuming, and scholarly specialist in defense analysis. He did not challenge the administration's major foreign policy assumptions and was not a key figure in formulating Middle East policy.

The middle level of the Middle East team was distinguished by internal camaraderie. William Quandt, who had been Harold Saunders's deputy for a time during the Nixon administration, became the key Mideast specialist at the NSC, and Saunders became the assistant secretary of state for the Near East in early 1978. Their close relationship reinforced the united front in State and the NSC. The views of other key officials were also compatible: Deputy Secretary of State Warren Christopher, the two under secretaries of state for political affairs—the pragmatic Phillip Habib and then David D. Newsom whose positions were similar to the NEA's. Robert Hunter, a close associate of Mondale, replaced Quandt, who left the government in mid-1979. Since Vance was strongly influenced by his aides at State, their consensus was important in shaping his approach.

If the new president had been previously exposed to the issue on a practical political basis (for example, if he had served in Congress), he might have come to understand the different views on Arab-Israeli matters in the United States and he might as a consequence have included in his entourage individuals with different perspectives, as previous presidents had done. But Carter did not understand that genuinely different views existed among experts! Rather, he believed that the pro-Israeli perspective was primarily political and emotional. This attitude was reinforced by the foreign policy intellectuals he had recently come to know and the bureaucrats he met upon assuming office. His fascination with these strategists did not lead him to be critical of their views.

Before it was tempered by events, the consensus at the outset of the administration was remarkably similar to the ideas Brzezinski and Vance had propounded before the election. Brzezinski, like many others in the administration, linked energy to the Arab-Israeli problem and so stressed the importance of Saudi Arabia.[15] Kissinger had concentrated on the Russians more and on the Third World less, but Brzezinski shared with Kissinger a deep-seated fear of another oil embargo. Kissinger had considered Egypt the key state in the Middle East and saw blocking Russian influence there as the central problem facing American policy. Brzezinski saw the key state as Saudi Arabia and energy as the central problem. Kissinger had a role for Israel to play; Brzezinski had little use for Israel in his plans.

The most important difference between the two foreign policy advisers was their stress on the Palestinian question. Kissinger did not forsee an imminent resolution. Brzezinski, on the other hand, was eager to settle the matter. In a 1974 article, he envisioned using American leverage over Israel "to decouple security from the possession of land," to make "minor rectifications" in the last 1967 West Bank–Israeli border, to achieve total Israeli withdrawals from a demilitarized Sinai Peninsula and Golan Heights, and to redefine the phrase "legitimate rights of the Palestinian people."[16] In 1975 he coauthored an article conceding that a Palestinian state would "probably" be PLO-dominated, but asserting that this state would be "inextricably bound" to Israel. In an optimism bordering on messianism, the article declared, "The relations with a neighbor formidable in economic development as well as in conflict would generate powerful Palestinian opinion in favor of cooperation." This statement showed little understanding of the hatreds in the Middle East. He and his coauthors also hinted that Israel should not be allowed to choose the Palestinians with whom to negotiate and implied that the Israelis should deal with the PLO.[17]

In writing on the Middle East, Brzezinski frequently made guarantees an integral element in the peace process, eventually reaching the concept of a Soviet-American commitment. This idea was expressed in the U.S.-U.S.S.R. statement two years later. He wanted to ensnare the Russians in the process lest, stranded outside the diplomatic framework, they support the Arab recalcitrants and block a resolution. To facilitate this approach, he advocated Soviet and American "participation in an international force patrolling safety zones on either side of the agreed frontiers."[18]

Before assuming office, Vance expressed views that were startlingly similar to those of Brzezinski. In a private memo to Carter in October 1976, he too favored guarantees and enlisting the aid of the Soviet Union "at an appropriate time." He also favored a basic tradeoff that would normalize relations "in exchange for return of most of the territories occupied by Israel in 1967." When Carter offered him the position of secretary of state, Vance stressed again the importance of Middle East negotiations and mentioned the "special urgency" that the energy crisis gave to finding a settlement and improving relations with the Arab states.[19]

This administration consensus was summed up in a doctrine that supplied the intellectual base for the Carter approach. Labeled by former Under Secretary of State George Ball, "How to Save Israel in Spite of Herself," the doctrine assumed that its proponents understood even better than the Israelis what was best for the Jewish state.[20] Carter's analysts argued that Israel should return to the 1967 borders because: (1) the Arab confrontation states are ready for peace, (2) the Palestinians deserve a homeland, and (3) a smaller Israel would ensure Middle East stability. Basic to this approach was the conviction that Israel could not have both territory and peace. Many argued that Israel must be pressured to accept the 1967 boundaries because, if there were no settlement, the Arab moderates would lose control (thereby diminishing American influence and allowing Russian reemergence), the Arabs would start another war, there would be another oil embargo, or all of the above. Those who championed these views argued that Israel's interests—and, conveniently, America's as well—would be secured by taking actions favored by the Arabs.

Many observers at the time identified the Brookings Institution Middle East report published in December 1975 as the intellectual basis of Carter's policy. Three of the Brookings group received high posts at the beginning of the administration: Brzezinski, Quandt, and Deputy for National Intelligence in the Central Intelligence Agency, Robert Bowie. A fourth, Philip Klutznick, became secretary of commerce during Carter's last year. But the report was ambiguous and its importance for later policy depended entirely on the people charged with implementing its ideas. Policies more pro-Arab or more pro-Israeli than Carter's might have been developed by different members of the Brookings team.

Although the Brookings report was vague on key issues because its participants differed, it broke significant new ground by taking a comprehensive approach (as opposed to Kissinger's step-by-step) and stressing the importance of phased territorial withdrawals. In a compromise between competing perspectives, the Brookings report urged resolving the Palestinian question and obtaining from Arab parties "evidence of progress toward the development of normal international and regional political and economic relations" in return for Israeli withdrawal to the 5 June 1967 lines "with only such modifications as are mutually accepted."[21] Except for the emphasis on normalizing relations between Arabs and Israelis, however, Carter's policy would probably have been similar if the Brookings report had never been written.

Brzezinski's more detailed ideas provided the framework in which Jimmy Carter felt at home. Carter's conservative Christian upbringing, combined with his engineer's training, predisposed him to believe that, for every problem, only one correct, just, and viable solution existed.[22] It was his duty to see that this "correct" solution was adopted. This peculiarly American bent of mind wrecked his energy program and almost ruined his credibility in Arab-Israeli diplomacy. In striving toward *his* just solution, Carter confronted Begin and Sadat, two strong-willed men with very different definitions of justice.

Carter's style had been demonstrated during his term as governor: inexperience, a passion for details, a preference for comprehensive solutions, serious difficulty in dealing with the legislature, suspicion of special interests, and greater success in the politics of election than in the politics of government.[23] Carter suffered from these limitations in handling the Arab-Israeli dispute.

The new president never completely overcame his inexperience. Though he had traveled to Israel in spring 1973 while still governor, he had never visited an Arab country and had never met an Arab leader before he was elected. Before 1977, Mideast leaders like Hussein and Rabin were more experienced than Carter in dealing with U.S. policy and personnel.

Carter's predilection for comprehensive solutions was reflected in his desire to resolve the Arab-Israeli problem. First he sought a return to the Geneva Conference. Then he sought to widen Arab participation in the Sadat initiative. Next he made an attempt to broaden Camp David. It is ironic that Sadat and Begin forced an administration favoring a comprehensive solution to sponsor an agreement that came perilously close to a separate Egyptian-Israeli accord and that seemed to preempt a comprehensive peace.

Carter's passion for details was reflected in his near-total immersion in every aspect of Mideast negotiations until the March 1979 Egyptian-Israeli peace treaty. In the critical negotiations at Camp David and the peace treaty discussions, Carter himself played the key role for the United States. Even when he appointed a special negotiator for the subsequent autonomy talks (first Robert Strauss and then Sol Linowitz), this representative reported directly to him rather than to the secretary of state. No other president so involved himself in the intricacies of Arab-Israeli negotiations. Carter seemed impelled by his own strong religious beliefs, including a fascination with the Holy Land.

Soon, however, Carter encountered the disadvantage of close involvements. Other presidents, more distant from the diplomatic fray, could give advice and dissent in the course of negotiations. Carter, however, was personally committed and emotionally engaged, and there was no one above him to provide perspective and arbitration. Only at the summit could his decision-making style overcome these disadvantages.

Finally, Carter's most vexing problem as chief executive—his inability to make loyal allies and form strong coalitions—hindered his Middle East policy. This president never seemed to understand politics as the art of the possible. Rather, he tenaciously sought to impose his views on others. Carter showed a shocking lack of finesse in manipulating political rewards and punishments, as suggested by the poor timing of the Mideast arms package in 1978. As his dealings with Congress attest, he was not effective in the art of personal persuasion. He was hindered by his evident distaste for taking actions or making statements for political reasons with which he personally disagreed. As a result, he failed to win over the pro-Israeli lobby in spite of his monumental success in achieving the Egyptian-Israeli peace treaty.

Although some of his summit meetings failed spectacularly, one reason for Carter's major success was his almost mystical belief in face-to-face contact with other leaders, an attitude perhaps influenced by his religious tradition of personal witness. This faith is reflected in his decisions to convene the Camp David talks and to embark on a sudden trip to the Middle East in early 1979 to conclude the peace treaty between Egypt and Israel. The fascination with personal contact is also exemplified by the importance he placed on his impressions after meeting with Arab and Israeli leaders in 1977: favorable toward Sadat and Assad, and negative toward Rabin and Begin. At Camp David, Carter sensed a special bond between the three leaders that those not at the conference could not comprehend.[24]

In attaining the success of Camp David and an Egyptian-Israeli treaty, Carter reversed his usual modus operandi. He pursued something less than comprehensiveness, used his penchant for detail and personal involvement to advantage, and persuaded both Sadat and Begin to accept critical compromises. Able to concentrate on only one problem for thirteen days, he drew upon the advantages of his working style without bringing any deficits into play.

As has often been noted, few presidents' wives have had the influence of Rosalynn Carter; she even attended a variety of key meetings. Her position on Mideast issues was not made public; it is known that in 1977 she served as the informal channel between the president and an emissary who contacted Yassir Arafat to gain an understanding with the PLO.[25]

Carter did not deal effectively with peripheral crises that arose from the independent actions of his associates. Brzezinski frequently irritated the Jewish community; his brother Billy Carter took large "loans" from the Libyans; Bert Lance, former director of the Office of Management and Budget, was reported to have close financial ties to Saudi interests, and Andrew Young made sweeping statements about administration policy. Carter did not cap or control these controversies before they erupted into full-scale crises.

To a large extent Carter's difficulties in Middle East politics, as in other arenas of presidential leadership, resulted from continuous failures to make clear where his administration actually stood. As on the Palestinian question, Carter proved a master at contradictory statements. Although his attitudes toward Arab-Israeli issues remained fundamentally consistent, he rephrased his views so often that supporters and opponents were confused. His willingness to allow subordinates to present their own views added to the confusion.

Despite his clumsiness, however, Carter did convey a sincere concern for Palestinian grievances. During the election campaign he had been more forthright on this issue than any previous presidential candidate:

> Ultimately the legitimate interests of the Palestinians are going to have to be recognized. I would not negotiate with the PLO, nor would I try to force Israel to do that, until I was convinced that the Palestinians do recognize Israel's right to exist in peace in the Middle East. After that, negotiations could proceed to meet the needs of the Palestinians.[26]

Carter's obvious sincerity on this issue convinced Sadat that he could serve as an "even-handed" mediator between Egypt and Israel.[27]

The Palestinians became a way to deal with the controversy and blame that had embroiled the Democrats over civil rights and Vietnam. For Carter, Vance, Brown, Brzezinski, and others, support for Palestinian rights became a means of moving beyond old contentions and identifying with Third World aspirations.[28] Vance had been deputy secretary of defense at the outset of the Vietnam War; Brown had been secretary of the Air Force during the same period. Brzezinski had served on the Policy Planning Staff of the State Department in the Johnson administration as a defender of the war. Carter had not only supported the war but had been slow to join the civil rights movement. In fact, Georgians were surprised when he proved a tolerant governor. By resolving the Palestinian dilemma once and for all, the new Democratic administration would show the world that America had truly been born again.

Throughout his term, Carter saw no contradiction between his commitment to Palestinian rights and his oft-expressed support for Israel. He told fifty Jewish leaders in July 1977 that he would "rather commit political suicide than hurt Israel" and he undoubtedly meant it.[29] He continued to believe that good intentions would triumph.

Carter's relations with the pro-Israeli camp were thus tinged with self-righteousness. Rather than attempting a genuine dialogue with Israel's supporters, he sought to impose his views on them. When he achieved an Arab-Israeli peace, he seemed to think, his pro-Israeli critics would recognize the correctness of his approach. Chastened, they would return to his support.

The problem faced by Carter in dealing with Israel's backers was that they wanted more than presidential visions of what was best for Israel—especially when these visions seemed closer to those of the State Department than to their own. Jews had been a traditional partner in the Democratic coalition since 1932, and they expected to influence Carter on Middle East policy.

However, the administration's foreign policy decision-making structure was distinguished by the absence of any senior official who saw Israel as a valuable ally of the United States. Although they were genuine supporters of Israel, the two highest ranking Jews in the White House—director of the domestic policy staff, Stuart Eizenstat, and the first Counsel, Robert Lipshutz—had responsible domestic positions, no foreign policy experience, and little previous connection with the Democratic pro-Israeli coalition. The vice president, noted for his pro-Israeli views in the Senate, occupied a weak position. Like most vice presidents, Mondale had to dance to his boss's tune. Even his close ties to the deputy director of the National Security Council, David Aaron, did not significantly increase the leverage of the pro-Israeli forces.

Because Carter came to understand through bitter early experience that Middle East policy could cause political fallout, Hamilton Jordan—the president's most trusted lieutenant—became engaged as an adviser. But Jordan also had no foreign policy background, only the skill to present positions more persuasively. Thus, there was no one in the administration to challenge or augment the shared policy assumptions about the Middle East that prevailed at the White House and the State Department.

After much public criticism from friends of Israel, Carter in summer 1978 appointed Edward Sanders, a Los Angeles attorney and an active national Jewish leader, as an adviser on Middle East affairs to both the president and the secretary of state. Sanders took different positions on the Arab-Israeli dispute from the Carter foreign policy team, but confronted a unified administration. Unlike Feldman, McPherson, and Garment, he had no other responsibilities in foreign or domestic policy to bring him into the mainstream.[30] Nevertheless, Sanders secured the confidence both of the Jewish community and the president. His eighteen months in office, mid-1978 to early 1980, marked a relatively quiet period in the administration's relations with American Jews. He was followed during the last months of the term by Al Moses, a Washington lawyer. Robert Strauss—previously chairman of the Democratic National Committee, in 1979 chief Mideast negotiator, and ultimately the chairman of Carter's reelection campaign—frequently advised against pressuring Israel. Sol Linowitz, who succeeded Strauss as chief Mideast negotiator, also sought better relations with Jerusalem.

When Mondale, Eizenstat, Jordan, Sanders, or Strauss attemped to modify administration strategy, they were only marginally successful.

Carter, especially because of his new fascination with foreign policy, was influenced by attitudes prevailing in the wake of the October 1973 War. His involvement in the Trilateral Commission was particularly important. Virtually all the policy-level officials were members (Carter, Mondale, Vance, Brzezinski, Harold Brown, and the first Treasury secretary, Michael Blumenthal). Founded by David Rockefeller and Zbigniew Brzezinski, the commission sought to promote the international market system as led by the United States, Western Europe, and Japan. Most commission members saw the Arab-Israeli dispute as a major nuisance that should (and could) be eliminated. It had already thrown the world economy into chaos as a consequence of the policies that had led to the Yom Kippur War. It might provoke a collapse of the international banking system if the Arabs, angry and humiliated, acted together with malice. Men who were concerned with the smooth operation of international commerce were inclined to be exasperated with Israel's tough foreign policy.[31]

The president treated the Middle East as his key foreign policy issue from the very beginning of his tenure. As Hamilton Jordan said in a late 1978 news broadcast interview, "There's not a single issue, domestic or foreign policy, that the President has spent more of his time and energy and resources on than his quest to bring peace to the Middle East."[32] On secondary topics, there is room for diverse opinions, but on an issue with which the president is personally identified and on which detailed policy has been developed, other views are seldom welcomed. In both the Carter and Eisenhower administrations, domestic pro-Israeli influences were thwarted in part by the president's strong personal views, but in Carter's case, the president himself bore the political costs. The process that led to Carter's single-mindedness can be understood by comparing how other presidents handled high priority concerns.

Such a comparison suggests that every president has an area of rigidity in the conduct of foreign policy. To Truman it was the Soviet Union; to Eisenhower, China; to Kennedy, Cuba; to Johnson, Vietnam; and to Nixon, Cambodia. In each case, the sensitive policy issue had become critical in the latter part of the previous administration; the new team assumed office ready to correct the mistake of its predecessor. On these issues, no dissent was allowed—agreement became a litmus test of loyalty to the new president. Individuals who differed with the president were fired, transferred, or allowed to resign: Henry Wallace under Truman, the State Department's "old China hands" under Eisenhower, Chester Bowles under Kennedy, a variety of officials under Johnson (of whom Robert McNamara was the most prominent), and a number of younger National Security Council officials who disagreed with Nixon on Cambodia. Under Carter, Mark Siegel, Hamilton Jordan's political aide and Carter's liaison with the Jews, became the first high official to resign and the first ever to resign over policy toward Israel.[33] The Johnson and Nixon administrations, less tolerant of dissent than Carter, had allowed fundamental differences on the Middle East. In fact, dissent over Arab-Israeli policy had been traditional. But previous presidents had not been preoccupied with the issue; it had not been central to their conduct of foreign policy; and it had not been the object of their "rigidity syndrome."

The key officials who dominated the American government under Carter were veterans of Vietnam; their personal lives had been seared by the experience. It was as though the Young Turks and the Old Guard of the Vietnam era had united in an attempt to erase the memory of that blemished episode by producing peace in the Holy Land. The irony of their crusade was overwhelming. Under both Johnson and Carter, a Southern president, inexperienced in foreign affairs, preoccupied with an overriding issue, possessed of a moral fervor, impatient of dissent, and handicapped by broken campaign promises, sought to apply a unanimous strategy to poorly understood foreign cultures. Brzezinski and Vance on the Arab-Israeli issue were analogous to Walt Rostow and Dean Rusk, who were equally stubborn about a specific policy in Vietnam. In each case the responsible officials saw themselves as political martyrs in a righteous cause.

It is also striking that in this century three Southern presidents, all high-minded and idealistic in their approach to foreign policy, were brought to political ruin over one issue in world affairs: Wilson on American participation in the League of Nations, Johnson on Vietnam, and Carter on the Middle East (the combination of the Arab-Israeli, Iranian, and Afghan issues). In each case key officials who did not accept the prevailing premises left office. Wilson's first secretary of state, William Jennings Bryan, resigned over differences with the president's policy of neutrality; his second secretary of state, Robert Lansing, resigned after he and the president had stopped speaking over issues such as the Versailles peace settlement and Wilson's handling of Congress's role in the U.S. entry into the League of Nations. Secretary of Defense Robert McNamara's growing doubts over Vietnam strategy led to his departure near the end of the Johnson administration. Vance's moderate reaction to the Soviet invasion of Afghanistan, conciliatory approach to the Iranian hostage situation, and his dogged focus on a comprehensive Arab-Israeli policy even in an election year led him to resign immediately after the disastrous raid to free the Iranian hostages in April 1980. All of these well-intentioned men—and many others in their respective administrations—might have avoided isolation and exile if their presidents had been more willing to consider differing views.

Because of the wide interest in the Arab-Israeli issue and the obvious domestic implications, Carter's administration did include officials who disagreed on his approach to the Arab-Israeli dispute. However, they were confronted by a unified decision making team with which the president agreed. They could therefore do little more than occasionally moderate specific policies recommended by State and the NSC.

The Rush to Geneva

Carter had barely settled into the Oval Office when it became clear that he intended to deal extensively with Arab-Israeli matters. Administration spokesmen immediately began speaking about the importance of progress towards a settlement in 1977. Vance went to the Middle East in mid-February on his first trip abroad as secretary of state. The administration was soon engaged in conflicts with the Israelis over arms sales policy. These disputes were caused in part by the strong influence of mid-level bureaucrats in a new administration and in part by Carter's bias against arms sales as a primary tool of foreign policy.

Thus, despite oral promises made by Kissinger, Carter vetoed the sale of

$150 million worth of Israeli-built Kfir jets to Ecuador. For the Israelis, the deal was actually worth much more because of likely future sales in South America and elsewhere. While Carter and the Israelis argued, the Ecuadorians began negotiations with the French and Russians.[34]

The administration also cancelled the sale to Israel of concussion bombs. There was much talk at the time about the evil nature of this weapon; the president even announced a study to consider the elimination of concussion bombs from the American arsenal. The administration's arguments about arms control were undercut, however, when it failed to abrogate President Ford's sale of sophisticated Maverick air-to-ground missiles to Saudi Arabia, a deal opposed by Carter during the campaign. The administration rationalized the apparent contradiction on the grounds that concussion bombs might be used against civilians, but the political signal was that the new administration thought it could exercise arms control over Israel but not Saudi Arabia.[35]

By May the administration had produced a presidential review memorandum on arms-sales policy (PRM 12, which led to a Presidential Directive—PD-13) that provided for strict controls on arms sales, coproduction agreements, and transfer of high technology with exceptions for the NATO and ANZUS Pact countries and Japan but not for Israel. Since Israel was planning to expand its defense industry, this memorandum (if allowed to stand) would have severely constricted those plans and would have had detrimental effects on both the Israeli defense effort and economy. The document also contradicted Carter's campaign statements that assistance to Israel had to be guaranteed if negotiations with the Arabs were to be successful. Now Carter officials were using arguments identical to those employed by Ford—that a lid had to be put on Israeli aid during delicate negotiations with the Arabs. After pleas from Mondale and Eizenstat and strong congressional pressure (especially from Senators Humphrey, Case, Church, and Javits), Carter did reinstate Israel as a favored arms recipient.[36]

Meanwhile, the administration proved more responsive to anti-Israeli business interests in the Middle East than had been anticipated. Thus, the State Department found it necessary to complain about controversial Israeli drilling in the Gulf of Suez, and muted its support for antiboycott legislation, which the campaigning president had declared "is not a matter of diplomacy or trade with me, it's a matter of morality."[37] Carter's tendency to turn diplomatic issues into moral principles that he could not then uphold repeatedly hampered his conduct of foreign affairs.

As these relatively minor controversies swirled about the president in his first months, greater attention was paid to his statements and to his exploratory meetings with Mideast leaders. Kissinger's rhetoric had been subordinate to behind-the-scenes negotiations, but for Carter words themselves were important. This proved unfortunate, because Carter did not employ words with subtlety or precision. Carter's meetings in the spring with Rabin, Sadat, Hussein, Assad, and Crown Prince Fahd of Saudi Arabia allowed him to present publicly and privately his administration's plans for Mideast diplomacy. Yet these occasions thrust Carter himself too early into formulation of policy details. Nixon and Ford had left initial discussions with foreign leaders to trusted aides like Kissinger, Rogers, and Sisco, with the president providing approval and sometimes a different perspective at an appropriate juncture. Moreover, as in the Rogers Plan, previous presidents had carefully avoided being personally identified with controversial new ideas until they had been tested before the American public and with foreign governments. Keeping preliminary discussions preliminary also provided opposing American groups and foreign emissaries an opportunity to intervene before positions had hardened. With Carter's close involvement in making and presenting policy, this avenue for accommodating dissent was closed.

Prime Minister Rabin's visit on 5 March exemplified the dangers of the new method. Upon Rabin's arrival, Carter declared that peace negotiations between the Arabs and Israelis should lead to "defensible borders," a code phrase that usually implied Israel should not withdraw from all the territories captured in 1967. In private discussions, however, the Israeli prime minister discovered to his surprise that the U.S. president was not signaling agreement with Jerusalem's territorial claims. Carter led the first administration prepared to accept the goal of full peace between the Arabs and Israelis. The price of peace, however, would be nearly complete Israeli territorial withdrawals and an unprecedented recognition of Palestinian rights, perhaps even the entry of the PLO into the discussions.[38] Thus, Carter accepted the Israeli version of peace but opposed them on the subjects of territories and Palestinians. When Carter talked in a general way about making public statements on his positions to restore confidence in the presidency, Rabin thought he was indicating that he would not reveal his policies immediately. A promise to that effect was expressed by Vance and Mondale later in the day.[39]

Carter's statement on defensible borders was on the public record, however, and at a news conference the next day, while the Israeli prime minister was still in Washington, he was pressed to explain what he meant. To the astonishment of all, Carter discussed his views in detail, including references to "substantial withdrawal of Israel's present control over territories" and some "minor adjustments in the 1967 borders." Now Carter appeared closer to the Arab position on territories. The phrase "minor adjustments in 1967 borders" had a specific meaning in Mideast diplomacy, a meaning very much at odds with the phrase "defensible borders." Carter, perhaps ignorant of this distinction, seemed to be contradicting himself. What Carter meant to suggest was that for a few years Israel might maintain defense lines, forces, or monitoring stations beyond legal and recognized borders.[40]

The new president dropped an even larger bombshell a week later. He stunned even his closest aides by announcing at a town meeting at Clinton, Massachusetts, "There has to be a homeland provided for the Palestinian refugees. . . ." Although Carter appeared to be endorsing a Palestinian state, he further explained his position while returning to Washington on the presidential plane. "I think some provision has got to be made for the Palestinians, in the framework of the nation of Jordan or by some other means."[41] Other than affirming a new U.S. interest in the Palestinian question, that left the issue even cloudier. Was Carter advocating a Palestinian state, a province within a Jordanian federation, or what?

Confusion over what the new president meant led to further statements and more mystery. On 17 March he shook hands with the PLO representative to the U.N., argued on 8 April that the Palestinians "must be represented by a surrogate or by them directly" at a Geneva Conference, and on 12 May was arguing that there could not be "any reasonable hope for settlement of the Middle East question . . . without a homeland for the Palestinians." But "there is a chance that the Palestinians [presumably the PLO] might make moves to recognize the right of Israel to exist. And if so, this would remove one of the major obstacles toward further progress." At the end of the month, 25 May, the president caused a furor when he mistakenly declared, "All the United Nations resolutions have contemplated a homeland for the Palestinians. And this is obviously something that will have to be accommodated."[42] The president was obviously confused. Several General Assembly resolutions that the United States had opposed had supported a Palestinian state, but Security Council Resolution 242, the basis for U.S. policy, did not.

These incidents led to growing consternation among Israel and its supporters. What was Carter actually planning? In order to allay these fears, Vice President Mondale was appointed to deliver a speech clarifying administration policy in mid-June. The effect was exactly the opposite. Mondale assumed that the Arab states desired peace, announced that Israel would have to "return to approximately the borders that existed prior to the war of 1967, albeit with minor modifications as negotiated among the parties," and mentioned as necessary in settlement discussions "the possibility of some arrangement for a Palestinian homeland or entity—*preferably* in association with Jordan." This left open the possibility of the United States supporting a Palestinian state. Mondale tried to ease Israel's fear of returning to the 1967 frontiers with a provision that for a period after an agreement, Israel would hold defense lines beyond its recognized boundaries for security. Unlike the president's frequent extemporaneous remarks, these statements had been carefully prepared beforehand. For the first time, the administration presented a coherent and well-developed policy in contrast with the random torrent of statements that had preceded them. Israel's supporters were more alarmed than ever. Was Carter offering another Rogers

Plan? Senator Jacob Javits (R.-N.Y.) addressed this question on the Senate floor, criticizing "Mondale's blueprint" in advance of the Geneva Conference, claiming it would raise "Arab expectations and Israeli fears, thereby inviting failure."[43]

Mondale's speech only confirmed approaches taken by the president several weeks earlier in his meetings with President Assad of Syria and Crown Prince Fahd of Saudi Arabia. Although Assad had taken the most extreme anti-Israeli views of any leader Carter had met, the president exulted that "for many years he has been a strong supporter in the search for peace . . ." Carter praised Assad's "unique role" in the march for peace, the "trust of the Palestinians in him," and "his sacrificial effort to bring peace to Lebanon." Carter also compared himself to Assad in their farming backgrounds and whippings by "stern but fair fathers." These comments were not mere public relations; they reflected the administration's belief that Syria could play a constructive role in a settlement. The administration's hope to admit the PLO to the peace process was evident when Carter praised Assad "because of his ability to bring together different peoples who in the past have been unfriendly toward one another and at odds."[44] Assad, the only radical Arab leader who had participated in the disengagement accords, would have to do just that for Carter's strategy to succeed.

In late May, meeting with Fahd, Carter commented publicly on the central role of Riyadh in his administration's concept of U.S. economic and political needs:

> I've said several times since I've been President of our country that I don't believe there is any other nation with whom we've had better friendship and a deeper sense of cooperation than we've found in Saudi Arabia.
>
> There have been many times unpublished when we saw a particular problem, either in our country or around the world, and as soon as this need became known by the leaders of that great country, the need has been met in a quiet but very effective and friendly way."[45]

Praising Saudi oil and financial strategies as "responsible and unselfish," Carter declared, "It is very valuable to us to understand and to preserve and to strengthen this important friendship." In their private meetings, Fahd argued in favor of a PLO state.* To the optimistic Carter team any and all solutions were possible among the moderate leaders of the area. They saw many positive ties between the United States and the Saudis. They thought Saudi Arabia was producing more oil than "perhaps would be best for them." Saudi investments in the

---

* In 1979 Carter stated that no Arab leader had ever advocated in private an independent Palestinian state, but William Quandt, who was present at several of the key meetings with Fahd, forcefully claims that the president was wrong and that Fahd had done just that in May 1977 (*Saudi Arabia in the 1980s*, 58–59).

United States were huge; they had already become "one of our largest customers" and the trade relationship was growing. No wonder the president concluded at the end of Fahd's visit, "So far as I know, between ourselves and Saudi Arabia there are no disturbing differences at all."[46] This statement reflected a monumental naïveté about the differences between the two countries and their roles in the world.

After only four months in office, Carter had released an unusually large number of statements about the Middle East. He had revealed that the peace effort in the area was crucial to him and would be central to his presidency, a priority that combined an optimistic Christian charity with economic and political calculation. Carter's comments revealed a president who was an unguided missile in public. No matter how carefully he was briefed by his aides in the intricacies of Mideast politics, no one could ever be certain what he would say before the microphones.

By the time he met with Fahd, Carter was faced with a new Mideast figure, Menachem Begin. The Carter administration had not anticipated his victory in the May elections. Begin's Likud platform called for permanent Israeli retention of the West Bank, which conflicted with Carter's plans for a Palestinian homeland. Therefore, in late June the State Department issued a formal statement pointedly reminding the new Israeli government that "no territories, including the West Bank, are automatically excluded from the items to be negotiated."[47] That led to a torrent of charges from Israel's supporters—including many congressmen—that the administration had again acted in a one-sided fashion. With this latest furor, the president had had enough; during an ensuing news conference, he barred further detailed public discussion of a Mideast settlement before the visit of Prime Minister Begin in mid-July.[48] The President used the intervening time to bolster his position with American Jewish leaders. He held a White House meeting where he spoke forcefully of his commitment to Israel.[49]

The new Israeli prime minister arrived after tremendous media hoopla. The public meetings were warm, with each leader being careful to heap praise on the other. In private Carter made clear his desire for a Geneva Conference as rapidly as possible, and Begin presented a paper outlining his government's positions on procedures for convening a conference and defining Israel's borders. In these discussions Begin treated Carter to a lecture complete with vivid maps of the West Bank showing how vulnerable Israel had been before the 1967 War. Begin insisted that the West Bank (he used the terms Judea and Samaria) not fall under foreign control, although he did not insist on an affirmation of Israeli sovereignty.[50] His view on the contours of a peace settlement was far from the Carter administration's. But the immediate problem was convening a Geneva Conference.

During their discussions, Carter cautioned Begin against establishing new Israeli settlements on the West Bank, an issue which repeatedly brought the two governments into contention. Carter opposed all settlement activity, although he conceded that it would be preferable for Begin to expand existing settlements rather than establish new ones. Upon his return to Jerusalem, the Israeli prime minister grasped this loophole in Carter's injunctions and legalized three existing (and previously unauthorized) settlements. In response, Carter and Vance decried the Israeli action and labeled Israeli settlements "illegal" and a serious "obstacle to peace."[51] The goodwill of the Begin visit quickly dissipated.

The administration feared any Israeli action that the Arabs might interpret as an obstacle to peace because it believed that a crucial period had arrived. When Secretary of State Vance journeyed back to the Middle East in early August to try resolving procedural problems for a new Geneva Conference, he tackled the problem of devising a formula that would include generally accepted Palestinian representatives. Sadat sought specifics from the U.S. delegation on what the United States expected of the PLO.[52] The Saudis hinted that the PLO could moderate its policy if properly encouraged. Vance wrote a possible paragraph for PLO attendance while meeting with Crown Prince Fahd in the resort city of Taif. The paragraph suggested that the PLO accept Resolution 242 with the reservation that it did not adequately reflect Palestinian aspirations. A high-ranking PLO official was in Taif at the same time, and discussions of possible amendments proceeded through the Saudi intermediaries.[53]

Both Carter and Vance made statements to encourage the PLO to accept Resolution 242. In an interview with *Time* in early August, Carter declared that his administration "would immediately commence plans" to talk with the PLO if it accepted *either* Israel's right to exist *or* U.N. Security Council Resolutions 242 and 338 as a basis for negotiations. Previously, he had adhered to Kissinger's 1975 agreement insisting on *both* conditions. With Vance negotiating in Taif, Carter declared from his home in Plains, Georgia, "If the Palestinians should say, 'We recognize 242 in its entirety but we think the Palestinians have additional status other than just refugees,' that would suit us okay."[54] Meanwhile, in speaking to newsmen in Taif, Vance telescoped his own requirements of the previous February by saying that PLO acceptance of Resolution 242 would mean that they were recognizing "the right of Israel to exist in a state of peace within secure and recognized boundaries," and that they would thereby be revoking their Convenant which called for an end to the existence of Israel.[55]

Thus Carter and Vance made it clear that they would deal directly with the PLO if it accepted Resolution 242, even with a qualifier concerning Palestinian rights. As Carter said on 10 August, there has to be "some solution to the question of the enormous numbers of Palestinian refugees who have been forced out of their homes and who want to have some fair treatment."[56] In this offhand remark made on vacation, Carter revealed that he accepted the Arab, not the

Israeli, interpretation of what had occurred in 1948. The Palestinians had always claimed that they fled their homes to save themselves from massacre at Israeli hands. The Israelis had always claimed that the Palestinians fled at the behest of cynical leaders who promised to reward them with Jewish land after the "inevitable" Arab triumph over the Zionists. Since he had nothing to gain by taking sides in this emotionally-charged historical dispute, Carter was presumably unaware of the implications.

These statements from the administration's highest officials should have elicited a positive PLO response, but the Palestine National Council rejected these overtures at the end of August. At one point Arafat sent a secret message to Washington through a prominent American educator whom the administration was using as intermediary. The PLO chief said that his organization would accept the American overture only in return for guaranteed American backing of a PLO state.[57] But no one in the Carter administration would guarantee the outcome of negotiations or risk confrontation with Israel or its supporters for unconditional PLO demands. Wracked by internal dissension and under pressure from Assad who feared that a major PLO concession would diminish his own influence, Arafat and the PLO finally reiterated their refusal to accept U.N. Resolution 242.[58] Again Arab divisions had thwarted an American initiative.

Temporarily blocked by this refusal, the administration continued to insist on Palestinian representation at a reconvened Geneva Conference. There were critical meetings in Washington in mid-September with the new Israeli foreign minister, Moshe Dayan, who later called the atmosphere "ugly."[59] A particularly acrimonious session occurred with Carter and Mondale privately in the president's study. The American leaders complained bitterly about Israel's settlement policy in the occupied areas. "You are more stubborn than the Arabs, and you put obstacles on the path to peace," Carter angrily told the Israeli foreign minister. According to Dayan, "Whenever the President showed signs of calming down and holding an even-tempered dialogue, Mondale jumped in with fresh complaints which disrupted the talk." Carter and Vance made it clear to the Israelis that the United States expected Israel to withdraw to the pre-1967 borders on all fronts, with only "slight changes" on the West Bank, an area that would be reconstituted as a "Palestinian entity" linked to Jordan.[60] This session disturbed the Israelis; the United States and Israel seemed to be heading toward a major international conference on the Middle East with top American leaders in sharp disagreement with Israel. Even Vice President Mondale, considered the most sympathetic among senior Carter officials, had been swayed or led to take a hard line toward the Israelis by pressure within the administration.

Dayan's first round of talks in the United States was followed by mutually disparaging leaks from both sides. The Americans complained about Israeli settlement policy, Israel's rigid position on the format for the Geneva Conference, and the grandiose public statements of Ariel Sharon. Dayan complained that the Americans harped on the settlements as if they were the sole cause of the Arab-Israeli dispute. He also resented America's flirtation with the PLO and the vague U.S. assurances concerning security guarantees. Why wouldn't Washington make a specific commitment to Israel?[61]

The meeting between Carter, Mondale, and Dayan produced still more misunderstandings on Israeli settlements. Carter and Brzezinski thought Dayan had promised that new settlements would be small and limited to military camps. Vance thought that Dayan had promised no civilian settlements for at least a year. Dayan claims that he referred only to the next six planned settlements. By 26 September, Vance and several aides informed Dayan that the administration did not want any new settlers on the West Bank. Dayan reneged on the whole deal, a message not understood by the administration since there was no written and signed document on the subject between the two sides.[62]

By late September, U.S. policy had faltered. A Geneva format acceptable to Israel, the Arabs, and the Russians simply could not be found. Israel insisted on meeting separately with each of its Arab neighbors: Egypt, Syria, and Jordan. Palestinian representatives but not members of the PLO would be included in the Jordanian delegation. Egypt was apparently willing to accept this arrangement. The other Arabs (and the Soviets) sought a united Arab delegation for *all* discussions.[63] If the conference broke into subcommittees, they would concern themselves with functions—borders, guarantees, refugee rights, and the like—and not bilateral, nation-to-nation issues. This approach, the Syrian plan, implied that the Syrians, Egyptians, Jordanians, and Palestinians made up one Arab state. This was manifestly not the case. Worse, the Syrian plan would give the radical Syrians and Palestinians a veto over every decision of the conference. If Egypt could not make peace with Israel unless Hafez Assad approved the terms, the conference would fail.

To placate the Syrians, Vance put forward a third compromise plan. Each Arab country would discuss its grievances with Israel separately, but a united delegation would approve the comprehensive agreement at the end of negotiations. Vance's compromise failed to solve the fundamental problem in Syria's proposal, however, and left murky the question of Palestinian representation. Israel rejected the Vance plan but agreed in principle to meet with a united Arab delegation.[64] However, the substantive negotiations would be handled in the bilateral talks with each Arab country, and any agreements reached would be valid with or without the endorsement of the united Arab delegation. It seemed all but impossible to get Arabs and Israelis to agree even on how to talk about peace.

Meanwhile, after talks between Vance, his aides, and several Russian officials in Washington and at the U.N., the administration accepted a Soviet initiative for a joint statement. It was designated as the basis for reconvening the Geneva Conference and was issued on 1 October. In this document the United States accepted for the first time the phrase *legitimate rights of the Palestinian people*, once viewed as Arab code for displacing Israel with a Palestinian state. The administration, which had previously used the term *interests*, obviously did not endorse the Arab interpretation. The communiqué also called for representatives of the "Palestinian people" to participate in a Geneva Conference, advocated "normal peaceful relations on the basis of mutual recognition of the principles of sovereignty, territorial integrity, and political independence," and suggested a role for Soviet and American guarantees as part of any settlement.[65]

Two factors had contributed to the administration's interest in a joint statement with the Soviet Union. First, the initial Russian position had been less extreme than the U.S. team expected. The Soviets had dropped requirements that the PLO participate, that a Palestinian state come into existence, and that Israel withdraw to its old borders. Second, key officials believed that a U.S.-Soviet agreement would lead to Soviet cooperation in coaxing Syria to drop its insistence on a veto over every decision at Geneva.[66] The communiqué was a tactical device for advancing the objective on which the administration had focused its Mideast diplomacy: convening a Geneva Conference.

The communiqué therefore had not been carefully weighed beyond the State Department. Vance pulled it out of his pocket and presented it to the president during a short break in discussions with Latin American leaders over the Panama Canal treaties. Carter approved it despite objections raised by David Aaron. When Brzezinski learned of the statement, he thought it might pressure Begin to be more conciliatory. No consideration was given to consulting Congress or handling domestic repercussions of the communiqué. Hamilton Jordan, the president's principal aide responsible for selling controversial foreign policy programs (such as the Panama Canal treaties) to the Congress and the public, was not even consulted.[67]

The magnitude of this miscalculation was clear as soon as the communiqué was issued. The PLO welcomed it; the Israelis denounced it. At home, a political firestorm erupted as editorial and congressional critics charged that the administration—for no apparent reason—had invited the U.S.S.R. back into the center of the Mideast diplomatic scene. Not one senator or congressman rose to defend the administration, which was widely seen as catering to the Russian and Arab positions. After American officials had worked successfully for years to reduce Russian influence over the Mideast peace process and in the area as a whole, critics could not understand why the administration had suddenly invited Moscow to return. In addition, the flat Israeli rejection appeared to foreclose further diplomatic progress.[68]

To smooth over the controversy, Carter asked for a meeting with Dayan on the night of 4 October. The Israeli foreign minister was about to embark on a national speaking tour denouncing administration policy wherever he went. Now the Israelis had gained a politically stronger position.

The meeting, which lasted past 2 A.M., included blunt exchanges between Carter and Dayan before the president departed around midnight. Carter told the Israeli foreign minister that he would hold to his "word of honor" not to impose a peace on the Israelis, but he would not refrain from pressuring Israel over the key disputed issues. The president argued that Israel was placing obstacles to peace and a Geneva Conference by objecting to the presence of Palestinians and the PLO and by refusing to negotiate with a united Arab delegation. Carter complained that Israel had shown less flexibility than Egypt and Jordan, and he wrangled with Dayan over the extent of future Israeli withdrawals.[69]

Despite the tough talk, neither Israel nor the United States could afford continued acrimony. Israel depended on the United States, and the Carter administration sought to rebottle the political genie released by the U.S.-Soviet communiqué. Thus, the outcome of the evening's negotiations was an Israeli-American working paper for a Geneva Conference format that committed both sides to a conference in which Israel would sit with a unified Arab delegation, including Palestinian Arabs at the outset. The working groups in which peace treaties would be negotiated would be bilateral, however. This represented a return to the format already accepted by the Israelis, but they now agreed to the participation of a Palestinian delegation in determining the future of the West Bank and Gaza. A special West Bank and Gaza working group would include Israel, Jordan, Egypt, and the Palestinian Arabs. Begin had already agreed in August that Palestinians who were not known to be members of the PLO could participate in the Geneva Conference.[70] The Palestinians who would be acceptable to the Israelis were discussed in great detail during the meeting. Although Dayan agreed not to "inspect credentials," the U.S. team assured him that Israel would have a list of names beforehand and would be able to reject any Palestinian representatives. A discussion of difficult cases ensued, and the principle emerged that anyone would be approved who had participated in the political life of the West Bank or Gaza and was not imprisoned. Meanwhile, Dayan agreed that no one at the meeting could prevent acceptable Palestinian representatives from checking with PLO members if they chose to do so.[71]

These secret discussions resolved the issue of Palestinian representation for the United States and Israel but did not resolve the Syrian objections to the Geneva format. The Syrian position hardened after the U.S.-Israel working paper was released in early October. Following immediately the political fiasco of the Soviet-American communiqué, the working paper conveyed an image of administration vacillation and weakness. Carter's Geneva diplomacy seemed stalemated.

The Soviet-American communiqué was ill-conceived from the beginning, given Israeli suspicion of the U.S.S.R. and Russian reluctance to pressure the Syrians. In the end, the incident only irritated and further alienated Israel's supporters in the United States, alarmed Sadat, and disillusioned the radical Arabs when Carter backed down.

Sadat Takes Charge

The administration's preoccupation with comprehensiveness and Geneva had led it to discount another diplomatic route that had been developing for months. Sadat had become disenchanted with his Arab brethren, especially the Syrians, and disillusioned with the slow discussions over a format for the Geneva Conference. When Begin assumed office, he used Moroccan King Hassan to inform Sadat in detail of a Libyan-backed conspiracy against Sadat's government. Sadat was stunned, especially after the details proved accurate. Israeli intelligence had saved him from possible death at the hands of another Arab leader. Israeli Labor governments had previously conveyed such information to the United States for handling as it wished.[72] Later, Romanian leader Ceausescu, who had met with Begin in late August, convinced the Egyptian leader that the new Israeli prime minister was strong and determined enough to make peace.

Sadat had decided on a bilateral agreement with Israel prior to Geneva.[73] During meetings with Vance in Egypt in August, Sadat stunned the secretary by taking him aside during the discussions and showing him a draft of a peace treaty with Israel. The Egyptian president then swore Vance to absolute secrecy and proceeded to write his fallback position in the margins, while suggesting that the administration encourage Israel to produce a draft of its own. The administration did get a draft from the Israelis, and eventually a set of principles from the Jordanians and even two paragraphs from the Syrians.[74] Meanwhile, Sadat authorized a secret meeting between Egyptian deputy premier Hassan Tuhami and Dayan, held at the palace of the King of Morocco in Rabat in mid-September. Although Dayan later denied it, Tuhami reported to Sadat that the Israeli foreign minister had told him Egypt would receive all of Sinai if it agreed to a peace treaty with Israel. Accurate or not, this supposed promise would color future negotiations.[75]

Syrian opposition continued to prevent agreement on a format for a Geneva Conference. During a mid-October breakfast, the desperate Carter decided to write Sadat asking that he take the initiative to save the peace process. Quandt was ordered to write a first draft, and the president finally sent the letter in his own handwriting.[76]

Sadat's first idea was to suggest that the five permanent members of the U.N. Security Council meet in Jerusalem with Israel, Syria, Jordan, Egypt and the PLO to settle the Arab-Israeli dispute. Washington discouraged the concept and Sadat later thought better of it. On the way home from a trip to Iran and

Saudi Arabia in early November, the Egyptian president decided to go to Jerusalem himself. Thus, on 9 November before his parliament, he departed from his prepared text to announce his willingness to address the Knesset in Jerusalem if that would help bring peace.[77]

Begin's initial reaction was disbelief. But after Sadat reaffirmed his commitment in an interview with CBS anchorman Walter Cronkite, Begin issued a formal invitation through the auspices of the United States. The stage was set.

Sadat's trip to Jerusalem on 19 November 1977 revolutionized the context of Mideast diplomacy. His address to the Israeli Knesset was broadcast to a world audience of hundreds of millions. Sadat was seen shaking hands with Israel's leaders, exchanging gifts with Golda Meir, visiting Yad Vashem, Israel's memorial to the victims of the Holocaust, and granting relaxed joint interviews with Prime Minister Begin to the American media. He had quite literally extended the hand of friendship to Israel and with one deft stroke seized the initiative in Arab-Israeli diplomacy and rendered irrelevant the U.S. move for a Geneva Conference.

Administration officials observed these developments with excitement and frustration. Although they had sought a breakthrough in negotiations, they had never conceived that Sadat would take such a bold step. Since October 1973, the United States had been central to negotiations. This administration, which had regarded the Mideast as its top priority, now found itself on the sidelines; Sadat had not even informed the United States before his dramatic announcement. Indeed, after Sadat had said he would be prepared to go to Jerusalem, U.S. Ambassador Eilts in Cairo phoned to tell him that if he were not serious he should issue a retraction.[78] The State Department was concerned that Sadat's action would impede Arab unity and sabotage a Geneva Conference. Washington also worried about Sadat's failure to inform the Saudis in advance. Key officials fretted: Sadat was too optimistic that a quick agreement would follow his trip and he had provided no negotiation mechanism to follow his initiative. Thus, the administration failed to show the enthusiasm that might have been expected.

No rapid behind-the-scenes agreements were reached during Sadat's visit. In fact, the two sides discovered that they were still far apart on all major issues. The Israelis pointed out to Sadat that some mechanism for continuing discussions would be necessary; in response, Sadat soon invited all parties to the dispute to a "preparatory" conference in Cairo. The United States, however, was clearly unenthusiastic. The administration delayed its response to Sadat an embarrassing seventy-two hours. In the end only the United States, Egypt, and Israel agreed to attend, demonstrating once again that Egypt was the only Arab country ready for negotiations. No major Arab country endorsed Sadat's actions.[79]

The dichotomy between the administration's goals and the new realities was obvious when Secretary of State Vance arrived in the Mideast in December. He said repeatedly, "Our goal remains a comprehensive settlement." Still, Vance made progress. Upon arriving in Israel from Egypt, the American team informed the Israelis that Sadat would conclude a bilateral peace agreement with Israel as long as it was accompanied by a general "declaration of principles" that covered the Palestinian problem and defined an approach to negotiations with the other Arab states.[80] The conceptual basis for Camp David had been laid.

Since Sadat had visited Jerusalem, Begin had been pressured to make a counterconcession. As the Cairo Conference was about to begin, he announced suddenly that he had completed his plans and would fly immediately to present them in Washington before informing Sadat. His decision was bizarre. For thirty years the Israelis had insisted on direct negotiations and now that the opportunity had arrived, their prime minister rushed to Washington for approval. Begin demonstrated by this action that America so dominated Arab-Israeli peacemaking that he dared not make a major proposal without American support. Begin's belief that American backing would strengthen his hand in dealing with the Egyptian leader was also clear.

The problem for Begin, however, was that the Carter administration was uncertain about its role. By running to Washington for support against his negotiating partner, Begin started a game that Egypt could also play. If Begin could seek U.S. backing, Sadat could do the same for *his* ideas. Thus Begin revived the United States' active involvement. A three-cornered relationship rapidly emerged in Begin's talks with Carter and his aides.

The Israeli prime minister arrived in an air of mystery, since U.S. officials did not know the content of his proposal. Begin presented a plan for Israeli recognition of Egyptian sovereignty over the Sinai in return for a peace treaty. He wanted to retain Israeli settlements and air bases in the area of the Sinai closest to Israel. He also sought to keep Israeli control over Sharm El Sheikh to prevent another blockade of the Straits of Tiran.[81] However, what most attracted Washington's attention was a plan by which the residents of the West Bank and the Gaza Strip would establish "administrative autonomy," elect their own council, and choose between Israeli and Jordanian citizenship. The question of sovereignty over the area would be left open; Israeli and "other claims" would continue and be reviewed five years later. The American officials who listened to Begin were particularly interested in these ideas and encouraged him to proceed. They did not entirely agree, but they thought Begin's proposals a good basis for discussion. Begin, however, did not understand the doubts behind the American interest. Vance had been too polite; Begin misunderstood him and believed that the secretary had acquiesced in the Israeli plan. Brzezinski, for his part, quizzed Begin about the specifics of the plan, commenting that a Palestinian "Basutoland" would not be acceptable.[82]

Begin tried to turn the mild administration response to his own benefit. Despite his bellicose image and hard-line rhetoric, the Israeli prime minister loved formal gatherings and craved a place in history as a peacemaker. On this particular trip he desperately needed American support to bolster his own credentials in peacemaking as a balance to Sadat's dramatic visit. Given what he interpreted as favorable private comments, Begin was relieved to state publicly that he had American backing for his proposals. Carter even labeled them "constructive." The president was sufficiently encouraged to phone Sadat and recommend another Begin-Sadat meeting, a suggestion accepted by the Egyptian leader.[83] In order to counter any impression that this was a joint U.S.-Israeli plan, the State Department rapidly pointed out that Washington was not endorsing the proposal and was willing to accept any plan agreed to by Egypt and Israel. Upon his return to Israel, Begin presented his plan for the first time to the Israeli Cabinet, whereupon several amendments were made.[84]

Begin then traveled to Ismailia to meet with President Sadat on Christmas Day, confident that he spoke with American backing and optimistic that a deal could be struck. The meeting was formally correct but largely unproductive. Sadat was displeased that Begin was not offering total Israeli withdrawal from the Sinai, but he agreed to accept the autonomy concept, whereupon Egyptian Foreign Ministry aides persuaded their president to change his mind.[85] In the end, the two sides agreed to convene a military committee in Cairo and a political committee in Jerusalem to move the negotiations forward. In retrospect, however, Ismailia marked the end of the idealistic hope that an early agreement could be reached after Sadat's visit to Jerusalem. Sadat and Begin would not meet again until the Camp David summit.

Begin and Sadat's failure brought the United States back to center stage in the peace process. Three days after the Ismailia summit, Carter gave another controversial interview to network television correspondents. Carter had often alienated Israel and its supporters with his comments; this time he severely annoyed President Sadat by proclaiming that Begin's proposal was "certainly . . . a realistic negotiating position" and saying, "Prime Minister Begin has taken a long step forward in offering to President Sadat and indirectly to the Palestinians, self-rule." Then he opposed Sadat's support for "an independent [Palestinian] nation." These remarks seemed to move Carter closer to Begin and Sadat voiced his disappointment to reporters.[86] As it happened, Carter was about to embark on an extensive trip to several of Brzezinski's "new influential" states—Poland, Iran, India, and Saudi Arabia—as well as France and Belgium. A stopover to see Sadat at Aswan was quickly added to reassure the Egyptian leader. The result was an "Aswan Declaration," which stated that the Palestinian question must be resolved "in all its aspects." Carter and Sadat agreed, "The resolution must recognize the legitimate rights of the Palestinian people and enable the Palestinians to participate in the determination of their own future."[87] Although Begin approved the statement, the incident again made the administration seem to be swaying between the Egyptians and Israelis.

This was not surprising. The administration was both under countervailing pressures and uncertain of its next move. Supporters of Israel had proclaimed the Egyptian initiative as the development on which the United States should concentrate. They believed a separate Egyptian-Israeli peace possible and desirable.[88] However, traditional supporters of the Arab cause or of a more even-handed policy—when they recovered from the shock of Sadat's visit—argued that Sadat could not and would not act alone and that the principal objective of U.S. policy should be to involve as many Arab parties as possible to lessen intra-Arab pressure on the Egyptians. These analysts called for sweeping Israeli concessions in response to President Sadat's trip to Jerusalem.[89]

In addition to these pressures, the president had been attempting to reconcile his preference for comprehensiveness with Sadat's visit, which had led back to bilateral, step-by-step diplomacy. Trying to resolve the apparent contradiction between the two approaches, Brzezinski sought to place U.S. policy in perspective. In a news interview, the national security adviser suggested that the Arab-Israeli issue was like a series of concentric circles in which each circle further involved the parties. To Brzezinski the first circle consisted of Israel and Egypt plus the United States; the second circle involved moderate Palestinians and Jordanians; the third circle encompassed Russia and Syria.[90] Administration officials, still uncertain when and how they would reach Geneva, were still trying.

The inner circle began to collapse, however, in the three weeks between the Ismailia summit and the convening of the political committee in Jerusalem. Israel's ever-provocative agriculture minister, Ariel Sharon, announced plans for expanding the Sinai settlements and sent in television crews and bulldozers to demonstrate his point. Meanwhile, Sadat and Egyptian newspapers escalated attacks on Israel, and Begin soon complained that the Egyptian press had called him a "shylock."[91]

To salvage the will for peace, Secretary of State Vance delicately set the agenda and arrived for the political talks scheduled to begin on 17 January. But the Egyptian attitude had already worsened. When Egyptian foreign minister Muhammad Ibrahim Kamel arrived at Tel Aviv Airport, he delivered a hard-line speech demanding Israeli agreement to complete withdrawals from the territories captured in 1967 and to establishment of a Palestinian state on the West Bank and the Gaza Strip. After agreeing privately with Kamel to limit political rhetoric, Begin nevertheless responded with a tough speech at the first formal dinner. He refused to redivide Jerusalem, withdraw from all occupied territories, or accept a Palestinian state. Begin inadvertently insulted the Egyptian foreign minister by calling him a "young man," a derisive term to Egyptians. That was enough for Sadat, who abruptly ordered his negotiating team home and promptly delivered a bitter speech to his People's Assembly on 21 January. Begin replied in equally strident tones to the Israeli Knesset two days later. Egyptian–Israeli rhetoric had returned to its familiar pattern: each leader justified his own actions and blamed the other side for the breakdown in negotiations (which would not resume until July). Meanwhile, Sadat left the military committee in Cairo intact, but despite Defense Minister Weizman's popularity with the Egyptians and his inclination to deal with broader questions, his forays with his aides to Egypt did not yield substantive progress.[92]

From the Carter administration's perspective, these events represented disaster. After a year of effort, a comprehensive Arab-Israeli settlement seemed more distant than ever. Sadat's trip to Jerusalem had preempted the reconvening of a Geneva Conference, and now the Egyptians had withdrawn from the talks that resulted from the trip. What next? The most obvious option was to get Sadat to return to the talks. He was therefore invited to Washington for a weekend at Camp David with the president in early February.

On the eve of the doomed Jerusalem talks, Carter had suggested that he and Sadat viewed the Middle East "about identically" and he reiterated his position that Israeli settlements in occupied territories were "illegal" under international law.[93] Carter and Vance had been upset by Sadat's sudden suspension of the Egyptian-Israeli dialogue, but they were more concerned that Sadat would abandon the peace process altogether. Israel's supporters called on the president to press Sadat back to the talks and additional compromises. But after his stunning journey to Jerusalem, Sadat had become an international superstar, canonized by the American media as a great leader and man of peace. Sadat shrewdly exploited his new status and prepared appeals before the court of American public opinion, as the Israelis had done so well for so many years. Sadat's strategy was to persuade the administration, the Congress, and the American people that Israel's position was unreasonable. The Egyptian president hoped thereby to weaken Israel's hand by diminishing its support in the United States. America, he still believed, "held ninety-nine percent of the cards" in the Arab-Israeli dispute.

The two presidents met for two days. Although the discussions began on a negative note when Sadat threatened to resign if his peace initiative collapsed entirely, the concern expressed by the American negotiators won him over.[94] The meetings also reinforced fundamental administration attitudes. Thus, when Sadat insisted that the United States must become a "full partner" in the talks, his plea fell on receptive ears. Carter promised to become more involved and secretly promised arms aid.[95] He also promised an American plan that would evolve after a complex U.S. strategy was played out. Sadat would produce a peace proposal that Begin would reject, producing the need for an American proposal. Sadat would initially take a hard line that he could then moderate in response to American pressure, thereby painting Begin as unreasonable. The United States was in effect colluding with the Egyptians to confront the Israelis. Sadat's tough stance until Camp David, then, can in part be attributed to his playing a role assigned by Carter. However, the strategy unraveled. The Egyptians did not produce an adequate proposal; and Sadat may have misunderstood the American design and reacted more harshly than intended. Camp David then overtook the need for a U.S. plan.[96]

The Carter-Sadat talks resulted in private briefings and public statements in which leading officials placed the United States closer to the Egyptian position. Carter attacked the Israeli settlement policy, emphasized the need to solve the Palestinian problem, and called for Israeli withdrawal from the West Bank. Vance drew a storm of protest from Jerusalem when he said that the settlements in the Sinai "should not exist" and that the West Bank and Gaza should become a Palestinian homeland linked to Jordan.[97]

When Dayan visited Washington soon after Sadat, Carter told him that he and the Egyptian president were anxious to have King Hussein enter the peace talks. Therefore, a proposed Egyptian-Israeli declaration of intentions should include Israel's agreement to withdraw from the West Bank. The Begin government maintained that Resolution 242 did not apply to all fronts and so Israel need not withdraw from the West Bank. The Carter administration made it absolutely clear that it expected such an Israeli withdrawal, with only "territorial adjustments for security reasons" permitted.[98]

The Triple Arms Sales Package

Thus, the Begin and Carter governments were again at loggerheads when a new arms sales controversy disrupted the movement toward peace.

For months the administration had confronted three related problems. First, in 1975 Kissinger had informally promised Israel 50 F-15s and formally promised to consider selling advanced equipment "such as the F-16 fighter." The Israelis had already received permission to purchase the first 25 F-15s and were now seeking the other 25, along with 150 F-16s. Second, the Saudi Air Force had outdated planes and an inflated budget. Kissinger had promised the Saudis their choice of new fighters and, under the influence of enthusiastic U.S. Air Force officers, Prince Fahd requested the F-15, America's finest, when he visited Washington in May 1977. At the time the administration attempted to discourage Fahd, but various bureaucratic studies urged the Saudi sale.[99] When Carter traveled to Saudi Arabia in January 1978, he had found the Saudis nervous because of Sadat's visit to Jerusalem. They had pleaded for the planes and Carter acquiesced. Finally, the Egyptians sought 120 F-5Es as a reward for cutting themselves off from the Soviet Union since 1973 and creating the peace initiative.

The key problem with these sales was political. There was no serious congressional opposition to selling Israel planes, and in the euphoria after Sadat's trip to Jerusalem, no successful opposition could be anticipated for the Egyptian sale. However, the sale to Saudi Arabia was likely to arouse stiff protest. Here was an administration, morally opposed to major arms sales abroad, selling America's most sophisticated fighter to a backward country just beginning to build its own military force. The Saudis had taken a stern, uncompromising attitude toward Israel, conspicuously refusing to endorse Sadat's initiative despite American urging. In addition, Carter himself had strongly opposed sophisticated arms sales to the Saudis during the presidential campaign. Referring to the then-controversial sale of Maverick missiles to Saudi Arabia, he had declared, "No Administration which was sensitive to the climate in the Middle East could let the sale go forward."[100] He had also argued that it was not the time to supply "strike weapons" to Egypt: "With its vast population and deep poverty, Egypt needs housing and jobs and health care far more than offensive weapons such as tanks and planes and missiles."[101]

Sadat's dramatic trip to Jerusalem had obviously changed Washington's attitude toward Egypt. But why did Carter change his mind on arms sales to Saudi Arabia? His administration believed that keeping the Saudis' trust was crucial. The Saudis could harm the United States if they took unfriendly actions. As Vance said in announcing the sale, Saudi Arabia "is of immense importance in promoting a course of moderation in the Middle East—with respect to peace-making and other initiatives—and more broadly, in world affairs, as in petroleum and financial policy."[102]

In other words, the decision to sell arms to the Saudis was made for much broader reasons than a Saudi military need for the F-15 and, as Vance stated clearly, the decision was directly related to the administration's global philosophy. Indeed, Vance has since revealed that as early as his first meeting with the president after the election, both men were prepared to furnish military equipment to moderate Arab states as long as it did not upset the military balance.[103]

The sales to the three countries were announced as a package deal in an attempt to paralyze the pro-Israeli lobby.[104] Congress would have to approve or reject the entire sale—either all three countries would receive the arms or none would. The administration proposed selling Saudi Arabia all 60 planes that it had asked for, while Israel and Egypt would each receive about half of their request. (Egypt would get 50 out of 120 requested F-5Es; Israel, 75 out of 150 requested F-16s; 15 out of 25 requested F-15s.)

The American Israel Public Affairs Committee immediately announced that it would seek to block the sale. Overwhelming House opposition quickly emerged. Since under a law revised in 1976, the sale could be vetoed if both Houses opposed it within thirty days, all parties quickly focused on the Senate. Although considerable opposition was soon evident, the administration was well-organized. The president let it be known that he would brook no internal opposition. Even before the announcement, one of Israel's leading Senate supporters, Abraham Ribicoff, was won over to the administration policy.[105] The pro-Israeli lobby also had tradition working against it—it had never blocked a sale to an Arab country. The sale of mobile antiaircraft missiles to Jordan had been altered in 1975, but that was due in large measure to the skepticism of the Joint Chiefs. This time there was no effective opposition from within the U.S. government.

The triple arms sale revealed the unity in Carter's decision-making system for Mideast issues. After the shock of the Soviet-American communiqué, the administration had resolved to amend its decision making. High-level officials concluded that a political firestorm had erupted not because the policy was incorrect or based on false assumptions, but because key officials had failed to consult beforehand with American Jewish leaders, key congressmen, and even some of their own colleagues. Hamilton Jordan's role in formulating foreign policy was elevated after this reevaluation, but the basic approach to the Middle East did not change.

The new method broadened consultation with outsiders, but the alterations were procedural rather than substantive, the consultations perfunctory rather than genuine. The arms sale decision percolated through Washington for weeks before it was announced. Opponents outside the administration were "consulted"—that is, they were warned politely. But within the administration, the only arguments revolved around numbers, not objectives. The Arms Control and Disarmament Agency and the Division of Program, Analysis, and Evaluation, Office of the Secretary of Defense, opposed the sale to Saudi Arabia. Some bureaucrats, especially in the Near East Bureau of the State Department, favored the sales to the Arabs but opposed weapons for Israel. No agency or individual took up the AIPAC case against selling F-15s to Saudi Arabia and F-5Es to Egypt or its advocacy of selling Israel all the F-15s and F-16s it had requested. Thus, the pro-Israeli lobby had no bureaucratic ally.[106]

Administration officials believed the decsion-making apparatus had touched base with all major views. One journalist reported shortly after the announcement,

> The process for reaching their decision over the sales embodied the best features of the Administration's open, collegial and sometimes chaotic approach to policy-making—the effort to expose Mr. Carter to a wide range of departmental views. As such, the decision is said to offer a revealing example of how the Administration's loosely structured mode of doing business differs from that of the Nixon-Ford period, when decisions were made in a much more rigid and hierarchical framework.[107]

Thus, openness and chaos (in contrast to Kissinger's authoritarian style) were equated with care and breadth in decision making. This procedure was assumed to guarantee optimal results, but key officials did not realize that the conclusions reached were foreordained, since all participants agreed on the assumptions underlying the decisions. The vaunted "open consideration of options" was in reality only a debate over details, such as how many planes to sell to each country and how to convince Congress.

The heated public debate over the sale revolved around the future of Saudi-American relations and the Mideast military balance. Proponents of the sale argued that it would increase Riyadh's confidence in the United States, encourage Saudi support for the peace process, and lead to decisions keeping oil production high and prices low.[108] The argument proved effective but not prophetic, for within a year the Saudis opposed Camp David and helped triple oil prices. The arguments against the sale were more diffuse, which is one of the reasons that opponents ultimately lost. Led by AIPAC, this group focused on the threat to Israel and the unreliability of the Saudis—their failure to support the peace process, their participation in the 1973 oil embargo, and their poor security and huge numbers of foreign workers, which might allow U.S. technology to reach the Russians.[109] The problem with this position was that in the short term the planes did not seem threatening to Israel—they were not even to be delivered for three or four years. Arguments based on the Saudis' unreliability had the disadvantage of being purely negative. In short, the proponents provided a plan in which the plane sales fit; the opponents argued against the sale without showing specifically and convincingly how U.S. policy might proceed if the president's arms package were defeated.

The political debate lingered through the spring. Submission of the sale to Congress had been delayed several weeks after the original announcement in mid-February while the Senate considered the Panama Canal treaties. There were further delays while Congress recessed and the administration waited for emotions to settle after the television miniseries, *Holocaust.* In the end the president agreed to sell an additional twenty F-15s to Israel and Secretary of Defense Brown wrote Senator Sparkman, the chairman of the Foreign Relations Committee, promising that the Saudis would not request nor would the United States sell external fuel tanks, refueling air tankers, or bomb racks that would allow the Saudi F-15s to be used as bombers, increasing their threat to Israel.[110] With these assurances, the Senate voted 54-44 in favor of the arms for the three countries.

This hard-fought campaign, pursued on the airwaves and in the cloakrooms of the Capitol, severely damaged the president's Jewish support. At the end of the campaign, senior administration officials were reported to have boasted that they had "broken" the pro-Israeli lobby. The president, who was bitterly irritated by the debate, never fully recovered politically from this episode.[111]

The more important consequence of the prolonged F-15 battle, however, was damage to the peace process. Almost four months were lost. Meanwhile, developments had further strained American-Israeli relations. In February, after

President Sadat's departure, the administration invited Prime Minister Begin to Washington for a meeting in mid-March. On the eve of the meeting, however, the PLO raided Israel, attacking a busload of Israeli civilians and killing thirty-six. This led to a large-scale Israeli incursion into South Lebanon to weaken the PLO bases south of the Litani River. The president pressured Begin to withdraw. Yet another U.N. peacekeeping force was established by a U.N. Security Council Resolution sponsored by the United States—over Israeli objections—to resolve the crisis quickly before Begin arrived for his now-delayed visit. Begin thus could not discuss a settlement of the Lebanese issue with Carter before he arrived in Washington. The president intentionally presented him with a fait accompli: a U.N. force already authorized to replace the Israelis.[112]

When the prime minister arrived, Carter confronted him on his posture toward the Palestinians and the West Bank. With the Middle East arms package annoying Begin and Israel's Lebanon incursion annoying Carter, the atmosphere was acrimonious.

For weeks the president and his aides had declared publicly that U.N. Resolution 242 applied to all fronts including the West Bank. During a private meeting with the Israeli negotiating team, Carter bluntly demanded whether the Israeli government agreed that the withdrawals demanded in Resolution 242 applied to the West Bank. The Israelis told him at great length that their military would withdraw from Arab populated areas under Begin's autonomy proposal but never from the entire West Bank and Gaza Strip. That position did not satisfy the president. He stated that during a five-year transition period, the Israelis should neither open new settlements nor expand existing ones. He opposed Israeli political control over the West Bank and Gaza after the transition, demanding that the area residents be permitted to choose whether they would join Israel or Jordan or retain the status quo.[113] Carter did propose that, however er the residents voted, Israel should maintain advanced military outposts in the areas and that some border changes should occur. He agreed with Israel only in its opposition to a Palestinian state. He also contended that Israel should give up the Sinai settlements. He angrily told the stunned Israeli negotiating team that if they would incorporate these views in a declaration of principles, he believed they would be acceptable to Sadat.[114]

The Israelis did not believe that Sadat had accepted the notion of a partial Israeli withdrawal from the West Bank and Gaza, nor were they convinced that he had dropped his demand for a Palestinian state. They were ready to allow individuals, even a majority of the populace, to become Jordanian citizens but they would not permit the residents to effect a Jordanian takeover of the West Bank and Gaza. They believed, in any case, that self-determination would lead to a PLO state.[115] Not surprisingly, no formula acceptable to the United States and Israel emerged from the meetings.

The open tension between the United States and Israel was in pointed contrast to the harmonious end of Sadat's trip in February. Criticism of the Israeli negotiating stance spread throughout Washington, initiated by the president himself as the talks ended. The day after his meeting with Begin and his aides, the president met with the Senate Foreign Relations Committee where he presented a detailed critique of the Israeli position.[116] As a result, opposition to the Israeli government rose even in the American Jewish community, although the official leadership continued to give public support. The administration's attempt to enlist American Jews to pressure Israel, however, was undermined by its tough posture—especially on the arms package. Most Jewish leaders were horrified at Saudi Arabia's buying the F-15s and were in no mood to increase Israel's burdens.[117]

The United States and Egypt continued to take similarly critical attitudes toward Israeli proposals. During the weeks that the triple arms sale drama escalated, the Carter administration demanded that the Israelis allow the West Bank and Gaza to come under Arab control after a transition period of five years. The Israelis adamantly refused. This phase of negotiation ended in late June when the Israeli Cabinet responded to Carter's written questions about Israel's negotiating stance on the West Bank. Carter publicly criticized the Israeli answers. He had praised Sadat's attitude as "very constructive" a few days earlier.[118] Despite this positive description, the president knew that the Egyptians' proposals were not viable either.[119] Carter's tactics kept Sadat dependent on American mediation and the Israelis defensive but alienated. The administration groped for a new vehicle to reach a breakthrough.

Despite the turmoil, there were hopeful signs. All three sides still intensely sought an agreement. Alfred Atherton, named U.S. mediator in Middle East negotiations in February, traveled between Cairo and Jerusalem. The Israeli military committee representatives remained in Cairo and Israeli defense minister Weizman continued his frequent trips to Egypt, where Sadat remained cordial, a situation that would have seemed incredible a year earlier. Many Israeli ministers had also been impressed with Sadat's moderate response to Israel's invasion of Lebanon.

Even the Israeli-American relationship was less strained than it appeared in March. Begin returned to the United States at the end of April to celebrate Israel's thirtieth anniversary. If only for political reasons, Carter gave him a warm reception, promising: "We will never waiver from our deep friendship and partnership with Israel and our total absolute commitment to Israel's security."[120] For all their present differences, the United States and Israel still had a "special relationship."

The talks took a new direction in mid-July when the Egyptian and Israeli foreign ministers met with Secretary of State Vance at Leeds Castle in England. It was the first Egyptian-Israeli meeting at this level since January, when Sadat had broken off the Jerusalem talks.

The negotiators had before them the Israeli and Egyptian formal proposals—on which both sides profoundly disagreed. However, Vance successfully broke down social barriers by sponsoring a dinner at which all three delegations dined together and by conducting informal conversations with Dayan and Kamel. At least the two sides were beginning to address each other's needs. Dayan suggested to Vance that a breakthrough could occur if the future of the West Bank were decided after the five-year transition had already begun. Kamel was responsive to Israel's security requirements during the projected transition. Substantive progress may have been negligible, but Vance thought he had an agreement to return to the Middle East in two weeks for more talks.[121]

By now, however, irritations were mounting between Egypt and Israel. Sadat had angered Begin by meeting with the Labor party head, Shimon Peres, in Austria in early July. Shortly thereafter he had also met again with Weizman, but the defense minister's optimistic report on this talk was greeted skeptically by the Cabinet in Jerusalem. After all, the Egyptians had presented hard-line proposals at Leeds and Sadat had made several hostile public statements.[122] Begin abruptly and publicly rejected Sadat's suggestion for a goodwill gesture, the immediate return of two key Sinai locations, the town of El Arish and Mt. Sinai. For his part Sadat evicted the military committee from Cairo after receiving reports on the Leeds conference. He began talking of terminating the U.N. peacekeeping force in the Sinai when it came up for renewal in October, and, for good measure labeled Begin "the only obstacle" to peace in the Middle East.[123] Then he abruptly canceled Egyptian participation in the discussions that Secretary of State Vance was preparing to lead. Sadat asserted that only an Israeli commitment to withdraw from the territories captured in 1967 would lead to more peace talks.

The Carter administration was alarmed by this collapse of the negotiations. The president's legislative program was in growing disarray and his own popularity had plummeted.[124] Meanwhile, Sadat's Jerusalem visit had reduced his key foreign policy priority, a comprehensive Middle East peace, to an Egyptian-Israeli dialogue. As even that achievement seemed about to disintegrate, Carter officials feared another Mideast war would ensue with disastrous potential for ruptured relations with Saudi Arabia, an oil embargo, an intensified energy crisis, and reduced American influence in the area. Sadat had been promised an American proposal, but there was little chance Begin would accept it. American-Israeli relations had reached a new low. Carter distrusted many people in his own administration, who he thought were "only too eager to share information with the Israelis." Brzezinski wondered if the administration had the political strength to confront Israel.[125] Much of the administration's domestic leverage on the issue had been dissipated by the arms sale.

Despite the crisis in negotiations, Carter was confident that peace could be achieved if dramatic steps were taken. He decided to invite both Begin and Sadat to a trilateral summit at Camp David. Many officials informed of the president's decision were dismayed, especially at State. The venture would probably fail, they worried, and further undermine the president's political position at home and his reputation abroad. It would be a disaster for American Middle East policy. The president, however, remained determined.[126]

Secretary of State Vance traveled to the Mideast in early August to present both Begin and Sadat with secret and sealed handwritten letters from the president inviting them to the summit. Begin accepted immediately. So did Sadat. William Quandt of the NSC then returned to Jerusalem with the secret message from Sadat that he accepted the invitation unconditionally and that the Israeli prime minister could ignore his public talk of an October 1978 deadline to the discussions and a possible withdrawal of the U.N. peacekeeping force in the Sinai.[127] The stage was set for the most dramatic Middle East meeting in which an American president had ever engaged.

Camp David

Shortly after all three leaders helicoptered to Camp David with their aides on Tuesday, 5 September, they released a statement, originally drafted by Rosalynn Carter, asking for divine assistance in their deliberations. With that announcement a news blackout descended over the summit, which some believe is responsible for its success. By agreement Jody Powell served as press spokesman for all three delegations. The participants had even agreed that to prevent leaks no one in any delegation could leave during the conference. In this informal setting, with no formal schedule or protocol of dress, the participants retreated to produce a framework for Mideast peace. The meetings were hardly a traditional summit, because the three heads of state did not meet together as a group after the first two days. Both the Egyptians and Israelis worked in separate meetings with the Americans. In fact, the Egyptians and Israelis could not even telephone each other. Their calls were routed through the U.S. delegation.[128]

In this activity the central figure remained Jimmy Carter. His mastery of detail and great stamina saved the negotiations time and time again. After the president, Cyrus Vance played the most significant role in negotiations. Brzezinski was less prominent in critical decisions, just as he played a lesser role in the specifics of Mideast policy. Most of the drafting and redrafting was undertaken by both State and NSC staffs.

There were two key phases to Camp David: the first week when the Egyptian and Israeli leaders negotiated directly, and the second period, which began Saturday night, 9 September, when the discussions refined successive American drafts. Despite the informality and entertainments such as movies, tennis, and billiards, the atmosphere through most of the conference was extremely tense. Begin and Brzezinski, the two former Poles frequently at odds, engaged in a fiercely competitive chess tournament.

After preliminary bilateral meetings on Tuesday, the first session was held between Sadat, Begin, and Carter on Wednesday afternoon, the second day. Although Carter had hoped the conference might end with a peace treaty, Sadat cautioned at the first meeting that details would take too long, so the three leaders decided to work out an overall agreement that could then be transformed into a peace treaty, "perhaps three months later."[129]

At this meeting Sadat presented a detailed peace plan that could not have begun the talks more negatively. He had secretly informed Carter that it was the work of his hard-line aides and was intended as a sop to the Arab world, not a take-it-or-leave-it offer to Israel. Attempting to limit the damage, Carter warned Begin beforehand to expect a tough opening Egyptian position.[130] Indeed, the new Egyptian plan was tougher than anything they had proposed since Sadat traveled to Jerusalem. It demanded complete Israeli withdrawals from territories captured in 1967, the redivision of Jerusalem, the right of Palestinian refugees to return to their points of origin, even in pre-1967 Israel, and Palestinian self-determination. The Egyptians preferred a "national entity" linked to Jordan. Israel would be expected to compensate Arabs for any damage caused by its armed forces in the past. Egypt would not exchange ambassadors or normalize relations with Israel. Sadat took ninety minutes to read the full text of his document. Although Begin was alarmed, the meeting ended in surprising good will, with Begin and Carter joking about the Israelis accepting the plan in toto.[131]

At the second meeting between the three leaders on Thursday, 7 September, Begin responded point by point to Sadat's plan, demonstrating its unacceptability to Israel. This resulted in angry and heated exchanges between the two men during two meetings that day. Most of the Israeli delegation at this stage believed the conference would break up. They thought only to stay long enough to protect their image with the American government and with American public opinion.[132]

Although Carter agreed with Begin that Sadat's document was "extremist," the president ignored it and hoped for continuation of the conference so that the United States could produce compromises. But Sadat's proposals appeared firm. Begin would not accept Carter's recommendation that he freeze new West Bank and Gaza Strip settlements, and he vehemently opposed Sadat's idea (which Carter had consistently supported) for a Palestinian national entity linked to Jordan. Begin would not even consider relinquishing the Sinai settlements. (Carter could not persuade Sadat to allow an Israeli presence in some form.) The meetings between Begin, Sadat, and Carter were so unproductive that from then on the three did not meet. This increased Carter's importance.

After Carter met separately with Sadat and Begin on Friday, the talks entered a new phase. Although the United States had presented no specific proposals yet, an American draft had been in development for months. In preparation for meetings of the aborted political committee the previous January, the

American team had worked on a framework for Arab-Israeli peace. Initial ideas had been shared with Sadat in February and with Begin at the disastrous March meeting. By the time of the Leeds conference, these ideas were discussed directly and simultaneously with both parties. In preparation for Camp David, this work on a draft document continued at a two-day session on a Virginia estate and in an extensive meeting at the White House. Thus, when the initial discussions foundered, the American team had a document that it could amend and produce if needed. An American draft refined by Saunders, Quandt, Lewis, and Eilts was ready by midday Saturday. Carter was also provided with an annotated text indicating the likely Egyptian and Israeli reactions to each item.[133]

This draft dealt hardly at all with the Sinai but with principles of withdrawal, Palestinians, the West Bank, and the thorny issue of the "source of authority," or sovereignty, on the West Bank. It referred to Israeli withdrawals in accordance with U.N. Resolution 242. Carter added the words, "to the 1967 lines with minor adjustments." Since this approach was obviously unacceptable to the Israelis, perhaps he believed that he could later delete the phrase in return for an Israeli concession. Vice President Mondale, however, convinced the president that, once the phrase was inserted, the Egyptians would never allow it to be excised.[134]

On Sunday, Carter, Begin, and Sadat visited nearby Gettysburg. Shortly afterward Carter, Mondale, Vance, and Brzezinski met with Begin, Dayan, Weizman, and Aharon Barak (Israel's attorney general) so that the Americans could present their draft. The president read to the Israelis the seventeen-page document, clause by clause, with additional oral explanations. He expected to present the draft with Israeli comments to Sadat that evening, but to Carter's chagrin Begin refused to comment on the document until he had consulted with colleagues. He and his aides returned after dinner with a multitude of complaints, which led to an angry exchange between the Israelis and the Americans lasting until 3:00 A.M. The Israelis still refused to withdraw from the Sinai settlements and to give up the Sinai airfields. They would not freeze settlements on the West Bank. They refused to accept a phrase referring to the inadmissibility of acquiring territory by war, fearing it would lead to their withdrawal from the Golan Heights and the West Bank. When Carter pointed out that the language was from the preamble to U.N. Resolution 242, Begin objected that he was only repeating what had been Israel's position for eleven years. "Maybe that's why you haven't had peace for eleven years," Carter snapped. The Israelis would not accept the right of Palestinian self-determination, fearing it would lead to a PLO state. They suggested instead that the future of the West Bank be settled by a committee of Palestinian Arab residents of the West Bank and Gaza, the Egyptians, the Israelis, and the Jordanians. The only major American suggestion that they accepted was the notion that Israeli forces could remain in the West Bank beyond the five-year transition period.[135]

After the meeting, the president asked Dayan to walk him back to his cabin. They talked until 4:00 A.M., and out of the conversation a personal rapport developed that proved important as the summit moved toward a climax. The president, however, was disgusted with Begin, whom he described to his wife as a "psycho."[136]

Carter had asked for formal Israeli comments on the draft by 10:00 A.M. Monday. To save time that morning, the Israelis' handwritten notes were bicycled up a hill to Carter and Vance, who reviewed the suggestions and, when appropriate, sent them to U.S. officials for rewriting and refining, whereupon each section was typed up within a few minutes. The Egyptians watched this process with growing alarm, fearing that they were to be presented with an Israeli-American fait accompli. It was only after Carter met with Sadat that the Egyptians realized that they too could react to an American draft.[137]

Sadat hinted that he would leave the conference if this was Israel's final word. Shortly thereafter, Carter found Ezer Weizman in his cabin trying to take a nap. Carter told him of Sadat's negative reaction and implied that the United States agreed with Egypt: Israel should agree to withdraw its Sinai settlements and abandon its airfields. Later in the day Carter conveyed the same message to Dayan and Barak. Sadat repeatedly refused to consider anything but total Israeli withdrawal; he even rejected the idea of replacing one Israeli airfield with an American base.[138]

In their private meeting that Monday morning, Carter had obtained Sadat's agreement to a new procedure that proved to be the turning point of the conference. The Egyptian president agreed to separate the Sinai issue from the general framework dealing with the West Bank and Gaza. For the rest of the conference, there were two sets of negotiations: one on the Sinai agreement led by Carter and the other on the general Palestinian framework led by Vance.[139] The idea of separating the two issues was the president's. He then studied detailed maps of the Sinai and wrote a draft agreement, including projected dates of withdrawal and demilitarized zones. Carter soon gained Sadat's basic approval with only minor changes. Sadat also told Carter secretly that, if necessary, he would agree to allow Israeli settlers and airfields to remain in the Sinai for three years.[140]

Still the Israelis refused to agree to withdraw from the Sinai settlements and airfields; and the two sides were also far apart on details of a general Palestinian framework. In order to calm the situation, the American delegation promised a new draft. On Tuesday, 12 September, Carter met with Sadat during the day, the Israeli delegation for dinner, and afterward with Begin. At this meeting the Israeli prime minister discussed a final communiqué, suggesting that the conference would soon end in failure.[141] But following this pessimistic note, the discussion turned more productive. Carter, for example, agreed to delete the "areas obtained by war" phrase. Begin agreed to be more definite about deciding the future of the West Bank after five years.

Having temporarily mollified Begin, Carter on Wednesday asked each delegation to send one legal adviser to work with him and Vance on the details of another draft. Begin selected Aharon Barak, who was highly respected by all three delegations and a particular favorite of the American team. Sadat sent Osama al-Baz, a leading Egyptian legal expert and diplomat involved in the peace effort from the beginning. The four spent most of the ninth day at Camp David in conference together. Each successive draft, however, contained articles objectionable to one side or the other.[142]

It is an irony of Camp David that the American team found Sadat easier to deal with than Begin but found Israeli subordinates more amenable than their Egyptian counterparts. Al-Baz created more obstacles than Barak. Carter opposed al-Baz's demand that an Arab flag fly over the Temple Mount, but he also wanted Israel to accept Sadat's insistence on relinquishing the Sinai settlements. After many hours of exhausting discussion with Barak and al-Baz, Carter saw Begin on Wednesday evening, the thirteenth. The president called the prime minister outside from where he was viewing a film and pled for Israeli withdrawal from the settlements. Begin refused.[143]

Thus, by Thursday, the tenth day of the conference, the settlements loomed as the critical obstacle. Carter and Weizman had been urging Sadat to meet with Moshe Dayan from the beginning of the conference. Sadat did not trust the famous Israeli military hero and had never met with him alone but finally agreed. Although he had encouraged the meeting, Carter feared it might only make matters worse at this critical stage and warned Dayan not to discuss the key issues. But Sadat quickly launched into just such a discussion, convincing Dayan that Egypt would never accept an agreement unless Israel evacuated the settlements.[144]

When Dayan, Weizman, and Barak met with Carter late Thursday, Carter told them they would have to choose between the Sinai settlements and peace. In response, Dayan suggested that withdrawal from the settlements required a vote of the Cabinet and the Knesset. This was a hint that he had changed his mind and now believed Israel should withdraw, but Carter failed to understand the significance of his remarks.

By Thursday afternoon, the Israelis had received the second major American draft of the Palestinian framework. When Vance went to Begin's cabin for the Israeli reply, he had instructions to be "quite tough." The Israelis felt the draft improved upon the earlier version, but Begin still thought its formula would result in a Palestinian state. Since the American team had concluded the Egyptians would accept nothing less, Vance was infuriated.[145]

The U.S. delegation feared that the process had become endless. On

Friday morning Carter sent a note to Begin and Sadat informing them that the conference would end on Sunday whether or not agreement had been reached. The president told Dayan that he would report on the conference to Congress and the American people on Monday. It was clear that he would blame Israel for any breakdown.[146]

Minutes later Carter learned that Sadat had prepared his delegation to depart and had asked for a helicopter to Andrews Air Force Base. Sadat was bitterly discouraged by what he perceived as Dayan's uncompromising stance and by the resignation of Egyptian foreign minister Kamel and two of his aides the previous evening. For Sadat, Kamel's resignation was a disaster. How could he hope for Arab backing if he could not even maintain the support of his foreign minister? Carter immediately went to the Egyptian president and asked him to remain. He told Sadat that a unilateral departure would harm U.S.-Egyptian relations and their personal friendship, ruin Sadat's peace initiative, and lead to his being blamed for the breakdown and to the end of the Carter presidency. Carter feared a major Soviet victory in the Mideast if Sadat departed. Sadat feared that the concessions he had already made would be used against him by the Israelis in future negotiations. Carter answered the Egyptian president's concerns by suggesting that none of the agreements reached at Camp David would remain in effect if any part of the proposals was rejected by either Egypt or Israel. On this basis Sadat agreed to stay.[147]

The Egyptians had insisted that they would not have normal diplomatic relations with Israel until it had totally withdrawn from the territories captured in 1967, but now Sadat agreed to exchange ambassadors within nine months of signing the peace treaty. Carter also persuaded Sadat on Friday morning to delete the clause on the "inadmissability of the acquisition of territory by war," which so offended Begin. This compromise meant that Israeli commitments to withdraw from the Sinai were further separated from any concessions that might be made on the Golan Heights, the West Bank, and the Gaza Strip.

Meanwhile, pressure from all sides mounted against Begin. He still would not agree to dismantle the Sinai settlements. With Dayan also threatening to leave, one of the Israeli delegates suggested phoning Ariel Sharon and enlisting his support for withdrawing the settlements. A few hours later Begin was stunned by Sharon's support for Israeli withdrawal from the Sinai if that was the only step blocking agreement.[148] Still Begin held back.

As far as the airfields were concerned, Secretary of Defense Brown—who played a subsidiary role in the conference except on military matters—arranged a deal with Weizman by which the United States would rebuild Israeli airfields in the Negev, providing an American guarantee that they would be built on time and would not devastate Israel's overheated economy.[149]

The Saturday discussions concentrated primarily on the Palestinian question. Although Begin did not participate, most of the Israelis were involved in the intense negotiations. In one critical meeting Dayan produced a possible compromise by reminding everyone of the Israeli-American working paper that he had concluded with Carter the previous October. That paper distinguished between Israeli-Jordanian peace negotiations (that is, between two states) and discussions—not peace agreements—with the Arabs over the West Bank and Gaza. The Israeli team used this distinction to avoid establishing any basis for a Palestinian state.[150]

On Saturday night, Carter and Vance met with Begin, Barak, and Dayan to discuss the remaining issues. The moment of truth had come. Begin announced that he would allow the Knesset to decide on total withdrawal from the Sinai—including the settlements—and party discipline would not be imposed. He also accepted wording that he had previously opposed on "recognition of the legitimate rights of the Palestinian people," although he still rejected any reference to "national rights" that might imply an independent state.[151]

It had already been agreed that several issues still in dispute or peripheral to the agreements would be handled in side letters. For example, in these letters Begin promised to submit the Sinai settlements issue to the Knesset, and Sadat reiterated diplomatically what he had stated even more bluntly to Carter and Vance: that without a favorable Knesset vote, he would not honor his concessions at Camp David. Sadat also agreed to handle the West Bank and the Gaza Strip on behalf of the Arabs "following consultation with Jordan and the representatives of the Palestinian people." Now Israel would be protected if Jordan and the West Bank Palestinians refused to participate.[152]

Two issues even more difficult—Jerusalem and Israeli settlements on the West Bank—had been left until the end of the conference. Tired and anxious to reach an accord, negotiators handled both issues in ways that later created American-Israeli dissension. From the start of the conference, the Americans had wanted Israel to freeze all settlements in the West Bank from the end of the Camp David summit until the end of the autonomy talks. After arguing for hours at the fateful Saturday night meeting, Carter finally asked Begin to sign a letter promising not to establish settlements "during the negotiations"—by which he meant the autonomy negotiations—and in the future to establish them only as "agreed by the negotiating parties." Begin said he would think it over and Sunday afternoon handed Carter a note saying he would not establish settlements during the "agreed period of negotiations [three months] for the conclusion of the peace treaty." But Carter and Vance thought that Begin had committed himself to the president's proposal of the previous night. Carter had already informed Sadat that Israel would freeze settlements "during the negotiations." Indeed, Sadat said two days after the summit that he too had understood Begin's commitment to mean three months, but he may have expected both the peace treaty and the autonomy discussions to be handled by then. At one point some Israelis told Brzezinski that they thought both sets of negotiations could be completed in three months. At any rate the issue was not clarified until after the conference, because the side letters were not included in the agreements originally signed Sunday evening.[153]

The Jerusalem issue was left until Sunday, and it almost prevented an agreement. On Sunday morning Begin and Carter seemed to have agreed on a formula that Jerusalem would remain "undivided." Yet at lunch Mondale showed Dinitz a letter from Carter that was to be delivered to Sadat. The letter stated that the United States considered East Jerusalem to be occupied territory. Since the document was to be included in the accords, the Israelis thought that they would thereby be agreeing in principle to withdraw from East Jerusalem. Dinitz told Mondale that the Israelis would not sign any document with such a proviso, and an Israeli-American meeting was quickly convened.

Carter and Dayan launched into a furious exchange. The president insisted he had promised Sadat and would not retreat. Carter was clearly under severe pressure, but he allowed Vance and Barak to try for a new formula, which they produced within the next hour. Under the new arrangement, Egypt, Israel, and the United States would all include letters stating their positions on Jerusalem. The American letter would simply restate the positions taken previously by U.S. ambassadors at the United Nations. Sadat agreed. The last major stumbling block had been removed.[154]

At 11:00 P.M. the two frameworks reached at Camp David were signed in an emotional ceremony at the White House. Sadat was somber and had privately insisted on signing the broader "framework for peace in the Middle East" before the "framework for the conclusion of a peace treaty between Israel and Egypt." The basic compromise of the latter agreement included a phased Israeli withdrawal from all parts of the Sinai, including Israeli settlements and airbases, to be completed within three years of concluding the treaty in return for normal diplomatic and commercial relations between Jerusalem and Cairo. In addition, U.N. forces and limited force zones would separate the armies of the two states.

The other agreement established the context for settling the West Bank/Gaza Strip issue. Under its terms, a five-year transition administration would be established by a committee consisting of Egypt, Jordan, and Israel; West Bank and Gaza Palestinians might participate on the Egyptian and Jordanian delegations. This committee would arrange for full autonomy in these two territories by an administrative council to be "freely elected by the inhabitants of these areas to replace the existing Israeli military government." Under the accords, security during the transition period would be provided in three ways: (1) the Israeli armed forces in both the West Bank and Gaza Strip would withdraw to "specified security locations"; (2) "a strong local police force" would be established, that might include Jordanian civilians; and (3) the borders were to be patrolled by joint Israeli and Jordanian units.

By the third year of the five-year transition period, negotiations would begin among the four parties (the Israelis, Egyptians, Jordanians, and representatives of the West Bank/Gaza administrative council) to determine the final disposition of the West Bank and Gaza Strip. Meanwhile, the Israelis, Jordanians, and administrative council representatives would negotiate a final Jordanian-Israeli peace treaty. At the end of the process, the elected representatives of the West Bank and Gaza would vote on the new arrangements. The five-year transition, however, would not begin until the administrative council had been established and inaugurated. If serious delays occurred in arranging for elections, the part of the accords applying to the Gaza Strip and the West Bank could become academic.[155]

The Aftermath of Camp David

These accords represented the most dramatic progress any president had made on the Arab-Israeli dispute. With varying emphasis and differing tactics, every president since Eisenhower had tried to bring the Israelis and Egyptians together in an agreement that would guide future American action in the area. Jimmy Carter had done it. But he had accomplished the feat by compromising his philosophy and approach to the conflict. Carter and his aides had firmly believed from the outset that Sadat would never agree to a separate peace with Israel, but the formulations that emerged from Camp David were closer to a separate peace than to Carter's goal of a comprehensive solution including the Palestinians. Carter's key decision at Camp David had been to separate the Sinai issue from the more general framework. This decision—rooted in the pressure to reach some agreement—superceded the administration's strategy for a comprehensive settlement.

Within the American camp, the participants differed on which of the two frameworks to stress. Carter seemed torn. Signs of the resulting conceptual schizophrenia were soon seen in debates with the Israelis over the settlements question, in the unsuccessful effort to gain Saudi and Jordanian support for the Camp David accords, and in the president's own renewed stress on comprehensiveness after the conference. Even during the summit, Carter rejected Vance's appeals to delete Begin's amendments to the Palestinian sections. The American delegation finally persuaded Sadat to accept Begin's proposed changes, some at the last minute. The Americans also persuaded Sadat to agree not to have the two frameworks binding legally, which meant that an Egyptian-Israeli deal could be consummated before the autonomy talks had been completed. On this issue there were divisions in both the Egyptian and American camps. Members of Sadat's delegation, especially al-Baz, were so upset by the decision to delete linkage that they appealed to their American counterparts to persuade Sadat to reintroduce it. American officials were sympathetic, but Carter would not allow the linkage question to be reexamined.[156]

Camp David succeeded in part because each of the three leaders could not bear the consequences of failure: Carter, because he had staked his reputation on it and feared a Mideast war if the conference broke up; Begin, because failure could destroy the Israeli-American relationship; and Sadat, because he would not admit that his peace initiative had been a mistake and he saw no acceptable alternative to agreement. It is not surprising that differences arose once the conference ended.

The settlements issue brought those conflicts into clear focus. Traveling by plane to New York City, Begin was stunned to hear that Brzezinski had asserted that Israel had agreed to a long-term freeze on settlements.[157] On Wednesday, 20 September, Saunders, on behalf of the State Department, formally rejected the Israeli side letter, which declared that Israel would freeze settlements for the three months when the peace treaty was being negotiated. Carter and Vance insisted that at the crucial Saturday night meeting Begin had agreed not to establish new settlements during the autonomy talks, which would likely last much longer than the peace treaty negotiations. However, Barak's notes backed Begin's version of his commitment. It is simply not plausible that Barak—soon to become an Israeli Supreme Court justice and recognized by Carter for his integrity, moderation, and precision—would have been wrong about such a critical point. Yet the issue created bitterness between Carter and Begin, just as it had before Camp David. The president later accused the Israelis of "using the settlements on the West Bank and the East Jerusalem issue to prevent the involvement of the Jordanians and Palestinians."[158] For this reason Carter subsequently blamed Begin's "broken promise" for the Jordanian and Saudi refusal to back Camp David.[159]

Carter's failure to pinpoint Begin's commitment on settlements was his greatest error of the conference. The controversy over what Begin had actually promised at the meeting on the last night of the conference reveals again that oral agreements are meaningless. In this case Carter and Vance seem to have misunderstood Begin, in part because their post-Camp David strategy depended on a commitment from Begin, one that he never made.[160] True to Begin's interpretation of the promise he had made, however, he did not initiate new settlements for three months.

Both Begin and Carter made statements that exacerbated the other side's bitterness. Under pressure on the settlements, Begin declared to a Jewish audience in New York that he would maintain a military presence on the West Bank even after the five-year transition period. The administration answered with statements and leaks to reinforce its version of Begin's commitment to a settlements freeze.[161]

The Arabs overwhelmingly rejected the Camp David accords. A few days before Camp David, Carter's Middle East experts warned him that other Arab states would not support an agreement that did not resolve the Palestinian question in some satisfactory way. During the summit, however, Carter was convinced that the Saudis and the Jordanians would back the accords and he so assured Sadat.[162] Carter's aides were skeptical; some thought he had a secret commitment from King Hussein. After the conference, Vance left for Saudi Arabia, Jordan, and Syria, but each rejected his pleas for endorsement.[163]

Just as he was about to leave the United States, Sadat met with Ambassador Eilts aboard his plane. Sadat had been in a foul mood, barking at his aides as well as berating the ambassador over the American failure to produce Saudi support for the accords. "You promised to deliver the Saudis," he is reported to have complained. "Now, we're really in trouble."[164]

Over the next several weeks the Arabs prepared to coordinate their opposition to the accords at a meeting to be held in Baghdad during November. In order to reduce Egypt's isolation and the opposition from the Arab world, Carter clarified what he meant by a comprehensive peace:

> There are three elements that any Arab leader cannot, in good conscience, endorse or avoid. One is the matter of sovereignty over the West Bank, Gaza Strip. And of course, when I say "Arab leaders," I am including President Sadat. The other one is the question of eastern Jerusalem and control of the Moslem holy places by Moslems. And the third one is the resolution of the Palestinian question . . . in all its aspects.[165]

To the Israelis and their American supporters, Carter's statement compromised the whole basis of negotiations by predicting (and thereby seeming to accept) a hard Arab line. How could any Arab leader, including Sadat, take a more conciliatory stance than the U.S. president? Carter seemed to be suggesting new and tougher U.S. demands on Israel. Since the Israelis would not accept these positions, the prospects of post–Camp David success had just declined. American efforts to assuage the Arabs feelings alarmed the Israelis. Although Prime Minister Begin gained strong support from the Knesset for the Camp David accords, including withdrawals from the settlements, he was bitterly criticized by some of his closest and oldest associates for having agreed to leave the Sinai entirely.

Thus, opposition to Sadat in the Arab world and to Begin in Israel eroded the conciliatory atmosphere of Camp David. Nonetheless, all sides were optimistic as the delegations reconvened at Blair House in mid-October to work out the last details of an Egyptian-Israeli peace treaty. Vance led the American team; Dayan and Weizman, the Israeli; the new defense minister, General Kamal Hassan Ali, the Egyptian. The Americans were concerned that Arab rejection of Camp David would undermine Sadat's willingness to make peace. Carter told both delegations that he was anxious for quick agreement, preferably before the Baghdad Conference convened in two weeks.[166]

A now familiar process had begun, one distinctive of the Carter administration. The Arabs pressed the United States which in turn pressured the resisting Israelis. The result—as at Camp David—was compromise. In this case the process would take six months.

The Blair House conference opened with discussion of a draft treaty prepared by the United States, which was revised after the American team had consulted with each side. The most important early disagreements included the question of linkage, with the Israelis resisting Egyptian suggestions that the peace treaty be tied to the autonomy negotiations. The Egyptians in turn resisted Israeli efforts to have this treaty take priority over other obligations; the Israelis feared that previous anti-Israel treaties with the other Arab states would draw the Egyptians into a future Arab-Israeli war. There were other problems, too, such as timing the exchange of ambassadors and the establishment of diplomatic relations and arranging a peacekeeping force if the Soviets vetoed a U.N. commitment.[167] In addition, the Israelis sought financial assistance for their withdrawal from the Sinai, including the transfer of airbases and the relinquishing of Sinai oil and settlements. For this they turned to the United States.

A more fundamental problem, however, was created by the structure of these talks. Their Washington location permitted the administration to offer legal and political expertise in devising formulas to bridge the gap separating the two sides, but Sadat and Begin, the two principal figures, were not present. Their absence meant that both delegations needed home approval for any concessions or agreements. This arrangement led to misunderstandings and disappointments, especially since the new relationship between the two nations was at best delicate and both leaders were under severe political pressure from opponents.

The talks extended from October twelfth to twenty-first. For most of this period Vance was in southern Africa, and Atherton replaced him as head of the U.S. delegation; Brzezinski played a more prominent role than usual. The secretary of state had been a prime American negotiator at Camp David, and no one present enjoyed Vance's influence with both delegations. By 17 October, the talks had stalled and Carter invited each delegation to the White House for separate discussions. When this approach did not work, the president came to Blair House two days later for a working luncheon with both delegations at once. At this session he recommended compromises to both sides that gave new impetus. When Prime Minister Begin received Dayan's report, he ordered his foreign and defense ministers home for the weekly Sunday Cabinet meeting, and on Friday, the twentieth, Dayan informed his Egyptian and American colleagues that they would be leaving on Saturday night. Carter insisted that the two Israeli ministers come to the White House that afternoon. He informed them that he hoped they would take a draft treaty for their Cabinet's approval! Dayan later commented, "I enjoyed watching Carter in all his obdurate persistence. He was like a bulldog whose teeth were fastened on his victim."[168]

But Carter's persistence produced results. After a meeting with the Egyptians, he met later that evening with an expanded Israeli delegation until 11 P.M. He met with the Egyptians at 7 A.M. the next morning. Then Carter insisted the three delegations meet together. Five hours later they produced a new and agreed formulation (based on the seventh American draft) for consideration by their respective governments.

The Israeli Cabinet approved the draft in principle, while adding amendments and provisos on several issues. Their most important concern was the linking of the treaty with the Palestinian question.[169] Nonetheless, several Cabinet ministers criticized Dayan and Weizman for being too flexible. Meanwhile, the Egyptians were also examining and amending the draft. Just as the Israelis sought to make certain that the treaty and the Palestinan issues were kept apart, the Egyptians were trying to join the two. Linkage was vital to avoid the appearance of a separate peace with Israel.

Coinciding with these developments, a new Israeli-American controversy erupted with immediate effect on the talks. In early October, King Hussein had questioned the Carter administration on what the Camp David agreements meant for the future of Jerusalem, the settlements, and the eventual sovereignty of the West Bank and Gaza. The administration was desperate to engage Hussein in the negotiations to support Sadat and facilitate a resolution of the Palestinian question. Therefore, answers were prepared and the president personally edited a draft written by Saunders and Michael Sterner.[170] The Israelis protested that these topics were to be covered in negotiations; unilateral American statements might prejudge the results. When they received a copy of the response on the third day of the Blair House Conference, they were incensed. In their view, the United States had stuck to its pre–Camp David positions even where the accords reflected compromise. For example, the document suggested to the Jordanian king that both settlements and "limited numbers of Israeli security personnel" in the West Bank and Gaza would remain "if agreed to by the parties." This implied that the Arab negotiators would have veto power. That appalled the Israelis, who thought they had made clear at Camp David that they regarded their settlements and some military force (however redeployed) in the West Bank and Gaza Strip as permanent. Despite the soft wording of American answers, both the Saudis and the Jordanians dismissed the Camp David agreements.

When he traveled to the area to deliver the answers to Hussein, Saunders told the Palestinian leaders on the West Bank that they should support autonomy because it offered them an opportunity to administer their territory apart from Jerusalem. He said the United States did not believe that Jerusalem should be entirely in Israel's hands.[171] In response, the Begin government announced that it would expand some existing settlements in the West Bank and conveyed its intent at some unspecified date to move the prime minister's office to East Jerusalem (an act it subsequently did not take). These actions did not technically contravene the Camp David commitments, but nonetheless infuriated Jimmy Carter, who cabled a strong protest to Begin. Carter remained annoyed with the Israelis through the next several weeks. Vance announced he was "deeply disturbed."[172]

Begin's reactions to Saunders's statements and Carter's reaction to Begin occurred while Dayan and Weizman were in Israel getting conditional Israeli approval of the draft treaty. When they returned to Washington a bare five days after their departure, the mood had changed radically. The Egyptians at first refused to see the Israelis. When they did agree to meetings, both sides discovered that their previous stands had hardened. The Saunders's exercise had backfired. Rather than securing Saudi and Jordanian participation in the talks, it had only provoked the Israelis into taking tough steps, which in turn alarmed the Egyptians.

Begin then compounded the problem by accepting a long-standing invitation to visit Canada. This took him away from Israel during the next crucial negotiating phase of the Blair House Conference. He also visited New York City before and after his Canadian trip, providing more occasions for his combative personality to annoy American officials. Begin again maneuvered himself into the position of target for American pressure.

The prime minister's first stopover in New York caused several problems. First, Carter, who was there to campaign for the Democratic mayoral candidate, had no plans to see Begin because of his displeasure over the West Bank settlements. The media magnified the apparent snub into a major story and Carter was forced into a short "hug and hello" session with Begin at the apartment of Democratic party activist, Arthur Krim. In New York Begin astonished both Israeli and American negotiators by declaring at a session with Vance that the Israelis sought only a loan and not grant aid for their move out of the Sinai, even though Washington had already agreed to help pay for the transfer of the airfields![173] Two days later the Israeli prime minister had to reverse himself after an outcry in Israel over the huge cost of the withdrawal. This left American officials frustrated and angry. Begin also was still trying to change the draft preamble that linked the Palestinian question with the treaty, but Vance held firm, arguing that any changes could lead to counterdemands from both Egypt and Israel. Besides, American officials were at least as intent on linkage as the Egyptians in order to show the Saudis and Jordanians that the Camp David process was viable.[174]

Meanwhile, the Baghdad Conference, attended by all Arab states except Egypt, denounced the Camp David accords and voted to punish Egypt. If a treaty with Israel were signed, the Arab League headquarters would be moved from Cairo, Egypt would be suspended from the league, and a boycott of Egyptian companies dealing with Israel would be imposed. Secret agreements on additional sanctions were also approved. This development alarmed both the Egyptian and American delegations. Sadat called key delegates home, and the

Israelis—growing more apprehensive that they would be forced into concessions to compensate Egypt for Arab rejection of Camp David—discussed bilateral issues with U.S. officials on such matters as U.S. involvement in the treaty process, guarantees covering a multinational force in the Sinai, and the oil question.[175]

The Egyptian delegation did indeed return with new demands. The bottom line now was Sadat's insistence on a much tighter linkage between the Palestinian question and the peace treaty to appease his Arab critics. He wanted a specific timetable for autonomy negotiations, elections, and Israeli military withdrawal before the peace treaty would be implemented. The Israelis, of course, sought the opposite formula. They wanted to be certain the Egyptian-Israeli treaty was implemented before they made specific moves on the West Bank and Gaza. Meanwhile, the Israelis quarreled with the Egyptians and Americans over coverage of Israel's oil losses after the Sinai withdrawals and Egyptian requests, backed by the United States, for unilateral gestures (such as an early return of the Sinai town of El Arish) that might bolster Sadat's status in the Arab world. With the Americans worried over negative Arab reaction, Sadat over his isolation, and Israel over continued pressure, the Blair House meetings were doomed.

The talks with Begin on his way home from Canada broke no new ground and the Blair House Conference ended the day after he returned to Jerusalem. Two weeks later, with Sadat hardening his demands, the Begin government suddenly accepted in toto the very draft that it had sought to amend a month earlier.[176] It added the proviso, however, that a proposed side letter with a timetable for elections in the West Bank and Gaza must be altered so that the normalization of Egyptian-Israeli relations would not depend on the implementation of autonomy. In response, the Egyptians and Americans accused the Israelis of trying to renege on their Camp David commitment to the Palestinians, accusations the Israelis hotly denied. According to the Camp David accords, autonomy required the cooperation of the Jordanians and West Bankers, but the Israelis pointed out in their own defense that linkage would make realization of the treaty dependent on hostile parties.

The three-month target date set at Camp David for ending the peace treaty discussions (mid-December) was approaching with no breakthrough in sight. The atmosphere of the talks was further clouded by the emerging Iranian crisis as the shah's government faced street demonstrations in the country's main cities. The shah seemed to have lost control. Meanwhile, the administration worried about Saudi oil price and production decisions, a concern that intensified when OPEC (with Saudi acquiescence) raised prices 14.5 percent. The Saudis never explicitly linked this move to their displeasure with the Camp David accords, but it nevertheless reminded the nervous administration of Saudi leverage over the United States.[177]

As tensions in the Middle East itself rose, the importance of concluding the peace treaty increased. The positions of the parties might harden further, and the administration also needed a success to bolster America's weakening position in the area. That meant an agreement by the target date of 17 December in a form that would appease some Saudi and Jordanian objections. In the administration's view, the treaty needed to be linked in some way to the Palestinian question.

In an effort to break the logjam, Carter sent Vance to Cairo and Jerusalem on 10 December. The results were disastrous. Vance traveled first to Cairo and produced several "interpretive notes" and "legal opinions" to be attached to the treaty. In effect, these were Egypt's new demands. Among other things, Sadat insisted that the exchange of ambassadors between Egypt and Israel should occur only after autonomy had been initiated, at least in Gaza. The Israelis argued that this position retreated from the Camp David accords, which stated that full diplomatic relations would be established after Israel's interim withdrawal from the Sinai, scheduled for nine months after the treaty was signed. Vance, in defending Sadat's changed stance, argued that the Egyptian president was entitled to alter his position because his concession had been offered at Camp David in response to an accelerated Israeli withdrawal from El Arish that the Israeli Cabinet had subsequently rejected. It was clear that Sadat realized the importance of ambassadorial exchange to Israel and was using it to tighten the linkage question.[178]

When Vance failed to gain Israeli acceptance of the new Egyptian side notes on the treaty, a drama ensued with striking similarities to March 1975. Shortly after the secretary's plane had left the Tel Aviv airport, a "senior official" aboard blamed the Israelis for the impasse.[179] As in March 1975, a public outcry that the administration was one-sided erupted from Israel's supporters and the press. Critics claimed that Vance had presented Israel with a fait accompli after meeting with Sadat.

The administration soon witnessed a classic example of the pro-Israeli forces in high gear. Leading American Jews and their allies attacked the administration's operating style in statements, articles, and meetings.[180] Unlike 1975, however, no reassessment or a prolonged conflict followed. Despite the acrimony and tension, it was clear that all three sides still sought an accord. Within ten days the administration had arranged a meeting in Brussels with Vance, Dayan, and the new Egyptian prime minister, Mustapha Khalil. The meeting kept the negotiations going and demonstrated again the parties' mutual interest in a resolution as well as the Egyptians' concern about their growing isolation.

From mid-December 1978 to mid-January 1979, American foreign policy makers were occupied with a host of other issues. The administration surprised everyone with the announcement that the United States would normalize relations with China. Speculation ran high that the SALT II agreement would soon be finalized. In the Mideast, the shah was forced to leave Iran. The administration dispatched the secretary of defense to Saudi Arabia to show U.S. military support and staged a demonstrative "fly-in" of a dozen F-15 fighters. Billy Carter's comments on Jews and Israel embarrassed the president.

It was difficult to keep the Egyptian-Israeli talks at the top of the administration's agenda. In the last two weeks of January, Atherton and the State Department legal adviser Herbert Hansell went to Israel and Egypt in a vain effort to get agreement on the side notes. The only result of Atherton's talks in Israel was a new set of interpretive notes, and these were more acceptable to Israel. Now it was the Egyptians' turn to feel that they had been presented with a fait accompli. They played the Israeli role of the previous month and rejected the new agreement out of hand, which led Atherton to abandon *both* sets of notes. The parties were back to where they had been after the Blair House Conference. The Egyptians, however, suggested a new trilateral meeting. At the beginning of February, Carter invited Khalil and Dayan to join Vance at Camp David for another effort to reach agreement.

When this second Camp David meeting convened in the fourth week of February, the Ayatollah Khomeini had become the new Iranian leader. The events in Iran and the continuing harsh reaction in the Arab world to the Camp David accords still weighed heavily on the negotiations. It was likely that the final agreement could be reached only at a summit meeting, which the president had suggested he would call if "Camp David II" did not work.[181]

It is therefore not surprising that this meeting between Vance, Dayan, and Khalil failed. The Egyptians now refused to exchange ambassadors and continued to demand that the treaty be linked to Palestinian autonomy. The suspicious Israeli Cabinet kept Dayan and his team on a tight reign. The tireless American negotiators produced their own proposals, but the Israelis rejected them. At the end of the meetings, Carter, Vance, and Brzezinski met with Dayan and Khalil on Sunday afternoon, 25 February.[182] The president made it clear that he wanted an agreement within ten days. With the shah's fall, the Mideast had become too volatile to allow further delay in the treaty negotiations. (Saudi Crown Prince Fahd had refused the previous week to come to Washington, apparently fearing identification with the United States as it handled the peace treaty negotiations. To make matters worse, a war had broken out between the two Yemens.) With every passing day the possibility of failed negotiations increased.

The president planned to invite Begin and Sadat to another summit, but the Egyptian leader would not attend, saying that Khalil would have full authority to conclude a treaty on Egypt's behalf. Sensing a trap, Begin refused to attend without Sadat, but to soften the blow for Carter, he indicated that he would meet the president alone to discuss the treaty. With no options left, Carter phoned Begin and asked him to the White House for a private meeting, and he insisted that Begin come almost at once. Thus, four days after "Camp David II" had dissolved, Begin arrived in Washington.

At first the meeting appeared to add to the growing gloom. Begin spoke defiantly in public and private, suggesting that the United States had compromised its role as evenhanded mediator by supporting Egyptian positions. As the meetings appeared headed for disaster, however, U.S. officials presented the Israeli prime minister with new proposals for the treaty. Begin reacted favorably and passed them on for positive action by his Cabinet.[183] But several issues remained in dispute. Carter later recalled the situation was of such "desperation" that only a presidential trip might turn stalemate into success.[184] The president made the decision to fly almost immediately to Israel and Egypt to reach final agreement on the treaty. His advisers, stunned by this idea, all opposed it except for Brzezinski and Jordan.[185]

In this tense atmosphere Carter arrived in Egypt on Thursday, 8 March, four days after his meetings with Begin had ended. In discussions with Sadat, the president agreed yet again to amend the proposals approved by Begin in Washington. Upon their arrival in Jerusalem Saturday evening, the American party was optimistic. But Carter soon discovered that Begin would not accept Sadat's amendments and the atmosphere quickly changed. As Carter told Begin at their private dinner Saturday night, he wanted a treaty signed before he left Israel, for Sadat had agreed to join them. But the Israeli leader surprised him by insisting that any agreement must be presented to the Knesset first. Having risked his personal prestige by taking the trip, Carter now used that investment to pressure the Israelis. The president argued he could not afford to fail.[186] Through the first day of the Jerusalem meetings—Sunday, 11 March—Carter pressed for rapid agreement. Begin resisted.

Carter was accompanied by the major players on Middle East policy making, including Vance, Brzezinski, Brown, Atherton, Saunders, Quandt, Hamilton Jordan, and others. The large American team met for most of the day with their Israeli counterparts with no discernible progress. Despite the availability of the U.S. Mideast policy makers and the unprecedented presidential pressure for an agreement, the meetings were interrupted by ceremonial occasions. On Sunday morning, Carter had to visit several symbolic locations in Jerusalem. Since Sunday evening negotiations were interrupted by a gala dinner, tbe Israeli Cabinet met all night to make up lost time. At noon on Monday, Carter, Begin, and opposition leader Peres delivered speeches to a special session of the Knesset. These ceremonies only added to the fatigue and the tension.[187] When diplomatic finesse was required, the Israeli and American teams were exhausted.

The problems raised in combining negotiation and ceremony were apparent in the events of Monday morning, the twelfth. After the all-night meeting broke up at 5:30 A.M., the Cabinet agreed to several compromises. Most important was the Blair House Conference proposal (which the Cabinet had rejected in October) of an early Israeli withdrawal from El Arish in return for an early exchange of ambassadors. These concessions did not satisfy the impatient U.S. delegation, because American officials realized that time was running out on the president's trip and all outstanding disputes had not yet been settled. At a rushed meeting Monday morning with the Israeli Cabinet, Carter supported Egypt's call for a special relationship with Gaza and demanded that the Israelis allow Egyptian liaison officers there. The Israelis feared that this step might lead to claims of sovereignty over the district. They also insisted that Egypt promise to continue selling Israel oil from the wells being returned under the treaty.[188]

The Israeli Cabinet met alone later in the day and then with several top Americans. Carter had frequently phoned Sadat, but Vance had refused to fly to Cairo as had been planned because the secretary believed that the Egyptian leader would reject the latest proposals. The irritation of the negotiators in Jerusalem intensified. The Israelis resented what they regarded as false American leaks blaming their negotiating stance for the disappointing lack of progress. The American delegation resented the cumbersome Israeli procedures, the seemingly endless Cabinet consultations, and the haggling over every word. Carter found Begin peculiarly reluctant to conclude the treaty, almost as though a lifetime of struggle had made it difficult for him to confront peace, especially Palestinian autonomy.[189] By 6:30 Monday evening the last scheduled Israeli-American meeting had broken up in failure. The president was scheduled to leave the next morning.

The turning point came just when the talks appeared to have collapsed. Several Cabinet ministers decided that the opportunity for an Egyptian settlement could not be lost and the president could not be embarrassed by failure. Since only the Gaza issue and the oil supplies remained as obstacles, the ministers resolved to make new suggestions on the oil problem. Dayan phoned Begin, who had barely slept since Carter's arrival forty-eight hours earlier and was about to retire for the night. He authorized his foreign minister to see Vance. Dayan and Vance then spent several hours together, with Vance checking frequently with Carter. At about 3:30 A.M. the secretary and Brzezinski awoke the president with new formulations proposed by the staff.[190]

Vance met again with Dayan for breakfast. New proposals prepared by the American team and based on the overnight discussions would give Israel the right to purchase oil directly from Egypt. If oil were unattainable from any other sources, the United States would guarantee Israel's oil supply for fifteen years. As far as Gaza was concerned, Dayan convinced the American team that there was no need for liaison officers in Gaza: the Egyptians would have access to the area as part of normalization. By including most of these issues in side letters only and deferring some issues for the autonomy discussions, agreements were finally reached. At a breakfast meeting between Begin and Carter, attended by their respective foreign secretaries, the two leaders confirmed the basic understanding.[191] When Carter left Israel, it appeared that the mission had failed. After he stopped over to see Sadat at Cairo International Airport, he amazed the world by announcing a peace treaty. Sadat had accepted all proposals agreed to between Carter and Begin. The Israeli Cabinet then voted its acceptance. The process was complete.

Or almost complete. Arrangements were made for Sadat and Begin to sign the treaty in Washington at the end of March with Carter as witness. But obstacles remained. Only at the last minute were the final touches placed on the U.S.–Israeli Memorandum of Understanding by which the United States gave Israel a security guarantee if Egypt violated the treaty. Begin and Sadat agreed in Washington that Israel would withdraw earlier from El Arish and the oilfields in return for guaranteed permission to purchase Sinai oil.[192]

The final treaty between Egypt and Israel resembled the original Camp David accords except for alterations necessitated by the refusal of the Jordanians and the West Bank Palestinians to participate. Letters attached to the treaty confirmed that the United States would participate as a "full partner" in the talks with Egypt and Israel over the future of the West Bank and the Gaza Strip. These talks had a "target date" of one year to prepare the "modalities for establishing the self-governing authority." Israel stipulated in detail that its forces would withdraw from the western half of the Sinai within nine months after the treaty documents were exchanged, and Egypt agreed to exchange ambassadors the following month. Israel committed itself to withdraw completely from the Sinai by the end of three years. In return, the Carter administration requested and received approval from Congress for $5 billion in supplemental economic and military assistance to the two countries, of which only about $1.2 billion was in the form of grants rather than loans.[193]

At the celebration dinner on 26 March in a tent on the White House lawn, President Carter seemed fully aware of Arab opposition. He said in his toast, "We hope that the Palestinians and others will soon join us in our efforts to make this treaty the cornerstone of a comprehensive peace, a true and a lasting peace, a just peace for the entire Middle East. I welcome and invite those who have so far held back—for whatever motive they might honor—to join us in the future. The way is long and the way is hard, but peace is the way."[194]

Carter thus expressed the anomaly of his administration's Middle East record. At each juncture it had sought a comprehensive settlement only to be thwarted by Arab disputes, other Arabs' hostility to the Sadat peace initiative, and Israeli fears that Egyptian-Israeli agreements would founder on the Palestinian issue. Carter had been forced to choose the possible immediate step instead of the preferable comprehensive approach. The notion of a Geneva Conference had been replaced by an Egyptian-Israeli initiative; at Camp David comprehensiveness had been subordinated to the Egyptian-Israeli arena. In the treaty negotiations, the same process had started again, with the focus on linkage and an autonomy timetable giving way to vaguer formulations accommodating Israeli fears.

Even now the paradox of Carter policy remained. The president's invitations to join the peace process were not heeded. Sadat soon found himself the victim of Arab efforts to isolate Egypt politically and economically. Egypt was suspended from the Arab League, Arab economic aid was aborted, and eighteen Arab states threatened to break diplomatic relations.[195] The administration had believed that Saudi Arabia was crucial to a comprehensive solution, but its close relationship with Riyadh was now unraveling. The Saudis were dismayed with America for sponsoring an Egyptian-Israeli treaty and they were alarmed over Washington's inability to save the shah of Iran. The United States was irritated over the tripling of oil prices during 1979.[196] Meanwhile King Hussein's traditionally cordial relations with U.S. presidents deteriorated to their lowest point when the king refused to join the peace process.

The Egyptian-Israeli peace treaty called for another round of negotiations at the end of May on autonomy for the West Bank and Gaza. Yet, the gargantuan efforts that had been necessary to achieve the treaty had tired all three parties. Leaders in Cairo and Jerusalem saw themselves as having taken huge and largely unappreciated risks for peace—Israel by its willingness to give up assets such as oil fields, air bases, and settlements and Egypt by its willingness to risk alienating other Arab states. As for the Carter administration, it was exhausted by treaty negotiations and the continuing turmoil in Iran.

Carter could not continue to devote so much of his attention to Arab-Israeli matters. The president could not be the administration's principal Middle East operations officer. Therefore, for the next round of talks dealing with Palestinian autonomy, Carter appointed his special trade representative, Robert Strauss, as a "super-ambassador" reporting directly to him. Strauss, however, was inexperienced in Middle East diplomacy and had a serious bureaucratic conflict with the secretary of state over who would have prime authority. Begin and Sadat, accustomed to personal presidential intervention in their negotiations, might not settle for less. Meanwhile, the administration struggled with inflation, energy, Iran, the SALT II treaty, and the 1980 elections. Would it be able to complete the next stage of Arab-Israeli diplomacy?

Autonomy

In the autonomy talks between the United States, Israel, and Egypt which began in late May 1979, the administration was soon tested. The basic problem now confronting the Carter team was inherent in the Camp David accords. The accords provided a means for continuing talks on the Palestinian question, even if the Camp David parties remained the only negotiators, but the concept was flawed. Since Egypt could not speak for the Palestinian residents of the West Bank, its ability and incentive to make viable concessions was limited, especially as its isolation from the Arab world grew. Because Israel was not actually negotiating with the Palestinians but was making concessions to a third party, any Israeli compromises were open to criticism by the various competing Palestinian factions. Since this meant that no one could guarantee the Palestinians' adherence, Israel's incentive for concessions was sharply curtailed. Both the Egyptians and Americans at Camp David had been desperate to show other Arabs that Palestinian negotiations would continue. The projected autonomy talks helped avoid the appearance of an Egyptian-Israeli separate peace, but the talks were severely impeded when the Jordanians and the West Bank Palestinians refused to participate.

In the talks, Egypt was impelled to take a tough stance toward autonomy, hoping to end its isolation in the Arab world. Sadat favored granting such wide latitude to a Palestinian council that it could well have led to an independent state. The Israelis attempted to limit the independent powers and jurisdiction of the Palestinian representatives as much as possible. The Carter team, basically sympathetic to the Egyptian view, sought a strategy to broaden the talks and include the Palestinians, perhaps even the PLO.

In pursuing a new strategy in summer 1979, the administration faced countervailing pressures. On the one hand, it continued to be concerned about the Saudis and key officials believed that a Palestinian initiative was necessary to calm them. The Iranian revolution had nearly cut off Iranian oil production, and in the ensuing panic buying on the oil spot markets, gas lines and soaring prices spread across the United States. The administration won an increase in Saudi production. Less than a month later, one anonymous high-ranking official warned that unless there was noticeable progress toward an autonomy agreement in the next ten weeks, "the West is likely to face increased pressures on its oil supplies."[197] On the other hand, any initiative on the Palestinian question would likely be fought by Israel and her supporters.

Carter, who after Camp David had compared the PLO to Nazis, Communists, and the Ku Klux Klan in early August reversed the analogy and said the Palestinian issue was like the "civil rights movement here in the United States."[198] The White House later claimed that the president had been misinterpreted—he had not referred explicitly to the PLO—but many of Israel's supporters saw this as a renewed flirtation with the PLO, an implication heatedly denied by Vice President Mondale on Carter's behalf. At the same time Israeli-American tensions rose because of Israel's settlements policy in the West Bank and its air raids on Palestinian bases in Lebanon. To allay the concerns of the pro-Israeli lobby, Carter stated, "I am against any creation of a separate Palestinian state. . . ."[199]

As usual, the Carter team feared Saudi oil pressure more than pro-Israeli domestic constraints; further, key officials were committed to progress on the Palestinian question. The administration's Mideast team—including Carter—

next tried for a suitable amendment of U.N. Resolution 242, which had drawn PLO objections because it referred to the Palestinians only as "refugees." The strategy was deceptively simple: instead of merely vetoing an upcoming Kuwaiti-sponsored U.N. resolution calling for a Palestinian state, the United States would negotiate a resolution that it could accept, calling for "Palestinian rights." This would then lead to PLO acceptance of the resolution. Then the Carter administration could deal with the PLO and still be true to the 1975 promise to Israel not to deal with the organization until it recognized Resolutions 242 and 338 and Israel's right to exist. Under this strategy the PLO would ultimately enter the talks.

The new Mideast negotiator, Robert Strauss, however, opposed the proposed modification of Resolution 242 on the grounds that it would only complicate his efforts and would not prove useful. Strauss was attuned to the objections of Israel's supporters because of his political background as a former chairman of the Democratic National Committee. Nonetheless, on his first trip to the area in early August, he was instructed to present the proposal with U.S. endorsement to both Israel and Egypt, which he did—unenthusiastically. The idea was opposed by both Begin and Sadat. The administration was then forced to kill the plan.[200]

The matter would have ended with the Strauss trip except that the Israelis, who monitored the activities of the PLO representative Zehdi Labib Terzi at the United Nations, discovered that Ambassador Young had spoken to him at the home of the Kuwaiti ambassador. The Israelis assumed that the United States was pursuing its new initiative and feared that Young's meeting signaled a major change in U.S. policy. It was not the independent-minded Young's first secret session with a PLO representative.[201]

Young had gone to this meeting on his own: no official in Washington had sanctioned his action. When queried, he first claimed that the incident had not occurred, then suggested that the meeting had been accidental, and finally admitted to Secretary of State Vance that he had gone to the apartment to smooth negotiations for a possible U.N. Security Council resolution on the Palestinians.[202]

Vance was furious. Not only had the U.N. ambassador held an unauthorized meeting at a critical moment in a crucial arena of U.S. foreign policy, but he had then lied about it when asked directly. The secretary told the president that Young's actions were intolerable; if Young remained at his post, Vance would resign.[203] The president had developed a close personal relationship with Young, whom he deeply admired and was loathe to fire lest his standing with American blacks be hurt. The presidential election was less than fifteen months away, and Carter had needed overwhelming black support to give him victory in the southern states in 1976. Under the circumstances, however, he had no choice but to let Young resign.

The incident was the beginning of a gradual estrangement between Vance and Carter, and it damaged Carter's image with both Jews and blacks, prime elements of his Democratic coalition. The president's reluctance to blame Young directly made it seem that Israel or American Jews—not Carter or Vance—had precipitated Young's resignation. Although untrue, this impression caused a political uproar among American black leaders. Many called for a PLO role in peace talks or even a PLO state as a demonstration of solidarity for Young, who, shortly after resigning, had labeled American refusal to talk to the PLO "kind of foolish" and called the Israeli government "stubborn and intransigent."[204] Not surprisingly, American Jewish leaders resented the president's handling of the incident, his failure to denounce Young's errors publicly, and his failure for six weeks to make clear that Young's resignation was not due to pressure from the Israeli government or the American Jewish community. Many Jewish leaders believed that the president's inaction had exacerbated their relations with American blacks. This nightmare of ethnic politics left a residue of bitterness at home and delayed the administration's embarking on another major diplomatic initiative in the autonomy talks. Further delay occurred in early November when Strauss relinquished his post to head the president's reelection campaign and was replaced by Sol Linowitz.

Before the administration could develop another initiative on autonomy in fall 1979, however, its Middle East policy was staggered by a double blow from Iran and Afghanistan. The administration's approach to the area had assumed that answering the Palestinian question and achieving a comprehensive settlement of the Arab-Israeli dispute would be enough to preserve stability. The overthrow of the shah and the tripling of oil prices during 1979, both unrelated to Israel, challenged its philosophy and strategy. These challenges intensified when sixty-six Americans were taken as hostages in the U.S. embassy in Teheran on 4 November and when the Soviets launched an invasion of Afghanistan on 26 December. These events created an entirely new agenda that occupied the administration until its final moment, when the hostages were at last released. The Middle East would remain the top priority, but henceforth there would be concern about an "arc of crisis" extending from Ethiopia to Pakistan. It was ironic that as this administration achieved the greatest American diplomatic victory in the Middle East, other regional conflicts began overshadowing its success.

The twin crises in Iran and Afghanistan moved the American media and public in a pro-defense, anti-Soviet direction. This "toughness" issue helped Carter retain the nomination against Senator Edward Kennedy's challenge, but in the fall the same issue worked in Ronald Reagan's favor.

In the midst of growing crisis, the administration continued to stumble. The U.N. vote on Israeli settlements on 1 March 1980 epitomizes the problems faced by presidents in dealing with the Arab-Israeli dispute. To attract broader support for the Camp David agreements, the administration decided to negotiate acceptable language for a proposed U.N. Security Council resolution initiated by Arab moderates Jordan and Morocco. This resolution would berate Israel for its settlements policy on the West Bank. When similar resolutions had been proposed during the Carter administration, the United States had abstained. U.N. Ambassador Donald McHenry, whose views were if anything more pro-Palestinian than Young's, argued forcefully in favor of a "yes" vote. At the Friday morning breakfast on 28 February, Vance pressed for presidential approval of an affirmative American vote.[205] Mondale, on the campaign trail, and Hamilton Jordan, who might have flagged political problems at home, were not present at the meeting. Edward Sanders, who would not have been at the breakfast but would likely have heard of the initiative, had left the administration by then. The president, therefore, heard only from the diplomatic advisers who wanted an olive branch for the anti-Camp David Arabs.

The compromise resolution considered by the president that morning contained many phrases that not only condemned Israeli settlements policy but also repeatedly used the phrase "including Jerusalem." The president, however, recalled that the Jerusalem issue had almost blocked agreement to the Camp David accords on the last day of the summit and that he had promised Begin that the issue of Jerusalem would be resolved in later negotiations. He ordered that the delegation vote affirmatively only if all references to Jerusalem were deleted; otherwise the United States would abstain. The next day Vance called Carter and told him that all references to Jerusalem had been deleted and so the president authorized an affirmative vote. Neither realized that some references to Jerusalem were still there because a communications breakdown had occurred between the secretary of state, the middle levels of the State Department and the U.N. delegation. State Department officials had told Vance that there was nothing in the resolution that had not been included in U.S. government statements in the past, especially statements by U.N. representatives. Therefore, when McHenry and Saunders gained the removal of wording in a paragraph that had particularly bothered Carter, they thought that it was now acceptable and so informed Vance. Since the president did not ordinarily read the exact text of U.N. resolutions, the United States voted with the other members of the Security Council on Saturday, 1 March, calling upon Israel "to dismantle the existing settlements and in particular to cease, on an urgent basis, the establishment, construction and planning of settlements in the Arab territories occupied since 1967, including Jerusalem."[206]

This tough anti-Israel language created a furor, but controversy became debacle when Carter admitted two days later that the affirmative vote had been an error. He tried to explain what had actually happened, saying, "The United

States' vote in the United Nations was approved with the understanding that all references to Jerusalem would be deleted. The failure to communicate this clearly resulted in a vote in favor of the resolution, rather than abstention."[207]

The administration's credibility with both Israel and the Arabs was shattered. Carter hoped to defeat his challenger, Edward Kennedy, in the New York primary, only three weeks away, and there end Kennedy's candidacy. Many assumed the president admitted the error only to placate the large numbers of Jewish voters in the New York Democratic Party, but the president also was surely concerned that the vote could lessen his "credibility as a mediator" and diminish U.S. influence on the Israelis as the target date for the completion of the autonomy talks drew near. The U.N. vote became a political disaster that worsened Carter's already tense relations with Israel and its supporters. There was little trust left between the White House and American Jews.[208]

When Secretary of State Vance testified on Capitol Hill just a few days before the New York primary, he made matters worse for the president. He stated that U.S. policy had not changed after all, that the Carter administration believed Israeli settlements to be "contrary to international law and an impediment to the successful conclusion of the Middle East peace process." On Jerusalem, he admitted under senatorial questioning that the administration regarded the eastern part of the city as occupied territory. Although Vance's statements were indeed accurate, they reminded Israel's supporters of the tough pressure Carter had frequently used on Israel, and Vance's tone made it appear that the U.N. vote revealed the administration's true policy, notwithstanding its subsequent repudiation. Actually, Vance had refused the president's request that he renounce the policy leading to the vote.[209]

Carter was as furious at Vance as he had been at the original 1 March foul-up, for both incidents emphasized the differences between his administration and Israel.[210] Politically, Carter paid a heavy price for the U.N. vote, its repudiation, and the Vance testimony. Kennedy exploited the issue skillfully, reversed his losing position in the polls, and won the New York primary handily. This victory in a major state enabled him to preserve his candidacy until the convention, which further weakened Carter in the fall race against Reagan. Most analysts agreed that the president would have won the primary except for the controversial U.N. vote that reminded Jewish voters of Carter's tough stand against Israeli settlements and in favor of Palestinian rights rather than his successful negotiation of the Egyptian-Israeli treaty.[211] The incident illustrates the dangers of an informal "Tuesday lunch/Friday breakfast" setting for major decisions. The vote typifies the administration's tendency to alienate political supporters, give contradictory signals, and take great political risks to involve Arabs in the peace process. The incident also dramatizes the major role that Arab-Israeli issues can play in key states during U.S. elections.

The 1 March 1980 vote and its repudiation was not the last administration effort to engineer a breakthrough in the autonomy talks, but it was the last dramatic enterprise and the last time the administration blew its lines on the Mideast stage. Vance had presented the administration's case clearly a month earlier:

> There is no doubt but that the Palestinian question remains the most troubling issue in the Arab-Israeli relationship. It does make it more difficult to draw together in a cooperative effort the moderate Arabs and the United States in dealing with the threats and problems which we face in the region and we must therefore continue to pursue and indeed intensify our efforts to try and find a solution to the Palestinian issue in all of its aspects.[212]

In the autonomy talks, the administration could not settle conflicting Israeli and Egyptian interpretations of the Palestinian council. Israel preferred an administrative body, and Egypt insisted on an authority vested with "full powers of self-governance." Questions of security, water, land (including settlements), and voting by East Jerusalem Arabs also remained. The May 1980 target date came and went without results, even though the administration earnestly sought to keep the talks going despite crises. For example, in July the Knesset voted to reaffirm a united Jerusalem as the Israeli capital and Sadat postponed the autonomy talks in protest. Finally, the administration announced that the president would convene another summit with Begin and Sadat if he were reelected. Meanwhile, Vance resigned at the end of April following the abortive Iranian rescue operation and was replaced by Senator Edmund Muskie. Although no major policy changes resulted, Vance's experience was missed in the autonomy talks.[213]

By fall the election campaign prevented any diplomatic initiatives, and Iraq's attack on Iran presented yet another Mideast crisis. Linowitz continued to negotiate quietly with Begin and Sadat, reaching confidential understandings with both, but in the atmosphere of an election campaign no delicate negotiations could be completed.[214] The controversy over his brother Billy's Libyan involvement further undermined Carter's credibility with American Jews and with many non-Jews as well. Many American Jews feared that Carter would pressure Israel on the Palestinian question if he were reelected.

Conclusion

Carter's dream of settling the Arab-Israeli dispute was thwarted in midcourse. He was the first president, however, whose record was likely to be judged by his accomplishments in the Middle East. The Egyptian-Israeli peace treaty was his notable diplomatic achievement, but Iran and Afghanistan symbolized his inability to deal with direct challenges to the United States. Meanwhile, the autonomy negotiations dragged on, dramatizing Carter's frustration over the Palestinian question.

In Mideast engagements, this president had been guided by an innovative global philosophy, which by the end of his term seemed inadequate for the complexity of events. This inadequacy was magnified by frequent communication snafus. Unlike administrations in which the president was forewarned by internal dissension, Carter was often blinded by the astounding philosophical consensus among his advisers. Rarely had a president been so closely identified with a philosophy that was refuted by events abroad. Carter's presidency became a peculiar testing ground for concepts derived from Vietnam and applied with particular vehemence to the Mideast. Carter's policies represented the culmination of past efforts and the origin of new challenges. The Egyptian-Israeli peace treaty represents an Arab-Israeli settlement that six previous presidents had failed to achieve, but Carter nevertheless did not get the comprehensive peace he had set out to accomplish. The rise of anti-American Islamic fundamentalism in Iran, the hostage crisis, the Iran-Iraq war, the Soviet invasion of Afghanistan—these foreshadowed a wider conflict that the Carter team, with its focus on the Palestinian question, was ill-equipped to address. In the end, Carter's single-mindedness in the Middle East had produced both stunning success and failure. His mission was left only partially complete because of crisis in the area and rejection at home.

9

STARS AND IDEAS
The Key to U.S. Policy Formation

This discourse on the formulation of U.S. policy dealing with the Arab-Israeli dispute brings us to ask, finally, how can we explain the record? Why does policy evolve as it does and who is responsible for the course of events? In short, what lessons are to be learned from almost four decades of American experience? On the one hand, these years have been filled with common perceptions and consistent concerns. On the other hand, new policies have been offered to meet a changing set of problems. Are there any discernible patterns? How do we account for a changing policy within a static framework?

Factors of Continuity

Certainly, there have been continuities that reflect the American style in foreign affairs and a consensus on U.S. interests.

1. Although their emphases have differed, American leaders have consistently sought to prevent Soviet expansion, limit Arab radicalism, promote Arab moderates and pro-American governments throughout the area, and preserve both petroleum supplies and the sea-lanes and pipelines through which oil is shipped to the West.

2. No matter how high tensions between the two governments might rise, no administration since 1948 has wavered from a fundamental commitment to the security and survival of the State of Israel.

3. American leaders have consistently assumed that they knew better than other involved statesmen how to provide for the peace and security of the

region. In the decade after the Second World War these attitudes were manifested in a mild anticolonialism toward the British and French, culminating in the Suez Crisis. In the 1970s Henry Kissinger's shuttle diplomacy and Jimmy Carter's critical role in consummating the Egyptian-Israeli peace treaty reinforced a sense that the future of the area would be determined by American plans. The effect of these presuppositions was to encourage a consistent unilateralism in American diplomacy, undergirded by a belief that America's allies had made errors that the United States would not repeat.

4. All American leaders were affected by the formative experience of the immediate postwar period, which culminated in the establishment of the state of Israel. Since the struggle over Israel's birth coincided with the United States' first sustained involvement in the Middle East and since the issue occasioned intense public interest, Americans tended to see the Middle East as the Arab-Israeli arena. The assumption prevailed that resolving this dispute would solve other problems faced by the United States in the area, such as the expansion of the U.S.S.R., Arab radicalism, or the instability of energy supplies. This belief resulted in various peace plans and overtures designed to organize the Arab states against communism among other "higher" objectives.

5. Because of this concentration on the Arab-Israeli dispute, administrations consistently ignored the potential impediments to U.S. policy arising from other sources in the area. Thus, conflicts within the Arab world often upset American plans and policies—from the Baghdad Pact to the Yemen War to the Camp David formulation, from Eisenhower's Johnston Plan to Kennedy's Johnson Plan to Carter's design for a Geneva Conference. Moreover, American experiences in the Middle East have not prepared U.S. leaders to deal with conflicts other than those involving the Arab-Israeli issue. Therefore, in the 1950s, struggles between Iraq and Egypt for supremacy in the Arab world were viewed as part of the global confrontation between capitalism and communism. Similarly, being outside the Arab-Israeli focus, the turmoil in the Persian Gulf after the British departure in 1971 was not anticipated. The implications of an Iranian upheaval in 1978–79 and the Soviet invasion of Afghanistan in 1979 were not at first understood because of long experience with the shah and with a neutral government in Kabul.

Alternative Models

This pattern of consistent objectives and perceived interests does not explain why individual decisions have been made by successive American leaders nor does it account for the changes in those policies. Recent analysts have offered three approaches to fill the gap: systems theory, bureaucratic and organizational models, and pluralist theory.

Systems Theory

Systems theory stresses the economic and military strength of the states that confront one another in any given period. It explains developments by the interaction of these states and their balance of power rather than by focusing on internal developments within particular countries. According to this approach, the system changes when the number or power of major states alters, resulting in new rules governing the system.[1]

In American policy toward the Middle East, an emphasis on the international system identifies the external constraints on the United States. Although the system has evolved gradually, remaining substantially the same, government policies have changed and often quite dramatically. If the international system could explain these changes, if leaders were largely reacting to outside events, then major regional developments such as the overthrow of regimes, diplomatic initiatives by individual states, and wars would account for new directions pursued by policy makers. Indeed, many authors do argue that crises explain changes in American policy.[2]

Yet the pattern that emerges clearly from this study is that crises do not alter the basic policy of an administration. Rather, the administration adapts to changes in the regional environment in light of its existing attitudes. While crises frequently increase the priority of the Middle East so that new tactics are devised, fundamental changes occur only when the next administration takes office. Thus, Eisenhower and Dulles opposed British, French, and Israeli policy in the Middle East from the outset—long before Suez; they met the Czech-Egyptian arms deal with the Aswan Dam offer instead of with hostility to Nasser because a strengthened Egyptian-American relationship was central to their Mideast policy. The Suez crisis itself was followed by the Eisenhower Doctrine— an updated and diluted version of their original notion, the Baghdad Pact. Rethinking the consequences of Suez and adjusting to the new conditions created by the crisis and the new direction of Egyptian policy occurred only when the Kennedy administration arrived. Similarly, the Johnson administration muddled through in its Middle East policy after June 1967. With the exception of the U.N. mission negotiating U.N. Security Council Resolution 242, an act that did not involve top levels of the administration, there were no major initiatives. Rather, the Nixon administration entered office with an agenda for the area; and its experiences during the first term were epitomized by the three Rogers plans. Even before 6 October 1973, its strategy was in place and Kissinger was pursuing it. The Egyptian and Syrian attack gave him and an anxious Nixon the opening they were seeking. In response to the Mideast and energy crises, the basic policy innovations on issues such as the Palestinians, a comprehensive peace, and the U.S.S.R. awaited the advent of the Carter administration. That new policy team in turn was so preoccupied with convening a Geneva Conference that it had difficulty adjusting to Sadat's Jerusalem trip.

Thus, what explains American policy after a crisis are the assumptions and attitudes held by U.S. policy makers before the external event. Systems theory is not borne out by the history of the period. Each situation demanded reaction, but the leaders had wide latitude in their choice of tactics. Their prior strategy and assumptions, not the conditions surrounding the external event, explain how they reacted. Thus, to understand American policy toward the Middle East, it is a necessary but insufficient first step to assess the power of the United States, its limits and advantages, the existence, location, and military and economic power of all involved states. These are continuing constraints. If systems theory does not fully explain how and why policy is formulated, we must turn inward—toward the American context itself. Here the two other theories may prove useful.

Bureaucratic and Organizational Theories

Decision-making theories often stress bureaucratic and organizational factors in explaining why the United States acts as it does.[3] "Where you stand depends upon where you sit" has become the motto of a generation of scholars who emphasize the policy constraints epitomized by the permanent civil service and agencies with their own interests. This study indeed confirms the extraordinary power of the bureaucracy and its influence over the context in which every president views foreign policy. Invariably, each new administration is greeted with papers and plans, especially from the State Department, suggesting how the new leadership should conduct Mideast policy and adjust to the "realities" of decision making. These ideas often differ from the president's campaign promises. Secretaries of state are influenced at least in part by the arguments of the Near East Bureau, even if they did not agree with its assumptions before taking office.

As often noted in the literature and confirmed in this study, bureaucracies are slow to implement and even apt to sabotage policies with which they disagree; they have greater latitude when the policy is of lesser priority and the president is less involved. Examples abound. Under Truman we can cite the Morrison-Grady Plan, the attempts to undermine United States support for partition, the 1948 arms embargo, trusteeship, backing of the Bernadotte Plan, delays in de jure recognition of Israel. Examples under Eisenhower include the bureaucratic infighting between those who favored an Egypt-first strategy and those boosting the Baghdad Pact, the conflict that followed the CIA's warnings that a Soviet arms deal with Nasser was imminent, and its attempts to dilute John Foster Dulles's reaction when the deal was announced. Under Kennedy the Near East Bureau sought to keep the Johnson Plan alive even after the president had "buried" it, while under President Johnson the Near East Bureau and the Pentagon sought to undermine the "Red Sea Regatta" supported by the president during the May 1967 crisis. Under Nixon the conflict between Rogers and Kissinger unleashed massive bureaucratic infighting to gain presidential backing of the Rogers Plan, to prevent a new Phantom arms deal with Israel, and to neutralize Israeli accusations that the Egyptians had broken the cease-fire in August 1970. Under Ford a proposed 1975 arms deal with Jordan was set back when Congressional testimony revealed that the Joint Chiefs favored a smaller sale. Earlier in the year, many diplomats tried unsuccessfully to persuade Ford and Kissinger to turn to a more comprehensive approach. Under Carter bureaucratic initiatives helped create the communications gap between the president and his secretary of state over the 1 March 1980 U.N. Security Council vote censuring Israel.

Opponents of the State Department or NSC bureaucracy can sabotage or alter specific policies as well. Examples include Niles's circumvention of the presidential decision against lobbying for partition at the U.N. in 1947, the Air Force initiative during the Yom Kippur War in preparing an airlift to Israel in case it was ordered, and Strauss's unenthusiastic presentation to Begin and Sadat of the presidential plan for revising U.N. Resolution 242 in summer 1979.

We have also seen that bureaucratic interests, functions, and roles can change over time. In the 1950s the CIA's Mideast covert operations under Kermit Roosevelt had extraordinary latitude, while relations between the Defense Intelligence Agency and the Israelis were extremely close between 1967 and 1973. There was prevailing skepticism in the Pentagon (led by a hostile secretary of defense) over the birth of Israel in 1947 and 1948. Twenty years later that negativism turned positive as Israel used Western equipment against Russian arms to defeat the Arabs, provided important information to the United States during the Vietnam War, and bore the major responsibility for the closing of the Suez Canal, making Soviet assistance to the North Vietnamese more difficult. By the late 1970s, that prevailing attitude had been reversed again because of some officers' resentment at the generous U.S. resupply effort of scarce equipment to Israel during October 1973 and because new needs in the Persian Gulf increased interest in bases on Arab soil and arms sales to moderate Arab regimes.

This ample catalog of bureaucratic activity and influence might suggest that the bureaucratic model best explains U.S. policy for dealing with the Arab-Israeli dispute. Yet over the years most officials involved with Mideast policy have been critical of successive U.S. administrations. They will complain about their lack of influence even to the most casual acquaintance. Typical is Johnson's 1968 Phantom arms sale to Israel in which the Washington bureaucratic community (except for the chairman of the Joint Chiefs of Staff) was united against the deal and the president still ruled against them. Even during the Dulles era, in a period of alienation from Israel, most officials dealing with the

Middle East criticized the administration's policy, particularly its preoccupation with the communist menace. Since the Truman era, many bureaucratic agencies have repeatedly but unsuccessfully opposed the amount of aid to Israel. It is worth remembering that, despite prodigious efforts, bureaucrats did not permanently block U.S. support for partition or recognition of Israel or Eisenhower's support for the Baghdad Pact or Nixon's expansion of arms shipments to Israel and acceptance in 1970 of Israeli accusations of Egyptian cease-fire violations. Nor did they succeed in dissuading Kissinger from returning to shuttle diplomacy in 1975. The 1 March 1980 vote was in the end revoked by Carter.

Thus, bureaucratic influence is deceptive. The "permanent government" is able to influence principal policy makers, to mold options through papers and cables, and to delay or facilitate implementation. But the bureaucracies are themselves often divided, the interests and roles of some agencies change over time, and, whatever their influence, the context and direction of policy is set by higher officials. Bureaucrats usually succeed better in delaying or accelerating policy formulation and implementation than in making decisions. Examining bureaucratic preferences over the years would not explain U.S. policy toward the Middle East. The bureaucracy is a constraint rather than a source of policy change.

Pluralist Theory

The frustration of many in the bureaucracy leads us to the third explanation, one rooted in pluralist theory—namely, that the influence of pro-Israeli interest groups (especially the American Jewish community in presidential and congressional elections) shapes U.S. policy toward the Arab-Israel dispute.[4] The accounts in this volume demonstrate clearly that this assumption is false. Domestic politics affects the timing and handling of decisions more than their actual content. Presidents try to avoid antagonizing Israel's supporters in an election year, especially a presidential year. They will delay decisions or manipulate announcements so that they receive credit for favorable actions. Yet they make decisions generally for reasons of state, largely unrelated to domestic politics and often in defiance of domestic groups.

Examples abound from this study.

1. In 1948 the Zionists and their allies did not prevent trusteeship from being proposed nor could they undo the United States' arms embargo to the entire area, an action that clearly favored the Arabs. Truman recognized Israel because the Jews there had created a fait accompli, which the United States was as powerless to prevent as were the British. Domestic politics determined only the timing and announcement of the decision, not its content. The president told his secretary of defense in 1946 that he would not be influenced by the Zionists or by oil.

2. Eisenhower repeatedly defied Israel's supporters and won, most spectacularly during the Suez crisis as the presidential elections were being held and in the February 1957 speech to the nation that insisted on complete Israeli withdrawal from the Sinai.

3. Kennedy sold Hawk anti-aircraft missiles to Israel because the British and French did not have comparable sophisticated equipment to counter the Russian weapons that the Egyptians were receiving, but he was careful to let the information leak during the 1962 congressional campaign.

4. Johnson accelerated military sales to Israel because the United States had increased aid to Jordan, not because of domestic politics. In the May 1967 crisis Johnson acted cautiously and hestitantly, despite entreaties from Israel's supporters for some clear action to lift the Egyptian blockade of the Straits of Tiran. Later, Johnson sold Phantom jets to Israel at the height of the 1968 presidential campaign because the Russians would not agree to an arms limitation arrangement for the area, but he was sure to have the announcement made before the election.

5. Kissinger points out that Nixon frequently wished to oppose Israel's supporters to show his independence of domestic politics, but he often acted in ways advocated by Israel's backers for geopolitical reasons (as in the airlift in October 1973). Nixon's notes to Kissinger, as they have been revealed, are filled with demands to confront rather than accommodate the "Israel lobby." Thus, the Rogers Plan, the delays in selling Phantom jets to Israel in 1969 and 1970, the limited peace initiative of 1971—all were pursued in the face of varying domestic pressures.

6. Similarly, Ford pursued a highly publicized and unpopular "reassessment" of U.S. Mideast relations in early 1975 to press Israel toward negotiations. When Ford and Kissinger decided to return to the Egyptian-Israeli negotiations, many who favored a comprehensive approach blamed the pro-Israeli forces, especially because they had just persuaded seventy-six senators to sign a letter endorsing their position. Yet the decision was actually made in spite of the letter (it annoyed Ford) because Sadat and Rabin sought another accord and because Ford and Kissinger did not believe that comprehensiveness or any other alternative would succeed.

7. No president, however, confronted Israel's supporters as repeatedly and as publicly as Jimmy Carter. When faced with a clear conflict between his and his advisers' views on the one hand and those of Israel's supporters on the other, he almost always opposed Israel's backers. Examples include Carter's declarations on a homeland for the Palestinians and the importance of Israeli territorial withdrawals, his overtures to the PLO, his tough stance on Israeli settlements in occupied territory, the sale of sixty-two F-15s to Saudi Arabia in 1978, his blaming Israel for the failure to reach a peace treaty in December 1978, the effort to rewrite U.N. Resolution 242 in summer 1979 and the 1

March 1980 U.N. vote. Carter sometimes did modify his initial policy preferences, but in each case he was moving primarily to keep Menachem Begin's government from cutting off particular negotiations in progress. Domestic pressures beset this president, but their effects on his policies were muted.

Most presidents were annoyed at times with pro-Israeli groups (Truman, Eisenhower, Nixon, Ford, Carter). Some regarded them with cautious cordiality (Kennedy, Johnson). All treated the pro-Israeli lobby as a political force to be reckoned with.

Friends of Israel around the country and in Washington have created a positive atmosphere toward Israel on Capitol Hill. Their task has been facilitated by the readiness of many congressmen to be sympathetic for various reasons: ideology, impact of the Holocaust, perceived personal political advantage, and the support of Israel traditional in U.S. politics. But how have these activities and sympathies affected the policy of successive administrations? By helping to create a pro-Israel environment in Washington, these activities may have slowed policies antagonistic to Israel and favorable to the Arabs. The fact remains that broad pro-Israeli statements by congressmen have not prevented disputes between every administration and the Israelis. Congress has been largely irrelevant to U.S. participation in the Mideast peace process.

The leverage exercised by Congress has been on aid for Israel. Congress has never blocked an arms sale to an Arab country, but both houses have regularly increased the amounts of aid to Israel above administration requests and have influenced arms sales favorably for the Jewish state. For example, both Johnson and Nixon used congressional pressure to justify sending Phantom jets to Jerusalem despite bureaucratic hostility. Carter increased the number of F-15s to be sold to Israel as a result of bargaining with Congress over the 1978 Mideast arms package.

Individual congressmen have lobbied hard for particular issues or for assistance favored by Israel. Congressmen from the same party as the president have often urged him to help Israel lest their party suffer. Conversely, congressmen from the opposition have often used the Israeli issue as a political club against the president. Seen in isolation, this activity is impressive, even awesome. However, when the pattern of decision making within the executive branch is studied, it becomes clear that individual decisions are ordinarily made for reasons unrelated to domestic politics and then packaged so as to flatter the administration.

These factors begin to explain why the pro-Israeli lobby is universally (and incorrectly) thought to have great leverage if not a determining impact on U.S. Mideast policy. First, most observers assume that the activities of the pro-Israeli forces will influence the executive branch, especially because they have an impact on Capitol Hill. Second, all parties involved have an interest in perpetuating the myth. Jewish leaders and activists use it to promote their work.

Congressmen use it to demonstrate their own contribution to the Israeli cause and their services to their constituents. Presidents find the legend useful to suggest that they heed those who advocate Israel's cause, especially when they do not.

The myth is even more useful to opponents of Israel. Bureaucrats and corporate officials find it enormously helpful in explaining to the Arab officials and businessmen with whom they deal in the Middle East why U.S. policy has not been more sympathetic to Arab demands, interests, or whims. Implicitly, they say don't blame America (or our friends in America) to the detriment of our relations; blame the Zionists and let's get on with the matter at hand. Only when the myth is taken to its logical extreme and erupts in antisemitism, with accusations of ubiquitous Jewish control of American institutions, do most participants shrink from its implications. Denunciations of extremism routinely follow, but the inaccurate perception of policy formulation remains. A typical example is the reaction to the statement by the late Joint Chiefs chairman George Brown in 1974 that Jews controlled the banks and media in the United States.

Just as many frustrated bureaucrats have concluded that Jewish groups are responsible for America's policy toward the Middle East, many of Israel's supporters think that U.S. policy is heavily influenced by commercial interests. That assumption is equally false. Oil companies and other groups with commercial interests have sought to lobby congressmen, but commercial interests have been more concerned with their own benefits (such as securing favorable tax write-offs) than with influencing specific Mideast policies. However, huge arms sales to Arab states (especially Saudi Arabia) after the mid-seventies interested many corporations because of potential profit from the sales or the fear a congressional veto would adversely affect present or future contracts. By the late 1970s these corporations were often aligned with the growing number of pro-Arab organizations in Washington on these issues, but their actions only strengthened an administration and bureaucracy predisposed in their direction for other reasons—concerns about energy supplies, a desire for Mideast bases and enthusiasm for arms sales. The corporations did not produce changes in policy; if Carter had decided not to sell F-15s to Saudi Arabia, they could not have altered the decision.

Through the years, the interested sector of the corporate community has maintained contacts with bureaucratic officials dealing with the Mideast. Many officials in both business and government have served together abroad on Mideast matters, but the corporation executives most frequently preached to the converted and only reinforced established views. In the end they were no more effective in their quieter approach than their more public opponents within the pro-Israeli camp.

Congress, like the international system and the bureaucracy, constrains any administration. Congressmen rarely influence specifics; on aid issues their influence is greatest, on the intricacies of diplomacy, least. Congressmen and the lobbies that try to influence them provide part of the context in which policy is made. But the role of domestic institutions is analogous to that of states in the international system: they shape the environment confronting decision makers. Domestic constraints, like external ones, may change over time but do so only gradually (as with the rising or declining importance of oil, the perceived threat of the U.S.S.R., the rise of an "Arab lobby," or the changing image of Israel). Normally, domestic and external constraints are part of the givens that any decision maker must confront.

The Presidential Elite

Against those who look to structures to discern fundamental realities, I believe that American foreign policy can be understood only by studying the ideas, the attitudes, and the experiences of the "people at the top." It may be useful to study trends in American politics and society, but unless we understand the purposes of key policy makers, we will miss the reasons that changes occur as they do. The system, the bureaucracy, Congress, and interest groups account for the continuity of American policy in relation to the Arab-Israeli dispute, but it is the presidential elite that generates change. Therefore, in trying to understand why the United States acts in a particular way at any point, the approach of key policy formulators in Washington must be investigated. Other decision makers would not necessarily have conducted policy in a similar manner, even when facing the same problems.

An analysis of the administrations that have conducted Arab-Israeli policy shows us that when the players change, the policies change. Roosevelt made opposing promises to the Zionists and Arabs; he did not press the British, and, as was his style, he often pursued policy through procrastination. When Roosevelt addressed the Palestine Mandate, duplicity coexisted with consistency. His successor was as straightforward as he was inconsistent. Truman was ready to make demands on London and thereby, within limits, involve the United States in the Palestinian question for the first time. Roosevelt had a clearer sense of direction, often acting as his own secretary of state. Toward Palestine he was concerned not to alienate either the Arabs or the British. Truman, by contrast, had a specific objective—helping Jewish refugees—even if he had problems with both the Arabs and London. Yet he had little understanding of how to achieve his objective; by consulting advisers with different views and perspectives over time, he produced sudden lurches in U.S. policy.

To Roosevelt and Truman, the Arab-Israeli issue had been peripheral, but Eisenhower and Dulles saw the area as central to containing international communism. The Baghdad Pact, the Aswan Dam offer, the Suez crisis, the Eisenhower Doctrine, and the intervention in Lebanon were some of the results of the increased importance they gave the area. Similarly, a new policy toward both Israel and Nasser's Egypt came about only because the Kennedy administration entered office with a different perspective, one that favored promoting U.S. relations with a number of emerging Third World nationalists anxious to remain neutral between East and West. When Johnson assumed the presidency, he brought to the Oval Office admiration for Israel mixed with interest in promoting relations with the more conservative and pro-Western Arab regimes.

The Johnson administration, traumatized and preoccupied with Vietnam, could not deal in depth with the changed Middle East after the Six-Day War. Nixon, by contrast, came to office determined to rebuild U.S. relations with the Arab world and displace Soviet influence with American dominance. At first constrained by competing world issues, his chief foreign policy aide, Henry Kissinger, ultimately achieved these objectives by carefully isolating specific issues in the Arab-Israeli problem after the October 1973 war. That was not enough for Jimmy Carter, who entered office zealously committed to achieving a comprehensive solution of the Arab-Israeli problem, a deemphasis on competition with the U.S.S.R., a determination to address the Palestinian question directly, and an overriding concern with the energy crisis.

In all of these cases, the old adage, "a new broom sweeps clean," applies: a new foreign policy team brings with it new global philosophies and tactics. These approaches may be rooted in the personal or professional experiences of leading officials, in the attitudes prevailing at selected think tanks and universities, or in the concerns of particular corporations, bureaucracies, or interest groups in which the new leaders previously participated. In this psychological era, many writers concentrate on the dynamics of perception—or the "operational codes" of individual leaders—in explaining international developments.[5] Yet this study demonstrates that the presidential elite governs with policy ideas and a philosophy that create the environment in which it makes decisions. For example, Truman was caught between the Soviet threat as he saw it and the peripheral problem of doing something for Jewish refugees in Palestine. Eisenhower and Dulles shared a concern for the global onslaught of the "Sino-Soviet bloc" and sought to organize the Arabs to withstand it. Expressing a more "progressive" outlook, Kennedy aimed to make U.S. policy more appealing to nationalists like Nasser; and Johnson embarked on a global crusade against international communism that became mired in Vietnam, leaving little time for concern with the Middle East. Nixon and Kissinger gave the Middle East a key place in their calculations for a new balance of power, while Carter saw the area as an opportunity for a new foreign policy that would stress human rights and economic interdependence. In each case the tactics and responses to events flowed from the philosophical approach of the top players of the administration. As John Lewis Gaddis argues, "There exist for presidential administrations certain 'strategic' or 'geopolitical' codes, assumptions about American interests in the world, potential threats to them, and feasible responses, that tend to be formed either before or just after an administration takes office, and barring very unusual circumstances tend not to change much thereafter."[6]

As the ultimate authority, the president is the critical actor in any period because his interests and concerns set the tone, and he selects the major officials and the roles they play in particular policy decisions. Without sharing his global view, they are not likely to remain in power (for example, Henry Wallace under Truman; Chester Bowles under Kennedy; Charles Yost under Nixon). Yet officials often disagree on how the predominant global perspective applies in the Middle East, especially when the area is given low priority. Thus, Marshall and Acheson were secretaries of state greatly admired by Truman but they differed with him markedly on the Arab-Israeli dispute. Similarly, Rusk and Johnson viewed Vietnam similarly but Israel very differently.

Many writers suggest that there is an optimal way of organizing the presidency so that decisions can be made effectively.[7] Yet this study shows that the organization of the presidency is less important than the caliber of the key figures and the relations between them. The president not only determines who participates in decisions, but how many officials, where and how. He selects the cabinet, the White House staff, all major national security figures, and his own personal advisers. This selection is especially important in the Middle East, because White House officials from Clark Clifford to Henry Kissinger to Walter Mondale have frequently differed with State Department representatives. Policy toward the Arab-Israeli dispute has often provoked major confrontations: Henderson versus Niles and Marshall versus Clifford under Truman; Komer versus Feldman under Kennedy; Arthur Goldberg and Eugene Rostow versus Rusk and Battle under Johnson; and most spectacularly, Rogers versus Kissinger under Nixon. When presidents like Eisenhower and Carter held particularly strong and well-developed views on the Middle East, however, these debates among subordinates have been limited. Thus, what has mattered more than the decision-making system of the administration has been the personalities of the critical officials, the relations between them, and—most important—their individual views on Middle East policy.

In this light the greatest changes in U.S. policy occur when administrations are altered and a complete new foreign policy team assumes office. Since the president selects the policy elite, a new president creates a new foreign policy team. In other words, the more players change the more policies change.[8] Not since 1928 has a new president been elected from the same party as his predecessor (Hoover after Coolidge). As confirmed by the Mideast experience, the greatest changes in policy perspectives occur when a new president assumes office from a different party, as happened under Eisenhower, Kennedy, Nixon, and Carter.

Three vice-presidents in the post-1945 period have entered the Oval

Office suddenly and therefore presided over more limited transitions: Truman, Johnson, and Ford. Because Truman's ascendency coincided with a period of enormous change in international and domestic affairs and Roosevelt's death occurred at the outset of a new term, this transition most closely resembled a normal change of government. With Johnson and Ford, the changes were more subtle. Johnson brought greater conservatism and sentimental attachment to Israel and less skill in foreign affairs than Kennedy showed. Although most of the key foreign policy advisers remained, at least for a time, the political and intellectual atmosphere altered. The transition from Nixon to Ford, with Kissinger at the helm, made the least difference of all the administrations studied. Nixon, even while preoccupied with Watergate, knew his foreign policy goals, including a need for frequent diplomatic success during the Watergate crisis. Ford, by comparison, had no such vision or pressure; Kissinger's Mideast diplomacy became more cautious during his presidency.

Power is measured in any administration by access to and influence with the president. Therefore, when personnel change within a presidency, the difference can greatly affect the conduct of foreign affairs. The greater the status and influence of the departing official, the more important the change. Thus, when Christian Herter replaced the dying Dulles in early 1959, the result was a quieter, less dynamic and volatile Mideast policy than had been conducted previously in the Eisenhower period. Forrestal's departure as secretary of defense in early 1949 removed one of the firmest opponents of a Jewish state within the higher echelons of the Truman administration. Marshall was not so opposed to establishing the State of Israel as was Acheson. Nixon's first secretary of defense, Melvin Laird, was more fearful than James Schlesinger that America's support for Israel might lead to military involvement. Kissinger's replacing Rogers in September 1973 prepared the way for a unified decision-making approach on the eve of the Yom Kippur war. There was nothing inevitable about specific policies; other advisers might have pursued different strategies by different methods.

Conclusion

We thus see that in American policy dealing with the Arab-Israeli dispute, policy changes within a static framework. The international system, the bureaucracy, Congress, and interest groups account for the constant picture, but they limit policy; they do not define it. Only by examining the attitude of the presidential elite do we understand why and how policy changes. Directions do not ordinarily change within an administration (unless there is a major shift of personnel), even when outside events would seem to demand major new approaches. Rather, policy changes occur when a new administration enters, because this is the time when the largest number of personnel, including the highest ranking officials, change. Most studies deal with one crisis, one decision, or one period of time. By dealing with one issue over many administrations, we can see more clearly the effect of different presidential elites.

Every president enters office with a global and regional philosophy. As events develop during the presidency, the chief executive is affected not only by his previous attitudes but by his White House advisers, his informal contacts within and outside government, and the chief foreign policy officials of the administration. Because no president can deal only with the Middle East, those officials shape his views when he is involved with other matters. Yet the president selects his advisers and all of them emerge from a particular philosophical milieu, whatever the differences among them on specific policy questions. It is the relationship among these advisers, their policy positions and their relative power within the administration, that determine policy more than the formal decision-making system used by the president for international affairs. This study demonstrates that factors such as Congress, domestic groups, bureaucracies, and crises have less significance in determining the content of U.S. policy toward the Arab-Israeli dispute. Perhaps the most important influence of all groups and agencies is the political perspective that they have given policy makers. Battling for the hearts and minds of the American elite has been the true subject of the Arab-Israeli war for Washington.

POSTSCRIPT
Reagan—the First Three Years

The first three years of the Reagan administration confirmed the principal arguments of this volume. The broad contours of policy are clear even before most of the memoirs of the major participants are written. Certainly documents are not available; interviews with scholars and in-depth assessments by journalists have not been carried out, and oral histories have not been recorded. Nevertheless, the Reagan administration's foreign policy seems likely to be remembered as one with a distinct philosophical perspective, formulated by a passive and even uninvolved chief executive who was surrounded by competing and frequently changing players.

The Carter Legacy

In order to understand the domestic constraints on Reagan and Carter's influence on his initial success, it is necessary to look back at the Democratic party during the presidential campaign of 1976. The foreign policy community of the Democratic party was divided into four factions. The first two groups were composed of mostly older individuals who had supported the Vietnam War; the second two were made up of younger persons who had opposed the Vietnam experience or turned against it early on.

The first group consisted mostly of middle-aged men with previous government experience, men like Vance, Brzezinski, Warnke, Ball, and Brown. Many had served during the Vietnam War years and rejected the decisions and assumptions of the 1960s. Some carried a sense of guilt from the war. Aspiring to reenter government service, they sought to avoid the negative historical judg-ment pinned on their former superiors by authors like David Halberstam in *The Best and the Brightest.*[1]

The magazine *Foreign Affairs,* published by the Council on Foreign Rela-tions, represented the views of this group. Its editor, William P. Bundy, was a former assistant secretary of state for Far Eastern affairs. In substantive foreign policy matters, it had a tendency to stress North-South rather than East-West relations. Generally accommodationist toward the third world, this group fa-vored the reorientation of policy toward Black Africa, greater sensitivity to the Organization of Petroleum Exporting Countries (OPEC), and sympathy for the fulfillment of Palestinian aspirations in the Middle East while insuring Israel's minimum security needs.

The second faction was affected very differently by events in the 1960s and 1970s, especially Vietnam and the October 1973 War. Its members in-cluded notables like Henry Jackson, Daniel Patrick Moynihan, and Norman Podhoretz, editor of *Commentary,* whose magazine upheld this group's views. These individuals were concerned with the East-West conflict and the potential threat of Soviet communism to American interests. They focused on the lack of civil and political rights in the Third World, advocated increases in the Ameri-can defense budget, were suspicious of OPEC, skeptical of the new fascination with Third World nationalism, supportive of Israel, antagonistic toward the Soviet Union and dubious about detente, and either unaffected by Vietnam or not prepared to see the war as an error.

The third group was younger than the other two. Many of its members were associated with the McGovern campaign in 1972 or shared the foreign policy ideology of that short-lived political effort. This faction was more intense-ly oriented toward the Third World than its older counterparts in the first group; its major themes included conciliation toward the Third World and OPEC, realignment in Africa, amelioration of the Palestinian condition, and deem-phasis of the Communist threat. The journal that reflected this group's views was *Foreign Policy,* whose editor, Richard Holbrooke, participated in the Carter campaign and later became assistant secretary of state for Far Eastern affairs. Other representative members of the group included Anthony Lake, who be-came head of the Policy Planning Staff; Leslie Gelb, who became assistant secre-tary of state for political military affairs; Charles William Maynes, who became head of the International Organization Bureau; and Richard Moose, who be-came assistant secretary of state for African affairs.

The fourth faction was a hybrid. Its proponents shared some of the views of each of the other groups. The *New Republic* under Martin Peretz was the magazine most representative of its approach. Walter Mondale was the group's most illustrious member, but foreign policy specialists who might have served in key posts were difficult to find. While sensitive to the economic and political problems of the Third World and intensely concerned about the fate of the blacks in Southern Africa, this group was also pro-Israel, suspicious of OPEC, and skeptical of many Third World initiatives in the United Nations. Toward the Soviet Union, it took a middle-of-the-road stance, concentrating on human rights issues and arms limitation.

The origins of Carter's plight can be found in the way he originally organized his presidency. His connections with the Trilateral Commission and alliances made during the presidential primaries provided him with a collection of presidential advisers who represented primarily the first and third factions. The *Commentary* and *New Republic* groups remained outside the foreign policy consensus of the administration. This particular selection of advisers, combined with heightened ideological tensions within the Democratic party after Vietnam, gave the Carter team its remarkable singleness of purpose.

This combination of groups meant that the Middle East would be viewed from a particular perspective: oil, North-South issues, and Palestinians would be emphasized. It also meant that from the outset the administration had no key foreign policy specialists who saw Israel as a valuable asset to American interests.

As I have suggested before if Carter had been previously exposed to the issue on a practical political basis (in Congress for example), he would have been aware of the different views on Arab-Israeli matters in the country. He would consequently have been careful to include on his staff individuals of different perspectives. But Carter did not understand that there were experts who held different views. Rather he thought that the pro-Israeli stance was primarily emotional and political. No one around him challenged the prevailing assumptions and perspectives of the Democratic party factions that took power in January 1977. By 1980, the *Commentary* group supported Reagan; the *New Republic* endorsed John Anderson.

Domestic Constraints

Ronald Reagan began his presidency with an impressive coalition of domestic support on Middle East issues. He garnered a comparatively large Jewish vote for a Republican (39 percent). This achievement can be explained in part by his long-standing backing of Israel and also by his predecessor's political ineptitude. Jimmy Carter had made Jewish voters afraid that he would treat Israel severely if reelected. Further, Jewish support for Reagan was reflected by the neoconservative thrust toward his candidacy. He was also aided by the votes that Anderson took from Carter. The election of 1980 was the first since 1920 in which the Democrats had not received at least 50 percent of the Jewish vote.[2] Reagan also had strong backing from pro-Israel evangelical groups such as the Moral Majority.

If pro-Israel groups voted for Reagan in unusual numbers, he did not lose the traditional support given Republican candidates by the business community. Entrepreneurs with new ties to the principal oil producers, especially Saudi Arabia, could be confident that they had a friend in the White House. Although Reagan was not so vocal in support of the Saudis as one of his 1980 Republican opponents, John Connally, he was appalled by the Carter administration's handling of the fall of the shah. He saw the Saudis as staunch anti-Communists and friends of the United States and was always sensitive to the concerns of major businesses active in the area.[3]

Reagan's hand was strengthened by the unexpected Republican capture of a majority in the Senate, his persuasiveness with Congress, and his abilities as the "Great Communicator" with the American people. Yet his advantages were severely tested in 1981 by the controversial $8.5 billion sale of five AWACS jets to Saudi Arabia. In this conflict, the pro-Israel lobby waged a rigorous campaign that pitted it against the growing strength of the pro-Arab lobby. It opposed a coalition consisting of Arab-Americans, the national security bureaucracy, and corporations with interests in Saudi Arabia, particularly those that stood to profit from the sale. For the first time these companies involved their employees and subcontractors in a lobbying effort.[4] The scales were tipped in favor of the AWACS sale by the president's forceful intervention. Without him, opponents of the sale would certainly have won.

One unexpected consequence of the AWACS battle was increased political activity among American Jews in response to their defeat in Congress. Pro-Israeli political action committees burgeoned. Stronger efforts were mounted to defeat congressmen perceived as pro-Arab. Contributions to AIPAC increased, as did its visibility, staff, and membership. The administration could not ignore the forces it had inadvertently unleashed.

The American intervention in Lebanon provided another major constraint on the administration's Middle East policy. Congress used the War Powers Act to retain close scrutiny over the marine contingent that was part of the multinational peacekeeping force in Beirut for eighteen months. After the American role escalated to military support of the Gemayel government in mid-1983, congressional leaders negotiated a delicate compromise with the administration, allowing the marines to remain in Beirut for another eighteen months. Congressional support unraveled after the 23 October terrorist bombing of marine headquarters at Beirut airport. Finally, with a growing number of congressmen calling for withdrawal, the president ordered the marines to redeploy offshore. Administration spokesmen, especially Secretary of State Shultz, later blamed congressional sniping for the failure of U.S. policy in Lebanon.[5] Reagan's political advisers were also affected by domestic considerations; taking advantage of his divided foreign policy team, they urged him repeatedly in late 1983 and early 1984 to withdraw.

External Constraints

Like its predecessors, this administration had to confront many unanticipated developments in the Middle East. (1) It expected a breakthrough in the autonomy talks before the April 1982 withdrawal of Israeli forces from the Sinai, but Anwar Sadat's assassination in October 1981 halted progress. (2) It received a series of shocks from an activist Israeli government in 1981: the destruction of the Iraqi nuclear reactor in June, the bombing of Beirut in July, and the imposition of Israeli law on the Golan Heights in December. (3) The most significant crisis faced by the Reagan team during the first three years was the Israeli attack on Lebanon in June 1982. (4) As the Iran-Iraq War varied in intensity, administration concern fluctuated. It could afford to be somewhat more relaxed about this war because U.S. dependence on Mideast oil supplies had diminished. Energy concerns shifted from long-term oil shortages to the possibility of a short-term supply cutoff because of an Iranian blockage of the Strait of Hormuz or an attack on the Saudi oil fields. (5) Concern remained about the spread of Shiite fundamentalism, fears that intensified when Anwar Sadat was assassinated by Muslim fanatics.

The Reagan administration had a distinct philosophy but employed vague tactics, so that it was susceptible to the ebb and flow of external events. Many of its decisions were reactions to specific developments in the region rather than parts of an overall strategy. Like many of its predecessors, it arrived with a policy formulated to respond to the crisis of the previous administration. In this case the crisis had occurred in the Persian Gulf with the fall of the shah, the Iranian hostage crisis, and the Soviet invasion of Afghanistan. Yet the Arabs and Israelis were seen as instruments to be used in resolving the new problems confronted by the United States in the region. The Reagan administration, no less than its predecessors, thought that a peaceful settlement would strengthen U.S. interests in the area. It sought to submerge Arab-Israeli issues in an overall strategy for containing Soviet expansion. Since the administration was divided over how to achieve its objectives, and particular governments often proved unwilling to cooperate, the effect of external constraints on policy was intensified.

Philosophy

Few presidents have come to office with as specific a vision of the world as Ronald Reagan. The basic tenets of his policy could not have been more divergent from the principles of the Carter era: staunch anticommunism, antagonism to the Soviet leadership, deemphasis on the Third World as an object of U.S. concern, and a commitment to a dramatically increased defense budget. The Reagan administration saw the Soviets as responsible for U.S. problems worldwide and therefore was more prepared to use conventional force to thwart Russian aims as it perceived them.

To Reagan, the Soviet Union was the true source of evil in the world. Many in the administration believed that the United States could not ignore the nature of the Soviet system and the oppression of its people. In a 1983 speech referring to the Soviet Union, Reagan declared, "Let us pray for the salvation of all those who live in that totalitarian darkness—pray they will discover the joy of knowing God. But until they do, let us be aware that while they preach the supremacy of the state, declare its omnipotence over individual man and predict its eventual domination of all peoples on Earth—they are the focus of evil in the modern world."[6]

As suggested by this statement, the president's vision was organized around a few simple beliefs. For example, in February 1980, Reagan said of the Lebanese, "I can't see why they're fighting. After all, they're all Lebanese."[7] His problem arose when his basic premises did not adequately cover the issues he confronted. In response, he often continued to hold to his preconceived attitudes long after the facts ceased to justify them (as in his continued declarations into late 1983 that the United States would succeed in Lebanon), or else he walked away from the issue (as he did in Lebanon early in 1984).[8]

This "good versus evil" image of the world expressed in the president's rhetoric did not produce a set of specific policies, beyond global confrontation with the Soviet Union. It was not an accident that Reagan refused to issue a foreign policy manifesto as Carter had done at Notre Dame in 1977 or as Nixon and Kissinger had done in annual State of the World messages. Emphasizing his determination to thwart the U.S.S.R. wherever it threatened U.S. objectives might frighten the American public and Congress. Clearly, his actions in Lebanon and Central America disturbed many. On the other hand, to give the appearance of flexibility would compromise the president's cherished principles and possibly alienate his right-wing supporters. The administration maintained the purity of its philosophical perspective, compromising only under pressure on specific instances, such as China policy, Lebanon, the European oil pipeline, grain sales to the U.S.S.R., or a willingness to enter arms control talks.

This process was played out in the Middle East. The president entered office determined to square the circle of previous U.S. policy toward the area. The administration planned to provide incentives to both the Israelis and Arabs so they would join the effort to block Russian expansion in the area. Reagan, who had gone further than any previous major candidate in celebrating the Jewish state as an important strategic asset to the United States, would offer the Israelis unprecedented cooperation and increased military assistance. Meanwhile, the Arabs, especially the Saudis, would be fortified with arms so that they could contribute to the effort. Each side would acquiesce in U.S. support for the other because of the assistance they were to be provided.

As early as February 1981, Reagan's first secretary of state, Alexander Haig, was explaining, "We feel it is fundamentally important to begin to develop a consensus of strategic concerns throughout the region among Arab and Jew and to be sure that the overriding danger of Soviet inroads into this area are not overlooked." By September he was arguing that the strategic consensus already existed ("still in embryo but nonetheless existent"); otherwise, he claimed, a cease-fire achieved in Lebanon the previous month would not have been possible. Haig talked about organizing the area from Pakistan to Egypt, possibly even including formerly pro-Soviet Iraq.[9]

One problem with this approach was that little consideration was given to the possibility that the Arabs and Israelis might not accept the deals being proffered. Despite Haig's confidence, there was little chance that either would suddenly abandon its regional conflict to confront the U.S.S.R.

Another problem with a philosophy that is firm in objective and vague in tactics is that it leads to opposing interpretations. In the Carter administration, tactical differences had existed between Vance and Brzezinski on policy toward the U.S.S.R., but a high degree of consensus was maintained on the Middle East. The Reagan administration's broad philosophical objectives offered less specific guidance. Opportunities for disagreements were enhanced because concerted direction from the top was lacking, particularly on Middle East issues. While Reagan and Haig's concept of strategic consensus included an important role for Israel in the continuing conflict with the U.S.S.R., Secretary of Defense Caspar Weinberger's approach did not.

Like Haig, Weinberger was barely in office when he began expounding on the new approach to the Middle East. He declared that Saudi Arabia would make "an important contribution" to the security of all nations in the area, including Israel, and "will promote our efforts to create a strategic consensus in the Southwest Asia region."[10] He argued publicly that the United States should strengthen its relations with Riyadh to discourage further Soviet intervention following recent Western setbacks in Iran and Afghanistan. Weinberger was perhaps influenced by his work in the Bechtel construction corporation, which had regularly held large contracts with Saudi Arabia. To the defense chief, ironically, not unlike many liberal Carter officials, U.S. security interests in the region demanded close relations with the Arabs. Therefore the United States could not pursue practical programs with Israel. Weinberger's interpretation of the Reagan strategic consensus was that "friendly" Arab states should be mobilized against the Soviet threat. In contrast, Haig's original approach encompassed a broader coalition of countries that included Israel.

Decision Making

Ronald Reagan, like his predecessor, was inexperienced in the intricacies of foreign policy. There the similarities ended. Jimmy Carter was exposed to ideas and personalities at the Trilateral Commission; Reagan was initiated in foreign policy matters at Stanford's Hoover Institution, where he was an honorary fellow.[11] Reagan did not immerse himself in the details of particular issues, neither did he work long hours. He was well-known for lack of mastery over finite material—even for errors in press conferences. Reflecting his personal confidence, Reagan usually made judgments with less hesitation than his predecessors. However, when his assumptions were challenged by complex issues such as Lebanon, he tended to put off facing the demanding reality.

This pattern may have originated in Reagan's commitment to his overall set of beliefs, which paradoxically further isolated him from the policy process. This president rarely delved further into material about which he knew little; he learned primarily from what he observed and heard rather than from what he read. One reason that he was so effective in communicating his ideas was that he was genuinely and emotionally committed to them. Rather than seek new ideas, Reagan sought information that would reinforce those he already had. Therefore, when aides wanted him to change policy, they tried to show that the policy they were advocating was consistent with his previous approach, even when it was not.[12] Except in some crises or when a fundamental decision required a choice between his feuding assistants' competing views, Ronald Reagan generally remained aloof. After making decisions, he would usually not remain closely involved. He rarely pressed initiatives and never followed up to control a disparate decision-making system. His predispositions served as general guidelines, and he, in turn, preferred situations in which his aides reached a consensus among themselves. Although this style encouraged disputes among his assistants, he hated to deal with conflict among them or the need to remove anyone from office.

Much of his information came from the palace guard at the White House, a situation which offered fewer opportunities for key foreign policy officials to deal with him directly. Subordinates could assume that, within the limits set by Reagan's "cabinet government," the chief's preferences would not be rigorously enforced. Except when instructions were extraordinarily specific, they had considerable latitude to implement policy as they saw fit. (For example, during the administration's early months, while Haig was privately trying to soothe ruffled Israeli-American relations, Weinberger would denounce Israeli actions on television or announce policies that Haig had not yet had an opportunity to warn the Israelis about.)[13]

Given Reagan's passivity, the best way to assure a smooth foreign policy decision-making system was for a vicar or czar to emerge in the Republican tradition of Dulles and Kissinger. Alexander Haig understood this reality.[14] His attempts to preside over foreign policy as the administration's preeminent figure cost him his job after seventeen frustrating months in office. Instead, the decision-making approach of the administration remained chaotic. If policy changes when the players change, the constant turnover of key foreign policy figures led to a lack of consistency. In the first three years, there were three successive constellations of decision makers—the first through 1981; the second emerged by mid-1982; the third developed during late summer and early fall of 1983.

Although Weinberger retained the defense portfolio during the first three years, the original team also included Haig and Richard B. Allen as national security assistant. This post was purposely limited to avoid a repetition of the Vance-Brzezinski and Rogers-Kissinger conflicts. Allen reported to Edwin Meese, the counselor to the president, rather than to the president himself. His staff was often maligned and his influence constrained. Since Haig and Allen had little respect for each other, wherever possible the secretary of state tried to keep the NSC staff out of the policy process.[15] Allen, at first a favorite of the pro-Israeli forces, moved toward the Weinberger perspective during the AWACS conflict.

On the Middle East, the acute philosophical differences between Haig and Weinberger dominated early decision making. The defense secretary consistently favored arms sales for Arab states, in part because he saw such sales as important for the corporations involved and in part because he thought they were critical to keeping these states secure and close to the United States.[16] Although the president shared Haig's view of the importance of the Israelis, Weinberger was closer to Reagan personally. Therefore, these two key cabinet members stalemated each other. It was not Reagan's style to press trusted aides who acted independently. As happened with Haig and Weinberger, at times he would side with both of two conflicting parties over an extended period, thus adding to the confusion of policy.[17]

The administration's ambassador to the United Nations, Jeane Kirkpatrick, took a position similar to Haig's on the value of Israel. She was admired by Reagan and, like Weinberger, she retained her post. As with her predecessors, however, her location in New York kept her on the periphery of decision making.

In January 1982, Deputy Secretary of State William P. Clark replaced Allen at the NSC. The move was engineered by Baker and Deaver in an attempt to bring order to the chaos of foreign policy formulation.[18] Clark had no foreign policy experience before 1981. He progressively tilted toward Weinberger's view that Israel was a growing nuisance and must be taught to behave if American interests in the Middle East were to be advanced. This position was strengthened when George P. Shultz replaced Haig in mid-1982. Like Weinberger, Shultz had been a high-level official of the Bechtel corporation.

In summer 1982, a stable approach toward the Middle East was established with the second decision-making team in place. It was reinforced by Phillip C. Habib, the president's negotiator in the area since the spring 1981 Syrian missile crisis in Lebanon. Moreover, Habib was the only key official left in the administration with practical experience in Mideast diplomacy. An accomplished diplomat, he had been Vance's undersecretary of state for political affairs until a heart condition forced his resignation. As an American of Arab descent who had grown up in a Jewish neighborhood of Brooklyn, his credentials for the position were impeccable. He enjoyed the confidence of both the president and the secretary of state.

This team remained in charge of Mideast diplomacy from mid-1982 to mid-1983. However, another new constellation of forces began to take shape in July 1983 when Habib was replaced by Robert McFarlane, a tough former marine colonel. McFarlane was originally appointed counselor of the State Department by Haig and held views on the Middle East similar to those of his former chief. He had moved to the NSC with Clark and became his deputy, a post he retained when he also assumed the duties of Middle East negotiator. When Clark was forced out by Baker and Deaver and became secretary of the interior in November 1983, McFarlane was appointed NSC adviser when Clark and Meese prevented Baker from assuming the post.[19] McFarlane in turn was replaced as Middle East negotiator by the former secretary of defense, Donald Rumsfeld.

The third constellation of forces had now taken shape, but on substantive Mideast issues it resurrected the Haig-Weinberger split. The new balance of forces in the administration allowed McFarlane, Shultz, Kirkpatrick, Rumsfeld, and Undersecretary of State for Political Affairs Lawrence Eagleburger to support the original idea of closer strategic ties with Israel and a tough posture toward Syria. The other group was led by Weinberger, the Joint Chiefs, and the diplomats of the Near East Bureau. They wanted to rely on links with moderate Arabs and opposed closer ties with Israel, increased military involvement in Lebanon, and confrontation with Syria. However, there was no concerted opposition in the administration to increased arms sales to Arab states.

Future historians will spend much time sorting out the chaos created by the musical chairs of the Reagan decision-making process. In no previous administration had the turnover of major foreign policy personnel been so rapid or extensive, a turnover occurring on lower levels as well. Haig appointed several key figures in the State Department bureaucracy who had views on the Middle East similar to his own. They included foreign policy specialist Paul Wolfowitz as director of policy planning, Harvey Sicherman as speech writer, Sherwood Goldberg as chief of staff, Richard Burt as director of political military affairs, former Senator James Buckley as undersecretary of state for security assistance, Elliot Abrams as assistant secretary of state for human rights, and Meyer Rashish as undersecretary of state for economic affairs. Given Haig's views, this constellation of forces might have been viewed as a temporary departure from the conventional State Department perspective, but then Shultz subsequently reinforced Haig's original position with appointments like Peter Rodman, a former Kissinger aide, as chief of the policy planning staff.

Shultz entered office when opposition to the Israeli invasion of Lebanon was running extraordinarily high in Washington, even in Congress. The former secretary of the treasury and economics professor did not have a record of working sympathetically with Israeli officials and their American supporters as Haig did. But neither was Shultz like Weinberger, a corporate technician with single-minded opposition to Israel. Most important, he did not have some of his predecessors' patience with the vagaries of Arab politics. Thus, when Syria refused to accept the 17 May 1983 Israeli-Lebanese accord, Shultz shifted his position closer to Haig's. When friendly Arab states were unwilling to support the Reagan Plan or failed to gain Syrian acquiescence to the accord, Shultz was disillusioned with their frustrating inconsistency. While he opposed Israel's withdrawal from the Shouf mountains near Beirut in September 1983 and resisted congressional pressure to move the U.S. embassy to Jerusalem in 1984, after mid-1983 he increasingly favored closer ties to Israel. In adopting this new posture, Shultz was undoubtedly influenced by Undersecretary Lawrence Eagleburger who was a particularly strong advocate of strategic cooperation with Israel.

Haig, Shultz, and Weinberger demonstrate how important the chief of a department can be despite the ingrained attitudes of a bureaucracy. Through his appointments and the natural bureaucratic tendency to mimic the chief of the moment, the secretary can set a tone that changes at least the higher echelons of a department's views. Well-entrenched views in an agency like the Near East Bureau may not be altered, but the importance of the agency will decline as NEA did under Haig and belatedly under Shultz.

White House staff positions were uniquely important in the administration's foreign policy formulation. None of the three key aides, White House Chief of Staff James Baker, Deputy Chief of Staff Michael K. Deaver, or the president's counselor Edwin Meese, had close ties to American Jews or previous foreign policy experience. Their backgrounds were especially important because this group controlled much information reaching the president, a particularly powerful tool in dealing with the usually distant Reagan.

In the past, White House advisers had frequently sided with Israel for political reasons. However, the searing AWACS experience turned several officials against Israel. There was no counterweight to balance or diffuse this resentment. The "Jewish portfolio," when held at all, was assumed by figures peripheral to the central decision-making process. Jewish Republican leaders had difficulty finding a representative. The one Jew in the kitchen cabinet, the late Theodore Cummings, served for a time as ambassador to Austria before his death in April 1982. Another Californian, Albert A. Spiegel, commuted between Los Angeles and Washington for eighteen months, beginning at the height of the AWACS controversy in October 1981, before leaving over procedural and substantive differences. But as Israeli-American relations improved, so did the outlook of Reagan's pro-Israel associates. As a sign of the changing conditions, as the election drew closer in fall 1983, Baker grew more sympathetic to aid and cooperation with Israel and adamant that the marines be removed from Beirut.[20]

Vice President Bush's position in the decision-making process was mercurial. As part of the White House conflict with Haig, he was placed in charge of crisis management, which gave him an automatic foreign policy role. During the conflict over AWACS and at the start of the Lebanon War, he weighed in against the Israeli position. But it was not clear whether he had done so independently (as Haig's associates claimed) or because he had been ordered to do so by the White House (as he later claimed). Bush does not appear to have played a major role in Mideast policy making except during crises. At these times, his influence was often inconsistent, shifting preferences as conditions changed.[21]

Above this chaotic and almost constantly changing constellation of forces stood the president—affable but distant; optimistic, gracious, guileless, undemanding of his aides. Harking back to his career in Hollywood, he held a romantic view of Israel as a vibrant democracy. As he often told Jewish audiences, he was deeply affected by movies he had seen while still in the army of American forces entering the concentration camps. As a presidential candidate in 1976, he had celebrated the dramatic Israeli rescue of hijacked hostages at Entebbe: "They were acting the way America used to act."[22] Four years later he had become an apostle of Israel as a strategic asset. Writing in the *Washington Post* in August 1979, he stated,

> The fall of Iran has increased Israel's value as perhaps the only remaining strategic asset in the region on which the United States can truly rely . . . Only by full appreciation of the critical role the State of Israel plays in our strategic calculus can we build the foundation for thwarting Moscow's designs on territories and resources vital to our security and our national well-being.[23]

At his first news conference as president-elect, he reviled the PLO as a terrorist organization.[24] In private conversations, especially with Jews, he often quoted from Hal Lindsey's *The Late Great Planet Earth*, stunning his listeners with analogies between Biblical references and contemporary events. In fall 1983, speaking by telephone with AIPAC's chief, Thomas A. Dine, about the situation in Lebanon, he said, "We've got to find a settlement there. You know, I turn back to your ancient prophets in the Old Testament, and the signs foretelling Armageddon, and I find myself wondering if—if we're the generation that's going to see that come about. I don't know if you've noted any of the prophecies lately, but, believe me, they certainly describe the time we're going through."[25]

That was the ideological Ronald Reagan. The practical Ronald Reagan welcomed the support of Arab regimes opposed to the Soviet Union and assumed that the Israel he so respected would always be a compliant ally. But although Israel's prime minister Menachem Begin was congenial ideologically with Reagan, he was also fiercely independent. The new president was unprepared for the repeated frustrating shocks that Begin presented to him. By summer 1982, he was commenting to aides, "Boy, that guy makes it hard for you to be his friend."[26] During tense moments in Israeli-American relations in 1982, there proved to be bounds beyond which Reagan would not go in opposing Israel. The Israeli invasion of Lebanon made a deep impression on him because he suspected that the Jerusalem government sought to keep a part of the country. After it agreed in May 1983 to withdraw totally if Syria would also withdraw, his original positive perception of Israel returned.

Reagan also had a practical bent toward the peace process. Even during the campaign he had spoken on occasion about the possibility of a peace settlement that would return Jordanian sovereignty to the West Bank. Reagan no less than Eisenhower, Nixon, and Ford hoped for an Arab-Israeli settlement that would permit greater concentration on the Soviet threat. Despite his harsh rhetoric toward the Russians and his reputation of being trigger-happy, he was uncomfortable with conflict—conflict over policy, among his aides, or among America's friends. Annoyed when forced into tense situations, he was often bothered by Prime Minister Begin's activist policies, culminating in the attack on Lebanon. His problems with Begin ironically made him more willing to consider U.S. participation in a peacekeeping force in Lebanon. It also predisposed him to consider the kind of initiative that Shultz later pressed him to endorse in his own name.

Thus, the patterns observed throughout this book also are found in the Reagan administration. The president's beliefs, working habits, style, and choice of advisers set the framework of his policy. Every administration brings its own philosophy into office. It has a plan for reacting to a crisis that occurred during a previous administration. It wants to bring about a peace settlement between the Israelis and the Arabs. Its philosophy causes it to be surprised by regional developments but it nevertheless reacts in light of its preconceptions. It is affected by the particular cacophony of domestic constraints operating on it. The degree of continuity and agreement among the president and his key advisors affects the content of policy, especially in light of the particular president's ability to orchestrate his advisers' disputes and channel their activities.

In the Reagan administration, poor direction, rapid turnover of key personnel, and deep internal division were not a recipe for a strong record. That record will have to be fully assessed in future years. However, the three key events of the first three years were the conflict over the sale of AWACS to Saudi Arabia, the enunciation of the Reagan Plan, and the war in Lebanon. Each illustrated the problems that presidents face in trying to choose between conflicting claims both at home and abroad. Each also illustrates the problems that arise when an administration has a philosophy it is not able to turn effectively into specific policies and when it is continually divided internally.

AWACS

Every administration has confronted the option of selling arms to Arab states. Thus, each has had to face immediate conflict among opposing pressures.

None, however, has confronted the problem so immediately and dramatically as did the Reagan team. The controversy illustrated the weaknesses in its philosophy toward the area and in its decision-making approaches. It affected relations with both the Saudis and Israelis and engaged competing American parties on both sides.

It had been widely anticipated that the Reagan administration would quickly move to sell Saudi Arabia sophisticated equipment in addition to the sixty-two F-15s sold by the Carter administration in 1978. Israel would be compensated with increased military and economic assistance. Indeed, the Carter administration had already made a commitment to the Saudis before it left office.[27] Although a preliminary decision had been made a month earlier, the crucial NSC meeting to consider the sale of an Airborne Warning and Command System (AWACS) to Saudi Arabia occurred on 1 April, the day after Reagan was shot. Vice President Bush sought guidance for a disabled president. Weinberger was on the offensive. Haig "supported the sale of an airborne warning and surveillance system in principle" but he was skeptical about the five AWACS aircraft then being considered. However, the secretary of state was reeling from a series of defeats and embarrassments following his famous "I'm in control here" comment at the White House in the aftermath of the assassination attempt and the loss of crisis management direction to Bush.[28]

While Haig was inhibited by his problems, a vehement Weinberger persuaded the NSC to sell the sophisticated equipment for the F-15s and five AWACS jets to Saudi Arabia. The Begin government had appeared to acquiesce in the sale of F-15 add-ons in order to facilitate smooth relations with the new administration. It expected Reagan's administration to be more philosophically congenial and practically sympathetic than its predecessor, especially given the esteem in which Israel was held by both the new president and secretary of state. Yet the sale of AWACS jets to Saudi Arabia was more than it could accept. Israel's supporters in America were horrified that such an advanced intelligence tool with a possible combat role would be placed under Saudi control. Administration efforts to convince a skeptical Congress that the sale was wise forced months of national debate in which Israel and its supporters were progressively seen as the enemy by many on the Reagan team, especially domestic policy advisers. Although the administration was unified in support of the AWACS sale, the conflict strengthened Weinberger and his allies at the Pentagon, NSC, and Near East Bureau at the expense of Haig and his appointees at State. The Joint Chiefs of Staff, especially the Air Force, were forcefully in favor of the sale.[29]

Yet administration victory was by no means assured. During the first months of the administration, Reagan and his key White House aides devoted themselves to domestic issues, gaining a reputation of formidable effectiveness with Congress in the process. Belatedly, they realized that Allen and the State Department were losing the AWACS battle and with it the Reagan team's vaunted omnipotence with Congress. Under Baker's direction and with Reagan's determination, the administration turned to the fierce battle in the Senate. Proponents of the sale promoted the slogan, "It's Reagan or Begin."[30] Indeed, the president himself suggested at a 1 October press conference, "It is not the business of other nations to make American foreign policy."[31] The slam at Israel and its supporters was clear. Sadat's assassination on 6 October intensified senators' apprehensions that regional instability would increase if the sale was not approved. To satisfy wavering senators, Reagan adopted the tactic used by Carter and Brown in the F-15 battle: a letter enumerating constraints on the Saudis that the administration would impose (but that the Saudis themselves never explicitly accepted).[32] In the end the administration won by a vote of 52 to 48.

Problems with Israel

The AWACS battle left a residue of bitterness on both sides, especially because AWACS was not the only controversy eating away Israel's relationship with the administration. In every presidency, the problems between Jerusalem and Washington have been confronted in light of the administration's approach to the region. When Israel was seen as burdensome, as under Eisenhower and Carter, tensions were approached as inevitable, even necessary—a bother but not unexpected. It has proved more difficult for presidents like Truman, Johnson, and Ford to handle problems with the Israelis because tensions did not fit into their expectations. Until it reversed course in mid-1983, the Reagan administration provided the most extreme example of this pattern, because part of the administration led by the president expected harmony and the remainder led by Weinberger promoted distance. Only the early Nixon years (before Kissinger's carrot and stick policy prevailed) even came close to the pattern of the Reagan era. Certainly, both the Nixon and Reagan administrations were bitterly divided, with chief executives hesitant and somewhat remote on the issue. However, Reagan was emotional, even sentimental, more like Truman, Johnson, and Ford than Nixon.

When Israel destroyed the Iraqi nuclear reactor in June and retaliated against terrorist attacks by bombing Beirut in July, both Haig's strategic consensus doctrine and Weinberger's regional anticommunism were threatened. The administration not only deplored Israel's actions, it suspended shipments of F-16 aircraft due for delivery and approved the U.N. Security Council's condemnation of Israel. Suspending delivery of equipment already sold to Israel was unprecedented; the last time any such action had been taken by an administration was Eisenhower's temporary suspension of economic aid in October 1953. Even after the shipments were resumed, the president's attitude was increasingly negative and tensions between Jerusalem and Washington continued.[33]

Haig had hoped to persuade Begin to acquiesce in American initiatives, but by now both sides were disillusioned. Begin resented not being invited to meet the new president until after the Israeli elections of June 1981. The Reagan team resented Begin's preemptory actions, which compromised the coordination integral to strategic consensus. Begin always acted at awkward moments. The Iraqi raid occurred three days after he saw Sadat; the Beirut raid came two days after a Begin-McFarlane meeting in Jerusalem that tried to set relations back on an even keel and while Reagan and Haig were in Ottawa for an allied economic summit meeting.[34] The Israelis thus appeared obdurately insensitive to American needs.

When Reagan and Begin met at the White House for the first time in September, matters only worsened. Begin's pensive emotionalism did not match well with Reagan's more relaxed style, and a major misunderstanding over AWACS embittered the president. Reagan thought he had a commitment from Begin to state his opposition to the AWACS sale only when asked. Yet when Begin was questioned by the congressional foreign relations committees about his opinion of the sale, he spoke definitively against the president's proposal. Reports that reached the furious Reagan gave the impression that Begin had initiated lobbying against the sale. Haig investigated and discovered that this was not true; Begin had indeed kept his promise. Reagan was not mollified.[35]

Reagan and Begin's meetings established the basis for a strategic cooperation agreement between the two countries, which Reagan and Haig were prepared to conclude if they won the AWACS vote. However, even this accord became a source of tension. Weinberger opposed an agreement with Israel. Since his department would have to implement any decision, he stalled while Haig continued to press for an agreement. Finally, Ariel Sharon, Israel's new defense minister, came to Washington in late November and negotiated a diluted version of the strategic cooperation agreement with Weinberger. It took the form of a Memorandum of Understanding. Dramatizing his lack of enthusiasm, Weinberger would not even allow photographers at the signing session. Because the memorandum would upset the Arabs, the administration presented it as quietly as possible. The Likud government on the other hand trumpeted the agreement as a major achievement, a way of salvaging its relations with the United States in the wake of the AWACS debacle.[36]

According to the memorandum, strategic cooperation was not to be used against any states in the region but rather "against the threat to peace and security of the region caused by the Soviet Union or Soviet-controlled forces from outside the region introduced into the region." Proposed mutual activities included joint military exercises, joint readiness activities, cooperation in research and development, and defense trade.[37]

Immediately after the agreement was announced, opposition was voiced by many in Israel. Begin and Sharon were forced to defend the accord, which embodied an idea that at least in theory had been an objective of Israeli foreign policy since Ben Gurion's day. Opponents objected not to the concept itself, however, but to the clauses in the document that publicly pitted Israel against the U.S.S.R. in the context of U.S.-Soviet tensions.[38]

A few days later Begin caused a political earthquake when he unexpectedly announced and then ramrodded through the Knesset a bill applying Israeli law to the Golan Heights. Although Begin's action seems difficult to explain, he had plenty of time to plan strategy during a hospital stay of several weeks just before the move. He may well have sought to neutralize his right-wing domestic opponents, who were vociferously demanding that Israel not withdraw from the Sinai in April 1982.[39]

Whatever his reasons, Begin typically did not take into account (or at least miscalculated) the American reaction. To Reagan and company, this was another example of Begin's propensity for ignoring American concerns. From the U.S. point of view, Begin's timing again was terrible. The new memorandum had been concluded seventeen days earlier, and Washington was preoccupied with the imposition of martial law in Poland just one day before.[40]

Therefore, the dismayed administration suspended the agreement. It also suspended substantive peripheral agreements to the memorandum that covered indirect aid to Israel.[41] The administration was thus as insensitive to Begin's problems as he had been to theirs. It saw strategic cooperation with Israel as either a sop to Israel's interests or a club to use against it. The administration totally undercut Begin in a primary foreign policy objective and in the debate he had been waging with opponents of the accord.

The prime minister reacted with the type of tirade that had made him infamous in the West and a hero in Israel. In addition to stating that the United States had no moral right, in light of its behavior in Vietnam, to punish or preach to Israel, he referred to what he called "an ugly anti-Semitic campaign" in connection with the administration's battle to win Senate approval for the AWACS sale to Saudi Arabia. "Are we a vassal state of yours? Are we a banana republic? Are we fourteen-year-olds who, if we misbehave, we get our wrists slapped?" He also said that he interpreted the U.S. action as tantamount to a cancellation of the accord.[42]

With the United States and Israel unable to accomplish their objectives toward each other, the attention of both governments turned to the scheduled 25 April 1982 final Israeli withdrawal from the Sinai. In late January, Secretary of State Haig made one final but fruitless effort to conclude the autonomy talks before the withdrawal.[43] A period of uncertainty descended over the Middle East as Washington and Cairo sought to avoid providing an excuse for Begin to cancel the departure. Despite the misgivings of a vocal minority, Israel completed its withdrawal from the Sinai precisely on schedule.

Flirtation with Jordan

The U.S. interest in arms sales to Arab states remained a source of tension with Israel. In response to Weinberger's approaches, the Saudis made it clear that they would not agree to any form of strategic consensus. Neither would they allow U.S. bases on their soil. Pentagon officials then maintained that further sales of sophisticated equipment to Riyadh would lead to an increased U.S. presence there since servicing such materiel required large numbers of technicians and specialists.

When administrations believe that relations with particular Arab regimes are deteriorating, they often focus on other Arab leaders who they hope will help them reverse the trend. When their initial approach fails, they turn to alternatives. Thus, Roosevelt, Eisenhower, and Carter all saw the Saudis as potential major allies, only to be subsequently disillusioned. Kennedy, like Eisenhower before him, flirted with Nasser's Egypt; Carter turned to Sadat's Egypt after the other Arab states rejected Camp David. In its search for surrogates, the United States has always had great difficulty in sidestepping conflict within the Arab world. In all this, the Reagan administration was archetypical. After its initial disappointment with Saudi Arabia, it tried to build Jordan into an alternative.

In early 1982 Weinberger traveled to Saudi Arabia, where disagreements caused an all-night meeting with the Saudi defense minister. He left realizing that the Saudis would not cooperate as he had anticipated. The defense chief immediately began to speak of increased arms aid to Jordan. Over the next year this led to administration proposals for advanced arms aid and a Jordanian rapid deployment force.[44] The strategy was to continue strengthening the Saudi military while creating this Jordanian force to assist Saudi Arabia and other Persian Gulf states. Another factor reinforcing the new focus on Jordan was administration concern in spring 1982 about Iran's successes against Iraq, a fear that reemerged each time Teheran launched an offensive in the war with Baghdad.

Lebanon: U.S. versus Israel

Any administration is judged by its handling of a major crisis; it is a test of its philosophy, personnel, and decision making. A crisis response is a culmination of previous policies and not an occasion for new ideas. The handling of Lebanon 1958, the Jordanian Civil War, Suez, the Six-Day War, and even October 1973, illustrate this pattern. It was also clearly evident in the Lebanon War. The Reagan administration's response exemplified the inconsistency and divided voice by which the administration had become distinguished by June 1982. For the first time a major official, Secretary of State Haig, resigned at the height of an Arab-Israeli crisis, an event that he later claimed had aborted a rapid solution.

The Lebanon issue, of course, did not emerge de novo in 1982. In 1976 U.S. mediation had achieved a tacit understanding between Syria and Israel. This "agreement" was revealed in February 1983 by former Prime Minister

Rabin. Under its terms, Jerusalem would not challenge Damascus and Lebanon if (1) Syrian troops did not proceed south of a "red line" defined precisely by the Israelis, (2) the Syrians did not deploy ground-to-air missiles on Lebanese territory, and (3) Syria did not conduct aerial attacks against targets in Lebanon.[45] This agreement was observed by both sides until April 1981, when Israel shot down two Syrian helicopters over Mt. Lebanon in reply to a Phalangist cry for help in opposing a major Syrian attack. The Syrians promptly responded by placing ground-to-air missiles in Lebanon. Begin threatened to destroy them immediately, but cloud cover delayed retaliation. This gave Haig time to convince the prime minister that U.S. diplomacy might solve the problem for him.[46]

The president responded to this Syrian missile crisis by appointing Phillip Habib as his special negotiator. Through the next several months, Habib endeavored to get Damascus to remove the missiles. Despite Washington's protest, the Israelis strengthened his hand by concentrating more troops on their Lebanese border. But the PLO, whose strength in Lebanon was growing, represented an even more serious problem for the Israelis. During summer 1981, the number and intensity of shooting incidents between the PLO and Israel increased. For the first time PLO shelling mounted direct threats against Israeli settlements in the Galilee, which called their future viability into question.[47]

In late August, Habib, with the aid of the Saudis, was able to negotiate a cease-fire. This achievement had several consequences. First, Saudi assistance reinforced the administration's commitment to the sale of AWACS jets. Second, the new administration was further convinced that diplomacy was effective in the Middle East. Third, Habib's status rose, especially with the president.

Despite the administration's confidence, the agreement only delayed hostilities. Incredibly, it did not prevent the PLO from adding to its military strength in the south. As the PLO moved more artillery and the latest Russian Katyusha rockets into southern Lebanon over the next several months, Sharon prepared for war. He planned to resolve Israel's problems in Lebanon with one military operation. It would destroy the PLO force in the south, help the Phalangists destroy PLO headquarters in Beirut, and remove the Syrian missiles, perhaps even push the Syrians out of Lebanon, gaining a better bargaining position for Israel in the West Bank. Finally, he hoped to take advantage of the August 1982 Lebanese elections so that Israel's ally, Phalangist military leader Bashir Gemayel, would become president. Sharon thought this would lead to a second Arab-Israeli peace treaty.[48]

By May 1982 reports of Sharon's plans were widespread in both Israel and Washington. On a trip to the United States, Sharon announced publicly that Israel would enter Lebanon if the PLO broke the cease-fire. Haig cautioned him that a PLO breach of the cease-fire would have to be unquestionable. Haig did not try to persuade Sharon not to attack under any circumstances, because he was anxious to repair relations with Israel and was not as opposed as many of his colleagues to a quick Israeli strike in southern Lebanon. A bloodying of the PLO and quieting of the Israel-Lebanon border might facilitate diplomatic progress.[49] In early spring, Haig had sent a proposal to the White House suggesting an "internationalization" of the Lebanon conflict. Several European countries would engage in a search for a solution in an international conference. Clark, in his new post at the NSC, had shelved the idea, but Haig still hoped for a diplomatic breakthrough.

It is possible that the secretary was not as tough as he might have been with Sharon because an imminent PLO violation of the cease-fire was not anticipated. Moreover, it was not clear that Sharon's plan for military action would gain the support of Israel's Cabinet. Most important, the administration wanted to concentrate on Begin rather than on the much disliked Sharon. It was thought that the prime minister's visit in June would offer ample time to discuss Lebanon, to renew strategic cooperation, to request serious discussions of autonomy and possible Israeli concessions, and to consider Israel's new security assistance requests. However, after the meeting with Sharon, cautious aides persuaded Haig to send a letter to Begin reiterating the dangers of war, just in case there had been a misunderstanding.[50]

That a misunderstanding occurred despite Haig's precautions is testimony to Sharon's single-mindedness and the poverty of the Israeli-American dialogue in 1982. Israel's key leaders were convinced that Washington had given them a green light to enter Lebanon. Their confidence was based on the conversation between Haig and Sharon and another between the secretary and the new Israeli ambassador to Washington, Moshe Arens. The uncertain consequences of poor communication between the two governments over the previous eighteen months were just beginning. In his memoirs Haig declares repeatedly that he was constantly cautioning Israeli officials against intervening in Lebanon; but he did not threaten sanctions or pressure if Israel acted. In this sense his warnings were similar to Johnson's before the Six-Day War and just as ineffective; Haig used a phrase similar to Johnson's, that Israel would be alone if it acted.[51]

On 3 June 1982 a terrorist attack on the Israeli ambassador in London by Palestinians who were not PLO members led Israel to bomb PLO targets in Lebanon in retaliation. In response, the PLO forces in southern Lebanon unleashed a major artillery attack against northern Israel, the heaviest ever inflicted on Israel's civilian areas. The Israelis promptly invaded on 6 June. Instead of limiting themselves to the zone forty kilometers from the frontier as had been widely expected, both in Israel and the United States, the Israeli forces pushed forward, advancing to within sight of Beirut by 11 June.[52]

On 9 June, Israel destroyed the Syrian missile emplacements in Lebanon. Israeli forces were clearly in the ascendency, but the Reagan entourage—traveling in Europe for a series of state visits and a seven-nation economic summit—

was furious both at the timing and substance of Israel's actions. For once the entire Reagan team was unified in pressing for an immediate cease-fire. Haig arranged a cessation of hostilities between Israeli and Syrian forces independent of the PLO. He reportedly conveyed a warning to Israel from the U.S.S.R. about the dire consequences of further attack on the Syrians.[53]

In his military campaign, Sharon was acting on his own, often without Israeli Cabinet approval and sometimes even without the knowledge of the prime minister. At first, however, it was difficult to argue with success. By 11 June Israeli troops had cut off West Beirut, closed the Beirut-Damascus road, and connected with Phalangist forces, trapping the PLO's military and political leadership. The Phalangists, however, did not act against the PLO units independently as the Israelis had hoped. Over the next two months, the question confronting the Israelis was whether they would have to march into Beirut's Moslem sector or whether Habib could arrange a safe-passage agreement for the PLO fighters to leave.[54]

In this situation, Haig was the only key administration figure who still opposed a tough stance toward the Israeli prime minister. He was particularly concerned that the PLO would be encouraged to remain in West Beirut if the United States pressured Israel. Begin was due to arrive at the White House on 21 June. Clark asked Bush, Weinberger, CIA Director William Casey, Kirkpatrick, and the Joint Chiefs of Staff for their opinions about how to treat him, in an effort to circumvent the secretary of state. As Clark anticipated, all those solicited differed with Haig's more delicate approach. This advice persuaded Reagan to be tougher with Begin. However, Reagan's bland style, his difficulty in handling personal confrontations, and Begin's obtuse intensity prevented the tough message from getting through. When Reagan spoke publicly about a U.S.-Israel "common understanding" and the need to withdraw all foreign forces from Lebanon, the two governments appeared closer than was actually the case.[55]

Thus, the public image of what had happened between Reagan and Begin reinforced Haig's strategy but countered that of the president and most of his advisers. Nevertheless, the secretary of state was still torpedoed by Bush, Weinberger, and Clark. Bush and Weinberger led a delegation that flew to Riyadh after the death of Saudi King Khalid on 14 June; they told their hosts that the United States would not allow Israel to enter West Beirut.[56] Clark conveyed a similar message to the Saudi ambassador in a meeting with him on 22 June.[57] These messages were bound to encourage the PLO to stand firm.

As these events suggest, the conflict within the administration's foreign policy team had reached the breaking point. By now Haig's opponents included Bush, Weinberger, Kirkpatrick, Clark, and the White House troika of Baker, Deaver, and Meese. The secretary of state was in conflict with the Middle East assistant secretary, Nicholas Veliotes, whom he had decided to replace. Even Haig and Kirkpatrick, who agreed fundamentally on the Middle East and Israel, took diametrically opposed positions on the Falklands crisis the previous March and April.[58] After the internal conflict generated by the situation in the Falklands, the just-concluded European trip, and the controversy with the allies over their aid for the Soviet pipeline to Western Europe, Clark, Deaver, and Baker would soon have forced Haig to resign regardless of the war. But the crisis exacerbated the tensions and illustrated how serious the chasm had become. On 14 June Haig informed the president that he planned to resign after the November congressional elections because Reagan would not grant him the authority he felt he required. He could not even get the president's approval of an urgent cable of instructions to Habib in the midst of the crisis because of Clark's interference.[59] When Haig's complaints continued, Clark arranged a rare meeting alone between the secretary of state and the president on 24 June, and later that day Reagan accepted a letter of resignation that was never actually submitted. That the change to Shultz as secretary of state was announced in the middle of a Mideast crisis is testimony to the intensity of the conflict within the administration.[60]

Clark phoned Shultz in London to tell him that the president was about to offer him the post of secretary of state. It is an irony of history that the NSC adviser knew of Shultz's whereabouts because he had phoned Clark before leaving for England to complain about the administration's soft treatment of Israel. His appointment signaled that the United States would be less sympathetic to Israeli efforts in Lebanon. Since Shultz had stated publicly in fall 1980 that his one area of disagreement with Reagan was on the approach to Israel, the Arabs had ample reason to anticipate U.S. pressure on Israel in the weeks ahead.[61]

But Haig had one last chance to achieve a quick end to the crisis. While vacationing in West Virginia in early July, he arranged a deal through the Saudis by which the PLO force would leave Beirut and move to Syria. He phoned the California White House on Sunday, 3 July, to inform them. Whether or not this quick settlement would have worked remains conjectural because that night Haig was abruptly relieved of his duties.[62] However, if there was a chance of success, we are reminded again of the dangers of shifting the key foreign policy adviser in the middle of a crisis.

On 6 July Reagan agreed "in principle to contribute a small contingent" of U.S. troops as part of a multinational force for "temporary peacekeeping" in Beirut. The die was cast. The Soviets and Syrians, who had been feuding bitterly over responsibility for the Syrian military defeat by the Israelis, responded to the prospect of U.S. entry into the Lebanese thicket by resolving their differences.[63] Arafat became more emboldened. On 9 July the Syrians rejected the plan to transfer PLO forces to Syria.

Lebanon now settled into weeks of violent stalemate. Both sides were trapped. The PLO leadership would not be forced out of West Beirut, but it could not leave on its own power. The Israelis hesitated to enter West Beirut because they did not want to suffer casualties or to alienate the Americans. But remaining on the outskirts of the city was a public relations disaster. Unlike the British in the Falklands or the United States in Grenada, the Israelis could not close Lebanon to the foreign press. No political analysis could overcome nightly pictures of dead bodies, partially destroyed buildings, suffering civilians, and falling bombs. Throughout the summer, protests over specific Israeli actions were continually heard from the White House, Congress, already unfriendly sectors of the foreign policy community, and even Jewish groups.[64]

While the fighting continued, Habib negotiated one broken cease-fire after another. He tried to arrange a deal to allow the PLO leadership to evacuate Beirut unhindered. As the weeks passed, Sharon became convinced that Arafat would never agree to withdraw as long as he believed that the United States would restrain Israel. Therefore, on 4 August he ordered a thrust by Israeli armored units into West Beirut under the cover of heavy artillery fire.[65] This attack caused a heated exchange of messages between Reagan and Begin. It also led to the PLO's rapid acceptance of Habib's major points on 6 August. By 9 August, Israel had accepted his plan "in principle." Yet there was still no final agreement. Therefore, in one of the most controversial moves of the war, Sharon ordered Israeli warplanes to bombard West Beirut on 12 August, a bombardment that continued for eleven hours.[66]

The president was disgusted. By now, he was deeply suspicious of Israeli actions. He too had been moved by the media coverage, especially a photograph of a baby that lost its arms printed in the *Washington Post*. (Actually the picture was deceptive and UPI issued a correction the following month; the baby's arms were bandaged after being burned in a PLO attack on East Beirut and he was recovering satisfactorily.)[67] With cameras capturing the session, the president telephoned Begin on 12 August expressing U.S. "outrage" and demanding an end to the attacks. Indeed, he told Begin that "the symbol of this war is becoming a baby without arms."[68] When the prime minister phoned back to confirm that "a complete cease-fire" had been implemented, it appeared that American leverage on the Israelis had been profound. Again, the images were deceptive. Sharon had exceeded his authority and the Israeli Cabinet had ordered him to end the raids before the president's call.[69] Nonetheless, the image of U.S. control of Israeli actions was reinforced, making the United States susceptible to Arab pressure. If Washington possessed such authority over Israeli policy, why not exercise it more frequently?

American-Israeli contacts became increasingly bitter and Israel's determination to force the PLO leadership to leave Beirut was now intensified. Despite the bombings of 12 August (or perhaps because of them), an agreement for the peaceful departure of the PLO forces and Syrian troops in West Beirut was rapidly concluded. On 19 August President Reagan announced that eight hundred U.S. marines would join with French and Italian forces in protecting the

PLO fighters as they departed for various Arab destinations. Three days later Bashir Gemayel was elected president of Lebanon by the country's weakened parliament.

The successful and rapid removal of PLO forces from West Beirut encouraged a false sense of stability. Bashir Gemayel was not the United States' first choice to attempt rebuilding the country. Yet it was recognized that his close relationship with the Israelis might induce them to withdraw. He could at the same time attempt to reestablish connections with the surrounding Arab states.

The Reagan Plan

With Lebanon temporarily quiescent, the administration's attention turned to the Palestinian question. Every new administration since Eisenhower has presented a peace plan for the Arab-Israeli dispute early in its first term. The results were the Johnston Plan, Dulles's August 1955 speech, the Johnson Plan, the Rogers Plan, and Carter's comprehensive conception of a Geneva Conference. Reagan was no different from other presidents in hoping to achieve a Mideast peace. In Reagan's case a special incentive operated that had not been present previously: his predecessor had successfully sponsored an Egyptian-Israeli settlement. If Carter could succeed with Cairo, why couldn't Reagan with the Palestinians?

Shortly after the administration assumed office, the final Israeli withdrawal from the Sinai seemed threatened by a Soviet veto of the U.N. peacekeeping force that had been prescribed under the 1979 Egyptian-Israeli peace treaty. The administration was forced to waste precious weeks in fall 1981 to bring about a multinational force with the Europeans as a substitute.[70] In Haig's view, one positive effect of engaging the Europeans was to prevent an independent initiative by them and to commit them indirectly to the Camp David process. However, this time might have been devoted to the autonomy discussions; by the time the Sinai multinational force negotiations were complete, Sadat was dead.

As early as August 1981, Haig had informed the president that a secret contact had been made with the PLO through an intermediary who said that Yassir Arafat was ready to recognize Israel's right to exist and to enter into negotiations. When nothing came of the contact, Haig assumed the matter had ended. Assistant Secretary of State Nicholas Veliotes continued to deal through John Edwin Mroz of the Institute of East-West Affairs until June 1982, when the contacts were suspended because of the Israeli invasion of Lebanon.[71]

After Sharon met with Haig about his plans in May, NEA and the Pentagon proposed that the United States recognize the PLO. By July, when it was besieged in Beirut, the PLO was demanding American recognition as the price for its departure. This position had strong support in the U.S. bureaucracy. On their trip to Saudi Arabia, Bush and Weinberger informed the Saudis that the administration would not let Israel determine U.S. policy and that its approach to the area would soon change.[72] Shultz stated at his confirmation hearings before the Senate Foreign Relations Committee, "The crisis in Lebanon makes painfully and totally clear a central reality in the Middle East: the legitimate needs and problems of the Palestinian people must be addressed and resolved—urgently and in all their dimensions."[73] The Saudi and Syrian foreign ministers presented the PLO case more directly to the president at the same time.[74] Reagan told the Arab diplomats that he would not recognize the PLO, but he promised to address the Palestinian issue after the PLO fighters left Beirut. Thus, several weeks after the Israeli invasion, the president secretly promised that he would embark on an initiative on behalf of the Palestinians to compensate the Arabs for Israel's actions.[75]

Shultz initiated a policy review during which he consulted specialists inside and outside the State Department. This review concluded that the PLO was at a point of maximum weakness, offering a unique opportunity for an initiative on the Palestinian question. Since Israel had less to fear from a defeated PLO, there would be less excuse for failure to make major concessions. State Department experts advised the immediate pursuit of this program lest Arab radicals and Soviet influence resurface. They also feared that Israeli settlement activity on the West Bank would soon make any attempt at permanently settling the Palestinian situation obsolete.[76] Moreover, the Arabs were preparing for a summit meeting at Fez, Morocco, in early September, and high-level administration officials believed the meeting would be highlighted by wholesale condemnations of the United States for its failure to prevent Israeli actions in Lebanon.

At the end of August, Veliotes was sent secretly to Jordan for discussions with King Hussein about U.S. proposals for the West Bank. He had developed a close relationship with the Jordanian monarch while he was U.S. ambassador in Amman under Carter. Veliotes returned to Washington confident that the king would support (perhaps within seventy-two hours) a publicly delivered American plan and that this support would strengthen Arab moderates at the forthcoming Arab summit.[77] (It is worth recalling that the famous Rogers Plan for the Middle East, enunciated by Secretary of State Rogers a dozen years earlier, was also presented shortly before an Arab summit.)

In light of these considerations and concern about a possible leak from Israel, on the night of 1 September President Reagan delivered a surprise speech on the Middle East. He presented American ideas on the final shape of a Palestinian settlement, which were quickly labeled the Reagan Plan. Barely mentioning Lebanon, the president rejected both an independent Palestinian state and

Israeli sovereignty over the West Bank and Gaza. Instead he argued, "Self-government by the Palestinians of the West Bank and Gaza in association with Jordan offers the best chance for a durable, just and lasting peace." The president also called upon Israel to freeze all settlement activity on the West Bank. At the last minute he personally added a paragraph suggesting that Israel could not be expected to return to the narrow and indefensible frontiers it had endured during the nineteen years before 1967.[78]

Before the speech, Shultz phoned Haig to ask for his support of the initiative. Haig refused. Then he went public with his criticism, calling the proposal for a freeze on West Bank settlements "a very serious mistake."[79] The Reagan Plan would never have been presented had Haig remained secretary of state—one more dramatic example of the effect that personnel change has on U.S. Mideast policy.

The plan was undiplomatically rejected by Prime Minister Begin and his Cabinet because it compromised their claims to Israeli sovereignty over the West Bank and Gaza and differed from their interpretation of the Camp David accords. They also thought it would lead to a PLO state on the West Bank, thus endangering Israel's vital security. The harsh rejection was yet another public relations disaster for the Israeli government.[80]

Several American Jewish leaders—concerned by the Begin government's conduct during the war, the tough image Israel had acquired over the previous several months, and the poor reception of Begin's abrupt rejection—were fearful of alienating a president who had placed his own name on the Mideast plan and a Congress that appeared supportive. Emboldened by the Labor party's willingness to consider the plan, these Jewish leaders attempted to present a perspective different from that of Israeli government policy. They noted the plan's positive elements, such as its emphasis on defensible borders for Israel.[81] The Reagan administration had made these statements possible by avoiding any condemnation of Israel for rejecting the plan. However, many observers incorrectly took the differences in style between the Likud government and some American Jewish leaders as a sign of an impending break between Israel and American Jewry.

As the administration well understood, the favorable response to its plan in the United States was as irrelevant as Begin's rejection if the Arab states did not endorse it and if King Hussein, who publicly praised the plan, still refused to negotiate directly with Israel. Contacts with Saudi Arabia and Jordan led administration officials to anticipate that the president's proposals would preempt an Arab plan at the summit.[82] They were soon disappointed. In the meeting at Fez, the Arab states offered a plan of their own rather than accept the Reagan proposals. Shaped by the need to find consensus among sharply differing views and to contain the radicals' bitterness over Arab failure to assist the PLO in Lebanon, the Fez Plan offered a very different perspective on the future of the area than its American counterpart. It called for the creation of an independent

Palestinian state with Jerusalem as its capital and again labeled the PLO the "sole legitimate representative" of the Palestinians. Markedly different from the Camp David agreements, this plan envisioned immediate Israeli withdrawal from the West Bank and Gaza followed by a period "not longer than several months" during which the area would be under the control of the U.N. (where Arab influence was determining). Then, a PLO state would be established. But would that state coexist with Israel or replace it? On this point the plan was cryptic, calling for "the drawing up by the Security Council of guarantees for peace for all the states of the region, including the independent Palestinian state."[83] In this key clause, Israel was not mentioned, but U.S. officials clung to the hope that the phrase "all the states of the region" included Israel.

The summit's actions were hardly the authority sought by Hussein for negotiating on behalf of the Palestinians for the future of the West Bank and Gaza Strip. Through the next several months, he negotiated with Arafat for some arrangement that would permit him to proceed. These discussions between two former enemies intensified Israeli bitterness at an American policy whose initial success seemed to depend on the goodwill of Yassir Arafat. It was inconceivable that the Israelis would offer concessions if they thought that the West Bank would be taken over by the PLO, which they feared would happen even if the initial arrangement was a federation with Jordan. Of course, the administration was confident that Hussein would manipulate Arafat rather than vice-versa. As events after 1 September amply demonstrated, however, the king had not survived thirty years of rule because he was bold. Hussein was too weak to act without a favorable Arab consensus. By relying on Jordanian participation, the administration had placed itself on a tenuous limb indeed.

In retrospect, the Reagan Plan failed because the fear of leaks prevented detailed preliminary discussions with Israel, because the probable Arab and Israeli reactions to an American plan were not accurately anticipated, and because the risks of failure were not evaluated. In particular, the future perils in Lebanon were not adequately understood. As the president noted in his speech, the last of the PLO forces had left West Beirut. Weinberger, who had opposed the entry of the marines in the first place, pulled them out on 10 September, fifteen days ahead of schedule. Habib supported him, fearing the marine presence would become permanent.[84] Yet the Syrians and the PLO still remained in the north of the country around Tripoli and in the east in the Bekaa Valley. The Israelis were located in the south and center sectors of the country. All three were surrounded by violently warring Lebanese factions.

The negotiations for withdrawal of all foreign forces would never have been easy, but the Reagan Plan increased the difficulties. Israel and Syria both had a pressing interest in withdrawals because they were overextended. Although Israel could shell Damascus at will from its posts in Lebanon, mounting casualties and economic considerations militated in favor of early withdrawal.

Syria had been defeated and needed a respite. But the Reagan Plan gave both sides reason to delay their departure from Lebanon—to deflect attention from the Palestinian question. The Likud government feared increased American pressures on Israel to make the compromises anticipated in the president's plan. Assad worried that concentrating on the Palestinian question would result in bypassing the Golan Heights problem and leave Israel permanently in control there.

The Reagan Plan expanded the administration's agenda, making it difficult to handle either Lebanon or the Palestinians. Both dilemmas were made more difficult when Bashir Gemayel was assassinated on 14 September, only five days after the enunciation of the Fez Plan. Since the multinational force had already been withdrawn, Begin, Sharon, and Foreign Minister Shamir immediately moved their forces into West Beirut despite the cease-fire agreement. Their goal was to capture or destroy huge caches of arms and the two thousand Palestinian terrorists suspected of having remained behind in Beirut.[85]

The results were disastrous. The Israelis allowed Phalangist forces into the camps of Sabra and Shatila where, instead of confronting guerrilla fighters, they killed hundreds of civilians. When the Israeli press began to reveal what had happened, widespread protests developed in Israel. The opposition called for an independent commission of inquiry to investigate the cause of the massacres. Begin first refused, and criticism mounted against Israel. In the United States criticism was acute from Israel's friends, particularly American Jews. When Begin reversed himself a week later and the commission was appointed and began to operate, dissatisfaction with Israel began to abate in the U.S. public arena.[86]

The Reagan administration's major reaction to the massacres was to reorganize the multinational force and order the marines back to Beirut. American officials were guilt-ridden that the multinational force had been withdrawn prematurely and that guarantees of safety for Palestinian residents of Beirut had not been kept. The Reagan Plan had reflected a sympathy for the Palestinians that was running high in the administration and was only intensified by the killings in Beirut. As Shultz told the U.N. General Assembly on 30 September, Israel must yield territory to gain peace; the "Palestinian claim is undeniable" to "a place with which they can identify."[87]

The Reagan administration, however, was quickly becoming hostage to its own plan. It could not take any action that might adversely affect the ongoing Hussein-Arafat talks. If Israel could be pressed to withdraw from Lebanon, Hussein would have evidence of American seriousness. The king subsequently made Israeli withdrawal a precondition for his entering the talks.[88]

Thus, in December Reagan, Bush, Shultz, Clark, Habib, and Kenneth Dam, deputy secretary of state, all attempted to persuade Congress not to increase aid to Israel in order not to send the wrong signal to the Arabs.[89] However, despite its assumption that Israel had lost support over Lebanon, the administration was soundly defeated. The stunning reversal of Jerusalem's previously sagging fortunes on Capitol Hill can be attributed to three developments in fall 1982. (1) Many in Congress believed that Israel had redeemed itself by establishing the commission of inquiry; (2) King Hussein still had not agreed to enter talks on the Reagan Plan, which dulled the effect of Israel's rejection; and (3) several critics of Israel were defeated and new supporters elected in the 1982 congressional elections, demonstrating continued political advantages in supporting Israel.

As we have often noted in this study, Congress is the branch of government most attuned to political winds. This was shown again when a majority in the House (followed in the Senate) signed a letter opposing sophisticated arms sales to Jordan. Thus, when Reagan met Hussein in Washington in December, he told the king that a squadron of F-16s would be forthcoming only when he joined the talks. Reagan also secretly gave Hussein a letter stating that if the king would only agree to enter the talks, the United States would pressure Israel to freeze settlements. As a further reassurance to the king, Reagan promised to put forward an "American draft" at the negotiations. Several weeks later, however, the president may inadvertently have undercut Hussein when he secretly told a Saudi emissary that the Reagan Plan's term "association" between the West Bank and Jordan could also mean "confederation." A confederation is a link between two countries, implying possible U.S. acceptance of an independent Palestinian state. Under this interpretation, the president would have given a greater concession to the Saudis than to Hussein.[90]

Progressively, the talks with Arafat became entangled in competing Arab tactics and objectives, with radical PLO factions seeking to prevent an understanding between Hussein and Arafat. On 10 April Hussein announced his failure to reach agreement with Arafat on a joint approach to the Palestinian question. Despite secret American commitments, he was not prepared to enter negotiations without an accord with the PLO chief. The program envisioned by the Reagan Plan had collapsed. Once again an American Mideast initiative was sacrificed on the altar of intra-Arab rivalry.

Lebanon: U.S. versus Syria

With the Reagan Plan stymied, the focus of U.S. activity in the region remained Lebanon. The United States had never before confronted such an acute or prolonged Arab-Israeli crisis. Compounding the unprecedented difficulties, American troops were involved for the first time. No administration had ever been tested under comparable conditions. I have argued that personnel turnover creates policy instability. Two secretaries of state, two NSC advisers, and three Mideast negotiators served from mid-1982 to late 1983. These changes were matched by truly stunning U.S. alterations from peacekeeper to combatant, from opponent to ally of Israel, and finally from engagement to withdrawal.

The new president of Lebanon, Amin Gemayel, appeared a more tractable figure than his late brother. Unlike Bashir he had never been so close to the Israelis. When Israeli officials tried to persuade him to sign a separate peace treaty with Israel, the United States opposed it. American officials were in no mood to see Israel rewarded for its misdeeds. Besides, an Israel-Lebanese peace treaty would further divide Lebanon and certainly threaten the Reagan Plan because it would lead to new tension in the Arab world, perhaps culminating in a boycott of Lebanon and the country's isolation. Instead, the administration offered Gemayel economic and military aid and proposed to train his army. Presented an escape from the unpalatable choice between Syria and Israel, Gemayel and his advisers concluded that the protection of a superpower eager to come to their aid was far preferable. By October 1982, the United States had become the key power behind the Lebanese government.[91]

Habib now moved to coordinate Israeli-Lebanese talks. The anticipated outcome was an agreement for Israeli withdrawal from Lebanon, followed by Syrian acquiescence. The talks were scheduled to begin on 7 November but did not convene until 28 December. During these crucial weeks, the Lebanese and Israelis contested the site of the talks—the Lebanese demurring on holding them in Jerusalem. One reason for the delay was that the Israelis and the Lebanese were secretly concluding an agreement. However, Sharon foolishly leaked it to the press to the utter dismay of Gemayel and the sheer astonishment of Habib who did not know about the secret negotiations. By all available accounts, this agreement was not substantially different from the accord reached in May 1983.[92] Nonetheless, the talks quickly reverted to formal negotiations mediated by Habib. Then the Israelis and Lebanese spent months arguing over whether the outcome would form an Israeli peace agreement with a second Arab nation or would be only a security arrangement.

While the Israeli, Lebanese, and American participants argued, the Syrians rearmed with massive Russian assistance and eight thousand Soviet advisers. In the eighteen months after their forces had been smashed, Syrian forces were augmented by $2.5 billion of the latest Russian equipment, over $1 billion of which was paid for directly by the Saudis. Their prewar force was doubled and substantially upgraded. In January 1983, for example, U.S. intelligence officials revealed that the Soviet Union had supplied Syria with new long-range SAM-5 ground-to-air missiles, which sharply increased Syrian air defense capabilities. This was the first time these missiles had been placed outside the U.S.S.R.[93]

While these developments were occurring, U.S.-Israeli relations were still tense. Sharon and Weinberger had been feuding for months over Israel's terms for sharing the military information gained during the Lebanon war. Weinberger even rejected an agreement reached by a Pentagon team sent to

Israel.[94] The American defense chief also refused to set up a liaison committee to coordinate contacts between neighboring Israeli and American military forces near Beirut. He feared that the Arabs might think that the two countries were coordinating their actions. By early 1983 this had led to a series of confrontations between the two forces. One particularly dramatic incident was on 2 February when an American marine drew his pistol to halt three Israeli tanks that seemed to be heading toward the American lines.[95]

This incident marked the low point of Israeli-American relations over Lebanon. The report of the massacre commission was released several days later, leading to Sharon's resignation and his replacement by Moshe Arens. The new defense minister moved quickly to resolve existing disputes with Washington. He removed all conditions for sharing secrets with the United States and simply informed Weinberger that the information would be handed over. He also issued new orders to Israeli soldiers to observe restraint toward the marines near Beirut.[96] Since his objectives in Lebanon were more limited than Sharon's, Arens also moved to concentrate on security issues in the continuing talks. To all of these moves, the administration reacted with relief.

Events moved quickly to reverse the assumptions on which the administration had operated toward the area since Shultz had taken office. The secretary of state began to conclude that relations with Israel would have to improve if administration policy in the Middle East was to succeed. In April, the week after Hussein refused to enter negotiations with Israel on the Reagan Plan, a terrorist bomb damaged the U.S. embassy in Beirut and caused heavy casualties. As in Gemayel's assassination, Syrian complicity was palpable.[97]

The administration's policy toward the region was unraveling. Four days after the embassy bombing, Shultz traveled to the area to pursue a Lebanese-Israeli accord that Habib and his assistant Morris Draper had been unable to conclude. The secretary of state's visit was a success. An agreement was reached on 4 May and signed on 17 May. It terminated the state of war between the two countries, created liaison offices, established the basis for discussions on the normalization of relations, created a security zone in southern Lebanon where Israeli and Lebanese patrols would operate for at least two years, and included the withdrawal of Israeli troops. But the agreement would be effected only if Syria also agreed to remove its troops from Lebanon. However, Assad declared that the accord merely ratified Israel's gains in Lebanon. "Camp Reagan" and "an advance copy of Camp David," the Syrian press called it.[98] When Syria refused to withdraw, the United States was stuck backing an agreement that could not be implemented.

In response, the administration's policy was transformed almost overnight. The president and his secretary of state realized too late that it was Syria, not Israel, that would not withdraw voluntarily from Lebanon.[99] As Assad became more obdurate, the Israeli-American relationship steadily improved. The administration renewed permission for Israel to purchase seventy-five F-16 jets embargoed since the beginning of the war. There would be much more to come.

In Lebanon, America's embrace of Gemayel unintentionally gave the regime a false sense of confidence. The Lebanese government used U.S. backing to avoid making compromises with its domestic foes. As the U.S. embassy in Beirut had predicted, a broad accord with Israel led to further opposition by Lebanon's Moslems. The Syrians took advantage of this growing opposition to Gemayel within Lebanon and attempted to undermine the accord.[100] Assad influenced events by supporting Lebanese factions opposed to the Gemayel government and by aiding PLO rebels against Arafat. The Syrian president refused to see Habib, whom he blamed for the Lebanese-Israeli agreements. Since Habib's thesis that Syria would withdraw following an agreement had now been proven fallacious, Reagan replaced him with McFarlane, who had entry into Damascus but believed that Assad only understood the language of force.[101]

It was not long before McFarlane's theory was tested. The Israelis were exhausted and disheartened by their Lebanese experience—their economy shattered, casualties mounting, domestic dissent at an all-time high. The war now claimed its most prominent Israeli victim, Menachem Begin. His health failing, still mourning the death of his wife in the previous November, and sickened by the failures of the war and the deteriorating economy, Begin announced his resignation. With diplomatic progress now seemingly hopeless, the Israeli public and army pressed for unilateral withdrawal from the Shouf mountains near Beirut.

The administration, however, cautioned the Israelis not to withdraw. When their determination to pull out became clear, it sought to delay them. Finally, on 3 September, because Lebanese factions could not agree on a post-Israeli disposition of forces and Gemayel refused to coordinate with Jerusalem, the Israelis began their withdrawals. Syrian-backed Druze militiamen immediately gained control of most areas evacuated by the Israelis. With the Lebanese army seemingly helpless to stop them, McFarlane, over the objections of the marine commander in Beirut, ordered naval guns offshore to fire on Druze positions. During the weeks after America joined the Lebanese fray, U.S. marines at the Beirut airport progressively became targets for militiamen opposed to Gemayel.[102] U.S. forces had completed their evolution from peacekeepers to combatants.

At first the new strategy seemed to work. A cease-fire was arranged and the stage set for Lebanese reconciliation talks in Switzerland. The administration reached a compromise with Congress that allowed an eighteen-month extension of the marine presence. Yet these signs of progress were a mirage. On 23 October the marine headquarters in Beirut was attacked by a terrorist on a suicide mission driving a truck filled with explosives. He killed 241 marines and navy personnel. The death blow to the U.S. role in the country had been delivered.

This devastating attack occurred when the administration was in the midst of a major dispute over its future strategy. Weinberger maintained his usual opposition to any escalation of the American role in Lebanon and to any expansion of the U.S. relationship with Israel. McFarlane, Shultz, and Eagleburger, however, supported a tough stance against Syria and had been horrified by the signs of diminished Israeli will under the new prime minister, Yitzhak Shamir. They prepared to increase aid to Israel and to resurrect the strategic cooperation agreement suspended almost two years earlier.[103]

A few days before the truck-bombing, the National Security Council gathered to discuss National Security Decision Direction 111, which included a plan to improve relations with Jerusalem. Before the president, Shultz argued in favor and Weinberger against the new policy. As the NSC met in an emergency session that grim Sunday afternoon in October to monitor the consequences of the bombing of marine headquarters, the argument between Weinberger and Shultz continued. Later in the week Reagan informed McFarlane that he had decided in favor of Shultz's approach and signed the NSC directive. Eagleburger went immediately to Israel to discuss the new policy. As an indication of the administration's seriousness, he informed the Israelis that they would be allowed to use U.S. aid in building a new Israeli jet fighter, the Lavie.[104]

The outcome of these discussions was a visit to Washington by Shamir and Arens in late November. Before their arrival, the middle levels of the State Department and Pentagon debated how to approach greater cooperation with Israel. The Near East Bureau and the Pentagon still tried to halt certain measures. Even after the president had publicly supported a new relationship with Israel, Chairman Vessey of the Joint Chiefs publicly asserted that strategic cooperation with Israel was a bad idea. He argued that Israel's goals were different from those of the United States: "We don't need to be siding with either the Israelis or the Syrians in trying to reestablish Lebanon."[105] Finally, the two competing bureaucratic groups compromised. Shamir and Arens were offered a broad commitment to strategic cooperation. A joint Israeli-American political-military group was established to work out details of the new program. It began functioning at the beginning of 1984 without any indication of how proponents in the administration could overcome the Pentagon's reluctance to implement the policy. The president also agreed to provide new grant aid in deference to Israel's growing debt burden and to lay a basis for an American-Israel free trade area, whose details would have to be negotiated and then approved by Congress.[106]

The administration's abrupt return to its original conception of relations with Israel did not change the situation in Lebanon: aborted reconciliation talks, a weakening government position, military defeats, the increasing power of Syria and its clients. As further indication of the Syrians' growing strength, the PLO rebels whom they supported forced Arafat to leave ignominiously from

Tripoli in November, his second humiliation in a year. In December and January, U.S. carrier-based combat planes and offshore gunners unsuccessfully tried to stop the advance of Syria's Lebanese allies.

Back in Washington a rising chorus—from a military commission to congressional liberals—called for the marines' withdrawal. By the end of January 1984, the Lebanese army had split and collapsed. The Shiites and Druze had retaken West Beirut and Gemayel's government seemed near disintegration. The president accused his Democratic foes of being "ready to surrender." The marines were placed in Lebanon "in the interest of our own national security." "We have vital interests in Lebanon, and our actions in Lebanon are in the cause of world peace." Reagan declared, "If we get out it also means the end of any ability on our part to bring about an overall peace in the Middle East."[107] Then he ordered the redeployment of the marines offshore.

Behind the scenes he compromised among his competing advisers. Shultz favored the increased use of offshore firepower to defend Gemayel. Weinberger wanted the marines removed. The president ordered both, but he was soon forced to circumscribe the offshore attacks because they were ineffective and they were causing civilian casualties that aroused domestic protests. This time Weinberger won the internal conflict. The real victor, however, was the White House political team led by Baker, which was the only faction that wanted both an improvement in relations with Israel and a withdrawal from Lebanon.

In the Middle East, the United States was seen as having failed to back its allies. Several moderate Arab states anxiously distanced themselves from Washington. Standing next to Reagan at the White House in early 1984, Egypt's president Mubarak called on the United States to deal directly with the PLO. Hussein, bitterly disappointed, said of Washington, "You've obviously made your choice and your choice is Israel and support of Israel."[108] Reagan was thus forced to withdraw a proposal to sell lethal Stinger hand-held ground-to-air missiles to Jordan. Then Gemayel abrogated the 17 May agreement with Israel, reflecting Syria's control over Lebanon's affairs. The Israelis were left questioning the value of peace agreements with Arab states, especially in light of deteriorating relations with Egypt after the Lebanon war.[109]

Conclusion

The president demonstrated that the complement to his philosophical rigidity was tactical flexibility. Reagan's approach to the Middle East was a combination of emotion, ideology, lack of knowledge, and instinctive political acumen that made him so difficult for analysts to comprehend. He could proclaim a united pro-American Lebanon vital to U.S. interests in one month (January 1984) and then act as if the country did not exist the next. He presided over periods of Israeli-American tensions unusual even in the checkered history of relations between Jerusaalem and Washington and yet later approved new levels of assistance to Israel. He took responsibility for the establishment of the first genuine strategic relationship with Israel but left the Pentagon leadership, which would have to implement agreements, opposed. His administration sponsored the largest single arms sale in history to an Arab state (AWACS to Saudi Arabia) against bitter domestic opposition and then was unable to gain Saudi cooperation for U.S. diplomatic and political-military initiatives. He reveled in rebuilding American military might and failed to use arms effectively in Lebanon. He was preoccupied with the expansion of Soviet arms and influence and then watched helplessly as Russian involvement escalated in Syria. He reviled the PLO yet saved its leadership from destruction.

Ronald Reagan seemed blind to these contradictions. He used the actor's ability to reassure and convince to compensate for a lack of policy expertise and managerial skill in the area of foreign policy. But as with other presidents before him, his attitudes, style, and advisers dominated his administration. However frustrating were Reagan's experiences in the Middle East during his first three years, his efforts and their results were consistent with the history of the U.S. relationship to the Arab-Israeli dispute. There have been occasional moments of spectacular success—U.N. Resolution 242 in 1967, the Kissinger shuttle, the Camp David accords, and the Egypt-Israel peace treaty. Unfulfilled objectives, however, have been the norm: from trusteeship proposals to the Baghdad Pact; from the Johnson and Rogers Plans to autonomy and the Reagan Plan. The frequent Arab-Israeli wars testify to the inability of American leaders to mold regional developments to their designs and interests. Where Reagan forged new ground was in deploying U.S. troops during an Arab-Israeli crisis in an effort to stabilize a particular government. The experience of the marines in Lebanon substantially contributed to U.S. consternation in the region. But U.S. policy makers have always had to tread cautiously through the political minefields of intra-Arab tensions and Arab-Israeli conflicts. Since the fall of the shah, Iranian-Arab tensions have added a dangerous new element.

The difficulty of dealing with this region has put increasing pressure on America's leadership as it attempts to advance U.S. interests there. While it is impossible to predict the nature of future American efforts, the Arab-Israeli issue seems certain to continue to fascinate and at times frustrate. It will continue to occupy the attention of America's highest-ranking officials. Their handling of this problem undoubtedly will continue to reflect their global philosophy and the quality of their decision making and leadership.

ABBREVIATIONS USED IN NOTES

DOHC: John Foster Dulles Oral History Collection (Princeton University)

DSB: *Department of State Bulletin* (Washington, D.C.)

FBIS: Foreign Broadcast and Information Service

FRUS: Foreign Relations of the United States Diplomatic Papers (Washington D.C.: U.S. Government Printing Office)

JOHI: Lyndon Baines Johnson Oral History Interviews (Austin, Texas)

KOHI: John F. Kennedy Oral History Interviews (Boston)

MEPS: *Middle East Policy Survey*

MNC: *Multinational Corporations and United States Foreign Policy,* hearings, 94th Cong., 1st Sess., 1975

MNOC: *Multinational Oil Companies and U.S. Foreign Policy* (Washington, D.C.: U.S. Government Printing Office, 1979)

NER: *Near East Report* (Washington, D.C.)

NYT: *New York Times*

PC 1976: *The Presidential Campaign 1976* (Washington, D.C.: U.S. Government Printing Office, 1979)

PPP: Public Papers of the President (Washington, D.C.: U.S. Government Printing Office)

YKW: (London) *Sunday Times, The Yom Kippur War* (Garden City, N.Y.: Doubleday, 1974)

NOTES

Chapter 1. The Process

1. Reuben Fink, *America and Palestine* (New York: Herald Square Press, 1944), 20. Adams added, "Once restored to an independent government and no longer persecuted they would soon wear away some of the asperities and peculiarities of their character, possibly in time become liberal Unitarian Christians." Quoted in Peter Grose, *Israel in the Mind of America* (New York: Alfred A. Knopf, 1983), 6.

2. Frank E. Manuel, *The Realities of American-Palestine Relations* (Washington, D.C.: Public Affairs Press, 1949), 72.

3. Sen. James Abourezk, "The Relentless Israeli Propaganda Machine" (New York: Penthouse International, 1978; distributed by Arab Information Center, New York), 3.

4. Alvin Rosenfeld, *The Plot to Destroy Israel: The Road to Armageddon* (New York: G. P. Putnam's Sons, 1977), 174.

5. Philip J. Baram, *The Department of State in the Middle East, 1919–1945* (Philadelphia: University of Pennsylvania Press, 1978), 49, 52, 327–28.

6. Congressional Quarterly, *The Middle East: U.S. Policy, Israel, Oil, and the Arabs*, 4th ed. (Washington, D.C.: Congressional Quarterly, 1929), 97.

7. For a more complete discussion of religion and U.S. Mideast policy, see Steven L. Spiegel, "Religious Components of U.S. Middle East Policy," *Journal of International Affairs* 36 (Fall-Winter 1982–1983): 235–46.

8. Richard N. Lebow, "Woodrow Wilson and the Balfour Declaration," *Journal of Modern History* 40 (December 1968): 521.

9. Manuel, 163.

10. Lebow, 517–18.

11. Ibid., 522–23; Grose, 66–69.

12. Manuel, 167; Grose, 66–71, 82–89.

13. Selig Adler, "Franklin D. Roosevelt and Zionism: The Wartime Record," *Judaism*

21 (No. 83, 1972): 270. For a more complete and detailed account, see Henry L. Feingold, *The Politics of Rescue* (New Jersey: Rutgers University Press, 1970), 99–109.

14. Adler, 265; *Foreign Relations of the United States Diplomatic Papers*, vol. 5, 1944 (Washington, D.C.: United States Government Printing Office, 1965), 88–91. (Hereafter cited as FRUS.)

15. Adler, 266; *New York Times*, 16 October 1944; author's interview with Emmanuel Celler. (Hereafter cited as NYT.)

16. Grose, 115, and chap. 6.

17. William A. Eddy, *F.D.R. Meets Ibn Sa'ud* (New York: American Friends of the Middle East, 1954), 34.

18. Joseph B. Schectman, *The United States and the Jewish State Movement* (New York: Herzl Press, 1966), 110.

19. Howard M. Sachar, *Europe Leaves The Middle East, 1936–1954* (New York: Alfred A. Knopf, 1972), 454.

20. Adler, 268.

21. Schectman, 112–13; Charles L. Gellner, *The Palestine Problem*, Public Affairs Bulletin, No. 50 (Washington, D.C.: Library of Congress Legislative Reference Service, 1 March 1947), 115.

22. Robert J. Donovan, *Conflict and Crisis, The Presidency of Harry S. Truman, 1945–1948* (New York: W. W. Norton, 1977), 312; FRUS, 1945, 704–705.

23. Sachar, 454.

Chapter 2. Truman

1. See, for example, John Snetsinger, *Truman, The Jewish Vote and the Creation of Israel* (Stanford: Hoover Institute Press, 1974), 35, 116.

2. Snetsinger, 35–38. Also see Arthur Abramson, *The Formulation of American Foreign Policy towards the Middle East during the Truman Administration, 1945–1948*. Ph.D. diss., Department of Political Science, University of California, Los Angeles, 1981. Chap. 1, pp. 101–4.

3. Zvi Ganin, *Truman, American Jewry and Israel, 1945–1948* (New York: Holmes and Meier, 1979), 157–58, and Bernard Postal and Henry Levy, *And the Hills Shouted for Joy* (New York: David McKay Company, 1973), 321–22; Clark M. Clifford, "Recognizing Israel: The Behind-the-Scenes Struggle in 1948 Between the President and the State Department," *American Heritage*, April 1977, 4–14.

4. Hadley Cantril, *Public Opinion, 1935–45* (Princeton: Princeton University Press, 1951), 386.

5. The Gallup Poll, *Public Opinion, 1935–48*, vol. I (New York: Random House, 1972), 554.

6. Eddy, 37. The date of October 1945 for the meeting reported here is suspect, because Eddy claims it was "after the elections" and none were held that year.

7. Abramson, 409–13, 428; Dean Acheson, *Present at the Creation* (New York: Signet, 1969), 240.

8. Snetsinger, 18: Acheson, 240–41.

9. NYT, 13 June 1946 (Annual Labour Party Conference at Bournemouth, 12 June 1946), p. 14.

10. John M. Blum, ed., *The Price of Vision: The Diary of Henry A. Wallace, 1942–46* (Boston: Houghton Mifflin, 1973), 607.

11. Truman to Wise, 6 August 1947, o.p. 204-misc., Truman Library.

12. Donovan, 320.

13. Blum, 607.

14. Harry S. Truman to Stephen Wise, 1 June 1943, Robert Wagner Papers, George-town University, Washington, D.C., quoted in Snetsinger, 15.

15. Based on Niles's papers cited in Abram L. Sachar, *The Redemption of the Un-wanted: From the Liberation of the Death Camps to the Founding of Israel* (New York: St. Martins/Marek, 1983), 190–91; author's interview with Herbert Fierst.

16. Preliminary report to the president on displaced persons in Germany and Austria, the Harrison Report, August 1945, *Department of State Bulletin* 13 (September 1945): 456–63. (Hereafter cited as DSB.)

17. FRUS, 1945, 737–39; Truman, *Years of Trial and Hope*, vol. 2 (Garden City, N.Y.: Doubleday, 1956), 138–39.

18. Ian J. Bickerton, "President Truman's Recognition of Israel," *American Jewish Historical Quarterly* 58 (December 1968): 190.

19. Ganin, 81.

20. Donovan, 319.

21. Ganin, 82; Nahum Goldmann, *The Autobiography of Nahum Goldmann: Sixty Years of Jewish Life* (New York: Holt, Rinehart & Winston, 1969), 232–36.

22. Ganin, 90–94.

23. NYT, 7 October 1946, p. 1; Acheson, 239–40.

24. Donovan, 320–22.

25. FRUS, 1947, 1300.

26. James Forrestal, *The Forrestal Diaries*, ed. Walter Millis (New York: Viking, 1951), 357.

27. FRUS, 1947, 1153–58; author's interview with Loy Henderson.

28. Bickerton, 205.

29. Truman, 140; Acheson, 233, 241.

30. FRUS 9 October, 1947, 1177–78.

31. FRUS, 1947, n. 7, p. 1158.

32. FRUS, 1947, 1167; Clifford, 6–7.

33. Abramson, 346; author's interview with Herbert Fierst.

34. Frank J. Adler, *Roots in a Moving Stream: The Centennial History of Congregation B'nai Jehudah of Kansas City* (Kansas City: The Temple Congregation of B'nai Jehudah, 1972), 209, 433; Donovan, 327; Ganin, 138; Acheson, 242–44.

35. For the correspondence on the Negev incident, see FRUS, 1947, 1267–72. For the reaction of Johnson and Hilldring, see FRUS, n. 2, p. 1271. According to Eban, after Hilldring answered the phone, Johnson left the meeting in the middle of his talk for about twenty minutes to speak with the president. Abba Eban, *An Autobiography*, (New York: Random House, 1977), 94–95.

36. FRUS, 1947, 1284.

37. Truman, 158.

38. Dan Kurzman, *Genesis 1948: The First Arab-Israeli War*, (New York: New American Library, Signet Books, 1972), 36–40; and FRUS, 1947, 1287–92; Grose, 248–54.

39. Walter Millis, in collaboration with E. S. Duffield, ed., *The Forrestal Diaries* (New York: Viking, 1951), 344.

40. Donovan, 328–31.

41. Abramson, 356–58; Henderson, who was constantly opposed to Niles's activities, bitterly resented the latter's independence. Author's interview with Loy Henderson.

42. Donovan, 331.

43. FRUS, 1947, 1309.

44. As demonstrated in FRUS, 1947, 1319–21.

45. FRUS, 1947, 1177–78, 1249, 1300–1301; Shlomo Slonim, "The 1948 American Embargo on Arms to Palestine," *Political Science Quarterly* 94 (Fall 1979): 496–97. For evidence of Truman's opposition to sending arms to the Near East, see FRUS, 1948, 598.

46. FRUS, 1947, 1315, 1322–28; Slonim, 499.

47. Leonard Slater, *The Pledge* (New York: Simon and Schuster, 1970); author's interview with Oscar Gass.

48. Robert H. Ferrell, *Off the Record: The Private Papers of Harry S. Truman* (New York: Harper and Row, 1980), 65–66.

49. FRUS, 1947, 1177–78.

50. Donovan, 331.

51. FRUS, 1948, 556–66, 617–18, 637–40.

52. Bickerton, 220–21.

53. FRUS, 1948, 592–99.

54. Abramson, 382–83.

55. See "Proposed United States Policy," in Clifford Memo to Truman, 8 March 1948: FRUS, 1948, 693–95.

56. FRUS, 1948, 695–96.

57. FRUS, 1948, 687–96. Grose, who stresses the importance of Niles's absence, also argues that Clifford was provided with arguments and material by a high-level group of American Zionists and Palestinian Jews, including Ben Cohen, David Ginsburg, Robert Nathan, and Eliahu Elath (264–71).

58. FRUS, 1948, 697, 749.

59. Ibid.

60. FRUS, 1948, 730.

61. Truman, 161; Bickerton, 217; Donovan, 375.

62. Donovan, 376.

63. Author's interview with Dean Rusk.

64. Abramson, 417–22.

65. Abramson, 423–27; Postal and Levy, 319–20; Donovan, 376; Grose, 277–78, 285–86.

66. FRUS, 1948, 755. Slonim (507–8) points out that a powerful argument used by the State Department to gain Truman's continued approval of the embargo was that chances for an imminent Palestine truce would be impeded. Then, the Security Council called for a truce after Department efforts, which served as an excuse for continuing the embargo.

67. Donovan, 378.

68. FRUS, 1948, 832; Trygve Lie, *In the Cause of Peace: Seven Years with the United Nations* (New York: Macmillan, 1954), 169–73.

69. FRUS, 1948, 832.

70. FRUS, 1948, 873–74; 886–89; author's interview with Dean Rusk.

71. Ganin, 175–78; Grose, 282–84.

72. Postal and Levy, 322; FRUS, 1948, 893.

73. Postal and Levy, 328.

74. Postal and Levy, 327.

75. FRUS, 1948, 935–36.

76. FRUS, 1948, 966.

77. FRUS, 1948, 966–67.

78. Donovan, 376–77.

79. FRUS, 1948, 976.

80. Ibid.; Clifford, 8–10.

81. FRUS, 1948, 974–75.

82. Author's interview with Clark Clifford; Clifford, 12.

83. Author's interview with Eliahu Elath.

84. Clifford portrays Lovett as having changed his mind about recognition (Clifford, 10–11, 13), but this is not confirmed by Lovett's memorandum of his conversations. See FRUS, 1948, 1005–7. Lovett, however, did seem prepared to acquiesce in White House preferences. Author's interview with Loy Henderson.

85. FRUS, 1948, 1006–7.

86. FRUS, 1948, 993; Phillip C. Jessup, *The Birth of Nations* (New York: Columbia University Press, 1974), 289, 280–81; author's interview with Raymond Hare. Loy Henderson told the author that he was responsible for Israel's receiving the lower level of recognition, de facto, rather than the higher level, de jure.

87. FRUS, 1948, 993; 1949, p. 681; and Snetsinger, 135.

88. FRUS, 1948, 878–79.

89. FRUS, 1948, 1007.

90. Snetsinger, 132, argues the opposite: "The evidence is overwhelming, not only in the official statements but also in the record of behind-the-scenes maneuverings, that the President was deliberately and calculatingly playing politics with this explosive issue." See also FRUS, 1948, 633; Donovan, 386; and Bickerton, 199–200. Author's interview with Fraser Wilkins.

91. Alfred Steinberg, *The Man from Missouri: The Life and Times of Harry S. Truman* (New York: G. P. Putnam's Sons, 1962), 308.

92. Kurzman, 144–50, 515, 547; Nadav Safran, *From War to War: The Arab-Israeli Confrontation, 1948–1967* (New York: Pegasus, 1969), 96; FRUS, 1948, 1571.

93. George T. Mazuzan, *Warren R. Austin at the U.N., 1946–1953* (Kent, Ohio: Kent State University Press, 1977), 99; *Time*, 5 February 1951, 16.

94. FRUS, 1948, 1117–19, 1120–21, 1140, 1178–79, 1300–1301, 1131–32 (Clifford called Lovett on 22 June and told him the decision had been made). For discussion of Jacobson's effort to help with the loan, see Adler, *Roots in a Moving Stream*, 212–13, 219; author's interview with Eliahu Elath.

95. FRUS, 1948, 1172.

96. FRUS, 1948, 982.

97. FRUS, 1948, 1415 (my italics).

98. FRUS, 1948, 1037.

99. FRUS, 1948, 1313.

100. FRUS, 1948, 1300–1301.

101. FRUS, 1948, 1513.

102. FRUS, 1948, 1136, 1172.

103. FRUS, 1948, 1367–68.

104. FRUS, 1948, 1363, 1437–38.

105. FRUS, 1948, 1420.

106. FRUS, 1948, 1485–86.

107. Jacobson, diary entry, 28 September 1948.

108. FRUS, 1948, 1430, 1437–38; Leonard Mosely, *Marshall, Hero for Our Times* (New York: Hearst Books, 1982), 426–29.

109. FRUS, 1948, 1430, 1437–48.

110. FRUS, 1948, 1448–49, 1463.

111. FRUS, 1948, 1490.

112. FRUS, 1948, 1509, 1512–14.

113. FRUS, 1948, 1512–14.

114. Public Papers of the President, 1948, 913. (Hereafter cited as PPP.)

115. FRUS, 1948, 1528.

116. FRUS, 1948, 1535.

117. FRUS, 1948, 1600.

118. FRUS, 1948, 1565–67.

119. FRUS, 1948, 1565–67.

120. FRUS, 1948, 1595, 1607–09, 1610–12, 1625, 1622.

121. James G. McDonald, *My Mission in Israel, 1948–1951* (New York: Simon and Schuster, 1951), 116–17; FRUS, 1948, 1704.

122. PPP, 1948, 913.

123. FRUS, 1948, 1681; author's interview with Eliahu Elath. Grose points out that "as late as March 16, 1948, the Joint Chiefs of Staff believed that the dominant Labor Party of the Jewish Agency 'stems from the Soviet Union and its satellite states and has strong bonds of kinship in those regions, and ideologically is much closer to the Soviet Union than to the United States'" (259).

124. FRUS 1950, 658–61; Adler, *Roots in a Moving Stream,* 221–22.

125. Author's interview with I. L. Kenen; FRUS, 1949, 957; I. L. Kenen, *Israel's Defense Line: Her Friends and Foes in Washington* (New York: Prometheus Books, 1981), 75.

126. Adler, *Roots in a Moving Stream,* 223, quoting original Truman memo to budget director.

127. FRUS, 1949, 1072–74.

128. FRUS, 1949, 1109.

129. FRUS, 1949, 1250, 1261, 1272, 1297, 1325.

130. Jacobson, diary entry for 28 September 1948.

131. Ibid., entry for 5 May 1950.

132. FRUS, 1950, 167–168; author's interviews with Raymond Hare and George McGhee.

133. Acheson, chap. 58; author's interview with George McGhee.

134. See Clark Clifford, "Factors Influencing President Truman's Decision to Support Partition and Recognize the State of Israel," Annual Meeting of the American Historical Association, 28 December 1976.

135. FRUS, 1948, 1633.

136. FRUS, 1948, 1131–32.

Chapter 3. Eisenhower

1. Hal Lehrman, "American Policy and Arab-Israeli Peace," *Commentary* (June 1954), 550.

2. Judah Nadich, *Eisenhower and the Jews* (New York: Twayne Publications, 1953), 18.

3. *Department of State Bulletin,* 15 June 1953, 831. (Hereafter cited as DSB.)

4. Membership in the Zionist Organization of America dropped from 250,000 in 1948 to 87,000 in 1963, reflecting the loss of interest in pro-Israel political activity. Ernest Stock, *Israel on the Road to Sinai, 1949–1956; with a Sequel on the Six Day War, 1967* (Ithaca: Cornell University Press, 1967), 142, Kenen, 66–68 and 80–83.

5. Steven Fred Windmueller, *American Jewish Interest Groups: Their Role in Shaping United States Foreign Policy in the Middle East. A Study of Two Time Periods: 1945–1948, 1955–1958.* Ph.D. diss., University of Pennsylvania, 1973, 95; Kenen, 92–94; Stock, 57–59.

6. Interview, Roderic L. O'Connor, John Foster Dulles Oral History Collection, Princeton University, 2 April 1966, 32 (hereafter cited as DOHC); Kenen, 106–7.

7. Peter Lyon, *Eisenhower: Portrait of the Hero*, (Boston: Little, Brown, 1974), 546; William Bragg Ewald, Jr., *Eisenhower the President: Crucial Days, 1951–1960*, (Englewood Cliffs, N.J.: Prentice-Hall, 1981), 171; Blanche Wiesen Cook, *The Declassified Eisenhower: A Divided Legacy* (Garden City, N.Y.: Doubleday, 1981), 220–21.

8. Robert J. Donovan, *Eisenhower: The Inside Story*, (New York: Harper and Row, 1956), 67; Robert H. Ferrell, ed., *The Eisenhower Diaries* (New York: W. W. Norton, 1981), 220–21.

9. Donovan, *Eisenhower: The Inside Story*, 67.

10. Henry A. Byroade, "Facing Realities in the Arab–Israeli Dispute," DSB, 10 May 1954, 711–12.

11. Department of State Memorandum of Conversation between U.S. and British Diplomats, "The Eden Talks" (30 January–1 February 1956), 7.

12. Eisenhower, *Waging Peace*, 74.

13. Ibid., 99.

14. Author's interview with Philip Klutznick; Louis Gerson, *John Foster Dulles: The American Secretaries of State and Their Diplomacy* (Lawrence: University of Kansas Press, 1964), 25.

15. Dwight D. Eisenhower, *Crusade in Europe* (Garden City, N.Y.: Doubleday, 1948), 128; Eisenhower, *Waging Peace*, 114.

16. Dwight D. Eisenhower, PPP, 29 April 1954, 436.

17. Diary of the President, 8 March 1956, 1. Unless otherwise noted, all diary extracts and unpublished documents are taken from the collections of the Dwight D. Eisenhower Library, Abilene, Kansas.

18. Ibid. 1–2.

19. Dwight D. Eisenhower, PPP, 7 January 1954, 9; Ewald, 155.

20. Diary of the President, 13 March 1956, 2.

21. Dwight D. Eisenhower, PPP, 31 March 1954, 367.

22. Interviews, DOHC: Stewart Alsop, 4 February 1966, 29; Robert Bowie, 30 August 1964, 10; Richard M. Nixon, 5 March 1965, 38; Roderic L. O'Connor, 98.

23. Byroade, 70.

24. Letter, Eisenhower to Winston Churchill, 29 March 1956, p. 2. See also Robert A. Divine, *Eisenhower and the Cold War* (Oxford: Oxford University Press, 1981), 73.

25. White House Memorandum of Conference with the President, 21 November 1956, 4:00 P.M., p. 3.

26. Miles Copeland, *The Game of Nations* (New York: Simon and Schuster, 1969), 62; Lyon, 552–53; Wilbur Crane Eveland, *Ropes of Sand: America's Failure in the Middle East*, (New York: W. W. Norton, 1980), 356.

27. Nadav Safran, *Israel, the Embattled Ally*, (Cambridge, Mass.: Belknap Press, 1978), 352.

28. White House Memorandum of Conference with the President, 28 March 1956, 4:30 P.M., p. 2.

29. Notes of Bipartisan Congressional Meeting, 20 February 1957, 8:30 A.M., p. 3.

30. George V. Allen, "United States Policy in the Middle East," DSB, 31 October 1955, 685–86.

31. John Foster Dulles, "Report on the Near East," DSB, 15 June 1953, 834.

32. Herman Finer, *Dulles over Suez: The Theory and Practice of His Diplomacy* (Chicago: Quadrangle Books, 1964), 392.

33. Dwight D. Eisenhower, PPP, 28 October 1953, 717.

34. Memorandum of Conversation with the President, 14 July 1958, 11:25 A.M., p. 1.

35. Bernard Shanley, DOHC, 14 July 1966, 25.

36. Interviews, DOHC: Peter Lisagor, 3 February 1966, 37; Robert Murphy, 19 May, 8 June 1965, 20; Joseph Sisco, 12 August 1966, 25; Robert Bowie, 13; Richard Nixon, 19; Bernard Stanley, 18.

37. Gerson, 106.

38. Roderic L. O'Connor, DOHC, 76; Michael Reiner, *Reactions of the Organized American-Jewish Community to the Sinai Campaign 1956–1957*, Master's thesis (in Hebrew), Brandeis University, 1976, 124–27.

39. Andrew Berding, *Dulles on Diplomacy* (Princeton, N.J.: Van Nostrand, 1965), 100.

40. Robert Silverberg, *If I Forget Thee O Jerusalem* (New York: Pyramid, 1972), 510.

41. Byroade urged Nahum Goldmann to form the Conference of Presidents after "he had received representatives of Jewish organizations five times in five days during one week." See Kenen, 111; Goldmann, 324–25.

42. Richard Neustadt, *Alliance Politics* (New York: Columbia University Press, 1970), 105; Roderic L. O'Connor, DOHC, 31–32; Robert Murphy, DOHC, 13.

43. Author's interview with Maxwell Rabb.

44. Sherman Adams, DOHC, 15 August 1964, 3.

45. Emmett John Hughes, DOHC, 22 April 1965, 24.

46. DOHC, Robert Murphy, 17; DOHC, Roderic L. O'Connor, 37–38.

47. Michael Yizhar, "The Eisenhower Doctrine: A Case Study of American Foreign Policy Formulation and Implementation." Ph.D. diss., New School for Social Research, 1969, 36.

48. Eugene Black, DOHC, 15 July 1964, 2; Copeland, 59–62.

49. Townsend Hoopes, *The Devil and John Foster Dulles* (Boston: Little, Brown, 1973), 326; Copeland, 138; Eveland, 134–38; Leonard Mosely, *Dulles: A Biography of Eleanor, Allen, and John Foster Dulles and Their Family Network* (New York: Dial Press, 1978), 386–87.

50. Safran, *From War to War*, 102.

51. Kennett Love, *Suez, the Twice-Fought War* (New York: McGraw-Hill, 1969), 182–86; John Foster Dulles, "Anglo-Egyptian Agreement on the Suez Base," DSB, 9 August 1954, 198.

52. Jefferson Caffery to Secretary of State, Department of State Incoming Telegram, 11 April 1953, 11:25 A.M.; Department of State Memorandum of Presidential Conversation with Egyptian Ambassador, 4 May 1953, p. 1.

53. Love, 194.

54. Paul Jabber, *Not by War Alone: Security and Arms Control in the Middle East* (Berkeley and Los Angeles: University of California Press, 1981), 152.

55. Ibid., 154–55.

56. Carl McCardle, DOHC, December 1969, 108–9.

57. Copeland, 152.

58. Jabber, 1955; author's interview with Kermit Roosevelt.

59. Jabber, 155–57.

60. John Foster Dulles, DSB, 9 July 1954, 90.

61. John Foster Dulles, "Report on the Near East," DSB, 15 June 1953, 10.

62. Stock, 65.

63. John Foster Dulles, "Statement on Israel," DSB, 28 October 1953, 589–90; Hal Lehrman, "Arms for Arabs—and What for Israel?" *Commentary*, November 1954, 424.

64. Byroade, "The Middle East in New Perspective," DSB, 26 April 1954, 632, 630.

65. Lehrman, "Arms for Arabs—and What for Israel?" 424; and Lehrman, "American Policy and Arab-Israeli Peace," 552–53.

66. Ibid.

67. White House Memorandum of Conference with the President, 28 March 1956, 4:30 P.M., p. 2.

68. Lehrman, "Arms for Arabs—and What for Israel," 427.

69. Ibid., 426–27; Hoopes, 320–21.

70. Hoopes, 326.

71. Eveland, 147; Copeland, 156–57; George V. Allen, DOHC, 29 July 1965, 14.

72. Hoopes, 326; Eveland, 146–48; Copeland, 157.

73. Hoopes, 325; Eisenhower, *Waging Peace,* 24.

74. DSB, 30 November 1953, 749.

75. Safran, *From War to War,* 46–47; Stock, 65; Michael Brecher, *Decisions in Israel's Foreign Policy* (New Haven: Yale University Press, 1975), 193.

76. Gerson, 254; author's interview with Francis H. Russell.

77. John Foster Dulles, "Entering the Second Decade," DSB, 3 October 1955, 526; Russell, DOHC, 6 April 1966, 6–7; author's interview with Francis H. Russell.

78. Hoopes, 324; Copeland, 166; Eveland, 144–45.

79. For a detailed discussion of the arms issue, see Jabber, 128–72, especially 170–72; Hoopes, 327.

80. Eisenhower, *Waging Peace,* 24; Love, 282, Copeland, 156.

81. DSB, 4 October 1955, 604.

82. Love, 100; Hoopes, 327; Donald Neff, *Warriors at Suez* (New York: Linden Press, 1981), 88–90.

83. Neff, 107.

84. "The Eden Talks," 12, 9.

85. White House Memorandum of Conference with the President, 28 March 1956, 4:30 P.M., pp. 1–2.

86. Love, 307–310, 308; Eveland, 157–59; author's interview with James Eichelberger. For details of the Anderson mission, see Ewald, 194–98.

87. Love, 304–308; Lyon, 507–508.

88. Interviews, DOHC: Eugene Black, 15 July 1964, 7; Dwight D. Eisenhower, 28 July 1964, 31; Herbert V. Prochnow, 11 July 1966, 30; Robert Bowie, 29; also Finer, 39–40.

89. Interviews, DOHC: John W. McCormack, 12 February 1966, 12–13; James P. Richards, 23 September 1965, 16–28; George V. Allen, 30; "The Eden Talks," 8.

90. Diary of the President, 13 March 1956, pp. 1–2.

91. Love, 305; author's interviews with Robert Bowie, Loy Henderson, and Francis Wilcox; Herbert Parmet, *Eisenhower and the American Crusades* (New York: Macmillan, 1972), 481.

92. Hoopes, 337; author's interview with Loy Henderson.

93. Eisenhower, *Waging Peace,* 31–32; Love, 322; author's interviews with Loy Henderson and Kermit Roosevelt.

94. Interviews, DOHC: Herman Phleger, 21 July 1964, 43; Robert Bowie, 39–41; Herbert V. Prochnow, 39; Francis H. Russell, 13; Dillon Anderson, 39; Love, 117; Eisenhower, *Waging Peace,* 31; author's interview with Robert Bowie.

95. Interviews, DOHC: Herman Phleger, 43; Robert Bowie, 30, 39–41; Herbert V. Prochnow, 39; Francis H. Russell, 13; author's interviews with Robert Bowie, Loy Henderson, and Kermit Roosevelt.

96. Eisenhower, *Waging Peace,* 32; Hoopes, 338; Love, 325–26; interviews, DOHC: Robert Bowie, 39–41; Herman Phleger, 43; Herbert Prochnow, 39; Francis H. Russell, 13.

97. Eisenhower, *Waging Peace,* 31; Sir Roger Makin, DOHC, 5 June 1964, 31; author's interview with Robert Bowie.

98. Robert Bowie, DOHC, 28; Love, 322; Hoopes, 339; Eisenhower, *Waging Peace*, 33.

99. Dillon Anderson, DOHC, 13 June 1966, 35–37; Neff, 259–60.

100. Interviews, DOHC: George V. Allen, 29 July 1965, 36; John B. Hollister, 6 May 1964, 49; James R. Wiggins, 9 August 1965, 10; Eugene Black, 15.

101. Dwight D. Eisenhower, DOHC, 34; Lyon, 735; Eveland, 193–94.

102. Diary of the President, 28 March 1956, pp. 1–2.

103. Love, 376.

104. White House Memorandum of Conference with the President, 30 October 1956, p. 4.

105. Gerson, 284.

106. Dwight D. Eisenhower, DOHC, 31; Neustadt, 13.

107. Hoopes, 348–53. For a slightly different view of Eisenhower's and Dulles's divergence, see Ewald, 211–13.

108. Notes of Bipartisan Congressional Meeting, 12 August 1956, 12:00 P.M., pp. 2, 5, 7, 8.

109. Robert Bowie, DOHC, 35; Love, 448; Lyon, 703; Rt. Hon. Sir Anthony Eden, *Full Circle* (London: Cassell, 1960), 524–26.

110. Love, 387.

111. For a more detailed study of Dulles's plan (SCUA) see Chester L. Cooper, *The Lion's Last Roar: Suez, 1956* (New York: Harper and Row, 1978), 125–30; Neff, 304–22; Love, 419.

112. Love, 441, 445–46.

113. Neustadt, 20; Hoopes, 368; Robert Murphy, *Diplomat among Warriors* (Garden City, N.Y.: Doubleday, 1964), 388.

114. Brecher, *Decisions in Israel's Foreign Policy*, 264.

115. White House Memorandum for the Record, 15 October 1956, p. 1; Love, 448.

116. Love, 489.

117. Neustadt, 22.

118. Eisenhower, *Waging Peace*, 56–57; telephone call, Secretary of State to Allen Dulles, 29 October 1956, 10:22 A.M.

119. John Emmet Hughes, *The Ordeal of Power: A Political Memoir of the Eisenhower Years* (New York: Atheneum, 1963), 212.

120. Parmet, 473; Eban, 209–11.

121. White House Memorandum of Conference with the President, 29 October 1956, 7:15 P.M., pp. 2–3.

122. Ibid., 3, 1, 4.

123. White House Memorandum of Conference with the President, 29 October 1956, 8:15 P.M., p. 1.

124. Brecher, *Decisions in Israel's Foreign Policy, 277–78.*

125. *White House Memorandum of Conference with the President, 29 October 1956, 7:15 P.M.,* pp. 2–3; Eisenhower, *Waging Peace,* 73; Admiral Arthur W. Radford, DOHC, 8 May 1965, 65.

126. White House Memorandum of Conference with the President, 30 October 1956, pp. 3–4, 1.

127. Telephone call, Dulles to Eisenhower, 30 October 1956, 2:17 P.M., p. 3.

128. NYT, 2 November 1956, p. 4.

129. Finer, 446–47; Hoopes, 381–62; Richard M. Bissell, DOHC, 7 September, 1966, 27.

130. DSB, 12 November 1956, 754; Finer, 394–97; Love, 562; Hoopes, 378–80.

131. Hoopes, 380–81; Herman Phleger, DOHC, 41.

132. Neustadt, 24–25; author's interview with Kermit Roosevelt.

133. Author's interview with Maxwell Rabb; Richard M. Bissell, DOHC, 26–27.

134. Eisenhower, *Waging Peace*, 58; see also Eveland, 229.

135. Eisenhower, *Waging Peace*, 89–90; Love, 614; Sherman Adams, *First Hand Report* (New York: Harper and Brothers, 1961), 258.

136. Brecher, *Decisions in Israel's Foreign Policy*, 284; Love, 610–15; Murphy, 391.

137. Eisenhower, *Waging Peace*, 91; Robert Murphy, DOHC, 44.

138. Brecher, *Decisions in Israel's Foreign Policy*, 286; Love, 614; Eisenhower, *Waging Peace*, 91.

139. Brecher, *Decisions in Israel's Foreign Policy*, 286.

140. Love, 651–52; White House Memorandum of Conference with the President, 20 November 1956, 5:30 P.M., p. 2, and 21 November 1956, 4:00 P.M.

141. Brecher, *Decisions in Israel's Foreign Policy*, 295; Eban, 234–36.

142. Love, 666; Department of State Memorandum, William B. Macomber to Secretary of State, 22 February 1957; Phone call to Secretary of State from Arthur H. Dean following latter's talk with Abba Eban, 24 February 1957.

143. Love, 666.

144. Eisenhower, *Waging Peace*, 384–85.

145. Brecher, *Decisions in Israel's Foreign Policy*, 297; Eisenhower, *Waging Peace*, 185; Finer, 476. Recently declassified documents reveal the intricacies of the U.S.-Israeli negotiations; see Department of State telephone messages from Arthur H. Dean to the Secretary of State following talks with Israeli Foreign Minister Meir and Israeli Ambassador Abba Eban, 11 February 1957, 18 February 1957, 19 February 1957, 20 February 1957.

146. Love, 665.

147. Eisenhower, *Waging Peace*, 185–86.

148. Notes of Bipartisan Congressional Meeting, 20 February 1957, p. 2.

149. Eisenhower, *Waging Peace*, 186.

150. Adams, 284; Notes of Bipartisan Congressional Meeting, 20 February 1957, pp. 4, 5, 6.

151. Ibid., p. 6, 7, summary of notes.

152. Brecher, *Decisions in Israel's Foreign Policy*, 299; telephone calls: Ambassador Lodge to Dulles, 25 February 1957, 3:51 P.M.; Dulles to Israeli Minister Reuven Shiloah, 25 February 1957, 4:41 P.M.; Dulles to Dag Hammarskjold, 25 February 1957, 4:00 P.M. and 5:48 P.M.; Dulles to Ambassador Abba Eban, 25 February 1957, 5:34 P.M.; Dulles to Ambassador Lodge, 25 February 1957, 6:08 P.M.

153. Telephone calls, Dulles to Ambassador Lodge, 26 February 1957, 1:19 P.M., Department of State Memorandum for Secretary of State from Arthur H. Dean, 26 February 1957. For the Israeli perspective on these negotiations, see Eban, 245–56.

154. Theodore Draper, *Israel and World Politics: The Roots of the Third Arab-Israeli War* (New York: Viking Press, 1968), 21–22; Finer, 487.

155. Finer, 488; Brecher, *Decisions in Israel's Foreign Policy*, 300; author's interview with Henry Cabot Lodge.

156. Privately, Eisenhower immediately reassured the Israeli prime minister that the United States would support "the united effort by all of the nations" to bring about stable and tranquil conditions in the Middle East. Department of State Outgoing Telegram, Eisenhower to Israeli Prime Minister, 2 March 1957, 2:00 P.M., pp. 1–2.

157. Notes of Bipartisan Congressional Meeting, 20 February 1957, pp. 2, 3.

158. Eisenhower, *Waging Peace*, 189.

159. Diary of the President, 28 March 1956, p. 2; 8 March 1956, p. 2; 10 April 1956.

160. White House Memorandum of Conversation with the President, October 6, 1956, p. 2.

161. Cablegram, President to John Foster Dulles, 12 December 1956, p. 1.

162. Ibid., 2–3.

163. Eisenhower, *Waging Peace,* 120.

164. White House Memorandum of Conference with the President, 21 November 1956, 4:00 P.M., p. 2.

165. White House Memorandum of Conference with the President, 23 November 1956, 12:00 P.M., p. 2.

166. Cablegram, Eisenhower to Dulles, 12 December 1956, p. 2.

167. Notes on Presidential–Bipartisan Congressional Leadership Meeting, 1 January 1957, 2:00–5:50 P.M., pp. 3, 6; see also Dwight D. Eisenhower, *Waging Peace,* 178.

168. Notes on Presidential–Bipartisan Congressional Leadership Meeting, 1 January 1957, 2:00–5:50 P.M., pp. 3, 4.

169. Yizhar, 46–56.

170. Ibid., 67, 69–71.

171. Copeland, 215–16.

172. Yizhar, 68.

173. Finer, 504; Deanne Heller and David Heller, *John Foster Dulles: Soldier of Peace* (New York: Rinehart and Winston, 1960), 285.

174. Camille Chamoun, DOHC, 28 August 1964, 45–46.

175. Author's interview with Philip Klutznick; Kenen, 139.

176. Safran, *Israel, the Embattled Ally,* 373.

177. Eisenhower, *Waging Peace,* 194–95. This episode is dealt with at length by Yizhar, 151–74; see also Eveland, 245.

178. Department of State Memorandum for the President, 20 August 1957, p. 1.

179. Eisenhower, *Waging Peace,* 198.

180. Malcolm Kerr, *The Arab Cold War: A Study of Ideology in Politics* (London: Oxford University Press, 1965), 10.

181. Eisenhower, *Waging Peace,* 262, 265.

182. *Los Angeles Times,* 12 February 1976, p. 9: report on original version of Victor Marchetti and John D. Marks, *The CIA and the Cult of Intelligence* (New York: Alfred A. Knopf, 1980), portions of which—including this section—were later deleted by court order at the behest of the CIA.

183. Eisenhower, *Waging Peace,* 265–66; Yizhar, 172–73; Hoopes, 433.

184. Camille Chamoun, DOHC, 28 August 1964, 13; Briefing notes (by Allen W. Dulles), Meeting at the White House with Congressional Leaders, 14 July 1958, 2:30 P.M., p. 3.

185. Department of State Memorandum for the Record, "Meeting re Iraq," 14 July 1958; Eisenhower, *Waging Peace,* 270; Hoopes, 435; Edward Weintal and Charles Bartlett, *Facing the Brink* (New York: Charles Scribner's Sons, 1967), 4.

186. Department of State Memorandum for the Record, "Meeting re Iraq," 14 July 1958, pp. 1–2.

187. Briefing notes (by Allen W. Dulles), Meeting at the White House with Congressional Leaders, 14 July 1958, 2:30 P.M., p. 5.

188. Camille Chamoun, DOHC, 33–34; Lyon, 773: Copeland, 239. Also see Eveland's eyewitness account of events in Lebanon in *Ropes of Sand,* 277–99.

189. White House Memorandum of Conference with the President, 15 July 1958, 11:25 A.M.; Department of State Outgoing Telegram, Eisenhower to Shah of Iran, 19 July 1958, 7:07 P.M., Memorandum of Conference with the President, 23 July 1958, 3:00 P.M.

190. Eisenhower, *Waging Peace,* 274.

191. Jacob Javits, DOHC, 2 March 1966, 13; Nadav Safran, *The United States and Israel* (Cambridge: Harvard University Press, 1963), 262.

192. Confidential interview with author; Eisenhower, *Waging Peace*, 278; Lyon, 824–25; William Quandt, "Lebanon, 1958, and Jordan, 1970," in Barry M. Blechman and Stephen S. Kaplan (eds.), *Force without War: U.S. Armed Forces as a Political Instrument* (Washington, D.C.: The Brookings Institution, 1978), 238.

193. White House Memorandum of Conference with the President, 15 July 1958, 11:25 A.M., p. 1.

194. Eisenhower, *Waging Peace*, 272.

195. Robert Murphy, DOHC, 404–8; 485–509.

196. Robert Murphy, DOHC, 410; Eisenhower, *Waging Peace*, 290.

197. Agency for International Development, *U.S. Overseas Loans and Grants and Assistance from International Organizations*, 1 July 1945–20 September 1979, p. 19; Kenen, 143–44.

198. Weintal and Bartlett, 5. See also Memorandum of Conference with the President, 23 July 1958, 3:00 P.M.

199. Author's interview with Raymond Hare.

200. White House Memorandum of Conference with the President, 23 July 1958, 3:00 P.M., pp. 1, 2.

201. Department of State Memorandum of Conversation with Foreign Secretary Lloyd, 17 July 1958, 3:30 P.M., p. 1.

202. White House Memorandum of Conference with the President, 23 July 1958, 3:00 P.M., pp. 2–3.

Chapter 4. Kennedy

1. Chester Bowles, "A Look at the Middle East Today," DSB, 7 May 1962, 765–66.

2. Author's interview with Myer Feldman.

3. Ernest Barbarash (Zionist Organization of America), *John F. Kennedy on Israel, Zionism and Jewish Issues* (New York: Herzl Press, 1965).

4. NYT, 3 July 1957, pp. 1, 5; private file made available to author; Kenen, 135–37.

5. Confidential sets of minutes made available to author; Kenen, 155–56.

6. Silverberg, 551–52.

7. Author's interview with Philip Klutznick.

8. Barbarash, 60.

9. Author's interview with Philip Klutznick.

10. Oral History Interview with Myer Feldman for the John F. Kennedy Library. (Hereafter cited as KOHI.) Between 23 January 1966 and 21 September 1968, Myer Feldman taped fourteen separate interviews for the JFK Library. Those interviews are unedited.

11. *Washington Post*, 13 April 1963, p. A6. The letter, from Under Secretary of State for Political Affairs Averell Harriman to Congressman Farbstein, claimed that the alarm over German scientists in the U.A.R. was exaggerated and even suggested that they diminished Egyptian dependence on the Soviet Union. According to Ambassador Barbour, Meir was concerned more about the impression the letter made on the public than about whether or not it indicated a change of U.S. policy. Barbour to Rusk, Department of State Incoming Telegram, 18 April 1963, 5:00 P.M.

12. National Security Council Memorandum, Robert Komer to McGeorge Bundy, 30 April 1963.

13. See, for example, John F. Kennedy, PPP, 11 January 1962, 12; ibid., 13 March 1962, 214–15.

14. Myer Feldman, KOHI.

15. John Badeau, *The American Approach to the Arab World* (New York: Harper and Row, 1968), 83.

16. Airgram from Chester Bowles to Kennedy, Rusk and Hamilton, 21 February 1963, included in Mordechai Gazit, *President Kennedy's Policy toward the Arab States and Israel* (Tel Aviv: Shiloah Center for Middle Eastern and African Studies, 1983), 80.

17. In a letter to the Israeli prime minister, Kennedy expressed his hope for ultimate peace in the Near East, adding, "Throughout this period, the United States Policy has consistently included among its objectives the security and progress of Israel . . . The maintenance of Israel's integrity and independence and her economic progress will continue to engage our full support." Letter from President Kennedy to David Ben Gurion, 13 June 1962. Unless otherwise noted, all unpublished documents used in this chapter can be found in the John F. Kennedy Library.

18. Barbarash, 65–66.

19. I. M. Destler, *Presidents, Bureaucrats and Foreign Policy* (Princeton: Princeton University Press, 1972), 100–104.

20. Department of State Memorandum for McGeorge Bundy, "U.S. Position on Jerusalem," 31 May 1962.

21. Author's interview with Myer Feldman; Myer Feldman, KOHI.

22. Richard J. Walton, *Cold War and Counterrevolution: The Foreign Policy of John F. Kennedy* (New York: Viking Press, 1972), 4–10; Fred Khouri, *The Arab-Israeli Dilemma* (Syracuse, N.Y.: Syracuse University Press, 1968), 304–5.

23. Myer Feldman, KOHI.

24. DSB, 20 November 1961, 858.

25. Author's interview with Robert Komer: Badeau, 94–95, 136; Gazit, 16–19.

26. John S. Badeau, KOHI, 25 February 1969, 9–10; John F. Kennedy, PPP, 7 June 1962, 461.

27. *Near East Report* 6, no. 20 (25 September 1962): 1 (hereafter cited as NER); Myer Feldman, KOHI, 462–63.

28. Text of the two letters reproduced in *Middle Eastern Affairs*, November 1962 (New York: Council for Middle East Affairs, 1962), 269–75.

29. NER 6, no. 20 (25 September 1962): 1.

30. Myer Feldman, KOHI, 465–72.

31. John C. Campbell, "American Efforts for Peace," in *The Elusive Peace in the Middle East*, ed. Malcolm Kerr (Albany, N.Y.: State University of New York Press, 1975), 280–82.

32. John Jernegan, KOHI, 12 March 1969, 26; Gazit, 25; author's interview with Phillips Talbott.

33. Myer Feldman, KOHI.

34. John S. Badeau, *The American Approach to the Arab World*, 123–24; Weintal and Bartlett, 38–41; Myer Feldman, KOHI, 502–7; author's interview with Robert Komer.

35. John S. Badeau, *The American Approach to the Arab World*, 133–35.

36. Ibid., 141–44.

37. Ibid., 144–45.

38. Weintal and Bartlett, 43–45.

39. Badeau, *The American Approach to the Arab World*, 144.

40. Ibid., 145.

41. Myer Feldman, KOHI, 508; author's interview with Robert Komer; John S. Badeau, KOHI, 24; author's interview with Robert Komer.

42. John S. Badeau, KOHI, 26–27.

43. Myer Feldman, KOHI.

44. Robert Komer, Memorandum for Record, 14 January 1963.

45. Memorandum of Presidential Conversation with Israeli Foreign Minister Meir, 27 December 1962, 10:00 A.M., p. 5.

46. Myer Feldman, KOHI, 523.

47. Memorandum of Presidential Conversation with Israeli Foreign Minister Meir, 27 December 1962, 10:00 A.M.

48. Michael Brecher, *Decisions in Israel's Foreign Policy*, 210–19; Myer Feldman, KOHI, 515–20; Letter from John F. Kennedy to Ben Gurion, 13 June 1962, included in Gazit, 95–96.

49. Shimon Peres, *David's Sling* (New York: Random House, 1970), 93.

50. Myer Feldman, KOHI, 526.

51. Author's interview with Myer Feldman; Department of State Outgoing Telegram, Rusk to Tel Aviv, 18 August 1962, 8:48 P.M.; Department of State Incoming Telegram, Feldman to President, Rusk, and Grant, 19 August 1962, 6:46 P.M.; Peres, 99; Theodore Sorensen, *Kennedy* (New York: Harper and Row, 1965), 558; Gazit, 43.

52. Chester Bowles, *Promises To Keep: My Years in Public Life, 1941–1969* (New York: Harper and Row, 1971), 371–72.

53. Peres, 93; Memorandum of Presidential Conversation with Israeli Foreign Minister Meir, 27 December 1962, 10:00 A.M., p. 3; Department of State Memorandum of Conversation between Joseph Johnson, Shimon Peres, Avraham Harmon, Mordechai Gazit, 2 April 1963; Department of State Incoming Telegram, London to Secretary of State, 28 March 1963, 6:00 P.M. Gazit believes that a contributing factor in the Hawk missile sale was the fear that Israel might turn to the nuclear option to restore the military balance. Both Gazit and Shlomo Aronson see this American fear as a reason for the beginning of serious U.S. military aid to Israel in the Kennedy and Johnson administrations although I have found no evidence to support this claim. Gazit, 44, 117–18; Shlomo Aronson, *Conflict and Bargaining in the Middle East* (Baltimore and London: Johns Hopkins University Press, 1978), 39–45.

54. John Jernegan, KOHI, 12 March 1969, 16–17; author's interview with Roger Davies; Department of State Incoming Telegram, Damascus to Rusk, 27 September 1962, 2:00 P.M.

55. Department of State Incoming Telegrams, Beirut to Secretary of State, 28 September 1962, 3:00 P.M. and Damascus to Secretary of State, 27 September, 2:00 P.M.

56. Author's interview with Philip Klutznick; NYT, 27 September 1962, p. 1.

57. Department of State Outgoing Telegram, Rusk to Foreign Ambassadors, 27 September 1962, 3:02 P.M.; Gazit, 43.

58. John S. Badeau, KOHI, 12. However, the U.A.R. ambassador told a State Department official that the United States should "not be deceived by the mildness of comments of UAR officials re missiles for Israel . . . [and] could expect delayed but severe reaction." The problem lay not with Nasser but with the U.A.R. army. Department of State Outgoing Telegram, Ball to Cairo, 29 September 1962, 5:34 P.M.

59. Department of State Incoming Telegram, Badeau to Rusk, 21 September 1962, 12:39 A.M. Badeau later commented, "Having chosen the mess of potage we should not be surprised at bitter taste . . . Our hitherto successful approach to Nasser on basis of quiet diplomacy and frank statement intentions seriously imperilled by this incident." Department of State Incoming Telegram, Badeau to Rusk, 29 November 1962, 2:00 P.M.

60. Department of State Incoming Telegrams: Jones to Rusk, 21 September 1962, 10:53 A.M.; Amman to Secretary of State, 27 September 1962, 5:41 P.M.; Stevenson to Rusk (Re: Iraq), 2 October 1962, 6:41 P.M.; Jerusalem to Secretary of State, 4 October 1962, 10:33 P.M.

61. John F. Kennedy, PPP, 13 April 1963, 307.

62. Mordechai Gazit interview with Myer Feldman, cited in Gazit, 46. The president told Feldman he had decided to sell tanks to Israel but he died ten days later without proceeding further. The discussions began again under Johnson.

63. Myer Feldman, KOHI, 544–47.

64. Ibid., 573–86.

65. Memorandum of Presidential Conversation with Israeli Foreign Minister Meir, 27 December 1962, 10:00 A.M., p. 6.

66. Ibid., 7–8.

67. Not yet declassified letter from President Kennedy to Prime Minister Eshkol, cited in Gazit, 47.

68. Ibid.

69. Barbarash, 26.

70. Ibid., 57.

71. Myer Feldman, KOHI, 399–401, 567; Dean Francis Sayre, KOHI, 25 June 1964, 10–12.

72. David P. Forsythe, *United Nations Peacemaking: The Conciliation Commission for Palestine* (Baltimore: Johns Hopkins University Press, 1972), 124–25; Myer Feldman, KOHI, 402–6.

73. Forsythe, 126.

74. Ibid., 127–28; author's interview with Joseph Johnson.

75. Author's interview with Joseph Johnson; see also *Jerusalem Post,* 29 November 1961, p. 1.

76. This description is based on a U.N. document cited in Forsythe, 128, 129.

77. Ibid., 130.

78. Ibid., 130; Department of State Incoming Telegram, Tel Aviv to Rusk, 22 January 1963, 8:09 A.M.

79. Forsythe, 130–31.

80. Ibid., 125–26; author's interview with Joseph Johnson.

81. Department of State Incoming Telegram, Barbour to Rusk, 12 April 1962, 7:41 A.M.

82. Forsythe, 125–26.

83. Author's interview with Roger Davies.

84. Author's interview with Joseph Johnson; Memorandum for the President from Dean Rusk, 7 August 1962; Feldman, KOHI, 407–9.

85. Department of State Outgoing Telegram, Ball to Tel Aviv, 16 August 1962; Department of State Incoming Telegram, Tel Aviv to Rusk, 17 August 1962, 1:26 P.M.; Feldman, KOHI, 407, 409.

86. Department of State Incoming Telegram, Feldman to the President, Rusk, and Grant, 19 August 1962, 6:46 P.M.; Feldman, KOHI, 537.

87. Department of State Incoming Telegram, Feldman to the President, Rusk, and Grant, 19 August 1962, 6:46 P.M.; Department of State Outgoing Telegram, Rusk to Feldman, 20 August 1962, 12:55 P.M.

88. Feldman, KOHI. The question of Israel's nuclear capability was a concern during the Kennedy and Johnson administrations but was ignored by Nixon and Kissinger until the October 1973 war. See Aronson, 118.

89. Department of State Outgoing Telegram, Rusk to Feldman, 20 August 1962, 12:55 P.M.

90. Department of State Incoming Telegram, Feldman to Rusk, the President and Grant, 21 August 1962, 9:11 P.M., pp. 2–3.

91. John S. Badeau, KOHI, 11–12.

92. Department of State Outgoing Telegram, Secretary of State to Cairo, 22 August 1962.

93. Department of State Incoming Telegram, Badeau to Rusk, 16 October 1962, 1:33 P.M.; author's interview with Myer Feldman.

94. Myer Feldman, KOHI, 419–21; John S. Badeau, KOHI, 11–12.

95. Myer Feldman, KOHI, 425–28.

96. Ibid., 426–28.

97. Author's interview with Joseph Johnson.

98. Forsythe, 132–34; Joseph E. Johnson, "Arab vs. Israeli: A Persistent Challenge to Americans," *Middle East Journal* 18 (No. 1, Winter 1964): 10.

99. Forsythe, 135–37.

100. Ibid.

101. Ibid., 138–39.

102. Memorandum, Conversation with Israeli Foreign Minister Meir, 27 December 1962, p. 7.

103. Department of State Incoming Telegram, Barbour to Rusk, 3 April 1963, 6:00 P.M.

104. Department of State Outgoing Telegram, Rusk to American Embassies in Amman, Beirut, Cairo, Damascus, Tel Aviv, 13 April 1963, 5:30 P.M.

105. Johnson, "Arab vs. Israeli," 10–11.

106. Ibid., 11–12; Forsythe, 135.

107. Johnson, "Arab vs. Israeli," 12.

108. Forsythe, 130–31; Department of State Incoming Telegrams, Tel Aviv to Rusk, 22 January 1963, 8:09 A.M., and 3 April 1963, 6:00 P.M.

109. Memorandum for Mr. McGeorge Bundy (briefing material), 5 February 1963.

110. Author's interview with Robert Komer.

111. Myer Feldman, KOHI, 432–33. Although available evidence does not substantiate the point, Moshe A. Gilbo'a claims that the Israelis were pressured to accept the Johnson plan in exchange for Hawks. The prime minister said publicly that he refused to allow Israel to be destroyed from within. See Gilbo'a, *Six Years—Six Days: Origins and History of the Six Day War* (in Hebrew) (Tel Aviv: Am Oved Publishers, 1969), 31.

112. Author's interview with Roger Davies.

Chapter 5. Johnson

1. See for example George Liska, *Imperial America: The International Politics of Primacy* (Baltimore: Johns Hopkins Press, 1967); Zbigniew Brzezinski, "The Implications of Change for United States Foreign Policy," DSB, 3 July 1967, 19–23.

2. Lyndon B. Johnson, PPP, 13 November 1966, 1378; 4 June 1968, 680.

3. See NER 11, no. 17 (22 August 1967): 66; also Nadav Safran, *From War to War*, 167–69; Robert H. Trice, "*Domestic Political Interests and American Policy in the Middle East: Pro-Israel, Pro-Arab, and Corporate Non-governmental Actors and the Making of American Foreign Policy, 1966–1971,*" Ph.D. diss., University of Wisconsin, 1974, 133.

4. John P. Leacacos, *Fires in the In-Basket: The ABC's of The State Department* (Cleveland and New York: World Publishing, 1968), 81–82.

5. Harry McPherson, 5 December 1968, tape 1, pp. 21–22 (my italics), Lyndon Baines Johnson Library Oral History Interview. (Hereafter cited as JOHI.)

6. Author's interview with Ephraim Evron and Harry McPherson.

7. Lyndon B. Johnson, PPP, 11 May 1966, 497.

8. Ibid., 21 October 1966, 1241.

9. See Seyom Brown, *The Faces of Power* (New York: Columbia University Press, 1968), 358.

10. See for example, Lyndon B. Johnson, PPP, 28 May 1965, 593.

11. See for example, DSB, 8 November 1965, 736–37.

12. Brown, 336–37.

13. Nasser's speech at Port Said, broadcast on Radio Cairo, 23 December 1964, cited in William B. Quandt, *U.S. Policy in The Middle East: Constraints and Choices* (Santa Monica: Rand Corporation, 1970), 38.

14. Author's interview with Lucius Battle.

15. Quandt, *U.S. Policy*, 37–38.

16. Komer memo to Bundy, 6 April 1965, in the Lyndon Baines Johnson Library.

17. Lyndon B. Johnson, PPP, 10 September 1968, 949.

18. Ibid., 1 June 1964, 732.

19. Ibid., 2 August 1966, 796.

20. Ibid., 14 April 1964, 462.

21. Author's interview with Harry McPherson.

22. Author's interviews with Ephraim Evron and Yehuda Avner.

23. Lyndon B. Johnson, PPP, 7 January 1968, 19.

24. Author's interview with Harry McPherson; author's confidential interview.

25. Lyndon B. Johnson, PPP, 10 September 1968, 947.

26. Author's confidential interview with a former CIA official.

27. Jonathan Trumbull Howe, *Multicrises* (Cambridge: MIT Press, 1971), 362–67; William B. Quandt, *Decade of Decisions* (Berkeley and Los Angeles: University of California Press, 1977), 52.

28. Joseph Sisco, JOHI, 6 November 1971, tape 1, pp. 12–14.

29. Earl G. Wheeler, JOHI, 21 August 1969, tape 1, pp. 8–9.

30. John P. Roche, JOHI, 16 July 1970, tape 1, p. 63.

31. Earl G. Wheeler, JOHI, 7 May 1970, tape 2, p. 16.

32. Lucius Battle, JOHI, 5 December 1968, tape 2, p. 26; Earle J. Wheeler, JOHI, 21 August 1969, tape 1, p. 6; Clark Clifford, JOHI, 7 August 1969, tape 4, p. 6.

33. Lucius Battle, JOHI, 5 December 1968, tape 2, p. 26.

34. Clark Clifford, JOHI, 15 December 1979, tape 5, p. 19.

35. Ibid.

36. Author's interview with Daniel Henken.

37. Clark Clifford, JOHI, 14 July 1969, tape 3, pp. 24–25; 7 August 1969, tape 4, p. 31.

38. Morton H. Halperin, "The Decision to Deploy the ABM: Bureaucratic and Domestic Politics in the Johnson Administration," *World Politics* 25 (no. 1, October 1972): 90–95.

39. Lucius Battle, JOHI, 14 November 1968, tape 1, p. 42.

40. Harry McPherson, JOHI, 16 January 1969, tape 4, p. 22.

41. Confidential files made available to the author; Eban, 460.

42. Harry McPherson, JOHI, 16 January 1969, tape 4, p. 22.

43. Author's interview with Ambassador Walworth Barbour.

44. Harry McPherson, JOHI, 16 January 1969, tape 4, p. 37.

45. Eban, 460.

46. Harry McPherson, JOHI, 16 January 1969, tape 4, pp. 36–37; author's interviews with Harry McPherson and Herman Edelsberg.

47. John P. Roche, JOHI, 16 July 1970, tape 1, pp. 63–66; author's interview with John P. Roche.

48. Department of State outgoing telegram 5592, 29 May 1964, to U.S. ambassador in Cairo.

49. State Department paraphrase of Nasser letter in Rusk memo to LBJ, 12 August 1964.

50. Rusk memo to LBJ on the second McCloy mission, 12 August 1964, State Dept. Doc. 77a, p. 1.

51. Peres, *David's Sling*, 103.

52. Confidential documents made available to the author by Israeli sources.

53. Peres, 103–107; Gilbo'a, 41.

54. Peres, 105–6.

55. Ibid., 103, confirmed by confidential Israeli source; Gilbo'a, 41.

56. Peres, 104; Safran, *From War to War*, 167–69.

57. Weintal and Bartlett, 129; for newspaper accounts of these events, see NYT, 21, 31 January; 11, 13, 18 February; 4 March; and 14, 16 May 1965.

58. Komer memorandum on Harriman mission to Israel, 26 February 1965, State Dept. doc. 4880, pp. 1–7.

59. Komer memorandum of conversation with Harriman, 26 February 1965, State Dept. doc. 4880, p. 4.

60. Komer memorandum of conversation with Harriman, 25 February 1965, A.M. State Dept. doc. 4878, p. 3.

61. Ibid.

62. Author's interview with Moshe Bitan.

63. Komer memorandum of conversation with Harriman, 2 February 1965, State Dept. doc. 4880, p. 4.

64. See Komer memorandum of conversation with Harriman, 25 February 1965, P.M., State Dept. doc. 4879, pp. 2–3.

65. Komer memorandum of conversation with Harriman, 26 February 1965, State Dept. doc. 4880, pp. 4–7.

66. Peres, 107.

67. Rusk memo of conversation with Talbott, State Dept. memo. 1080, 20 April 1965, P.M., pp. 3–5. Talbott-Nasser meeting, NYT, 19 April 1965, p. 10; Talbott-Eshkol meeting, NYT, 22 April 1965, p. 9; Talbott return to Washington, NYT, 25 April 1965, p. 2.

68. Rusk memo of conversation with Talbott, pp. 2–3.

69. Department of State memo of conversation between Talbott and Harman, 19 May 1965 P.M., p. 4.

70. U.S. Department of Defense, *Military Assistance Facts*, May 1966, 21; *Military Assistance and Foreign Military Sales Facts*, May 1973, 19.

71. Trice, 227, 277.

72. State Department background paper, "Informal visit of President Zalman Shazar of Israel."

73. Ibid., 2.

74. Komer memo to Lyndon B. Johnson, 14 March 1964; Trice, 234–35.

75. Author's interview with Lucius Battle; Quandt, *Decade*, 38.

76. Draper, 36–37; Gilbo'a, 78.

77. DSB, 16 November 1966, 974–78.

78. Lucius Battle, JOHI, 14 November 1968, tape 1, p. 36.

79. Lucius Battle, JOHI, 5 December 1968, tape 2, pp. 36–37.

80. Lucius Battle, JOHI, 14 November 1968, tape 1, pp. 30, 33; author's interview with Richard Nolte.

81. Bernard Lewis, "The Consequences of Defeat," *Foreign Affairs* 46 (July 1967): 322; Eban, 318.

82. Lyndon Baines Johnson, *The Vantage Point: Perspectives of the Presidency 1963–69* (New York: Holt, Rinehart & Winston, 1971), 290.

83. Ibid.

84. Michael Bar-Zohar, *Embassies in Crisis: Diplomats and Demagogues behind the Six-Day War* (Englewood Cliffs, N.J.: Prentice-Hall, 1970), 40–41.

85. Brecher, *Decisions in Israel's Foreign Policy*, 375; Bar-Zohar, 56, 107; Quandt, *Decade*, 42.

86. Brecher, *Decisions in Israel's Foreign Policy*, 375; Quandt, *Decade*, 43 fn.

87. Gamel Nasser, speech published in *Al-Ahram* (Cairo), 23 May 1967, reprinted in Draper, app. 9, p. 214.

88. Eban, 118; Brecher, *Decisions in Israel's Foreign Policy*, 378; Gilbo'a, 127, 132.

89. Quandt, *Decade*, 43; Brecher, *Decisions in Israel's Foreign Policy*, 381.

90. Lyndon Baines Johnson, PPP, 23 May 1967, 561–63.

91. Trice, 138; American Israel Public Affairs Committee (AIPAC) asked Congress to reaffirm America's Near East commitments; cf. Trice, 216, n. 14; NER 11, no. 11 (29 May 1967): 41–42.

92. Johnson, 291–92; Brecher, *Decisions in Israel's Foreign Policy*, 384; Bar-Zohar, 99; Eban, 368.

93. Bar-Zohar, 105; Gilbo'a, 146.

94. Author's interview with A. Yariv; see also Draper, 88, and Brecher, *Decisions in Israel's Foreign Policy*, 386, for slightly different versions.

95. The cable to Eban was written by Aviad Yaffe (the prime minister's political aide), Shlomo Argov, and Yariv. The cable to Harman was prepared the same day by Jacob Herzog and Yitzhak Rabin. The confusion was not clarified with the United States until much later, after the war. Letter of clarification, Aharon Yariv to author, 17 June 1984.

96. Quandt, *Decade*, 49.

97. Brecher, *Decisions in Israel's Foreign Policy*, 387; Draper, 89–90.

98. Eban, 350–51; Winston Burdette, *Encounter with the Middle East* (New York: Atheneum, 1969), 253; Bar-Zohar, 196, claims that even before Eban arrived, in a Thursday afternoon meeting, Harman had already expressed his dismay to Rostow and Battle at the deliberate pace of American activity in putting together an international flotilla.

99. Bar-Zohar, 109; Brecher, *Decisions in Israel's Foreign Policy*, 387.

100. Brecher, *Decisions in Israel's Foreign Policy*, 390; Eban, 351–53; Gilbo'a, 148.

101. Bar-Zohar, 98, 117; Burdette, 253–54.

102. Quandt, *Decade*, 51.

103. Ibid., 52.

104. Ibid.

105. Brecher, *Decisions in Israel's Foreign Policy*, 390–91; Eban, 353; Gilbo'a, 148; Burdette, 254–55; author's interview with Ephraim Evron.

106. Original Evron cable reproduced in Brecher, *Decisions in Israel's Foreign Policy*, 390–91; see also Burdette, 255.

107. Johnson, 293.

108. Earle G. Wheeler, JOHI, 7 May 1970, tape 2, pp. 22–23.

109. Author's interview with John P. Roche.

110. Earle G. Wheeler, letter to author, 13 May 1975.

111. Eban, 358.

112. Johnson, 293; author's interview with Dean Rusk.

113. Bar-Zohar, 140; Eban, 359.

114. Quandt, *Decade*, 52.

115. Eugene Rostow, JOHI, 2 December 1968, p. 18.

116. John P. Roche, JOHI, 16 July 1970, tape 2, p. 68.

117. Bar-Zohar, 139; Eban, 368–69.

118. Eban, 370; Brecher, *Decisions in Israel's Foreign Policy*, 398; Gilbo'a, 200.

119. Eban, 370; Brecher, *Decisions in Israel's Foreign Policy*, 400.

120. Brecher, *Decisions in Israel's Foreign Policy*, 400.

121. Johnson, 294.

122. Howe, 151.

123. Author's interview with Lucius Battle.

124. Eugene Rostow, JOHI, 2 December 1968, p. 18.

125. Author's interview with Dean Rusk.

126. Author's interview with Townsend Hoopes.

127. Quandt, *Decade*, 56–57.

128. Bar-Zohar, 99; Howe, 63–64; *Congressional Record*, Senate, vol. 113, pt. 10, 23 May 1967, pp. 13481, 7222; House, vol. 113, pt. 11, 25 May 1967, pp. 14191, 14249, 14270; author's interview with I. L. Kenen; Lucius Battle, JOHI, 14 November 1968, tape 1, p. 44; Kenen, 196.

129. Draper, 105; Quandt, *Decade*, 46.

130. DSB, 19 June 1967, 927. Brecher, *Decisions in Israel's Foreign Policy*, 414n.; U Thant called for a "breathing spell" on 29 May 1967; Goldberg spoke on 31 May 1967; NYT, 30 May 1967, p. 1.

131. Johnson, 295–96; Howe, 66.

132. Johnson, 295.

133. Johnson, 295; author's interview with Ephraim Evron.

134. John P. Roche, JOHI, 16 July 1970, tape 1, p. 64.

135. Brecher, *Decisions in Israel's Foreign Policy*, 414; Howe, 54–55; Rusk stressed preference for multilateral action, NYT, 2 June 1967, p. 1.

136. Brecher, *Decisions in Israel's Foreign Policy*, 414; Bar-Zohar, 159–60.

137. Howe, 57–58, 67, 70–71.

138. Author's interview with John P. Roche; Lucius Battle, JOHI, 5 December 1968, tape 2, p. 4.

139. Brecher, *Decisions in Israel's Foreign Policy*, 417; Walter Laqueur, *The Road to Jerusalem: The Origins of the Arab-Israeli Conflict, 1967* (New York: Macmillan, 1968), 125, 141.

140. See Draper, 109, for a similar argument; Gilbo'a, 191; Aronson, 71–75; Brecher, *Decisions in Israel's Foreign Policy*, 425.

141. Eban, 394.

142. Quandt, *Decade*, 58.

143. Lucius Battle, JOHI, 5 December 1968, tape 2, p. 5.

144. Quandt, *Decade*, 57.

145. Author's interview with Lucius Battle.

146. Mohamed Heikal, *Nasser: The Cairo Documents* (London: New English Library, 1972), 221. Heikal emphasizes Nasser's desire to avoid war.

147. Draper, 67; Walter Laqueur, *The Israel-Arab Reader* (New York: Bantam Books, 1969), 186; Eban, 379–80.

148. Brecher, *Decisions in Israel's Foreign Policy*, 420.

149. Johnson, 296; Quandt, *Decade*, 59.

150. Johnson, 297.

151. Author's interviews with Dean Rusk and author's confidential interview.

152. Earle G. Wheeler, JOHI, 7 May 1970, tape 2, p. 25; Lucius Battle, JOHI, 5 December 1968, tape 2, pp. 3–9.

153. Lucius Battle, JOHI, 16 December 1968, tape 1, p. 44; author's interview with Dean Rusk.

154. Johnson, 298; Howe, 91–93.

155. Bar-Zohar, 260; Eban, 421; Johnson, 301. Rostow claims that Johnson wanted the Israelis to defeat the Syrians but "not to take too much time." Author's interview with Eugene Rostow.

156. Johnson, 302; author's confidential interview; Quandt, Decade, 63; Howe, 104–6.

157. Earle G. Wheeler, JOHI, 7 May 1970, tape 2, p. 24.

158. "Meet the Press" interview with Robert McNamara quoted in Howe, 102–3; DSB, 26 February 1968, 27.

159. Johnson, 301–3; Howe, 104–7; Eban, 422.

160. Eugene Rostow, JOHI, 2 December 1968, p. 34.

161. Quandt, Decade, 62; author's interview with Eugene Rostow.

162. Lucius Battle, JOHI, 14 December 1968, pp. 38–39.

163. Howe, 367; Draper, 112; for other accounts of this story, see Howe, 93–94.

164. For example, Nadav Safran, Israel: The Embattled Ally, 417–18; Quandt, Decade, 71.

165. Author's confidential interview.

166. Ibid.

167. Lyndon Baines Johnson, PPP, 19 June 1967, 633.

168. Ibid.

169. Johnson, 483.

170. Author's confidential interview with a former CIA official. Leacacos, 334; Arthur S. Lall, The UN and the Middle East Crisis, 1967 (New York: Columbia University Press, 1968), 312; Eban, 442–45; Lawrence I. Whetten, The Canal War: Four-Power Conflict in the Middle East (Cambridge: MIT Press, 1974), 47–48; Gideon Raphael, "U.N. Resolution 242: A Common Denominator," New Middle East, June 1973, 28–29; Theodore Draper, "Road to Geneva," Commentary, February 1974, 25–27; Goldberg, DSB, 21 August 1967, 262–65; Gideon Raphael, Destination Peace: Three Decades of Israeli Foreign Policy (New York: Stein and Day, 1981), 177–82.

171. Eban, 448–49.

172. Joseph Sisco, JOHI, 6 November 1971, 14.

173. Lall, 255; Draper, "Road to Geneva," 27; Quandt, Decade, 55.

174. Author's interviews with Eugene Rostow, Arthur J. Goldberg, and Dean Rusk; Eugene Rostow, "The American Stake in Israel," Commentary, April 1977, 44–45; Arthur J. Goldberg, "The Road to Peace in the Middle East," Worldview (February 1974), 8–9.

175. Author's interview with Jack O'Connell; Quandt, Decade, 65; Henry Kissinger, White House Years (Boston: Little, Brown, 1979), 345; Draper, "Road to Geneva," 27.

176. Lyndon Baines Johnson, PPP, 30 March 1968, 467.

177. Yitzhak Rabin, The Rabin Memoirs (Boston: Little, Brown, 1979), 139.

178. Rabin, 140; author's interview with Dean Rusk.

179. Rabin, 140; Campbell, 287.

180. Rabin, 138–41; Campbell, 287–89; House Committee on Foreign Affairs, 10 January 1969, 19–20.

181. Eugene Rostow, JOHI, 2 December 1968, 35.

182. *Gallup Opinion Index*, Report 25, July 1967, 5.

183. Rabin, 64–66; 132.

184. Trice, chaps. 3 and 4.

185. Author's confidential interviews with two former CIA officials.

186. Confidential interview with author; author's interviews with Ephraim Evron and Harry McPherson.

187. Lyndon Baines Johnson, PPP, 8 January 1968, 20–21.

188. Marshal Amnon Hershberg, "Ethnic Interest Groups and Foreign Policy: A case study of the activities of the organized Jewish community in regard to the 1968 decision to sell Phantom jets to Israel" (Ph.D. diss., University of Pittsburgh, 1973), 199; Quandt, *Decade*, 67; author's interviews with Amos A. Jordan and Lucius Battle.

189. Author's interviews with John P. Roche and Harry McPherson; Quandt, *Decade*, 67.

190. Ibid.; author's interviews with Ephraim Evron, Lucius Battle, and a former CIA official. Ambassador Barbour told the author that he believed that some in the Pentagon were opposed because there was a shortage of Phantoms due to a higher-than-expected attrition rate in Vietnam.

191. Trice, 232; NYT, 28 September 1968, p. 1.

192. Earle G. Wheeler, letter to the author, 29 May 1975.

193. Hershberg, 30, 37, 128–37, 196.

194. NER 12, no. 18 (3 September 1968): 70–71; NER 12, no. 19 (17 September 1968): 74–75; Kenen, 218–21.

195. Author's interview with I. L. Kenen; Hershberg, 28–29; NER 12, no. 19 (17 September 1968): 75.

196. Trice, 234; also cited in NYT, 19 July 1968, p. 2; Kenen, 218–19; NER 12, no. 15 (23 July 1968): 59.

197. Hershberg, 32–33; author's interview with I. L. Kenen; Kenen, 218; NER 12, no. 16 (6 August 1968): 64.

198. Author's interview with I. L. Kenen; Kenen, 219.

199. Hershberg, 32–33; Kenen, 219.

200. Rabin, 131, and Hershberg, 34, offer slightly different details; NER 12, no. 19 (17 September 1968): 74–75.

201. Hershberg, 36; see Rabin, 131, for a different version.

202. Hershberg, 36–37.

203. This account was taken from Hershberg, 32–40. The quotations referring to the announcement are based on Neil Sheehan, "Rusk ordered to talk to Israel on Phantom Jets," NYT, 10 October 1968, as quoted in Hershberg, 40.

204. Trice, 236–41; Hershberg, 27; Rabin, 130–31.

205. Eban, 459; Rabin, 141; Hershberg, 40–41.

206. Rabin, 141–42; Quandt claims that Warnke sent Rabin a letter explaining that nonintroduction of nuclear weapons meant "no production of a nuclear device" after Rabin explained the phrase more vaguely (67).

207. Rabin, 142.

Chapter 6. Nixon

1. John B. Kelly, *Arabia, the Gulf, and the West* (New York: Basic Books, 1980), 332, 336–40; Kissinger, 373.

2. DSB (24 February 1969), 159; (14 April 1969), 305; (5 May 1969), 387; (16

February 1970), 173; (1 June 1970), 693; see also Richard Nixon, PPP, 18 February 1970, 152–55.

3. Kissinger, 178, 763, 1103; Richard Nixon, RN: The Memoirs of Richard Nixon (New York: Grosset and Dunlap, 1978), 345 (hereafter cited as Nixon memoirs).

4. Nixon memoirs, 343.

5. Nixon memoirs, 435.

6. Ibid., 481.

7. Eban, 463.

8. Kissinger, 564, 559.

9. William Safire, Before the Fall (New York: Doubleday, 1975), 564–66.

10. According to NBC News, in 1968 Humphrey received 81 percent of the Jewish vote and Nixon received 17 percent: Congressional Quarterly Weekly Report (29 November 1968), 3218. In 1960 Nixon received 18 percent of the Jewish vote. See Stephen D. Isaacs, Jews and American Politics (New York: Doubleday, 1974), 152.

11. Isaacs, 570–75; Richard Reeves, "McGovern, Nixon, and the Jewish Vote," New York Magazine, 14 August 1972, 26; see also "The Chosen Party" (30) and "Is Nixon Kosher?" (2) of the same issue; in an interview with the author, Leonard Garment emphasized Nixon's concern with the Jewish vote; author's interview with Lawrence Goldberg.

12. Safire, 575; NYT, 6 August 1974.

13. Nixon memoirs, 481.

14. NYT, 2 June 1970.

15. Nixon memoirs, 482.

16. Marvin C. Feuerwerger, Congress and Israel (Westport, Conn.: Greenwood Press, 1979), 41; NER 14, no. 2 (21 January 1970): 51–52; no. 7 (1 April 1970): 71; no. 10 (11 May 1970): 81; no. 12 (10 June 1970): 121–22; NYT, 2 June 1970, p. 10, featured a full-page letter from the American Jewish Committee supporting U.S. sale of Phantoms to Israel, accompanied by supporting letters from several senators; Congressional Record, Senate, vol. 115, pt. 29 (17 December 1969): 39630; 116, pt. 7 (24 March 1970): 8825; pt. 13 (3 June 1970): 18287; House, 115, pt. 29 (22 December 1969): 40930–31; 116, pt. 12 (14 May 1970): 15661; pt. 7 (23 March 1970): 8552, 8589, 8641, 4648; and (24 March 1970): 9018, 9019, 9115, 9124; see also House Resolutions 479 and 511, Congressional Record, House, 116, pt. 4 (24 February 1970): 4596. Also Kenen, 237–43.

17. Kissinger, 371; Safire, 566–67; author's interview with Leonard Garment.

18. Nixon memoirs, 355–56, 477; Kissinger, 43; Morton H. Halperin, Bureaucratic Politics and Foreign Policy (Washington, D.C.: Brookings Institution, 1974), 287.

19. Senate Committee on Foreign Relations, Subcommittee on Multinational Corporations, Multinational Corporations and United States Foreign Policy (94th Cong., 1st Sess., 1975), pt. 7: 517, 525, 528.

20. Anthony Sampson, The Seven Sisters: The Great Oil Companies and the World They Made (New York: Viking, 1975), 205–6, 247; Robert Engler, The Brotherhood of Oil: Energy Policy and the Public Interest (Chicago: University of Chicago Press, 1977), 63.

21. Engler, 62; Sampson, 247.

22. Shoshana Klebanoff, Middle East Oil and U.S. Foreign Policy (New York: Praeger, 1974), 229; John M. Blair, The Control of Oil (New York: Pantheon Books, 1976), 184–85; author's interviews with Jack Sunderland and Howard Page.

23. Nixon memoirs, 346.

24. Kissinger, 564.

25. Ibid., 350.

26. Richard M. Nixon, PPP, 25 July 1969, 549, 551; Nixon memoirs, 394.

27. Kelly, 303–4, 308–9. Kelly argues that the American oil companies (especially Aramco) opposed pressures on London to remain because of past British competition with them.

28. Richard M. Nixon, PPP, 1 July 1970, 558; Edward F. Sheehan, *The Arabs, Israelis, and Kissinger* (New York: Reader's Digest Press, 1976), 18, 19; Rabin, 172.

29. Author's interview with Warren Nutter; Quandt, *Decade*, 120.

30. Nixon memoirs, 340.

31. Kissinger, 40; Tad Szulc, *The Illusion of Peace: Foreign Policy in the Nixon Years* (New York: Viking Press, 1978), 14, 18; Kissinger, 48.

32. Kissinger, 48.

33. Ibid., 918; Nixon–Frost interview, NYT, 13 May 1977, p. A9.

34. Nixon memoirs, 339; Kissinger, 26, 31, 47.

35. Nixon memoirs, 339, 433.

36. Nixon–Frost interview, NYT, 13 May 1977, p. A9.

37. Nixon memoirs, 433; Kissinger, 26.

38. Kissinger, 341.

39. Insight Team of the London *Sunday Times*, *The Yom Kippur War* (New York: Doubleday, 1974), 23. (Hereafter cited as YKW.)

40. Kissinger, 376.

41. Nixon memoirs, 477.

42. Kissinger, 349–50, 376–77.

43. Nixon memoirs, 477; Kissinger, 348, 559.

44. Kissinger, 348.

45. Moshe Dayan, *Story of My Life* (Jerusalem: Steimatzky's Agency, 1976), 336; author's interview with Warren Nutter. Nutter, Laird's head of the International Security Agency, who did not have a major policy role, took a similar view.

46. Andrew Glass, "Nixon Gives Israel Massive Aid but Reaps No Political Harvest," *National Journal* 4 (no. 2, 8 January 1972): 58.

47. NYT, 11 December 1970, p. 2; 12 December 1970, p. 16; Robert Eastbrook, news analysis, *Washington Post*, 12 December 1970, p. A98; Charles W. Yost, *History and Memory* (New York: W. W. Norton, 1980).

48. Marvin Kalb and Bernard Kalb, *Kissinger* (Boston: Little, Brown, 1974), 188.

49. Safire, 574.

50. Rabin, 165, 168; Kissinger, 369, 372.

51. Rabin, 131–34; author's interview with Leonard Garment.

52. Heikal, 175; Richard Nixon, PPP, 8 August 1974, 628.

53. Safire, 567; Rabin, 132, 134, 153, 185, 244; Golda Meir, *My Life* (New York: G. P. Putnam's Sons, 1975), 390, 392, 430; author's interview with Leonard Garment: Dayan, 369.

54. Kissinger, 370, 371, 372–73.

55. Rabin, 208, 153; Nixon memoirs, 786.

56. Kissinger, 563, 564.

57. Nixon memoirs, 477.

58. Kissinger, 564; see also ibid., 559–60, 563–64; Nixon memoirs, 179; on Suez, see also Kissinger, 347.

59. Nixon memoirs, 481; Kalb and Kalb, 191–94; Safire, 568–69, 392.

60. Nixon memoirs, 481.

61. Ibid., 482.

62. NYT, 8 December 1968, p. 9; 10 December 1968, p. 1; 11 December 1968, p. 10; 12 December 1968, p. 1; author's interview with William Scranton.

63. Kissinger, 51; Dayan, 369–70; Kenen, 238–40.

64. Richard M. Nixon, PPP, 27 January 1969, 18.

65. Kissinger, 352, 559.

66. Kissinger, 351–52.

67. Ibid., 353.

68. Kalb and Kalb, 189; Quandt, *Decade*, 83–87; Szulc, 93–97; Safran, *Israel: The Embattled Ally*, 433–34; Bernard Reich, *Quest for Peace: United States–Israel Relations and the Arab-Israeli Conflict* (New Brunswick, N.J.: Transaction Books, 1977), 103, 105.

69. Rabin, 96.

70. Eban, 463; Kissinger, 357.

71. NYT, 28 March 1969, p. 14; DSB, 14 April 1969, 305.

72. Kissinger, 353; Rabin, 168; Trice, 255; NYT, 14 February 1969, p. 38; see also references in n. 16 above; Kenen, 238–40.

73. Glass, 59; Meir, 383.

74. Kissinger, 358, 354, 361. For an account critical of Kissinger and sympathetic to Rogers's initiatives, see Seymour Hersh, *The Price of Power: Kissinger in the Nixon White House* (New York: Summit Books, 1983), 203–49, 402–14.

75. Kissinger, 367–69.

76. Ibid., 367–69, 370–72.

77. Rabin, 153; NYT, 28 September 1969, p. 32; author's confidential interview; Richard M. Nixon, PPP, 25 September 1969, 74.

78. Rabin, 154; confidential files made available to author; author's interview with Theodore Tanenwald.

79. Nixon memoirs, 478; Rabin, 151; Meir, 387, 391; NYT, 26 September 1969, p. 1; 27 September 1969, p. 1.

80. Rabin, 153–54, 156; Kissinger, 370–71.

81. For a similar conclusion, see Szulc, 92; Trice, 259–61; NYT, 24 March 1970, p. 16; Hersh, 218–19.

82. Kissinger, 372.

83. Whetten, 75–78; Trice, 171–74; Safran, *Israel: The Embattled Ally*, p. 435.

84. Trice, 174–80; NYT, 22 December 1969, p. 1.

85. William Rogers, *A Lasting Peace in the Middle East: An American View; an Address by Secretary of State William P. Rogers before the 1969 Galaxy Conference on Adult Education* (Washington, D.C.: U.S. Government Printing Office, 1970); Mahmoud Riad, *The Struggle for Peace in the Middle East* (New York: Quartet Books, 1981), 111.

86. NYT, 21 December 1969, p. 1; 22 December 1969, p. 1; Trice, 174–75; Kissinger, 376; Quandt, *Decade*, 91.

87. Seymour Hersh claims, quoting Sisco (who confirmed the story to the author), that Kissinger saw the speech and wrote substantive comments on it. Hersh also claims that Kissinger pretended he had not participated in order to embarrass Rogers before the president. Hersh's account of Kissinger's maneuver seems contrived. Certainly Kissinger had been aware of State Department preferences for months. In his memoirs, Kissinger reports that he knew Rogers would deliver the speech. Even if he did have an advance copy and had commented on it, Kissinger was certainly not part of the State Department team during this period or in harmony with it. See Hersh, 220; Kissinger, 374.

88. Kissinger, 374; Trice, 174–75.

89. Rabin, 163–64; Richard M. Nixon, PPP, 18 February 1970, 119, 120, 154, 180.

90. Trice, 187–89; Richard M. Nixon, PPP, 26 January 1970, 18.

91. Nixon memoirs, 479.

92. Rabin, 159–61; Kissinger, 376, 377; NYT, 22 December 1969, p. 1. Hussein met

secretly with Israeli leaders at least eleven times between 1967 and 1977. The meetings were held in a limousine in the desert, on a boat in the Gulf of Aqaba, in London, in Israel. There have been various reports about them. See, for example, Moshe Dayan, *Breakthrough* (New York: Alfred A. Knopf, 1981), 35–37; Judith Miller, "King Hussein's Delicate Balance," *New York Times Magazine,* 22 April 1984, 30; confidential interview with author.

93. Rabin, 165, 167; Eban, 465.

94. Rabin, 167; Eban, 465.

95. Mohamed Heikal, *The Road to Ramadan* (New York: Ballantine Books, 1975), 83–90; Anwar el-Sadat, *In Search of Identity* (New York: Harper and Row, 1979), 197; Riad, 113, 119–20, 124–25.

96. Kissinger, 562.

97. Ibid., 563; NYT, 24 March 1970, p. 16; NER 14, no. 6 (17 March 1970): 67–68.

98. Trice, 245–47; Richard M. Nixon, PPP, 30 January 1970, 37; NYT, 31 January 1970, p. 14; Nixon memoirs, 480; Kissinger, 560–67.

99. NYT, 3 March 1970, p. 1; Trice, 245–52; Safire, 556, 567.

100. Trice, 245–54; Nixon memoirs, 480; Kissinger, 565; NYT, 4 March 1970, p. 3.

101. Anthony Sampson, *The Arms Bazaar* (New York: Viking Press, 1977), 177; Rabin, 169–73; Meir, 382; Kissinger, 483, 569, 571, 576; Nixon memoirs, 480; Riad, 119.

102. Kissinger, 568; Rabin, 169–70.

103. Rabin, 171.

104. Ibid., 172.

105. Kissinger, 566–70; Rabin, 169–74; Eban, 466–67; Trice, 264–66.

106. Kissinger, 571.

107. Ibid., 569–72.

108. Ibid., 570–71; Rabin, 173–74.

109. Max Frankel, news analysis, NYT, 2 May 1970, p. 6; Kalb and Kalb, 192; Kissinger, 483; Riad, 125–26.

110. Kissinger, 573.

111. Eban, 466; Rabin, 175; Kissinger, 572.

112. NYT, 2 June 1970, p. 12; Trice, 256.

113. Kissinger, 571, 575–79; Meir, 385; Rabin, 177.

114. Kissinger, 579–80; NYT, 3 July 1970, p. 1.

115. NYT, 4 July 1970, p. 1; 6 July 1970, p. 8; Kalb and Kalb, 193.

116. Richard M. Nixon, PPP, 1 July 1970, p. 558; NYT, 31 July 1970; Trice, 222.

117. Kissinger, 580, 582; Szulc, 315.

118. Aronson, 123; Safran, *Israel: The Embattled Ally,* 443; Kissinger, 585. For other points of view, see Eban, 468, and Riad, 150–52. Riad (141) writes that Egypt accepted the American proposal anticipating that Washington would then put greater pressure on Israel.

119. Brecher, *Decisions in Israel's Foreign Policy,* 493; Whetten, 117; Szulc, 317; Aronson, 112–23.

120. Nixon memoirs, 482.

121. Rabin, 179–85; Eban, 468–69.

122. Whetten, 131; NYT, 17 August 1970, p. 4; Rabin, 185; Nixon memoirs, 482.

123. Kissinger, 588–89; Nixon memoirs, 484; for a slightly different version, see Riad, 150–54.

124. Kissinger, 590, 591; author's interview with Ray Cline; NYT, 4 September 1970, p. 1; Szulc, 320.

125. Kissinger, 593; Szulc, 320, 324; Trice, 206–207; NYT, 2 September 1970, p. 1.

126. *Congressional Record*, Senate, 116, pt. 23 (1 September 1970): 30723–24.

127. Nixon (memoirs, 483) gives the crisis in Jordan as the reason for his reversal on military aid to Israel, but his decision was actually made in response to Egyptian violations before the crisis in Jordan intensified; Kissinger, 597–600; Eban, 467–68.

128. NYT, 8 September 1970, p. 17; 14 September 1970, p. 21; 21 September 1970, p. 11.

129. Kissinger, 602, 605–6, 620–21; Frank Van der Linden, *Nixon's Quest for Peace* (Washington, D.C.: Robert B. Luce, 1972), 83; David Schoenbaum, "Were We Masterful . . . or Lucky?" *Foreign Policy* 10 (Spring 1973): 173; Kalb and Kalb, 199. Hersh (235–36) claims that Kissinger reaffirmed the order and later called the defense secretary to find out why it had not been carried out. Hersh's evidence on Kissinger's involvement is, however, weak. For further evidence of the differences between Kissinger and Laird, see Henry Brandon, *The Retreat of American Power* (Garden City, N.Y.: Doubleday, 1973), 211.

130. Kissinger, 606–7, 611; Kalb and Kalb, 206.

131. Kissinger, 606.

132. Ibid., 602–4; see 621 for the names of WSAG principals.

133. Ibid., 607.

134. NYT, 13 September 1970, p. 1; 26 September 1970, p. 1; 27 September 1970, p. 1; 30 September 1970, p. 1.

135. Kissinger, 610, 612; Szulc, 326, 327.

136. Kissinger, 614. According to NYT, 19 September 1970, p. 8, Nixon told the editors, "The United States is prepared to intervene directly in the Jordanian war should Syria and Iraq enter the conflict and tip the military balance against government forces loyal to Hussein."

137. Kissinger, 614–15.

138. *Congressional Record*, Senate, 116, pt. 24 (22 September 1970): 32993–94; see also editorial, NYT, 21 September 1970, p. 42, warning against provoking an "explosion of Arab nationalism"; Nixon memoirs, 481; Kissinger, 614–17.

139. Nixon memoirs, 485–86; Kissinger, 632–39.

140. Kissinger, 618–19; Nixon memoirs, 483.

141. NYT, 23 September 1970; p. 18; Kissinger, 619, 621.

142. Ibid., 619–22; quotations are from 622.

143. Ibid., 622.

144. Ibid., 623; Rabin, 187–88; Nixon memoirs, 485.

145. See Rabin, 186–89, for an account slightly different in detail.

146. Kissinger, 622–25.

147. Ibid., 626.

148. Rabin, 188.

149. Kissinger, 629; Kalb and Kalb, 207; *Washington Star*, 23 September 1970.

150. Kissinger, 630; Hersh, 246; Brandon, 133–38.

151. See, for example, D. Schoenbaum, "Were We Masterful . . . ," 171–81. For a more positive assessment of the U.S. response to the crisis, see Alan Dowty, "The U.S. and the Syrian-Jordan Confrontation, 1970," *Jerusalem Journal of International Relations*, Winter-Spring, 1978, 172–96. Brandon, 133–38. A vehement, but nonacademic, critique of Nixon and Kissinger's handling of the crisis is provided by Hersh (234–49). He argues that Nixon was bent on punishing the Soviets for refusing an early summit and on proving his mettle in a confrontation with the Russians before the Moscow summit. Hersh complains that both Nixon and Kissinger were prone to blame the Soviets for any world affairs problem, when in reality Moscow urged restraint on its clients in this case.

Hersh also believes that the White House relied exclusively and wrongly on Jordanian and Israeli intelligence. He suggests a CIA role in preparing Jordanian forces and complains that Nixon and Kissinger sought a "cheap" Cuban missile crisis to demonstrate their powers vis-à-vis the Soviets.

152. Kissinger, 625. Many sources that I interviewed in 1974 and 1975 did not know that this decision had been made by the president and Kissinger.

153. Quandt, *Decade*, 126; G. Matthew Bonham, with Michael Shapiro and Thomas Trumble, "The October War: Changes in Cognitive Orientation toward the Middle East Conflict," *International Studies Quarterly*, March 1979, 14–17.

154. Quandt, *Decade*, 127; Kissinger, 618, 631; Kalb and Kalb, 208.

155. Rabin makes it clear that the president's conduct during the crisis assured him that Israel could trust Nixon's assurances; Rabin, 189–92; Sadat, 280, 286, 287; Riad, 154–57.

156. Support for Israel in the 91st Congress was so overwhelming that it is rare to find statements critical of Israel. Pro-Israel senators were sufficiently well organized to obtain immediate authorization for arms sales on credit to Israel in fall 1970. This was achieved by working around the usual channel, the Senate Foreign Relations Committee, whose chairman, J. William Fulbright, was critical of massive arms sales to Israel. See *Congressional Record*, Senate, 116, pt. 23: 30713. For a scholarly examination of the relationship between Israel and the U.S. House of Representatives in this period, see Marvin Feuerwerger, *Congress and Israel.*

157. NYT, 29 September 1970, p. 15; Szulc, 33; Trice, 763–64; see also Feuerwerger, 42.

158. Kissinger, 1277; Rabin, 192–92; YKW, 44; Eban, 472–73; for citation of Jarring's questions and the Israeli and Egyptian replies, see NYT, 10 March 1971, p. 8.

159. Rabin, 193–94; Eban, 475; see NYT, 13 March 1971, p. 1, for an account of Rogers's statements to the Senate Foreign Relations Committee on 12 March.

160. Kissinger, 1279.

161. Rabin, 195; Kissinger, 1279; Richard M. Nixon, PPP, 25 February 1971, 285–92.

162. All sides agree on this. See Rabin, 193–95; Sadat, 280, 286, 287; Heikal, *Road to Ramadan*, 141, 152–56; Kissinger, 1279, 1283.

163. Rabin, 191; Kissinger, 1281; Riad, 187.

164. For varying accounts of Sadat's position, see Sadat, interview, *Newsweek*, 22 February 1971; Kissinger, 1281; Rabin, 193; Sadat, 279; Heikal, *Road to Ramadan*, 114; Riad, 187; Eban, 473.

165. Sisco characterized the Sadat Plan as "serious and concrete"; compare Rabin, 193; Brandon, 122–24; and Eban, 473–74. See also NYT, 10 February 1971, p. 10, for further State Department views.

166. See Rabin, 195–99, for an account of Kissinger's repeated attempts to force Israel to clarify its proposals; Kissinger, 1281. For accounts of the Senate sessions, see Whetten, 154, 170; Rabin, 197; NYT, 13 March 1971, p. 1.

167. See Rabin, 197–200, and Eban, 473–76, for an example of differing interpretations within the Israeli government; for Egyptian explanations for the diplomatic failure, see Sadat, 286; Heikal, *Road to Ramadan*, 115; and Riad, 182–89. See also Kissinger, 1282.

168. Kissinger, 1282.

169. Brandon, 122; see Sadat interview in *Newsweek*, 13 December 1971, 43; Heikal, *Road to Ramadan*, 115. For Riad's account of Rogers's visit, see 197–202.

170. Brandon, 122–23; Eban, 475; NYT, 8 May 1971, p. 1.

171. Heikal, *Road to Ramadan*, 132; Rabin, 201.

172. Brandon, 124; Whetten, 183.

173. Kissinger, 1283.

174. Heikal, *Road to Ramadan*, 138; Sadat, 282–84; Safran, *Israel: The Embattled Ally*, 460. For the text of the treaty, see NYT, 28 May 1971, p. 2.

175. Kissinger, 1284–85; see Richard M. Nixon, PPP, 1 June 1971, 691, for Nixon's statement of 1 June expressing similar views; Hersh, 409.

176. Kissinger, 1285. Riad cites Egyptian dissatisfaction in March 1971 with delays in the delivery of Soviet weapons (191–92).

177. For the text of Kraft's column, see *Washington Post*, 27 June 1971, p. 23; also, Kissinger, 1284; author's interview with Donald Bergus; Heikal, *Road to Ramadan*, 141; Riad, 203–204; for a slightly different version, see Hersh, 409–10.

178. Whetten, 191; *USIS Bulletin*, no. 120 (29 June 1971).

179. Kissinger, 1284; Sadat, 286; Heikal, *Road to Ramadan*, 141; Riad, 205; NYT, 30 June 1971, p. 3.

180. For Sadat's statement on this, see NYT, 24 July 1971, p. 3; also, Heikal, *Road to Ramadan*, 141, 156; Safran, *Israel: The Embattled Ally*, 460–61. Ironically, Secretary Rogers was the first to use the phrase *year of decision* with reference to the Middle East; see DSB, 11 January 1971, 43.

181. Kissinger, 1285.

182. Ibid.

183. Whetten, 162–66; Riad, 205.

184. Trice, 268, 288; Whetten, 191–92; Brecher, *Decisions in Israel's Foreign Policy*, 508; Aronson, 147–149.

185. Quandt, *Decade*, 145.

186. See Trice, 270, for an analysis of this relationship.

187. Rabin, 201; author's interview with Mahmoud Riad. For public statements by Sadat expressing disillusionment with Rogers, see NYT, 17 September 1971, p. 13; 13 December 1971, p. 22; *Newsweek*, 13 December 1971, 44; Heikal, *Road to Ramadan*, 141; Riad, 209–10. Typically blaming Kissinger, Hersh (404–5) believes, citing the views of Bergus and CIA station chief Eugene Trone, that an agreement could have been reached that summer because he thinks Sadat was willing to consider a possible deal. Since serious negotiations did not begin, the notion that they would have been successful remains speculation.

188. For Rogers's statement, see DSB, 25 October 1971, 442–44; see also DSB, 6 December 1971, 649; 20 December 1971, 698. See also Kissinger, 1289; Quandt, *Decade*, 146.

189. Kissinger, 1283, 1289.

190. Ibid., 1286, 1288.

191. Kissinger, 1289–92, includes a long discussion of these "back channel" talks.

192. Rabin, 211–212.

193. For various points of view on these Soviet pledges, see Sadat, 226, 228–231, 287; Heikal, *Road to Ramadan*, 159–60; Kissinger, 1289; Trice, 269; Aronson, 153; Whetten, 211; Riad, 227.

194. Immediately following the announcement of the Soviet pledge, Senator Scott of Pennsylvania called for increased sales of Phantom jets to Israel, emphasizing the Soviet threat. Scott's resolution was endorsed by 77 senators. A supporting speech by Senator Symington of Missouri emphasized the threat of the Soviet MiG-25 Foxbat which had recently been deployed in Egypt. Two weeks later, the House advanced a resolution endorsed by 233 representatives calling for renewed jet shipments to Israel and adherence

to U.N. Resolution 242. *Congressional Record,* Senate, 117, pt. 28 (15 October 1971): 36366–69; House, 117, pt. 29 (28 October 1971): 38128–29. Congressional response also included an unbudgeted $85 million in economic assistance and $580 million in economic and military aid to Israel in fiscal 1972; see Trice, 269.

195. Trice, 270; Aronson, 153; Szulc, 441; NYT, 28 October 1971, p. 18; Whetten, 209.

196. Glass, 57; Trice, 271; NYT, 24 November 1971, p. 1.

197. Rabin, 207–208.

198. Kissinger, 1290. For Sadat's role in these efforts, see NYT, 3 February 1972, p. 1; 18 February 1972, p. 8, and *Newsweek,* 13 December 1971, 47; Riad, 223.

199. Kissinger, 1288; author's interview with Daniel Henken; NYT, 14 January 1972, p. 1; Heikal, *Road to Ramadan,* 170; Sadat, 227; YKW, 53.

200. Author's interview with Warren Nutter, 22 May 1975; Quandt, *Decade,* 145; Brandon, 124; Kissinger, 573, 575.

201. Kissinger, 1289–90; Trice, 270.

202. Kissinger, 1287; Rabin, 201.

203. Nixon memoirs, 786; Kissinger, 1285.

204. Author's interview with Harold Saunders; Aronson, 154; YKW, 54; Brandon, 127; NYT, 7 July 1972, p. 1 (feature article discussing the 1972 Jewish vote).

205. See McGovern's statement of Mideast policy, NYT, 3 March 1971, p. 8, in which he favored "internationalization" of Jerusalem. Also, Isaacs, 182–97; Safire, 570–78.

206. Stewart Alsop, "Why is Israel for Nixon?" *Newsweek,* 10 July 1972, 100; Isaacs, 192; NYT, 3 October 1972, p. 33.

207. Rabin, 232–33; NYT, 7 July 1972, p. 1.

208. *Congressional Quarterly Weekly Report,* 11 November 1972, 2949 (figures provided by NBC's sample of 1,500 precincts); George H. Gallup, *The Gallup Poll: Public Opinion 1972–1977* (Wilmington: Scholarly Resources, 1978), vol. 1 (14 December 1972): 76–78.

209. Rabin, 212, 217; Kissinger, 1290.

210. Kissinger, 1247; Rabin, 214; Eban, 480; Sadat, 229; Heikal, *Road to Ramadan,* 166–87, especially 176–77. Heikal claims that the summit communiqué was a major factor in Sadat's decision to expel the Russians from Egypt. See also Riad, 229.

211. Sadat, 230; YKW, 56–58.

212. Kissinger, 1293, 1295; Heikal, *Road to Ramadan,* 203. Heikal claims that he and Sadat were not eager to meet with Kissinger largely because they were not sure in their own minds what Egyptian strategy should be (*Road to Ramadan,* 204).

213. Kissinger, 1296.

214. For examples of attitudes at the time, see Eban, 479–80; Brandon, 127; NYT, 19 July 1972, p. 1; *Time,* 14 August 1972, 33; *U.S. News,* 14 August 1972, 45.

215. Kissinger, 1295, 1300.

216. Nixon memoirs, 786.

217. Kissinger, 1294–95; author's confidential interview.

218. Ibid., 1295.

219. See Rogers's statements in DSB, 1 February 1971, 134–35; 29 March 1971, 444; NYT, 17 March 1971, 18; Whetten, 71–72, 156.

220. Sadat, 287; Kissinger, 1248, 1294–95, 1297.

221. Rabin, 208.

222. Nixon memoirs, 787; NYT, 10 November 1972, p. 20.

Chapter 7. Nixon and Ford

1. Henry Kissinger, DSB, 29 October 1973, 535; 10 December 1973, 701; 21 July 1975, 90; 6 October 1975, 493–500; 27 October 1975, 609. Also, Richard Nixon, DSB, 7 July 1974, 3, and Joseph Sisco, DSB, 8 July 1974, 56.

2. For a representative sample of "doomsday" articles on the oil crisis see interview with W. J. Levy, *Business Week*, 2 March 1974, 60; "Petrocurrency Peril," *Time*, 17 June 1974, 83; W. J. Levy, "Oil Cooperation or International Chaos," *Foreign Affairs*, July 1974, 690; "Will Western Allies Go Broke?" *U.S. News and World Report*, 29 July 1974, 22–23; "Oil Crisis: It threatens to bring down the West," *U.S. News and World Report*, 14 October 1974, 23–24; P. Lewis, "Getting Even: the Effect of Oil Prices on World Monetary Systems," *New York Times Magazine*, 15 December 1974, 13.

3. *Commerce America*, 13 July 1973, 44–51; 22 July 1974, 48; 1 August 1977, 27–37, 48. Source: U.S. Department of Commerce, International Monetary Fund, and International Financial Statistics.

4. Ibid., 1 August 1977, 27–35. See also *Commerce Today*, 24 June 1974, 21–22. This magazine ran a series of articles in 1974 describing the lucrative Near East Market.

5. U.S. Senate Committee on Foreign Relations, Subcommittee on Multinational Corporations, *Multinational Oil Companies and U.S. Foreign Policy* (Washington, D.C.: U.S. Government Printing Office, 1975), 141–44. (Hereafter cited as MNOC.)

6. *Time*, 23 June 1975, 17–20; NYT, 30 June 1975, p. 1. These articles also discuss the Arab lobby.

7. Sadat met with businessmen and reporters and with delegations from both the U.S. Senate and House. For sample accounts of these meetings, see NYT, 28 January 1975, p. 3; 20 September 1975, p. 10; 18 April 1976, p. 3; 15 November 1976, p. 2 and 19 November 1976, p. 1.

8. Author's interviews with Granville Austin, Warren Nutter, and James Schlesinger.

9. Author's interview with Ray Cline. See also YKW, 113.

10. Author's interview with Ray Cline.

11. Author's interviews with Watt Cluverius and James Schlesinger; author's confidential interview. See also analysis by Drew Middleton, NYT, 21 October 1976, p. 11.

12. *Washington Post*, 13 November 1974, p. A9. Brown's retraction was printed the next day, p. A1.

13. Sheehan, 232; George H. Gallup, *The Gallup Poll: Public Opinion, 1972–77*, vol. 4 (Wilmington Scholarly Resources, 1978), 4–7 April 1975; May 1975, pp. 8–10; October 1975, p. 5.

14. Janice J. Terry and Gordon Mendenhall, "1973 Press Coverage of the Middle East," *Journal of Palestine Studies*, Autumn 1975, 120–33. AFL-CIO Secretary-Treasurer Lane Kirkland called the Arab oil cartel's policy "blackmail": NYT, 12 September 1974, p. 30, and the AFL-CIO later called for legislation to prohibit oil imports from countries that participated in the 1973 embargo; NYT, 24 January 1975, p. 1.

15. MNOC, 126, 150; Blair, 264; Kelly, 379–458; V. H. Oppenheim, "We Pushed Them," *Foreign Policy*, Winter 1976–77, 40–49.

16. NYT, 22 November 1973, p. 1; 24 September 1974, pp, 1, 12; 3 January 1975, p. 2; *Time*, 20 January 1975, 21. For Kissinger's "strangulation" warnings, see DSB, 27 January 1975, 101, and 10 February 1975, 172–73. Defense Secretary Schlesinger also issued warnings: NYT, 7 January 1974, p. 1, and 15 January 1975, p. 10.

17. George H. Gallup, February 1974, p. 4; NYT, 23 December 1973, p. 18; MNOC, 150.

18. *Business Week*, 17 March 1975, 24; NYT, 18 December 1975, p. 5; 14 March 1976, pt. 4, p. 2; 4 September 1976, p. 2; 8 September 1976, p. 3.

19. Carter attacked the Arab boycott and the Ford administration's response to it in speeches on 6 September 1976 and 30 September 1976. See *The Presidential Campaign 1976* (Washington, D.C.: U.S. Government Printing Office, 1979), vol. 1, pt. 2, pp. 711, 835–36 (hereafter cited as PC 1976). Ford responded in a speech on 9 September 1976 and during a press conference on 20 October 1976. See PC 1976, vol. 1, pt. 2, pp. 815, 951–54. The Rosenthal-Bingham Antiboycott bill was approved 25 September 1976, but with large differences between the House and Senate versions. Efforts to appoint conferees were thwarted by Senator Tower of Texas and Congress adjourned before a conference committee could be appointed. Thus, the bills died. See *Congressional Quarterly Almanac, 1976* (Washington, D.C.: Congressional Quarterly, 1976), 257; NYT, 26 September 1976, p. 52; 30 September 1976, p. 61.

20. Edward Luttwak, "The Defense Budget and Israel," *Commentary* February 1975, 27–37. Sixty-one articles appeared in technical U.S. military journals in 1974 on the tactics and hardware of the Yom Kippur War. Twenty-four additional articles appeared in 1975. See *The Air University Library Index to Military Periodicals* (Maxwell Air Force Base, Ala.: Air University Library, 1974, 1975).

21. NYT, 22 May 1975, p. 1.

22. Nixon memoirs, 787.

23. Carter called for a "clear, unequivocal commitment without change to Israel," PC 1976, vol. 3, p. 104; also see PC 1976, vol. 1, pt. 1, p. 440. Ford made several promises in a speech to the B'nai Brith convention on 9 September 1976. These included no imposed solution, no one-sided concessions, consultation with Israel, and diplomatic protection for Israel in the U.N. See PC 1976, vol. 1, pt. 2, p. 815.

24. Paula Stern, *Water's Edge: Domestic Politics and the Making of American Foreign Policy* (Westport, Conn.: Greenwood Press, 1979). The Jackson amendment was finally passed as part of the Trade Bill in late 1974.

25. Author's interview with Harold Saunders; Henry Kissinger, DSB, 11 February 1974, 142.

26. Sheehan, 169; Quandt, *Decade*, 202, 209; Bonham, Shapiro, and Trumble, 3–45.

27. "A New Hard Line on Oil," *Newsweek* 7 October 1974, 49–52; Robert W. Tucker, "Oil: the Issue of American Intervention," *Commentary*, January 1975, 21–32, and Tucker's reply to critics, *Commentary*, March 1975, 45–56; Terry and Mendenhall, 120–33; Edward Friedland, Paul Seabury, Aaron Wildavsky, *The Great Detente Disaster: Oil and the Decline of American Foreign Policy* (New York: Basic Books, 1975), 185–90.

28. *Vital Speeches* (1 December 1974), 102–7.

29. Nixon memoirs, 277, 927.

30. Kissinger, Address to National Press Club, DSB, 24 February 1975, 237–49; Assistant Secretary of State for Economic and Business Affairs Thomas Enders, Speech to Senate Foreign Relations Committee, DSB, 10 March 1975, 312–17.

31. NYT, 9 June 1974, p. 1; Stephan Hayes, "Joint Economic Commissions as Instruments of U.S. Foreign Policy in the Middle East," *Middle East Journal* 31 (No. 1, Winter 1977): 16–30; *Commerce America*, 1 August, 1977, 27–35; NYT, 7 September 1974, p. 1; 11 January 1977, p. 5. On the latter date the NYT noted that the Saudis had contracted for $12 billion in U.S. arms between 1950 and 1976, but only $1.6 billion worth had been delivered by the end of 1976.

32. DSB, 18 February 1974, 178.

33. DSB, 7 July 1975, 19. Interview also published in *U.S. News and World Report*, 23 June 1975.

34. Kissinger, *Years of Upheaval* (Boston: Little, Brown, 1982), 616, 634.

35. Ibid., 1249.

36. Ibid., 939.

37. Ibid., 664.

38. See H. R. Haldeman, *The Ends of Power* (New York: Times Books, 1978), 175–80.

39. See Nixon's interview with David Frost, NYT, 13 May 1977, p. A9. Kissinger questions Nixon's account of the John Connally appointment. He also claims that but for Watergate he would have left office by the end of 1973, although he admits that even he does not know if he would have carried out his plan to depart. See *Years of Upheaval*, 6–8.

40. Kissinger drew criticism from some in the Jewish community in the United States and from right-wing Jews in Israel. See, for example, Eban, 559–60, Matti Golan, *The Secret Conversations of Henry Kissinger* (New York: Quadrangle 1976), 151, and Sheehan, 173, 183, for descriptions of Kissinger's trials at the hands of some of his fellow Jews.

41. Heikal, *Road to Ramadan*, 141, 203. Meir, 442–45; Dayan, *Story of My Life*, 443; Rabin, 258, 261; Eban, 599.

42. Theodore Draper, "Appeasement and Detente," *Commentary*, February 1976, 27–38.

43. MNOC, 141–44; NYT, 19 September 1973, p. 65; 30 June 1975, p. 10; see also the Mobil advertisement in NYT, 21 June 1973, p. 18; *Newsweek*, 14 April 1975, 52–53; *Time*, 12 May 1975, 39; Gerald Ford, *A Time to Heal* (New York: Harper and Row, 1979), 247.

44. Edward N. Luttwak and Walter Laqueur, "Kissinger and the Yom Kippur War," *Commentary*, September 1974, 33–41; Szulc, 735–38; Kalb and Kalb, 465–78.

45. Ford, 308–9.

46. John Hersey, *Aspects of the Presidency* (New Haven, Conn.: Teiknor and Fields, 1980), 227, 229; Ford, 150.

47. Ford, 355, 129.

48. Hersey, 144–45. Ford denies that he was inexperienced in foreign affairs; see Ford, 128–29.

49. Ford, 5, 6.

50. Hersey, 144.

51. *Congressional Record*, 90th Cong., 2d sess., vol. 114, pt. 2 (7 February 1968): 2424; 92d Cong., 1st sess., vol. 117, pt. 10 (4 May 1971): 13352–56.

52. See, for example, ibid., 90th Cong., 2d sess., vol. 114, pt. 2 (7 February 1968): 882; ibid., 92d Cong., 1st sess., vol. 117, pt. 29 (27 October 1971): 37856.

53. Ibid., 90th Cong., 2d sess., vol. 114, pt. 2 (7 February 1968: 883; ibid., 91st Cong., 2d sess., vol. 116, pt. 28 (19 November 1970): 38255; ibid., pt. 14 (9 June 1970): 19006; ibid., pt. 28 (19 November 1970): 38260.

54. Ibid., pt. 4 (24 February 1970): 4616.

55. Ford's speech at Beechwood, Ohio, 14 February 1972; Gerald R. Ford, PPP, 1974, 64.

56. Ford's speech at Kfar Silver Hillel dinner, 6 June 1971.

57. NER, 5 May 1971, 70.

58. Ford, 140, 183, 290.

59. Ibid., 245. On Ford's first working day as vice president, he met with the Israeli defense minister, Moshe Dayan. Lavish in his praise of Kissinger, he stressed the importance of Israel's aiding the United States in the search for peace. Dayan, *Story of My Life*, 457.

60. International Institute of Strategic Studies, *Strategic Survey, 1974* (London: I.I.S.S. Press, 1975), 15; Anthony Cordesman, "The Arab-Israeli Balance: How Much is too Much?" *Armed Forces Journal International*, October 1977, 32–39; Gregory Copley, "The Concept of Israel as a Major Red Sea Power," *Defense and Foreign Affairs Digest*, no. 3 (1977), 12–14.

61. Ford, 246.

62. Author's confidential interviews.

63. Leslie Gelb discusses Schlesinger's view of detente and his differences with Kissinger, NYT, 4 August 1974, pt. 6, p. 8. Also see NYT, 16 July 1974, p. 18, and 8 November 1975, p. 2, regarding differences between the two.

64. Nixon memoirs, 924, 926–27, 1024–25; Ford wrote, "I must also admit that his aloof, frequently arrogant manner, put me off" (324).

65. John Osborne, *The Fifth Year of the Nixon Watch* (New York: Liveright, 1974), 127.

66. NYT, 9 December 1975, p. 9; 7 October 1975, p. 1; and 18 December 1975, p. 1.

67. Ibid., 19 October 1976, p. 26.

68. Author's interview with James Schlesinger; Szulc, 738. Also see Ford, 321–22.

69. Ford, 247, 286.

70. Kalb and Kalb, 467.

71. Golan, 241.

72. NYT, 26 April 1974, p. 2.

73. Nixon memoirs, 765.

74. Ibid., 786.

75. Kissinger, *Years of Upheaval*, 211–12.

76. Nixon memoirs, 787.

77. Kissinger, *Years of Upheaval*, 211.

78. Sheehan, 25; Heikal, *Road to Ramadan*, 204–7; Sadat, 238; Kissinger, *Years of Upheaval*, 212–16.

79. Rabin, 214.

80. Ibid., 216.

81. *Washington Post*, 2 March 1973, p. 1; Sheehan, 25–26.

82. YKW, 62; Sadat, 241; Quandt, *Decade*, 159; Kissinger, *Years of Upheaval*, 224–25.

83. Golan, 145.

84. Ray S. Cline, "Policy without Intelligence," *Foreign Policy* (Winter 1974–75), 121–35, especially 131–33.

85. Kissinger, *Years of Upheaval*, 220.

86. Nixon memoirs, 880–81. For the text of the treaty, see NYT, 23 June 1973, p. 8.

87. NYT, 13 June 1977, p. A-11; Nixon memoirs, 884–85.

88. Sadat, 238; Heikal, *Road to Ramadan*, 12–15; YKW, 492; DSB, 23 July 1973, 132.

89. MNOC, 134; DSB, 24 December 1973, 771–72; "Multinational Corporations and United States Foreign Policy," Hearings, 94th Cong., 1st sess., 1975, vol. 5, p. 12 (hereafter cited as MNC).

90. MNOC, 124; Kelly, 335.

91. Kelly, 336–39; Sampson, *Seven Sisters*, 214.

92. MNOC, 125. It is ironic to compare the arguments of the Israelis and the oil companies during the early 1970s. Both maintained that the Arab demands would escalate if they attempted to compromise. In each set of negotiations, the State Department urged the party facing Arab pressure to make concessions. The Israelis were more successful than the oil companies in resisting both Arab and State Department pressures because they were less trustful and because security is a less negotiable commodity than profit.

93. MNOC, 127.

94. MNOC, 132.

95. Kelly, 348; MNC 5: 18–19, 87–91, 140–43, 149–51.

96. MNC 5: 4.

97. Oppenheim, 24–58; "The Kissinger-Shah Connection," 60 Minutes, 4 May 1980 (transcript).

98. Sampson, Seven Sisters, 14–16; MNOC, 133–39; Blair, 262–64; Kelly, 356–78.

99. NYT, 23 February 1970, p. 14; 8 December 1971, p. 11; 16 May 1973, p. 6; 12 June 1973, p. 1; 2 September 1973, p. 1; MNOC, 121.

100. MNC, 7: 534.

101. M. A. Adelman, "Is the Oil Shortage Real?" Foreign Policy, Winter 1972–73, 69–108; James E. Akins, "The Oil Crisis: This Time the Wolf is Here," Foreign Affairs, 1 April 1973, 462–91.

102. MNC, 7:504.

103. MNC, 7:33, 509.

104. NYT, 21 June 1973, p. 30.

105. MNC, 7:512; NYT, 3 August 1973, p. 37.

106. Ibid., 4 August 1973, p. 31; 8 August 1973, p. 23; 10 August 1973, p. 30.

107. Author's confidential interview with Pentagon official who claimed that the NSC had produced a series of memos in July and August 1973 calling for more "daylight" between Washington and Jerusalem.

108. Kelly, 390–91. Evidence that the warnings had no effect on key officials can be found in the following statements: Richard Nixon, DSB, 4 June 1973, 788; Joseph Sisco, DSB, 7 July 1973, 31 and 27 August 1973, 310; William Casey, DSB, 30 July 1973, 190–94 and 3 September 1973, 324–25; William Rogers, DSB, 10 September 1973, 352. Nixon's first public acknowledgment that Mideast oil supplies might be a problem came on 5 September 1973 in a news conference; see Richard Nixon, PPP, 1973, 734–35.

109. Cline, "Policy Without Intelligence," 132.

110. Author's interview with Ray Cline; YKW, 56, 71; YKW, 104; Bonham, Shapiro, and Trumble, 7–8.

111. DSB, 23 April 1973, 487.

112. Ibid., 21 May 1973, 635; Richard Nixon, DSB, 4 June 1973, 783–89; Joseph Sisco, DSB, 2 July 1973, 31 and 27 August 1973, 310; William Rogers, DSB, 20 August 1973, 352.

113. Richard Nixon, PPP, 5 September 1973, 736.

114. Ibid.

115. Bonham, Shapiro, and Trumble, 14–15; Alan Dowty, "The Impact of the 1973 War on the U.S. Approach to the Middle East," paper read at conference, Leonard Davis Institute for International Relations, Hebrew University, Jerusalem, Israel, 9–11 July 1979, p. 3; and "U.S. Decision-Making Under Stress: 1973," paper read at Moscow International Political Science Association Congress, 12–18 August 1979; author's interviews with Ray Cline and Matthew Bonham.

116. Kalb and Kalb, 455–56; Kissinger, Years of Upheaval, 453; Heikal, Road to Ramadan, 7; Sheehan, 28.

117. Kissinger, Years of Upheaval, 871.

118. CIA Bulletin, quoted in the Washington Post, 13 September 1975, p. A5. See also the Watch Committee report, 6 October 1975, 9:00 A.M., printed in The Village Voice, 16 February 1976, 78, n. 305.

119. YKW, 112–13.

120. Nixon memoirs, 920; Henry Kissinger, DSB, 29 October 1973, 537. See Kissinger, Years of Upheaval, 459–67, for a thorough discussion of the intelligence errors for which Kissinger uncharacteristically accepts some of the blame.

121. Author's confidential interview with Pentagon intelligence official; Kalb and Kalb, 457.

122. Author's interview with James Schlesinger; NYT, 13 May 1977, p. A 11.

123. Kalb and Kalb, 460, 464; Golan, 41.

124. Kalb and Kalb, 455; Szulc, 728; Bonham, Shapiro, and Trumble, 14–15; Kissinger, *Years of Upheaval*, 465.

125. Heikal, *Road to Ramadan*, 7, 16; Sheehan, 28.

126. NYT, 13 May 1977, p. A 11.

127. Sadat, 246; Heikal, *Road to Ramadan*, 12, 14–15; YKW, 269, 492; William B. Quandt, "Soviet Policy in the October 1973 War," *Rand Corporation*, R-1864-ISA, May 1976.

128. Kalb and Kalb, 463; Quandt, *Decade*, 167–68; Sadat, 238; YKW, 62; *Newsweek*, 9 April 1973, 44–46.

129. Kalb and Kalb, 459–61; Golan, 41–42; YKW, 129. In *Years of Upheaval* (450–59), Kissinger gives a detailed account of his actions on 6 October.

130. Kissinger, *Years of Upheaval*, 477; Dayan, *Story of My Life*, 460–61; Meir, 427; YKW, 124–25; Kalb and Kalb, 460–61; author's interview with Kenneth Keating.

131. Eban, 502; Golan, 41; Quandt, *Decade*, 169–70; YKW, 129; Kalb and Kalb, 460, 464.

132. Kissinger, *Years of Upheaval*, 470; Quandt, *Decade*, 174–75.

133. Author's interview with Ray Cline; YKW 424. See Kissinger, *Years of Upheaval* (471–72) for a detailed discussion of his rationale for the initial proposal to seek Soviet acquiescence for a return to the status quo ante.

134. *Time*, 1 July 1974, 31.

135. Kissinger, *Years of Upheaval*, 490; Kalb and Kalb, 464; YKW, 272–73; William Quandt, "Kissinger and the Arab-Israeli Disengagement Negotiations," *Journal of International Affairs* 29 (no. 1, Spring 1975): 36–38; author's confidential interview.

136. Nixon memoirs, 921.

137. Ibid., 922.

138. Author's interview with James Schlesinger; Szulc, 735; Nixon memoirs, 922.

139. Author's interview with James Schlesinger.

140. Dowty, "U.S. Decision Making under Stress: 1973," 5.

141. Nixon memoirs, 921; Kissinger, *Years of Upheaval*, 469; Safran, *Israel: The Embattled Ally*, 481.

142. Whetten, 250–51.

143. Dayan, *Story of My Life*, 408–9; Whetten, 264–65; YKW, 188–89.

144. Kissinger, *Years of Upheaval*, 492.

145. Quandt, *Decade*, 176–78, and "Soviet Policy in the October 1973 War," 16, 20–21; Kissinger, *Years of Upheaval*, 493–96.

146. YKW, 270, 281.

147. Kalb and Kalb, 467.

148. Kissinger, *Years of Upheaval*, 485–86; Kalb and Kalb, 465; Szulc, 736.

149. Nixon memoirs, 922.

150. Luttwak and Laqueur, 33–41; Szulc, 735–36; Kalb and Kalb, 467; Sheehan, 37.

151. YKW, 276–85; Szulc, 735–36; Kissinger, *Years of Upheaval*, 498–506.

152. Author's interview with James Schlesinger; Nixon memoirs, 924; Kalb and Kalb, 467; Szulc, 735–36; Quandt, *Decade*, 175.

153. Author's interview with James Schlesinger; author's confidential interview; Admiral Elmo Zumwalt, USN (ret.), *On Watch* (New York: Quadrangle, 1976), 434, 441; Alan Dowty, *Middle East Crisis: U.S. Decision Making in 1968, 1970, and 1973* (Berkeley and Los Angeles: University of California Press, 1984), chap. 4.

154. Nixon memoirs, 924.

155. *Time,* 1 July 1974, 33.

156. DSB, 12 November 1973, 586; 19 November 1973, 624.

157. Kissinger, *Years of Upheaval,* 485; Kalb and Kalb, 464–77; Golan, 45–62; Quandt, *Decade,* 175, and "Kissinger and the Arab-Israeli Disengagement Negotiations," 36–38. Also, Zumwalt, 433–35; Szulc, 735–36. Szulc and Zumwalt are both highly critical of Kissinger's policy.

158. Author's interview with James Schlesinger; NYT, 11 October 1973, p. 1.

159. Author's interview with James Schlesinger; Quandt, *Decade,* 183; Kalb and Kalb, 474, 476–77; Luttwak and Laqueur, 37; Szulc, 737. In his memoirs, Kissinger says that "the conflict over the charters" was primarily responsible for the delays. *Years of Decision,* 520.

160. Letters from Martin Peretz and Jacob Stein (Chair of the Conference of Presidents of Major American Jewish Organizations), *Commentary,* December 1974, 4–17; author's interview with James Schlesinger; Quandt, "Soviet Policy in the October 1973 War," 15–16; Quandt, *Decade,* 178–80.

162. Nixon memoirs, 924; Dayan, *Story of My Life,* 444.

163. Dayan, *Story of My Life,* 411–12, 425–27; Kalb and Kalb, 464–65; NYT, 13 May 1977, p. A8. Kissinger (*Years of Upheaval,* 493) says that "he rejected the offer out of hand and without checking with Nixon"; Meir, 430–31; Golan, 47–48.

164. YKW, 280; Quandt, *Decade,* 182; Kissinger, *Years of Upheaval,* 509; Eban, 514–15; Golan, 66–67; Michael Brecher, *Decisions in Crisis* (Berkeley and Los Angeles: University of California Press, 1980), 214–15.

165. YKW, 281; Sadat, 256–58; Heikal, *Road to Ramadan,* 229; Golan, 67.

166. Golan, 67; YKW, 281–82; Quandt, *Decade,* 182; Kissinger, *Years of Upheaval,* 510–11; Eban, 516. Kissinger's anger at the British can be inferred by reading between the lines of his discussion of the incident (*Years of Upheaval,* 516–17).

167. Quandt, *Decade,* 183; YKW, 275, 282–83, 412; Kissinger, *Years of Upheaval,* 512–13; Safran, *Israel: The Embattled Ally,* 483–89; Aronson, 178–79.

168. Author's interview with James Schlesinger.

169. Nixon memoirs, 927; Kissinger, *Years of Upheaval,* 514–15.

170. David Frost's interview with Richard Nixon, NYT, 13 May 1977, p. A8.

171. Meir, 431; Quandt, *Decade,* 184; Dayan, *Story of My Life,* 421–22; Nixon memoirs, 927–28; Theodore H. White, *Breach of Faith* (New York: Reader's Digest Press, 1975), 168.

172. Kissinger, *Years of Upheaval,* 709.

173. Author's interview with James Schlesinger.

174. Kissinger, *Years of Upheaval,* 520; YKW, 284.

175. For an excellent survey of the American Jewish community's response to the Yom Kippur War, see Daniel V. Elazar, "Overview," in *The Yom Kippur War, Israel and the Jewish People* ed. Moshe Davis (New York: Arno Press, 1974), 3–35. See also NYT, 8 October 1973, p. 1; 10 October 1973, p. 20; 12 October 1973, pp. 16, 19; 13 October 1973, p. 13; 14 October 1973, p. 113; 15 October 1973, p. 17; 19 October 1973, p. 21; 19 October 1973, p. 31; 22 October 1973, p. 14.

176. Kalb and Kalb, 464–77; NYT, 15 October 1973, p. 21; author's interview with Richard Perle.

177. Author's interview with James Schlesinger; Kalb and Kalb, 479; Luttwak and Laqueur, 39. See Kissinger, *Years of Upheaval,* 520, for a detailed rationale for the airlift.

178. Quandt, *Decade,* 185.

179. Nixon memoirs, 930; Quandt, *Decade,* 190; Kissinger, *Years of Upheaval,* 534–35.

180. YKW, 318; Quandt, *Decade*, 188; NYT, 18 October 1973, p. 1, and 22 October 1973, p. 1.
181. Chaim Herzog, *The War of Atonement* (Boston: Little, Brown, 1975), 203–207; Whetten, 266–67; YKW, 289–300.
182. MNOC, 145; Kelly, 399.
183. MNOC, 140–44; Sampson, *Seven Sisters*, 250; Kelly, 395; MNC, 7:571.
184. MNOC, 144.
185. Sampson, *Seven Sisters*, 252; MNC, 7:449, 547.
186. *Washington Post*, 9 January 1975, p. A8.
187. MNC, 7:514.
188. MNOC, 144, 145; MNC, 7:515; Sampson, *Seven Sisters*, 253; Kelly, 399.
189. Heikal, *Road to Ramadan*, 237; Sadat, 258–59.
190. Author's interview with James Schlesinger.
191. The dispute over what Kissinger said to Dinitz at this crucial juncture is indicative of the distrust that had been growing between the U.S. and Israel since the beginning of the war. Kissinger says he told Dinitz that Israel would have forty-eight hours to conclude operations. Dinitz remembers the limit as seventy-two hours (forty-eight hours from the time Kissinger was to arrive in Moscow). In the event, Israel had about sixty-six hours from the moment Kissinger communicated the timetable to Dinitz to the moment the cease-fire took effect (Kissinger, *Years of Upheaval*, 453); author's interview with Simcha Dinitz; author's confidential interview; Kalb and Kalb, 482; Golan, 75.
192. Kissinger, *Years of Upheaval*, 548.
193. Nixon memoirs, 934; White, 266.
194. Ibid., 267.
195. Ibid., 259–71; Nixon memoirs, 969; author's interview with Leonard Garment.
196. Kissinger, *Years of Upheaval*, 550–52.
197. Heikal, *Road to Ramadan*, 244–45; YKW, 379.
198. Kissinger believed that the wording would require direct face-to-face talks (*Years of Upheaval*, 554) and seems not to have considered that it was vague enough to allow the Arabs to construe it as proximity talks or (as it turned out) shuttle diplomacy. For text of resolution, see DSB, 12 November 1973, 604.
199. YKW, 380; Kissinger complains that Israel failed to inform him of its military progress while he was in Moscow. When he tried to notify the Israelis of the terms of the cease-fire, mysterious "technical malfunctions" delayed the message. He claims this badly damaged his credibility with the Israelis. But Kissinger apparently had no intention of asking Israel whether it would accept the cease-fire. He intended to present Israel with a Soviet-American fait accompli in any case (*Years of Upheaval*, 558–89).
200. Sadat, 264–65; Heikal, *Road to Ramadan*, 244; Kalb and Kalb, 485.
201. Dayan, *Story of My Life*, 443; Golan, 85; YKW, 387; Eban, 532; Nixon memoirs, 936; Kissinger, *Years of Upheaval*, 569.
202. Dayan, *Story of My Life*, 441–42; YKW, 394–98; Whetten, 290–91.
203. Kalb and Kalb, 486; Quandt, *Decade*, 194; Kissinger, *Years of Upheaval*, 572.
204. Kalb and Kalb, 487; YKW, 399; Kissinger, *Years of Upheaval*, 572; Sheehan, 37.
205. YKW, 402. The text of Resolution 339 can be found in Kissinger, *Years of Upheaval*, 1247.
206. Kissinger, *Years of Upheaval*, 582–84; Nixon memoirs, 938–39; author's interview with Ray Cline; "Policy without Intelligence," 123–28; Kalb and Kalb, 488; Quandt, "Kissinger and the Arab-Israeli Disengagement Negotiations," 33.
207. Cline, "Policy without Intelligence," 127; Kalb and Kalb, 490.
208. Kissinger, *Years of Upheaval*, 581.

209. Kissinger, *Years of Upheaval,* 589; Kalb and Kalb, 490, 497.

210. Kalb and Kalb, 492; Szulc, 747; Scott D. Sagan, "Lessons of the Yom Kippur Alert," *Foreign Policy,* Fall 1979, 172; Nixon memoirs, 937–40.

211. Lucius Battle, "Peace—Inshallah," *Foreign Policy,* Spring 1974, 121.

212. Cline, "Policy without Intelligence," 133.

213. Theodore Draper, "The United States and Israel: Tilt in the Middle East?," *Commentary,* April, 1975, 30; Author's interview with James Schlesinger.

214. Sheehan, 376; author's confidential interview; Sagan, 171–72.

215. Author's interview with James Schlesinger.

216. Kissinger, *Years of Upheaval,* 591; Kalb and Kalb, 492.

217. Dayan, *Story of My Life,* 448; Golan, 88; Kalb and Kalb, 501; YKW, 433; Sheehan, 37; *Ma'ariv* (Tel Aviv), 2 November 1973; Donald Neff, Letter to the editor, *Commentary,* September 1975, 20; Eban, 537.

218. Golan, 89; Sheehan, 37; Draper, "The United States and Israel," 30; see also Kissinger, *Years of Upheaval,* 602–5; David Frost interview with Richard Nixon, NYT, 13 May 1977, p. A8.

219. DSB, 12 November 1973, 594; YKW, 433; Dayan, *Story of My Life,* 448; Kissinger, *Years of Upheaval,* 604–11.

220. A partial exception is Eisenhower's aim of gaining British, French, and Israeli withdrawals in 1956.

221. Richard M. Nixon, PPP, 26 October 1973, 900.

222. Nixon memoirs, 938–39; Quandt, *Decade,* 185. For excerpts from Kissinger's cables to Sadat, see Kissinger, *Years of Upheaval,* 522–23, 583, 588.

223. Golan, 85; Kissinger, *Years of Upheaval,* 610–11.

224. Nixon memoirs, 1012; Sheehan, 57.

225. Golan, 103; Sheehan, 41.

226. Sheehan, 41; Quandt, *Decade,* 214–15.

227. Nixon memoirs, 942–43.

228. Golan, 105; Quandt, *Decade,* 215; Kissinger, *Years of Upheaval,* 622; Sheehan, 41; YKW, 438–39.

229. Richard Valeriani, *Travels with Henry* (Boston: Houghton Mifflin, 1979), 197.

230. Oriana Fallaci, "Kissinger: An Interview with Oriana Fallaci," *The New Republic,* 16 December 1972, 21.

231. Kalb and Kalb, 510; Kissinger, *Years of Upheaval,* 643–44.

232. Kalb and Kalb, 504; Sheehan, 50; Eban (538) says that Meir brought a six-point plan to Kissinger on 1 November; Kissinger, *Years of Upheaval,* 641–43.

233. Sadat, 291; see Kissinger, *Years of Upheaval,* 636–51, for a lengthy description of Sadat's character.

234. Ibid., 642.

235. Sheehan, 234; Valeriani, 310.

236. Sheehan, 71; see also Kissinger, *Years of Upheaval,* 656–66, esp. 661. Actually, Marx's father converted to Christianity. Karl Marx was baptized at age six and raised as a Christian. He wrote on the subject of Christianity before turning to atheism.

237. Kissinger, *Years of Upheaval,* 1057, 750–53; Golan, 120–21, 124.

238. Dayan, *Story of My Life,* 454–56; Quandt, *Decade,* 221.

239. Nixon memoirs, 986.

240. Ibid., 987.

241. *Washington Post,* 22 December 1973, p. 1.

242. Roy E. Licklider, "The Failure of the Arab Oil Weapon in 1973–1974," *Comparative Strategy* 3, no. 4 (September 1982): 365–80. Later, of course, Arab hopes would be dashed when the embargo would be lifted without a timetable for Israel's withdrawal

from all territories occupied in the 1967 war. In this sense the embargo would fail, and it would add to Arab disillusionment. Meanwhile, the embargo succeeded in shifting the attention of the American government after the October 1973 War. See Heikal, *Road to Ramadan*, 28–82.

243. Sheehan, 97; Quandt, *Decade*, 223; Kissinger, *Years of Upheaval*, 784–85.

244. Quandt, *Decade*, 222. For an excerpt from one of the letters, see Kissinger, *Years of Upheaval*, 759; see also 775.

245. Eban, 542, 544; Golan, 126–27; Sheehan, 108, 126; Kissinger, *Years of Upheaval*, 770, 790.

246. Golan, 127; Sheehan, 108.

247. Golan, 132; Sheehan, 106; Quandt, *Decade*, 223.

248. Golan, 136–37.

249. Dayan, *Story of My Life*, 464; Golan, 156–57.

250. Kalb and Kalb, 352–53; Sheehan, 107–12; Golan, 157–58; Quandt, *Decade*, 226–29; Kissinger, *Years of Upheaval*, 810–15.

251. Dayan, *Story of My Life*, 466; Kalb and Kalb, 536–38; Sheehan, 109–10; Brecher, *Decisions in Crisis*, 319; Golan, 165. Kissinger says that the idea of an American plan was Sadat's (*Years of Upheaval*, 825).

252. Henry Kissinger, DSB, 14 January 1974, 23.

253. For text of agreement, see NYT, 19 January 1974, p. 7.

254. Golan, 175; for discussion of the "secret" memoranda with Egypt and Israel, see NYT, 21 January 1974, p. 6, and 22 January 1974, p. 1.

255. Golan, 144–46.

256. David Pollock, *The Politics of Pressure: American Arms and Israeli Policy Since the Six Day War* (Westport, Conn.: Greenwood Press, 1982), 180–81. The Ford administration won a fight to include a $100 million "special use fund" under the Foreign Assistance Act of 1974, which passed 18 December 1974 (S 3394). The administration indicated it would use the money for Syria, and ultimately it agreed to a $58 million loan to improve Syrian water and irrigation systems. *Congress and the Nation* (Washington: Congressional Quarterly, 1977) vol. 4, p. 858.

257. NYT, 18 January 1974, p. 32; *Los Angeles Times*, 18 January 1974, pt. 2, p. 6; *Chicago Tribune*, 19 January 1974, p. 10.

258. DSB, 28 January 1974, 78; 11 February 1974, 138.

259. Kissinger, *Years of Upheaval*, 945–49; Quandt, *Decade*, 231.

260. Sheehan, 116; Quandt, *Decade*, 232; Kissinger, *Years of Upheaval*, 975.

261. Kissinger, *Years of Upheaval*, 973. Quandt, *Decade*, 238.

262. Quandt, *Decade*, 236.

263. DSB, 8 April 1974, 368.

264. Golan, 182–85.

265. Valeriani, 286–308.

266. Quandt, *Decade*, 236.

267. Kissinger, *Years of Upheaval*, 1045.

268. Quandt, *Decade*, 240; Kissinger, *Years of Upheaval*, 1071.

269. Valeriani, 298, 300–301.

270. Golan, 195.

271. Sheehan, 124.

272. Valeriani, 301; Quandt, *Decade*, 243; Golan, 201; Sheehan, 126; Kissinger, *Years of Upheaval*, 1050–52, 1066, 1070–71, 1083–84.

273. See N. A. Pelcovits, *Security Guarantees in a Middle East Settlement* (Beverly Hills: Sage Publications, 1976), for a scholarly examination of the effects of these guarantees. Zeev Schiff, "Dealing with Syria," *Foreign Policy* 15 (Summer 1984): 97, claims that

there was a secret agreement that Assad "would prevent the Palestinians from conducting terrorist activities from Syrian territory on the Golan Heights."

274. Nixon memoirs, 1017.

275. Bob Woodward and Carl Bernstein, *Final Days* (New York: Simon and Schuster, 1976), 214–15; Nixon memoirs, 1006.

276. For text of this agreement, see NYT, 15 June 1974, p. 12.

277. Nixon memoirs, 1014; Sheehan, 133; Quandt, *Decade*, 248; Kissinger, *Years of Upheaval*, 1134.

278. Sheehan, 132; Quandt, *Decade*, 246; Kissinger, *Years of Upheaval*, 1127.

279. Nixon memoirs, 1015; Quandt, *Decade*, 248.

280. Nixon memoirs, 1008.

281. Ibid., 1018.

282. Valeriani, 305; Woodward and Bernstein, 219; Kissinger, *Years of Upheaval*, 1132; Nixon memoirs, 1016; author's interview with Dan Patir.

283. Nixon memoirs, 1012.

284. Ibid., 1008.

285. Golan, 217; Sheehan, 148–49; Quandt, *Decade*, 248. Kissinger makes it clear that he *preferred* Israeli negotiations with Jordan before the next round with Egypt (*Years of Upheaval*, 1138).

286. For activities of the PLO and its recognition by various countries, see NYT, 9 June 1974, p. 3; 3 July 1974, p. 3; 13 July 1974, p. 1; 19 July 1974, p. 2; 4 August 1974, p. 6; 3 September 1974, p. 1; 8 October 1974, p. 4; 29 October 1974, p. 1.

287. NYT, 13 July 1974, p. 1.

288. Ibid., 12 July 1974, p. 3; Kissinger, *Years of Upheaval*, 627–29, 1138–41. Kissinger was further reinforced in this view by two secret meetings he authorized with PLO officials in November 1973 and March 1974. His representative in these talks was Lieutenant General Vernon A. Walters, then deputy director of the CIA.

289. Golan, 218–19; Quandt, *Decade*, 255.

290. Quandt, *Decade*, 256; Golan, 222.

291. Joseph Sisco, DSB, 1 July 1974, 13.

292. NYT, 7 August 1974, pp. 102, 3. In an interview with the author, former Prime Minister Rabin said the Israeli government was inhibited in its negotiations with Jordan at this time because the position of the radicals cast a shadow over any agreement that might have been reached. Rabin said he felt that the radical Arabs were out to eliminate Jordan entirely.

293. On Nixon's flirtation with a comprehensive strategy, see *Years of Upheaval*, 202, 211–12, 550–52; on threats to cut off aid to Israel, see 202–203, 759, 792, 1071, 1078–79; author's interview with James Schlesinger.

294. Kissinger, *Years of Upheaval*, 759, 804, 830–33, 881, 948–49, 1122.

295. Ford, 213–19.

296. Ibid., 183.

297. Rabin, 245–56; NYT, 13 September 1974, p. 8; 14 September 1974, p. 3.

298. Rabin, 247.

299. Ford, 183; Rabin, 245–47.

300. NYT, 23 September 1974, p. 13; 4 November 1974, p. 15; Sheehan, 148; Quandt, *Decade*, 256–57.

301. NYT, 29 October 1974, p. 1; 30 October 1974, p. 1; Quandt, *Decade*, 257.

302. NYT, 11 November 1974, p. 1; 13 November 1974, p. 1.

303. Rabin, 250.

304. Text of Ford news conference of 29 October 1974, DSB, 25 November 1974, 738. See also Golan, 227.

305. Rabin, 245; Golan, 228–29; Sheehan, 157; Quandt, *Decade,* 261.
306. Golan, 233–34; Quandt, *Decade,* 263–64, 267–68.
307. Golan, 232.
308. Ibid., 264; Sheehan, 156.
309. Golan, 176. See NYT, 3 October 1974, p. 1, for an analysis of the military balance one year after the October War.
310. Sheehan, 161–62.
311. Rabin, 253, 255. See also Rabin's remarks at news conferences, NYT, 24 March 1975, p. 14, and 29 May 1975, p. 6. For a less partisan view of why the talks collapsed, see Quandt, *Decade,* 266; for the Egyptian position, see Sadat, 293–95.
312. Sheehan, 159–61.
313. Rabin, 256.
314. Golan, 237; Sheehan, 159.
315. Sheehan, 160; Quandt, *Decade,* 266; Golan, 239–40; Sadat, 294; Rabin, 257.
316. Ibid., 255.
317. Ibid., 257, 258–61; Golan, 240–41; for an example of the senior official's remarks, see NYT, 24 March 1975, p. 1.
318. Rabin, 261; Sheehan, 165; author's interview with James Schlesinger.
319. Ford, 247.
320. Ibid., quotations from 246–47.
321. Ibid., 245; Sheehan, 174; Quandt, *Decade,* 270. In several news interviews, Ford discussed his options; see NYT, 22 April 1975, p. 4, and 25 April 1975, p. 3.
322. Rabin, 254.
323. Golan, 242. Gerald Ford, DSB, 10 February 1975, 179; 17 February 1975, 220; 3 March 1975, 267; 28 April 1975, 535; 26 May 1975, 676.
324. Sheehan, 173; Quandt, *Decade,* 270; NER 19, no. 13 (26 March 1975): 53; no. 15 (9 April 1975): 61; no. 16 (16 April 1975): 69; no. 20 (14 May 1975): 85; no. 16 (16 April 1975): 69; no. 20 (14 May 1975): 85; no. 22 (28 May 1975): 93–95.
325. NYT, 23 May 1975, p. 8. For the text of the latter, see *Congressional Record,* vol. 121, pt. 12 (22 May 1975): 15959.
326. *Congressional Record,* vol. 121, pt. 12: 16078; pt. 13: 16539.
327. Ford, 287–88.
328. NYT, 1 May 1975, p. 3; 2 May 1975, p. 1; 3 May 1975, p. 3; 5 May 1975, p. 3; 6 May 1975, p. 3; 7 May 1975, p. 3.
329. Ford says, "Always before, American Presidents had met with the Israelis first" (287), but the assertion is inaccurate. At the beginning of his own term, for example, he met with Hussein before Rabin. Even with the Egyptians, Nixon had met with Fahmy the day before he met with Meir after the October War.
330. Sheehan, 167, 176–77; Quandt, *Decade,* 271; Ford, 290; Golan, 244.
331. Sheehan, 177; Rabin, 261; Ford, 291.
332. Rabin, 268; NYT, 14 July 1975, p. 1.
333. Rabin, 269–70.
334. Sheehan, 184.
335. Golan, 245; Quandt, *Decade,* 272. Rabin (267) says the Israeli Cabinet *did* approve the line Rabin drew in Washington, but shortly thereafter the Egyptians rejected it.
336. Rabin, 270; Sheehan, 188.
337. Rabin, 272, 274; Quandt, *Decade,* 274; Sheehan, 189.
338. Sheehan, p. 190. For text of agreement, see Sheehan, 245–57.
339. NYT, 2 September 1975, p. 16; Article 2; Article 7; Sheehan, 245, 247.
340. Ford, 308–309.
341. NYT, 18 September 1975, p. 4.

342. Ibid. Former Prime Minister Rabin later argued that only Kissinger's promise not to recognize or negotiate with the PLO prevented the Carter administration from bringing the PLO into the negotiating process (author's interview with Yitzhak Rabin).

343. NYT, 17 September 1975, p. 16; Sheehan, 257.

344. Ford, 309; "mind boggling" is Sheehan's phrase (190).

345. NYT, 10 September 1975, p. 1. However, in an interview with a Kuwaiti paper, Sadat denied any secret clauses. Ibid., 9 October 1975, p. 4.

346. Ibid., 3 March 1976, pp. 1, 3; Sheehan, 194.

347. Golan, 250–51; see Assad's comments in the *Foreign Broadcast and Information Service*, 10 September 1975, pp. H 1–8, and 1 December 1975, pp. H 1–7 (hereafter cited as FBIS).

348. NYT, 22 July 1975, p. 4; 26 July 1975, p. 8 (witnesses were Admiral Elmo Zumwalt and Joint Chiefs of Staff Chairman George Brown); 20 September 1975, p. 1; NER 19, no. 30 (23 July 1975): 127–28; no. 31 (30 July 1957): 129–30.

349. NER 19, no. 37 (10 September 1975): 158; see also no. 38 (17 September 1975): 163.

350. NYT, 7 September 1975, pt. 4, p. 16.

351. Joseph Kraft column, 4 September 1975; see, among other sources, *Los Angeles Times*, 7 September 1975, pt. 10, p. 4.

352. NYT, 1 October 1975, p. 14; *Congressional Record*, vol. 121, pt. 24 (1 October 1975): 31193–94.

353. *Congressional Record*, vol. 121, pt. 25 (9 October 1975): 32751. Author Edward Sheehan was also sharply critical (Sheehan, 191). On the actual additional cost, see Quandt, *Decade*, 279.

354. See, for example, Representative Biaggi's comments in *Congressional Record*, vol. 121, pt. 22 (10 September 1975): 28520. For Pentagon uneasiness about Israeli arms requests, see NYT, 18 September 1975, p. 3; 20 September 1975, p. 7. Sheehan says that Secretary of Defense Schlesinger led the opposition to the arms sales (Sheehan, 198–99), but in an interview with the author Schlesinger said he opposed the reassessment in the first place because it delayed crucially needed decisions on F-15 and F-16 production lines. Clearly, however, resentment against arms shipments to Israel had been brewing in the Pentagon for several months. See "Pentagon officials say increased arms shipments to Israel leave some military units short," in *Washington Post*, 21 January 1975, reprinted in the *Congressional Record*, vol. 121, pt. 1 (23 January 1975): 1106–7.

355. NYT, 1 October 1975, p. 15; 19 October 1975, p. 5; Sheehan, 196.

356. NYT, 25 September 1975, p. 1.

357. "The Palestinian Issue in Middle East Peace Efforts," Hearings, Special Subcommittee on Investigations, Committee on International Relations, House of Representatives, 93d Cong., 1st sess., 1976, p. 178, 180.

358. Quandt, *Decade*, 278; NYT, 11 November 1975, p. 14; 15 March 1976, p. 31; Sheehan, 213.

359. NYT, 8 January 1976, pt. 4, p. 2; NER 19 (no. 49, 3 December 1975): 209; 19 (no. 50, 10 December 1975): 214; 20 (no. 2, 14 January 1976): 5; 20 (no. 3, 21 January 1976): 10; author's confidential interview.

360. DSB, 19 April 1976, 528.

361. Rabin addressed Congress on 28 January 1976. See DSB, 23 February 1976, 228–31, for the text of his speech; for the text of Sadat's speech to Congress on 5 November 1975, see DSB, 24 November 1975, 728–31.

362. NYT, 29 October 1975, p. 3; 8 March 1976, p. 1.

363. Ibid., 8 February 1976, pp. 1, 18; 4 March 1976, pp. 1, 6; 5 March 1976, p. 3; 9 March 1973, p. 11; 15 March 1976, p. 1.

364. Ibid., 5 March 1976, p. 3; 9 March 1976, p. 11; 20 March 1976, p. 7; 3 April 1976, p. 2; 15 April 1976, p. 11.

365. Rabin, 276–77. Ford notes, "In the end, I approved a larger increase than the Pentagon recommended" (308–309).

366. Rabin, 278.

367. NYT, 4 April 1976, p. 5; 8 April 1976, p. 1; 29 April 1976, p. 7; 8 May 1976, p. 1; Quandt, *Decade,* 280.

368. NER 20, no. 19 (12 May 1976): 80–82.

369. *Foreign Military Sales and Military Assistance Facts,* December 1970 (Washington, D.C.: Defense Security Assistance Agency, 1980), 2, 8; NYT, 6 January 1977, p. 2; 2 September 1976, p. 12; 4 September 1976, p. 5. See also NER 20, no. 24 (16 June 1976): 103; no. 28 (14 July 1976): 119; no. 36 (8 September 1976): 153; no. 37 (15 September 1976): 155–56, for details and critique of the entire proposal.

370. See testimony of Colonel William Fifer, U.S. Army, in "Proposed Foreign Military Sales to Middle Eastern Countries," Hearings, International Relations Committee, U.S. House of Representatives, 94th Cong., 2d sess., 1977, 38–46.

371. Ibid., 15.

372. Alan Dowty, University of Notre Dame, in "U.S. Arms Sales Policy," Hearings, Committee on Foreign Relations, U.S. Senate, 94th Cong., 2d sess., 1977, 85.

373. Sampson, *The Arms Bazaar,* 331–37.

374. NER, 20, no. 10 (6 October 1976): 167.

375. See Kissinger's public comments, DSB, 2 February 1976, 131–32; 23 February 1976, 217; 1 March 1976, 268; 5 May 1976, 571.

376. Quandt, *Decade,* 283.

377. See Saunders, "The Palestinian Issue in Middle East Peace Efforts," 186; Quandt, *Decade,* 283; Sheehan, 213; Schiff, 97–100.

Chapter 8. Carter

1. According to a CBS News exit poll of 14,636 voters, Carter received 68% of the Jewish vote, 1 percent higher than the historical norm for a Democratic candidate. See NYT 4 November 1976, p. 25.

2. See NYT, 30 October 1977, p. 1, for a concise analysis of Carter's strained relations with the U.S. Jewish community. See also Ibid., 12 November 1978, p. 27, for the results of a poll showing that even after Camp David a majority of Jews gave Carter an unfavorable performance rating while Democrats as a group gave the president favorable marks by more than two to one. See also Zbigniew Brzezinski, *Power and Principle* (New York: Farrar, Straus, Giroux, 1983), 88–110, for a detailed treatment of the administration's troubles with American Jews.

3. NYT, 23 May 1980, pp. A1, D7; William Quandt, *Saudi Arabia in the 1980s* (Washington, D.C.: Brookings Institution, 1981), 132–33.

4. William Quandt, who served on the National Security Council under Carter, argues that "Despite their wealth, the Saudis are not very powerful" (Quandt, *Saudi Arabia in the 1980s,* 155). He concedes that a tendency to overestimate Saudi oil power strained U.S.-Saudi relations during the late 1970s when in fact Saudi oil decisions were seldom directly linked to American foreign policy moves.

5. Jimmy Carter, PPP, 1977, 956–57.

6. Such as the turmoil in the Horn of Africa in 1977 and 1978, the 1978 invasion of Zaire by Cuban-backed rebels, the South Yemeni invasion of North Yemen in early 1979, and most important, the Russian invasion of Afghanistan in December 1979.

7. Brzezinski, *Power and Principle*, 53–54.

8. Jimmy Carter, PPP, 1977, 961.

9. Ibid., p. 956.

10. Ibid., p. 957.

11. Zbigniew Brzezinski, "Recognizing the Crisis," *Foreign Policy*, Winter 1974–75, 67.

12. Jimmy Carter, PPP, 1977, 1006.

13. Brzezinski, *Power and Principle*, 245, 275, 278.

14. Ibid., 42.

15. Brzezinski, "Recognizing the Crisis," 69–70.

16. Zbigniew Brzezinski, "A Plan for Peace in the Middle East," *New Leader* 7 July 1974, 9.

17. Zbigniew Brzezinski, Francois Duchene, and Kiichi Saeki, "Peace in an International Framework," *Foreign Policy*, Summer 1975, 3–17.

18. Ibid., 12.

19. Cyrus Vance, *Hard Choices* (New York: Simon and Schuster, 1983), 32, 447–48.

20. George W. Ball, "How to Save Israel in Spite of Herself," *Foreign Affairs*, April 1977. See also Stanley Hoffmann, "A New Policy for Israel," *Foreign Affairs*, April 1975; and Richard H. Ullman, "After Rabat: Middle East Risks and American Roles," *Foreign Affairs*, January 1975.

21. Brookings Institution, *Toward Peace in the Middle East: Report of a Study Group* (Washington, D.C.: Brookings Institution, 1975), 2.

22. For a fascinating and predictive analysis of Carter's procedure-oriented philosophy of government, see Jack Knott and Aaron Wildavsky, "Jimmy Carter's Theory of Governing," *Woodrow Wilson Quarterly*, Winter 1977, 49–65.

23. Ibid.; and Steven Brill, "Jimmy Carter's Pathetic Lies," *Harper's*, March 1976, 77–88. For a thorough but abrasively anti-Carter critique of Carter's governorship, see Victor Lasky, *Jimmy Carter: The Man and the Myth* (New York: Richard Marek, 1979), esp. chaps. 4, 5, 6.

24. Comments by former President Jimmy Carter at a Middle East Consultation of the Carter Center of Emory University, 6–9 November 1983.

25. Brzezinski, *Power and Principle*, 32–33, 105, 241. See also Rosalynn Carter, *First Lady from Plains* (Boston: Houghton Mifflin, 1984).

26. *Chicago Tribune*, 8 May 1976, p. 10.

27. See Sadat's speech to the People's Assembly, 23 January 1978, printed in FBIS, 24 January 1978, p. D 1–23.

28. See Tom J. Farer, "The United States and the Third World: A Basis for Accommodation," *Foreign Affairs*, October 1975.

29. NYT, 7 July 1977, p. 1.

30. NYT, 20 October 1979, p. 28; author's interview with Edward Sanders.

31. Reflective of an approach popular among many Trilateral Commission members before 1977; see Brzezinski, Duchene, Saeki, 3–17. Note that in addition to Brzezinski, one author is European and another Japanese.

32. Hamilton Jordan, *Face the Nation*, CBS-TV, 12 November 1978. Similarly, Carter wrote in his memoirs, "I spent more of my time working for possible solutions to the riddle of Middle East peace than on any other international problem" (Jimmy Carter, *Keeping Faith* [New York: Bantam, 1982], 429). See also Rosalynn Carter, 237–38.

33. NYT, 11 March 1978, p. 16, and Tom Wicker, commentary, NYT, 12 March 1978, sec. 4, p. 19.

34. NYT, 16 February 1977, p. 7.

35. See NER 21, no. 8 (23 February 1977): 29; Brzezinski, *Power and Principle*, 91–92.

36. NYT, 25 April 1977, p. 11, and 9 May 1977, p. 6; NER 21, no. 20 (18 May 1977): 77, 79; Brzezinski, *Power and Principle*, 92–93.

37. Regarding the drilling, see NYT, 15 February 1977, p. 1; 16 February 1977, p. 7. For antiboycott stands, see the testimony of Cyrus Vance before the Senate Banking Committee, NYT, 1 March 1977, p. 1, and NER 21, no. 8 (23 February 1977): 29; no. 9 (2 March 1977): 33; no. 13 (30 March 1977): 49; no. 15 (13 April 1977): 57. For Carter's statement, see second presidential debate, 6 October 1976, reprinted in PC 1976, 115.

38. Rabin, 294; Carter, *Keeping Faith*, 279–80; Brzezinski, *Power and Principle*, 90–91.

39. Rabin, 298–99. Brzezinski says that Rabin pressed Carter not to speak on the subject, but Carter did not commit himself to withhold comment (*Power and Principle*, 91).

40. Jimmy Carter, PPP, 9 March 1977, 342; Carter, *Keeping Faith*, 280–81.

41. Jimmy Carter, PPP, 1977, 387; some later described this Clinton statement as the "Balfour Declaration of the Palestinian People." NER 21, no. 50 (14 December 1977): 217; Brzezinski, *Power and Principle*, 91; NYT, 18 March 1977, p. 10.

42. Jimmy Carter, PPP, 1977, 601, 861, 862, 1012.

43. Mondale's speech was reprinted in DSB, 11 July 1977, 41–46 (italics added); Javits's speech printed in *Congressional Record*, 95th Cong., 1st sess., 123, pt. 17 (27 June 1977): 20947–49.

44. Jimmy Carter, PPP, 1977, 842, 845.

45. Ibid., p. 1006.

46. Jimmy Carter, PPP, 1977, 1007, 1011.

47. NYT, 28 June 1977, p. 6.

48. Carter's news conference, 30 June 1977, Jimmy Carter, PPP, 1201.

49. Brzezinski, *Power and Principle*, 97; Carter, *Keeping Faith*, 290; NYT, 7 July 1977, p. 1.

50. Carter, *Keeping Faith*, 290–91; Brzezinski, *Power and Principle*, 100; Vance, 181–83.

51. Carter, *Keeping Faith*, 291. For Carter's statements, see Jimmy Carter, PPP, 30 July 1977, 1393–94, and 23 August, 1977, 1489; for Vance's statements see DSB, 22 August 1977, 233.

52. Author's interview with Harold Saunders; NYT, 3 August 1977, p. 1.

53. Vance, 188–89; by Martin Indyk, *"To the Ends of the Earth": Sadat's Jerusalem Initiative*, Harvard Middle East Papers, no. 1 (Center for Middle Eastern Studies, Harvard University, 1984), 33; author's interview with Harold Saunders; NYT, 9 August 1977, p. 1.

54. *Time*, 8 August 1977, 25; Jimmy Carter, PPP, 1977, 1460.

55. DSB, 12 September 1977, 340; Vance, 188–89; Brzezinski, *Power and Principle*, 103.

56. Jimmy Carter, PPP, 1977, 1470.

57. Brzezinski, *Power and Principle*, 105 (the emissary was apparently Landrum Bolling, then the director of the Lilly Foundation); Vance, 188 (the idea of an American guarantee was also raised by King Khalid); author's interview with William Quandt.

58. See Brzezinski, *Power and Principle*, 105 for details of the behind-the-scenes attempts to communicate with the PLO; NYT, 27 August 1977, p. 3; author's interview with William Quandt. See also the American Friends Service Committee, *A Compassionate Peace in the Middle East* (New York: Hill and Wang, 1982), 49.

59. Brzezinski, *Power and Principle*, p. 106; Dayan, *Breakthrough*, 64.

60. Dayan, *Breakthrough*, 59–60, 62–63.

61. Ibid., 60–65. Sharon was the Israeli general with responsibility for settlements in the first Begin government as agriculture minister.

62. Dayan, *Breakthrough*, 60; Brzezinski, *Power and Principle*, 107; Carter, *Keeping Faith*, 292; Vance, 191.

63. Dayan had hinted to the administration that Israel might be prepared to accept a unified delegation at the start of the talks but still insisted that the talks be held at the bilateral level. Brzezinski, *Power and Principle*, 107; Vance, 190.

64. Dayan, *Breakthrough*, 65; Vance, 191; Brzezinski, *Power and Principle*, 107.

65. For the text of the communique, see NYT, 2 October 1977, x. A 16. See also Vance, 463–64.

66. Carter, *Keeping Faith*, 293; Vance, 191–92; Brzezinski, *Power and Principle*, 108, 110; author's interview with William Quandt; see also an October 1976 memo submitted by Vance to Carter (Vance, 488).

67. Brzezinski, *Power and Principle*, 108, 110; author's interview with David Aaron.

68. For a description of the response of the major Jewish organizations, see NYT, 4 October 1977, p. 1. Those speaking against the communiqué in Congress included Senators Javits, Packwood, Danforth, and Brooke (*Congressional Record*, 95th Cong., 1st sess., 123, pt. 25: 32455, 32465, 32475); and Representatives Frenzel and Bingham (Ibid., 32619, 32833). The following week Senators Schweicker, Wallop, and Dole spoke out against the administration (ibid., pt. 26: 33103, 33419, 33426). See also NER 21, no. 40 (5 October 1977): 167, for the responses of Henry Jackson, Edward Koch, and Daniel Moynihan; and NER 21, no. 41 (12 October 1977): 172, for the responses of Alan Cranston, Frank Church, and James Blanchard. See also *Time*, 17 October 1977, 24–28, for a vivid account of the response of the pro-Israel lobby to the communiqué, and the *National Review*, 28 October 1977, 1216–17, for an editorial denouncing the inclusion of the Soviets in Mideast diplomacy.

69. Carter, *Keeping Faith*, 294; Dayan, *Breakthrough*, 68–70; Brzezinski, *Power and Principle*, 108–9.

70. Dayan, *Breakthrough*, 70–71; NYT, 6 October 1977, p. A 12; Vance, 193–94; Brzezinski, *Power and Principle* 109–10. Begin accepted the concept of Palestinian representation during Vance's talks in Israel in August; NYT, 21 August 1977, p. 1.

71. Author's interview with William Quandt; Dayan hints at this point in *Breakthrough*, 70–71.

72. Sidney Zion and Uri Dan, "The Untold Story of the Mideast Peace Talks," *New York Times Magazine*, 21 January 1979, 22.

73. Dayan, *Breakthrough*, 87; Eitan Haber, Ze'ev Schiff, and Ehud Yaari, *The Year of the Dove* (New York: Bantam, 1979), 13, 14. Dayan says Sadat told him personally about the bilateral decision (*Breakthrough*, 88).

74. Author's interview with William Quandt; Indyk, 31.

75. In Dayan's account of this first secret meeting, Tuhami repeatedly solicits this promise from Dayan, but Dayan agrees only to "report" this request to Begin (*Breakthrough*, 51–52).

76. Brzezinski, *Power and Principle*, 110; Carter, *Keeping Faith*, 295; author's interview with William Quandt.

77. Brzezinski, *Power and Principle*, 111; Vance, 194; author's interview with William Quandt; Dayan, *Breakthrough*, 87; NYT, 10 November 1977, p. 3. For the full text of Sadat's speech, see FBIS, 10 November 1977, p. D-20.

78. Indyk, 68–69; Dayan, *Breakthrough*, 89.

79. For the text of Sadat's speech, see NYT, 21 November 1977, 17. The Sultan of Oman supported Sadat's trip in a statement on 20 November (*FBIS*, 21 November 1977,

p. C-1). The other Arab states' reactions ranged fron noncommital (Jordan and Saudi Arabia) to vitriolic denunciation (Libya, Iraq, and the Palestinian groups). See Ibid., 14–23 November 1977.

80. Cairo news conference, 10 December 1977, DSB, January 1978, 40. See also 11 December news conference in Jerusalem (Ibid., 42), and his remarks at Andrews Air Force Base upon his return (Ibid., 46). Dayan, *Breakthrough*, 98.

81. Haber, et al., 108; Vance, 198–200.

82. Haber, et al., 110–11; Ezer Weizman, *The Battle for Peace* (New York: Bantam, 1981), 120; Vance, 198–200; Brzezinski, *Power and Principle*, 115–20.

83. NYT, 18 December 1977, p. 1.

84. Vance, 202; Dayan, *Breakthrough*, 102. See NER 22, no. 1 (4 January 1978): 3, for the amended version of the Begin autonomy proposal approved by the Israeli Cabinet, 23 December 1977; NYT, 4 December 1977, pp. 1, 4.

85. Author's confidential interview; Haber et al., 123.

86. Carter's interview, printed in Jimmy Carter, PPP, 1977, 2190; Sadat's remarks, reported in NYT, 30 December 1977, p. 1.

87. For the text of the Aswan Declaration, see DSB, February 1978, 12.

88. See, for example, "Rethinking Policy Objectives," in NER 21, no. 48 (30 November 1977): 209.

89. Brzezinski, *Power and Principle*, 111–13.

90. Interview with Zbigniew Brzezinski, "Issues and Answers," American Broadcasting Company, 10 December 1977; Brzezinski, *Power and Principle*, 113–14.

91. The author of the "Shylock" article was Mustafa Amin, writing in *Al-Akhbar* in late December immediately after the Ismailia Conference. Begin referred to Amin's article in his 23 January address to the Knesset. See FBIS, 24 January 1978, p. N-5.

92. Weizman, 148–89, esp. p. 168. Weizman argues that the nature of the Egyptian government, with all the important decisions made by one man, made progress impossible without Sadat's participation.

93. Jimmy Carter, PPP, 1978, 62.

94. Carter, *Keeping Faith*, 307–308; Brzezinski, *Power and Principle*, 243–44; Vance, 203–205. Dayan says Carter mentioned this threat in their 16 February 1978 talk (*Breakthrough*, 119). Brzezinski writes in his memoirs, "While Sadat's comments were a shock to us, I could not suppress a sneaking suspicion that this was a bluff designed to elicit some sort of U.S. commitment" (*Power and Principle*, 243).

95. NYT, 9 February 1978, p. 1; author's interview with William Quandt.

96. Author's interview with William Quandt; Brzezinski, *Power and Principle*, 244, 249; author's confidential interview.

97. NYT, 11 February 1978, p. 1. Carter reiterated his stance on the West Bank, 9 March; See Jimmy Carter, PPP, 1978, 491. Also NYT, 11 February 1978, p. 4; 13 February 1978, p. 1, 10.

98. Dayan, *Breakthrough*, 119.

99. NER, 22, no. 4 (25 January 1978): 14; NYT, 28 February 1978, p. 2; author's confidential interview.

100. Question and answer session, Conference of Presidents of Major Jewish Organizations, Boston, Mass., 30 September 1976, printed in NER, 6 October 1976, 169.

101. Address, New York Synagogue Council, minutes of the meeting, 1 April 1976.

102. DSB, March 1978, 37.

103. Vance, 32.

104. Brzezinski, *Power and Principle*, 248.

105. Author's confidential interview.

106. Author's confidential interview; NER 22, no. 6 (8 February 1978): 21; no. 7 (15 February 1978): 25–26; no. 8 (22 February 1978): 29; no. 9 (1 March 1978): 33; NYT, 28 February 1978, p. 2.

107. Richard Burt, "The Mideast Plane Sales Package: How U.S. Decision Was Reached," NYT, 28 February 1978, p. 2.

108. The most comprehensive single statement of the administration's arguments was a memorandum written by Douglas J. Bennet, Jr., Assistant Secretary for Congressional Relations, U.S. Department of State, and sent to the House Committee on International Relations. See Congressional Record, 95th Cong., 2d Sess., vol. 124, pt. 3: 3903. A similar memo on the Egyptian sale can be found Ibid., pt. 6: 6894. See also NYT, 16 May 1978, pp. 1, 12, for quotes and summaries of the administration's arguments.

109. See AIPAC's memo on the Saudi plane sale in the Congressional Record, 95th Cong., 2d Sess., vol. 124, pt. 3: 3900, and also AIPAC's memo on the Egyptian sale, Ibid., pt. 6: 6893.

110. See Carter's letter in Congressional Record, 95th Cong., 2d sess., vol. 124, pt. 10: 13628, and Brown's letter to Sparkman, Ibid., 13627.

111. NER 22, no. 21 (24 Mary 1978): 91; Brzezinski, Power and Principle, 248.

112. Carter, Keeping Faith, 310–11; Vance, 208–209. The Security Council voted 19 March. Begin arrived 21 March.

113. Carter, Keeping Faith, 311–12; Dayan, Breakthrough, 125.

114. Carter, Keeping Faith, 312; Vance, 210; Dayan, Breakthrough, 126.

115. Dayan, Breakthrough, 125–26; Haber, et al., 191. Begin had equated "self-determination" with "Palestinian State" as early as 4 January. (NYT, 5 January 1978, p. 3.)

116. Carter's criticisms were explicit. He attacked Israel for refusing to give up its Sinai settlements, refusing to concede that Resolution 242 applied to the West Bank, and refusing to agree to a plan for interim self-rule in the West Bank and Gaza. NYT, 24 March 1978, pp. A 1, 10; Brzezinski, Power and Principle, 246–47.

117. NYT, 27 March 1978, pp. 4 and 5. See also Anthony Lewis, commentary, p. 27; Carter, Keeping Faith, 313; Brzezinski, Power and Principle, 249.

118. Carter praised Sadat on 22 June (NYT, 23 June 1978, p. 2) and called the Israeli response to his questions "disappointing" in his 26 June news conference (Jimmy Carter, PPP, 1978, 1179).

119. Brzezinski, Power and Principle, 249.

120. Jimmy Carter, PPP, 1978, 813.

121. For accounts of the Egyptian plan presented at Leeds Castle, see Dayan, Breakthrough, 141–46; Haber, et al., 201–202, 209–13; NYT, 26 June 1978, p. 1; Vance, 215–16.

122. Weizman, 330–31; 335–36.

123. NYT, 23 July 1978, p. A 1; Haber, et al., 214.

124. A New York Times/CBS poll taken in August showed Carter with one of the lowest approval ratings of any president since the polls were first taken. NYT, 22 September 1978, p. 5. See also Gallup Opinion Index, July 1978, 1–4, which documents the steep decline in Carter's approval rating.

125. The ever-cautious Vance hinted "time is running out" on 20 July (NYT, 21 July 1978, p. 1) and warned on 17 August that "a new conflict in the Middle East could severely damage the security of our own country" (DSB, 1978 October 13). Carter warned congressional leaders that failure to make progress could result in war. Brzezinski, Power and Principle, 250–52, 256.

126. Carter, Keeping Faith, 317; Brzezinski, Power and Principle, 252; Rosalynn Carter, 239.

127. Author's interview with William Quandt.

128. Carter, *Keeping Faith*, 317, 319, 331; Vance, 219; Weizman, 343.

129. Carter, *Keeping Faith*, 344.

130. Carter, *Keeping Faith*, 342–43; Brzezinski, *Power and Principle*, 256.

131. Carter, *Keeping Faith*, 340, 345; Dayan, *Breakthrough*, 161–62.

132. Weizman (341) admits that he was so dubious of success at Camp David that he began preparing to explain the failure almost before he arrived. He even began to talk of mass rallies to defend Israel's position.

133. Carter, *Keeping Faith*, 364–69; Vance, 215–16; 220; author's interviews with Harold Saunders and William Quandt.

134. Carter, *Keeping Faith*, 370–71; Dayan, *Breakthrough*, 164–65; Haber et al., 250–51; author's interview with William Quandt.

135. Carter, *Keeping Faith*, 374–78; Brzezinski, *Power and Principle*, 260; Vance, 220–21; Dayan, *Breakthrough*, 164, 167–68; Weizman, 364; Haber et al., 251.

136. Carter, *Keeping Faith*, 378–79. See also Dayan, *Breakthrough*, 176, referring to a later talk between the two. See also Brzezinski, *Power and Principle*, 262.

137. Author's interview with William Quandt.

138. Carter, *Keeping Faith*, 379, 380–83; Haber et al., 253–54; Weizman, 366–67. See also Hermann Frederick Eilts, "Improve the Framework," *Foreign Policy*, Winter 1980–81, 5–6.

139. Eilts, 5; author's interview with William Quandt. As early as February 1978, after his meeting with Sadat, Carter began to think about the possibility of a separate Israeli-Egyptian peace treaty (Brzezinski, *Power and Principle*, 244).

140. Author's interview with William Quandt; Brzezinski, *Power and Principle*, 262; Weizman, 367–68.

141. Carter, *Keeping Faith*, 386; Haber et al., 257.

142. Carter, *Keeping Faith*, 382; Brzezinski, *Power and Principle*, 269; Dayan, *Breakthrough*, 156; Weizman, 370–71; Haber et al., 259.

143. Carter, *Keeping Faith*, 388–89; Haber et al., 260–61.

144. Dayan, *Breakthrough*, 171–72; Carter, *Keeping Faith*, 391.

145. Brzezinski, *Power and Principle*, 266–67; Dayan, *Breakthrough*, 174.

146. Carter, *Keeping Faith*, 391; Dayan, *Breakthrough*, 172–73.

147. Carter, *Keeping Faith*, 391–93; Brzezinski, *Power and Principle*, 271–72.

148. Weizman says Dayan was actually packing his bags at the same time the Egyptians were (Weizman, 369–70); Haber et al., 265; See also Zion and Dan, 38.

149. Haber et al., 275; Weizman, 371.

150. Dayan, *Breakthrough*, 175–76, 197. Dayan felt it important to emphasize repeatedly that boundaries on the West Bank would only be discussed with Jordan, a sovereign state, and not with the Palestinian inhabitants.

151. Weizman, 372; Carter, *Keeping Faith*, 396–97.

152. Side letters are printed in DSB, October 1978, 10–11, and Dayan, *Breakthrough*, 328–30.

153. Dayan, *Breakthrough*, 185, 186–87; Vance, 225, 228–29; Carter, *Keeping Faith*, 397; Brzezinski, *Power and Principle*, 270, 273; FBIS, 20 September 1978, p. D-1; Eilts, 8.

154. Weizman, 373; Carter, *Keeping Faith*, 399; Haber et al., 274; Dayan (*Breakthrough*, 179) gives much of the credit for hammering out a compromise to Aharon Barak.

155. For text of accords, see DSB, October 1978, 7–11.

156. Eilts, 4–5; author's confidential interview.

157. See *Washington Post*, 20 September 1978, p. A 1. Brzezinski clearly believed that Begin had agreed to this. See Brzezinski, *Power and Principle*, 270, 273; Carter, *Keeping*

Faith, 397; Vance, 228; author's interview with Edward Sanders who was with Begin in the plane.

158. Carter, *Keeping Faith*, 409; Vance, 228; author's confidential interview. Carter was frequently lavish in his praise for Barak. For example, he describes him as "outstanding" and "a real hero of the Camp David discussions" (*Keeping Faith*, 382).

159. Comments by former President Carter at a Middle East Consultation of the Carter Center of Emory University, 6–9 November 1983. Carter thought that Begin's posture on the settlements had caused Hussein, who was in London during the conference, to fly back to Jordan instead of seeing Sadat on the way home.

160. Dayan's account (*Breakthrough*, 181–88) is detailed and persuasive on this point. Carter (*Keeping Faith*, 397) and Vance (228) contradict Dayan directly. See also *Washington Post*, 20 September 1978, p. A 1, and 28 September 1978, p. A 25; Brzezinski's 24 September interview on ABC's "Issues and Answers," reprinted in NER 22, no. 39 (27 September 1978): 177. According to Hermann Eilts, who was then U.S. ambassador to Egypt, the absence of a long-term West Bank settlements freeze was the single most objectionable aspect of the Camp David agreements for the Palestinians and moderate Arabs. Failure to obtain such a freeze "destroyed the last chance of obtaining moderate Arab support" (Eilts, 8). Brzezinski agrees, noting that the "worst failure" at Camp David "lay in not obtaining Begin's clear-cut acquiescence to a freeze on settlements activity" (*Power and Principle*, 273).

161. *Washington Post*, 20 September 1978, p. A 1. In his speech to the Knesset, Begin also pledged there would be "no plebiscite on the West Bank, and no Palestinian State" (Ibid., 26 September 1978, p. A 12). Ibid., 28 September 1978, p. A 25.

162. Carter, *Keeping Faith*, 384–85; Eilts, 9, 14; author's interview with Harold Saunders; author's confidential interview.

163. Author's confidential interview; Brzezinski, *Power and Principle*, 274; *Washington Post*, 23 September 1978, p. A 1; Vance, 229–31.

164. Author's confidential interview.

165. Jimmy Carter, PPP, 1978, 1780. A similar statement by Carter is quoted in *Breakthrough*, 187.

166. Dayan, *Breakthrough*, 205.

167. Haber et al., 285. Sadat confirmed on 22 October that the linkage issue was still one of the primary areas of dispute between Egypt and Israel. Dayan implied the same in remarks in Jerusalem the next day. *Washington Post*, 23 October 1978, p. 1. Dayan examines this issue at length in *Breakthrough*, 207–9, 219–20.

168. Carter, *Keeping Faith*, 407–408; Dayan, *Breakthrough*, 211–17, 218, 220–21.

169. Dayan, *Breakthrough*, 228; *Ha'arez*, 31 October 1978, p. 1, reprinted in FBIS, 1 November 1978, p. N 3; the Jerusalem Domestic News Service, in FBIS, 2 November 1978, p. N 2, says the question of Israel's access to Sinai oil was also a major issue. The *Washington Post*, 27 October 1978, p. A 14, emphasizes the linkage issue only.

170. Author's interview with Harold Saunders; Michael Sterner was deputy assistant secretary of state.

171. Dayan, *Breakthrough*, 202, 227–31. For the text of Hussein's questions, see FBIS, 17 October 1978, pp. F 3–5. The American answers were never fully released, but see Carter, *Keeping Faith*, 408–9. See also FBIS, 20 October 1978, p. F 1, and 23 October 1978, p. N 11, for reports from the Jordanian and Israeli media of Saunders's statements to the Palestinians.

172. *Washington Post*, 27 October 1978, pp. A 1, 14.

173. Jerusalem Domestic News Service, 2 November 1978, in FBIS, 3 November 1978, p. N 1. *Washington Post*, 4 November 1978, pp. A 1, 17.

174. Carter, *Keeping Faith*, 404–11; Brzezinski, *Power and Principle*, 276–77; Vance, 233, 237–38.

175. For text of the first Baghdad Communiqué, see FBIS, 6 November 1978, pp. A 13–15; Dayan, *Breakthrough*, 233–34.

176. Carter, *Keeping Faith*, 411; Vance, 239.

177. The decision was announced on 17 December and took effect on 1 January 1979; author's interview with William Quandt; Quandt, *Saudi Arabia in the 1980s*, 116.

178. Vance, interview on NBC's "Meet the Press," 17 December 1984, printed in DSB, January 1979, 16. Egyptian prime minister Mustafa Khalil attempted on 22 December to make the entire concept of ambassadorial exchange contingent on Israel's willingness to permanently freeze West Bank settlements (Dayan, *Breakthrough*, 254).

179. NYT, 16 December 1978, pp. 1, 3.

180. See NYT, 17 December 1978, p. A 3 for an article describing the reactions of American Jewish groups to Vance's accusations. See also page E 20 of the same issue for a *New York Times* editorial criticizing the administration's intemperance. William Safire criticized the administration in his column the next day (Ibid., 18 December 1978, p. A 19), and outgoing Israeli ambassador Simcha Dinitz criticized Carter's "ultimatum" to Israel before the Conference of Presidents of Major American Jewish Organizations on 18 December (Ibid., 19 December 1978, p. A 5). For a sampling of congressional criticism leveled against the administration, see NER 22, no. 51 (20 December 1978): 234.

181. Vance, 242.

182. Carter, *Keeping Faith*, 413; Vance, 243; Haber et al., 292; see especially Dayan's account of his Washington meeting with Carter and Khalil on 25 February 1979 (*Breakthrough*, 264–66).

183. Carter, *Keeping Faith*, 416; Haber et al., 293. Carter (*Keeping Faith*, 414) notes that "Begin's purpose seemed to be to convince us that Israel should be the dominant military power in the area, and that it was our only reliable ally in the Middle East."

184. Carter, *Keeping Faith*, 416; Dayan, *Breakthrough*, 268–69.

185. Brzezinski, *Power and Principle*, 280–82. According to Brzezinski, Carter had been considering withdrawing from active involvement in the Mideast peace process, but Begin so angered him that he changed his mind. The president also suspected that Begin was stalling so that Carter would be defeated in the 1980 elections.

186. Haber et al., 299; Dayan, *Breakthrough*, 272; notes of meetings in Jerusalem provided to author by Edward Sanders.

187. See Carter, *Keeping Faith*, 417–26, for detailed accounts of the Carter shuttle; also, Dayan, *Breakthrough*, 269–78.

188. Dayan, *Breakthrough*, 273, 274–77; NYT, 14 March 1979, p. 1; Haber et al., 299.

189. Carter, *Keeping Faith*, 420–21, 424.

190. Vance, 249–51.

191. Vance, 249–50; Dayan, *Breakthrough*, 275. Carter (*Keeping Faith*, 424–25) describes this as a climactic moment, when Begin finally accepted the "Egyptian-American proposal."

192. NYT, 27 March 1979, p. 1; Dayan, *Breakthrough*, 279–80.

193. NYT, 26 March 1979, p. A5; NER 23, no. 16 (18 April 1979): 76.

194. Jimmy Carter, PPP, 26 March 1979, 523.

195. NYT, 1 April 1979, p. 1; for the text of the final communiqué of this second Baghdad Summit, see FBIS, 2 April 1979, pp. A 1–8; of these eighteen Arab states,

fifteen actually broke diplomatic relations with Egypt: *Facts on File* (New York: Facts on File, 1979), 4 May 1979, 319.

196. For an informed discussion of United States–Saudi relations during this period, see William Quandt, *Saudi Arabia in the 1980s*, 126–35.

197. The increase was announced 11 July 1979. NYT, 12 July 1979, p. A 3, 2 August 1979, p. A 1.

198. Carter had made the anti-PLO remarks at a town meeting in Aliquippa, Pa., 23 September 1978 (Jimmy Carter, PPP, 1978, 1612); his more favorable comments were reported in NYT, 1 August 1979, pp. A 1, D 2.

199. NYT, 12 August 1979, p. A 1.

200. Brzezinski, *Power and Principle*, 438–40; NYT, 20 August 1979, p. A 1; 23 August 1979, pp. A 1, 11.

201. Author's interview with David Aaron.

202. Author's interview with Edward Sanders.

203. NYT, 18 August 1979, p. 1; author's interview with Edward Sanders.

204. NYT, 20 August 1979, p. A 1.

205. Author's interview with Edward Sanders; confidential reports made available to the author; Carter, *Keeping Faith*, 492–93; Brzezinski, *Power and Principle*, 441–42.

206. Carter, *Keeping Faith*, 492–93, NYT, 5 March 1980, p. A 12; author's interview with Harold Saunders. Brzezinski says he told Vance to "transmit the revised text to the President or at least speak to him personally to be sure" before he gave the go ahead (*Power and Principle*, 441). For text of resolution, see NYT, 5 March 1980, p. A 12.

207. Jimmy Carter, PPP, 4 March 1980, 427.

208. Carter, *Keeping Faith*, 493–94; Brzezinski, *Power and Principle*, 442.

209. For the text of Vance's opening statement, see DSB, May 1980, 62. For a transcript of the entire hearing, see Senate Committee on Foreign Relations, *U.S. Middle East Policy*, United States Senate, 69th Cong., 2d sess., 20 March 1980. Brzezinski, *Power and Principle*, 442.

210. Brzezinski, *Power and Principle*, 442–43.

211. NYT, 26 March 1980, p. B 5, notes that "Jewish voters, angered over the Administration's March 1 vote at the United Nations on Israel's settlement policy, went nearly four to one for Mr. Kennedy . . . the Jewish vote . . . provided the base for Mr. Kennedy's overall statewide margin . . ." See also an election post-mortem (Ibid., 9 November 1980, p. 36) that drew much the same conclusions. Carter (*Keeping Faith*, 493–94) also believes that he would have won the New York and Connecticut primaries but for the U.N. vote on Jerusalem.

212. House Committee on Foreign Affairs, *Foreign Assistance Legislation for Fiscal Year 1981*, pt. 1, 96th Cong., 2d sess., 5 February 1980, p. 18.

213. J. C. Hurewitz, "The Middle East: A Year of Turmoil," *Foreign Affairs*, Winter 1980, 571; Carter, *Keeping Faith*, 494–96, Vance, 253–55. See also Secretary Muskie's statement of the issues in DSB, 9 June 1980, 3.

214. Author's discussion with Sol Linowitz at Middle East Consultation of the Carter Center of Emory University, 6–9 November 1983.

Chapter 9. Stars and Ideas

1. For examples of systems theory in international politics, see Morton Kaplan, *System and Process in International Politics* (New York: Wiley, 1957); Richard Rosecrance, *Action and Reaction in World Politics* (Boston: Little, Brown, 1963), and Kenneth Waltz, *Theory of International Politics* (New York: Addison-Wesley, 1979).

2. See, for example, Charles Hermann, *Crisis in Foreign Policy* (Indianapolis: Bobbs-Merrill, 1969), and Glenn Paige, *The Korean Decision* (New York: Free Press, 1968). The most complete work on the effect of crises in decision making has been done by Michael Brecher. See, for example, *Decisions in Crisis* (Berkeley and Los Angeles: University of California Press, 1980).

3. See, for example, Graham Allison, *Essence of Decision* (Boston: Little, Brown, 1971), and Morton Halperin, *Bureaucratic Politics and Foreign Policy* (Washington, D.C.: Brookings Institution, 1974).

4. On pluralist theory, see, for example, Lester Milbrath, "Interest Groups and Foreign Policy," in *Domestic Sources of Foreign Policy*, ed. James Rosenau (New York: Free Press, 1967); and, for a classic view, David Truman, *The Governmental Process* (New York: Alfred A. Knopf, 1964). See also Abdul Aziz Said, ed., *Ethnicity and U.S. Foreign Policy* (New York: Praeger, 1977); Mancur Olson, *Logic of Collective Action, Public Goods, and Theory of Groups* (Cambridge: Harvard University Press, 1971); Theodore J. Lowi, "Making Democracy Safe for the World: National Politics and Foreign Policy," in Rosenau, 295–331.

5. See, for example, Robert Jervis, *Perception and Misperception in International Politics* (Princeton, N.J.: Princeton University Press, 1976); Nathan Leites, *The Operational Code of the Politburo* (New York: McGraw-Hill, 1951); and Alexander L. George, "The 'Operational Code': A Neglected Approach to the Study of Political Decision Making," *International Studies Quarterly* (June 1969): 190–222.

6. John Lewis Gaddis, *Strategies of Containment* (New York: Oxford University Press, 1982), ix.

7. See I. M. Destler, *Presidents, Bureaucrats and Foreign Policy: The Politics of Organizational Reform* (Princeton, N.J.: Princeton University Press, 1972), and Alexander L. George, *Presidential Decision Making in Foreign Policy: The Effective Use of Information and Advice* (Boulder, Colo.: Westview Press, 1980).

8. For an analysis of the effect of leadership transition, see Valerie Bunce, *Do New Leaders Make a Difference?* (Princeton, N.J.: Princeton University Press, 1981). See also Amos Perlmutter, "The Presidential Political Center and Foreign Policy: A Critique of the Revisionist and Bureaucratic-Political Orientations," *World Politics* 27, no. 1 (October 1974): 87–106, for a discussion of the consensus in foreign policy formulation built around the president's "court."

Chapter 10. Postscript: Reagan

1. David Halberstam, *The Best and the Brightest* (New York: Random House, 1972).

2. NYT, 5 November 1981, p. 1; Isaacs, 151–53.

3. *Middle East Policy Survey*, 12 September 1980. Hereafter cited as MEPS.

4. See *Congressional Quarterly*, 22 August 1981, 1523–30; Steven Emerson, "The Petrodollar Connection," *New Republic*, 17 February 1982, 18–25.

5. DSB, November 1983, 24–26.

6. Ronald Reagan, PPP, 8 March 1983, 369. President Reagan was addressing the National Association of Evangelicals in Orlando, Florida.

7. MEPS 2 (29 February 1980): 4.

8. Steven R. Weisman, "Will the Magic Prevail?" *New York Times Magazine*, 29 April 1948, 43–49.

9. NYT, 5 February 1981, p. 1; 6 September 1981, p. 16.

10. NYT, 29 September 1981, p. 1.

11. NYT, 22 December 1980, p. D 14.

12. Weisman, 48.

13. Laurence T. Barrett, *Gambling with History: Reagan in the White House* (New York: Doubleday, 1983), 221–22; Alexander Haig, *Caveat* (New York: Macmillan, 1984), 167–93.

14. Haig, 53, 58. At his first news conference as secretary of state, Haig stated: "I was assured by President Reagan personally that I will be his chief administrator, if you will, and I use the term vicar."

15. For examples, see Barrett, 225–31; Haig, 58.

16. See for example, NYT, 4 February 1981, p. A7; 29 September 1981, p. 1; 7 February 1982, p. 1; 14 February 1982, pp. 1, 8; 11 February 1982, p. 14; 10 February 1982, p. 7; 7 February 1982, p. 13.

17. Barrett, 222–23.

18. Barrett, 231–33.

19. Francis X. Clines, "James Baker: Calling Reagan's Re-election Moves," *New York Times Magazine*, 20 May 1984, 56, 66.

20. Ibid., 58.

21. Author's confidential interview.

22. Weisman, 42. Reagan did not actually enter the concentration camps, as he sometimes embellished the story. See also NER 28, no. 6 (10 February 1984): 20; *Los Angeles Times*, 6 July 1976, p. 6; *Washington Post*, 5 March 1984, p. A2.

23. *Washington Post*, 15 August 1979, p. 25.

24. NYT, 7 November 1980, p. 16; MEPS 19 (7 November 1980): 4. Reagan spoke similarly as a candidate; see MEPS 15 (12 September 1980): 1.

25. Bernard Gwertzman, "Reagan Turns to Israel," *New York Times Magazine*, 27 November 1983, 64. Reagan spoke in the same way in an interview with the author in December 1978.

26. Barrett, 271.

27. Haig, 174–75; Barrett, 264–65.

28. Haig, 177–79; Barrett, 268.

29. Haig, 179; MEPS 29 (10 April 1981): 3–4; Barrett, 268–69. In September, a group of Israeli military observers was taken on a flight in an AWACS jet by the Pentagon in order to calm Israeli fears. The effort backfired when it reinforced Jerusalem's opposition to the sale. See Haig, 187; NYT 26 August 1981, p. 12.

30. This phrase was initially coined by Saudi lobbyist Fredrick Dutton and was soon echoed by senior administration officials. See MEPS 40 (25 September 1981): 1; Haig, 186, 190.

31. Reagan also said, "We will not permit [Saudi Arabia] to become another Iran." See Ronald Reagan, PPP, 1 October 1981, 867; Haig, 190.

32. Haig, 188; MEPS 43 (6 November 1981): 3.

33. Haig, 183–86; *Congressional Quarterly*, 18 July 1981, 1318; 25 July 1981, 1351; MEPS 34 (19 June 1981): 2–4. Haig also discussed the increased tensions between the United States and Israel at this time; see Haig, 321.

34. Having just met with Begin, Sadat was embarrassed in the Arab world by the Israeli bombing of Osiraq; MEPS 34 (19 June 1981): 2.

35. Haig, 187–88; MEPS 40 (11 September 1981): 2; Barrett, 273.

36. For the text of the Memorandum of Understanding, see DSB, December 1981, 45–46; and FBIS, 1 December 1981, I/1. Weinberger would allow the signing to take place only privately; see NYT, 1 December 1981, p. 1. For American and Israeli presentations of and responses to the memorandum, see Barrett, 276; and FBIS, 1 December 1981, I/2; 3 December 1981, I/1–5.

37. DSB, December 1981, 45–46, article I of the memorandum; also see NYT, 1 December 1981, p. A 14.

38. For Sharon's defense of the memorandum, see FBIS, 2 December 1981, I/2; 3 December 1981, I/5. For Begin's responses in support of the memorandum, see FBIS, 11 December 1981, I/3; For internal Israeli opposition to the memorandum, see FBIS, 1 December 1981, I/4–5; 2 December 1981, I/3–4; 3 December 1981, I/6–10.

39. Although almost universally reported as annexation, the action was actually a legal step short. It was not annexation because, formally, only Israeli law was applied; the Golan Heights were not declared Israeli territory. See Dan Bavly and Eliahu Salpeter, *Fire in Beirut: Israel's War in Lebanon with the PLO* (New York: Stein and Day, 1984), 230–31.

40. Haig, 328.

41. Ibid.

42. FBIS, 21 December 1981, I/1–3.

43. Haig, 326–30; NYT, 28 January 1982, p. 1; 20 January 1982, p. 5.

44. NYT, 13 February 1982, pp. 1, 8; 4 May 1982, p. A6; MEPS 49 (12 February 1982); Haig, 333. This Jordanian strike force was formally known as the "Joint Logistic Planning Project" between the U.S. and Jordan.

45. Zeev Schiff, "The Green Light," *Foreign Policy* 50 (Spring 1983): 75–76.

46. Ibid., 75; MEPS 31 (8 May 1981): 1–2; Barrett, 269.

47. Schiff, "The Green Light," 76; Bavly and Salpeter, 17.

48. Haig, 331; Schiff, "The Green Light," 76–77, 78; Itamar Rabinovich and Jehuda Reinharz, eds., *Israel in the Middle East* (New York: Oxford University Press, 1984), 350–51.

49. Haig, 318, 333–35; MEPS 43 (6 November 1981): 2–3; Schiff, "The Green Light," 80–81.

50. Haig, 330, 334; Schiff, "The Green Light," 81–82.

51. Haig also met the previous February with Israeli chief of military intelligence, Yehoshua Saguy. Haig, 188, 326–27, 332–33; Ze'ev Schiff and Ehud Ya'ari, *Israel's Lebanon War* (New York: Simon and Schuster, 1984), 67–77.

52. Haig, 335–38; FBIS, 7 June 1982, I/2–3; Barrett, 279–80; Bavly and Salpeter, 136–37; Schiff, "The Green Light," 82–83.

53. NYT, 1 March 1984, p. A 10.

54. Bavly and Salpeter, 84, 99–100.

55. Barrett, 245, 282–83; Ronald Reagan, PPP, 21 June 1982, 799.

56. Author's confidential interview.

57. Haig, 343–44.

58. Haig, 268–70; Barrett, 237–42. Also see MEPS 34 (18 June 1981) for Haig's and Kirkpatrick's differing perspectives on the Israeli bombing of Osiraq.

59. Haig, 310–11.

60. For details of his resignation, see Haig, 313–14; Barrett, 245–50.

61. Barrett, 248; NYT, 20 November 1980, p. B 12.

62. Haig, 348–51.

63. Ronald Reagan, PPP, 4 July 1982, 876; NYT, 7 July 1982, pp. 1, A6; Haig, 351.

64. There has been a continuing debate about the role of the media in summer 1982. See for example, Joshua Muravchik, "Misreporting Lebanon," *Policy Review,* Winter 1983; Bavly and Salpeter, 135–50; Roger Morris, "Beirut—and the Press—Under Siege," *Columbia Journalism Review,* November/December 1982; Rita J. Simon, "The Print Media's Coverage of the War in Lebanon," *Middle East Review,* Fall 1983; Martin Peretz, "Lebanon Eyewitness," *New Republic,* 2 August 1982.

65. NYT, 4 August 1982, p. 1.

66. See, in sequence, NYT, 7 August 1982, pp. 1, 4; 11 August 1982, p. 1; 13 August 1982, p. 1.

67. *Washington Post,* 2 August 1982, p. A 16; Bavly and Salpeter, 139, 149; Muravchik, 12.

68. Barrett, 284.

69. NYT, 13 August 1982, pp. 1, 6. A written message from the president expressing outrage arrived at the time the Israeli Cabinet met to order the cease-fire. It ordered the cease-fire, however, three hours before the president's call and appears to have been reacting to concerns that Sharon had exceeded his authority rather than to the president's message. The timing and sequence of events was:

  6:00 A.M.—Air raid begins.

  2:00 P.M.—Cabinet decides to end the raids; the president's message had just arrived.

  5:00 P.M.—Cease-fire in effect.

  5:10 P.M.—Reagan reaches Begin by phone.

  5:40 P.M.—Begin calls Reagan to inform him that the cease-fire had begun.

70. Haig, 327.

71. Author's confidential interview; NYT, 19 February 1984, pp. 10, 14; 23 February 1984, p. 10.

72. Author's confidential interview. Haig, in *Caveat,* writes, "The foreign policy bureaucracy, overwhelmingly Arabist in its approach to the Middle East and in its sympathies, saw the crisis as an opportunity to open direct negotiations between the U.S. and the PLO" (334).

73. NYT, 14 July 1982, p. A 12.

74. MEPS 61 (30 July 1982): 4.

75. Author's confidential interview.

76. Barrett, 284; MEPS 60 (16 July 1982).

77. MEPS 63 (10 September 1982): 2.

78. DSB, September 1982, 24–25; Barrett, 285.

79. NYT, 15 September 1982, pp. 1, A 12.

80. NYT, 2 September 1982, pp. 1, A 10; FBIS, 1 September 1982, I/1–2; *Congressional Quarterly,* 3 September 1982, pp. 1, 8. The Israelis were also reacting to secret "talking points" that they had received; these alarmed them more than the plan itself because of their greater detail; see NYT, 9 September 1982, p. 14; MEPS 63 (10 September 1982): 1–4; and Barrett, 245.

81. Barrett, 286; NER 26, no. 37 (10 September 1982): 179–81.

82. Author's confidential interview.

83. For the text of the Fez Plan, see FBIS, 10 September 1982, A 17–18.

84. Thomas L. Friedman, "America's Failure in Lebanon," *New York Times Magazine,* 8 April 1984, 37.

85. NYT, 16 September 1982, pp. 1, A 12; Bavly and Salpeter, 152.

86. For details of the commission's report and Sharon's removal, see Bavly and Salpeter, 154–62.

87. Friedman, 37; DSB, November 1982, 8.

88. NYT, 5 November 1982, pp. 1, 6; 2 March 1984, p. 10; MEPS 71 (14 January 1983): 1–2.

89. NER 26, no. 50 (10 December 1982): 243; no. 53 (31 December 1982): 255; MEPS 69 (3 December 1982): 1, 3.

90. Karen Elliot House, *Wall Street Journal,* 14 April 1983, p. 1, 16; 15 April 1983, p. 1.

91. *Los Angeles Times*, 11 March 1984, p. 1; Friedman, 37.

92. These meetings actually had their antecedent in a secret and unsuccessful meeting between Begin and Bashir Gemayel late in summer 1982 (Bavly and Salpeter, 199–200). Schiff, "Dealing with Syria" (106), claims that the Lebanese were actually talking to the United States and the Syrians during this period without Sharon's knowledge and therefore Habib was not surprised. He also denies the existence of a secret agreement. Even if he is correct, Sharon's statements exacerbated Lebanese-Israeli distrust.

93. Stockholm International Peace Research Institute, *Yearbook* (New York: World Armament and Disarmament International Publications Service, Taylor and Francis, 1983), 364; NYT, 15 January 1984, p. 6.

94. NYT, 22 March 1983, p. A 12; MEPS 74 (25 February 1983): 4.

95. Gwertzman, 86; Friedman, 37. In February the Joint Chiefs of Staff presented a paper recommending U.S.-Soviet collaboration against Israeli aggression in Lebanon. It even suggested the possibility of armed combat between the United States and Israel. See MEPS 51 (12 March 1982): 1.

96. NYT, 22 March 1983, p. 1; MEPS 75 (11 March 1983): 2–3; 76 (25 March 1983): 3–4; 77 (8 April 1983): 4.

97. DSB, June 1983, 62–64; MEPS 78 (22 April 1983): 4.

98. Ibid., 55–57; FBIS, 7 September 1982, H3.

99. Bavly and Salpeter, 222–23. Assad had told Shultz and Habib that Syria would withdraw if they negotiated an agreement.

100. Friedman, 37, 40.

101. NYT, 12 February 1983, p. 5; 6 July 1983, p. A7; 7 July 1983, p. 1; MEPS 85 (29 July 1983): 2–3.

102. Gwertzman, 88; Friedman, 44.

103. Gwertzman, 63.

104. Ibid.

105. General John W. Vessey, Jr., interview, 6 November 1983, *Meet the Press* (Washington, D.C.: Kelley Press, 1983), 3; MEPS 91 (11 November 1983): 1–2; NYT, 28 November 1983, pp. 1, 10–11.

106. NYT, 28 November 1983, pp. 1, 10–11.

107. Ronald Reagan, PPP, 3 February 1984, 163; DSB, February 1984, 8; Ronald Reagan, PPP, 23 October 1983, 1482; February 1984, 164.

108. NYT, 15 March 1984, p. A 10.

109. For Egypt's responses to Israel after the Lebanon War, see FBIS, 9 June 1982, D/1–6; and Bavly and Salpeter, 124–27.

INDEX

Subheadings are arranged in two sequences: first, by general topic, alphabetically; second, by presidential administration, chronologically.

American Israel Public Affairs Committee (AIPAC)
conflict-centered concerns of, 6–7
formation of, 52
Johnson administration, 161, 162
Ford administration, 231–33, 308–10
Carter administration, 347–49
Reagan administration, 398, 406
American Jewish Committee, 6, 13, 18
American Jewish community
conflict-centered concerns of, 6–7
influence of, on electoral process, 7
and policy formation, pluralist theory
of, 388–89
Kennedy administration, 95–97
Johnson administration, 120, 161
Nixon administration
and decision making process, 229–30
as domestic constraint in, 168–69, 220–22
and emergence of Kissinger, 213
and energy crisis, 243
and Rogers Plan, 187–88, 194
and Yom Kippur War, 249, 275
Ford administration, 231–32, 303–4, 309–10
Carter administration
and arms sale package controversy, 347–49, 351
and Camp David aftermath, 368
as domestic constraint, 316–17
and Geneva Conference, planning for, 334
and Palestinian autonomy, 376, 378
Reagan administration, 397, 398, 408–9
American Jewish Congress, 18
American Legion, 161, 162
American Mideast Educational and Training Services, Inc. (Amideast), 8
Americans for Democratic Action, 161
Americans for Middle East Understanding, 8
Americans for Near East Refugee Aid, 8
American Zionism. See Zionism
American Zionist Council, 52
Amideast, 8
Amit, Meir, 146

Anderson, John, 397
Anderson, Robert B.
Eisenhower administration, 67, 68
Johnson administration, 143–44
Nixon administration, 187
Angleton, James, 221
Anglo-American Committee of Inquiry, 22–23
Anti-Defamation League of B'nai B'rith, 6, 222, 310
ANZUS (Australia–New Zealand–United States) Pact countries, 330
Aqaba, Gulf of, 78–80, 138, 140, 144, 145, 148
Arab boycott of Israel, 222, 310
Arab embassies in U.S., 9
Arab League
and Eisenhower administration, 65
and Johnson administration, 155
and Nixon administration, 186
and Ford administration, 288
and Carter administration, 366, 373
Arab League Information Office, 9
Arab lobby, 8
Arab nationalism, 51, 87–91
Arab refugees. See Palestinian question
Arab states
Eisenhower administration, 2
Johnson administration, 121–23, 153–58, 159
Nixon administration
and decision making in, 178–80
and philosophy of, 173, 224–26
and Rogers Plan, 183, 186–87, 188
and Yom Kippur War, 245, 247, 249, 257
Carter administration
and Camp David aftermath, 362–64, 366–67, 372, 373
as external constraint in, 317
and Geneva Conference planning, 337
and Sadat initiative, 341
Reagan administration
and decision making in, 406–7
and Lebanon, Syrian presence in, 428
and philosophy of, 400–401
and Reagan Plan, 419, 420

Arab-Western defensive arrangement,
  62–66
Arafat, Yasir
  Ford administration, 288
  Carter administration, 325, 336
  Reagan administration
    and Lebanon, Syrian presence in,
      426–28
    and Reagan Plan, 418, 421–23
Aramco (company)
  Truman administration, 18
  Nixon administration, 170, 242–43,
    258, 259
Arens, Moshe, 414, 425, 427
Arms aid
  to Arab states, 159
  to Ecuador, 329–30
  to Egypt
    from Czechoslovakia, 65–66
    from Soviet Union, 107, 108, 189,
      190, 208, 239, 247, 253
    Eisenhower administration, 64
    Ford administration, 307
    Carter administration, 346–53, 372
  to Iraq
    from Soviet Union, 107, 108
    Eisenhower administration, 61
  to Israel, 233
    from Soviet Union and the West,
      39
    from West Germany, 132
    Kennedy administration, 107–8
    Johnson administration, 131–32,
      134–35, 159–61
    Nixon administration, 169–70, 185,
      189–92, 195–96, 203, 208, 210–
      12, 238, 248, 250–55
    Ford administration, 301, 307–8
    Carter administration, 330, 346–53,
      372
    Reagan administration, 409, 426,
      427
  to Jordan
    Johnson administration, 132–33,
      159
    Ford administration, 303–4
  to Lebanon, 135
  to Libya
    from France, 170, 190
    Johnson administration, 135

  to Middle East
    embargos on, 30, 158–60
    Tripartite Declaration limits on, 47
  to Morocco, 135, 154
  to Saudi Arabia
    Kennedy administration, 104
    Johnson administration, 135
    Nixon administration, 226
    Ford administration, 308–10
    Carter administration, 330, 346–53
    Reagan administration, 407–9
  to Syria, 247, 424
  to Tunisia, 35
  to United Arab Republic, 163
  Carter administration, memoran-
    dum/directive on, 329–30
Arms Control and Disarmament Agency,
  348
Assad, Hafez
  Nixon administration, 201, 227, 272,
    276–81
  Ford administration, 303, 305, 311
  Carter administration, 325, 331, 333,
    336
  Reagan administration, 422, 425, 426
Aswan Dam, 66–71, 178
Aswan Declaration, 343
Atherton, Alfred (Roy)
  Nixon administration, 238, 269
  Ford administration, 236, 300, 309
  Carter administration, 351, 364, 369,
    370
Austin, Warren, 33, 34, 36, 40
Australia, 73, 109, 145
Australia–New Zealand–United States
  (ANZUS) Pact countries, 330
AWACS sale, 407–11
Azores, 253, 256

Ba'ath party, 201
Bab El Mandeb straits, 270
Badeau, John, 100, 101, 103, 104, 109,
  114
Baghdad Conference, 366–67
Baghdad Pact, 62, 67, 84, 85, 88, 91
Baker, James, 404, 405, 409, 415–16,
  428
Balfour Declaration, 11–12
Ball, George
  Johnson administration, 126, 140